"In this volume the three authors have succeeded where many have failed. They have brought their talents together in an exceptional way to give a clear and dispassionate account of a notoriously contentious subject. In doing so, they have provided a lucid analysis of the actions of all the parties involved. But equally importantly, they have gone to the heart of the matter through their sympathetic, yet critical understandings of the opposing narratives that have fuelled this conflict for so long. It is a book that will enlighten those who come fresh to the subject, as well as those who want to study further the inner workings of the Arab-Israeli conflict and the chances of its resolution."– *Charles Tripp,Professor of Politics, School of African and Oriental Studies, University of London, UK*

"This extraordinary work about the Arab–Israeli conflict is both brilliant and unique. The three authors are eye-witnesses. They represent both the Arab and Israeli perspectives. They once even served in armies that opposed each other. But now they have come together to thoughtfully explore the many dimensions – from geo-strategic interests to the human factor – of the world's most volatile region. Arabs and Israelis is an exceptional contribution to understanding a tragic, troubling and costly conflict. It also provides tremendous insights that will help understand how to solve it." – *Robin Wright*, Author of Rock the Casbah: Rage and Rebellion across the Islamic World

"If there is anything more contentious than the Arab-Israel conflict, it is the history of the conflict. Rather than try the impossible task of writing the one true story, the authors give us a fair reading of the accounts that various participants believe. Furthermore, they have related the stories and events to powerful theories of international politics. The result is a signal achievement that deserves a wide readership."– *Robert Jervis, Adlai E. Stevenson Professor of International Politics, Columbia University, USA*

"No single author could write this book with its richness of multiple perspectives on a topic of such controversy as the Arab-Israeli conflict. These three distinguished scholars – one from Israel, one from Palestine, and one from Egypt – produce a unique work of scholarship. Particularly for those new to the topic, this is the book to start with. It informs and explains, without the propagandistic overtones that often find their way into such volumes."– *William B. Quandt, Professor Emeritus, University of Virginia, USA*

"An outstanding book written by some of the best scholars who have immersed their scholarly careers on the subject matter of the Arab-Israeli conflict. This is a must read that carefully contextualizes the nuances of the conflict according to different political dynamics across time and space. Students, policy makers, and academics have much to learn from this very valuable and insightful book."– *Amaney A. Jamal, Associate Professor of Politics, Princeton University, USA*

"The major strength of this textbook is its attempt to cover the unfolding events of the conflict from the three perspectives: Jewish/Israeli, Palestinian, and Arab, and by placing these events within a broader regional and international context. It is innovative and will be used by many scholars as a prime textbook because of its refreshing approach."– *Asher Kaufman, Associate Professor of History and Peace Studies, Notre Dame University, USA*

"The competing narratives are a terrific addition… it is a thoughtful and engaging way to present the material, and encourages critical thinking and discussion."– *Kimberly Jones, Head Advisor, International Affairs and Middle East Studies, Northeastern University, USA*

Arabs and Israelis

Conflict and Peacemaking in the Middle East

Abdel Monem Said Aly

Chairman of the Board, CEO and Director, Regional Center for Strategic Studies, Cairo

Shai Feldman

Director, Crown Center for Middle East Studies, Brandeis University, Waltham, MA

Khalil Shikaki

Director, Palestinian Center for Policy and Survey Research, Ramallah

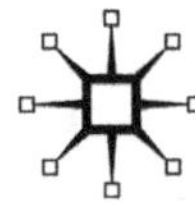

First published 2013 by
PALGRAVE MACMILLAN

Palgrave Macmillan in the UK is an imprint of Macmillan Publishers Limited, registered in England, company number 785998, of Houndmills, Basingstoke, Hampshire RG21 6XS.

Palgrave Macmillan in the US is a division of St Martin's Press LLC, 175 Fifth Avenue, New York, NY 10010.

Palgrave Macmillan is the global academic imprint of the above companies and has companies and representatives throughout the world.

Palgrave® and Macmillan® are registered trademarks in the United States, the United Kingdom, Europe and other countries

ISBN 978-1-137-29082-3 ISBN 978-1-137-29084-7 (eBook)

DOI 10.1007/978-1-137-29084-7

This book is printed on paper suitable for recycling and made from fully managed and sustained forest sources. Logging, pulping and manufacturing processes are expected to conform to the environmental regulations of the country of origin.

A catalogue record for this book is available from the British Library.

A catalog record for this book is available from the Library of Congress.

Contents

Preface

The writing and publication of this book comprises the most complex and demanding project ever undertaken by Brandeis University's Crown Center for Middle East Studies since its establishment in 2005. It also constitutes one of the most salient expressions of the Center's commitment to pursuing a *balanced and dispassionate* approach to the study of the contemporary Middle East. While reflecting this broad sustained commitment, however, this book would have never seen the light of day, were it not for the imagination, creativity, generosity and tenacity of one individual: Marcia Riklis of New York.

How did all this come about? In late 2004, one of the three co-authors of this book, Shai Feldman, was asked by the then-President of Brandeis University, Jehuda Reinharz to join Brandeis for the purpose of building a new Crown Center for Middle East Studies. Shai made his consent conditional on the university accepting his philosophy regarding this challenging endeavor: namely, that in its research, writing, and other activities the Crown Center will pursue a balanced and dispassionate approach to the Middle East. As this principle was approved, Shai's next step was to ensure its implementation by asking the other two of us, Abdel Monem Said Aly and Khalil Shikaki, to join him as Senior Research Associates of the soon-to-be-created Crown Center.

Once all three of us agreed to join the new Center, we entered into detailed discussions about the possible content of such association. The talks yielded an agreement to teach a new class, *Politics 164a: Conflict and Peacemaking in the Middle East* – the first ever on this sensitive subject to be team-taught by an Israeli, a Palestinian and an Egyptian, who represents the broader Arab perspective. The class was to be unique not only in providing students an analytical framework for analyzing developments in the Arab-Israeli conflict but even more so in sensitizing students to the competing narratives that Israelis, Palestinian and Arabs more broadly have adopted over the years with regard to these developments. As at least two of us were to be in class every session, students were to have an opportunity not only to avail themselves of the texts that elaborate these competing narratives but also to acquire "a feel" for the texture of these stories.

A close friend of Shai and supporter of the Center, Marcia Riklis visited us at Brandeis sometime in the fall 2006 semester, when we first team-taught the class. Having witnessed the students' reaction to our approach, Marcia was very complimentary but raised a difficult question: Why do we limit exposure to this experience to the relatively small number of students attending our class? Is it not imperative, Marcia asked, that the insights to which our students are exposed would be placed at the disposal of a far larger audience by translating the class into a book?

Having some sense of how difficult such an endeavor may be, we at first resisted the suggestion. But Marcia was persistent and thus began the very long journey that led to the birth of this textbook. Since in addition to teaching the class at Brandeis every fall semester, all three of us were busy building and directing our respective research centers, we could not spend more than six or seven weeks every summer writing the book. Thus, its pregnancy extended that number of years.

And it was not only Marcia's vision and enthusiasm that allowed the completion of this book but also her generosity: it was she who provided the funds required to make this happen. Without her support this book would never have made it to publication.

In turn, the Crown Center itself, providing the framework and the environment for such a demanding project to be pursued in the first place, would not have been possible if it were not for the generous and consistent support provided by Lester Crown of Chicago. Lester and his brother-in-law, Charles (Corky) Goodman were also full partners to the Center's commitment to pursue a *balanced and dispassionate* approach, thus avoiding the acrimonious partisanship which has plagued the study of the Middle East for decades. They, like President Reinharz, also proved themselves to be courageous warriors, backing us without any hesitation or reservation when we were attacked by those who felt threatened by our approach.

Successively, two senior editors at Palgrave Macmillan believed in this project almost from its inception. The excitement of Kate Hanes was contagious and the enthusiasm and persistence of Jenna Steventon, Kate's successor as Head of Humanities in Higher Education, was intoxicating. Jenna saw the unique aspects of this book when others were skeptical. She was relentless in encouraging us not to give up even when the difficulties entailed in the on-and-off writing dictated by the competing pressures on our schedules sometimes looked insurmountable.

Alec McAulay and Felicity Noble, both also at Palgrave Macmillan, were of great help as well: Alec in undertaking the enormous task of copy-editing the entire manuscript and Felicity in obtaining permissions for using the photos and illustrations inserted in the text.

Equally supportive was Laura Gross who agreed to serve as the literary agent for this book. Her enthusiasm was also crucial to our ability to find the energy and "staying power" required to bring the project to completion.

We are also grateful to William Quandt at the University of Virginia, an eminent scholar and teacher of the modern Middle East, for the very helpful comments he provided on the first rough draft of a number of chapters of this book. Also helpful were comments we later received from Moshe Ma'oz, a great scholar of modern Syria at the Hebrew University in Jerusalem. Finally, we are truly indebted to the anonymous scholars who accepted Palgrave Macmillan's request to review the advanced draft of the manuscript. Their detailed and meticulous comments helped us make this book so much better.

During these many summers, we attempted to involve a large number of students in the process of conceptualizing, organizing and researching for this book. Indeed, their most important contribution was to help us ascertain what forms of presentation would be most understandable to students. We are indebted to these students for their helpful assistance to the project. They include: Ofir Abu, Zeynep Civcik, Karim Elkady, Sarah Feuer, Keren Fraiman, Ari Jadwin, Cory Julie, Jim Kahler, Jonathan Miller, Jason Olson, Joshua Shifrinson, Jonathan Snow, and Rafi Stern. Most extensive was the research assistance provided in 2011–12 by Jasmine Gothelf.

Many thanks are also due to the Crown Center's two Associate Directors, Naghmeh Sohrabi and Kristina Cherniahivsky, and to the Center's administrator, Marilyn R. Horowitz, for the support they provided during the many years it took to complete this project.

Finally, we are particularly grateful to our wives, Valorie Kopp-Aharonov, Wafa Shikaki, and Molly Toukan for permitting their husbands to spend many summers, weeks and weekends writing this book. In the process, they became close friends as did their husbands, making the nearly impossible – enjoyable.

Abdel Monem Said Aly
Shai Feldman
Khalil Shikaki
Waltham, MA October 2013

About the Authors

Abdel Monem Said Aly

Dr. Abdel Monem Said Aly has been the Chairman of the Board and CEO of Al Masry Al Youm Publishing House in Cairo since February 2013, and the Chairman of the Board, CEO, and Director of the Regional Center for Strategic Studies in Cairo since January 2012. He is also a Senior Fellow in the Crown Center for Middle East Studies at Brandeis University. He was the President of Al Ahram Center for Political and Strategic Studies in Cairo in 2009–2012 and the Chairman of the Board and CEO of Al Ahram Newspaper and Publishing House in 2009–2011. He was a member of the Board at Al Ahram Institutions from 1999 to 2005 and the Director of Al Ahram Center for Political and Strategic Studies in Cairo from 1994 to 2009. He obtained his BA from Cairo University (1970) and his MA (1979) and PhD (1982) in Political Science from Northern Illinois University. He worked at the Ahram Center since 1975 as a researcher, senior researcher, head of the international relations research unit, and deputy director. He was a research fellow at the Brookings Institution in Washington, DC in 1987 and again in 2004, and a research fellow at Harvard University's Belfer Center for Science and International Affairs in 2003. From 2007 to 2011 he was a Senator in the Egyptian Shura Council (the Consultative Assembly). In 1990–1993 he served as political advisor to the Amiri Diwan of the State of Qatar. He contributes opinions and commentaries regularly in Arabic newspapers and other media forums in Arabic and in English. From 1997 to 2011 he was the anchor for the Egyptian TV weekly program *Wara Al Ahdath* (*Behind Events*), and from 2002 he has been the political analyst of Orbit Television program *Ala Alhawa* (*On Air*). His most recent major publication is *State and Revolution in Egypt: The Paradox of Change and Politics* (Waltham, MA: Crown Center for Middle East Studies, Brandeis University, January 2012).

Shai Feldman

Shai Feldman is the Judith and Sidney Swartz Director of the Crown Center for Middle East Studies and Professor of Politics at Brandeis University. He is also a Senior Fellow and a member of the Board of Directors of Harvard University's Belfer Center for Science and International Affairs. In 2001–2003, Feldman served as a member of the UN Secretary General's Advisory Board on Disarmament Matters. In 1997–2005, Professor Feldman served as Head of the Jaffee Center for Strategic Studies at Tel Aviv University. He has been a Senior Research Associate at the Jaffee Center since its establishment in late 1977. In 1984–87, he was director of the Jaffee Center's Project on US Foreign and Defense Policies in the Middle East and, in 1989-94, he directed the Center's Project on Regional Security and Arms Control in the Middle East. In 1994, he was a Visiting Fellow at the Washington Institute for Near East Policy and, in 1995–1997 he was a Senior Research Fellow at Harvard University's Belfer Center for Science and International Affairs (BCSIA). Educated at the Hebrew University in Jerusalem, Professor Feldman was awarded his PhD by the University of California at Berkeley in 1980. His numerous publications include five books: *Israeli Nuclear Deterrence: A Strategy for the 1980s* (New York: Columbia University Press, 1982); *The Future of U.S. – Israel Strategic Cooperation* (Washington, DC: The Washington Institute for Near East Policy, 1996); *Nuclear Weapons and Arms Control in the Middle East* (Cambridge, MA: MIT Press, 1997); *Bridging the Gap: A Future Security Architecture for the Middle East* (Lanham, MD: Rowman & Littlefield, 1997 – with Abdullah Toukan (Jordan); and, *Track-II Diplomacy: Lessons from the Middle East* (Cambridge, MA: MIT Press, 2003 – with Husscin Agha, Ahmad Khalidi, and Zeev Schiff).

Khalil Shikaki

Khalil Shikaki is a Professor of Political Science and director of the Palestinian Center for Policy and Survey Research (Ramallah, Palestine). Since 2005 he has been a Senior Fellow at Brandeis University's Crown Center for Middle East Studies. He received his BA and MA in Political Science from the American University in Beirut and in 1985 he received his PhD in Political Science from Columbia University. He taught at several Palestinian and American universities including al-Najah National University, Birzeit University, the University of Wisconsin (Milwaukee), and the University of South Florida (Tampa). In 1996–1999, Dr. Shikaki served as Dean of Scientific Research at al Najah National University in Nablus. In the summer of 2002 he was a Visiting Fellow at the Brookings Institution in Washington, DC. In 1998–99, jointly with Dr. Yezid Sayigh, Shikaki led a group of more than 25 Palestinian and foreign experts to assess the process of Palestinian institution-building. The result was a report titled *Strengthening Palestinian Public Institutions* (New York: Council on Foreign Relations, 1999). Since 1993, Dr. Shikaki has conducted more than 200 polls among Palestinians in the West Bank and the Gaza Strip and, since 2000 he conducted dozens of joint polls among Palestinians and Israelis. His research has focused on the peace process, Palestinian state-building, public opinion, transition to democracy, and the impact of domestic Palestinian politics on the peace process. He is the co-author of the annual report of the *Arab Democracy Index*, published annually by the Arab Reform Initiative. His other publications include *Public Opinion in the Israeli–Palestinian Conflict: The Public Imperative During the Second Intifada*, with Yaacov Shamir (Bloomington: Indiana University Press, 2010), and *The Israeli-Palestinian Peace Process: Oslo and the Lessons of Failure* (East Sussex: Sussex Academic Press, 2002), co-edited with Robert Rothstein and Moshe Ma'oz.

List of Illustrations

Figures

Table

Select Chronology: Key Moments in the Arab–Israeli Conflict, 1516–2012

1516	Beginning of Ottoman rule over Palestine
1798	French invasion of Egypt
1805	Birth of modern Egypt under Muhammad Ali Pasha
1830	Brief Egyptian conquest of Palestine
1834	Revolt of Jerusalem, Nablus and Hebron against Egyptian Rule
1839	*Tanzimat* reforms in the Ottoman Empire
1881	Pogroms in Russia and Ukraine
1882	Beginning of the *First Aliyah*; Beginning of British occupation of Egypt
1894	Trial and conviction of French Jewish officer, Alfred Dreyfus
1886	Theodore Herzl's publication of *Altneuland* and *The Jewish State*
1987	First Zionist Congress meets in Basel, Switzerland
1901	Meeting between Herzl and Ottoman Sultan Abdulhamid II
1904	Beginning of the *Second Aliyah*; Establishment of *Hashomer*
1908	New Ottoman constitution allowing publication of newspapers in Palestine
1914	Beginning of the First World War
1915	Hussein–McMahon Correspondence
1916	Great Arab Revolt against the Ottomans begins; Sykes–Picot Agreement concluded
1917	British conquest of Palestine; Britain issues the Balfour Declaration; Russian revolution
1919	Weizmann–Faisal Agreement; Beginning of the *Third Aliyah*; Founding of *Ahdut Ha'avoda*; Founding of the Palestinian Arab Congress and the Arab Executive Committee (AEC)
1920	Founding of the *Histadrut* and the *Haganah*; League of Nations at San Remo conference endorses the Balfour Declaration
1921	Violent Arab protests in Palestine; Haycraft Commission issues report
1922	Britain proposes creation of a Palestine Legislative Council
1924	Beginning of the *Fourth Aliyah*
1929	Beginning of the *Fifth Aliyah*; Second wave of major Arab violent protests in Palestine; Shaw Commission report, Hope-Simpson Report, and Passfield White Paper are issued; Founding of *Mapai*
1931	Founding of *Irgun* (or *Itzel*); General Islamic Conference for Support of the Palestinian Question meets in Jerusalem

1935	Izzeddin al-Qassam declares *Jihad* in northern Palestine and is killed by British near Jenin
1936	Eruption of the Arab Revolt in Palestine; Establishment of the Arab Higher Committee (AHC)
1937	Peel Commission Report is published; AHC is outlawed
1939	Woodhead Commission Report is published; St. James Round Table Conference held in London; McDonald White Paper is published; Second World War begins with German attack on Poland
1941	Hajj Amin al-Husseini meets with Adolf Hitler
1942	Zionist meeting in NYC declares goal of independent statehood
1945	Second World War ends; The Arab League is formed; Meeting between FDR and King Abdul Aziz Ibn Saud
1946	*Etzel* bombs Jerusalem's King David Hotel; Anglo-American Commission of Inquiry and Morrison–Grady Plan recommendations submitted; Winston Churchill delivers "Sinews of Peace" speech inaugurating the Cold War; TransJordan becomes the Hashemite Kingdom of Jordan
1947	Britain announces it will terminate Mandate over Palestine in May 1948; UN adopts Resolution 181; Arab–Jewish civil war erupts in Palestine; Ba'ath Party established in Syria; USA announces Containment Strategy
1948	Berlin Airlift; *Haganah* adopts Plan D; Israel declares Independence; Armed forces of Egypt, TransJordan, Syria, Iraq and Lebanon invade Palestine; UN mediator Count Bernadotte is assassinated; UN adopts Resolution 194; Palestinians declare All-Palestine Government (APG) in Gaza; Jericho Conference declares union of Jordan and Palestine
1949	Armistice agreements signed between Israel and Egypt, Syria, Lebanon and Jordan
1950	USA, Britain and France negotiate Tripartite Declaration to limit arms transfers to the Middle East
1951	King Abdullah of Jordan is assassinated; Iranian *Majles* votes to nationalize oil industry; Israel launches project to drain Hula Valley leading to Syrian attacks and Israeli retaliations
1952	Nasser and Free Officers stage revolution in Egypt
1953	CIA orchestrates removal of Iranian Prime Minister Mossadeq; Israel launches retaliation raid against Qibya, Jordan; US Secretary of State Dulles and senior CIA official Kermit Roosevelt visit Egypt; USA introduces Johnston Plan for division of water between Israel and Jordan
1954	Egypt and Britain negotiate British withdrawal of bases in Egypt; Israeli espionage and terrorism operation in Egypt (the "Lavon Affair") is uncovered
1955	Baghdad Pact is signed; Israel conducts Gaza Raid; Czech Arms Deal to Egypt is announced; USA offers to finance construction of the Aswan Dam
1956	Egypt nationalizes the Suez Canal; USSR offers to substitute for US financing of the Aswan Dam; French, British and Israeli leaders meet in Sevres, France, and later launch Sinai–Suez War; Syrians blow up the Kirkuk–Tripoli oil pipeline; USA presses Israel, Britain and France to withdraw from Egypt

1957 Israel completes withdrawal from the Sinai and Gaza; USA announces the "Eisenhower Doctrine"
1958 Egypt and Syria unify under "United Arab Republic (UAR)"; Revolution in Iraq ends Hashemite monarchy; USA intervenes militarily in Lebanon; USA launches "Atoms for Peace" program, supplies nuclear reactors to Israel and Egypt
1959 Fatah – the Movement for the Liberation of Palestine is created
1960 Construction of French-made nuclear reactor in Dimona, Israel is discovered
1961 UAR is dissolved; Israel conducts successful launch of rocket into space; US invasion of Cuba's Bay of Pigs fails
1962 Cuban Missile Crisis brings superpowers to the brink of a nuclear war; USA approves first major arms sale to Israel; Civil war in Yemen begins
1963 Revolution in Iraq brings Ba'ath to power; Israel launches National Water Carrier; President Kennedy is assassinated
1964 The Arab League establishes the PLO – The Palestinian Liberation Organization – and adopts military plan to confront Israel's National Water Carrier; Israel attacks Syrian efforts to divert its sources of water
1965 Jeddah Agreement stipulates end of the civil war in Yemen
1966 Syria and Egypt sign mutual defense pact; Arab League creates The Palestinian National Council; Israel launches retaliation raid against Samu, Jordan
1967 Major Syrian–Israeli air battle; Nasser orders Egyptian army into the Sinai; UN withdraws UNEF forces from Sinai; Nasser orders closure of the Straits of Tiran; Jordan and Egypt sign defense pact; Israel launches war, capturing the Sinai, Gaza, the Golan, the West Bank and East Jerusalem; Arab League adopts the Khartoum Resolution; UN Security Council adopts Resolution 242; Israel extends jurisdiction to East Jerusalem and begins construction of settlements in the Golan, the Sinai and the Jordan Valley; UN launches mediation by Swedish diplomat Gunnar Jarring
1968 Egypt launches War of Attrition; IDF engages Fatah and Jordanian Army units in Battle of Karamah
1969 War of Attrition escalates; Israel constructs the Bar-Lev Line and launches deep penetration bombings of Egyptian infrastructure; USSR deploys air-force and air-defense units in Egypt; Fatah gains majority of seats in the Palestinian National Council
1970 Cease-fire ends War of Attrition; USA launches peace initiative – the Rogers Plan; Jordanian army launches major attack on Palestinian groups and Syria begins to attack Jordan; Palestinian groups relocate to Lebanon; Fatah creates the Black September Organization and launches attacks against Israeli and Jordanian targets; Hafez Assad ousts Salah Jadid as Syria's leader; Nasser of Egypt dies and is replaced by Anwar Sadat
1972 Sadat expels the Soviet advisors from Egypt; King Hussein launches United Arab Kingdom to unify the East and West Banks
1973 Egypt and Syria launch surprise attack that begins the October War; Arab oil ministers ban oil shipments to the USA and the Netherlands; US nuclear forces are placed at Def Con-3 alert; War ends with adoption of UN Resolution 338; Egypt

	and Israel begin talks at km 101; Geneva Conference for Peace in the Middle East is convened
1974	Egypt–Israel and Israel–Syria disengagement agreements signed; OAPEC lifts the oil embargo; Palestinian National Council adopts the Provisional Program; Arab League Summit in Rabat declares the PLO as the "sole representative of the Palestinian People"; PLO Chairman Arafat addresses the UN General Assembly; Helsinki Final Act is adopted
1975	Second Egypt–Israel Disengagement Agreement signed
1976	Israel and Syria conclude "red lines" agreement on Lebanon; Local elections are held in the West Bank
1977	Israeli elections brings Likud to power for the first time – new Begin-led government is created; Soviet–American Communiqué is announced; Sadat conducts ground-breaking visit to Jerusalem; Begin reciprocates with a visit to Ismailiya; Egypt is expelled from the Arab League
1978	Carter and Sadat meet in Aswan; Begin–Sadat summit meeting hosted by Carter produces Camp David Accords
1979	Israel and Egypt sign peace treaty; Soviet Union invades Afghanistan; Revolution in Iran and the beginning of the 444-day Iran–USA hostage crisis
1980	Iraq invades Iran, beginning an 8-year war
1981	Israel bombs Iraqi nuclear reactor, Osiraq; Sadat is assassinated and is succeeded by Hosni Mubarak; Saudi Arabia proposes the Fahd Plan, later adopted by the Arab League as the Fez Plan
1982	Israel completes evacuation of the Sinai; Israel invades Lebanon; USA announces the Reagan Plan; Lebanese President Jumail is assassinated, leading to Maronites' massacre of Palestinians at the Sabra and Shatila refugee camps
1985	PLO and Jordan sign the Amman Accord
1987	King Hussein and Shimon Peres reach London Agreement; First Palestinian Intifada begins; Palestinian Muslim Brotherhood is renamed Hamas
1988	Iraq–Iran War ends; Jordan announces disengagement from the West Bank; PNC issues Palestinian Declaration of Independence, opens way to launching of US–PLO dialogue
1989	Fall of the Berlin Wall symbolizes end of the Cold War; Soviet Union's gates open to mass Jewish emigration
1990	Iraq invades Kuwait; USA reacts by building anti-Iraq coalition and moves over 400,000 troops to the Middle East
1991	First Gulf War is launched; Madrid Peace Conference is convened, leading to Arab–Israeli bilateral and multilateral talks
1992	Labor wins Israeli elections, leading to the creation of Rabin-led government
1993	Rabin conveys Israel's "hypothetical" consent to withdrawal from the Golan Heights; Israel–PLO Track-II negotiations result in the Oslo Accords
1994	Clinton-Assad meet in Geneva; Israel–Jordan Peace Treaty is signed; Israel and the PLO sign the Gaza and Jericho First Agreement; Arafat enters Gaza; first meeting between Israeli and Syrian army chiefs of staff is held

1995 Rabin is assassinated and is replaced by Peres; Israeli–Syrian talks at Wye River are launched; Israel–PLO Oslo-II Interim Agreement is signed; tension between Israel and Egypt erupts over the nuclear issue

1996 Israel and Turkey sign defense cooperation agreement; Hamas launches suicide bombings inside Israel; USA and Egypt host anti-terrorism conference in Sharm el-Sheikh; in first-ever Palestinian general elections, Arafat wins presidency; Israel launches Operation Grapes of Wrath in southern Lebanon; Labor led by Peres is defeated in Israeli elections and is replaced by Netanyahu-led Likud

1997 Israel and the PLO conclude the Hebron Agreement

1998 Israel and the PLO negotiate the Wye River Memorandum; Clinton visits Gaza to inaugurate international airport; Al-Qaida attacks two US embassies in Africa

1999 Labor defeats Likud in Israeli elections, resulting in Ehud Barak-led government; Summit in Sharm el-Sheikh revises implementation timeline of Wye River Memorandum; low-level Israeli-Palestinian permanent status negotiations begin

2000 Israeli–Syrian negotiations in Shepherdstown and Clinton–Assad summit meeting in Geneva both fail; Al-Qaida attacks USS *Cole* in Yemen; secret Israeli–Palestinian negotiations held in Stockholm are revealed; Israel withdraws unilaterally from South Lebanon; Camp David Summit attempts to reach Israeli–Palestinian permanent status agreement; Second Palestinian Intifada begins; Summit in Sharm eal-Sheikh fails to halt the Intifada; Further Israeli–Palestinian negotiations result in US articulation of Clinton Parameters for resolving the conflict

2001 Israeli–Palestinian negotiations held in Taba; Ariel Sharon-led Likud wins Israeli elections; Mitchell Commission submits report; Al-Qaida conducts massive terror attack on New York and the Pentagon; USA declares War on Terror

2002 Israeli Navy captures *Karin-A* ship carrying weapons and ammunition from Iran; Arab League adopts the Arab Peace Initiative (API); Israel launches Operation Defensive Shield, reoccupying all urban areas of the West Bank; Bush announces US support for Palestinian independent statehood; Arafat appoints Mahmoud Abbas to new position of Prime Minister

2003 Quartet announces roadmap to Israeli-Palestinian peace; US-led coalition invades Iraq

2004 Arafat dies

2005 Mahmoud Abbas wins Palestinian Presidential elections; Israel disengages unilaterally from Gaza; Sharon leaves Likud to form new Kadima party; Ahmadinejad is elected President of Iran; Thirteen Palestinian factions negotiate the Cairo Declaration

2006 Hamas wins Palestinian elections and forms government; Sharon suffers massive stroke and is replaced by Ehud Olmert; Hamas abducts Israeli soldier Gilad Shalit; Hezbollah cross-border attack begins Second Lebanon War; Hamas and Fatah negotiate Prisoners' Document

2007 Palestinian factions negotiate Mecca Accords; Hamas takes control of Gaza; Annapolis Conferences launches new Palestinian–Israeli negotiations; Israel bombs Syrian nuclear reactor

2008 Turkey facilitates Israeli–Syrian proximity talks; Egypt negotiates a six-month ceasefire between Hamas and Israel; Hezbollah occupies West Beirut; Hamas decides not to extend the ceasefire; Israel launches Operation Cast Lead; PA launches major security sector reform

2009 With speeches in Ankara and Cairo, Obama attempts major change of Muslims' and Arabs' view of the USA; Obama also attempts to persuade Israel to halt settlement construction; Iranian secret nuclear facility in Qom is discovered; Olmert resigns; Following new elections Netanyahu forms a Likud-led government; Fatah convenes Sixth Congress; Fayyad announces two-year plan for statehood

2010 Turkish-led flotilla attempts to break siege of Gaza; Obama states terms of reference for renewed Israeli-Palestinian negotiations

2011 Revolutions in Tunisia and Egypt oust President Zine El Abidine and Hosni Mubarak; Mass protests follow in Libya, Yemen and Bahrain; Tunisia holds first free elections; Abbas asks UN to admit Palestine as a Member State

2012 Hamas and Fatah reach Doha Agreement; Egypt holds first free elections; UNGA upgrades status of Palestinian Mission to Non-Member Observer State

Introduction

This textbook is devoted to the Arab–Israeli conflict – one of the most protracted of modern times. It has already lasted more than 110 years: a bitter struggle, involving states, peoples, movements and individuals. It has manifested itself in wars, revolts, uprisings, massacres and various types of violence and terror. It has involved the historical ingathering of a people to a land they regard as their ancient home and the uprooting and displacing of a people from a land they regard as their own, and the creation of a huge refugee problem that has so far lasted more than six decades. It involves conflicting narratives about history, national identities, land ownership, injustices and victimhood. Domestic forces and actors as well as international and regional dynamics have ensured the conflict's durability, with arms supplies and proliferation as well as national, historic and religious beliefs and ideologies adding fuel to the fire.

The process of accommodation that began in the aftermath of the 1973 War did alter the nature of the conflict. Indeed, at times the conflict seemed resolvable, as major breakthroughs were achieved, notably the peace treaties between Israel and Egypt in 1979 and between Israel and Jordan in 1994, as well as the partial deals made between the Palestinians and Israel beginning with the 1993 Oslo Accords. These breakthroughs transformed the conflict from an existential to a non-existential one, shifting the focus of the dispute to the terms required for co-existence: dividing the land, demarcating the borders and acknowledging, if not recognizing, national identities. Yet to date, these positive trajectories have proved insufficient to overcome the aforementioned forces accounting for the conflict's amazing resilience.

Arabs and Israelis: Conflict and Peacemaking in the Middle East is based on our team-taught class at Brandeis University entitled "Conflict and Peacemaking in the Middle East." The class offers students an opportunity to explore some of the most important developments in the history of the Arab–Israeli conflict from three perspectives simultaneously: an Israeli, a Palestinian, and an Egyptian representing a broader Arab perspective. The class and this resulting book are designed to sensitize students and readers to the different sides' competing narratives about the conflict and the later peacemaking efforts, and to offer a conceptual framework – a prism through which major developments in the conflict can be best understood. Writing this book together, we seek to place the insights we provide our students at the disposal of a broader community.

The book is designed to serve a number of purposes: first, to provide basic information about the evolution of the Arab–Israeli conflict and about the efforts to resolve it. In presenting this information we are cognizant of the potential gap between all three of us – men in their early 60s who have lived through a significant part of the history described in this book – and some of our prospective readers: young students to whom much of what has happened in the Middle East only ten years ago will seem like ancient history. Aware of this gap, we made every attempt to clarify what to us is often self-evident.

The second purpose of this book is to convey that almost every important development in the history of the conflict was seen differently by each of the important parties and to show *how* differently these events were seen. Each of these parties *interpreted* these developments differently, each *explained* these developments differently and each *told* themselves and their neighbors *a different story* about what had happened.

Indirectly, appreciation of this gap in narratives will also provide the reader with some sense of the difficulties in resolving the conflict. The premise here is that the wider the gap between the parties' interpretation of their past interactions, the greater the difficulties they face in reaching an understanding about the possible modalities of their future relations.

In emphasizing the narratives adopted by the parties to the conflict, we are sensitive to the fact that deciding what has been any party's narrative at any particular juncture requires a significant measure of generalization and possibly an equal measure of subjective judgment. This is because individuals and groups among each of the parties to the conflict have adopted somewhat different narratives about each important event. Describing a party's narrative, therefore, requires piecing together these varying narratives into a completed puzzle that, hopefully, represents some approximation of the party's collective narrative. However, this process is almost by definition highly subjective. This difficulty is further compounded by the fact that these narratives are rarely fixed or stable: the parties' understanding of the important developments in the conflict has evolved over time.

We are also aware that at different junctures narratives have served different functions. At times, they represented an honest attempt by the parties to interpret and understand developments as well as to explain their conduct in these developments. At other times, however, narratives have been offered to rationalize decisions made and, sometimes, even to camouflage the real reasons behind a party's behavior – that is, to hide what truly drove it to make the choices it made.

When possible we also hope to be able to sensitize readers to instances when parties have *changed their stories over time.* This raises an intriguing set of questions: given that narratives serve as an important weapon in national struggles, are parties more likely to feel that they can afford to change their narratives once they become more confident that their basic goals have been achieved? Is it only when parties' security and survival have been assured that they feel they can concede some of the more disputed aspects of their narrative? Also, does peace require that parties come to terms with the narratives they have adopted during the many years of conflict? Can the parties be expected to begin closing the gaps between their narratives during the peace-negotiations phase or, instead, only after they have resolved their conflict? Finally there is a fascinating question regarding the relationship between narratives and analyses: When can narratives be taken as a close approximation of analysis and when, instead, is there a wide gap between the parties' narratives and our own analysis?

In exposing the different *narratives* about the conflict and the efforts to resolve it we limit ourselves to the parties directly involved in the conflict: Israel, the Palestinians and key Arab countries. We refrain from investing equivalent resources and from devoting the requisite space to the narratives adopted by external parties – even important ones like the United States. We made this decision for two reasons: economy of energy and space; and the authors' premise that notwithstanding the importance of the external parties, the primary agency in affecting the developments in the conflict – and the primary responsibility for the fluctuations in the conflict and for the failure to resolve it – rests with the parties themselves.

Finally, this book also comprises an attempt to make a modest and indirect contribution to the study of international politics in the Middle East. It aims to achieve this by offering readers a conceptual framework – a three-level prism through which we believe the history of the Arab-Israeli conflict may be understood. We hope that this framework will provide readers a useful tool for understanding the events and developments we address. Should students find this to be the case, they may wish to apply this framework to other historical conflicts in the hope of gaining insights and a better understanding of their dynamics.

The book divides the history of Arab–Israeli interactions into twelve chapters to enable, together with a concluding chapter, a 13-week semester schedule to be followed. The textbook also includes many maps, charts, tables and various illustrations, including short biographies that will help students grasp the history of conflict and peacemaking in the Middle East.

Each chapter has an identical five-part structure: the first section provides a brief general description of the period covered – it addresses the questions: What characterizes this period? What distinguishes it from other periods in the history of the conflict? The second section offers a synopsis of the most important events and developments that have taken place during the period covered. It highlights facts that are not in dispute about the period addressed. The third section provides three narratives about the period: an Israeli, a Palestinian and a broader Arab perspective. Thus, this section tells the reader how each of the parties understood what happened during this period and what story it developed and marketed about these developments. The fourth section provides the three authors' analysis of what happened during the period addressed. It seeks to present an agreed interpretation of these events and developments. The final section provides some concluding remarks addressing the most important lessons that can be drawn from our examination of the period. At times, these will also include some comments about the extent to which the developments addressed and analyzed in the chapter foretell future milestones in the evolution of the conflict and in the attempts to resolve it.

Following the twelve chapters that span the history of the Arab-Israel conflict, the book concludes with some generic observations about the conflict and the failures thus far to resolve it. Thus, in this concluding chapter we offer some insights and observations regarding the most puzzling aspect of the conflict: its remarkable resilience. In it, we attempt to answer the following question: What is it about this conflict that has made it so immune to repeated and recurring efforts to resolve it?

The conceptual framework we offer in the fourth section of each chapter is merely an adaptation of the three-level prism for understanding international politics first introduced by Kenneth Waltz in *Man, the State, and War.*[1] Accordingly, we first search for *systemic* explanations: what dynamics of the international system and the regional subsystem that comprise the environments of Israel, the Palestinians and the Arab states can explain developments in their conflict? These systemic causes vary from major changes in the distribution of power in the global and regional arenas to other important developments in these realms that have impacted the region and the parties to the conflict.

The second level, *the State* in Waltz's paradigm, focuses on the *units* in conflict, their internal structure and domestic developments. This pertains to established states like Israel and Egypt as well as to major non-state actors like the Palestinians. Here we ask: What changes in the domestic scenes of the parties involved – their politics, economics and societies – have impacted and, therefore, may explain developments in their conflict?

The third and final level is what Waltz refers to as *Man* and we refer to as the *individual level.* But whereas Waltz focuses on the extent to which there is something about human nature that propels individuals toward war, we focus on the role of individual leaders in affecting fluctuations in the conflict. Thus we ask: Is there something about the personality of the leader without which the development analyzed would not have occurred and therefore cannot be explained?

The possible contribution of this book to the study of international politics will be limited by the fact that validating the conceptual framework offered here is not the primary purpose of this enterprise. Hence, we have made no systematic attempt to compare its explanatory power to that provided by alternative paradigms. However, at the end of each chapter we provided suggestions for further readings, thus allowing readers the means to explore other perspectives and to build upon the foundation we established in this book.

By exposing students to the important competing narratives about the Arab–Israeli conflict while also providing them a joint Israeli–Palestinian-Arab analysis of the most important developments in the conflict, we defy the "common wisdom" that it is impossible to produce balanced and dispassionate analyses of the Middle East.

Yet attempting to address the most important questions raised by the conflict requires a selection method and process: how were we to choose on what the *analytical* section of each chapter should focus – in other words, what requires an explanation? In making these choices we were outcome-driven. That is, we selected for study, focus and explanation those developments and events that we viewed as having had significant long-term impact on the resilience and intensity of the conflict. But this is easier said than done: there are no scientific criteria for deciding that a development was *very important.* Therefore, our choice of developments for analysis was based inevitably on a high degree of subjective judgment. In this, we did benefit from a measure of historical hindsight: the perspective of time provides some help in ascertaining that a development has had significant long-term implications for the conflict.

The book is, therefore, unique in at least three respects: first, in the attributes of the three authors, who represent very different but also complementary perspectives. We are three patriots – an Israeli, a Palestinian and an Egyptian. Two of us have served in our countries' armed forces during wartime; one of us even took part in major combat operations. Yet all three of us are social scientists, receiving our training from America's best institutions of higher learning. In later phases of our lives all three of us taught in America's finest universities and have researched in America's best think-tanks. Finally, for some three decades all three of us have taken an active if not a leading part in Arab-Israeli Track-II talks and negotiations – attempts by non-officials to help resolve the Arab–Israeli conflict. As such, we have been in touch often with our nations' leaders, giving us unique perspectives and insights into their modus operandi.

The second unique aspect of this book is the emphasis placed here on the narratives adopted by the parties to interpret developments in the conflict. This emphasis and the attempt we have made to separate the competing narratives from the historical account we provide, as well as from the analytical framework we offer, comprises a unique exercise in keeping these three separate. This separation is very rare; many existing texts about the conflict confuse the three, embedding narratives in the account of historical developments and offering explanations in a fashion that raises suspicions that they are intended to justify the behavior of one or more of the conflict's protagonists.

Finally, the analytical framework we offer places considerable emphasis on the effects of the international and broader regional environments on the course of the Arab–Israeli conflict and the efforts to resolve it. The importance of these broader contexts is often either overlooked or simply downplayed in existing accounts of the conflict. Students of international relations are bound to find this prism particularly appealing as it places the Arab–Israeli conflict in a broader perspective.

While we think that the structure we adopted in writing the book provides a unique perspective and an excellent framework for understanding the Arab–Israeli conflict, we are also aware of the structure's drawbacks and limitations. The most important of these is the risk of repetition. An important milestone in the history of the conflict may be examined from a number of perspectives across the structure of each chapter.

A degree of repetition is useful in assisting the reader to develop the ability to distinguish between history, narrative and analysis and to sensitize him or her to the need to do so. But we are aware that repetitions can make reading tedious – and we have done our very best to emphasize the different facets of each event in a non-repetitive way. However, we are also aware that despite our efforts to achieve such separation, the result is sometimes imperfect.

In order to devote space to exploring the different narratives and levels of analysis that we feel are so valuable to understanding the conflict, we have kept to a concise length the overviews of each period covered in the Main Developments sections. This has placed serious limitations on the level of detail which we can provide when describing these events – often omitting important social and economic dimensions. For this reason, we close each chapter with a list of suggested further reading for students who may be interested in exploring the developments covered in greater historical detail.

Similar limitations of space have also prevented us from fully exposing competing narratives about important developments *within* each of the protagonists' societies. In cases when parties were so internally divided that it became impossible to credibly present a single narrative as mainstream, we have elaborated the competing narratives. But these instances are rare – in most cases we were able to provide a coherent overview of the dominant narratives and avoid drowning our readers in a sea of detail. However when reading the narrative sections it is important for students to bear in mind that in many cases there will have been competing factions, and the dominant narratives should not be taken to reflect the only view in that party. In some but not in all cases students can read more about the competing narratives within each party in some of the suggested further readings.

Finally, some readers who would like us to have adjudicated the conflict by stating who we think were "the good," "the bad," and "the ugly" in its development and escalation, will remain dissatisfied with this text. Other readers who would have liked us to have ruled which party's narratives came closer to what we might think was the "real history," will be equally disappointed. This is the inevitable cost of our attempt to provide a balanced and dispassionate approach to understanding the conflict – a cost of which we are fully aware and gladly accept because its benefits far outweigh its shortcomings: allowing students to be confident in the knowledge that the information and analysis they are provided is not intended to serve any particular agenda but instead comprise an honest attempt to understand the conflict in all its complexities.

Note

1. Kenneth N. Waltz, *Man, the State, and War: A Theoretical Analysis*. New York: Columbia University Press, 1959; Second revised edition 2001.

1 The Formative Years

This chapter is devoted to the birth of the Arab national movement, its later offspring, the Palestinian national movement, and Zionism, the Jewish national movement. It follows the evolution and the clash of these movements from their inception at the end of the 19th century up to and including the Second World War. It focuses on the success of the Zionist movement and the failure of Palestinian Arabs to contain it.

The background to the emergence of the two movements is to be found in the most important historical development of late-19th-century Europe: the rise of nationalism. The idea of nationalism can be traced back to the 17th and 18th centuries. Its later spread throughout Europe and North America can be attributed to the growing economic and political maturity of societies, the impact of the European Enlightenment upon traditional values, and Napoleon's conquest of Europe. Nations' right to self-determination ignited calls for independence, decolonization, and, in a number of cases such as Italy and Germany, unification.

In the Middle East, the 19th and 20th centuries witnessed the rise of national feelings in defiance of two powerful forces: the long Ottoman rule, in which Islam had served for centuries as the cement holding the empire together, and the new injection of Western powers into the region.

The Industrial Revolution and its associated innovations – first and foremost the printing press – enabled the resurgence of the Arabic language to serve as the common basis of Pan Arabism. As a result, by the closing decade of the 19th century, nationalism in Europe had inspired the rise of Arab nationalism in Beirut, Damascus, and Cairo. Meanwhile, in Eastern Europe, nationalism was also associated with new and more violent forms of anti-Semitism, giving new impetus to the so-called "Jewish question": What would be the fate of Jews in inhospitable environments? The Zionist movement was established as an attempted response to this question by calling for a Jewish homeland.

Main Developments

The main developments of this era span the very end of the 19th century to the immediate aftermath of the Second World War. They include the decline of the Ottoman Empire and the rise of nationalism in the Middle East; the imposition of the British Mandate; the waves of Jewish immigration to Palestine; the resulting conflict between Jews and Arabs as well as between both and the British; attempts to address these conflicts through diplomacy; efforts by Jews and Arabs to develop state institutions in Palestine; and, finally, efforts to resolve the escalating Arab–Jewish conflict over Palestine through its partition.

The Rise of Arab Nationalism

The middle of the 19th century ushered in a unipolar world, centered on the industrial and naval might of Britain. The distribution of power in Europe changed somewhat in the 1870s with the rise of unified Italy and Germany, creating a multipolar system characterized by various levels of cooperation, competition, and conflict.

During this period the international system largely comprised three decaying empires – the Ottoman, the Russian, and the Austro-Hungarian – and four industrializing modern powers: Britain, Germany, France, and Italy. By the turn of the century, however, two non-European powers had gained powerful international standing: the United States and Japan. Together, these nine powers created a global multipolar system in which they competed for influence, resources, and colonies.

Within this new global order, Jewish and Arab self-realization was to be formulated and to mature over time. On the Arab side, the first significant milestone of the emerging national movement was the French invasion of Egypt in 1798. The invasion brought with it the benefits of the industrial revolution, particularly the printing press, which enabled the resurgence of the Arabic language. In turn, this resurgence drove the rediscovery of Islam in the Arabic language – a development that had eluded the region as long as it remained dominated by the Turkish tongue.

During the 19th century most of what later became known as the Arab world came under the influence of the European colonial powers while remaining legally under the jurisdiction of the Ottoman Empire.[1] Thus, emerging Arab nations found themselves under two different influences: the past, represented by a decaying Islamic empire, and the present, represented by waves of modernizers arriving from revolutionized Europe. These different influences placed Arabs under very different forms of colonization. Intellectually, they inspired resistance against both forms of domination: the old Ottomans and the modern European colonizers. This new discourse was amplified by the spread of education, press, and an increasing awareness of Arab past history and glory on one hand, and present underdevelopment and humiliation on the other.

The expression of this new discourse – the Arab *Nahda* (renaissance) – developed primarily in Egypt with the birth of its modern entity under Muhammad Ali Pasha, the *Wali* of Egypt (1805–42), and in mid-19th-century Lebanon and the Greater Syria region. There, the combination of the arrival of American missionaries and the reform policies enacted in the 1830s under Muhammad Ali's son, Ibrahim, who briefly conquered the territory during his father's failed attempt to take over the Ottoman Empire, had sparked a growth in education. This, in turn, fostered a revival of Arabic literature and language. With the arrival of the printing press, scholars like Nasif Yazeji and Butrus Bustani began circulating texts facilitating the study of classical Arabic works and thus planting the seeds of Arab national identity.

In the later part of the century, literary and scientific societies were founded, increasing the Arabs' knowledge of their own history and culture.[2] Politically, this Arab *Nahda* found expression in three modes of nationalism: first, Arab nationalism, which stressed that Arab peoples sharing cultural and historical ties should be unified under one Arab kingdom. Muhammad Ali Pasha and particularly his son Ibrahim Pasha, both of Macedonian origin, flirted with this idea, especially when the former invaded the Levant, Sudan, and Arabia (today's Saudi Arabia).[3] Yet, it was not until the Great Arab Revolt in 1916, conducted in collaboration with the British during the First World War, that the idea of an Arab kingdom seemed feasible for the first time.

The second mode was the separate nationalism of each Arab country. As the colonizing powers drew borders and frontiers, a sense of local association and self-realization was bound to develop. This was particularly true in Egypt which found in its pre-Arab and pre-Islamic past enough common ground to create Egyptian nationalism.

The third mode was Islamic nationalism, with the *Umma*, the Islamic nation, as a focus of self-identity, energized by modern means of communication and education. In reality, the interactions between the three modes of nationalism were tense and included various forms of accommodation, competition, and conflict. Yet all three were to take a part in the Arabs' confrontation with Zionism – the Jewish national movement.

Palestinian Society at the Turn of the Century

Ottoman rule over Palestine lasted from the late Middle Ages until the second decade of the 20th century (1516–1917). In 1831–1841, however, Palestine was occupied for a number of years by Egypt under Muhammad Ali and Ibrahim Pasha.[4] Though there was no political entity named Palestine, by the second half of the 19th century the Arabs of the area between the Mediterranean and the Jordan River could be distinguished from those of Syria or Egypt by dress, dialect, and customs.

Signs of the emergence of a separate Palestinian identity remained inconclusive, however, until the second decade of the 20th century. The first formative event of the history of the Palestinian people and in the formation of Palestinian identity was the 1834 revolt in the three main Palestinian cities of Jerusalem, Nablus, and Hebron against the repressive policies of conscription and taxation of Egyptian military rule. Yet, as late as the beginning of the 20th century, within the context of the rise of broader Arab nationalism and the struggle against the Ottomans, a Greater Syria movement won support among the elite seeking to unify Palestine and Lebanon into Syria to form a pan-Arab identity. Indeed, immediately after the arrival of British forces in Palestine and prior to the application of the Mandate, Palestinians' rising concern about the Balfour Declaration (see below) led them to demand to be united with the Arab state they hoped would be established in Syria.[5]

The military occupation of Palestine by Egypt under Muhammad Ali and Ibrahim Pasha first set the wheels in motion for integration of the Palestinian economy. The Egyptians also helped reform the economy by insisting on an increased proportion of monetary rather than barter transactions, and economic and other restrictions on Christians and Jews were eased.

Soon, however, with England's help, the Ottoman Sultan reasserted his power over the occupied land by forcing Ibrahim Pasha to concede the Levant in exchange for handing over the *wilayat* of Egypt to Muhammad Ali and his descendants by an Ottoman decree (*firman*). Though they now held a tighter grip on local affairs in Palestine, the Ottomans had to concede strategic power to the British across the region. In 1839, administrative reforms called the *Tanzimat* were declared throughout the Ottoman Empire, guaranteeing rights for all, regardless of religion. This was followed by edicts issued in 1856 and in 1858 that codified informal private land ownership. With the establishment of formal government connections and the subsequent civilian connections that led to European interest in trade in the region, Palestinians began to invest in cash crops, such as cotton, sesame, and oranges, to supply European, mainly British, factories and markets. Thus, with both increased trade and investment, by the start of the First World War the integration of the Palestinian economy was well under way.[6]

Throughout this period the policy of centralization was taking power away from rural sheiks, who had acted as tax collectors for the Ottoman rulers, and shifting it to the urban elite, especially on the Mediterranean coast. Because of the commoditization of land that followed from the 1858 edict, many large tracts were owned by absentee landlords who lived in the cities. With their power stemming from kinship ties to their rural base, the big landlords, along with artisans, merchants, and other notables, made up an urban class that established its hegemony over Palestine. Though most of the reins of power were held by the urban elite, there still existed deep connections to the rural classes who, at the close of the Ottoman period, still comprised most of the Palestinian population.[7]

Palestinian cultural life began to flourish in the second half of the 19th century with the introduction of the printing press in Arabic. Further momentum was gained when the Ottoman constitution of 1908 allowed ordinary citizens to publish newspapers. Among the first to be published in that year were *Al-Quds* (Jerusalem) and *al-Karmil*.[8] By the end of 1908, 15 newspapers were being published, with 19 more appearing by the beginning of the First World War.[9]

By 1890 Palestine's population stood at 532,000, of whom 42,000 were Jews: the rest of the population were Muslim and Christian Arabs. This was a significant change compared to 1800, when Jews comprised only 2 percent (6,700) of the total population of Palestine. The British census of 1922 registered 752,048 inhabitants in Palestine, consisting of 660,641 Palestinian Arabs, 83,790 Palestinian Jews, and 7,617 persons belonging to other groups.[10]

The increasing Jewish immigration to Palestine planted the early seeds of conflict. By the early 20th century strong opposition to Zionism, and evidence of a growing nationalistic Palestinian identity, were being expressed in Palestinian newspapers such as *al-Karmil* and *Filasteen*. The latter addressed its readers as "Palestinians" and focused its critique of Zionism on the failure of the Ottoman administration to control Jewish immigration.[11]

The Rise of Zionism – The Jewish National Movement

Zionist history began with two developments, at the two edges of Europe: East and West. In 1881 a new wave of violence, or *pogroms*, against Jewish communities took place in Russia and Ukraine. This led a growing number of Jews to conclude that their environment was unsafe and inhospitable.

Most Jews who reached this conclusion sought to emigrate – and many did – to North and South America. But a small number were energized by the idea of relocating to

Palestine. Thus, by the end of the 19th century, the first drips of emigration to Palestine took place, mostly to the urban areas of Jaffa and Jerusalem. However, it is also during this period that the first Jewish agricultural settlements were established in the land's rural areas.

POGROMS

The term *pogrom* stems from the Russian word *pogromit*, meaning "to destroy." Historically, it refers to violent attacks by local non-Jewish populations on Jews in the Russian Empire and in other countries. The perpetrators of pogroms organized locally (sometimes with government and police encouragement), raped and murdered their Jewish victims and looted their property. The first such incident to be labeled a pogrom was anti-Jewish rioting in Odessa in 1821.

Following the assassination of Tsar Alexander II, a new wave of particularly vicious pogroms swept southern Russia and Ukraine from 1881 to 1884, killing Jews and destroying their property. In a pogrom that broke out in Kishinev in 1903, 45 Jews were killed and many more wounded. In October 1905 a series of riots throughout southern Russia left 810 Jews dead in the course of 12 days.[12]

In the West, the trial of a Jewish officer in the French army - Alfred Dreyfus - brought a Jewish Austrian journalist, Theodore Herzl, to despair with regard to what was then the most common response to the "Jewish question" in Western Europe: namely, assimilation. Dreyfus, the only Jewish Captain in the French General Staff, was accused by anti-Semitic army officers and the press of spying on behalf of Germany by conveying French military secrets to the German Embassy in Paris.[13] He was convicted of treason in 1894 and sentenced to life imprisonment. In 1899 the case was reopened and, following another trial where he was found guilty with extenuating circumstances, Dreyfus was pardoned by the French president. However, the affair was a milestone, not only in the discrediting of the French army and the Third Republic, but also in the growth of anti-Semitism in France.

Herzl regarded the Dreyfus affair as a typical manifestation of deeply entrenched anti-Semitism in a society where Jews had made every effort to assimilate. This propelled him to write two books: *Altneuland* and *The Jewish State*. The books - the first fictional, the second a political manifesto - received considerable attention in Jewish communities in Europe. The resulting debate propelled a small number of Jews to gather in Basel, Switzerland, to discuss the feasibility of Herzl's ideas. The conference, held on August 29, 1897, later became known as the First Zionist Congress. It led to the first diplomatic venture of the embryonic movement: a May 1901 meeting in Istanbul between Herzl and Abdulhamid II, the Sultan of the Ottoman Empire. The purpose of the meeting was to obtain the Ottomans' consent to the creation of a Jewish homeland in Palestine - something Herzl failed to obtain.[14]

Waves of Jewish Immigration

The first practical step taken by the newly created Zionist movement was the relocation to Palestine of a small number of Jews in the framework of two emigration waves, and the establishment of small agricultural settlements there. Between 1890 and the outbreak of the First World War, in 1914, some 75,000–85,000 Jews migrated to Palestine.[15]

The first wave (the *First Aliyah*) of some 35,000 Jewish immigrants (1882–1903) consisted mostly of Russian Jews fleeing pogroms as well as a small number of Yemeni Jews.[16] The *Second Aliyah* (1904–14) comprised individuals fleeing Tsarist Russia. This group of some 40,000 immigrants had a more profound impact on the shape of the future Jewish state, bringing with them socialist ideas and establishing the first "collective" agricultural settlements (*kibbutzim*).

The *Third Aliyah* of 1919–23 also numbered 40,000 new immigrants. Sparked by continuing pogroms, this major wave consisted mainly of young East European Jews.

The *Fourth Aliyah* of 1924–29 was a result of increased economic hardships in Eastern Europe, the application of anti-Semitic policies in Poland, and strict immigration quotas applied by the United States. About 75,000–82,000 Jewish immigrants arrived in Palestine in this wave.[17] They were largely middle-class Jews, who brought with them modest sums of capital that permitted the Jewish community in Palestine some economic growth.

Beginning in 1929, and accelerated by the pressures on Jewish communities in Europe created by the Nazis' rise to power in 1933, the *Fifth Aliya*, which lasted until 1940, consisted largely of German Jews – many of them highly skilled professionals – along with a smaller number of Jews from Eastern Europe. Between 1933 and 1936 some 174,000 Jews took part in this immigration wave. By 1940, nearly 250,000 Jews had arrived, bringing the Jewish population of Palestine to some 450,000.[18]

The First World War

The years of the First World War were not conducive to advancing the Zionist project. The economic conditions in Palestine and the neighboring provinces of the Ottoman Empire were very harsh, with some locations, such as Beirut, suffering famine and disease. Foreign subjects were expelled from Palestine by the Ottoman authorities, including thousands of Jews, mostly of Russian origin. The Ottomans also ordered the evacuation of Jaffa and its new northern Jewish neighborhood, Tel Aviv. The combined effect of these measures was to reduce the Jewish population of Palestine from 85,000 in 1914 to only 56,000 by the end of 1917. Suffering similar hardships, the Arab population of Palestine declined by about 100,000 during the same timeframe.[19]

At the same time, what came to be known as The Great War also provided Zionists with a first opportunity to demonstrate their potential strategic utility to Britain – the power that now came to dominate the region – thus garnering London's favor. The Zionists did so in a number of different ways: first, as they anticipated the British Army's invasion of Palestine, a number of members of the Yishuv formed a spy network in the service of Britain's efforts to defeat the Ottomans.[20] The term Yishuv – the Hebrew word for "settlement" or "community" – will henceforth be used to refer to the Jewish population in Palestine prior to the founding of the state of Israel. Led by Sarah and Alexander Aronson the network provided intelligence to the British regarding the morale of the Turkish troops, troop movements, fortifications, and plans.[21]

Outside Palestine, Zionists volunteered to join the fighting on the British side, forming a military transport unit, *Gdud Nahagei Hapredot* [the Zion Mule Corps – ZMC]. The unit came about as a result of Zeev Vladimir Jabotinsky and Joseph Trumpeldor advocating a Jewish fighting force to join the British Army in liberating Palestine from the Turks.[22] Finally, and of more significant assistance to Britain's war effort, there was the contribution of Dr. Haim Weizmann, a distinguished chemist and a leader of the Zionist movement. Weizmann's invention of an efficient mode of production of acetone – a chemical substance that figured highly in the manufacture of explosives and thus in Britain's war effort – allowed him to play a key role in Britain's later decision to issue the Balfour Declaration.[23]

Yet the same Great War was also significant in demonstrating the Arabs' utility to the British effort. This was manifest in the Great Arab Revolt which Hussein, the Sharif of Mecca, launched in June 1916 against the Ottomans. Advised and supplied by a number of British officers led by T.E. Lawrence, the Arab Revolt contributed to Britain's war effort by causing the Ottomans to divert and tie down their troops, by disrupting the Hijaz Railway and by cutting Turkish supply lines and threatening their flanks. One result of this chapter in Arab–British partnership was that the primary agent for this relationship during the war, T.E. Lawrence, developed a network of special relationships with Middle East leaders that served Britain well for years to come.[24]

The British Mandate

The role of the Zionists and the Arabs in the Ottomans' defeat in the First World War led to a number of important developments following Palestine's conquest by the British, and the subsequent replacement of the Ottomans in the broader Near East by Britain and France. A set of competing, if not contradictory, commitments were made by the British to those whose support they had courted in order to achieve the Ottomans' collapse: the Arab peoples and the Zionist movement. The first of these was a promise made to Arab nationalists led by Sharif Hussein bin Ali (1854–1931) – the Sharif and Emir of Mecca from 1908 until 1917 – to facilitate the creation of an independent Arab state.[25] The promise was contained in a letter delivered to Hussein by the British High Commissioner, Sir Henry McMahon in 1915.

HUSSEIN–MCMAHON CORRESPONDENCE

The British High Commissioner Sir Henry McMahon and the Sharif of Mecca, Hussein, exchanged ten letters between July 1915 and March 1916. The correspondence began with a letter sent by Hussein's son, Abdullah, to McMahon, requesting British acknowledgment of Arab independence from Cilicia in the north to the Indian Ocean in the south and from the Mediterranean in the West to Iran in the East, as well as British approval for the establishment of an Arab Caliphate. Although the first British letter recognized an Arab Caliphate, it was ambiguous regarding the borders of the future Arab kingdom. Nevertheless, with some reservations regarding areas where Arabs did not comprise the majority and where British and French interests required "special measures of administrative control," in his letter dated October 24, 1915 McMahon accepted general Arab terms about the borders. The correspondence did not mention Palestine specifically, but rather the district (*wilaya* in Arabic) of Damascus that included eastern Palestine, which, according to one interpretation, was to belong to the future Arab kingdom. Others point out, however, that two days later, McMahon wrote a letter to the Foreign Office explaining that the promised territories to the Arabs only exclude "portions on the Northern Coast of Syria." Although according to this interpretation Palestine was not excluded, McMahon later claimed that indeed it was.[26]

Figure 1.1. The Middle East in the 1920s

The Hussein–McMahon correspondence was contradicted by the Sykes–Picot Agreement of 1916. The Agreement divided the Near East into spheres of influence and control between Britain and France, marking the borders between these prospective areas, including Syria, Lebanon, Transjordan, and Palestine. The correspondence was also contradicted by a second dramatic development – the November 1917 Balfour Declaration, in which Lord Arthur James Balfour, the British Foreign Secretary, declared a commitment of His Majesty's Government to the establishment of a national home for the Jewish people in Palestine.

An important later development during this period was the decision of the League of Nations' San Remo conference on April 24, 1920 to endorse the Balfour Declaration and to grant Britain and France a mandate to govern the areas carved out by Sykes and Picot – areas in the Near East which were part of the Ottoman Empire until the latter's collapse. The decision noted that implementing its promise to establish a home for the Jewish people was part of the British mandate in Palestine. The text was confirmed by the Council of the League of Nations on July 24, 1922.

THE SYKES–PICOT AGREEMENT

During the course of the First World War, Russia, Britain, and France made different and sometimes competing claims on the Ottoman territories. As Russia was the key to avoiding a German–Ottoman victory, the British promised it control over Istanbul and the Dardanelles. While France sought control over the southeastern portion of Anatolia, called Cilicia, northern coastal Syria, and Greater Lebanon, Britain had claims on Iraq, some parts of Palestine, and Jordan. In the secret agreement signed on January 3, 1916, by the first secretary of the French embassy in London, Francois Georges-Picot, and Sir Mark Sykes, War Minister Horatio Kitchener's personal representative, Britain and France agreed to divide the Middle East into spheres of influence and areas of direct control. Also drawn were the borders of Syria, Lebanon, Transjordan, and Palestine. The agreement provided France unconditional authority in Cilicia, coastal Syria, and Lebanon and a sphere of influence in mid and south Syria and Mosul. Britain was granted unconditional authority in Basra, Baghdad, and a sphere of influence in Jordan. Britain also received Haifa and Acre, but the rest of Palestine was to be placed under international administration.[27]

THE BALFOUR DECLARATION

On November 2, 1917 Foreign Secretary Arthur James Balfour wrote a letter to one of the leaders of the British Jewish community, Lord Walter Rothschild. Later known as the Balfour Declaration, the letter announced the British government's commitment to use its best endeavors for the establishment in Palestine of "a national home for the Jewish people." The letter also stipulated that "nothing shall be done which may prejudice the civil and religious rights of existing non-Jewish communities in Palestine, or the rights and political status enjoyed by Jews in any other country."[28]

Jewish–Arab Relations

During the second half of the 19th century, relations between Arabs and Jews in the area later called Palestine were generally calm – until 1882, when Jewish immigration and land purchases became organized and targeted. These purchases from Arab landowners forced Arab peasants – who were now replaced by Jewish laborers – to leave these lands. This, in turn, led to the first clashes between Arab peasants and Jews.[29]

In 1891 a statement signed by 500 Arab Jerusalemites was sent to Istanbul, complaining about Jewish immigration, land purchases, and arms buildup. It demanded that Jews not be allowed to own land in Palestine. By 1909, Palestinians also began to demand the cessation of Jewish immigration, and in 1910 local newspapers began to attack Arab landowners for selling land to Jews. Some articles accused the local Ottoman authorities in Palestine of facilitating Jewish land ownership. In 1913, Arab community-based groups began to organize to promote awareness of what they saw as the danger of Zionism. Also that year, concern emerged over the creation of special courts with jurisdiction over Jewish residents of Palestine, depicting this development as tantamount to the establishment of a "state within a state."[30]

Figure 1.2. Al Aqsa Mosque, 1918. *Source*: Library of Congress, LC-DIG-matpc-05603.

Parallel to the first signs of an emerging Arab–Jewish conflict over Palestine, initial efforts were made to defuse the clash created by the competing British commitments to the Arabs and the Zionists. In mid-1918, in what later became Transjordan, in late 1918, in London, and finally in January of 1919, at the Paris Peace Conference, Emir Faisal bin Al-Hussein bin Ali, representing and acting on behalf of the Arab kingdom of Hejaz,[31] and Dr. Haim Weizmann, representing and acting on behalf of the Zionist Organization, met and formulated the secret Weizmann–Faisal Agreement.[32] The agreement sought to harmonize the interests of Arab nationalists and Zionists at the postwar Paris Peace Conference. This was to be achieved by excluding Palestine from the nationalists' demand for an Arab state and by allowing Jewish immigration to Palestine, both in return for Jewish assistance in the establishment of the Arab state.

The agreement vaguely outlined the positive relationship to be held between the to-be-created Arab State and Palestine. It was to be implemented by the British, who were also to moderate all future disputes. The major concession Faisal made was allowing a Jewish homeland to be established in Palestine.[33] Faisal believed that his new pan-Arab nation could greatly benefit by securing Jewish-led and sponsored development for both the Arab state as well as the non-Jewish component of Palestine.[34] Faisal agreed to the implementation of the Balfour Declaration in Palestine, as well as to allow a massive influx of Jewish immigration into Palestine as long as the rights of local Arab farmers were secured and they received assistance in further developing their land. The remaining terms of the agreement stipulated that no

Figure 1.3. The Western (or Wailing) Wall, 1929. *Source*: National Archives.

religious discrimination was to be state-sponsored; all Muslim holy sites were to remain under Muslim control; the Zionist Organization would organize a commission to survey economic possibilities in all of the Arab state (and not just the potential of a Jewish state in Palestine) and would assist the Arab state in providing means for developing the land.[35] To the signed agreement, Faisal attached a handwritten note in Arabic which stipulated that the powers at the Paris Peace Conference had to agree to Arab independence or the attached agreement would be rendered void.[36]

The Arab state was never established in the way envisaged in the Weizmann–Faisal Agreement, and Faisal never acknowledged its existence. In fact, the opposite was the case: Faisal publicly called for Palestine to be part of Greater Syria and demanded an end to Jewish immigration. In a letter to Britain's General Allenby, he also denied that he ever agreed to a national home for the Jewish people in Palestine.[37]

These efforts at high-level diplomacy did not alleviate the concerns of the Arab population in Palestine. Their worries were heightened by a new wave of Jewish emigration following the Russian revolutions of February and October 1917. By April 1920, this new wave led to the first violent protest by Arabs in Palestine against the Zionist project. During the course of the riots, five Jews were killed and 211 were injured.[38] Smaller outbreaks of violence continued over the subsequent months.

In May 1921, larger-scale clashes broke out in the port city of Jaffa, eventually spreading to other towns as well. In this round of fighting, Arabs attacked Jewish homes and businesses, killing 47 Jews and injuring many more. In the associated confrontation with British forces, 48 Arabs were also killed.[39] In response, the British declared a state of emergency and set up a commission of inquiry to investigate the situation. The Haycraft Commission found that the Arabs had instigated the attacks, but that their actions were caused by their fears of the growing Jewish population in Palestine.[40] The result was a British decision to temporarily halt Jewish immigration to Palestine.

A second more violent wave of Arab protests took place in 1929 when disagreements regarding Jewish prayers at the Western Wall in Jerusalem provided the impetus for Arab riots against Jewish communities throughout Palestine, with the worst violence taking place in Hebron, Safed, and Jerusalem. In all, 133 Jews and 116 Arabs were killed and 339 Jews and 232 Arabs were wounded, and the Jewish communities in Hebron and Gaza were forced by the British to evacuate.[41]

Like the earlier outbreaks, the riots of 1929 were followed by an official commission of inquiry, the Shaw Commission. Its conclusions agreed with those of the Haycraft Commission: it found that Arab violence was caused by a fear of Jewish immigration and recommended that the British government rethink its policies regarding immigration and land sales. In turn, these findings led, in August 1930, to the commissioning of the Hope Simpson Report and the issuing at the same time of the Passfield White Paper, both stipulating that Jewish immigration to Palestine must be limited. Parallel to the growing manifestations of violent Arab reactions to the Zionist project, leaders of the Jewish and Arab communities in Palestine made initial efforts to explore whether their clash could be ameliorated.[42]

Whereas the first acts of violent protests against the Zionists were carried out by small ad-hoc groups, in 1935 the Syrian-born militant Sheik Izzeddin al-Qassam formed an organized armed group in northern Palestine and declared *Jihad* – holy war – against the British and the Zionists. The ascent of al-Qassam represented a qualitative change in the Arab response to Zionism and to the British Mandate in three ways. First, he posed a challenge to the traditional national leadership that sought to work with, rather than confront, the British. Second, al-Qassam argued that the British Mandate was the root cause of all the problems haunting the Palestinians and that only organized armed resistance against the British army, not diplomacy and non-violent protests, would bring the Mandate to an end. Finally, he brought Islam into the battle against the British and the Zionists; al-Qassam called for armed *Jihad* in the name of Islam, not in the name of Palestinian nationalism.

Institution-Building

The 1920s also witnessed the beginning of Zionist institution-building in Palestine. Some key precursors to these developments occurred in the first decade of the 20th century, when members of the *Second Aliya* founded the Jewish community's first self-defense organization, *Hashomer.* A second took place in 1919, when David Ben Gurion founded *Ahdut Ha'avodah* [the Unity of Labor], bringing together various socialist groups under a centralized leadership. A year later Ben Gurion created the *Histadrut*, which became the main labor union of the Yishuv.

In 1921 the British government officially recognized *Knesset Israel* [the Assembly of Israel] to serve as the main legislative body of the autonomous Jewish community under the Mandate. By the close of the decade, *Mapai* [The Workers of the Land of Israel Party], led by Ben Gurion, was to dominate the politics of the Yishuv and, later, that of the state of Israel until the late 1970s.

The 1920s also saw the first major expansion of Zionist security institutions. In 1920, the *Haganah* was created to serve as the clandestine mainstream Zionist militia. Originally small and without central authority, it expanded its role and ranks following the Arab riots of 1929, transitioning into a significant armed force. However, the defensive character of the organization led to friction amongst its ranks regarding the role of restraint in its practices. By 1931 some *Haganah* members, mostly associated with Jabotinsky's Revisionist Zionism Movement, broke off and formed the *Irgun* [National Military Organization in the Land of Israel, also known as *Etzel*] – a much smaller and more militant aggressive group.

The 1920s also witnessed important milestones in the establishment of the Yishuv's education institutions. Centralization of the elementary and secondary school system began in 1919, and throughout the decade institutions of higher education were founded in Haifa (The Technion, 1924) and Jerusalem (The Hebrew University, 1925).

Politically, the Yishuv experienced major developments throughout this period. The World Zionist Organization (WZO) now advised the Mandate government on the Yishuv's major economic, social, and other affairs. In the 1920s it underwent structural changes aimed at increasing the effectiveness of all Zionist institutions falling under its umbrella leadership. In 1929, this culminated in the creation of the Jewish Agency, which replaced the WZO as the Yishuv's main representative body in all dealings with the British Mandate authorities.

Palestinian institution-building began soon after the establishment of the British Mandate. In August 1922, the Mandate government had proposed a Palestinian constitution that stipulated the formation of a legislative council. The council was to enact laws which would be bound by the terms of the Mandate and would be subject to the approval of the British High Commissioner, who would also have the right to dissolve the council. The council was to have had 22 members: 10 would be nominated (six British and four Jewish) and 12 elected (eight Muslims, two Christians, and two Jewish). But Palestinians, who believed they constituted the overwhelming majority of the population, refused to comprise a minority in the proposed parliament and therefore called for a boycott of the council elections.

Palestinians had already formed the Palestinian Arab Congress, an elected assembly that convened seven times between 1919 and 1928. In turn, the congress created the Arab Executive Committee (AEC) and received de-facto recognition from the British Mandate authorities during most of its lifetime. The congress sought to avoid challenging the Mandate authorities, viewing Britain as a potential friend and ally, while affirming its rejection of the Balfour Declaration. Members of the AEC were elected in a secret vote; they were older politicians who had come to prominence through the Ottoman reforms of the mid-19th century. Those reforms enabled the formation of an elite cadre of landowners and office-holding notables, many of whom also engaged in commerce or control of large religious endowments. The congress dealt with the most important issues of the day, such as the relationship with the Mandate, the creation of the Jewish National Home and various legislative proposals. It acted as an executive and a legislature, issuing resolutions, declaring national strikes, sending envoys to other countries as well as to international organizations, collecting donations, launching anti-Zionist political and propaganda campaigns, and declaring positions on major events and developments.

HAJJ AMIN AL-HUSSEINI

Figure 1.4. Hajj Amin al-Husseini, 1929. Courtesy of the Library of Congress, LC-DIG-matpc-15737

Born in 1895 in Jerusalem to a prominent Palestinian Muslim family, Hajj Amin was a religious and a nationalist political leader. He studied at al-Azhar University in Cairo and, although he served in the Ottoman army, he later participated in the efforts to establish an Arab nation by joining the Arab revolt against the Ottomans. Observing the failure of the nationalists to establish a united Arab state and to confront the Zionist project, he sought to establish a separate Palestinian state. Al-Husseini's initial rise to prominence was orchestrated by the British: it was the first British High Commissioner who appointed him the Grand Mufti of Jerusalem in 1921, and, a year later, as President of the Supreme Muslim Council, a new body created by the British. As a member of Palestinian aristocracy, the British at first saw in him a force for stability and tranquility. For many years, he sought cooperation with the British in pursuit of a change in the Mandate policy though dialogue. In the meantime, he used his control of Palestine's Muslim religious institutions to incite hatred against the Zionists, eventually leading the 1936–39 Arab Revolt.

The Third Palestinian Arab Congress, meeting in December 1920, called for the formation of a Palestinian national government accountable to an elected parliament. The latter was to be elected by all who resided in Palestine prior to the outbreak of the First World War. The Fifth Congress rejected the 1922 British proposal for the creation of a legislative council, arguing that the proposed council – created within the terms of the Mandate – would not have the power to reject the establishment of a Jewish National Home. In other words, the AEC regarded the proposed council as an indirect endorsement of the Mandate and its missions, including the establishment of a Jewish home in Palestine.

Formally, the AEC was dissolved only in 1934, to be replaced in 1936 by the Arab Higher Committee (AHC). The AHC was established by Hajj Amin al-Husseini and Raghib al-Nashashibi, among others, to fill the vacuum left by the death of Musa Kazim al-Husseini and the earlier demise of the Palestine Arab Congress. This took place a few days after the eruption of the revolt of 1936–39 (see below) and the call for a general Arab strike. The strike, demanding an end to Jewish immigration and land sales to Jews, was initially called by local committees and workers in various towns, beginning in Nablus and spreading to Haifa and Jenin. Once established, the AHC coordinated and expanded the strike activities and articulated demands for the formation of a national government. Blaming it for the violence of the revolt, the British outlawed the AHC in 1937.[43]

The proposal to create a Legislative Council was reintroduced in the 1930s. In 1935 the British High Commissioner proposed the establishment of a 28-member Legislative Council: 12 elected members (eight Muslim, three Jewish, one Christian); eleven appointed members (two Muslim, five Jewish, two Christian, one Bedouin, and one businessman); and five official members of the Mandate authorities. The High Commissioner was to serve as its chairman. While the Zionists promptly rejected the proposal, the Palestinian Arab reaction was mixed, with most of the political parties accepting the idea in principle.[44]

What killed the proposal, however, was not the lack of an *Arab* consensus but rather the outcome of a debate in the *British* Parliament.[45] The debate ended with a rejection of the Colonial Office's proposal, first in the House of Lords on February 26, 1936, and then in the House of Commons on March 24.[46] To avoid upsetting the Arab side, the British invited a delegation of Palestinian leaders to London to discuss the proposal, but factional infighting among the Palestinian leadership delayed the trip, and when the revolt broke out in April, the Arab leaders decided not to send a delegation. The British reacted by publicly suspending the proposed creation of a Legislative Council.[47]

The Position of the Arab States

The first expression of collective support for the Palestinians by the neighboring Arab states came in 1931 in a meeting of representatives of 22 Arab states or proto-states: the General Islamic Conference for Support of the Palestinian Question. The meeting, held in Jerusalem, declared an Arab boycott of Jewish and British companies. The call for the conference was initiated by Hajj Amin al-Husseini and the Indian Muslim Leader, Shuwakat Ali. *Al-Wafd* – the national majority party of Egypt – was officially represented by a delegation led by Abdel Rahman Azzam. However, the delegation did not comprise an official representation of Egypt.[48] A separate meeting of these delegates called for the following: (a) the establishment of Arab unity; (b) a rejection of any plan for partitioning Palestine; (c) the formation of an Arab bank in Jerusalem; (d) the establishment of a university in Jerusalem.[49]

The Arab Revolt of 1936–39

Hitler's rise to power had by 1936 resulted in the largest wave of Jewish emigration to Palestine. It also led to the largest-ever rebellion by Palestine's local Arab population, which demanded independence from Britain and an end to British support of Zionist efforts. The rebellion was marked by Palestinian attacks against Jewish civilians and British soldiers and forceful British measures to suppress the violence. Some 5,000 Arabs, 415 Jews, and 101 British were killed in the clashes.[50]

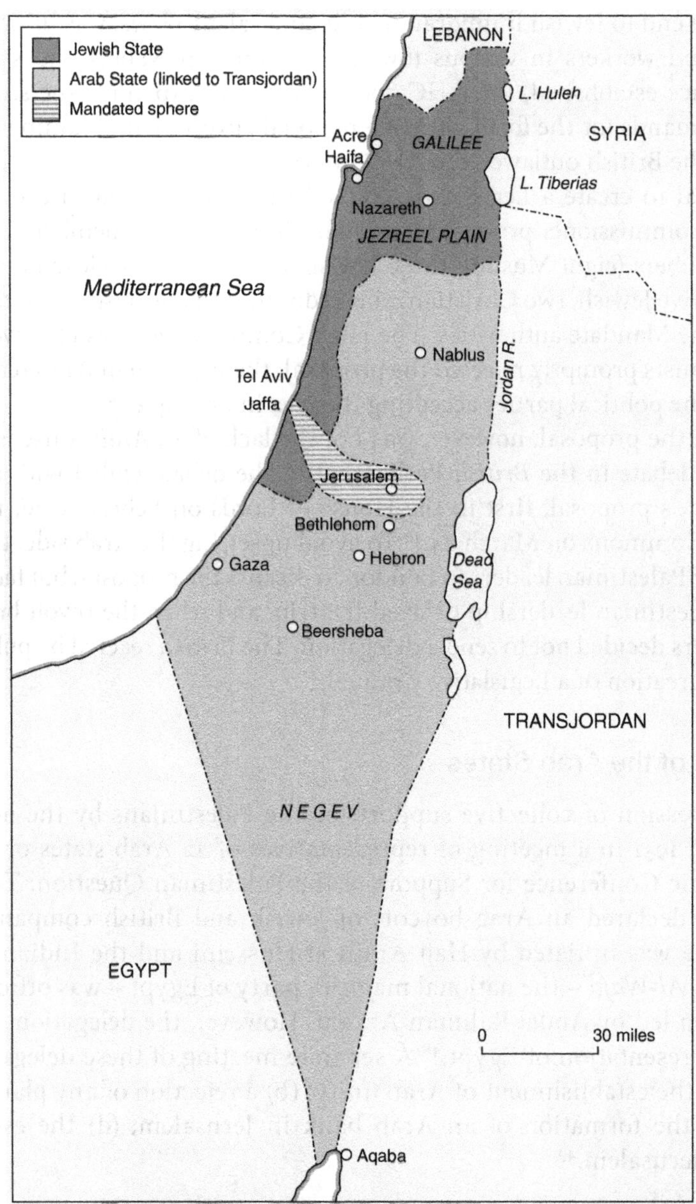

Figure 1.5. Map of Peel Commission Proposal, 1937

The revolt should not have been a surprise. After the death of al-Qassam in a clash with a British force near Jenin in November 1935, moderate nationalist members of the dissolved AEC told the British High Commissioner that they were losing influence over the public, and that, if Britain did not change its policy soon, radicals would take over the street and conditions would rapidly deteriorate.

Led by a younger generation of nationalists who felt that the Palestinians' traditional leadership was out of touch with the pulse of the street, the revolt turned to violence one month after its eruption. It quietened down in November 1936 after the Arab leadership called for an end to the strike. However, violence revived in September 1937 after the AHC rejected the Peel Commission's partition proposal and after the British sought to arrest the Mufti. The basic demands of the revolt were a cessation of Jewish immigration, prohibition of land sales to Jews, and the formation of a national government accountable to an elected representative council. More militant grass-root groups also demanded Palestine's independence as an Arab state.

The revolt led the British to apply harsh counterinsurgency measures. In September 1937 they ordered the dissolution of the AHC and arrested many of its leaders. Some, however, managed to escape, including the Mufti, who fled to Syria.

The 1936–39 revolt was disastrous for the Palestinians. About 10 percent of the Arab population of Palestine was either killed, injured, detained, or exiled by the British during its three years. The Palestinian economy was paralyzed and Palestinian military capacities were destroyed. Palestinians were disarmed: it was declared illegal for them to carry firearms, a ban the violation of which was punishable by death.[51]

The revolt also led to far closer cooperation between the British authorities and the newly created Jewish security forces. British army officers led by Colonel Orde Wingate now became engaged in training Zionist forces in counterinsurgency warfare.[52]

The outbreak of the violence in 1936 and the intensity of the subsequent Jewish–Arab confrontations also led the British Government to launch a reexamination of its overall strategy regarding Palestine. This reassessment was entrusted to a Royal Commission, chaired by Lord Robert Peel, which published a report in July 1937 recommending for the first time that Palestine be partitioned into two states: one Jewish, one Arab. The Arab state was to merge with Transjordan under Emir Abdullah. A third part, that would include Jerusalem, Bethlehem, and Nazareth, was to remain under British mandate. The Peel Commission also recommended that some "transfers" of Jewish and Arab populations should take place to ensure that the two states would be as homogeneous as possible.

The Arab Higher Committee rejected the Peel Commission's proposal, but the Arab Defense Party of Raghib Nashashibi accepted its recommendations. As a result, the latter was accused of cooperating with the British commission and with Emir Abdullah. The British considered Nashashibi a moderate while calling the Mufti a hard-liner and adopting a hostile view of the AHC.

While the Zionists accepted the Peel Commission's recommendations, the report's rejection by the Arab side led to another rethinking by the British government of its policy regarding Palestine. In May 1939, the Woodhead Commission published its report, recommending two different plans for partitioning Palestine into two states and a British mandatory zone. Plan A was similar if not largely identical to that proposed by the Peel Commission. Under Plan B, which was rejected by both sides, the size of the proposed Jewish state was to be reduced.

The rejection of the Woodhead Commission's proposals was followed by the failure of the St. James Round Table Conference of February–March 1939, during which the Jewish and

Figure 1.6. David Ben-Gurion. © Bettman/CORBIS

Arab delegates rejected the British proposal for resolving the conflict. This, in turn, led the British government to issue on May 17, 1939 a new statement of policy known as the *MacDonald White Paper*. It proposed the establishment of a unitary Palestine State of Arabs and Jews within ten years; a five-year plan of limited Jewish immigration to Palestine (up to 10,000 per year plus acceptance of another 25,000 as refugees); and severe restrictions on land transfers from Arabs to Jews in most parts of Palestine and a total prohibition of such transfers in other areas of Palestine.[53] The Zionist movement and the Arab Higher Committee rejected the offer, but the Nashashibi camp in the Committee favored its acceptance.[54]

Alongside the British government's effort to reconcile Zionist and Arab aspirations for Palestine as well its own conflicting commitments to the two sides, Arab leaders, some from inside Palestine but most from outside, also took part in intermittent contact with the leaders of the Yishuv in an effort to explore whether some understanding could be reached through direct talks. In Palestine, discussions were held between leaders representing the traditional Palestinian land-owning elite, like Musa Alami, and Zionist leaders, like Haim Weizmann and David Ben Gurion. Outside Palestine, efforts at engagement had been conducted by Zionist leaders and Emir Abdullah of Transjordan since as far back as 1937.[55] Similar talks were held by Zionist representatives and Egyptian Prime Minister Ismail Sidqi in August 1946.[56]

The Second World War

The Second World War led to another wave of Zionist–British cooperation in defense affairs. Following extensive negotiations with the British authorities, Yishuv leaders called upon the community's youth to volunteer for service in the British military. The policy adopted was that articulated by Ben Gurion, namely that Jews must "fight the White Paper as if there is no war, and fight the war as if there is no White Paper." The *Etzel* (the *Irgun*) at first accepted this priority, leading to the founding of yet another splinter group, *Lehi* [Fighters for the Freedom of Israel], called "The Stern Gang" by the British. *Lehi* leaders argued that the Zionists should continue the fight against British colonialism, despite the war.

Threatened by Britain's enemy – Nazi Germany – the Zionist movement and its institutions encouraged their youth to join the British armed forces in the fight against Hitler. But for this the Zionist organs extracted an important concession from the British authorities: after heavy advocacy by Haim Weizmann and Moshe Shertok (Sharett), youth recruited from the Yishuv, in addition to integrating in different units including the Royal Air Force, were also allowed to form a distinct unit within the British armed forces: the Jewish Brigade. This "reinforced brigade" was created in 1944, disbanded in 1946, and was composed of three infantry battalions largely made up of Palestinian Jewish units. After training in Egypt, the Jewish Brigade joined the Eighth Army and fought in Italy. In May 1945, they met Holocaust survivors for the first time and provided them with basic services, even smuggling some into Palestine.[57]

Earlier, within Palestine, units of the Yishuv's security forces – some trained by the British during the 1936–39 revolt – were integrated in British plans for guerrilla war against the Germans, in case General Erwin Rommel's forces were to defeat General Montgomery's forces in North Africa and then march on to Palestine. To combat this specific threat, the British and the *Haganah* jointly formed the *Palmach* [strike forces], a military unit designed to protect Palestine from Nazi invasion. Rommel's defeat led the British to disband the *Palmach*. However, its members, by now already well-trained, chose to defy the British order. Thus, the *Palmach* became an illegal armed force.

The Palestinian leadership was seen as opting for a different alliance during the war. With the Mufti meeting with Hitler in November 1941, the most prominent Palestinian leader had associated himself with Germany. Al-Husseini argued that Germany, unlike Britain and France, did not occupy or have designs for Arab land, had not deceived Arab nationalists as the British had, and, instead, recognized Arab and Palestinian aspirations to independence and self-determination. The Mufti's talks led to a November 1943 German statement supporting full independence for the Arab countries, including Palestine.

As news of the Holocaust began to spread during the final two years of the war, the Zionist movement began to articulate the demand for statehood more clearly. Earlier, on May 11, 1942, Ben Gurion proposed to place the quest for an independent state – and not simply a homeland, as promised in the Balfour Declaration – at the top of the Zionist movement's agenda. The location of the meeting where he proposed this – the Biltmore Hotel in New York City – represented another change in Zionist strategy: based on the assessment that the United States would emerge from the war as a very strong power, Zionist leaders now shifted the focus of their diplomatic efforts from London to New York and Washington, DC.

In the immediate aftermath of the War, the Arab states took the first steps toward the Arabization of the conflict – their assumption of primary responsibility for defeating the Zionists' designs. Thus, when in 1945 the League of Arab States was formed, it placed the question of Palestine at the top of its agenda. And in 1946, when Arab prime ministers met in Bludan in Syria, they took it upon themselves to appoint the members of the second Palestinian AHC and agreed that if the Palestinians were to fail to defend themselves, the Arab states would have no choice but to intervene militarily against the Jews.[58]

Zionist leaders assumed as much. Hence, when Ben Gurion was given responsibility in December 1946 for the defense portfolio of the Jewish Agency Executive, he initiated a complete retooling of the Yishuv's security forces from those geared to combat an insurgency challenge – as presented by Palestinian Arabs during the 1936–39 revolt – to the kind of force structure and doctrine that would be needed in the event of a conventional military attack by the surrounding Arab states.

Narratives

The Zionist Narrative

The Zionist narrative envisaged the movement as one of national liberation, created in response to anti-Semitism. In the eyes of Zionists the pogroms of the late 19th century proved once again that the populations of Eastern Europe – particularly Russians, Ukrainians, and Poles – were unwilling to accept Jews into their fold. Zionists attributed the hatred of Jews to one aspect of Diaspora life: that Jews were a minority everywhere. Social-democratic Zionists added a second reason: namely that Jews were barred from owning and cultivating land. The latter dimension was seen as having forced Jews to become the merchant class: buying agricultural products from peasants and selling them in the marketplace. In the eyes of social-democratic Zionists, Jews were seen by their gentile neighbors as greedy middlemen who bought the peasants' products cheaply and sold them in the marketplace for a high price.

Zionists also assessed that all previous attempts to address "the Jewish question" had failed. Efforts to reduce friction with the general population by limiting Jewish residence to specific locations [*Tchum Hamoshav*] could not solve the problem for more than a small number of Jews. Yet attempts at assimilation proved equally futile: in the eyes of the Zionists, Jews were rejected irrespective of the efforts they made to integrate into the larger societies in which they resided.

Given the two predicaments that made Diaspora life untenable, social-democratic Zionists argued that Jews must undergo a twofold revolution: they must have a homeland in which they would comprise an absolute majority, and they must connect to the land by farming it, rather than exploiting its products. While the issue of location – where Jews would establish a homeland – was a subject of some debate, most Zionists believed that only the Land of Israel could attract the imagination of Jews and persuade them to leave their homes and communities for a location where they could eventually comprise a clear majority.

The Land of Israel

The centrality of the Land of Israel in the Zionist narrative was tied to the effects of the rise of nationalism in Europe during the 19th century on the unique manner in which Jews regarded Judaism. Zionists regarded Jews as united not only by their common religion but much more so by their common "nationhood." Accordingly, the conviction that Jews must establish their homeland in the Land of Israel was not necessarily tied to a belief in the Bible as a *religious* document and, therefore, to the belief that Jews had a God-given right to the Holy Land. After all, most social-democratic Zionists, who comprised the first immigration waves and thus the core of the Yishuv, as well as most if not all of the movement's forefathers, were secular. Rather, it was their belief in the Bible as an *historical* document and its role in keeping Jews together for two millennia that propelled them to conclude that no other venue should be considered acceptable for establishing a Jewish National Home.

Could the establishment of such a national home in Palestine take place other than at the expense of the local Arab population? The Zionist narrative regarding this issue evolved over time. The forefathers of the movement in the late 19th century saw the Land of Israel as uninhabited. This was exemplified by the statement, "A People without a land to a Land without a people."[59] Thus, the Jews' return would be relatively painless because the indigenous population was believed to be very small.

When as early as the first decade of the 20th century it became clear that Palestine was not uninhabited, two additional narratives became central to explaining how the potential cost to the indigenous population resulting from the Jews' return could be addressed. The first saw the local population as inseparable from that of the surrounding Arab societies. Thus, Zionists saw the Arabs as comprising one "people" and those among them residing in Palestine as comprising merely part of a larger whole. As such, if those among the local population who may suffer the consequences of the Jews' return would be relocated to any one of the surrounding Arab lands, this should not be considered a major dislocation.

Second, Zionists saw European Jews relocating to Palestine as bringing modernity to an arid and backward land. Modernity, Zionists argued, would increase dramatically the absorption capacity of the land – it would allow gainful employment to a far larger population. During the 1920s and 1930s, the area's absorption capacity became an increasingly central theme of Zionist narrative. It was then that successive British governments tasked commissions to review Jewish immigration to Palestine – commissions that often attempted to limit such immigration based on conservative estimates of the land's absorption capacity.

The second part of the Zionist assessment – namely, that anti-Semitism was also propelled by the fact that Jews in the Diaspora were forced to comprise the merchant class – informed the stipulation that when establishing their homeland, it was imperative that Jews reinvent themselves by reconnecting with the land. This would be done by Zionists becoming peasants and farmers, and thereby living a life similar to those whose hatred in the Diaspora they suffered. Accordingly, unlike the small number of Jews who settled in Palestine during the 19th century and employed Arab laborers, the Zionist immigrants of the early 20th century insisted on tilling the land themselves. Thus, Hebrew Labor – *Avoda Ivrit* – became the slogan of the *Second Aliya*. As Zionists saw it, the purpose was not to deprive Arab laborers of gainful employment. Rather, it was to create a "new Jew" who could substitute the Diaspora middleman's way of life by working as hard as the lowest-paid Arab laborer.

Competing Priorities

As for the Zionist movement's purposes, the dominant narrative of social-democratic Zionist leaders like Berl Katzenelson and David Ben Gurion envisaged these as encompassing the following objectives: (a) the ingathering of Jews from the Diaspora to the Land of Israel; (b) the establishment of a society based on superior values of equality and social justice; (c) the achievement of peace with all neighbors; (d) the salvation of the Land of Israel by settling its entirety.

Within the Zionist movement, this narrative was challenged by the Revisionists who aspired to achieve the same goals except in reverse order of priorities. Thus, Revisionists argued that the salvation of the Land of Israel should take precedence over other Zionist goals. They further argued that the current generation of Zionists lacked the right and legitimacy to give up any part of the Land of Israel, since historically and religiously this land belonged to the Jewish people through all its past and future generations.

These two narratives came into collision when in 1937 the Zionist movement and the Yishuv in particular were required to react to the recommendations of the Peel Commission Report. For the mainstream of the Zionist movement the main advantage of the commission's offer was that statehood would mean the sovereignty to pursue an independent immigration policy and hence the ability to offer Jews a safe refuge. Yet, the area offered by the Peel Commission for the prospective Jewish state was but a fraction of what the Zionists considered to be the boundaries of the Land of Israel. For the Revisionists, who saw the salvation of the Land as the movement's highest priority, and even for some social democrats like Katzenelson and Golda Meir, such a concession was unacceptable.

The triumph of the mainstream and the resulting acceptance of the Peel Commission's recommendations by the organs of the Zionist movement figured centrally in the making of another important aspect of the dominant Zionist narrative: namely, that their movement was pragmatic – willing to go to any length to avoid conflict by accepting compromise proposals – while their Arab adversaries were dogmatic: never willing to accept anything short of everything they wanted.

Britain's Role

The debate about the Peel Commission report later became connected to another dimension of the Zionist narrative: namely, Britain's role in the Zionist enterprise. In varying degrees the different factions of the Zionist movement saw the British government as having regretted the commitment it made in the Balfour Declaration. Accordingly Britain was seen as making every attempt to reconcile this commitment with its competing interests in the region: currying favor with the larger Arab population in Palestine – and even more so, among the population of the surrounding Arab states – in order to secure its interests and continued influence in the Middle East.

Thus, the dominant Zionist narrative regarding the British role in the aftermath of the Balfour Declaration was that of betrayal. In the Zionists' eyes, Britain reneged on its promise to establish a home for the Jewish people in Palestine by limiting the number of Jews who would receive certificates for entering and settling in Palestine and by denying the Yishuv the means to defend itself against its Arab opponents. Britain was seen as having prevented the Yishuv from building properly equipped and trained security forces and as conducting repeated intrusive searches in Jewish settlements for illegal arms caches.

Zionists' anger at this perceived betrayal peaked in the late 1930s and early 1940s after the British failed to implement the recommendations of the Peel Commission and during the run-up to the Second World War. When, against a background of Jews being increasingly subjected to atrocities in Europe, the British government decided instead to implement the recommendations of the Whitehead Commission by limiting Jewish immigration to Palestine and by sending the British navy to turn back boatloads of Jewish refugees trying to escape Europe's horrors, British behavior was viewed as nothing less than treacherous.

This perception was only reinforced by the behavior of the Mufti during the war. With the photos of his visits to Germany symbolizing what Zionists now perceived to be an alliance of Palestinian Arab nationalists with the Nazis while Britain was at war with Nazi Germany, it was difficult for the Zionists to understand why Britain was assisting their Palestinian opponents.

Al-Husseini's association with the Nazis led to another element in the evolving Zionist narrative; namely, that they were facing murderous if not genocidal opponents. Thus, Zionists now came to believe that the struggle with the Palestinians was existential not only because the Palestinian nationalists' aim was to oppose the creation of a Jewish state but also because the fanaticism of the Mufti implied that if the Arabs were to defeat the Yishuv, Jews residing in Palestine would experience nothing short of physical extermination.

The Palestinian Narrative

The single most important element of the Palestinians' narrative during this period is that they, not the Zionists, were the rightful owners of Palestine. As the descendants of the *Canaanites*, Palestinians remained in their land throughout history. The Palestinian narrative emphasized that throughout this long period, with the sole exception of the last few decades of Ottoman rule in the aftermath of the emergence of Zionism, Jews and Arabs lived together in peace and harmony.

Palestinians also defined themselves as Muslims who accepted and lived under Ottoman rule until the end of the First World War. Believing that Palestine was an Islamic land, with religious sites sacred to all Muslims, the conflict was at times framed by Palestinians as a religious one in which they defended Muslim holy sites against Jewish desecration. Thus, the Palestinian nationalist conflict took religious overtones as Palestinians came to believe that Zionist Jews sought to claim ownership of *al-Buraq*,[60] an Islamic sacred site called by Jews the Western or Wailing Wall. Palestinians describe the 1929 violence as an attempt to prevent Zionist Jews from claiming ownership of a Muslim sacred site, thus changing the status quo that had prevailed there for centuries.

In the immediate aftermath of the First World War, Palestinians also saw themselves as part of a proud Arab nation that was struggling collectively to end the yoke of colonialism and to build a unified and sovereign state. In this regard, their goal in the early 1920s was to become part of a large Arab state, rather than to build a state of their own. For the first Palestine Congress, which met in Jerusalem in 1919, the main motivation was to insure that Palestine would be part of the Arab state and that the Balfour Declaration would not be implemented. The goal was to communicate a unified Palestinian position to the great powers' 1919–20 Paris Peace Conference in which they would affirm rejection of the Balfour Declaration and demand the implementation of the Wilsonian principle of self-determination. Very soon, however, with neighboring Arabs preoccupied with their own state-building projects, and with Arab states coming under different colonial powers' rule and different local governments, Palestinians, too, came to demand their own independence and statehood.

Perceptions of Zionism

Zionism was viewed by Palestinians as nothing but a tool of British colonialism, and the goal of a Jewish homeland or state was seen as an imperialist attempt to weaken and divide the Arab nation. The colonial powers were viewed as aiming to implant a foreign entity in a critical area, separating the Arabs of Asia from the Arabs of Africa, thereby impeding Arab territorial contiguity. In this context, the Balfour Declaration was seen as an instrument of British control designed to extend Britain's rule over Arab lands.

Palestinians emphasized that they had no quarrel with Jews, who had lived in their midst and could continue to live in Palestine as equal citizens. Rather, it was the Zionists, not Jews, who were rejected because they represented an existential threat to Palestinian Arabs. By definition, Zionism meant for Palestinians their eviction from their homeland and their replacement with foreign settlers. Zionists, with their belief that Palestine was a "land without people" were viewed as determined to conquer and control Palestine for the Jewish people, "the people without land." Indeed, Zionists' aim was seen as extending beyond Palestine to cover the whole region between the Nile and the Euphrates. For this reason, Palestinians were unwilling to engage Zionists or the British in any political or economic scheme that was based on the Balfour Declaration or the Mandate, viewing both as carrying the seeds of Palestinian national destruction.

British Deception and Palestinian Institution-Building

The British were seen as having deceived Arab nationalists led by Sharif Hussein; the Sykes–Picot Agreement of 1916 and the Balfour Declaration one year later were viewed as contradicting the promises to facilitate the creation of an independent Arab state made by Sir Henry McMahon to Sharif Hussein in 1915. As Palestinians saw it, it was this British deception and the continued British efforts, in collaboration with the French, to divide the Arab world and to build a Jewish home in Palestine that eventually forced them to seek the support of Britain's enemy, Germany under the Nazis. Hajj Amin al-Husseini's efforts in this regard were seen as justified, but as in no way constituting endorsement of Nazi racist goals or ideology.

Palestinians rejected efforts to include them in the governing bodies of the British Mandate's administration, viewing such efforts as attempts to trick them into endorsing the goals of the Mandate, including that of building a national home for the Jewish people in Palestine. By taking this position, Palestinians were willing to sacrifice an important goal: building national institutions and government in preparation for independence. This made the Palestinian colonial experience different from all other Arab experiences. It is in this context that one should read the Palestinians' rejection of the British proposals, in 1922 and again in 1936, to create a legislative council.

By rejecting British institution-building proposals, Palestinians were willing to pay a heavy price, as they lost the ability to organize national elections, select representatives, and influence British public policy in Palestine. They did, however, search for alternative ways to achieve these goals through building a process of decision making based on the formation of national conferences, the election of an executive, and continued engagement with the British authorities. In fact, it was these bodies that took the decision to reject British institution-building proposals. For Palestinians, therefore, failure at institution-building was the unintended, but also the unavoidable, consequence of the need to protect a greater national interest: to deny legitimacy to the Zionist project in Palestine.

Failure to Prevent Partition

Suspicion of British intentions was also responsible in part for rejecting the idea of partitioning Palestine between Jews and Arabs. Palestinians believed that the British had no intention of allowing the emergence of a viable Arab state even if Palestinians agreed to partition. But most importantly, they believed that they had the historic and religious right to all of Palestine and that there was no moral reason for them to concede any part of it to those whom they regarded as European settlers. Indeed, they viewed the whole land of Palestine as *Waqf*, a religious endowment that can never be conceded to non-Muslims. They saw partition as equivalent to the stealing of their homeland, since they owned almost all of the land and constituted the greatest percentage of the population. The few Palestinian leaders who advocated a more flexible position found themselves isolated from the street and shunned by other leaders.

Ultimately the Palestinians' narrative attributed their failure during this period to the enormity of the challenge they confronted and the modest resources available to them. Theirs was a rural society confronting modern European settlers brought in by the greatest colonial power of the day. In Palestinian eyes, the Zionists were far superior in many components of power: education, political organization, social norms and access to money, arms, and training. Most importantly, the Zionists had a patron who facilitated their immigration to Palestine, allowed them to acquire land and arms and encouraged their state-building efforts by formally recognizing and engaging their elected institutions and leaders. The British Mandate was seen as seeking to divide Palestinians, as having refused to formally recognize their political institutions, and as denying them the ability to organize and train for the inevitable moment of armed conflict with the Zionists.

The Arab Narrative

The Arab reaction to the question of Palestine largely focused on opposition to the establishment of a Jewish state. Arab objections had intensified during the period of the British Mandate in Palestine, in the aftermath of the First World War and the 1919–20 Paris Peace Conference. With the San Remo Conference of April 19–26, 1920 announcing the adoption of the Balfour Declaration, Arabs concluded that the British and French Mandates in the region would support the creation of a Jewish state in Palestine. Arabs' general opposition to Zionism during this period was based on the increasingly important Arab nationalist ideas that were developed predominantly in the Levant and the Arab *Mashreq*.[61] These ideas launched and accelerated the anti-colonial nationalist movements in Egypt and Greater Syria, including Palestine.[62]

The termination of the Ottoman Empire in 1922 and of the Islamic Caliphate in Istanbul in 1924 intensified Arab emotions towards Palestine. In Arab eyes, the Mufti now became the symbol of Palestinian resistance for decades to come.[63] Between the two world wars, al-Husseini had focused Arab anger on the Jewish settlements, immigration, and land purchases. In 1929, renewed Arab protests in Palestine were also seen as connected with Arab disappointment with the unfulfilled promise to establish an Arab state in Greater Syria, a promise shattered when Britain ceded Syria and Lebanon to France in 1920. Al-Husseini then gained broader Arab support for his efforts to create a Palestinian state with Jerusalem as its capital.

Arab Nationalism and the Arab Revolt

The emergence of the idea of Arab nationalism was an important supporting factor in building an Arab collective awareness of the question of Palestine. Therefore, the Arab rejectionists fiercely opposing the settlement of Jews in Palestine had gained ground particularly in the Levant – in Syria and Lebanon – where the roots of Arab nationalism were developing. In Egypt the evolution of nationalism seemed to follow a different path. Egyptian nationalism focused on opposition to the British mandate, and its intellectual class emphasized Egypt's roots as a Mediterranean civilization and as an heir to the Pharonic civilization. Thus, up to and during the 1920s, Egyptians' conception of the Palestine question was still in its preliminary phase.[64] The first expression of collective support for the Palestinians came only in 1931 in a meeting of representatives of 22 Arab and Islamic states or proto-states.[65]

In 1933, as Hitler's rise to power resulted in increased Jewish immigration to Palestine, Arabs concluded that their efforts to curb such immigration by communicating their objections to the British authorities had failed. The resulting revolt of 1936–39 presented a portrait of anti-colonial resistance familiar to most Arab countries that were facing similar challenges. The Arab press that covered and reported the events in Palestine conveyed pictures and stories of oppression, raising Arabs' empathy toward the Palestinians. The latter were seen as facing not only the superior power of the British imperial army, but also a Zionist movement determined to take over the land of Palestine. Palestinian delegations toured Arab capitals to explain their peoples' dire situation and ask their Arab and Muslim brothers for help.

The Arab street reacted quickly to the events in Palestine, as civil society organizations mobilized resources to help the Palestinians.[66] Arab political movements, whether national or religious, raced to provide relief for the Palestinian victims of British and Zionist atrocities.

Political Parties' Reactions

The outbreak of the Second World War in 1939 galvanized Arab collective awareness of the question of Palestine. The majority of nationalists and Islamic movements, notably the Muslim Brotherhood in Egypt, were strongly opposed to the Jewish settlement in Palestine. However, other political players in the Arab intelligentsia, especially in Egypt, held positions that differed from the Arab mainstream and general public opinion. For them, Egypt's major problem was the British. They also believed that Egypt's development should receive priority over involvement abroad.

Aware of this debate, the Jewish Agency was said to have utilized the existence of wealthy privileged Jewish minorities in the Arab states to establish contacts with some major political players in these countries.[67] Meanwhile, in Transjordan, Emir Abdullah was said to have established direct contacts with the Jewish Agency in the framework of which the Agency succeeded in securing his support for partition. The grand bargain was to allow the annexation of the Arab lands in Palestine to Jordan.[68]

Analysis

At the birth of the Zionist movement in the late 19th century, Jews were a tiny minority in Palestine. Against all odds and barely fifty years later, Jews comprised a fully developed community there, a proto-state prepared to assume all the burdens of independent statehood. By contrast, all efforts by Arabs in general and Palestinians in particular to abort the project at its inception had failed. What accounts for the success of the Zionist movement and the failure of the Palestinians to thwart its designs?

The International and Regional Systems

At the *systemic level*, the international scene presented both opportunities and constraints for both sides. The decay and final collapse of the Ottoman Empire created a vacuum of political legitimacy that the colonial powers, particularly Britain and France, and the new emerging national movements of Jews and Palestinians, raced to fill. Thus, the forces of modernization and the reach of the industrial revolution that touched the Middle East released the new forces of nationalism and the pursuit of self-determination. This was particularly true for the Jewish national movement which, given its European origins, carried the traditions of European nation-state-building.

On the Arab side, the same forces, while touched by the same new modes of nationalism - local, Arab, and Muslim - but in competition and rivalry with Jewish nationalism, were born in societies that were still suffering from centuries of Ottoman decadence and backwardness. The dominance of the British Empire in collaboration with the region's local nationalisms - Arab and Jewish - gave Britain an opportunity to consolidate its dominance by issuing contradictory promises to all parties: the French, the Arabs and the Jews.

The Zionist movement benefited from the fact that during the First World War Britain felt it needed the assistance of Jews both inside and outside Palestine. Aside from the willingness of some Jews in Palestine to create a spy network in Britain's service, Zionists outside Palestine joined the fighting on the British side by forming a military transport unit. Even more important was Haim Weizmann's contribution to the production of acetone. Finally, the Zionist project also served Britain's interest by introducing an element of constant friction, thus channeling Arab attention away from opposition to Britain's rule and influence. In this respect the Zionist movement benefited from the British Empire's attempt to sustain itself through a policy of "divide and rule."

When the British finally recognized the threat posed by the large number of illegal weapons in Palestine, they decided to raid storage facilities used by both Arabs and Jews. But these raids barely put a dent in both sides' overall holdings.[69] So while both the Arabs and the Zionists stockpiled weapons during this period, the better-trained forces of the Yishuv gained the upper hand over the disorganized and ill-trained Palestinian irregulars.

The peak of Zionist–British cooperation in defense affairs took place during the Second World War. Many young Jews from Palestine were integrated in different units of the British armed forces, including the Royal Air Force, and some joined a distinct Jewish fighting unit: the Jewish Brigade. The benefit to the Zionist movement was that many young Jews now received training in conventional warfare and in the command and management of large military formations. This experience would prove extremely valuable immediately after the War as the Yishuv prepared for the possibility that its independence would be challenged by the armies of neighboring Arab states.

Another hindrance to Arabs' ability to resist the Zionist project was at the interface between the international and regional levels: the decision of Britain and France in 1916 to carve the Middle East into separate spheres of influence. This introduced another element of "divide and rule," as Arabs were now divided between the big powers' different spheres of influence, along the lines agreed upon by Sykes and Picot, making it difficult for them to unite in opposition to the Zionists.

Yet the systemic level held at least as many opportunities for the Arab side. First, it seemed that the Arabs were much more important than the embryonic Jewish community in Palestine in Britain's conflict with the Ottoman Empire during the First World War. Indeed it was the expectation that they would contribute to the British war effort and the desire to avoid Arabs contributing to the Ottomans that led to Britain's commitment to the Arab side in the form of the McMahon letter of 1915. Clearly, the Arabs could offer Britain what the Jews could not – large numbers in a strategic location: along the passage to India.

Neither was it a foregone conclusion that Zionists would be more successful in persuading the great powers of the legitimacy and justice of their claims. Certainly, they were aided by the existence of Jewish communities in Britain and the United States. Key British and American Zionists gave the movement access to the highest echelons in both governments, whereas neither country had a significant Arab community. Yet the British Jewish community was docile, ever-sensitive to its role in British society at large. The American Jewish community of the 1930s was also careful, fearing it would be accused of pushing the United States to enter a war in Europe, a war referred to by many isolationist opponents of intervention as "the Jews' War."[70]

By contrast, there was considerable public sympathy for the Arab cause, particularly in Britain. The Oriental Club in London was home to an important part of the British elite – former diplomats and Army officers who had served in Arab lands and had developed a fondness for Arab culture and language. While this was not necessarily the case in the United States, up to the outbreak of the Second World War it was not clear that Zionist diplomacy would win the Great Powers' support.

In the immediate aftermath of the war, the international arena had changed dramatically – the enormous effect of the Holocaust provided the Zionists with a huge moral advantage. To many in the United States and Europe the Holocaust provided the ultimate evidence and conclusive proof that the Zionist narrative of Jews' right to sovereign state independence was correct. For many in Britain and the United States this was coupled with remorse for their own failure both before and during the war to provide a refuge to Jews attempting to escape the Nazi horrors and to bomb the facilities of the Nazi death machine.

The enormity of the atrocities committed by the Nazis made the decision of Hajj Amin al-Husseini to seek the support of Germany against the British during the war nothing short of disastrous. In the immediate aftermath of the war, Palestinians were seen in many corridors in Britain and the United States as having sided with the perpetrators of the Nazi horrors.

The Palestinian Domestic Scene

At the *unit level* focusing on the parties' domestic scenes, both sides in the escalating conflict were highly fragmented. Palestinians were divided between their urban elite and the rural peasants, and their elite was divided between the more hard-line Husseinis and the dovish Nashashibis. Moreover, for a long time Palestinian leaders could not determine who the greater enemy was: the British Mandate or the Zionists.

Palestinian society was not prepared for a confrontation with either the British or the Zionists. Living for centuries under Ottoman rule, Palestinians had never had a political entity or political organization worth mentioning; their elite was fragmented and their national identity was weak. Urbanization and education were limited, while the peasantry dominated the landscape under the shadow of a significant absentee landownership. The resistance Palestinians were able to mount was, therefore, limited and fragmented.

The failure of the 1936–39 revolt had devastating consequences for Palestinians' ability to meet the challenges of the war period. While Zionists built a defense apparatus and acquired arms, Palestinians were leaderless, their economy destroyed and their society demoralized. Their rejection of the various partition ideas, their inability to relate to the British colonial power in a state-building manner, and their inability to build independent Palestinian institutions and rise above personal and family loyalties doomed their efforts to prevent the impending collapse.

During the period between 1918 and 1936, Palestinian leaders, including the Mufti, sought to maintain friendly relations with the British Mandate authorities despite their opposition to the Mandate and its terms, especially its commitment to implementing the Balfour Declaration. Representing this view, Boulus Shehadeh, a prominent Palestinian notable, wrote in the *Mirat al-Sharq* newspaper on September 26, 1925: "The only way for the [Arab] nation to succeed is by reaching an understanding and cooperating with the British government." But others, most prominently the Arab Independence Party, saw the British Mandate as the prime threat to Palestinian independence.

During the 1936–39 revolt such fragmentation peaked. In addition, the British expelled members of the elite who were considered competent and therefore a threat to their control.[71] As a result, Palestinian violence degenerated to a long series of uncoordinated actions.

The Palestinian decision to reject Britain's proposal to create a legislative council had far-reaching consequences for Palestinian institution-building, as the Palestinians lost the ability to organize national elections, select representatives, and influence British public policy in Palestine. Some Palestinian leaders, notably Awni Abdel Hadi, argued at the time that by rejecting the legislative council, the Palestinians denied themselves an important tool to limit Jewish immigration. But others argued that accepting the council would harm the goal of real independence and constitute an indirect acceptance of the Mandate and its mission.

By the mid-1930s, it was clear that Palestinian institution-building efforts had proved inadequate to meet the challenges that confronted them. Leaders of the Arab Congress were "older politicians," who had gradually lost contact with their masses. By the mid-1930s these older leaders were being challenged by younger politicians, such as Hajj Amin, who led the nationalist camp between 1936 and 1948. More importantly, family and tribal allegiances and rivalries plagued both the older and the younger leadership. For example, competition between al-Husseini and al-Nashashibi prevented the Arab Congress from meeting between 1928 and 1936. The vacuum was filled by several political parties and trade and labor unions.[72] The congress and its executive committee, however, were unable to lead, as they had no role in some of the major events during this period, including the major Jewish–Arab violence of 1929 and the 1936 revolt.

The Zionist Movement and the Yishuv

The Zionist movement and the Jewish Yishuv in Palestine were no less divided. At first, they were torn primarily between "diplomatic Zionism" and "practical Zionism" – those emphasizing the need to cultivate close relations with the colonial power, and those who called for focusing on the need to create "facts on the ground" through settlement activity. Later they became increasingly divided between the social democrats, who emphasized the need for statehood, and the Revisionists, who, though initially accepting of the mainstream position, later argued against conceding any part of the Land of Israel. In 1936–39 they were further divided between those who advocated harsh retaliation to Arab efforts to derail the Zionist enterprise, and those who called for *Havlaga* [restraint] in the face of such attacks.

During the Second World War, the Jewish Yishuv was torn between the social democratic mainstream that advocated cooperation with the British against the common Nazi enemy and the Revisionists who argued that the struggle for liberation from the British colonial rule should continue as if Nazi Germany did not exist. The internal debate turned violent when the former camp allegedly "informed on" Revisionists who planned attacks against the British forces in Palestine while the war went on and turned them in to the British authorities.

Accordingly, what accounts for the success and failure of the two movements seems to have had less to do with their relative internal fragmentation than with their relative progress or lack thereof in the realm of institution-building which enabled a mediation of differences and the integration of contending elements into a more-or-less coherent whole. In this process the two sides differed greatly. While the British encouraged both sides to develop proto-state institutions – hoping that these institutions would take care of all local matters, thus reducing the burden of the colonial authorities – the Jewish Yishuv took full advantage of these offers while their Palestinian neighbors did not.

As a consequence, when the British decided to leave Palestine, the Yishuv was fully prepared to take their place. Its institutions, formally under the umbrella of the Jewish Agency, paralleled those of a national government: every division, branch, and department of the agency had roles and missions equivalent to a government ministry. Hence, they could smoothly slide into their new role of running the institutions of state.

Hajj Amin al-Husseini

The relative success and failure of the Zionists and their Arab opponents can also be traced to differences at the *individual level*. The dominant Palestinian figure during this period, overshadowing all others, was Hajj Amin al-Husseini. With a leadership style that marginalized others, he failed to build coalitions with other national leaders. This contributed to greater leadership fragmentation and undermined efforts to create strong public institutions. His tendency to adopt hard-line views led to a Palestinian failure to take advantage of changes in British policy in the late 1930s, such as those exemplified in the 1939 White Paper – changes that would have ultimately served Palestinian purposes. His failure to build an effective military force and his tendency to underestimate the capacity of the Zionist forces led him to make grave strategic mistakes. Indeed, his support for violence against far more superior forces doomed all Palestinian efforts to abort the Zionist and British designs for Palestine.

Leading the Arab revolt in 1936, and emerging as its chief architect, al-Husseini openly supported violence during the revolt, sought an alliance with the Germans and abandoned any notion of a dialogue and cooperation with the British. But by then Palestinian violence was in no position to challenge what had meanwhile become a viable Zionist entity or to stand against a much more powerful British military. By allying himself with Nazi Germany during the war, in exchange for a German promise that Arabs and Palestinians would be granted independence after it, he tainted the Palestinian cause and seriously damaged if not totally destroyed any chance of international support for the Palestinians in the immediate postwar period.

Al-Husseini's rise to prominence had other negative consequences for Palestinian politics. Given his leadership style, his rise – taking place in a traditional, weak, and fragmented society – generated internal friction and elite rivalry, greatly weakening Palestinian institution-building. Most importantly, more than any other Palestinian figure during this period, Hajj Amin contributed to the formulation of an uncompromising Palestinian position, a position that rejected any and all compromises with the British or the Zionists over the future of Palestine. Thus, when in 1939 the British government presented a White Paper most favorable to the Palestinian side – a paper viewed as such by a number of Palestinian leaders – al-Husseini, already bitter and defeated, rejected it out of hand.[73]

Haim Weizmann

On the Zionist side, no person played as important a role and contributed more to the movement during its formative years than Dr. Haim Weizmann. The diplomatic effort to gain international support for the creation of a Jewish state was one of the two pillars of the Zionist project during this period – the other being settlement construction. In this context, gaining the commitment of Britain for the enterprise in the form of the Balfour Declaration was of critical importance. Yet the Declaration, as well as other forms of international support during the subsequent two decades, could not have been gained if it were not for Weizmann's unique attributes: his stature as a gifted scientist acting in Britain's interests during the First World War, as well as his outstanding diplomatic skills.[74]

Charisma, perseverance, dedication, openness to new, original, and often conflicting ideas, organizational capacity, and adaptability to changing political circumstances were only some of the attributes of Weizmann's personality. For the British elite, whose support he needed, Weizmann could display strong passion, even anger, and equal doses of charm. He could play to his listeners' emotions – manipulating British religious and cultural sentiments for the "Holy Land." He played to the mildly anti-Semitic premises of the British elite and other world leaders about the influence of Jews worldwide. Indeed, he excelled in manipulating such assumptions to advance the Zionist cause by enhancing his listeners' beliefs about Jewish influence. With a unique combination of dedication and audacity and the display of equal doses of emotions, rational thinking, and humor, Weizmann could win the support of the most skeptical, if not initially hostile, counterpart.[75]

Concluding Notes

This chapter traced the sources of the Arab–Israeli conflict by characterizing, portraying, and analyzing its formative years. It ascertained the emergence of the two national movements that came to clash over the land between the Jordan River and the Mediterranean: Arab nationalism which later gave birth to its specific Palestinian variety, and Zionism, the Jewish national movement. The roots of the two movements were very different: one expressing the desire of the area's inhabitants to gain freedom from Ottoman rule, the other seeking a solution to anti-Semitism – a dark offspring of the rise of nationalism in western, and especially eastern, Europe.

As the conflict between the two movements evolved and escalated, their competing narratives also began to crystallize. The common denominator of the two narratives was their main characteristic: mutual denial. The Arab national movement and, later, Palestinian nationalism denied any connection between the Jews and the area that has come be known as Palestine and which Jews saw as the Land of Israel. On its part, the Zionist movement denied that the Arabs who saw themselves as the indigenous population of Palestine had the right as a people to the same land. Thus, the two narratives were mutually exclusive, feeding a conflict that was increasingly measured in existential terms. In turn, this existential dimension contributed to making the conflict – even in its early days – so resistant to the efforts to resolve it, then and in decades to come.

The chapter also showed how the balance of power between Zionists and Palestinian nationalists changed to the latter's detriment during the first four decades of the 20th century. First, while both were caught in the web of contradictory promises that the British made to Arabs and Zionists in their effort to defeat the Ottomans during the First World War, the Zionist movement proved more successful in navigating its way between these competing British impulses. In this, Zionists were clearly aided by the victory of the Allies over the Axis in the Second World War and the enormous sympathy that their cause gained among the public and elites in western Europe, and especially the United States, as a consequence of the Holocaust.

Another important reason why the Zionist movement surged during the first half of the 20th century while the Palestinians failed to thwart its designs was the choices the two movements made with respect to the offers presented to them by the British Empire.

Both opposed central tenets of British policies: the Arabs rejected any idea of partitioning Palestine and the Zionists opposed any attempt to restrict immigration. But the Zionists gained by taking advantage of the British invitation to establish state-like institutions while the Palestinians lost by rejecting such offers on the grounds that they entailed formal acceptance of the British Mandate, which included the commitment to establish a national home for the Jewish people in Palestine.

But possibly the most important of all was the gap between the quality and skillfulness of the individuals who led the two camps: Haim Weizmann and David Ben Gurion were at once grand-strategists and pragmatic tacticians. By contrast, Hajj Amin al-Husseini seemed to ally the Palestinians with Nazi Germany, thereby losing any sympathy that they might otherwise have won among the victorious powers. Having failed earlier to build the institutions of state, having experienced even greater fragmentation than their Zionist opponents, and having been led by dogmatic leaders, it was not surprising that by the mid-1940s the Palestinians found themselves at a serious disadvantage.

Readings

Avineri, Shlomo *The Making of Modern Zionism: The Intellectual Origins of the Jewish State* (Basic Books, 1981).

Bickerton, Ian and Carla Klausner, *A History of the Arab–Israeli Conflict* (Prentice Hall, 2010) 15–73.

Caplan, Neil, *The Israel–Palestine Conflict: Contested Histories* (Wiley, 2010) 39–100.

Dowty, Alan, *Israel/Palestine: Global Political Hotspots* (Polity, 2012) 12–71.

Eisenberg, Laura Zittrain and Neil Caplan, *Negotiating Arab–Israeli Peace: Patterns, Problems, Possibilities* (Indiana University Press, 2010) 1–34.

Gelvin, James, *The Israel–Palestine Conflict: One Hundred Years of War* (Cambridge University Press, 2007) 1–115.

Khalidi, Rashid, *Palestinian Identity: The Construction of Modern National Consciousness* (Columbia University Press, 1997).

Kramer, Gudrun, *A History of Palestine: From the Ottoman Conquest to the Founding of the State of Israel* (Princeton University Press, 2011)

Lesch, David, *The Arab–Israeli Conflict* (Oxford University Press, 2008) 1–93.

Morris, Benny, *Righteous Victims: The History of the Zionist–Arab Conflict, 1881–2001* (Vintage, 2001) 37–160.

Shlaim, Avi, *The Iron Wall: Israel and the Arab World* (W.W. Norton, 2001) 1–27.

Smith, Charles D., *Palestine and the Arab–Israeli Conflict* (Bedford/St.Martin's, 2007) 12–164.

Tessler, Mark, *A History of the Israeli–Palestinian Conflict* (Indiana University Press, 2009) 1–122.

Historical documents

1648 Peace of Westphalia: available online at The Avalon Project at Yale Law School http://avalon.law.yale.edu/17th_century/westphal.asp.

The Balfour Declaration: Walter Laqueur and Barry Rubin, *The Israel–Arab Reader: A Documentary History of the Middle East Conflict* (Penguin Books, 2008), 16.

The British Mandate: Laqueur and Rubin, *The Israel–Arab Reader*, 30–36.

The McMahon Letter: Laqueur and Rubin, *The Israel–Arab Reader*, 11–12; full correspondence available online at http://www.mideastweb.org/mcmahon.htm (accessed April 22 2013).
The Peel Commission: Laqueur and Rubin, *The Israel–Arab Reader*, 41–43.
The Sykes–Picot Agreement: Laqueur and Rubin, *The Israel–Arab Reader*, 13–16.
The Weizmann–Faisal Agreement: Laqueur and Rubin, *The Israel–Arab Reader*, 17–18.
The White Paper: Laqueur and Rubin, *The Israel–Arab Reader*, 44–50.
Zionist Reaction to the White Paper: Laqueur and Rubin, *The Israel–Arab Reader*, 50–51.
The Haycraft Commission Report.
The Hope-Simpson Report: full text available online at http://www.mideastweb.org/hopesimpson.htm (accessed April 22 2013).
The Passfield–White Paper: full text available online at http://www.mideastweb.org/passfieldwp.htm (accessed April 22 2013).
Shaw Commission Report.

Notes

1. Albert Hourani, *A History of the Arab Peoples* (London: Faber and Faber, 2002), 265–267.
2. George Antonius, *The Arab Awakening: The Story of the Arab National Movement* (Philadelphia: J.B. Lippincott, 1938), 35–60.
3. Hourani, *A History of the Arab Peoples*, 273.
4. *Ibid.*
5. Moshe Ma'oz, ed., *Studies on Palestine during the Ottoman Period* (Jerusalem: Magnes, 1975) and Shimon Shamir, "Egyptian Rule (1832–1840) and the Beginning of the Modern Period in the History of Palestine," in *Egypt and Palestine: A Millennium of Association (868–1948)*, ed. Amnon Cohen and Gabriel Baer (Jerusalem: Ben-Zvi Institute for the Study of Jewish Communities in the East, 1984), 220–221.
6. Samih K. Farsoun and Christina E. Zacharia, *Palestine and the Palestinians* (Boulder: Westview, 1997), 21–48.
7. Salim Tamari, *Mountain Against the Sea: Essays on Palestinian Society and Culture* (Berkeley, CA: University of California Press, 2009), 4–10.
8. Mustafa Kabha, *Journalism in the Eye of the Storm: The Palestinian Press Shapes Public Opinion 1929–1939* (Jerusalem: Yad Ben-Zvi, 2004), 11 and 14.
9. Ami Ayalon, *The Press in the Arab Middle East: A History* (New York: Oxford University Press, 1995), 55.
10. See Roberto Bachi, *The Population of Israel* (Jerusalem: Institute of Contemporary Jewry, Hebrew University of Jerusalem [and] Demographic Center, Prime Minister's Office, 1974), 31–33 and 367–370; and *Palestine, Report and General Abstracts of the Census of 1922, Taken on the 23rd of October, 1922*, compiled by J.B. Barron (Jerusalem: Greek Convent Press, 1923).
11. Kabha, *Journalism in the Eye of the Storm*, 15.
12. Walter Laqueur and Barry M. Rubin, *The Israel–Arab Reader: A Documentary History of the MiddleEast Conflict* (New York: Penguin, 2008), 58–59 and 123; United States Holocaust Memorial Museum, "Pogroms," Holocaust Encyclopedia, http://www.ushmm.org/wlc/en/article.php?ModuleId=10005183 (accessed April 22 2013); Paul R. Brass, ed., *Riots and Pogroms* (New York: New York University Press, 1996); Jan T. Gross, *Fear: Anti-Semitism in Poland After Auschwitz: An Essay in Historical Interpretation* (New York: Random House, 2006); *Kielce –July 4, 1946: Background, Context and Events* (Chicago: The Polish Educational Foundation in North America,

1996); John D. Klier and Shlomo Lambroza, ed., *Pogroms: Anti-Jewish Violence in Modern Russian History* (Cambridge: Cambridge University Press, 1992); and Stanislaw Meducki, "The Pogrom in Kielce on 4 July 1946," *Polin: Studies in Polish Jewry*, 9 (1996), 158–169.

13. Catane, Moshe, "Dreyfus, Alfred", *Encyclopaedia Judaica*, ed. Michael Berenbaum and Fred Skolnik, 2nd ed. Vol. 6 (Detroit: Macmillan Reference USA, 2007), 18–19. Gale Virtual Reference Library.
14. See "The Turkish Factor", in Neil Caplan, *Futile Diplomacy*, vol. 1, *Early Arab-Zionist Negotiation Attempts, 1913–1931* (London: Frank Cass, 1983), 14–16 and Neville J. Mandel, *The Arabs and Zionism Before World War I* (Berkeley: University of California Press, 1976).
15. Laqueur and Rubin, *The Israel-Arab Reader*, 213; Tessler, *A History of the Israeli–Palestinian Conflict*, 185; *Great Britain, Palestine Royal Commission Report* [Peel Commission] (London: H.M. Stationery Office 1937), 300.
16. The term "Aliya" refers to an immigration wave. The literal translation of the word is "ascend."
17. Tessler, *A History of the Israeli–Palestinian Conflict*, 186.
18. The aggregate numbers presented in these paragraphs are based on data compiled from the following sources: Mitchell G. Bard, "British Restrictions on Jewish Immigration," *Jewish Virtual Library*, http://www.jewishvirtuallibrary.org/jsource/History/mandate.html (accessed April 22 2013); Arieh Avneri, *The Claim of Dispossession* (Tel Aviv: Hidekel, 1984), 28; Yehoshua Porath, *The Emergence of the Palestinian-Arab National Movement, 1918–1929*, vol. 1 (London: Frank Cass, 1974), 17–18; Aharon Cohen, *Israel and the Arab World* (New York: Funk and Wagnalls, 1970), 53; Great Britain Colonial Office, *Palestine: Report on Immigration, Land Settlement and Development* [and Appendix Containing Maps], compiled by John Hope Simpson (London: H.M. Stationery Office, 1930), 126; and Tessler, *A History of the Israeli-Palestinian Conflict*, 185–186.
19. Anita Shapira, *A History of Israel* (Waltham, MA: Brandeis University Press, 2012), 67.
20. Walter Gribbon and Aaron Aaronsohn, eds., *Agents of Empire: Anglo-Zionist Intelligence Operations 1915–1919* (Washington, DC: Brassey's, 1995), 1–10.
21. Shapira, *A History of Israel*, 69.
22. Originally called the Assyrian Refugee Mule Corps, the group was made up of Russian Jewish refugees from Ottoman Palestine who were living in refugee camps in Alexandria, and Sephardi Jews residing in Egypt. On his standard issue British Army uniform, each soldier wore a Star of David cap badge. However, instead of Palestine, the ZMC was sent to Gallipoli, Turkey, to supply the troops there. Though strictly defined as a support unit, due to the nature of the Gallipoli theater, the ZMC experienced as much bombardment as combat units serving in the same area. See Martin Watts, *The Jewish Legion and the First World War* (New York: Palgrave Macmillan, 2004), 20–47. With the arrival of ZMC veterans in England in 1916, Jabotinsky was able to convince the British government to form a Jewish fighting force, named the Jewish Legion, which comprised three battalions of American, British, and Russian Jews, along with a mix of other members from neutral or allied countries, which would help with the liberation of Palestine from the Ottomans. See Joseph B. Schechtman, "Jewish Legion," *Encyclopaedia Judaica*, ed. Michael Berenbaum and Fred Skolnik. 2nd ed. Vol. 11 (Detroit: Macmillan Reference USA, 2007), 303–306.
23. Jehuda Reinharz, *Chaim Weizmann: The Making of a Statesman* (New York: Oxford University Press, 1993), 77–81.
24. T.E. Lawrence, popularly known as Lawrence of Arabia, served in the British Military Intelligence Office in Cairo starting in 1915 and later went to the Hejaz and formed close relationships with Sharif Hussein and his son Emir Faisal. Jeremy Wilson, "T.E. Lawrence: a biographical summary," *T.E. Lawrence Studies*, May 10, 2011 http://telawrence.info/telawrenceinfo/life/biog_biog.shtml.

25. Sharif, or a descendent from prophet Mohamed, Hussein bin Ali proclaimed himself to be a Caliph of all Muslims. He ruled Mecca and the Hijaz area of the Arabian Peninsula until 1924 when he abdicated his kingdom and other titles to his son Ali after he was defeated by King Abdel Aziz Al Saud, the founder of the Saudi family rulers of Saudi Arabia today. Joshua Teitelbaum, *The Rise and Fall of the Hashemite Kingdom of the Hijaz* (New York: New York University Press, 2001).
26. Porath, *The Emergence of the Palestinian-Arab National Movement*, 322.
27. M.E. Yapp, *The Making of the Modern Near East* (Harlow: Pearson, 1989), 277.
28. Laqueur and Rubin, *The Arab–Israeli Reader*, 16.
29. Caplan, *Futile Diplomacy*; Neville J. Mandel, "Attempts at an Arab–Zionist Entente: 1913–1914," *Middle Eastern Studies* 1, 3 (April 1965), 238–267; and Mandel, *The Arabs and Zionism Before World War I*.
30. *Filisteen* wrote on May 29, 1912 of the impact of Jewish immigration on Palestinians: "the current hardships and increase in cost of living felt by us is due to the continuous increase in the number of Jewish immigrants who refuse to integrate into the general population and instead establish their own neighborhoods and markets." Raghib al Khalidi, one of the main Palestinian notables wrote in *Filisteen* around the same time (April 2, 1913) that "the waves of foreign immigration is drowning us." Najib Nassar, editor of *al Karmel* newspaper, wrote on September 19, 1913 that the Palestinians are in grave danger as their own existence "is threatened by another nation that has proved itself strong, alive, hardworking, and self-reliant." *Al Karmel* wrote on December 2, 1913 that Jewish separate life and commitment to a historic legacy was a threat. But concern about a Jewish homeland in Palestine did not become widespread until 1918 in the aftermath of the collapse of the Ottoman Empire and the issuance of the Balfour declaration. Tessler, *A History of the Israeli-Palestinian Conflict*, 148–150.
31. Faisal had also been given authority to speak for the Arabs of Palestine who, due to British constraints, were not allowed to attend. "[T]he authorization of Faysal to represent the Palestinians was sent by the Jerusalem MCA on the basis of a resolution favouring political unity, but insisting that Palestine must enjoy complete internal autonomy within the framework of that unity." Porath, *The Emergence of the Palestinian-Arab National Movement 1918–1929*, 85–86.
32. Faisal-Weizmann Agreement Preamble. "Document 8: Text of Agreement between Amir Faisal and Dr Chaim Weizmann, 3 January 1919," in Caplan, *Futile Diplomacy. Vol. 1*, 145–147.
33. Faisal later claimed that he made this concession because Weizmann specified that the Zionists did not wish to pursue an independent state. Ann Mosely Lesch, *Arab Politics in Palestine 1917–1939* (Ithaca, NY: Cornell University Press, 1979), 133–134.
34. "[Faysal] had been willing to parley with Weizmann in 1918 and 1919 in the hope of obtaining diplomatic and financial aid against French designs on Syria… [He] hoped for Zionist financial aid and diplomatic backing." Lesch, *Arab Politics in Palestine*, 132–134.
35. Antonius, *The Arab Awakening: The Story of the Arab National Movement*, 437–439.
36. Gudrun Krämer, *A History of Palestine: From the Ottoman Conquest to the Founding of the State of Israel*, trans. Graham Harman and Gudrun Krämer (Princeton: Princeton University Press, 2008), 160; Lesch, *Arab Politics in Palestine*, 133.
37. For details on Faisal's view of the Zionist project, see the interview he gave to the *Jewish Chronicle*, October 3, 1919, reproduced in Caplan, *Futile Diplomacy*, 153–157 and 157–159. On how Palestinians viewed the reports about a Faisal–Weizmann agreement, see also Musa Kazim al-Husseini's remarks from October 8, 1919 in Document 14, Caplan, *Futile Diplomacy*, 157–159.
38. Anglo-American Committee of Inquiry on Jewish Problems in Palestine and Europe, and United Nations General Assembly Special Committee on Palestine. *A Survey of Palestine: prepared in*

December 1945 and January 1946 for the information of the Anglo-American Committee of Inquiry (Washington, DC: Institute for Palestine Studies), 17.

39. *Ibid.*, 18.
40. Sir Thomas Waystaffe Haycraft, *Palestine: Disturbances in May, 1921.* Reports of the Commission of Inquiry with Correspondence Relating Thereto (London: H.M. Stationery Office, 1921).
41. Anglo-American Committee *et al., A Survey of Palestine*, 24.
42. David Ben-Gurion, *My Talks with Arab Leaders*, trans. Arych Rubinstein and Misha Louvish (New York: Third Press,1973); Neil Caplan, *Futile Diplomacy, vol. 2, Arab-Zionist Negotiations and the End of the Mandate* (London: Frank Cass, 1983); *Caplan, Futile Diplomacy,* vol. 1.
43. On the strike see Abd al-Wahhab Kayyali, *Palestine: A Modern History* (London: Croom Helm, 1978).
44. See, League of Nations, "Report by His Majesty's Government in the United Kingdom of Great Britain and Northern Ireland to the Council of the League of Nations on the Administration of Palestine and Trans Jordan for the year 1936." The report stated that "The Jewish leaders rejected [the proposals made by His Majesty's Government for the establishment of a Legislative Council in Palestine] uncompromisingly; the Arab attitude though critical was disposed to give them full consideration." http://unispal.un.org/UNISPAL.NSF/0/FD4D250AF882632B052565D2005012C3.
45. Yehoshua Porath, *The Palestinian Arab National Movement, 1929–1939: From Riots to Rebellion*, vol. 2 (London: Frank Cass, 1977), 152–155.
46. Martin Kolinsky, *Britain's War in the Middle East: Strategy and Diplomacy, 1936–42* (New York: St. Martin's Press, 1999), 51, n19.
47. Porath, *The Palestinian Arab National Movement, 1929–1939*, 156–157.
48. See Martin Kramer, *Islam Assembled: The Advent of the Muslim Congress* (New York: Columbia University Press, 1986), 123–141 and 192–194; Ralph M. Coury, "Egyptians in Jerusalem: Their Role in the General Islamic Conference of 1931," *The Muslim World*, Vol. 82, Issue 1–2, 1992, 37–54; Thomas Mayer, "Egypt and the General Islamic Conference of Jerusalem 1931," *Middle Eastern Studies*, 8, 3 (July 1982).
49. Tarek Al Beshri, *Al Harka Al Siyassiya Fi Misr 1945–1952* [The Political Movement in Egypt: 1945–1952] (Cairo: Dar Al Shourouk, 1981).
50. Rashid Khalidi, "The Palestinians and 1948: The Underlying Causes of Failure," in *The War for Palestine: Rewriting the History of 1948*, ed. Eugene L. Rogan and Avi Shlaim (New York: Cambridge University Press, 2001), 27; See also "British Mandate Arab Revolt 1936–39," *Palestine Facts*, http://palestinefacts.org/pf_mandate_riots_1936-39.php (accessed on July 30, 2010).
51. Rashid Khalidi, "Palestine Arab Revolt (1936–1939)," *Encyclopedia of the Modern Middle East and North Africa* (Detroit, MI: Macmillan Library Reference, 2004); Kayyali, *Palestine*; Porath, *The Palestinian Arab National Movement, 1929–1939*; Theodore Swedenburg, *Memories of Revolt: The 1936–1939 Rebellion and the Palestinian National Past* (Fayetteville, AR: University of Arkansas Press, 2003); and Theodore Swedenburg, "The Role of the Palestinian Peasantry in *the Great Revolt (1936–1939)," in Islam: Politics and Social Movements*, ed. Edmund Burke III and Ira M. Lapidus (Berkeley: University of California Press, 1988).
52. Benny Morris, *Righteous Victims: A History of the Zionist-Arab Conflict, 1881-2001* (New York: Vintage, 2001), 148–149.
53. Palestine: Statement of Policy [British 1939 White Paper], Cmd. 6019 (May 1939).
54. A. W. Kayyali, *Palestine. A Modern History* (London: Croom Helm, 1978), 221.
55. Avi Shlaim, *Collusion Across the Jordan: King Abdullah, the Zionist Movement, and the Partition of Palestine* (New York: Columbia University Press, 1988), 60.

56. Neil Caplan and Avraham Sela, "Zionist-Egyptian Negotiations and the Partition of Palestine, 1946 (Documents)," *The Jerusalem Quarterly*, 44, 1987, 21.
57. "Jewish Brigade Group." *Encyclopaedia Judaica*, ed. Michael Berenbaum and Fred Skolnik, 2nd ed. Vol. 11, 271–272.
58. Mohamed Heikal, *Secret Channels: The Inside Story of Arab–Israeli Peace Negotiations* (London: HarperCollins, 1996) 71; and Bayan Nuweihid Al-Hout, "The Palestinian Political Elite during the Mandate Period," *Journal of Palestine Studies*, 9, 1 (Autumn 1979), 88.
59. This refers to a statement attributed to Zionist leaders to the effect that Palestine was empty of (a) people and was therefore perfect for the Jews, (b) people without a place to call their own. There is some ambiguity, however, as to the original source of the phrase. Many attribute it to Israel Zangwill, a prominent British Zionist, who in fact did publish the phrase "Palestine is a country without a people; the Jews are a people without a country," but Adam M. Garfinkle tells us that Zangwill got this idea from Lord Shaftesbury, a British millenarian Christian earl, who, Zangwill says, was "literally inexact in describing Palestine as a country without a people." Another possible source for this phrase is John Lawson Stoddard, an American traveler and lecturer, who often lectured on Jerusalem and the Jews, and addressed Jews when in his book, published in 1897, he wrote "You are a people without a country; there is a country without a people." Adam M. Garfinkle, "On the Origin, Meaning, Use and Abuse of a Phrase," *Middle Eastern Studies*, 27, 4 (October 1991).
60. What the Jews call the "Western Wall" or "Wailing Wall", Palestinians call *al-Buraq*, after the Prophet's horse which Muslim traditions describe as having been tethered to the Wall during Mohammad's ascent to Heaven.
61. The "Mashreq", a word derived from the Arabic for east, is the area spanning from the western border of Egypt to the western border of Iran. The term is used to distinguish this area from the "Maghreb," a word deriving from the Arabic for west, which includes the countries of North Africa, excluding Egypt.
62. Tarek Al Beshri, *Al Harka Al Siyassiya Fi Misr 1945–1952* [The Political Movement in Egypt: 1945–1952] (Cairo: Dar Al Shourouk, 1981), 233.
63. Heikal, *Secret Channels*, 42–44.
64. *Ibid.*, 45.
65. *Ibid.* This took place in the framework of the General Islamic Conference of Jerusalem, which was held on September 4, 1931. Thomas Mayer, "Egypt and the General Islamic Conference of Jerusalem 1931," 311–322.
66. Thomas Mayer, "Egypt and the 1936 Arab Revolt in Palestine," *Journal of Contemporary History*, 19, 2 (April 1984), 275–287.
67. Heikal, *Secret Channels*, 69.
68. Heikal, *Secret Channels*, 64.
69. Anglo-American Committee, *A Survey of Palestine*, Table 5, 594. Between 1936 and 1945, the British collected from the Arabs only two machine guns, 28 submachine guns, 7,617 rifles, 4,891 pistols, 1,376 bombs and grenades, 375 rounds of small arms ammunition, and 3,924 rounds of shotgun ammunition. They collected even fewer items from the Zionists who used the training that the British had provided them to better conceal their weapons. Table 6, 595. Between 1936 and 1945 the British succeeded in capturing from the Zionists only one machine gun, eight submachine guns, 135 rifles, 365 pistols, 657 bombs and grenades, 12 shotguns, 53,128 rounds of small arms ammunition, and 3,614 rounds of shotgun ammunition.
70. For more information on the connection between isolationism and anti-Semitism see Edward S. Shapiro, "World War II and American Jewish Identity" *Modern Judaism*, 10, 1 (February 1990),

65–84; Geoffrey S. Smith, "Isolationism, the Devil, and the Advent of the Second World War: Variations on a Theme" *The International History Review* 4, 1 (February 1982), 55–89.

71. Rashid Khalidi, "The Palestinians and 1948," 27–28.
72. The five parties were the National Defense Party, established in 1934 by Raghib Nashashibi, the Palestinian Arab Party, established in 1935 by Jamal Husseini, the Independence Party, established in 1932 by Awni Abdel Hadi, the Reform Party, established in 1935 by Hussien Khalidi, and the National Bloc, established in 1935 by Abd al-Latif Salah.
73. Porath, *Emergence of the Palestinian Arab-National Movement, 1918–1929*; Zvi Elpeleg and Shmuel Himelstein, *The Grand Mufti: Haj Amin Al-Hussaini, Founder of the Palestinian National Movement* (Portland, OR: Frank Cass, 1993); Taysīr Jabārah, *Palestinian Leader, Hajj Amin Al-Husayni, Mufti of Jerusalem* (Princeton, NJ: Kingston Press, 1985); Philip Mattar, *The Mufti of Jerusalem: Al-Hajj Amin Al-Husayni and the Palestinian National Movement* (New York: Columbia University Press, 1992); Yehuda Taggar, The Mufti of Jerusalem and Palestine: Arab Politics, 1930–1937 (New York: Garland, 1986); Majid Khadduri, "The Traditional (Idealist) School – the Extremist: Al-Hajj Amin al-Husayni," in *Arab Contemporaries: The Role of Personalities in Politics* (Baltimore, MD: John Hopkins University Press, 1973); Yehoshua Porath, "Al-Hajj Amin al-Husayni, Mufti of Jerusalem: His Rise to Power and Consolidation of His Position," *Asian and African Studies* 7 (1971), 212–256; and Joseph B. Schechtman, *The Mufti and the Fuehrer: The Rise and Fall of Haj Amin el-Husseini* (New York: Thomas Yoseloff, 1965).
74. Reinharz, *Chaim Weizmann: The Making of a Statesman*, 77–81.
75. *Ibid.*, 436–439.

2 The Partitioning of Palestine: "*Nakba*" and Independence

This chapter in the history of the Middle East, and of the Arab–Israeli conflict in particular, begins in the immediate aftermath of the Second World War and ends in the immediate aftermath of the 1948 War. It witnesses a number of interrelated important developments: the UN's adoption of Resolution 181 stipulating the partitioning of Palestine; the Zionists' assertion of independence and the failure of Palestinian efforts to prevent the assertion; the decision of the neighboring Arab governments to take over the conflict by intervening militarily in Palestine; the total failure of Arab states' efforts to prevent the emergence of Jewish independence; and finally, the resulting Nakba – the "catastrophe" – the displacement of hundreds of thousands of Palestinians.

The fact that all these developments followed the Second World War was not accidental; in one way or another, these developments were all related to the different dimensions and consequences of the war. The most important and shocking of these dimensions was the Holocaust – the systematic extermination of some six million Jews by Nazi Germany – an event that created a broad international consensus that the survivors of the horror must be compensated, and that conditions must be created to ensure that the Jewish people would "never again" experience such horrors. In the aftermath of the Holocaust, the power of the Zionist case seemed almost self-evident to western publics.

An important consequence of Britain's bankruptcy, itself an outcome of the war, was its replacement as the leader of the free world by the United States. And America's President, Harry S. Truman, was now determined to compensate the Jewish people for the atrocities committed against them by facilitating Jewish immigration to Palestine.

On the world stage this period witnessed the imposition of the Iron Curtain – dividing Eurasia into two blocs: a free world and one that was not. In the Middle East, however, multipolarity continued to linger through much of this period. Thus, Israel's independence was recognized by both emerging postwar powers: the Soviet Union and the United States. Indeed, for a short period, the USSR became, indirectly, Israel's primary arms supplier.

Within this still multipolar framework, with the influence of Britain and France in the Middle East declining, the decolonization of the region accelerated. It was now that Syria and Lebanon became independent, joining other states that had gained this formal status earlier: Egypt, Jordan, Iraq, Saudi Arabia, and Yemen.

Another dimension of the Second World War that had a profound effect on the Middle East concerned the extent to which the war manifested the so-called "second industrial revolution." The massive expansion of armed forces was associated with the production of thousands of air, naval, and land platforms. The huge quantities of these highly mobile systems – fighters and bombers, frigates, destroyers and submarines, tanks, armored personnel carriers, and self-propelled artillery – consumed enormous quantities of fuel. As a result, oil became the most strategically important of all commodities, making the Middle East, harboring the largest of world oil reserves, a critically important region.

In a sense, then, the different consequences of the Second World War tended to balance one another, at least to some extent. What the international community regarded as minimum compensation deserved by the Jewish people for the atrocities they experienced at the hands of Nazi Germany was limited by the growing significance of oil: the Arab states' ownership of this strategic commodity meant that their priorities and sensitivities regarding the emerging Jewish state could not be ignored. Thus, while the United States now became a strong advocate of the right of the Jewish people to self-determination, this period also witnessed the beginning of American–Saudi friendship.

Another unique dimension of this period was that the strength of the alliance that won the Second World War enabled the effective use of the newly created United Nations as an important instrument of international relations. Yet to be subjected to the fierce competition and dividing lines of the Cold War, the UN produced the most important decisions regarding the Middle East.

Main Developments

The developments described in this section encompass the impact of the Second World War on the evolving conflict between Arabs and the Zionist movement; the main events that set in motion the "winds of war" – the background to the coming violent conflict; the eruption of Arab–Jewish violence; the preparations for wider war and the immediate pre-war events that precipitated its eruption; the phases of the 1948 War; and finally, the immediate outcomes of that war.

The Aftermath of the Second World War

In the global arena, the immediate aftermath of the Second World War witnessed the beginnings of a transformation from a multipolar to a bipolar distribution of power. Although the Cold War was still several years away, competition between the United States and the Soviet Union was already apparent in the burgeoning arms race in the Middle East. Paradoxically, the shift to a bipolar system was accompanied by the emergence of a multilateral system of diplomacy, represented by the United Nations. The new world body would play a major role in the region's crucial developments, including partition in 1947 and negotiating the armistice agreements following the 1948 War; from Resolution 181 determining that Palestine must be partitioned, to Resolution 194 calling for the return or compensation of Palestinian refugees. It also offered the conflicting parties a number of high-power mediators: from Count Bernadotte to Ralph Bunche.

The Second World War had left Britain's treasury empty, thus forcing it to withdraw from most areas "East of Suez." This included Palestine – a rather small part of the region but an area

Figure 2.1. Displaced Jewish Persons. British troops are guarding the train as Jews are transported from Hamburg docks to the Poppendorf Camp. 'Illegal immigrants' to Palestine on the ship 'Exodus 1947', they were sent back to Germany on the British troop transport ship, the 'Ocean Vigour'. *Source*: Chris Ware/Getty Images

whose control demanded more and more of Britain's dwindling resources. The withdrawal from Palestine was also spurred by the spiraling costs – including in human lives – associated with Britain's military presence there. A particularly horrific example of such costs were those associated with the *Etzel* bombing of the King David Hotel in Jerusalem on July 22, 1946 resulting in the deaths of 92 people. At the time, the hotel served as the Palestine headquarters of the British Mandate authorities.

The withdrawal of the Great Powers in and from the Middle East during and after the Second World War fostered the emergence of independent states in Jordan (1946), Syria (1946), Lebanon (1943), and Israel (1948). The formal termination of the French and British mandates reflected the broader trend of decolonization that took place throughout Asia and Africa, as direct European control over its former colonies gradually came to an end – a process that would continue until the mid-1960s. At the same time, the establishment of the Arab League in Cairo in 1945 fostered a new regional dynamic that acknowledged the independence of the individual Arab states while also emphasizing solidarity among them.

Perhaps the most glaring example of the impact of global developments on the Middle East was the influence of the Holocaust on the Zionist enterprise. The Jews in Palestine, like those around the world, were greatly affected by the trauma of the Holocaust, lending a new urgency to the Zionist project in Palestine.

Meanwhile, another outcome of the Second World War was gaining international attention: refugees. From 1945 to 1952 over 250,000 Jewish refugees lived in Displaced Persons (DP) camps throughout Germany, Austria, and Italy. In these camps, where living conditions were often harsh, Zionist youth groups emerged and developed agricultural training programs intended to prepare refugees for settlement in Palestine. From 1945

Figure 2.2. President Harry S. Truman.
© Bettmann/ CORBIS

to 1948 the frustrations and difficult conditions of the refugees in DP camps lent additional urgency to the push for a Jewish state, as more and more inhabitants of the camps chose Palestine as their preferred destination for resettlement. By 1952, more than 80,000 DPs were admitted into the United States; 136,000 resettled in Israel; and 20,000 in various other countries, such as South Africa and Canada.

In the immediate aftermath of the war, images of tens of thousands of refugees who survived the Nazi death machine and were now languishing in DP camps had a strong impact on Americans, including President Truman. This issue was first taken up by President Franklin Roosevelt in his February 1945 meeting with King Abdul Aziz Ibn Saud of Saudi Arabia. Truman now began pressuring the British to ease the restrictions on immigration to Palestine, in place since the 1939 White Paper, by granting certificates of entry to Palestine to 100,000 Jewish refugees – a figure exceeding the 1939 White Paper quotas.[1]

Clement Atlee, who had now replaced Winston Churchill as Britain's prime minister, refused to acquiesce.[2] Instead, he proposed the establishment of an Anglo-American Committee of Inquiry to look into the refugee question and make recommendations. The Committee traveled throughout Europe and the Middle East and issued a report calling for permanent UN trusteeship of the entire area of Palestine. The report also recommended the repatriation of 100,000 Jewish refugees from Europe and the lifting of the White Paper's immigration restriction. To implement this, Truman appointed Henry F. Grady, a career diplomat, to meet with Herbert Morrison, the British official in charge of Palestinian affairs, and instructed him to produce a suitable plan.

The resultant *Morrison–Grady Plan* issued in late July of 1946 laid the groundwork for the entry of 100,000 Jews into Palestine and called for the division of Palestine into three separate, autonomous regions – a British sector (accounting for half the territory, including Jerusalem), a much smaller Arab sector, and a Jewish area comprising less than 20 percent of the country. The Arabs and the Zionists both rejected the plan.[3]

By 1947, United States public opinion polls found that Americans favored the establishment of a Jewish state by a ratio of 2 to 1.[4] In October of that year, the repatriation of 100,000 refugees to Palestine had still not materialized, but President Truman for the first time publicly committed America to supporting the Jewish demand for statehood. Still, his administration remained deeply divided between those advocating the Zionist cause and those fearful that the birth of a Jewish state in the Middle East would only lead to conflict, thus jeopardizing America's other interests in the region. In the meantime, however, Zionist underground groups smuggled over 100,000 Jewish refugees from the DP camps to Palestine by 1948.[5]

The Run-Up to the 1948 War

In February 1947 Britain announced that by May of the following year it would be terminating its mandate over Palestine. The UN responded by creating a Special Committee on Palestine (UNSCOP). Officially boycotted by the Arab states, the Committee issued a report in September calling for the partition of Palestine into two separate states, one Jewish, the other Arab. The report later became the basis of UN Resolution 181 (see box) approved by the UN General Assembly on November 29, 1947. The resolution called for the partition of Palestine into an Arab state and a Jewish state, with international trusteeship over Jerusalem and its environs.

Under the 1947 UN partition plan, 56 percent of Mandate Palestine was designated to the Jewish state, while 43 percent was allotted to the Arab state. The city of Jerusalem was not to come under the sovereignty of either side; instead it was put under a "Special International Regime." The borders proposed by the plan were intended to make each of the states as homogenous as possible. Nevertheless, many Palestinians (438,000) were to reside in the proposed Jewish state – comprising some 45 percent of the state's population – while a much smaller number of Jews (10,000) would fall within the proposed Palestinian state, comprising only 1 percent of the latter's population of 828,000.[6]

The total population of Palestine in December 1946 stood at 1,972,000 of which Arabs constituted 1,364,000 and Jews 608,000.[7] That is, a year before the UN adoption of the partition resolution, the Arab population of Palestine comprised 68 percent of the total and owned about 85 percent of the land; the Jewish population comprised about one-third of the total and owned about 7 percent of the land.[8]

UNITED NATIONS RESOLUTION 181[9]

"The Mandate for Palestine shall terminate as soon as possible but in any case not later than 1 August 1948... Independent Arab and Jewish States and the Special International Regime for the City of Jerusalem, set forth in Part III of this Plan, shall come into existence in Palestine two months after the evacuation of the armed forces of the mandatory Power has been completed but in any case not later than 1 October 1948. The boundaries of the Arab State, the Jewish State, and the City of Jerusalem shall be as described in Parts II and III below.

The Constitutions of the States shall embody Chapters 1 and 2 of the Declaration provided for in section C below and include, inter alia, provisions for:... Guaranteeing to all persons equal and non-discriminatory rights in civil, political, economic and religious matters and the enjoyment of human rights and fundamental freedoms, including freedom of religion, language, speech and publication, education, assembly and association;"

The Zionist movement, through a vote by the enlarged Zionist General Council, accepted UNSCOP's partition proposal.[10] By contrast, the Arab and particularly the Palestinian reactions to the proposal were overwhelmingly and uniformly negative. In response to the UN vote, the Mufti declared from Beirut that UN Resolution 181 was "null and void."[11] In Syria, public opinion was strongly against the creation of a Jewish state in Palestine. As a result, the Syrian government came under pressure from all sides to take active measures to prevent Jewish statehood. Members of the Muslim Brotherhood in Syria and the Mufti initiated a campaign calling for the formation of an Arab army for the liberation of Palestine. Residents of Damascus went on strike and a crowd estimated at over 10,000 broke into the United States Legation, the Belgian Legation, and the Soviet cultural office. In Aleppo, 300 Jewish homes and 11 synagogues were burned and 76 Jews were killed by a rioting mob before order was restored.[12]

Not long after, what some have termed a "civil war" broke out between the Arabs and Jews living in mandatory Palestine. Each side attacked villages and roads, but the heaviest fighting occurred in Jerusalem, Jaffa–Tel Aviv, the coastal plain, Tiberias, the eastern Galilee, and Haifa.[13] By March 1948, roughly 6,000 volunteers from neighboring Arab states had joined the Palestinian militias, together constituting the Arab Liberation Army (ALA).[14] Attacking Jewish settlements, these forces also cut the road from Tel Aviv to Jerusalem, laying siege to the latter's Jewish neighborhoods.[15] In April, the Arab League began preparing for a coordinated attack to include forces from Iraq, Syria, Lebanon, Egypt, and Jordan.

Nevertheless, the broader Arab reaction to the UN partition plan of 1947 was not uniformly negative. Although Arab governments publicly opposed the plan, some Arab leaders privately expressed a willingness to accept it. For example, in his meeting with a Jewish Agency executive, Eliyahu Sasson, in August 1946 – more than a year before UN Resolution 181 was adopted – Arab League Secretary General Abd al-Rahman Azzam told Sasson that he saw partition as the only solution for Palestine, but could not suggest the move himself.[16] Similarly, in meetings with Zionist leaders such as Sasson, and later Golda Meir, Emir Abdullah of Transjordan expressed interest in exploring the idea of dividing Palestine as part of a broader plan to annex the Arab sector of Palestine (as well as Syria) to his kingdom.[17]

On the Zionist side, in March 1948, two months before the declaration of independence, in anticipation of an impending attack by Arab armies, the leaders of the *Haganah* produced a plan to defend the territory allotted to the Jewish state and to secure Jewish settlements outside the proposed state's boundaries. The operational objectives of *Tochnit Dalet* [Plan D] included "[s]elf-defense against invasion by regular or semi-regular forces," "freedom of military and economic activity within the borders of the [Hebrew] state and in Jewish settlements outside its borders," "preventing the enemy from using frontline positions within his territory which can easily be used for launching attacks," and "[a]pplying economic pressure on the enemy."[18] The drafters of "Plan D" assumed that in order to beat back the Arab armies, the Zionist forces would first have to subdue the Palestinian irregulars. To do this, they would have to gain control of the roads, which, at that time, were largely dominated by Arab villages and towns.

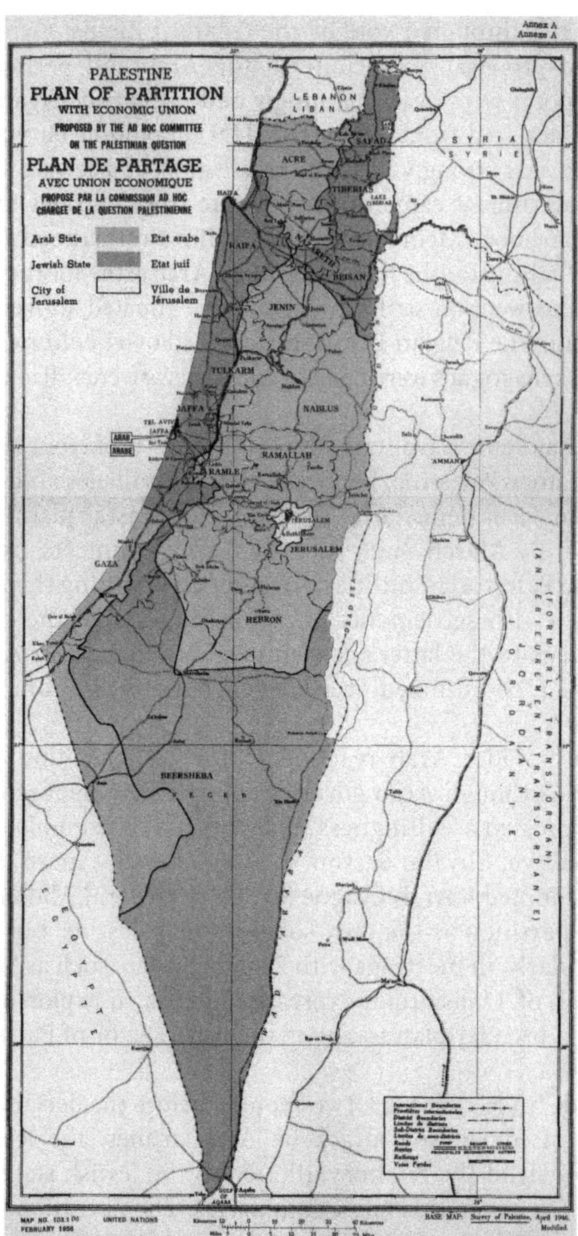

Figure 2.3. The official UN Partition Map

One of these battles, in the village of Deir Yassin on April 9, 1948, was to mark the major impact that "Plan D" had on the fate of the Arabs of Palestine. After having entered into a non-aggression pact with the *Haganah*, Deir Yassin was attacked by a joint *Irgun–Lehi* force that killed some 115–250 men, women, and children. The impact of the incident, however, far exceeded its physical dimensions. Broadcast by Arab radio, the story of Deir Yassin spread rapidly and terrorized Arabs in other towns and cities.[19]

From early April to Israel's declaration of independence on May 14, 1948, some of the fiercest battles took place as the *Haganah* launched another offensive, broke the siege of Jerusalem, captured territory allotted to the Jewish state under the 1947 UN partition plan, and secured Jewish settlements located outside the designated Jewish areas. The *Haganah* focused on capturing the Jerusalem corridor, with an eye to breaking the Arab siege on the Old City. By the time the Arab armies invaded in May 1948, Zionists had captured most of the territory allotted to them in the UN plan, as well as several areas not originally designated as part of the Jewish state. By mid-May, approximately 300,000 Palestinians left or were forced to flee their homes.[20]

Yet the surrounding Arab states were slow to decide to intervene militarily in Palestine. The UN's adoption of Resolution 181 led to a mid-December 1947 meeting in Cairo of representatives of Arab governments. It resulted in a decision to reject the UN resolution and to form a military committee to evaluate the Palestinian defensive needs. The sum of a million pounds Sterling was committed to the task. The meeting also decided to form the Arab Salvation Army to be headed by Fawzi al-Qawuqji.[21]

Figure 2.4. Emir Abdullah © Bettmann/CORBIS.

It was not until April 12, 1948 that the Arab League decided to send Arab military forces to Palestine. That day, an Iraqi military force entered Jordan for this purpose and soon thereafter Lebanese military units began some limited operations in northern Palestine. Yet even at that late point Egypt had not yet decided to go to war in Palestine. Pressure was put on Prime Minister Nuqrashi to adhere to the UNSC partition resolution by limiting the Egyptian involvement to material and moral support, and the provision of volunteers, instead of involving the Egyptian army in the war.[22] In the end, the decision to participate in the war was made by King Farouk, who, on May 11, 1948, ordered Haidar Pasha, the minister of war, to prepare the army for war.[23] After the Israeli declaration of independence on May 14, the armies of five Arab countries entered the war: Egypt, Jordan, Syria, Lebanon, and Iraq.[24]

The 1948 War

In a meeting of *Moetzet HaAm* [the National Council] in Tel Aviv on May 14, 1948 David Ben Gurion, acting in his capacity as chairman of the Executive Committee of the Jewish Agency for Palestine, declared the establishment of the State of Israel. In the following weeks, Ben Gurion moved to endow the newly-created state with a monopoly of force. The Israeli Defense Forces (IDF) were created, and all pre-state independent militias and semi-independent forces were ordered to disband or incorporate themselves into the newly created IDF. This was first applied to the opposition forces, the *Etzel* and *Lehi*. The *Etzel* was then seen as resisting the ordered incorporation by attempting to continue supplying its units with weapons and ammunition, and so, on June 20, 1948, Ben Gurion took the extreme measure of deploying the embryonic IDF artillery to sink the *Altalena*, a ship carrying these arms. Later, Ben Gurion moved to also disband the separate formations of the *Palmach* – the special forces created to defend the Yishuv during the Second World War.

The 1948 War began the day after Ben Gurion's declaration of independent statehood, when the British mandate in Palestine formally ended and the Arab states reacted to Ben Gurion's declaration by invading Palestine. The war proceeded in three main stages. Between May 15 and early July, Arab armies invaded Palestine but

Figure 2.5. David Ben Gurion declaring the establishment of the State of Israel. *Source*: Tal/Epic/Mary Evans.

Israeli forces managed to extend the territory under their control. Approximately 42,000 Jewish regulars and irregulars faced some 28,000 Arab troops from neighboring countries,[25] as well as some 2,000 Palestinian irregulars.

The Jordanian Arab Legion attacked in the Jerusalem area, capturing the Old City and positioning forces in Lydda and Ramle which were designated to be within the boundaries of the Palestinian state. Meanwhile, Egyptian army units entered from the south, reaching an area north of Ashkelon by May 29. Syrian forces attacked in the Jordan Valley and captured several Jewish towns and settlements before an Israeli counterattack forced them to partially retreat on May 23.[26] Lebanese units conducted a limited incursion into northern Galilee before being stopped on June 10 by an Israeli counterattack. An Iraqi contingent invaded south of the Syrian and Lebanese positions and captured several settlements before being forced to retreat. As of that point, the Iraqi force maintained mainly defensive positions in coordination with the Jordanian Arab Legion.[27] The first UN-mandated ceasefire came into effect on June 11 and lasted through July 7.[28]

The second phase of the war, lasting ten days, began on July 8. It saw Israeli forces capturing territory originally allotted to the Palestinian Arab state in the Galilee and the Tel Aviv–Jerusalem corridor. Forces of Jordan's Arab Legion stationed in Lydda and Ramle were withdrawn and redeployed in Jerusalem, where the fiercest fighting had taken place during the first phase of the war and where the Hashemite Kingdom was determined to maintain control.[29] Meanwhile, Egyptian forces had occupied considerable territory in the Negev, originally designated to the Jewish state.

The second truce held between July 18 and October. During this period, the UN mediator, Count Folke Bernadotte, submitted a proposal to end the fighting. The Bernadotte Plan would have redrawn the partition lines, allotting all of the Galilee to the Jewish state while attaching all of the Negev, as well as Lydda and Ramle, to Arab Palestine (which, significantly, was to be joined with Transjordan). Both the Arabs and the Zionists rejected Bernadotte's proposal, and, on September 17, the UN mediator was assassinated in Jerusalem by members of *Lehi*.[30]

Between October 1948 and January 1949 – the final phase of the war – Israeli forces expelled the Egyptian army from the Negev, including areas originally allocated to the Palestinian Arab state, extending their control into the Sinai desert. This compelled the Egyptian army, which was encircled in the Gaza Strip, to withdraw and accept a ceasefire on January 7, 1949.

The War's Immediate Aftermath

The armistice agreements signed by Israel and its Arab adversaries between February and July 1949 affirmed their consent to a ceasefire and established armistice lines which all parties agreed not to cross.[31] In addition, demilitarized zones were established along the Israeli–Egyptian and Israeli–Syrian borders. The agreements made clear that their provisions were not to be interpreted as delineating a "political or territorial boundary" or as affecting the "ultimate settlement of the Palestine question."

The Israel–Egypt armistice agreement, signed on February 24, 1949, resulted in the withdrawal of the IDF to a new border between the western Negev and the Sinai, leaving the Gaza Strip in Egyptian hands. The Israel–Lebanon armistice agreement, signed on

Figure 2.6. King Farouk of Egypt. *Source*: Library of Congress, LC-DIG-matpc-08368.

March 23, set the armistice line along the international boundary between Lebanon and Palestine, as defined by the 1947 UN partition plan.

The Israel–Transjordan armistice agreement, signed on April 3, left the Jordanian Arab Legion in most of the positions it held in the West Bank at the close of the war, most importantly in East Jerusalem including the Old City. Along the border separating East and West Jerusalem, several demilitarized "no man's land" areas were designated. In exchange for territory in the northern West Bank, Transjordan was forced to concede land in the southern Negev that Israel had captured after the second truce. Israel also received the territories of Wadi Ara and the "Little Triangle" (later known as simply "the Triangle"). Areas occupied during the war by Iraqi forces were now taken over by Jordanian forces, and a Special Committee was established to address outstanding issues such as "free movement of traffic on vital roads, including the Bethlehem and Latrun–Jerusalem roads; resumption of the normal functioning of the cultural and humanitarian institutions on Mount Scopus and free access thereto; [and,] free access to the Holy Places."[32]

Finally, the Israel–Syria armistice agreement, signed on July 20, stipulated Syrian withdrawal from territories captured in the war, including at least one town designated to the Palestinian state known as al-Himma. However, Israel was not to assert control – let alone sovereignty – over these territories. Instead, these areas were to become demilitarized zones and the issue of their sovereignty was to remain unresolved.[33]

In addition to the territorial results of the 1948 War, its dominant outcome was the displacement of Palestinians. While estimates of the number of Palestinian refugees following the end of the war vary from some 400,000 to nearly one million, UN calculations at the time indicated that some 711,000 Palestinian refugees lived outside Israel in the war's aftermath.[34]

The international community also responded to the Palestinian refugee crisis. On December 11, 1948, the United Nations General Assembly adopted Resolution 194, aimed at bringing about an end to hostilities. The resolution laid the groundwork for a process that would culminate in the armistice agreements of 1949. It repeated earlier calls for Jerusalem to be placed under international supervision, a stipulation that both the Israelis and the Jordanians rejected. Finally, the resolution stated that "refugees wishing to return to their

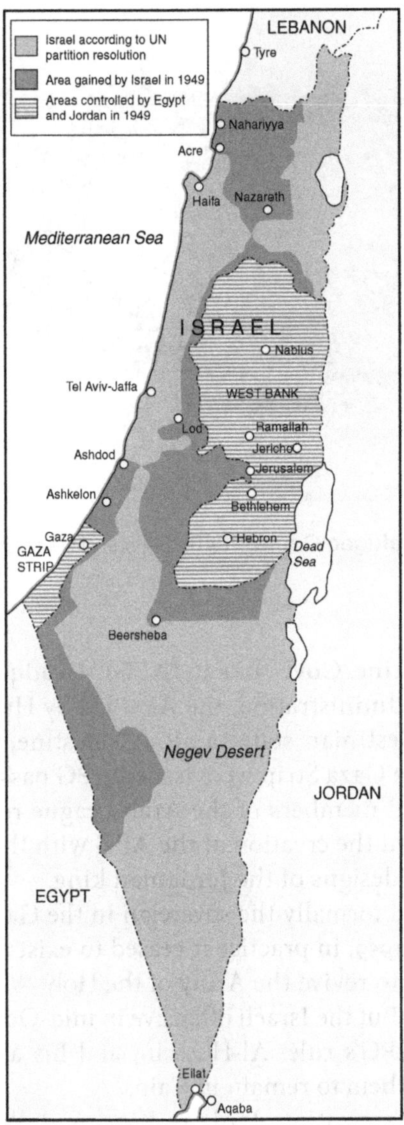

Figure 2.7. Partition vs. Armistice Lines: the 1949 Armistice Map

homes and live at peace with their neighbors should be permitted to do so at the earliest practicable date, and that compensation should be paid for the property of those choosing not to return and for loss of or damage to property which, under principles of international law or in equity, should be made good by the Governments or authorities responsible..."[35]

For their part, even before the war's end, the Arab states had begun to react to the Palestinians' disastrous predicament. On September 22, 1948, as the Israeli victory in the war began to seem imminent, the Arab League, led by Egypt, adopted a resolution

Figure 2.8. A Palestinian Refugee Camp, 1948. *Source*: United Nations Photo Library.

recognizing the All Palestine Government (APG). Headquartered in Gaza, which was under Egyptian military administration, the APG led by Hajj Amin al-Husseini, declared the establishment of a Palestinian state in all of Palestine, with Jerusalem as its capital. Accordingly, citizens of the Gaza Strip were issued APG passports.[36] With the exception of Jordan's King Abdullah, all members of the Arab League recognized the new state. King Farouk initiated and funded the creation of the APG with the hope that it would halt what he saw as the expansionist designs of the Jordanian king.

While the APG remained formally the sovereign in the Gaza Strip until President Nasser abolished it by a decree in 1959, in practice it ceased to exist after only three weeks. During this short period, it sought to revive the Army of the Holy War – irregular forces formed by the Arab High Committee. But the Israeli offensive in mid-October 1948 drove the Egyptians out of Gaza, ending the APG's rule. Al-Husseini and his associates were prevented from returning to Gaza, forcing them to remain in Cairo.

In response to the APG's creation, Jordan's King Abdullah convened four conferences between October 1948 and January 1949, attended by Palestinian and Transjordanian notables and civil servants. The Jericho Conference of December 1, 1948 proclaimed the union of Transjordan and Palestine under Abdullah's rule. In April 1950, elections were held for a new 40-member Chamber of Deputies – a parliament the seats of which were divided evenly between West and East Bank constituencies. On April 25, the Chamber ratified the unification of the two banks under a single Hashemite Kingdom of Jordan, and granted Jordanian citizenship to Palestinians residing in the West Bank.[37] As of that point the term "Palestine" was banned in all future Jordanian official documents and correspondence. Thus, in the aftermath of the 1948 War, all Palestinians with the exception of a small minority that remained in Israel came under the rule of neighboring Arab states.

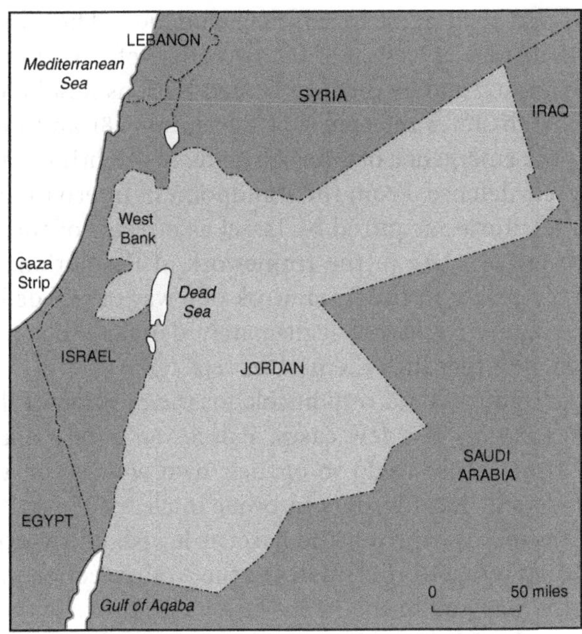

Figure 2.9. Jordan's Annexation of the West Bank

Narratives

The Israeli Narrative

The dominant Israeli narrative of this period consists of a number of components. First, that the Holocaust, as the most extreme manifestation of anti-Semitism, proved conclusively the justification of the Zionist cause: without a state of their own, Jews would be exposed to repeated atrocities, even if not always of the scale and horror administered by the Nazis. Moreover, in the absence of a state sovereign to determine its immigration policy, Jews escaping such atrocities would be denied refuge again, even by enlightened countries like the United States and Britain. Hence, Jews who could be saved would in fact be trapped, as they were in Europe between 1933, when the Nazis came to power, and 1942, when the Nazis began to implement the "final solution."

Second, that the Israeli triumph in 1948 provided the ultimate testimony to the justification of Jewish national independence. In the war, Israel suffered overall numerical inferiority, making it a grand struggle of "the few against the many." The Israeli side won the war by extracting from itself every bit of potential strength. The requisite motivation to do so was the outcome of total conviction that the only alternative to victory was another Holocaust, either immediately – that is, in the hands of the attacking Arab forces – or in the long run, because in the absence of Jewish statehood it would be impossible to prevent a similar calamity.

Third, that the War of Independence – resulting in the displacement of hundreds of thousands of Palestinians – was a direct outcome of the Palestinians' rejection of any compromise offered to them: a compromise between their needs and aspirations and those of the Jewish people and their right to self-determination. The clearest manifestations of these refusals were the Arabs' rejection of the two offers of partition presented to them: by the Peel Commission in 1937 and by the 1947 United Nations Resolution 181.

Fourth, since the Arab states rejected UN Resolution 181 and instead launched a war aimed at preventing the emergence of a Jewish state, the fighting waged by the Israeli side was clearly a war of self-defense. From the standpoint of international law and legitimacy this meant that the territories acquired by Israel as a result of the war – that is, beyond those allotted to the Jewish state in the framework of Resolution 181 – were gained not through aggression but rather in the framework of a war of self-defense. Hence, the Arab states and the Palestinians could not legitimately demand that Israel withdraw to the borders of a partition plan that they themselves rejected.

Fifth, that the Israeli side was not responsible for the creation of the Palestinian refugee problem. With the exception of a few cases, Palestinians were not forced to leave their homes; rather, they either chose to do so of their own volition or were encouraged to do so by Arab commanders or local leaders in order to clear the way for the invading Arab armies who were expected to wipe out the nascent Jewish entity expeditiously. Thus, the source of the Palestinian refugee problem lies in the Arab rejection of any compromise that could have avoided the war and in the Arab states' decision to launch a war of aggression against the newly born Jewish state. The problem was further rooted in the Palestinians' expectation that the Jewish community in Palestine would be quickly wiped out and in their judgment that in order to minimize their costs they must make way for the fighting Arab forces to do their job.

Finally, the invasion of Palestine by the Arab states made it impossible for Jews to continue to reside in these countries. Therefore, the war declared by the members of the Arab League also led to a massive displacement of Jews. In the immediate aftermath of the war and by the early 1950s, hundreds of thousands of Jews had no choice but to flee countries like Iraq, Morocco, Yemen, Egypt, and Tunisia. Hence, a balanced and fair view of the Palestinians' plight must take into account that they were not the only ones displaced by the 1948 War.

The Palestinian Narrative

The Palestinian narrative recognized that this was a period of monumental failure to gain self-determination, establish their own state and prevent the establishment of a Jewish state. Palestinians placed the responsibility for the outcome of these fateful years on Israel, Britain, and others but without neglecting their own. For the Palestinians, this period was a defining moment, closing a chapter of half a century of failed resistance to Jewish and British designs in Palestine. It was also a combination of a failure to assemble a unified nation, build effective national institutions, or engage in serious state-building.

The Nakba

The Palestinians saw Israel as responsible for their 1948 *Nakba*, or catastrophe, which to them meant the loss of their homeland to the Zionists or to the new state, Israel, which now came to control an even larger part of Palestine than that allotted to it by the UN partition plan. But they also saw others contributing to this outcome: Jordan, which annexed the area which in the war's aftermath came to be called the West Bank of Jordan, and Egypt, which placed the Gaza Strip under its military administration. Moreover, the *Nakba* in the loss of the homeland was not considered merely territorial. Most Palestinians lost their homes and property and were forced to live as refugees in camps inside historic Palestine, in the West Bank and the Gaza Strip, as well as in exile in neighboring countries, primarily Jordan, Lebanon, Syria, and Egypt.

Nakba also meant that the Palestinians now saw their leadership as totally decimated by the war – it was now forced to remain in exile or integrate into the new political entities, most notably the new Jordan that now controlled their destiny. Palestinians who now came under Israel's control were treated as second-class citizens. Placed under military administration with emergency regulations applied specifically to them, their land was confiscated and their movement was restricted. Many were forced to remain internal refugees, forbidden to return to villages and towns that they were forced to abandon during the fighting.

Rejection of Partition

In justifying their rejection of partition, Palestinians believed that the UN partition resolution inflicted upon them a great historic injustice. It gave a large part of their country to foreign, mostly Eastern European settlers, who had no rightful claim to the land: they were much fewer and owned only a fraction of the country's territory. Moreover, Palestinians believed that their rejection of partition did not justify the response of the Zionists, whom they saw as having initiated the armed hostilities before the arrival of the Arab armies on May 15th.

The Zionists, Palestinians believed, did not intend to settle for what the partition plan offered them. Instead, they were intent on expanding the borders of their state and "cleansing" the areas they wanted for their state of as many Palestinians as possible. Consequently, Israel was seen as fully responsible for the creation of the Palestinian refugee problem.

War and Defeat

For the Palestinians, the Zionists' war plans, military operations, tactics (e.g., use of artillery against civilians in villages and towns), and war propaganda (spreading rumors about impending Zionist attacks and probable annihilation of population) were purposefully aimed at forcing the indigenous population out of their homes and land so that new Jewish settlers could replace them and the new state would have a decisive Jewish majority.

Palestinians believed that the defeat was the outcome of their own weakness and the absence of their leadership on the eve of the war. The lack of a unified Arab command and the poor performance and inferior armaments of the Arab armies was no match for the superior Zionist forces. They believed that while the Arab people fully sympathized with them, the Arab regimes were under the influence of Britain, the main colonial power in the region, and that the aim of these leaders in ordering their armies into the war was not to liberate it for the Palestinians' sake but to secure for themselves control over the territory allotted by the partition resolution to the Arab state.

Uprooting and Marginalization

Palestinians further believed that their uprooting was deliberate. This being the case, and given international laws and norms including UN Resolution 194, Palestinians believed that all refugees and their descendants had the right to return to their original homes and properties or receive compensation if they so choose. They believed "occupation" of their homeland by "foreign settlers" gave them the morally legitimate and internationally sanctioned right to fight back by all means, including "armed resistance."

In Palestinian eyes, the aftermath of the 1948 War was characterized by deliberate efforts on the part of the Arab states to marginalize them, either because of intra-Arab rivalries and ambitions or because they saw the Palestinians as a threat to the stability of their relations with Israel after the signing of the armistice agreements. Thus Egypt and Jordan – the two countries in control of the remaining parts of historic Palestine – rejected the efforts by the exiled Palestinian leadership to declare the creation of a Palestinian entity or to establish state institutions.

Arab Narratives

Rejecting Partition

The Arab states rejected UN Resolution 181 for two main reasons. First, they believed that Palestine was an integral part of the Arab world and that, therefore, the Arab states had an obligation to support the Palestinians who had opposed the creation of a Jewish National Home in their country. Even before partition, the growing Jewish community in Palestine was viewed by the Arab states as posing an increasing threat to Arab control over, and the Arab character of, Palestine by purchasing land, building villages and towns, and establishing autonomous and effective institutions.

Second, the Arab states argued that the United Nations, a body which was created and controlled by the colonial powers (the United States and Western European countries), had no right to grant the Zionists any portion of their territory. The Arab states accused the Western countries of trying to soothe their conscience for the atrocities of the Second World War by paying their debt to the Jewish people with Arab land.[38]

Israel as Colonialism

The developments of the 1948 War reinforced the major facets of the Arab narrative that began developing in the early 1930s. The first major argument was that the support provided to the Zionists by the West, and especially by Britain and the United States, was an integral part of a larger colonial scheme. The scheme aimed to create a hostile state in the heart of the Arab land in an attempt to prevent Arab or Muslim unity. Thus, the Jewish state was perceived as a colonial arm of the West. It was viewed as an even broader attempt to spur a confrontation between the Zionists and the major national independence movements in the area. A powerful Jewish state was therefore intended to suppress any Arab anti-colonial resistance. Palestine was the connection between the East and the West of the Arab World. Hence, creating a non-Arab and predominantly non-Muslim alien state and placing it there would make any triumph of a major Arab state impossible.

The colonial goal was seen as building a purely Jewish state – not a Palestinian state that includes, in addition to its Arab majority, people with different affiliations of Islam, Christianity, and Judaism. The Arab anti-colonial narrative also viewed Jewish political and paramilitary organizations such as the *Haganah* and the *Irgun* as terrorist groups and gangs who committed atrocities and horrific acts of terror as a means of expelling the true inhabitants of Palestine. These terrorist groups would either force the transfer of Palestinians to other parts of the Arab world or establish a state based on racial discrimination, where Jews would enjoy all the privileges of a first class minority.

Finally, if the Jews failed to conquer all of Palestine, their last resort would be to accept a partitioning of the land in the framework of which they would constitute a majority in its better parts. Even so, the Jews' hope and aspirations to conquer the entire land would be merely postponed until they could populate the occupied land with a Jewish majority. Thus, all Zionist expansion projects were built on the same two constant pillars of expulsion and transfer. These projects would not end until the Zionists succeeded in building their Judaic state spanning the entire area, from the Nile to the Euphrates.[39]

Religious Conflict

Some Arab narratives about the conflict had powerful religious connotations, characterizing it as a war between Muslims and Jews over the Holy Land in Palestine. Other Arab narratives adopted a secular-nationalist and even leftist-Marxist orientation. In operational terms, Arab narratives saw Islam, the Arab world, and Arab masses as facing the onslaught of the combined forces of the West, the Jews, and all those who sought to gain world dominance and hegemony. The early recognition granted to the Zionist state simultaneously by both the United States and the Soviet Union – the two postwar superpowers – was seen as evidence of the superior forces with which Arabs were now confronted. The support provided by the West dating back to the Balfour Declaration, and now manifesting itself in support for the unjust partition plan, and the weapons provided to the Zionists before and during the 1948 War by the newly born Soviet bloc, were together taken as conclusive evidence that the entire world was conspiring to defeat the Arabs.

However, while this part of the Arab narrative assigned the blame for the Arab states' defeat to "others," another dimension of the narrative – focusing mostly on why the Arab side was defeated in the 1948 War – placed the blame squarely on the corrupt Arab leaders who failed to mobilize the necessary resources for the war and lacked the skill to manage the conflict. In Egypt, King Farouk was accused of acquiring defective weapons for his troops, purchased through corrupt arms deals. Jordan's King Abdullah was accused of "selling Lydda and Ramlah to the Zionists." Other Arab rulers were seen as being "soft" and lacking in determination to rescue the people of Palestine.

The Egyptian and Transjordanian Narratives

Within the general characteristics of the broader Arab narrative, in each of the Arab countries specific elements of this narrative were emphasized. For example, the Egyptian narrative assigned to the British special responsibility for Egypt's defeat. The British were viewed as having dragged Egypt into the war without any consideration for the extent to which Egypt was in fact prepared for the fight. Britain's ascribed motivation had to do with its dwindling standing in the aftermath of the Second World War and the corresponding rise of the United States. The competition between the two, and the United States' support for the creation of a Jewish state, compelled Britain to support the Arab side, including Egypt. But Britain's interest in maintaining its military presence in Egypt, including in the Suez Canal zone, was seen as dictating an interest that Egypt's military forces be kept weak and therefore dependent on the British. By encouraging Egypt to go to war, providing it with just enough weapons to enter the fighting, and then denying it the weapons and ammunition needed to avoid defeat, the British were viewed as gaining the resultant Egyptian postwar dependence they sought. In the war's aftermath Britain could credibly argue that Egypt was too weak to protect the Suez Canal.[40]

The Transjordanian narrative of this period is essentially King Abdullah's narrative.[41] As early as 1939, Abdullah (then an Emir under the British Mandate) had urged the Palestinians to accept the MacDonald White Paper, which would have created a state with a two-thirds Arab majority. Yet the Palestinians and Zionists ultimately rejected the British proposal. Abdullah saw himself as deeply devoted to the Palestinian cause but as constantly confronted and contradicted by forces in the Arab world that refused to deal pragmatically with the Zionists. During the 1948 War, Abdullah resented the fact that while Jordan's Arab Legion fought hard to retain control over Jerusalem, the Arab League gave its blessing to the establishment of an "All Palestine Government" based in Gaza. Not only did he see the APG as being under sponsorship of his Egyptian rivals, it was led by Hajj Amin al-Husseini, the Mufti of Jerusalem, whom Abdullah viewed as undermining the broader Palestinian cause.

When planning the 1948 War, Abdullah counted on Egyptian forces to conduct a northern thrust up through the Negev, and when this failed to take place, he felt personally snubbed by Egypt's perceived abandonment. Although he had been given the title of Commander in Chief of the Arab forces, Abdullah felt he was never fully entrusted to lead the Arab cause against the Zionists. He was reinforced in that belief by what he saw as the Arab countries' reluctance to commit the requisite forces, in size, form, and weapons stocks.

Abdullah opposed the internationalization of Jerusalem, believing it was his "duty to stand resolutely and firmly in the defense of the Arab character of the Holy City..."[42] During the first phase of the war, he urged the Arab states to uphold the ceasefire so that their armed forces could restock. Consequently, he found their breach of the ceasefire to be ill-advised and detrimental to the Arab cause. Accordingly, he explained that without sufficient arms and equipment, the Arab Legion had no choice but to withdraw from Lydda and Ramleh, paving the way for Israel's conquest of the two towns. More broadly, he attributed the failure of the Arab states to mount a successful attack against the Zionists in 1948 to the lack of a unified command and "sincere determination."[43] Regarding the merging of Jordan and the West Bank following the war, Abdullah believed the annexation was a restoration of the natural, patriotic bond between the Palestinians and their Jordanian brothers.

The Iraqi Narrative

The Iraqi narrative[44] for this period was characterized by disdain for the British, whom Iraqis saw as having abandoned the Arab cause; bewilderment at a perceived American hostility; and frustration at "the vacillation and weakness of the other Arab states, particularly Egypt and Saudi Arabia."[45] During the war, Iraqi soldiers sent to Palestine were under the command of Jordan's Abdullah, who is said to have assigned them a defensive role and to have prohibited them from attacking Israeli positions in the coastal plain or the Galilee (areas assigned to the Jewish state by the UN partition plan).[46] The limits placed on the Iraqi units frustrated many junior army officers and led Iraqis to resent the other Arab states for what they perceived as a lack of coordination and resolve to defeat the Zionists.

After the war, following attempts on the part of the Egyptian government to place some of the blame for the Arab defeat in the Negev on Iraqi inaction, Iraqi leaders like Nuri al-Sa'id and Salih Jabr retorted that Iraq was the Arab country that continued to advocate a unified, pan-Arab military strategy – a strategy the other Arab states had rejected. Iraqis felt similarly snubbed when their proposal for the imposition of an oil embargo following the war failed to gain traction among the other members of the Arab League. Up until the 1958 revolution, the Iraqi narrative continued to emphasize Iraq's uniqueness in its devotion to the pan-Arab cause and the detrimental role of the other Arab states in sabotaging Iraq's plan for coordinated Arab action.[47]

Analysis

Two dramatic interrelated developments characterizing this period require thorough explanations: first, what propelled the Arabization of the conflict? In other words, how and why was the Palestinian–Zionist conflict transformed into a Middle East-wide Arab–Israeli conflict? And second, what accounts for the outcome of the 1948 War? What explains the Arabs' political-military defeat and the Israelis' success in overcoming their potentially more numerous adversaries?

The Arabization of the Conflict

The Arabization of the Palestinian–Israeli conflict – the decision of the Arab states to "take over" the conflict – began with these states opposing the partitioning of Palestine and deploying their forces there in mid-May 1948. In the aftermath of the 1948 War, the Arab state system continued to eclipse the Palestine issue and to diminish the role of the Palestinians. Accordingly, Egypt and Jordan decided to assume control over the territories that were allotted to the Palestinian Arab state in the framework of the 1947 UN partition plan but were not conquered by Israel. In the case of Jordan, this eventually led to the annexation of the West Bank, including East

Jerusalem. Egypt refrained from annexing the Gaza Strip and it did not suppress Palestinian nationalist sentiments there. Yet, it applied its administration in Gaza, assumed total control of the area, and denied any Palestinian attempt at institution-building there.

Why was this policy adopted? Why did the Arab states send their forces to Palestine and why in the war's aftermath did they oppose Palestinian statehood and prevent the latter from establishing a state in the West Bank and Gaza? Why did Jordan move not only to annex the West Bank but also to de-Palestinianize it by relocating all important administrative institutions from Jerusalem to Amman, thus marginalizing the Palestinian dimension of the now expanded Transjordan?

The Regional System

At the systemic level, the decision to "Arabize" the Palestinian–Israeli conflict by sending forces to Palestine seems to have resulted from the anarchic nature of the Middle East sub-system as well as from the distribution of power within the region itself. With Britain's power in the Middle East diminishing and its ability to control developments in the region rapidly declining, the region increasingly resembled an anarchic realm. Within this anarchic realm, the UN stipulated, but could not enforce, its decision that two new states – Israel and Palestine – would emerge for the first time in history, with uncertain regional and international standing. As a result, the leaders of the region's constituent states faced an increasingly acute security dilemma, suspecting one another's intentions and designs, and fearing that their neighbors posed threats to their security and aspirations.

The effects of such anarchy were not mitigated by the attempt to introduce a sense of hierarchy in the form of the Arab League. While the League manifested an effort to institutionalize Arab nationalism and to provide a venue for managing Arab rivalries, it was too weak to erase these rivalries. Thus, although Arab publics seem to have believed that the League constituted an alliance, Arab elites were well aware that this was not the case.

In the absence of a party or institution capable of mitigating the effects of anarchy, Arab states were left to pursue self-help measures to insure their security and survival. This required first and foremost that none among them would strengthen at the expense of the other. Seen through this prism, the decision of Jordan, Egypt, and Syria to send military forces into Palestine in May 1948 was propelled at least as much by regional balance-of-power considerations – with each country acting to prevent the other from gaining a hold over the coveted land – as it was by the desire to erase or constrain the nascent Jewish state.

At the time, four pivotal states of the Middle East were competing for different levels of regional power: Egypt, Transjordan, Syria, and Saudi Arabia. Strategic and regional political objectives attracted the four to the question of Palestine, each with separate and different objectives, yet all efforts revolving around developments taking place in Palestine.

In Egypt, King Farouk, seeking final-status negotiations for independence from Britain, was advised to formalize an Egyptian policy towards his country's eastern boundaries, because it had strategic security interests in Palestine and the Levant in general. Compared to Saudi Arabia and Transjordan, Egypt at the time was the most powerful, stable, and developed state. Farouk also assessed that he might be able to fill the political gap created by the abolition of the Islamic caliphate by Turkey in 1924. With such ambitions, he could not possibly ignore the Palestinian question. Indeed, this also comprised the context of Egypt's support of the establishment of the Arab League.

In turn, King Abdullah of Jordan was eager to increase the size of his sparsely populated kingdom. By the eve of the 1948 War he had already lost hope of regaining influence in the Hejaz that his father once ruled, before Abdel Aziz al-Saud succeeded in taking over the Hejaz and Nejd and establishing his own Kingdom there. Syria was also beyond King Abdullah's reach as a result of the French interests there. It was not surprising, therefore, that he saw the UN proposal to partition Palestine as his last opportunity to expand the size of his kingdom.[48] In his contacts with the Jewish Agency, he did not show discomfort with the idea of a Jewish state on his borders. The two parties reached an understanding that met their interests: the Yishuv's *Haganah* forces would deploy in the parts of Palestine accorded by the UN partition plan to the Jewish State, while the Jordanian Arab Legion would take hold of the Arab side of Palestine and annex it to the kingdom.

As for Saudi Arabia, King Abdel Aziz had expressed to the United States his concerns about its support of Jewish immigration to Palestine. Saudi Arabia, therefore, had never accepted the idea of a Jewish state in Palestine. Yet, the Saudis seemed more threatened by the political maneuvers of Abdullah of Jordan who believed that the Hejaz was illegitimately taken away from his father. The Saudis also knew that the Jordanian king had contacts with the Jewish Agency and that he possessed a more modern and better equipped army than they did. Therefore, it was in the Saudis' interest to improve their relations with Egypt and to call for greater Egyptian engagement in Palestine so as to balance Jordan's ambitions.[49]

For its part, Egypt seems to have been motivated by the fear that Jordan intended to expand the Hashemite Kingdom at the Palestinians' expense and would then be able to project threats to the south. Thus Egypt feared that without formally endorsing partition, Jordan actually made a deal with the Zionists that gave it control over the Arab part of Palestine in accordance with the UN's partition plan. In turn, Jordan's Abdullah seemed to have feared that Syria harbored similar designs and that it intended to recreate Greater Syria, to initially include Syria, Lebanon, and large parts of Palestine and in the future Jordan as well.

These fears were merely mirror-images of similar concerns harbored in Damascus. Syria saw its involvement in the war in Palestine as necessary to maintain its recently acquired independence – a concern shared by Lebanon, another new and fledgling state[50] – and to prevent Jordan's Abdullah from fulfilling his expansionist designs. President Shukri al-Quwwatli of Syria was convinced that the war in Palestine would afford Abdullah a chance to destroy the Syrian republican regime and to substitute it with his Hashemite rule.[51] Syria was determined to thwart Abdullah's Greater Syria scheme by embracing the Arab League and building up the Arab Liberation Army into a force that could keep Abdullah in check.[52] Not surprisingly, each of these leaders developed ambitious plans as a way of aborting the perceived designs of their rivals.

For Egypt in particular, Palestine also had an international dimension: after the Second World War it saw Jewish settlement in Palestine as part of a plan by the Soviet Union to expand its influence to the Middle East. Egypt feared that if this plan were to materialize it would find the Soviets' long arm posing a serious threat along its eastern borders. This was deemed particularly threatening as Moscow was seen as following a policy of zero tolerance toward monarchies. Egypt further feared that this, in turn, would lead either to the prolonging of the British presence in the Suez Canal or the expansion of Soviet influence on Egyptian soil. These outcomes were equally unacceptable to Egypt.

Another important factor that seems to have propelled Arab states and non-state actors to enter the 1948 conflict was the vacuum created by the absence of a strong Palestinian actor, and the almost total absence of a credible Palestinian leadership or public institutions. The British did not prepare the Palestinians for statehood; they were far more interested in strengthening Jordan. Thus, as weak as the Zionists may have been perceived to be by the neighboring Arab states, these states could not count on the Palestinians to block the Zionists' designs.

In the aftermath of the 1948 War, Arab states' decision to evade the Palestinian issue seems to have been propelled by a different set of systemic factors: now that their weakness had been exposed and Israel's strength revealed, the national security of Egypt and Jordan as well as the security of their regimes required that the Palestinians be prevented from embroiling them in escalatory processes over which they would have no control.

Thus, while Jordan's decision to annex the West Bank seems to have been propelled largely by its grand designs for a greater Hashemite Kingdom, Egypt's decision to avoid annexing Gaza while assuming complete control over its territory seems to have been primarily motivated by the imperative of denying the Palestinians the option of embroiling Egypt in undesired escalation. These priorities were not offset by serious external pressures. Dominated by Egypt at the time, the Arab League did not push for independent Palestinian statehood. And despite its rivalry with Jordan, Egypt was more interested in stabilizing its armistice regime with Israel than in Palestinian state-building. Nor did any of the powers external to the region exert such pressure. Certainly Britain, who continued to exert considerable influence on Egyptian and Jordanian policies, did not favor such statehood. Instead it preferred that Palestine be partitioned, with some of it to be given to the Zionists and some to the Hashemite Kingdom.

For its part, the Palestinian leadership, in exile and further weakened by the outcome of the war, was not in a position to challenge the Arab takeover of the Palestine question. Notwithstanding the lip-service to the cause of Palestinian independence that it exercised in September 1948 with its endorsement of the All Palestine Government, Egypt did not want to relinquish control of the Gaza Strip to the Palestinians. Thus Arab decisions in 1948–49 sealed the fate of Palestinian state-building efforts.

The Arab States' Domestic Scenes

At the unit level, the weakness of the Palestinians had created a vacuum which was soon to be filled by states with ambitions and by an array of non-state actors who were committed to pan-Arab and pan-Islamic causes. In Syria, as already noted, support for the Palestinian cause was propelled in part by President Shukri al-Quwwatli's concern that a weak Syrian army would be no match for the Jordanian Arab Legion. In an effort to forestall perceived Hashemite threats to Syrian independence, Quwwatli reasoned that Syria's interest would be served by preventing a peaceful resolution to the Palestine question between Transjordan and the Zionists. However, given that Syria was a democracy at the time, Quwwatli was also accountable to public opinion, then strongly in favor of going to war to keep Palestine Arab.[53]

Within Arab societies – and especially in Egypt – there were important pan-Arab and pan-Islamic constituencies that adopted the Palestinian cause and which the regime, facing serious legitimacy problems, could not afford to ignore. This was primarily the case with Egypt's intellectuals as well as the Muslim Brotherhood (MB). The latter began sending volunteers to fight in Palestine before Israel's declaration of independence propelled the Egyptian state's military intervention. Such intervention was also demanded by an emotional media and an array of student groups and NGOs who adopted the Palestinian cause.

Indeed, most non-state actors in Egypt were strongly opposed to the partition plan and the establishment of the Israeli state. This position was to be expected in light of increasing awareness of Arab and Islamic values that developed even before the First World War.[54] The rejection of partition and the escalating hostilities towards the Zionists in Palestine were prominent components of the political rhetoric of Egyptian non-state actors. Yet each of these actors had a somewhat different rationale for rejecting partition and Jewish statehood.

Al-Wafd, the majority party, stood firmly in support of the Egyptian government's decision to go to war in 1948. Having become sympathetic to the Palestinian question in the early 1920s, it now saw Palestinians as facing the same forces of colonialism that Egyptians did, and as representing the same two values espoused by *al-Wafd*: Arab nationalism and anti-colonialism.[55] The Muslim Youth Association (MYA) – a branch of Mustafa Kamel's National Party – was equally opposed to the establishment of a Jewish state in Palestine.[56] *Hizb Misr al-Fatah* [the Young Egypt Party], now renamed the Egyptian Socialist Party, adopted a similar position, and was among the first to advocate militant resistance to the Zionists' goals in Palestine.[57]

The Muslim Brotherhood declared *Jihad* against Zionism in Palestine. For them, the conflict was religious in nature – between Muslims and Jews, with the latter being blessed by Christian crusaders and Western colonialists. Their support of the Palestinians began to evolve soon after the movement's creation in 1928 and it developed further when, during the revolt of 1936–39, it sent volunteers from among its members and Egyptian youth to fight in Palestine.[58]

Egyptian trade unions and professional associations (called "syndicates") also encouraged the government to participate in the war.[59] By contrast, the Democratic Front for National Liberation, a Marxist movement, argued that colonialism was the major enemy and that Arabs should therefore accept the partition plan and work hand-in-hand with the Zionists to expel colonialism from Palestine and the Middle East.[60]

Palestinian Internal Politics

Palestinian domestic affairs were equally important in propelling the decision of the Arab states to take over the conflict. In the first instance, the Palestinians' failure to build pre-state institutions created a vacuum which, had the Arab states failed to fill it, might have resulted in an even worse catastrophe. Indeed, the 1947 partition plan caught the Palestinians at their weakest moment. Fragmented and leaderless, they continued to suffer from the outcome of developments that contributed to their defeat in the 1936–39 revolt.

The Palestinians' internal weakness also explains the continued Arabization of the conflict in the aftermath of the 1948 War. Now the Palestinians' pre-state failures were compounded by the complete discrediting of their leadership. The Mufti was exposed as utterly ineffective. Worse still, much of the Palestinian elite found itself in exile, in countries that now considered taking over its cause. Elements of the Palestinian elite now found themselves weakened by their status as refugees in the West Bank, where they also faced rejection from Palestinians who were indigenous to the area. As a result, these leaders in exile were now vulnerable to the Hashemites' insistence that they adopt an Arab, not a Palestinian, identity

That the Palestinian national leadership was not up to the challenge was clearly reflected in the effort by the Mufti to establish a Palestinian government in the Gaza Strip and to declare statehood. The Arabs' defeat destroyed every basis for Palestinian statehood: its socioeconomic basis was shattered, its territorial basis was taken away, and in the absence of state structures or public institutions any attempt at independent statehood was doomed. Thus, while much of the resistance to independent Palestinian statehood came from Jordan and Egypt, it was the collapse of the Palestinian society and the lack of credibility of its leadership that made the idea irrelevant. As a result, the fragmented Palestinian public and most of its weak nationalist leadership went along with the annexation of the West Bank to Jordan, while Egypt's imposition of military administration and emergency laws in the Gaza Strip faced little or no resistance.

The Role of Leaders

At the individual level, attention should be focused on two monarchs, of Egypt and Jordan, who had different but very special and important interests in the Palestinian question. The main similarity between the two sovereigns was the political rhetoric they used when addressing the issue of the Arab and Islamic rights in Palestine, the urgency and importance they attached to defending the holy city of Jerusalem, and their responsibility as Muslim Arab leaders to defend the Arab land. Egypt's king preferred to be addressed during the crisis of Palestine as "al-Farouk," a title reserved in Islamic traditions for the second caliph Omar ibn al-Khattab, whose pious and just nature earned him the title of *al-Faruq* ("one who distinguishes between right and wrong"). In turn, Emir Abdullah of Jordan preferred to be described as the Protector of the Holy Mosque.

Jordan's Abdullah

The Hashemite royal family was torn between their noble origin and their sense of victimization. Having been pushed out of Hejaz by Saudi Arabia's King Ibn Saud, their dreams of a Greater Arab Kingdom were shattered. Abdullah and his Hashemite family had no choice but to try to establish a new kingdom. Indeed, having led the Great Arab Revolt during the First World War, they considered themselves entitled at least to Greater Syria. But when Abdullah conveyed his Greater Syria project to leaders of the Arab League, they did not welcome his ideas – resistance was led by Egypt, Syria, and Saudi Arabia. Hence, Palestine was the only territory open for King Abdullah to expand.

Now Abdullah perceived the Palestinian question as an opportunity that he should not miss. The Emirate of Transjordan was too small, remote, arid, and lacking in vital natural resources to fulfill his political ambitions. This was especially so compared to the possessions of his younger brother, Faisal, who was granted Syria and then Iraq as part of a settlement between Britain and France regarding their colonies.

Through contacts with powerful elements in the Jewish Agency, Abdullah sought and reached an understanding with the Zionist movement, committing him to supporting the establishment of a Jewish state on the lands allotted to the Zionists by the UN partition plan as long as he was permitted to annex the territories that the plan allotted to the Arab state, including the West Bank and the Gaza Strip.[61] This was meant not only to increase the size of Transjordan but also to provide it with a critically important seaport – an outlet to the Mediterranean. Through what he assessed were the Jewish Agency's contacts in Britain and the United States, Abdullah also hoped to secure greater financial assistance and political recognition for his kingdom.[62] Thus, Abdullah took charge of decisions that had the effect of marginalizing the Palestinians.

Egypt's Farouk

Egypt's King Farouk saw in Palestine a different opportunity. Farouk was a descendant of the Alaouite Dynasty that ruled Egypt since Muhammad Ali began to create modern Egypt in 1805. Ali and his successors sought a regional role for Egypt that extended beyond its borders. Ibrahim Pasha's expeditions to the *Mashreq* and to Arabia in the 1830s were propelled by a dream for Egyptian hegemony. The end of the Islamic caliphate in Turkey created a new dream: Fuad, the first King of Egypt (1917–36) and his son Farouk saw themselves as the rightful inheritors of the caliphate.

After the end of the Second World War, King Farouk focused on negotiating complete independence from Britain and the withdrawal of British forces from the Suez Canal. At the same time, a number of his close advisors argued that Palestine was the perfect candidate for extending Egypt's influence under these new circumstances. This, they stressed, could be done through the Arab League, established earlier under Egyptian auspices.[63] In this fashion, not only could Egypt's influence be extended, but – no less important – Jordan's expansionist designs could be checked.

Involvement in the Palestine issue also served Farouk's domestic interests. By the late 1940s Egypt's internal stability was shaky and Farouk's popularity was waning as his lavish and ostentatious lifestyle, as well as that of other members of his family, and his rumored addiction to gambling and womanizing, were increasingly scrutinized. At the same time, Egyptian public opinion was increasingly moving towards adherence to Arab nationalism and Islam. In such an environment, support for the Palestinian cause could gain Egypt's beleaguered King some much needed popularity.

Explaining Independence and Nakba

Turning to the second question – What accounts for the outcome of the 1948 War? – it is necessary to ascertain exactly what it is that requires explanation: Who won and who lost in 1948? Clearly, having obtained nearly all of its objectives, Israel emerged from the 1948 War as the great winner. It gained independence, it expanded its territory beyond that which was allotted to it by UN Resolution 181, and it ended up with a state that was far more homogeneous – nationally and ethnically – than would have been the case had the war not occurred.

The Palestinians were the great losers. Their *Nakba* consisted not only of the loss of their territory to Israel, Egypt, and Jordan but also of any hope for national independence. More than 700,000 Palestinians were displaced, and Israel, celebrating its new and relatively homogenous state, was not about to allow their return.

Another loser was Egypt: it failed to defend the territory allotted to the Palestinian state in the south. Worse still, it was on the Egyptian front that the newly born Israeli Defense Forces succeeded in carrying out their deepest incursion into an Arab state – well into the Sinai. By contrast, Jordan did not lose the war – it ended it with full control over the West Bank and it succeeded in defeating every Israeli effort to gain control over the Jewish Quarter of Jerusalem's Old City and the Hebrew University campus on Mount Scopus. Similarly, Syria was not defeated; indeed, it ended the war possessing territories east of the international border between Syria and Palestine.

What accounts for the Israelis' success but also for the different outcomes for the respective Arab players?

The International System

At the *global-systemic level* the international environment at the end of the Second World War could not have been more hospitable and favorable to the Zionist project. The Holocaust created broad international support for Jewish statehood, with Americans now expressing contrition at their own failure to open their doors to European Jews in the late 1930s. Now, United States occupation forces in Europe were pressing to alleviate the plight of hundreds of thousands of Jewish survivors who were crammed in Displaced Persons camps throughout the continent. And Britain, which was more sensitive to Arab concerns, was too weak and bankrupt to resist President Truman's resolve to support Jewish statehood.

The immediate aftermath of the Second World War provided a large window of opportunity to the Zionist enterprise in yet another way: despite the appearance of the Iron Curtain, the Cold War had yet to take hold, and during the second half of the 1940s the United States and the Soviet Union could still come together on specific issues. Both supported Jewish statehood, voted in favor of partitioning Palestine, and were the first to recognize the newly created State of Israel.

Importantly, the Soviet Union authorized and encouraged some of its new satellites in Eastern Europe to supply arms to Israel – thus indirectly becoming Israel's primary arms supplier. Motivated to create inroads in the Middle East, and anticipating that the social-democratic leaders of the Zionist movement would be receptive to Soviet influence, Stalin for a time decided to throw Russia's weight behind the Jewish state.

The distribution of international sympathy and support favoring Israel had a decisive influence over the regional balance of power. In the immediate postwar period, all force-balancing in the Middle East was external – relying on outside assistance. Indigenous arms manufacturing was years away; thus Arabs and Jews at this point were mere consumers, not producers, of the means of military power. And while it was not easy for the Jewish Agency to offset French and British military support for the offspring of their former empires, the converging interests of the United States and the Soviet Union produced a unique opportunity to do this successfully.

The Regional System

The balance of power at the *regional-systemic level* was also affected by the distribution of power between the region and its international environment. Although experiencing decolonization, the region's states during this period had far inferior power compared to their former colonizers. Consequently, the latter could easily set limits on the regional states' freedom of action. In this context, Britain's apparent insistence that the Arab armies were not to cross the lines marking the boundaries of the Jewish state according to the UN partition plan had a profound effect on Arab war plans – particularly on those of Jordan.[64]

Within the region, inter-Arab rivalries affected the distribution of power in a number of different ways. The most important of these was that while comprising "the few," the Israelis found themselves confronting a highly fragmented coalition of the Arab "many." Consequently, each of the Arab states engaged in the fighting did so in a bifocal manner, at once targeting Israel while at the same time ensuring that their rivals did not acquire undue gains in the war over Palestine. And, as noted earlier, while the Arab League attempted to introduce some cohesion and coordination into the Arab war effort – it could not overcome these centrifugal forces.

In turn, inter-Arab tensions resulted in the almost complete lack of coordination between the warring forces, making it practically impossible to use one country's forces to alleviate Israeli pressures on another. Worse still, Arab forces were not deployed and employed in a manner which maximized their military utility. Instead, they were positioned to ensure that their Arab rivals did not make gains at their expense.[65]

In addition, Egypt and Syria – and even more so, more distant Arab states which sent small expeditionary forces to fight in Palestine – faced serious logistical problems in confronting Israel. Indeed, some among the top echelons of the Egyptian military advised King Farouk against military intervention not only because in their estimate the Egyptian forces were weak but also because of concern about the long logistical lines entailed in fighting in far-away Palestine.

Within this broader context the numerically inferior Jews had a number of distinct advantages. First, they were highly motivated. Following the Holocaust, they saw Jewish statehood as providing the only guarantee against such atrocities recurring. Second, assessing that the Arabs' rejection of Jewish statehood meant that a grand struggle with the surrounding Arab states was inevitable, the leaders of the Yishuv began to overhaul the top echelons of its security forces, replacing those who had excelled in commando operations against the Palestinians (and, to a lesser degree, against the British) with individuals who had served in the allied armed forces during the Second World War and thus gained experience in commanding large conventional military formations.

Yet, not all Zionist forces demonstrated higher resolve and better training than their Arab counterparts – some Jewish soldiers were recruited soon after reaching Palestine, finding themselves in difficult battles before they could receive minimum military training or even master the Hebrew language enough to understand commands. Also, some of the Arab fighting forces were well equipped, well trained, and demonstrated a high degree of professionalism. This was particularly the case with the Jordanian Arab Legion which had been organized, exercised, and led by General Glubb, in line with the best of British military traditions. Still, the Jewish forces enjoyed overall qualitative superiority – an edge reflected in almost all the battles of the 1948 War.

The Yishuv's and the Palestinians' Domestic Scenes

At the unit level, the Jewish Yishuv in Palestine – and later the State of Israel – had a distinct advantage over its rivals. To be sure, the Yishuv was split along ideological, political, ethnic, and religious–secular lines. During the Second World War the sharpest of such differences concerned whether or not the Yishuv should violently resist Britain's continued Mandate or avoid such armed resistance as long as Britain was fighting Nazi Germany. In the last phase of the war the split was so sharp that during what was then called "the season," the mainstream *Haganah* went so far as to kidnap and interrogate *Etzel* members in order to extract information about the whereabouts of their leaders, some of whom they subsequently handed over to the British. They also provided the British secret police with some names of *Etzel* donors.[66]

Yet the disagreements, debates and splits within the Yishuv were mediated by a highly institutionalized structure. As a result, by the time Britain withdrew its forces and colonial authorities from Palestine, the Yishuv's bureaucracy was fully prepared to take its place.

By contrast, refusing to recognize the British mandate, the Palestinians rejected Britain's suggestion that they build institutions of their own, parallel to those of the Yishuv. Equally important, the splits within the Yishuv paled in comparison to the total fragmentation experienced by the Palestinian society. Dating back to the 1930s, Palestinians were split not only along religious and rural–urban lines, but also by allegiance to the different notable families at the top of their social structure.[67] More importantly, the British authorities reacted to the Arab revolt of 1936–39 by exiling many among the more talented of the Palestinian leaders. As a result, these leaders were absent from the scene when they were most needed – that is, when the British Mandate was coming to an end.

Arab States and Societies

Similarly weak were the societies of the surrounding Arab states that now invaded Palestine. First, most were still engaged in their own efforts to gain independence from their former colonizers. Consequently, they were unsure where they should focus their efforts: in confronting the British or against the Zionists. Second, their bureaucracies and institutions were fragile, ineffective and corrupt, leading to the failure to mobilize their national resources in a fashion commensurate to the challenge. Third, Arab state leaders were torn between considerations of national priorities and regime security. Thus, their ability and willingness to deploy military forces in Palestine were mitigated by their concern that these forces – upon which their regimes' security was based – would be weakened by the fighting in Palestine.

Egypt is a case in point – the Egyptian state was in no condition to go to war. First, it was still under British occupation, preparing itself for critically important negotiations aimed at gaining independence through Britain's complete withdrawal. In addition, it experienced growing instability, characterized and affected by a series of high-profile assassinations, such as that of Prime Minister Ahmed Maher in 1945. Riots and strikes were so broad and frequent during this period that even the Egyptian police went on strike.

Moreover, as pointed out earlier, the Egyptian ruling elite was completely divided over the Palestine issue. One group, favoring intervention due to populist, nationalistic, religious, and regional considerations, won the support of the Egyptian monarch. A second group opposed such intervention, arguing that it would prove a distraction from Egypt's more important priority: gaining full independence. This group was led by Prime Minister Fahmy al-Nuqrashi and his predecessor, Ismail Sidqi. It argued that Egypt had no vital interests in Palestine and that Egypt would be far better served by securing a deal with the Jewish Agency in the framework of which, in exchange for Egyptian recognition of the state of Israel, the Jewish Agency would use all its influence in Britain and the United States in support of Egypt's quest for independence.[68] In response to popular support for the Palestinian cause, this group suggested that while volunteers should be sent to conduct armed resistance in Palestine, the Egyptian government's role should be limited to offering training, weapons, and ammunition to these volunteers .[69]

Finally, the Egyptian military was in no condition to wage a war.[70] Its chain of command lacked the experience needed to lead and execute a regional war – it had not conducted military operations since 1931 – and its commander in chief, King Farouk, had no prior military experience.[71] The army lacked sufficient training, experience in battles, strategies, intelligence about their adversary, and, above all, weapons and ammunition. Indeed, the army's top commanders alerted the country's political leaders to all these shortcomings and stressed that, as a result, Egypt was in no position to intervene in Palestine.[72]

Egypt's political leadership did not seem to take the war seriously. Even King Farouk, who pressured his government to take the decision to fight, did not show in practice that he was serious about the war. Instead, Egypt's civilian leaders seemed to assume that the war would be political in nature and that Britain, the United States and the UN would intervene quickly to end the fighting.[73]

By contrast, the Jewish side saw the war literally as a matter of life and death. Its forces in Palestine were much more experienced and far better trained. Many of its officers participated in at least one of the two world wars, offering real-life experience of major combat operations. In addition, the Jewish Agency succeeded in mobilizing its financial, human, and political resources to win the required international cover and support. As a result, in terms of forces actually fielded, the Jewish side outnumbered all the Arab forces combined. Furthermore, during every truce reached, the Jewish side brought in more weapons and ammunition, advancing its operational strategies from the defensive to the offensive.[74]

The Leaders

At the individual level, Israel's triumph and the Palestinians' defeat was affected by the unique characteristics of a number of leaders within and outside the region who played a key role during this period. First among them was Harry S. Truman who, as President of the United States, prevailed over many advisors and cabinet members who believed that America's interests lay predominantly in the Arab Middle East and that Washington should, therefore, avoid antagonizing its potential allies in the region. The latter viewpoint saw the Arab states as possessing more people, space, and control of strategic positions such as the Suez Canal, the straits of Bab Al-Mandab, and Hormoz, on the sea lanes of the Mediterranean, the Red Sea, the Gulf, and the Indian Ocean. The Arabs, in addition, possessed more natural resources, particularly oil, access to which became a key to the allies' victory in the Second World War and, in the war's aftermath, to the livelihood of the industrial world. With American power and industrial base growing at a rapid pace, Arab oil had become essential for developing and sustaining America's new role in the world.

Truman's powerful personality and convictions drove him to override these strong geo-strategic considerations. He was resolute that in the aftermath of the Holocaust, America had a moral obligation to help the Zionist project. He gave this objective priority over conventional realist views of America's interest in the Middle East. The decision of the United States to throw its weight behind the creation of a Jewish state is largely attributable to the unique role played by Truman.

Ben Gurion

On the Israeli side, no single individual played as important a role in accounting for its success in the 1948 War as David Ben Gurion. Building on his experience in guiding the Zionists' response to the Arab revolt of 1936–39 by allying with Britain while also avoiding escalation through the policy of restraint, Ben Gurion played a key role in preparing the Yishuv forces for the challenges that awaited them in the immediate aftermath of Israel's declaration of independence.

Assuming responsibility for the Jewish Agency's defense portfolio in 1946, Ben Gurion understood that resistance to the Zionist project might soon shift from Palestinian insurgents to the conventional forces of the surrounding Arab states. Hence he undertook a massive intellectual enterprise – later called "the seminar" – in which he interviewed all ranking officers of the Yishuv's nascent security forces in an effort to assess these forces' readiness and ascertain what changes in doctrine and force-structure would be required to withstand the radically different challenge.

Ben Gurion's conclusion from these conversations was that the force-structure and defense doctrine of the Yishuv's security forces had to undergo a complete transformation. To do so, he demoted officers who had gained considerable experience and prestige in successfully countering Palestinian fighters and replaced them with men with British army experience in commanding large-scale conventional forces. Assuming that such a conventional confrontation might take place at any moment, Ben Gurion oversaw a massive clandestine effort to purchase surplus Second World War weapons stored in warehouses and abandoned military bases in different continents.

In addition, Ben Gurion understood that the prerequisite to Jewish sovereignty was that the new state had to enjoy a complete monopoly of force. The few, he argued, would never overcome the many if they were not totally unified. Accordingly, he coerced the different armed groups to dismantle their separate frameworks and integrate within the national forces of the new Israeli state.

Equally important was Ben Gurion's historical role in persuading his colleagues to declare Israel's independence on May 15, 1948 – a day after the British withdrew from their Mandate. Many, if not most, of his colleagues were hesitant and skeptical about the wisdom of such a declaration given the magnitude of Arab opposition to the enterprise. Naturally traumatized by the horrors that Jews had experienced only a few years earlier, some of them understandably feared that such a declaration by a weak Yishuv would result in its annihilation, and thus in another Holocaust.

While far from certain of the results of the expected military confrontation, Ben Gurion was convinced that the unique political and strategic conditions created by the immediate postwar environment created a "window of opportunity" which might never be replicated. In particular, he was worried that the massive international sympathy for the Jewish peoples' right to independent statehood would begin to decline once the psychological shock effect of the Holocaust on Western public opinion began to dissipate and the memory of its horrors faded.

Once the War of Independence began, Ben Gurion's personal role as the war's grand-strategist was felt in every important arena. Thus, he and military subordinates insisted that despite Israel's overall numerical inferiority vis-à-vis the invading Arab states, the newly created IDF would achieve both quantitative and qualitative preponderance at every point of engagement by exploiting its "internal lines" for rapid movement of forces from one area to another. In addition, Ben Gurion played a key role in determining where at each stage of the war the IDF should place its main effort and what risks it could take by thinning its forces and thus exposing itself in other fronts in order to achieve such force concentrations.

Concluding Notes

This chapter traced the Yishuv's victory in the 1948 War and the corresponding Arab defeat – the *Nakba* – and its offspring, the Palestinian refugee problem. It addressed the most important regional development on the eve of the war: the Arabization of the conflict – the decision of key Arab states to assume primary responsibility for attempting to thwart the Zionist movement's designs by opposing, first diplomatically and later militarily, the postwar United Nations plan to partition Palestine. The Palestinians disappeared as a central player in the conflict and would not assume such a role for some two and a half decades.

The Arabization of the conflict contributed greatly to making the Arab–Israeli conflict so resilient. No longer was this a struggle between two communities in Palestine. Instead, it became a conflict between states, embroiling much of the region. Moreover, at the community-to-community level, the contrast between the two sides' narratives now became sharper because of the creation of the Palestinian refugee problem. It is in this outcome that the Palestinian narrative of victimhood and abandonment was rooted – and the parallel Israeli narrative that denied any responsibility for the creation of the problem. These sharply differing narratives contributed their share to the further polarization of the conflict, making it resistant to any future efforts to address it.

This chapter also identified the most important determinants of the outcome of the first major clash between the Arab states and the Yishuv which, following May 15, 1948, became the State of Israel. It attributed this outcome to developments in the international system, the most important among them being the rise of the United States as a world power in the Second World War and the international sympathy that the Holocaust brought to the Zionist enterprise. An equally important factor was the Soviet Union's support, propelled by the socialist bent of key social-democratic leaders of the Yishuv, which gave Stalin hope that the future Jewish state might be brought into the Soviet orbit.

By contrast, the embryonic Arab states, which had already been divided by the colonial powers in the early decades of the 20th century, could not get their act together and unite in opposition to the Zionist designs. Equally important in determining their defeat was the limited commitment of Arab governments to the effort to defeat the Zionists. This, in turn, resulted from the collision between the requirements of defeating the Yishuv and other considerations to which their leaders at times attributed higher priority: concerns that their Arab counterparts might gain the upper hand in Palestine and hesitancy in committing military forces that might be needed to ensure their regime's security.

The fact that its neighboring states now became Israel's adversaries had direct, far-reaching, and almost immediate impact on its demography. Thus, as the region's states became increasingly inhospitable to their Jewish communities, mass immigration to Israel from countries spreading from North Africa to Iraq would not only contribute to the doubling of Israel's population in a span of only four years (1949–53), but would also change its composition: from a society dominated by European Jews to one busily absorbing hundreds of thousands of Jews from Arab countries, raised in a different culture and speaking a different language.

On the Arab side, the 1948 War had two equally important outcomes: first, the liberation of Palestine increasingly became the battle-cry of Arab nationalists. Used and abused, this battle-cry was to affect the Arab discourse for decades to come, deepening the conflict and making it apparently permanent. Second, the conflict with Israel, whose performance in the war earned it a reputation as a formidable foe, now meant that security considerations had to be given primacy by Arab states as well. In turn, this had far-reaching consequences for the domestic politics of these states as their militaries now became politically dominant. Thus, in Egypt and Syria, and later in Iraq, military rule became another important legacy of the 1948 War.

Readings

Bickerton, Ian and Carla Klausner, *A History of the Arab–Israeli Conflict* (Prentice Hall, 2010) 73–111.

Bowker, Robert, *Palestinian Refugees: Mythology, Identity and the Search for Peace* (Lynne Rienner, 2003).

Caplan, Neil, *The Israel–Palestine Conflict: Contested Histories* (Wiley, 2010) 101–130.

Dowty, Alan, *Israel/Palestine: Global Political Hotspots* (Polity, 2012) 72–112.

Gelvin, James, *The Israel–Palestine Conflict: One Hundred Years of War* (Cambridge University Press, 2007) 116–143.

Khalidi, Walid, "Plan Dalet: The Zionist Master Plan for the Conquest of Palestine," *Middle East Forum*, 37, 9 (November 1961), 22–28.

Lesch, David, *The Arab–Israeli Conflict* (Oxford University Press, 2008) 94–161.

Morris, Benny, *The Birth of the Palestinian Refugee Problem, 1947–1949* (Cambridge University Press, 1988).

Morris, Benny, 1948: *A History of the First Arab Israeli War* (Yale University Press, 2008).

Morris, Benny, *Righteous Victims: The History of the Zionist–Arab Conflict, 1881–2001* (Vintage, 2001) 161–258.

Pappé, Ilan, *The Making of the Arab–Israeli Conflict, 1947–1951* (IB Tauris, 2004).

Rogan, Eugene L. and Avi Shlaim (Editors), *The War for Palestine: Rewriting the History of 1948* (Cambridge Middle East Studies, Cambridge University Press, 2007).

Shlaim, Avi, *The Iron Wall: Israel and the Arab World* (W.W. Norton, 2001) 28–53.

Smith, Charles D., *Palestine and the Arab–Israeli Conflict* (Bedford/St.Martin's, 2007) 165–221.

Tessler, Mark, *A History of the Israeli–Palestinian Conflict* (Indiana University Press, 2009) 123–268.

Historical documents

The White Paper: Walter Laqueur and Barry Rubin, *The Israel–Arab Reader: A Documentary History of the Middle East Conflict* (Penguin Books, 2008), 44–50.

The Morrison-Grady Plan.

UN Special Committee on Palestine summary report: Laqueur and Rubin, *The Israel–Arab Reader*: 65–69.

UN General Assembly Resolution on the Future Government of Palestine: Laqueur and Rubin, *The Israel–Arab Reader*, 69–77.

Israel–Egypt Armistice Agreement: available online at The Avalon Project at Yale Law School http://avalon.law.yale.edu/20th_century/arm01.asp (accessed April 22 2013).

Israel–Lebanon Armistice Agreement: available online at The Avalon Project at Yale Law School http://avalon.law.yale.edu/20th_century/arm02.asp (accessed April 22 2013).

Israel–Transjordan Armistice Agreement: available online at The Avalon Project at Yale Law School http://avalon.law.yale.edu/20th_century/arm03.asp (accessed April 22 2013).

Israel–Syria Armistice Agreement: available online at The Avalon Project at Yale Law School http://avalon.law.yale.edu/20th_century/arm04.asp (accessed April 22 2013).
UN General Assembly Resolution 194: Laqueur and Rubin, *The Israel–Arab Reader*, 83–86.
UN General Assembly Resolution 181 (Partition): Laqueur and Rubin, *The Israel–Arab Reader*, 69–77.

Notes

1. Michael Oren, *Power, Faith, and Fantasy: America in the Middle East 1776 to the Present* (New York: W.W. Norton, 2007), 483.
2. *Ibid.*, 486–487.
3. *Ibid.*, 487.
4. *Ibid.*, 488.
5. *Ibid.*, 489.
6. These figures, based on data contained in the UNSCOP proposal, do not include an additional 90,000 Bedouins who would live in the Jewish state. Figures available at "Official Records of the Second Session of the General Assembly: Supplement No. 11: United Nations Special Committee on Palestine: Report to the General Assembly, Vol. 1," United Nations General Assembly, A/364, September 3, 1947, http://unispal.un.org/unispal.nsf/0/07175de9fa2de563852568d3006e10f3.
7. *Ibid.*
8. Population figures based on projections of the 1931 British census. See British Mandate: *A Survey of Palestine* Volume I, Chapter VI, p.144, Table 1. *A Survey of Palestine* (Volume II, Chapter XIV, 566, Table 2, offers land ownership figures for 1943. For Jewish land ownership, see Jewish National Fund, "Jewish settlements in Palestine, Jerusalem," March 1948, p. ii. Other sources include Tessler, *A History of the Israeli–Palestinian Conflict*. See also Map "Palestine Land Ownership by Sub-Districts" showing 1945 statistics, United Nations, August 1950: http://domino.un.org/maps/m0094.jpg.
9. "Resolution Adopted on the Report of the Ad Hoc Committee on the Palestinian Question," United Nations Security Council, http://www.securitycouncilreport.org/atf/cf/%7B65BFCF9B-6-D27-4E9C-8CD3-CF6E4FF96FF9%7D/IP%20ARES%20181.pdf.
10. Benny Morris, *Righteous Victims*, 182.
11. Tessler, *A History of the Israeli–Palestinian Conflict*, 261 (citing M.J. Cohen, *Palestine and the Great Powers* (Princeton: Princeton University Press, 1982), 339.
12. Gordon H. Torrey, *Syrian Politics and the Military, 1945–1958* (Columbus: Ohio State University Press, 1964), 103.
13. Morris, *Righteous Victims*, 191 and 196–204.
14. Tessler, *A History of the Israeli–Palestinian Conflict*, 263.
15. Charles D. Smith, *Palestine and the Arab–Israeli Conflict* (Boston: Bedford/St. Martin's, 2007), 199. See also Tessler, *A History of the Israeli–Palestinian Conflict*, 261.
16. Eliahu Sasson, *On the Road to Peace: Letters and Conversations* (Tel Aviv: Am Oved, 1978), 364–365.
17. *Ibid.*, 364–366; Shlaim, *Collusion Across the Jordan: King Abdullah, the Zionist Movement, and the Partition of Palestine*, 42–46 and 81–84. See also Yoav Gelber, *Jewish-Transjordanian Relations 1921–1948: Alliance of Bars Sinister* (London: Frank Cass, 1997), 195–217; Efraim Karsh and P. R. Kumaraswamy (eds.), *Israel, the Hashemites and the Palestinians: The Fateful Triangle* (London:

Frank Cass, 2003); and Ilan Pappé, *The Making of the Arab-Israeli Conflict, 1947–1951* (London: IB Tauris, 2004), 102–134.

18. Translation of Tochnit Dalet reprinted in Walid Khalidi, "Plan Dalet: Master Plan for the Conquest of Palestine," *Journal of Palestine Studies*, 18, 1 (Autumn, 1988), 24–33.
19. Smith, *Palestine and the Arab-Israeli Conflict*, 202–203; Benny Morris, *The Birth of the Palestinian Refugee Problem, 1947–1949* (New York: Cambridge University Press, 1987), 113–115. However, Benny Morris cites 250 Arab deaths. Sharif Kanaana of Bir Zeit University estimated in 1988 that only 107 villagers had died during the battle with another 25 executed afterwards; see Sharif Kanaana and Nihad Zaytuni; *Deir, Yassin, Destroyed Palestinian Villages Series* (Birzeit: Birzeit University Press, 1988), 5 and 57.
20. Conor Cruise O'Brien, *The Siege: The Saga of Israel and Zionism* (New York: Simon & Schuster, 1986), 282. See also Smith, *Palestine and the Arab-Israeli Conflict*, 203.
21. Mohamed Hassanein Heikal, *Thrones and Armies* (Al Urush wa Al Juyush)(Cairo: Dar Al-Shorouq, 1996, Seventh Edition). See also Ahmed Abdel Haleem, "Arab Experience in the War: Lessons and Results," *Al-Syassa Al-Dawliya*, Issue 133, July 1988, 100–101.
22. Fawaz A. Gerges, "Egypt and the 1948 War: Internal Conflict and Regional Ambition," in Eugene L. Rogan and Avi Shlaim (eds.) *The War for Palestine: Rewriting the History of 1948* (Cambridge: Cambridge University Press, 2001), 151–177.
23. On the same day, the Egyptian Senate decided unanimously to participate in the Palestine War. The President of the Senate sent a letter to Nuqrashi informing him of the Senate decision, and a similar letter was sent on the next day by the President of the House of Representatives (Majlis al-Umma [the Council of the Nation]).
24. Heikal, *Thrones and Armies*; Ahmed Abdel Haleem, "Arab Experience in War: Lessons and Results," 100–101.
25. These consisted of roughly 5,500 Egyptians; 6,000–9,000 Jordanians; 6,000 Syrians; 4,500 Iraqis; and a handful of Lebanese. Morris, *Righteous Victims*, 215 and 217.
26. Philip Robins, *A History of Jordan* (Cambridge: Cambridge University Press, 2004), 65; and O'Brien, *The Siege*, 291.
27. O'Brien, *The Siege*, 292; and Robins, *A History of Jordan*, 66.
28. O'Brien, *The Siege*, 294–296; and Robins, *A History of Jordan*, 67.
29. Robins, *A History of Jordan*, 67.
30. Tessler, *A History of the Israeli-Palestinian Conflict*, 273–274.
31. United Nations, Security Council, DOCUMENT S/1302/REV.1 1/ S/1302/Rev.1 3 April 1949 http://unispal.un.org/UNISPAL.NSF/0/F03D55E48F77AB698525643B00608D34.
32. *Ibid.*
33. Robert Rabil, *Embattled Neighbors* (Boulder: Lynne Rienner, 2003), 6.
34. Figure cited in the "United Nations General Progress Report and Supplementary Report of the United Nations Conciliation Commission for Palestine, Covering the period from 11 December 1949 to 23 October 1950," United Nations General Assembly, A/1367/Rev. 1, October 23, 1950, http://domino.un.org/unispal.nsf/9a798adbf322aff38525617b006d88d7/93037e3b939746de8525610200567883. See also, Morris, *The Birth of the Refugee Problem*, Appendix 1, 602–604.
35. For the text of UN Resolution 194, see "Resolutions Adopted by the General Assembly During Its Third Session," United Nations General Assembly, http://www.un.org/documents/ga/res/3/ares3.htm.

36. Avi Shlaim, "The rise and fall of the All-Palestine Government in Gaza," *Journal of Palestine Studies*, 20, 1 (Autumn 1990), 37–53; and Avi Shlaim, "Israel and the Arab Coalition," in Rogan and Shlaim, eds, *The War for Palestine*, 79–103.
37. Robins, *A History of Jordan*, 72–73.
38. Tessler, *A History of the Israeli-Palestinian Conflict*, 259.
39. See Mohamed Faisal Abdel Monem, *Palestine and the Zionist Invasion* (Cairo: Cairo New Library, 1970).
40. Heikal, *Thrones and Armies*, 95–108.
41. Based on King Abdallah ibn al-Husayn, *My Memoirs Completed* [al-Takmilah] (London: Longman, 1978).
42. *Ibid.*, 13.
43. *Ibid.*, 35.
44. In 1949 Iraq established a parliamentary inquiry to examine its actions during the war. The inquiry produced an official report, published in September 1949, entitled "Taqrir Lajnat al-Tahqiq al-Niyabiyya fi Qadiyyat Filastin" [Report of the Parliamentary Committee of Inquiry into the Palestine Question]. This report provides important insight into the Iraqi narrative of the war.
45. Charles Tripp, "Iraq and the 1948 War: Mirror of Iraq's Disorder," in Rogan and Shlaim, eds, *The War for Palestine*, 125–126.
46. *Ibid.*, 138.
47. *Ibid.*, 140.
48. *Ibid.*, 50–65; Heikal, *Thrones and Armies*, 31.
49. Heikal, *Thrones and Armies*, 31–36; Michael Doran, *Pan-Arabism before Nasser: Egyptian Power Politics and the Palestine Question* (New York: Oxford Universty Press, 1999), 94–155; Shafi Aldamer, *Saudi Arabia and Britain: Changing Relations, 1939–1953* (Reading: Ithaca Press, 2003), 105–158.
50. Avi Shlaim, "Israel and the Arab Coalition in 1948," in Rogan and Shlaim, eds, *The War for Palestine*, 82–83.
51. Joshua Landis, "Syria and the Palestine War: Fighting King 'Abdullah's 'Greater Syria Plan,'" in Rogan and Shlaim, eds, *The War for Palestine*, 178–179. See also Mary C. Wilson, *King Abdullah, Britain and the Making of Jordan* (Cambridge: Cambridge University Press, 1988), 151.
52. Landis, in Rogan and Shlaim, *The War for Palestine*, 178–179.
53. *Ibid.*, 180–201.
54. Tarek Al-Beshry, *The Political Movement in Egypt 1945–1952* (Cairo: Dar Al Shorouk, 1983), 233.
55. *Ibid.*, 242. Before being transformed into a political party, al-Wafd was a nationalist movement seeking independence from British occupation. When in the early 1930s Egyptians began to become aware of the Palestinian question as a result of the relocation of Palestinian political figures and students to Egypt and their subsequent publication of newspapers advocating their cause, al-Wafd began to express its support of Palestinian rights.
56. *Ibid.* Not only did MYA's political thought have an Islamic dimension, it was well connected, aware and informed about developments taking place in Palestine since it had several branches operating there, in Haifa, Jerusalem, and Jaffa. Thus, beginning in the early 1930s, it adopted a policy of actively supporting the Palestinian cause through fundraising and increasing awareness of the Egyptian public to Palestinian issues.
57. With strong ties with the Arab Palestinian Youth movement, the Egyptian Socialist Party was also the first Egyptian party to include in its manifesto a pan-Arab call for uniting the Arab states. And

it was the first to assemble units of volunteers to participate in fighting the 1948 War – units which were sent to the Syrian front.

58. Al-Beshry, *The Political Movement in Egypt*, 247.
59. *Ibid.*, 247–250. Predominantly opposed to the partitioning of Palestine, as early as in the 1937–1940 period, these syndicates held a series of conferences in support of the Palestinians: the Arab medical conference, the Arab educational conference, and the Arab agricultural conference.
60. *Ibid.*, 261–262. The other Egyptian Marxist movement, the Peasants and Workers Movement, strongly opposed Zionist policies in Palestine. It argued that Zionism was an arm of imperial colonialism aiming to distract Arabs from their national priorities by dragging them into a protracted confrontation between Zionists and Arabs.
61. See Avi Shlaim, *Collusion Across the Jordan: King Abdullah, the Zionist Movement and the Partition of Palestine.*
62. *Ibid.* See also Heikal, *Secret Channels*, 73–74.
63. Heikal, *Thrones and Armies*, 27.
64. Avi Shlaim, "Britain and the Arab–Israeli War of 1948," *Journal of Palestine Studies*, 16, 4 (Summer 1987), 50–76. Shlaim argues that the British worked closely with the Jordanians to prevent the establishment of a separate Palestinian state, in favor of a larger Jordanian state, thereby boosting Britain's strongest ally in the region.
65. Possibly the best example of this was Egypt's decision to divide its invading forces into two thrusts: one marching along the coast toward Tel Aviv; the other moving to the West Bank to be parked near Hebron. The latter column was not intended to strike a dagger at the heart of the newly created Jewish state; instead, it was apparently designed to insure that if the Israeli forces were beaten, the Hashemite Kingdom would not be in a position to reap the rewards all for itself. From Egypt's perspective, however, the same rivalry had different outcomes as the Jordanian Arab Legion practices seemed to have had devastating repercussions on the Egyptian Army. One example was the series of Jordanian withdrawals – for example, from Lydda and Ramle – which cleared the way for the Israeli forces' advance and permitted them to exert heavy pressures on the Egyptian front. Another was Jordan's refusal to help break the encirclement by the Israeli forces of the Egyptian units trapped in Faluja. See Gerges, "Egypt and 1948 War: Internal Conflict and Regional Ambition," 151–171.
66. Yehuda Slutzky, *Kitzur Toldot Hahaganah* [*An Abbreviated History of the Haganah*] (Israel: Enavi, 1986), 347–348.
67. See Rashid Khalidi, "The Palestinians and 1948," 12–36.
68. Heikal, *Secret Channels*, 69. See also, Heikal, *Thrones and Armies*, 36.
69. Heikal, *Secret Channels*, 74–75.
70. Heikal, *Thrones and Armies*, 50.
71. Gerges, "Egypt and 1948 War: Internal Conflict and Regional Ambition," 158–160.
72. Heikal, *Thrones and Armies*, 50 and 453–458. Egypt's military leaders, including the commander of Egyptian forces in Palestine, General Mohamed al-Muwaay, repeatedly complained to their political superiors that the army could not carry out the missions ascribed to it in Palestine. The army, he argued, lacked training, weapons, ammunitions, and proper transport. As a result of the latter, it was completely dependent on the British for logistics. It did not have enough troops to win the battle and it lacked the required intelligence about the enemy's plans and forces. But above all else, it lacked a war-winning strategy. See also Gerges, "Egypt and 1948 War: Internal Conflict and Regional Ambition," 156.

73. Heikal, *Thrones and Armies*, 47–48. This assessment was revealed when the commanders of the Egyptian army met with Prime Minister al-Nuqrashi – a meeting in which they pointed out that their army was not prepared for a fight. Nuqrashi's response was that the war was not going to be severe and that the military confrontations would be primarily conducted by the Jordanian Arab Legion.
74. Morris, *Righteous Victims*, 193, 217–218, and 223.

3 Under the Cold War: the 1956 Sinai–Suez War

This chapter centers on an early period in the Arab–Israeli conflict, focusing on the mid-1950s and particularly the 1956 Sinai–Suez war in which Israel joined Britain and France to attack Egypt. This period is characterized by the consolidation of the division that put Israel squarely in the Western camp while Egypt and a number of other Arab countries moved closer to the Soviet Union. The Palestinian issue remained, during this timeframe, subordinate to that of Arab players, primarily Egypt and Jordan, who then set the agenda for the Palestinians.

While the late 1940s and the early 1950s were characterized by the Arabization of the Palestinian–Israeli conflict – the eclipse of the conflict by the neighboring Arab states and, to a lesser extent, by the Arab world at large – by the mid-1950s the Middle East conflict found itself being waged under two umbrellas: a broader Arab framework that now adopted the banner of pan-Arabism; and the global Cold War waged by a coalition of Western powers led by the United States on the one hand, and an imposed Eastern Bloc alliance led by the Soviet Union on the other.

In the international system, the Cold War now became the dominant paradigm – affecting all important international interactions. In the Middle East the most important implication of the intensity of the Cold War was that almost every significant development in the region during this period was perceived in zero-sum terms: a gain by one side would inevitably be seen as the other side's loss. The United States and the Soviet Union now saw the Middle East as an important arena of their competition and organized themselves accordingly.

The Cold War also dominated the politics of the regional conflict and the pattern of alliances in the region during this period. Moreover, internally and regionally this period was marked by the rise of Nasserism in Egypt and the beginning of the rise of the Ba'ath in Syria. Another dimension of the same development was that revolutionary coups in the two countries increased the involvement and influence of the militaries in both. A similar development took place in Iraq after 1958.

A final facet of this period was the absence of the Palestinians as a political actor, as Jordan and Egypt viewed the Palestinians as a potential threat to stability. To achieve this goal Jordan incorporated the West Bank smoothly and when the Palestinian *Fedayyin* [guerrilla groups] appeared in the Gaza Strip in the mid-1950s, it was mostly under the watchful eyes of the Egyptians.

Main Developments

In the global arena this period was characterized by the settling in of a bipolar system characterized by the Cold War. By contrast, the Middle East witnessed a decolonization process that produced multiple centers of power. In the Arab–Israeli conflict these conflicting trajectories resulted in growing tensions between Israel and its neighbors – Syria, Jordan, and Egypt – culminating in the 1956 Suez–Sinai War. In the war, Israel allied itself with the ex-colonial powers, France and Britain, surprising their patron – the United States. The war gave rise to Egypt as a regional power, leading the Arab world under Gamal Abdel Nasser. In turn, this led to the further Arabization of the Arab–Israeli conflict, and the corresponding marginalization of the Palestinians, as Gaza came under Egyptian administration and the West Bank was absorbed by the Hashemite Kingdom of Jordan.

The Global Scene and the Middle East

The period following the 1948 War saw the broadening of the gap between the two superpowers and an increased focus by the United States and the Soviet Union on gaining regional allies. Former British Prime Minister Winston Churchill had framed the context of the conflict back in 1946 in his famous "Sinews of Peace" speech, in which he spoke of an "Iron Curtain" that had fallen across Europe, separating East from West.[1]

The United States conducted itself during this period under the "Truman Doctrine" – a containment strategy that included a pledge of support for "free peoples who are resisting attempted subjugation by armed minorities or by outside pressures" – a not-so-subtle reference to the Soviets.[2] In June 1948, in one of the first major conflicts of the Cold War, the Soviets blocked Western states from supplying West Berlin. The Western allies responded with the formation of the Berlin Airlift, effectively breaking the blockade. Then, in 1950, the first proxy battle between the superpowers took place as the United States sent a massive force and the Soviet Union sent fighter squadrons and other military specialists to fight on opposite sides of the Korean War.

In addition to internal political turmoil taking place in a number of Middle East states in the aftermath of the 1948 War, the early to mid-1950s also witnessed the collapse of the Tripartite Declaration – an agreement signed on May 25, 1950 by the United States, France, and Britain in an effort to stabilize the region. The agreement committed the three powers to prevent any attempts by the region's states to change the armistice lines by force, thus guaranteeing the borders of Israel as demarcated in 1949. The deal provided a major framework for arms sales to the Middle East. The three powers agreed that they would not provide Israel and the Arab states with weapons intended for use in an aggressive manner against one another.

By the mid-1950s, the United States also began to actively support an alliance between the two Western-allied countries bordering the Soviet Union: Turkey and Pakistan. After the two countries signed a limited defense cooperation agreement in 1954, in February 1955 Turkey and Iraq signed a similar but more binding Pact of Mutual Cooperation, better known as the Baghdad Pact. The agreement aimed to secure the defense of the Middle East against possible

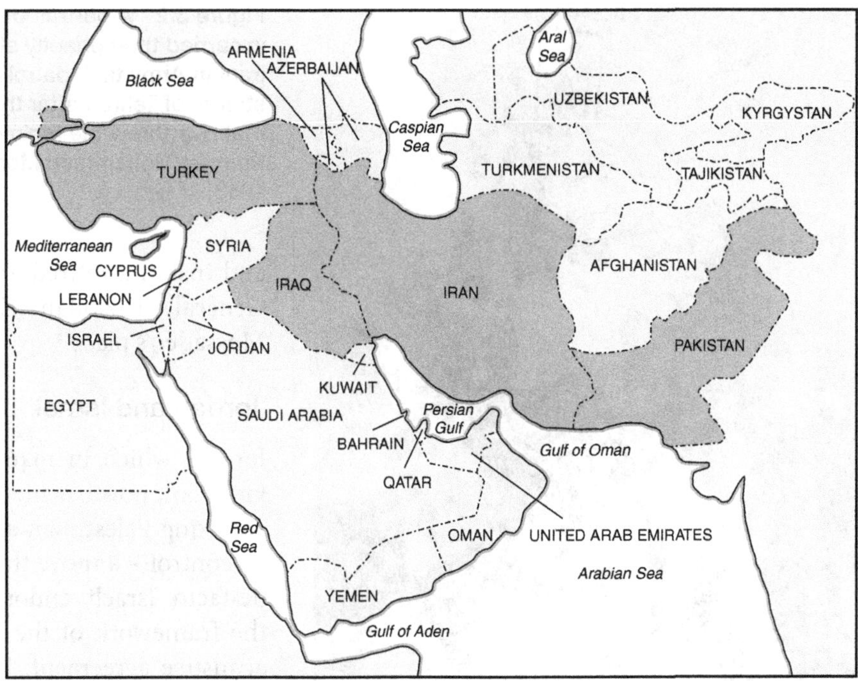

Figure 3.1. The Baghdad Pact, 1955

communist aggression and to improve economic cooperation among the signatories.[3] Soon Britain, Pakistan, and Iran joined the pact.

In Iran, Mohammed Reza Shah Pahlavi, the ruling monarch, bowed to public pressure in late April 1951 and appointed the reformist-minded Mohammad Mossadeq as prime minister. Once in office, Mossadeq, who had spent years in prison and political exile for his opposition to the Pahlavi regime, led a coalition of secular and religious nationalist groups known as the National Front. The Front aimed to nationalize Iran's oil industry, for years dominated by the Anglo-Iranian Oil Company (AIOC), which was Britain's largest overseas commercial interest. In the years following the Second World War, the AIOC had refused to meet the 50–50 profit share on which most oil agreements signed between the United States and oil producing countries were based.

Shortly before Mossadeq began his tenure, the Iranian *Majles* [parliament] voted to nationalize the country's oil industry. The AIOC responded by launching a boycott of Iranian oil, which was ultimately joined by the British government and American oil companies, straining further the already precarious Iranian economy. When President Dwight D. Eisenhower entered into office in January 1953, the United States increased its criticism of and opposition to Iran's nationalization plan, worried that it would affect the international market. It was equally concerned about signs that Mossadeq was edging too close to the Soviet Union. Together with its British counterparts, the CIA began coordinating a plan to remove Mossadeq from power. On August 19, 1953, pro-Shah crowds were incited to take to the streets

Figure 3.2 **A portrait of the Shah is carried triumphantly atop an Iranian Army tank patrolling the streets of Tehran after the coup that overthrew the regime of Premier Mohammed Mossadeq, 1953.** © Bettman/CORBIS

and install a retired army Major General, Fazlollah Zahedi, in Mossadeq's place.[4]

Jordan and Israel

Jordan, which in 1946 became a kingdom, now began a process of annexing Palestinian areas under its control – a move that received de-facto Israeli endorsement in the framework of the April 1949 armistice agreement. By the end of the 1948 War, Jordan controlled East Jerusalem and what was then known as Central Palestine, with a population of about 800,000. This area included the major cities of Hebron, Bethlehem, Nablus, Qalqilya and Tulkarm.[5] The annexation was rejected by most Arab countries, who also opposed the renaming of Central Palestine as the West Bank and the Jordanian ban on the use of "Palestine" in its official transactions. The latter steps also increased the Palestinians' suspicions and hostility toward King Abdullah's intentions, leading to his assassination on July 20, 1951 at the steps of the al-Aqsa Mosque in Jerusalem.

The following years witnessed efforts by Palestinians to infiltrate into Israel, mostly from the West Bank and Gaza. Some simply attempted to return to their homes or cultivate the land they left or from which they were expelled. However, by 1953 these infiltrations became more organized and violent, and Israeli retaliation raids became harsher and disproportionate, thereby escalating tension along border areas. In October 1953 one such Israeli raid targeted the Palestinian village of Qibya, destroying dozens of homes and killing 66 civilians. Alarmed by the increased tension, the Jordanians cracked down on Palestinians suspected of involvement in the violence. Although attacks from Jordan did not cease completely, by the mid-1950s they gradually subsided.

Syrian–Israeli Escalation

Tension on the Syrian–Israeli front was more serious. While on all other fronts Israel had gained territory in the 1948 war over what had been assigned to it in the 1947 UN partition plan, Syria actually ended the war in control of some areas that had been designated to the Jewish state. The Israeli–Syrian Armistice Agreement, brokered by UN mediator Ralph Bunche and signed on July 20, 1949, stipulated a Syrian withdrawal from this captured territory, creating three Demilitarized Zones (DMZs) totaling 66.5 square miles.[6] Farming was allowed in these DMZs, monitored by the United Nations Truce Supervision Organization (UNTSO). Disputes were to be adjudicated by Mixed Armistice Commissions (MACs) made up of representatives of the two countries and headed by a UN official.[7]

Interestingly, in the Syrian case, the signing of an Armistice Agreement was preceded by a Syrian proposal to bring about a comprehensive settlement with Israel – one which would have direct impact on Israel's conflict with the Palestinians. The bargain was proposed in April and May 1949 by Husni al-Za'im, the army Chief of Staff, who became the country's ruler following a coup on March 30 of that year. Za'im suggested a meeting with Israel's Ben Gurion to discuss a peace treaty. In the framework of the proposed agreement, Za'im expressed willingness to absorb some 250,000–300,000 Palestinian refugees within Syria. In exchange, he demanded that the international border be adjusted to give Syria control of the eastern banks of the Jordan River and of Lake Tiberias and that the two countries split control of the lake. Unsure of Za'im's standing and fearing a loss of control over Israel's water sources, Ben Gurion was unenthusiastic at first about the initiative. By the time Israel's premier warmed to the proposal, Za'im had been deposed in a bloody coup on August 14.[8]

After two years of quiet in the DMZs, following the signing of the armistice agreement – during which the main activities there were farming and the fortification of civilian settlements – tensions began to escalate on February 12, 1951 when Israel's Palestine Land Development Company (PLDC) launched work on a drainage project in the Hula Valley marshes, located in the DMZ north of the Sea of Galilee (or Lake Tiberias, or the Kinneret). The project was designed to drain the marshes in order to eliminate malaria in the area and to provide an additional 15,000 acres of farmland.

Objecting to the plan, Syria brought the matter to the UN Security Council. Meanwhile, on March 15, 1951 Arabs in civilian dress opened fire on Israelis working in the Hula area. Israel blamed Syria for the attack, while Syria claimed that the attack was carried out by "Arab landowners." Then, on April 4, Syrian soldiers killed seven Israeli policemen near al-Himma in the southern DMZ. Israel retaliated the next day with air strikes against the Syrian outpost and police station of al-Himma. A week later the Israeli air force shot down two Syrian planes.

As the UN Security Council deliberated the issue, violence continued. On May 2, Syrians attacked the Israeli post at Tel al-Mutillah, just beyond the DMZ, where fighting continued for four days during which Israel suffered 40 casualties and the Syrians many more. The Security Council called for a ceasefire on May 8, leading to a halt in the hostilities on May 11.[9]

On June 20, 1951 Israel announced that it would no longer participate in meetings of the Israeli–Syrian MAC as long as complaints involving the DMZs were on its agenda. Syria countered that it would not participate in MAC meetings that did not permit such complaints.[10] The resulting breakdown of the MAC's functioning increased tension in the area even further. These tensions now focused on disputes over sovereignty as well as over the controversial issue of water rights.

Following the disastrous performance of the Arab military forces during the 1948 War, a period of political upheaval had swept the region. Coups and uprisings, mostly orchestrated by military officers, took place in a number of countries, with Syria proving to be especially unstable. In 1949 alone, Syria experienced three different coups. The first of these, in March, was led by General al-Za'im, a sign of the growing influence of the Syrian army over the politics of the state.

The next coup, in August, was led by another military officer, Colonel Sami Hinnawi. His days in office were equally numbered, and in December, Colonel Adib al-Shishakli began a four-year reign. Though Shishakli initially allowed some role for Syria's traditional politicians, this came to an end in mid-1951, when he consolidated his position with a second coup in which the army assumed all political power.[11]

Shishakli gradually alienated many of his one-time supporters, leading to his forced resignation and exile in February 1954 at the hands of the army that he had made so central to public life. Syria then experimented with democracy once again, with elections held that year. Although it did not capture many seats, the Arab Socialist Ba'ath party, a recently formed conglomeration of the small Socialist party led by Akram Hourani and the Syrian Ba'ath party which had been established in 1947 by Michail Aflaq, ended up winning the election.[12]

The Ba'ath's mixture of socialism and pan-Arabism mirrored many of the themes that were laid out by Nasser in his takeover of Egypt. This shared rhetoric brought the two countries closer together, first through a military pact between the two countries signed in 1955, and later in the formation of the United Arab Republic in 1958.

Egypt, Britain and Israel

On July 23, 1952, Nasser and the *Zobat Ahrar* ("Free Officers") staged a revolution, forcing King Farouk into exile and, less than a year later, ending the monarchy and declaring Egypt a republic. The revolution was initially focused inward, introducing reforms in the areas of land ownership and education. Given Egypt's economic status – at the time, Egypt's economic development was more or less equal to that of Spain, Portugal, and Greece – Nasser's ambition was to make his country the strongest economic power in the region.

Nasser saw Egypt as located at the conjunction of three overlapping circles – an Arab circle, a Muslim circle, and an African circle – and thus endowed with a natural role as a regional leader. His charisma, lofty speeches, and calls for Arab unity struck a chord with Arab masses, and his popularity was unmatched amongst Arab leaders of his generation.

Early in 1954, Nasser began negotiating with Britain its final status in Egypt. During this period he had three objectives: to reach an agreement on Britain's final withdrawal; to rebuild Egypt's social, economic, and political fabric; and finally, to avoid a trap of colonialism such as defense pacts with the West.[13]

Nasser wanted Britain to withdraw its forces from the Suez Canal base where they had been stationed since 1882, when the British occupation of the country began. Even after Egypt gained formal independence in 1922 the British occupation persisted, though it was confined to the Suez Canal military base under the terms of a 1936 treaty. The base was of considerable strategic value for both Britain and the United States, and figured centrally in their plans for defending the Middle East.

Another sore point in Egyptian–British relations during this period was Britain's refusal to supply Egypt with weapons that it feared would be used against British forces in the Canal Zone – notwithstanding Egyptian insistence that they needed the arms to defend themselves against Israel.

Israel watched the negotiations between Egypt and Britain with deep apprehension. Its main concern was that the British forces' withdrawal from the Canal Zone would leave its borders with Egypt with no buffer.[14] To avoid this, Israel launched a major diplomatic effort to convince Britain to make withdrawal from its Canal bases conditional upon Egyptian commitment to complete freedom of passage through the Suez Canal.[15] At the same time, the United States and Britain actively explored the possibility of negotiating a peace agreement between Israel and Egypt, as well as the other Arab states.[16]

The Egyptian–British negotiations culminated in the Suez Canal Treaty of October 1954. Britain agreed to remove all troops from the Canal Zone within two years in exchange for the right to reenter the area in the event of an attack on the Arab states or Turkey.[17] This was a major victory for Egypt, since it effectively ended Britain's 72-year occupation.

In August 1954 the Egyptian government uncovered a plot in which some Egyptian Jews trained in Israel and France had been instructed to bomb American and British targets in an attempt to sabotage Egypt's relationship with the two powers. In Israel, the plot later became known as the "Lavon Affair" (named after the Israeli Defense Minister, Pinhas Lavon, who was later forced to resign because of the conspiracy). A month after the incident, Israel sent a ship, the *Bat Galim*, to test Israel's right to exercise free passage through the Suez Canal. The ship was stopped and its crew was arrested by the Egyptian authorities.[18]

Tension between Israel and Egypt also increased over developments in the Gaza Strip. Palestinian infiltrations from Gaza began in the early 1950s. As was the case with Jordan, Egypt's authorities at first tried to prevent such incursions in order to avoid jeopardizing the 1949 Egypt–Israel armistice regime. As these efforts failed, the cycle of infiltrations and Israeli retaliatory operations targeting facilities, including Egyptian facilities in Gaza, escalated. This reached an important climax in February 1955 with Israel's Gaza Raid in which 39 Egyptian soldiers were killed. By that time, Egypt's intelligence services had taken over much of the direction of the *Fedayyin* operations.[19]

The rising tension with Israel over the infiltrations from Gaza, the initial French arms transfer to Israel, and American reluctance to sell arms to Egypt all contributed to the making of the Czech arms deal announced by Nasser on September 27, 1955. In its framework, the Soviets, through their Czech satellite, agreed to supply Egypt with 230 tanks, 200 armored personnel carriers, 530 other armored vehicles, 100 self-propelled artillery, 500 other artillery pieces, 200 aircraft fighters, and a maritime group composed of destroyers, minesweepers, and three submarines.[20] The deal had a number of regional ramifications: first, it intensified the arms race between Egypt and Israel; second, it provided the Soviet Union with a presence in the Middle East which lasted for decades; and third, it placed the Arab–Israeli conflict on the Cold War agenda.

United States–Egypt Ties and the Road to Suez

Relations between Nasser's revolution and the United States had not begun badly. Before the July 1952 revolution, a number of its leaders tried to gain Washington's support. One of them, Ali Sabri, was permitted to use his contacts with the United States Assistant Air Attaché in Cairo to ask the Eisenhower administration to use its influence – in the event that a revolution took place – to dissuade Britain from intervening to support the king. After the revolution, American Ambassador Jefferson Caffrey is said to have expressed his intentions to do his best to help facilitate the British departure from Egypt. Nasser attempted to persuade Caffrey that the United States should supply Egypt with arms. This led to a visit to Egypt by Assistant Secretary of Defense William Foster with the aim of negotiating a possible $100 million arms sale. But the sale did not materialize.

In May 1953, United States Secretary of State John Foster Dulles visited Cairo in an attempt to convince Nasser to join a Western alliance against the Soviet Union. Nasser, however, was mainly interested in getting rid of the British military presence from Egypt. He argued that protecting Western interests did not require such bases and that, if provided with Western arms, Egypt could protect these interests and uphold its responsibilities.

In October 1953, the Eisenhower administration sent Kermit Roosevelt, a top CIA official, to establish a personal relationship with Nasser. This coincided with Nasser's interest in establishing a channel of communication with Eisenhower through the CIA. At that point Nasser had not refused to take sides in the Cold War. Indeed, in January 1954 Eisenhower sent a letter to President Muhammad Neguib – at that time still formally the leader of Egypt's new regime – explaining that Egypt could expect economic and military aid from the United States once an agreement with Britain was reached. On his part, to alleviate Western concerns about the possible ramifications of Britain's requested withdrawal from its bases in Egypt, Nasser is said to have agreed in early 1954 that under circumstances where the Soviet Union invaded an Arab state member of the Arab Mutual Security Pact or Turkey – circumstances Nasser thought unlikely – the base facilities could be made available to Britain for the purpose of repelling the invasion.[21]

The gap between the United States and Egypt widened after the March 1954 creation of a Middle East defense initiative which allied Turkey and Pakistan. The Arab Summit that convened in December 1954 adopted an Egyptian-inspired resolution instructing "Arab states not to hold any alliance outside the scope of the Arab League charter and not to join this alliance." The gap was further exacerbated when, in February 1955, Turkey and Iraq signed a similar but more binding Pact of Mutual Cooperation, known as the Baghdad Pact. Cairo would make every effort to thwart the proposed alliance.

The Soviet Union now offered to compensate Egypt for its efforts to oppose Washington's designs. The result was the Czech arms deal, which in Washington's eyes was a clear sign that Egypt was moving into the Soviet orbit. But the Eisenhower administration had not yet given up on the possibility of pulling Egypt away from the Soviets. Hence, in December 1955 it promised – together with Britain and the World Bank – to fund the construction of the Aswan Dam, the most ambitious project in the history of modern Egypt. However, the approval of the loan was made conditional on Egypt's undertaking of a set of commitments,

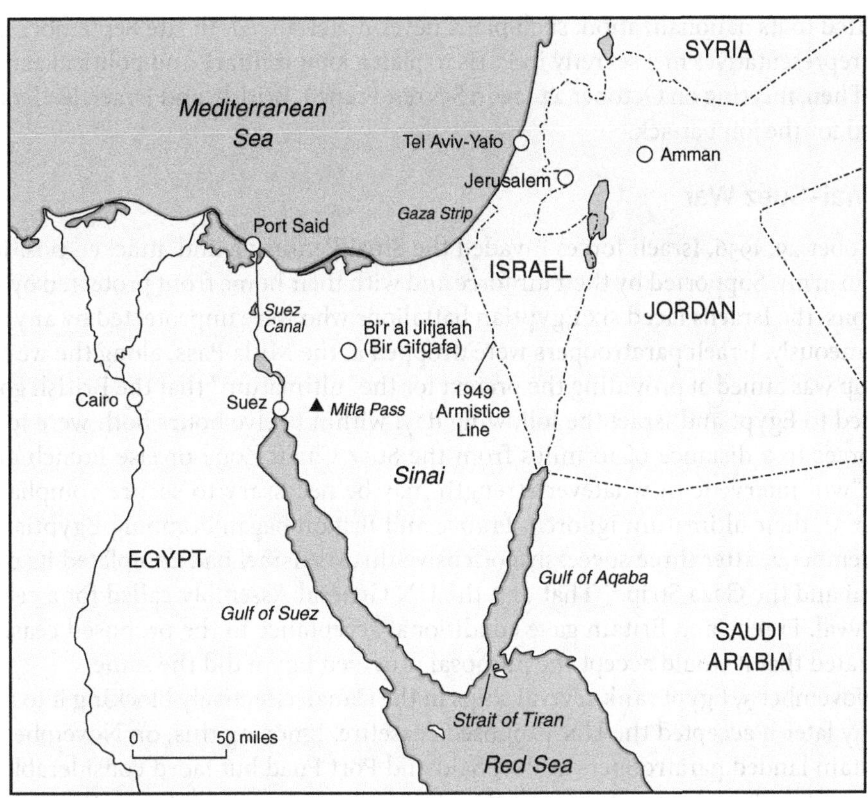

Figure 3.3. The Suez Canal, 1956

including a promise to open the work for the construction of the dam to competitive bids and to avoid taking additional loans.

Yet Egypt was also inclined to accept a Soviet offer made in June 1956 to help finance the Aswan Dam. This, alongside Egypt's decision to recognize the government of Communist China, led Dulles to announce on July 19 that the Egyptian economy would not be able to sustain the burden of building the Aswan Dam. Britain and the World Bank soon followed the United States "finding" with similar decisions to withdraw their offers to fund the project. In reaction, Nasser declared that Egypt would have no choice but to finance the Aswan Dam through the revenues generated by the Suez Canal. On July 26, 1956, Nasser announced that for this purpose Egypt would be nationalizing the canal.[22] United States–Egyptian relations completely ruptured over this nationalization.

Despite Egypt's promise to maintain free passage through the Suez Canal, Britain and France were deeply angered by Nasser's nationalization plan.[23] Britain soon began planning a military operation to reassert control of the canal. Eisenhower was less keen to use military force to achieve this, arguing that nationalizing the canal was within Egypt's sovereign rights.[24] Meanwhile, various plans were proposed to internationalize the Canal, but as Egypt remained committed to its nationalization, such plans never materialized. In late September, Israeli and French representatives met secretly in Paris to plan a joint military and political action against Egypt. Then, meeting on October 22–24 in Sèvres, French, British, and Israeli leaders gave final approval for the joint attack.

The Sinai–Suez War

On October 29, 1956, Israeli forces invaded the Sinai Peninsula and attacked positions of the Egyptian army. Supported by their air force and with their home front protected by French air squadrons, the Israelis faced six Egyptian battalions who were unprotected by any air cover.[25] Simultaneously, Israeli paratroopers were dropped at the Mitla Pass, along the western Sinai. The drop was aimed at providing the pretext for the "ultimatum" that the British government presented to Egypt and Israel the following day: within twelve hours both were to withdraw their forces to a distance of 10 miles from the Suez Canal Zone or else French and British troops "will intervene in whatever strength may be necessary to secure compliance."[26] On October 31, their ultimatum ignored, France and Britain began bombing Egyptian airfields. By November 2, after three successive offensive thrusts, Israel had completed its conquest of the Sinai and the Gaza Strip.[27] That day, the UN General Assembly called for a ceasefire and withdrawal. France and Britain gave conditional acceptance to the proposed ceasefire while Israel stated that it would accept the proposal provided Egypt did the same.

On November 3, Egypt sank several ships in the Canal, effectively blocking it to navigation, but a day later it accepted the UN-proposed ceasefire. Ignoring this, on November 6, France and Britain landed paratroopers at Port Said and Port Fuad but faced considerable Egyptian resistance. This led Moscow to issue a note to France, Britain, and Israel, threatening Soviet military action unless the parties agreed to abide by the proposed ceasefire.[28] At the same time, the United States exerted direct pressure on Israel to withdraw. In a November 7 letter to Ben Gurion, President Eisenhower stated: "It would be a matter of the greatest regret to all my countrymen if Israeli policy on a matter of such grave concern to the world should in any way impair the friendly cooperation between our two countries."[29] On November 12, Egypt accepted a ceasefire and the stationing of foreign observers in the Sinai, provided its sovereignty was not infringed.[30]

Meanwhile President Eisenhower assured British Prime Minister Anthony Eden that if Britain, France, and Israel were to accept the proposed ceasefire, the United States would stand by them and not leave them to face Soviet blackmailing alone. The United States also declared a state of emergency and stated publicly that it would forcefully resist any Soviet attempt to transport troops to the Middle East.

Eisenhower now became increasingly concerned that the crisis would result in growing Soviet influence in the region. Immediately after he was reelected on November 6, he asked Eden to quickly accept the ceasefire, noting his fears that "the red boy is going to demand the lion's share." As Britain was going through a financial crisis, Eisenhower threatened that the United States would not assist in saving the ailing British currency if Eden did not comply. Consequently, Britain and France both announced that they would cease all military operations in Egypt.[31]

Despite huge sympathy for Nasser's Egypt in the streets of most Arab states, the reaction of their respective governments was muted – limiting themselves to diplomatic and political support. Meeting in Beirut on November 13–14 Arab leaders called on the UN to implement its previous calls for a ceasefire and for the withdrawal of the attacking forces from Egyptian territories. The only concrete step in supporting Egypt was taken in Syria – blowing up the Kirkuk–Tripoli oil pipeline. This comprised the first use of oil as a weapon in the Arab–Israeli conflict. The explosion was executed by the Syrian intelligence agency, which was headed by Abdel Hamid a-Sarraj, a great admirer and supporter of Nasser. Whether the action was actually authorized by the Syrian government is unclear.[32]

On December 22, Britain and France withdrew their forces from the Canal Zone and were replaced by a United Nations Emergency Force (UNEF). By January Israel pulled back its forces from the Sinai Peninsula, but Israeli units continued to occupy Sharm el-Sheikh (overlooking the Straits of Tiran) and the Gaza Strip. In response to two UN resolutions of February 1957 "calling on Israel to complete its withdrawal behind the Armistice demarcation line without further delay," on March 7–8, 1957, Israeli troops completed their evacuation of Sharm el-Sheikh and Gaza, and on April 10 the Suez Canal was reopened.[33] UNEF then deployed along the western side of the Armistice Demarcation Line along the Gaza Strip and the Israeli–Egyptian border as well as in the Sharm el-Sheikh area. The latter deployment meant the opening of the Straits of Tiran to Israeli navigation.

In the War's Aftermath

Nasser, whose army deployed in the Sinai was militarily defeated by Israel, emerged from the confrontation victorious politically. He regained the Sinai Peninsula, confirmed the nationalization of the Suez Canal, and gained financing for his mega-project: the Aswan Dam. Yet for Israel, too, the outcomes of the 1956 War were not entirely negative. First, it ultimately produced a much more secure environment in the Sinai as well as along its border with Gaza – giving Israel some ten years of quiet which was only disturbed by the May 1967 crisis and the subsequent war. More enduring and consequential, however, was another outcome of Israel's decision to ally itself with France and Britain: the French decision to supply Israel with a nuclear reactor and other facilities required to obtain a full-fledged nuclear option.

While the Sinai–Suez War resulted in a huge blow to the prestige of Britain and France, Moscow's support of Egypt won it considerable praise and influence in various Third World countries. In the Middle East, the new bipolar world now replaced the old colonial system as the region had now become another theater of the Cold War. Regional powers, however, were not only a subject of the new global order – they also helped redefine it in ways commensurate with their interests.

Increasingly alarmed by Egypt's closer ties with the Soviet Union as well as by the threat Egypt posed to Arab monarchies, the Eisenhower administration decided in the aftermath of the Sinai–Suez War that a set of changes would need to be made in American strategy and policies in the Middle East. In December 1956, these new concepts were formulated as the "Eisenhower Doctrine," and on January 5, 1957 President Eisenhower officially unveiled the doctrine, receiving formal Congressional endorsement in March.

The doctrine called for the United States to provide economic and military assistance to countries threatened by other aggressive states in order to "secure and protect the territorial integrity and political independence of such nations, requesting such aid against overt armed aggression from any nation controlled by international communism."[34] The doctrine noted that the Sinai–Suez War resulted in a loss of prestige by Britain and France and that this, in turn, created a power vacuum in the region which "must be filled by the United States before it is filled by the U.S.S.R."[35] In addition to containing Russia, the doctrine also aimed at supporting the conservative Arab monarchies against the radical Arab regimes led by Nasser.

Offering generous economic and military assistance, the United States and Britain expected other regional countries to join the Baghdad Pact. However, President Nasser successfully thwarted such expectations by waging a successful campaign to persuade other Arab states to regard the pact as solely intended to increase the Western powers' influence in the Middle East.[36] Following the change in government in Iraq and its subsequent withdrawal from the pact, the alliance was renamed in 1959 the Central Treaty Organization (CENTO). Rather than becoming the envisaged regional collective security organization, it largely comprised a framework for United States-provided technical and economic assistance.[37]

Narratives

The Israeli Narrative

The Israeli narrative of this period was dominated by a deep sense of isolation and vulnerability and great fear of a second round of Arab–Israeli fighting. The doubling of Israel's population within a brief four-year period (1949–53) did not reduce the sense Israelis had that they were completely outnumbered. They saw themselves as facing adversaries that benefitted from huge populations, vast territory, and the associated strategic depth, and as surrounded by a large number of Arab states who enjoyed commensurate influence in the UN and other international institutions, as well as oil and its associated economic and political benefits. As a result, Israeli thinking during this period continued to be dominated by the notion that Israel comprised "the few" facing the Arab "many."

Israeli Vulnerabilities

Somewhat surprised by their success in the 1948 War, Israelis were convinced that the Arabs could not possibly accept the outcome and would, therefore, be determined to undo the results. Fear of such a "second-round" was grounded on an assessment that combined the ascribed Arab motivation to reverse the results of 1948 and the numerical advantage they would enjoy if such a war occurred. A third important element in Israel's estimate of its future prospects concerned the perceived fragility of its society. The doubling of Israel's population was achieved by immigration from many countries of different continents, with immigrants lacking a common language and a common culture. The hundreds of thousands of European Jews who came in the aftermath of the Second World War, many among them Holocaust survivors from DP camps who barely made it through the war's horrors, were now joined by an equal number of Jews who arrived from Arab countries.

Determined to settle every part of the land found in Israel's possession at the conclusion of the 1948 War, its government directed many of these immigrants to agriculture, a lifestyle and profession they had never experienced. Moreover, given Israel's very limited financial resources, these new immigrants were required to undergo this complete transformation under the most demanding physical circumstances. The result was an extreme sense of vulnerability.

One important consequence of this vulnerability was that Israelis viewed the infiltration of Palestinians in the early 1950s in nearly existential terms. In the most immediate sense it was feared that the new immigrants residing in Israel's frontier towns and villages – who had barely survived the transition from their former livelihood to agricultural – would simply not survive the challenge of repeated terror attacks. The fear was that this combined hardship would cause immigrants to flee their new dwellings and seek safer refuge in Israel's urban areas, thus negating its government's attempt to disperse its small population more evenly throughout the country's limited territory.

Thus, the morale of Israel's immigrant population – especially those residing in its frontier towns and agricultural settlements – now became a strategic issue. To avoid social disintegration, Israel believed it needed to project power internally and externally: internally in order to instill confidence in its weak population so that morale would not implode under the pressure of the recurring infiltration raids; and externally, to coerce the Palestinian infiltrators and those in the neighboring countries harboring them, assisting them, or simply tolerating them, to put a stop to their activities.

Retaliation Raids

In order to succeed in such coercion Israelis saw an imperative to launch retaliation raids in order to extract a heavy price from those whom Israel regarded as supporting or merely allowing these infiltrations. At first, the raids targeted primarily the Palestinian villages on the other side of Israel's borders with Jordan and Gaza, from which the infiltrators were believed to have originated. The purpose was not to locate and apprehend or liquidate the infiltrators – Israel's intelligence assets in these early years were far too limited to discover the terrorists' precise location. Instead, it was to persuade these villages to stop harboring terrorists by demonstrating that this would be associated with a heavy price-tag. Later, an increasing number of these raids targeted assets of the host countries – mostly military installations and personnel – with a view to compelling their governments to put a stop to the infiltrations. Being assaulted inside their borders by these violent infiltrators, Israelis saw themselves as acting in self-defense and thus as fully justified in using force – including harsh punitive raids – to bring these attacks to an end.

The logic of Israel's retaliation raids against Syrian targets involved two further factors. First, an additional dimension of vulnerability and asymmetry: the topographically inferior location of Israel's agricultural settlements along the Syrian frontier, relative to the Syrian positions which were located in the elevated Golan Heights. Second, Israel saw itself as fully justified in insisting on its right to farm the land in the DMZ because the territory in question was allotted to it in the 1947 UN partition plan. Israel also argued that as the successor to the Mandate authority, it had the rightful jurisdiction over the DMZ areas, since they had previously constituted areas delineated as being under Mandate control. Consequently it viewed Syrian attacks on Israelis attempting to farm these lands as acts of aggression. Israeli military operations against Syrian targets along the border areas were thus seen as merely an attempt to dissuade further Syrian attacks by demonstrating that such attacks would result in heavy costs.

Toward the mid-1950s, Israelis observed that the retaliation raids had two different results on the Jordanian and Gazan fronts. Whereas their raids seemed to have succeeded in persuading Jordan – itself weak, fragile, and vulnerable – to put a stop to Palestinian attacks, thus validating the logic of Israel's policy, it saw the same policy as having almost the opposite effect in the case of Egypt. In the latter case the host government, Egypt, seemed to have taken over the orchestration of the infiltration raids. This, in turn, was viewed in Israel as indicating that Egypt was preparing for the anticipated "second round," but since it was militarily too weak to confront Israel directly, it had turned instead to using Palestinian terrorists as its proxies. For this reason, Israeli retaliation raids against Egyptian military installations and personnel in Gaza were viewed as entirely justified.

Israel's view of Palestinians as the proxies of Arab states also played a role in its perception of the refugee issue. Israelis concluded that while the Arab states insisted that the rights of the refugees must be addressed, they in fact cared very little about the refugees' fate. Thus, they purposefully refrained from assisting the refugees and, indeed, resisted their resettlement so as to keep the issue alive. Accordingly, the Palestinians were increasingly seen as mere pawns in a cynical Arab power struggle against Israel.

Arab Hostility

For the Israelis, the 1955 Czech arms deal confirmed their assessment that Arab hostility was constant and high, and that the Arab states were determined to erase their humiliating military defeat in the 1948 War with a new round of conflict. Indeed, they viewed the deal as the next step in Egypt's plans to reverse the results of the 1948 War by building a military machine capable of matching and then overcoming Israel's military edge. Still, Israel was surprised by the dimensions of the deal and regarded it as unprecedented in its size, by the standards of the Middle East at the time.

Israel's failed initial attempts to respond to the Czech arms deal by persuading the United States to provide it with equivalent weaponry was seen by Israelis as evidence of their isolation and vulnerability. With its interests in the Arab world at large vastly surpassing its limited commitment to Israel, the United States was viewed as wishing to avoid being seen in Israel's company. Thus, in the competitive pursuit of allies, Israel viewed itself in a dramatically inferior position to that of its neighbors.

Israel's acute sense of isolation and vulnerability was also at the root of its approach to the issue of free passage in maritime waterways. Surrounded by hostile Arab states, Israel viewed the effort to deny its ships free passage to and from Asia – through the Suez Canal or the Straits of Tiran – as intended to strangle it. In arguing its case, Israel pointed to a clause in the 1888 Suez Canal Convention that required Egypt to keep the Canal open in times of war and in times of peace. Israel also disputed Egypt's claim that the armistice agreement amounted to no more than a cessation of hostilities and as thus allowing it to deny Israel free passage.[38]

The 1956 War

In this perceived environment, the joint attack on Egypt that France and Britain offered at the Sèvres summit was seen by Israel as an opportunity that it could not afford to miss. First, it allowed Israel to address its isolation by promising a long-term alliance with France. Although a power in decline in the aftermath of the Second World War, as a permanent member of the UN Security Council, France was still regarded in the mid-1950s as a formidable force in the international arena.

Second, in the absence of an American commitment to offset the Czech arms deal the proposed campaign promised to serve as a "preventive war" by enabling the destruction of Egypt's armed forces before they had time to fully integrate the huge quantities of advanced weaponry purchased from Czechoslovakia.

Finally, in light of the UN's perceived failure to enforce Israel's right of free passage through the Canal and Straits, the war offered an opportunity to reestablish Israel's rights – denied by Egypt since 1951 – by forcing the opening of these passages to Israeli vessels.[39]

In the years following the war, the Israelis judged it to have been a success. While forced to withdraw from the Sinai and the Gaza Strip by what they considered an inhospitable world environment, Israelis saw the war as having "bought" Israel ten years of quiet along its southern frontier. Egypt was seen as having been coerced into reining in the Palestinians in Gaza, preventing them from conducting any further cross-border attacks. Thus, between Israel's withdrawal from the Strip in February 1957 and the 1967 War, not a single attack against Israel was launched from Gaza.

Moreover, in Israeli eyes, the war resulted in a monumental defeat for the Egyptian army before it had a chance to integrate the weapons purchased from the Soviet bloc in the Czech arms deal. Also, the Straits of Tiran were reopened and freedom of navigation to Israel's southern port of Eilat was restored, remaining uninterrupted until the May 1967 crisis. The demilitarization of the Sinai Peninsula and its monitoring by UNEF units meant that Israelis won an important buffer, providing them with strategic depth and sufficient warning of any possible Egyptian aggressive designs.

Much more important, however, was that Israel now forged a strong alliance with France. Other than the ability to obtain essential advanced arms and munitions, the immediate benefit of the alliance was psychological, alleviating Israelis' sense of isolation. But the most enduring result of the alliance concluded in 1956 at Sèvres was a French-made nuclear reactor constructed near the southern town of Dimona – a pillar of Israeli strategic deterrence for decades to come.

For all these reasons, Israelis viewed the 1956 War as having been a success. For a while at least, the war's architects, David Ben Gurion and his young associates, IDF Chief of Staff Moshe Dayan and Deputy Defense Minister Shimon Peres, became mythical figures in the Israeli psyche and political discourse.

The Palestinian Narrative

In the aftermath of the *Nakba*, the 1948 defeat, the Palestinians saw themselves as helpless and leaderless, with Israel preventing them from returning to their homes after the war ended and the Arab states dictating their destiny. They saw both Egypt and Jordan, each for its own self-interest, as denying them the right to establish their own state and government in the areas remaining under Arab control. And while they realized that Arab countries had failed to defend them and while they saw themselves vulnerable and at the mercy of Arab regimes intent on maintaining stable conditions with Israel, the Palestinians still found comfort in identifying themselves as part of an Arab nation and hoped to make the liberation of Palestine the Arabs' most pressing task.

The Fedayyin

During this period, Palestinians saw Israel as an illegitimate entity and a mortal enemy, one that had stolen their land and resources and sought the destruction of Palestinian identity and national aspiration. The enemy, they believed, would not rest until it conquered the remaining Palestinian land and expelled its population. Neither peace nor coexistence were seen as conceivable with an enemy that was viewed as seeking their destruction. War was regarded as only a matter of time, requiring Palestinians and Arabs to be prepared for it. Consequently, Palestinians demanded that the Arab states make the liberation of Palestine their top priority, and that they should consider the use of force as the only means to redress the injustice of 1948.

Seeing themselves as merely doing the little they could to return to their homes and property, the Palestinians soon found themselves unable to do so, with many being shot on sight as they crossed the border, while others ended up in Arab jails, accused of attempting to destabilize the armistice regimes signed with Israel after the war. A small number of them joined armed groups and sought to fight back by attacking Israeli border towns, believing that Israel should not be allowed to easily swallow the Palestinian land it conquered during the war.

The early 1950s was a period in which small groups of armed Palestinians formed bands of *Fedayyin*, the earliest form of Palestinian armed resistance to the State of Israel. The infiltration attacks were an expression of the Palestinians' rejection of the status quo and their belief that their land could only be liberated through armed resistance. They sought to force Arab countries, especially Egypt and Jordan, to focus on their plight and to seek ways of addressing their needs. Palestinians in the Gaza Strip and in the West Bank were angry and disappointed with the inability of the Egyptian and Jordanian forces to defend or retaliate against Israeli attacks during 1953–56.

Annexation to Jordan

Although the annexation of central Palestine to Jordan and its renaming as the West Bank was accepted by most Palestinians residing in those areas, such a step was seen as temporary. The ultimate goal remained the liberation of occupied Palestinian land, after which an independent Palestinian state could emerge. Palestinians saw the annexation as providing them immediate political and socioeconomic benefits and as giving them political power, citizenship, and free movement. They therefore supported the annexation, despite their strong rejection of King Abdullah's efforts to erase the name "Palestine."

At the same time, Palestinians residing in the Gaza Strip and those associated with the Mufti, Hajj Amin al-Husseini, had long suspected King Abdullah's motivations and viewed him as complicit in their plight. For them, Abdullah, too, was an enemy who should be fought. The assassination of the king at the hands of one of the Mufti's followers indicated the strength of anger and hate directed at him. But Palestinians in the West Bank were alarmed by this development, fearing the destabilization that might follow.

Arab States' Role

Palestinians were especially worried about possible Arab–Israeli accommodation that might be based on the armistice regime established in 1949. The violent infiltrations of Israel were seen as one way of sabotaging such designs. Another was to keep the refugee problem alive as an obstacle to any peace deal at their expense. Despite the harsh conditions which refugees had to endure, it was seen as imperative that the refugee camps remain in place. Hence, Palestinians rejected offers to resettle refugees, for fear that this would entail abandoning their homeland or foregoing the goal of liberation. Refugee camps were seen as a daily reminder to all concerned, including the international community, that the plight of the Palestinians had not been addressed.

Palestinians saw salvation in Nasserism and pan-Arabism, particularly in the promise to unite the Arab world, especially its more revolutionary regimes, and confront Israel to restore Arab dignity and Palestinian rights. Military coups against pro-Western regimes were seen as assets enforcing a new pan-Arab force that was revolutionary and both anti-Israel and anti-West. The turn to the Soviet Union was perceived in a similar vein. Pan-Arabism viewed Israel as a tool of imperialism and as an enemy of all Arabs.

The 1956 War

The 1956 War was perceived by Palestinians as evidence of this view. More importantly, Israel's leading role in the war was seen as demonstrating beyond a shadow of doubt that Israel was not only a threat to Palestinians, but to all Arabs. By contrast, the Soviet Union was now perceived by Palestinians as an ally in the battle against Israel and its Western supporters.

The 1956 War and its outcome – with Israel being forced to retreat from areas it occupied during the war – convinced Palestinians that they had an Arab partner in a future war against a common enemy with the goal of liberating Palestine. With this conclusion, the idea that the Palestinians could now play the role of a vanguard and a catalyst began to take shape.

The Arab Narrative

The Arab narrative during this period was not different from that adopted during and immediately after the 1948 War. Israel was considered the primary threat to the Arab states;

hence, all Arab nations were urged to unite and place all their military, economic, political, and social resources under a single unified Arab command. In turn, these resources were to be directed against the Arabs' sole enemy, commonly referred to as the "so-called state of Israel." More often anti-Zionist rhetoric labeled Israel as a band of gangsters and conspirators who were manipulated by the world's imperial powers.

At the same time, a new rhetoric began to develop in the Arab street, targeting the region's "old regimes."[40] These regimes were depicted not only as the cause of the Arabs' failure in the 1948 War, but also as the tacit allies of Israel and the West. Thus, the defeat of 1948 was reinterpreted as resulting from structural deficiencies in Arab countries that could only be corrected by revolutionary and progressive regimes. The ascent of Arab militaries to power, particularly in Egypt and Syria, now began to mix the confrontation with Israel with issues related to the much deeper socioeconomic conditions of the Arab states. Repairing these malfunctions – a process to be led by the officers that had just taken power – was presented as a precondition for the inevitable victory over Israel.

Israel's "true nature" was soon to be defined as part of the neocolonial influence in the region – a depiction seen as confirmed by the assistance that Israel was attracting from Britain and France, the former colonial powers. In the case of the United States, the Arab narrative focused not only on the political support provided by the United States to Israel but also on the guarantee it gave to Israel's territorial integrity. Using the same prism, France and Britain were also seen as granting Israel necessary political and military support. Indeed, in Arab eyes, Israeli behavior in the demilitarized zones after 1949, the Israeli sabotage attempt in Egypt in 1954, the Israeli attack on Gaza in 1955, and finally the conspiracy against Egypt in association with France and Britain in 1956, all added up to prove Israel's imperial and expansionist character.

Egypt's Aswan Dam

The Arabs' parallel confrontation with the West was all too evident in the case of the Aswan Dam project – a project regarded as representing not only Egyptian but also broader Arab dreams of development and progress. When the Soviet Union declared its willingness to finance the dam, Arabs saw this as evidence that Moscow had become a natural and true ally, now providing weaponry, economic assistance, and a shared anti-imperialist stance.

Convinced that it was both politically and morally on the right side, Egypt regarded itself as fully justified in reacting to the World Bank decision – which merely masked an American decision to the same effect – to withdraw the commitment to fund the Aswan Dam project by nationalizing the Suez Canal. The canal ran entirely through Egyptian territory and hence it was Egypt's sovereign right to assert its control. Moreover, Egyptians were the ones who had dug the canal, under the most difficult circumstances. And since Egypt intended to keep the Canal open and free to international maritime navigation, other countries could not possibly object to its assertion of control over a company that had become a state within state. Indeed, Egypt now saw the logic of its move affirmed by the support it received from the Eastern Bloc, the Nonaligned Movement, the Islamic and Arab worlds, and even from a number of Western countries.

Relations with Israel

The Egyptian narrative stressed that it sought to avoid a confrontation with Israel over the Palestinian infiltrations but that it could not prevent refugees from crossing the border to return to their homes or to cultivate their land. Egypt also argued that it could not prevent its junior officers stationed in Gaza, who were sympathetic to the Palestinians' plight, aiding the latter. Thus, despite the official Egyptian policy of maintaining calm, these officers could not be prevented from encouraging rather than discouraging such infiltrations.[41] Nevertheless, Egyptians stressed that by mid-1954, their military began to openly crack down on those suspected as involved in the infiltration attempts, mostly Palestinians sympathetic to the Muslim Brotherhood.[42]

This policy changed only after the Israeli raid in February 1955 in which 39 Egyptian soldiers were killed. News of the raid and of its results coincided with reports of French arms transfers to Israel, which Egyptians saw as leading to the Czech arms deal. In light of these developments, by 1956, Egypt saw itself as justified in increasing its military presence in the Gaza Strip and in relaxing its restrictions on infiltration and the activities of what had by now become the *Fedayyin*.

Given these tensions, Egypt saw itself as entirely justified in preventing Israel from enjoying free passage in its waterways.[43] Egypt's legal argument relied in part on its interpretation of the 1888 Suez Canal Convention, which it viewed as authorizing Egypt to take any measures needed to protect its own security.[44]

The 1956 War

Equally important was the Egyptian understanding of the war's course and consequences. In Egyptian eyes, the Egyptian military was not defeated in the Sinai Peninsula – it simply withdrew its forces to defend the core of the homeland against the simultaneous attack by two world powers possessing some of the most advanced militaries: Britain and France. Moreover, Egypt saw itself as having stood its ground – especially in the battle of Port Said which now assumed mythical dimensions – until international pressures forced the former colonial invaders to withdraw.

Accordingly, not only in Egypt but also in the streets of almost every Arab country, Nasser was now hailed as a hero for having successfully deprived the two world powers of any meaningful gains. Britain was considered to have failed to reoccupy Egypt. France was seen as having failed to prevent Egypt from supporting Arab national liberation movements, particularly in Algeria. And Britain and France were viewed as having failed to reverse the nationalization of the Suez Canal. In turn, Israel was seen as having failed to occupy a slice of the Sinai or weaken Egypt, while Britain, France, and Israel were all seen as having failed to force a regime change in Egypt. Riding on this perceived success Nasser could now inspire Arab masses as well as some of the region's elites to revive the pan-Arab movement.

Syria

The Syrian narrative, justifying its violent opposition to the Hula project, was that under the Armistice agreement, the DMZ was a no-man's-land, and without a peace agreement establishing which country was the rightful owner of the land, no such projects should be undertaken. In addition, Israel's initiation of the 1951 project to drain the Hulu marshland would have harmed Palestinian Arab villages in the area. The Israeli decision, on March 30 of that year, to assert sovereignty over the DMZs led 800 inhabitants of the villages to be forcibly evacuated from the area. It was no surprise, then, that, beginning in 1951, Israel refused to attend the meetings of the Syrian–Israeli Mixed Armistice Commission. This refusal was viewed as constituting a flagrant violation of the General Armistice Agreement and as contributing to an increase of tension in the area. The UN Security Council strongly condemned the Israeli behavior in a resolution on May 18, 1951 as being "inconsistent with the objectives and intent of the Armistice agreement." Israel, therefore, was violating international law, the rules of the post 1948 arrangements, and the rights of Palestinians in their homeland.[45]

Jordan

Having characterized Israel as an imperial power waging war against Arab countries in order to take their lands and arrest their development and progress, it was necessary to keep the Palestinian cause alive in Arab political thought. For this reason, the Arab League and important Arab countries, particularly Egypt and Saudi Arabia, objected to uniting Jordan and the West Bank. The move was seen as intended to "liquidate" the Palestinian cause and as an example of Jordan's "royal" behavior that sought to enlarge a small, British-made, Arab state at the expense of Palestinian rights.

To counter this logic, Jordan argued that the Palestinian population expressed its preference for the unification of the West Bank and Jordan and that this was a step toward the Arab unity which had been a goal of the Great Arab Revolt led by the Hashemites in 1916. Jordan also argued that by inserting itself into the West Bank it was protecting Palestinian land from being taken over by Israel. Finally, it argued that the alternative – creating a Palestinian state – would not only break Arab unity apart, it would also create the conditions for Israeli hegemony over all Palestinian territories. Indeed, the connections and ties between the Palestinians and Jordan preceded even the inception of the Arab–Israeli conflict.

Analysis

This section focuses on identifying the causes of the most dramatic development of this period: the 1956 Sinai–Suez War.

The International System

At the *systemic level* this period provided conclusive evidence of the anarchic nature of the international system. The UN, having decided in November 1947 to create a Jewish state in Palestine and having failed in 1948 to provide safe implementation of its decision, now failed to enforce a peaceful implementation of the 1949 armistice agreements between Israel and its neighboring Arab states. Thus, the unfortunate distance between reality and the aspirations of the UN's founders to build an organization that could keep the peace.

Along Israel's border with Jordan and Gaza, the UN failed to prevent the spiral of Palestinian infiltrations into Israel and harsh Israeli retaliatory actions. Similarly, along the Syrian–Israeli border it failed to prevent the cycle of Israeli attempts to farm lands within the DMZ in the north, Syrian use of violence to prevent such farming and resulting Israeli military responses.

The UN also failed to enforce free passage through the international waterways of the Middle East, such as the Straits of Tiran. Nor was it able to arrest the rapidly evolving arms race in the region by providing some alternative to the collapsing limited arms control regime of the Tripartite Declaration. These failures, and the clear evidence of international anarchy that they represented, now produced a deep sense of insecurity that affected the calculations of almost every state in the Middle East.

The second systemic factor affecting the security environment leading to the 1956 War was the increased involvement of the United States and the Soviet Union in the region's affairs. An important consequence of this increased involvement was the extent to which developments in the region reflected the bipolar Cold War prism through which the two superpowers increasingly viewed anything occurring anywhere on the globe, including the Middle East. One example of this was the Soviet Union's attempt to acquire influence in the region through massive arms transfers as reflected in the Czech arms deal.

Yet the magnitude of the Czech deal, and the fear that the successful integration of the weapons supplied to Egypt's armed forces would alter the regional distribution of power, was propelling Israel to launch a "preventive" war before this occurred. This, as with France's supply of arms to Israel, illustrates the destabilizing effects of the major arms transfers by the external powers to their Middle Eastern clients in the framework of the global Cold War.

Another aspect of increased superpower influence during this period was the attempts made by the declining powers – Britain and France – to arrest the deterioration of their standing in the region. France feared that the Czech arms deal would inject confidence into Egypt's involvement in Algeria;[46] it responded by supplying Israel with equally impressive quantities of advanced weaponry. Britain's reaction to the nationalization of the Suez Canal was to combine with France in offering Israel a joint venture: a coordinated attack on Egypt.

France and Britain were both suffering post-colonial fear of losing their standing in world affairs. Britain considered Egypt's nationalization of the Suez Canal to be as threatening as Iran's earlier nationalization of its oil industry. It worried that these examples would inspire similar acts in other newly independent Third World countries with considerable British economic assets. Also, Britain's view of Nasser as a "Hitler on the Nile" reflected the impact of the Second World War on British political psychology, especially that of Prime Minister Anthony Eden, a prominent pre-war anti-appeaser and Churchill's wartime Foreign Secretary. The conclusion that the British reached was: as was the case with Hitler in the 1930s, dictators like Nasser had to be stopped before it was too late.

The case of France illustrates the interaction between global and regional developments. By arming Israel, France intended to put a check on Egypt's President Nasser, whose support for the struggles of the independence movements in Algeria, Morocco, and Tunisia threatened the French colonial forces still stationed in these countries. France was not only defeated in the Second World War, it also lost many of its colonies in Indo-China. But the war in

Algeria was seen as even more fateful, since Paris considered the country to be part of France. Nasser's nationalist and pan-Arab reach was viewed as threatening to tilt the war to France's detriment. Egyptian arms supplies to Algeria's National Liberation Front were viewed as strengthening its ability to fight for independence. [47]

The Middle East Region

At the *regional-systemic level*, the Middle East experienced all the maladies of the security dilemma: almost all measures taken by the parties to the conflict in an effort to increase their security could not but undermine the security of their neighbors. This, in turn, prompted the latter to take measures that in the end undermined the security of the state that initiated this chain reaction in the quest of increased security.

A clear reflection of the security dilemma was Israel's perceived imperative to put a stop to the Palestinian *Fedayyin* attacks. Israel regarded such attacks as threatening the overall distribution of power by presenting a serious challenge to the highly vulnerable Israeli society. Another aspect of the security dilemma prevalent in the Middle East at the time was mirror imaging and projection: in the early 1950s Ben Gurion was convinced that the Arab states could not possibly accept the results of the 1948 War and would launch "a second round" at a time convenient to them. In his view it was not just that the Czech arms deal would alter the distribution of power – he was convinced that Egypt would use its new strength to launch a war aimed at erasing the humiliation of its defeat in 1948. Ben Gurion believed that Israel must take self-help measures to thwart Egypt's plans. Thus, Israel's expectations that Egypt was harboring aggressive designs led to its own decision to take aggressive measures.

But neither could Egypt be sanguine about Israel. Having defeated the Egyptian army and having penetrated the Sinai in 1948 with a small population base of only some 650,000, Israel had doubled its population between 1949 and 1953. Coupled with the weapons that France provided Israel before the Czech arms deal and the aggressive "escalation dominance" strategy Israel pursued in the quest to suppress the *Fedayyin* attacks, it is easy to see why defense planners in Cairo would have been just as nervous about their northern neighbor as Israel was about Egypt's possible designs and the trajectory of its capabilities.

The most salient, and for Egypt the most painful, illustration of Israel's policy of "escalation dominance" was the February 1955 Gaza Raid. [48] The incident had a profound effect on the Egyptian governing elite's perception of Israel. No longer viewed as a neighbor kept sufficiently afar by the Sinai desert, Israel for the first time appeared as a menace, directly affecting Egypt's security and the safety and wellbeing of its servicemen.

The Gaza Raid also affected the priorities of Egypt's high command. Although it previously preferred to couple its opposition to British and French imperialism and colonialism with a military orientation to the United States, the Gaza Raid injected a new sense of urgency to finding a reliable source of arms. And since developing a defense relationship with the United States was seen as at best a long term project, Egypt's military leaders had no choice but to turn to the Soviet Union, which was only too happy to comply.

A different aspect of the *regional-systemic level,* without which Israel's role in launching the 1956 Suez–Sinai War cannot be understood, is the effects of the structural asymmetries in the region on Israel's national security strategy. The strategy, developed by Ben Gurion, was based on an extreme sense of vulnerability rooted in Israel's overall quantitative inferiority in all dimensions of national power – population, territory, the number of states and natural resources. To balance its neighbors' quantitative superiority Israel was to generate a qualitative edge – "quality opposite quantity" was the slogan adopted to describe this commitment.

The result of its limited population base was that Israel would not be able to sustain a large standing army without crippling its economy. Instead, it had to rely on a large reserve force that could only be mobilized for very short periods. The implication was that Israel could not sustain a long attritional war; instead, its doctrine had to be based on highly mobile, armored "wars of lightning."

The other impetus for this doctrine was Israel's narrow territorial base. Within such a narrow configuration Israel was deprived of strategic depth. It therefore lacked sufficient space for either tactical or operational withdrawals. Ben Gurion's conclusion was that Israel could not afford to wage war on its own territory; instead it was obliged to "deliver the battle to the enemy territory."

The large number of Arab states was seen as implying that Israel's neighbors enjoyed considerable strategic depth: while these states could be beaten again and again, they could not be brought to surrender. By contrast, defeat for Israel was seen as likely to terminate its existence.

The reliance on a "war of lightning" delivered to the enemy territory required a highly mobile force that would avoid absorbing the first attack. Rather, Israel would attack first, preemptively – before an enemy strike – or preventively, before any further deterioration in the balance of power occurred. Hence the logic of its decision to attack Egypt in 1956, before it was able to integrate the weapons it obtained through the Czech arms deal.

The Israeli Domestic Scene

At the *unit level*, the most important development in Israeli politics leading up to the 1956 War was the dispute between two schools that divided Israel's political leadership and governing elite during the first half of the 1950s: the split between the "activists" and the "diplomats." The "activists" were led by Ben Gurion, who in 1953 left government for a period of self-imposed "exile" in Kibbutz Sde Boker in the Negev. Ben Gurion returned to power gradually in 1955, first as minister of defense and later as prime minister.

When Ben Gurion left government, two of his lieutenants remained in command of Israel's defense community: IDF Chief of Staff, Lieutenant General Moshe Dayan, and Director General of the Defense Ministry, Shimon Peres. Both were strong advocates of responding to the *Fedayyin* attacks of the early 1950s by pursuing "escalation dominance." This school Arab hostility to Israel as high and constant and thus as unaffected by Israeli behavior. It believed that the only way to mitigate the guerilla threat was by effective dissuasion obtained through imposing very heavy costs on the villagers harboring the *Fedayyin* and on the governments hosting them and providing them safe havens.

The "activists" were opposed by the "diplomats" – a school led by foreign minister Moshe Sharett, who replaced Ben Gurion as prime minister in 1953, and by Israel's ambassador to the United States and the UN, Abba Eban. Sharett believed that Arab hostility was affected by Israeli behavior and that, therefore, Israel's responses to *Fedayyin* attacks should be measured. He and other members of this school argued that by responding disproportionately to such attacks, Israel was contributing to a cycle of escalation, as Arabs sought revenge and the IDF was compelled to react to Arab responses to its retaliation raids.

A different but equally important argument advanced by the "diplomats" was that the conventional forces of the neighboring Arab states posed a far greater threat to Israel's security and survival, that to counter this threat Israel needed the support of external powers, and that it should therefore refrain from horrifically violent retaliation raids that earn it nothing but international criticism. Abba Eban, who was at the receiving end of such criticism in Washington, DC and New York, was a strong advocate of the latter perspective.

This split in Israel's governing circles coincided with another dimension of Israel's domestic scene in its early days: the underdevelopment of its civil–military relations. While the legal structures created by the newly-born state placed its civilian authorities fully in command of its military, in practice this was not the case. The problem was exacerbated once Ben Gurion left government in 1953, since his successors, Sharett as prime minister and Pinhas Lavon as defense minister, had no prior expertise in military affairs and hence no self-evident defense credentials. As a result, they found it difficult to control the young and enthusiastic IDF officers – all strong advocates of "escalation dominance." The best example of the latter was the commander of the IDF's Unit 101 – a brash, daring young officer, Major Ariel Sharon. Absent sufficient control, these officers felt they could interpret liberally the authorizations they were provided by the country's civilian leaders. Consequently a number of retaliation raids resulted in far more Arab casualties than anticipated, thus contributing to the process of escalation.

IDF Chief of Staff Dayan was also a strong proponent of preventive war. Toward the mid-1950s, and especially after the magnitude of the Czech arms deal became known, Dayan believed in the necessity to act before the weapons received had been fully absorbed and integrated by the Egyptian army. Hence, he thought Israel should create an environment conducive to such an attack by initiating actions that would increase tensions with Egypt, primarily by reacting disproportionately to the *Fedayyin* raids, preferably against Egyptian targets in Gaza.

The conflict between "the activists" and "the diplomats" and the tension between some of the country's civilian leaders and its military were exacerbated in 1954 by Ben Gurion's gradual reinvolvement in the country's affairs and his later decision to return to power. Seeking to frame his return in policy terms, Ben Gurion escalated his criticism of his successors as timid, pressing them to respond forcefully to Arab attacks. Publicly, he discounted the importance of international criticism of the retaliation raids, arguing that "what counts is what the Jews will do, not what the gentiles will say."[49]

Reacting defensively to Ben Gurion's criticism, "the diplomats" felt compelled to demonstrate that they were no less patriotic or "hard-nosed" regarding the country's national security. As a result, they authorized more retaliation raids than would have otherwise been the case. At the same time, IDF officers advocating "escalation dominance" felt they had the support of the country's founding father. As a result, they felt legitimate in exceeding the instructions they received from Ben Gurion's successors – their formal civilian leaders. These internal dynamics contributed significantly to the ever-evolving escalation and thus to the creation of a regional environment conducive to the eventual war.

Egypt's Internal Politics

Egypt's domestic scene also contributed to the escalation. During the four years (1952–56) that preceded the war, Egypt had witnessed a dramatic if not total transformation: from a monarchy to a republic and from a multiparty political system to one-party system controlled by the former *Zobat Ahrar* [Free Officers] – army officers who toppled the old regime on July 23, 1952. The constitution of 1956 allowed for Nasser's election as the first president of the country and stipulated the formation of the National Union. By then Egypt had gone through processes of agrarian reform, redistribution of assets, and the Egyptianization of banks and foreign-owned or foreign-dependent institutions. Its new leaders also announced their intention of making Egypt an industrialized country.

But turbulence was not the only aspect of Egypt's domestic scene – another was the new confidence it displayed even in distant arenas. With its newly acquired high standing among newly independent states and especially among the non-aligned Afro-Asian countries that took part in the April 1955 Bandung Summit, with the Czech arms deal, and with the British leaving Egypt in June 18, 1956, the country felt it had reached a new phase in its history. The nationalization of the Suez Canal signaled Egypt's determination to control its resources and to become an example in this realm for other countries in the region as well as for a variety of national liberation movements in Africa and Asia.[50] This contributed to Israel's growing anxiety over Egypt's overall – political, as well as economic – ascendance and its possible effects on the distribution of power in the region.

One demonstration of Egypt's growing power was its embrace of the Palestinian struggle by orchestrating cross-border operations of the *Fedayyin* in response to Israel's "escalation dominance" policy. From Egypt's standpoint this was an attempt to place a price-tag on Israel's policy and to keep the Palestinian cause in a prominent place on the regional and international agendas. Depicting the *Fedayyin* as merely attempting to reclaim lands from which they were expelled by force was important for Egypt, not only in the Palestinian context but also in the framework of the decolonization climate that was then sweeping the world.

The Palestinians

On the Palestinian side, *unit-level factors* contributed their share to the march to the 1956 War. In the 1950s, the Palestinians were mostly subordinate to state actors.[51] The Mufti was no longer relevant and the All Palestine Government lost all relevance to Palestinians living in the Gaza Strip. For many years to come, Palestinian nationalist institution-building and activities were to take place mostly outside the boundaries of historic Palestine.

Leaderless, weak, fragmented, and under the full control of Egypt and Jordan, the Palestinian domestic environment lent itself to a multiplicity of responses. Some Palestinians took matters into their own hands, having lost all faith in their own leadership, by engaging in hundreds of individual and small group infiltration attempts. Given the armistice agreement limitations on Egyptian army deployment in the Gaza Strip, the Egyptians formed a small unit of Palestinian border police commanded by Egyptian officers to prevent these infiltrations.[52] But it was not until after Israel's raid on an Egyptian military outpost in Gaza in February 1955 that Egypt began to sponsor *Fedayyin* attacks into Israel.[53] By the mid-1950s, hundreds of Israeli casualties were reported and many more Palestinians were killed or injured in Israeli retaliations.

David Ben Gurion

At the *individual level*, the Israeli side was dominated during this period by the strong personality of David Ben Gurion. As the architect of Israel's grand strategy and national security doctrine and as the father of "the activists" school within Israel's governing circles, Ben Gurion inspired many of the actual measures taken by the IDF – measures that contributed to the escalation towards the 1956 War. While others in the Israeli policy elite – notably Peres and Dayan – played an important role in navigating Israeli policy, it was Ben Gurion's unique historical role as the country's leader in the struggle for independence that now made him pivotal to the adoption of a policy that pursued deterrence of terrorism based on "escalation dominance" with the associated risks that it would lead to war. And, uniquely among Israel's senior leaders, it was Ben Gurion's strong belief in the supreme importance of forging an alliance with France that created the conditions for the Sinai–Suez War.

Paradoxically, however, Ben Gurion's approach was primarily driven not by aggressive impulses but rather by deep pessimism and a profound sense of vulnerability. Indeed, Ben Gurion was far from certain that the Zionist project would or could succeed. Most of all he was uncertain as to whether the peculiar conglomerate referred to as the Israeli society at the time was resilient enough to sustain the hardships entailed in the difficult struggle. As noted earlier, it was this uncertainty that propelled Ben Gurion to advocate aggressive retaliation to *Fedayyin* attacks – uncertain that Israel's population was resilient enough to absorb such attacks.

Similarly, in 1956, the same sense of vulnerability led Ben Gurion to condition his consent to the French plan for a joint attack on Egypt on a prior French commitment to station air force squadrons in Israel, to defend against possible Arab air bombardments of Israel's vulnerable population centers. With this, Ben Gurion demonstrated both a grossly exaggerated assessment of Arab capabilities and a lack of confidence in the Israeli population's ability to sustain attacks.

The alliance with France demonstrated two other attributes of Ben Gurion's leadership. First, his capacity to identify opportunities: Ben Gurion was quick to realize that Nasser's involvement in Algeria provided Israel with a unique "French moment" – as Nasser was seen as a threat to both countries – a potential alliance that needed to be concluded and fortified by war if necessary, if it were to endure. And second, his capacity to identify young policy entrepreneurs and allow them significant leeway in exploring their ideas. Thus, while repeatedly questioning their rationale, Ben Gurion allowed Peres and Dayan to lay the foundations for the alliance with France which eventually led to the war.

Gamal Abdel Nasser

If during the period between the mid-1950s and the mid-1960s the cliché "larger than life" could be attached to any Middle East leader, Egypt's Nasser would have been the one. Although during the period leading to the 1956 War much of the force of his personality was yet to be revealed, during the 1954–56 period Nasser took a number of steps that placed him at the center and front of the world stage as a national liberation revolutionary. The nationalization of the Suez Canal, his ascribed commitment to Egypt's industrialization, his involvement in Algeria and his role in the non-aligned summit in Bandung, all fed into the escalation that led to the war by contributing to Israeli – as well as British and French – fears that they were facing a foe far more menacing than anyone else in the region.

Nasser saw his primary mission as that of releasing Egypt from colonialism and imperialism, so that for the first time in centuries it would be ruled by Egyptians. Since the confrontation with the colonial powers was extremely popular, it provided Nasser with a sense of empowerment. Externally, he now appeared as the first Egyptian leader to stand on the world stage side by side with such personalities as Nehru of India, Sukarno of Indonesia, and Tito of Yugoslavia, calling for a "Third World" position on the Cold War that would set it aside and release it from dependency on either the Western or Soviet Blocs.

Internally, Nasser sought to make Egypt Egyptian by reforming its education and health systems and by creating an industrial base for Egypt that would earn it a seat in the front row of the community of nations. A centerpiece of this plan was the building of the Aswan Dam – a long-held dream of Egyptians. The project was intended to generate electricity and help to quadruple the area that could be cultivated in Upper Egypt. The initial support for the project by the United States and the World Bank elevated Nasser's reputation as Egypt's nation-builder to that of Muhammad Ali, the founder of modern Egypt. Consequently, their later withdrawal of support was viewed by Nasser as an insult and as signaling that the world's dominant power would not accept a developed Egypt. His admiration for Musadek's nationalization of the oil companies in Iran came to Nasser's mind when he sought to compensate for the loss of American and World Bank support for the construction of the dam.

In his book *The Philosophy of the Revolution*, Nasser drew three circles for Egyptian foreign policy: Arab, African, and Islamic. In practice, based on his experience as a young Egyptian officer deployed in Palestine during the 1948 War, the first of these absorbed most of his attention. Hence his adoption of the Palestinian cause and support of *Fedayyin* attacks that now continued to escalate. His other revolutionary measures – nationalizing the Suez Canal and supporting the FLN insurgency in Algeria – now helped forge the Israeli–British–French alliance.

Indeed, it was fear of Nasser's extraordinary charisma and the rhetoric of "liberation from Western and colonial hegemony" with which he inspired broader Arab masses that caused Britain and France to view him as a mortal threat which had to be removed, thus motivating them to conspire with Israel to attack Egypt. These fears were only confirmed during the crisis when Nasser's speech at the al-Azhar Mosque on November 2, 1956, in which he declared "we will fight," became a transformative moment for Egypt and the region at large.[54]

Finally, Nasser also understood that the dynamics of the Cold War provided Egypt with an opportunity to maneuver between two blocs. He ascertained correctly the United States assessment that the old colonial powers were unsustainable and that their efforts to restore their previous standing in the region could not succeed. This gave him a unique opportunity to advance Egypt's interests by maneuvering between the United States' hope to gain influence in the Arab world and Moscow's willingness to support revolutionary regimes.

Concluding Notes

The period covered in this chapter encompasses a development that began on the eve of the 1948 War: the Arabization of the conflict. The Palestinians no longer comprised an important political factor; instead, the largest and most populous of the Arab states – Egypt – now began to spearhead the conflict with Israel. While Jordan and Syria were not inconsequential during this period – their clashes with Israel often occupied the attention of international organs – their role in determining the contours of the conflict was now dwarfed by that of Egypt.

Unsurprisingly, this dramatic change affected Israel's threat perception: its focus now shifted from Palestinian opposition to its project to the threat that Egypt's larger numbers and potential sources of powers posed to the Jewish state. Threatened by what it perceived as Egypt's plan to arm itself with massive quantities of Soviet weapons, Israel chose to join Britain and France in the 1956 Sinai–Suez War.

But the choice was not cost free, adding significantly to the persistence of the conflict. Gradually but surely, Israel made Egypt its enemy by attacking Egyptian targets in Gaza and later by invading the Sinai and forcing Egyptian forces to withdraw. Similarly, Egypt made Israel its enemy by transforming the Palestinian *Fedayyin* into an arm of its intelligence services and then orchestrating their attacks on the Jewish state. Thus, by mid-1955 the two countries found themselves locked in a fierce competition, unable or unwilling to arrest its escalation before it erupted into a full-scale war.

The escalation of the Egyptian–Israeli conflict seemed to be rooted in the enormous stakes associated with their struggle: both were playing on a very large chessboard. For Egypt, this period launched Nasser's post-revolution effort to establish himself as a regional leader. His conflict with Israel was both an outcome and a tool for establishing his credentials as a leader of the entire Arab world. For Israel, the war was first and foremost an opportunity to ally itself with two declining yet still important world powers. As such, Israel now became for the first, but not the last, time a player in the global scene.

Having abandoned its initial inclination to remain neutral, or at least non-aligned, in the rapidly escalating Cold War by declaring its association with United States' efforts in Korea in 1950, Israel now found itself subject to Washington's veto power. In the face of America's refusal to supply it with the means to balance Czech arms shipments to Egypt, Israel attempted to pursue its interests independently by allying itself with France, only to be rebuffed by the Eisenhower administration who would not tolerate such disobedience.

Finally, this period witnessed a further polarization of the two side's narratives. Israel's image as co-conspiring with the former colonial powers now became firmly imprinted in Egyptians' minds as well as in those of the broader Arab streets. Moreover, with British and French forces attacking their country's center core, Egyptians now saw the Israeli allies of the two former colonial powers for the first time as posing an existential threat to Egypt itself. In parallel, in the rapidly escalating Palestinian *Feddayin* attacks, Israel saw Egypt tying its fortunes to those who continued to deny Israel's existence: people who had no wish to reach any kind of accommodation with it.

Readings

Bickerton, Ian and Carla Klausner, *A History of the Arab–Israeli Conflict* (Prentice Hall, 2010) 112–131.
Caplan, Neil, *The Israel–Palestine Conflict: Contested Histories* (Wiley, 2010) 131–143.
Dowty, Alan, *Israel/Palestine: Global Political Hotspots* (Polity, 2012) 92–112.
Gelvin, James, *The Israel–Palestine Conflict: One Hundred Years of War* (Cambridge University Press, 2007) 171–172.
Lesch, David, *The Arab–Israeli Conflict* (Oxford University Press, 2008) 162–194.
Morris, Benny, *Righteous Victims: The History of the Zionist–Arab Conflict, 1881–2001* (Vintage, 2001) 259–301.
Shlaim, Avi, *The Iron Wall: Israel and the Arab World* (W.W. Norton, 2001) 54–185.
Smith, Charles D., *Palestine and the Arab–Israeli Conflict* (Bedford/St. Martin's, 2007) 222–258.
Tessler, Mark, *A History of the Israeli–Palestinian Conflict* (Indiana University Press, 2009) 269–335.

Historical Documents

The Baghdad Pact: available online at The Avalon Project at Yale Law School http://avalon.law.yale.edu/20th_century/baghdad.asp.
Eisenhower Doctrine: available online at The American Presidency Project http://www.presidency.ucsb.edu/ws/index.php?pid=11007&st=&st1=.
U.N. General Assembly 181 (Partition Resolution): Walter Laqueur and Barry Rubin, *The Israel–Arab Reader: A Documentary History of the Middle East Conflict* (Penguin Books, 2008), 69–77.

Notes

1. Winston Churchill, "The Sinews of Peace" speech, delivered March 5, 1946, at Westminster College in Fulton, Missouri.
2. Harry S. Truman, "Recommendation for Assistance to Greece and Turkey: Address of the President of the United States," 80th Congress, 1st Session, Document No. 171, March 12, 1947, Washington, DC http://www.trumanlibrary.org/whistlestop/study_collections/doctrine/large/documents/pdfs/5-9.pdf#zoom=100.
3. Behcet Kemal Yesilbursa, *The Baghdad Pact* (London: Frank Cass, 2005), 217.

4. Ervand Abrahamian, *Iran Between Two Revolutions* (Princeton: Princeton University Press, 1982); Mark J. Gasiorowski and Malcolm Byrne, eds., *Mohammad Mosaddeq and the 1953 Coup in Iran* (Syracuse: Syracuse University Press, 2004); Nikki Keddie, *Modern Iran: Roots and Results of Revolution* (New Haven: Yale University Press, 2003).
5. On April 24, 1950 a joint session of Jordan's parliament declared "its support for complete unity between the two sides of the Jordan and their union into one State, which is the Hashemite Kingdom of Jordan, at whose head reins King Abdullah Ibn al-Hussein, on a basis of constitutional representative government and equality of the rights and duties of all citizens." For the full text, see: "Jordanian House of Deputies and House of Notables, Resolution Annexing the West Bank and Jerusalem, Amman, 24 April 1950,"in *Documents on Jerusalem*, vol. 3 (Jerusalem: Passia, 1996), 7. See also, "Jordanian Annexation of West Bank – Resolution Adopted by the House of Deputies, Amman, 24 April 1950," Israel Ministry of Foreign Affairs website, http://www.mfa.gov.il/MFA/Foreign+Relations/Israels+Foreign+Relations+since+1947/1947-1974/10+Jordanian+Annexation+of+West+Bank-+Resolution+A.htm?DisplayMode=print.
6. Donald Neff, "Israel–Syria: Conflict at the Jordan River, 1949–1967," *Journal of Palestine Studies*, 23, 4 (Summer, 1994), 26–40.
7. *Ibid.*, 29. In an attempt to ensure the agreement of both Israel and Syria, Ralph Bunche wrote to both sides before the signing of the plan, informing them that in his interpretation, "Questions of permanent boundaries, territorial sovereignty, customs, trade relations and the like must be dealt with in the ultimate peace settlement and *not* in the armistice agreement."
8. Itamar Rabinovich, *The Road Not Taken: Early Arab–Israeli Negotiations* (New York: Oxford University Press, 1991), 65–110.
9. Michael Brecher and Jonathan Wilkenfeld, *A Study of Crisis* (Ann Arbor: University of Michigan Press, 1997), 272; N. Bar-Yaacov, *The Israeli–Syrian Armistice: Problems of Implementation, 1949–1966* (Jerusalem: Magnes, The Hebrew University, 1967), 76–111; Aryeh Shalev, *The Israel–Syria Armistice Regime, 1949–1955* (Boulder: Westview, 1993), 60–81.
10. Neff, "Israel–Syria: Conflict at the Jordan River, 1949–1967," 31.
11. Derek Hopwood, *Syria 1945–1986: Politics and Society* (London: Unwin Hyman, 1988), 33–36.
12. Amos Perlmutter, "From Obscurity to Rule: *The Syrian Army and the Ba'th Party,*" *The Western Political Quarterly*, 22, 4 (December, 1969), 827–845. For a comparison of Ba'ath and Nasserism, see Chapter 4, note 20.
13. Mohamed Heikal, *Suez Files:The Thirty Years War* (Cairo: Al Ahram Center for Translation and Publishing, 1986), 313–330.
14. Avi Shlaim, *The Iron Wall: Israel and the Arab World* (W.W. Norton & Company, 2001), 104–105.
15. Neil Caplan, *Futile Diplomacy, vol. 4: Operation Alpha and the Failure of Anglo-American Coercive Diplomacy in the Arab–Israeli Conflict, 1954–1956* (London: Frank Cass, 1997), 74.
16. Caplan, *Futile Diplomacy, vol.* 4, 73–95.
17. Wm. Roger Louis, "The Tragedy of the Anglo-Egyptian Settlement of 1954," in Wm. Roger Louis and Roger Owen (eds.), *Suez 1956: The Crisis and Its Consequences* (Oxford: Clarendon, 1989), 43–71.
18. Mohamed H. Heikal, *Cutting the Lion's Tail: Suez Through Egyptian Eyes* (New York: Arbor House, 1987), 48.
19. Yezid Sayigh, *Armed Struggle and the Search for State: The Palestinian National Movement, 1949–1993* (Oxford: Oxford University Press, 1997), 62–65; Mordechai Bar-On, *The Gates of Gaza: Israel's Road to Suez and Back: 1955–1957* (London: MacMillan, 1994), 11–12; Moti Golani, *Israel in Search of a War: the Sinai Campaign, 1955–1956* (Brighton: Sussex Academic Press, 1998), 1–11.

20. Ministry of Defense, Military Researches Agency, *The War of Tripartite Aggression on Egypt* (Cairo: Ministry of Defense, First Part, N/A), 19–26.
21. Anthony Nutting, *Nasser* (New York: E.P. Dutton, 1972), 68–69 and 72–77; Heikal, *Cutting the Lion's Tail*, 38–41 and 49.
22. Taha Abdel Aleem Taha, "Nationalization of the Suez Canal and the Suez War 1956: From Economic History to Political Economy," in Ra'ouf Abbas (ed.), *Suez War after 40 years* (Cairo: Al Ahram Center for Political and Strategic Studies, 1997), 244–245.
23. Keith Kyle, "Britain and the Crisis, 1955–1956," in Louis and Owen, *Suez 1956*, 111–112.
24. Bowie, in Louis and Owen, *Suez 1956*, 201.
25. Heikal reports that six brigades had been withdrawn from Sinai earlier in the year to train on their new Russian arms. See Heikal, *Cutting the Lion's Tail*, 184.
26. *Ibid.*, 184 and 198 fn. 2.
27. Heikal reports that Nasser had ordered Egyptian troops to withdraw from Sinai to avoid falling into an Israeli trap. *Ibid.*, 180.
28. John C. Campbell, "The Soviet Union, the United States, and the Twin Crises of Hungary and Suez," in Louis and Owen, *Suez 1956*, 246–247. Campbell reports that the day after the USSR issued its threat to France, Britain, and Israel, American intelligence informed British Prime Minister Eden that Washington believed the Soviet threat to be a bluff.
29. http://history.state.gov/historicaldocuments/frus1955-57v16/d414 .
30. Tessler, *A History of the Israeli–Palestinian Conflict*, 349.
31. Heikal, *The Suez Files*; Latifa Mohamed Salem, "International Stance on Aggression," in Ra'ouf Abbas (ed.), *Suez War after 40 years*, 278–279. [In Arabic]
32. Abdel Hamid Shalaby, "The Suez War, Fourty Years After," in Ra'ouf Abbas (ed.), *Suez War after 40 years*, 305–307 [in Arabic].
33. According to Fry and Hochstein, Israel's retreat from the territories occupied in the Sinai–Suez War was "slow and disputatious." Israel started retreating on November 15, 1956, after having agreed to the ceasefire more than a week earlier on November 6, 1956. By early January, Israel had yet to complete its withdrawal. Ben Gurion did not want to leave Gaza or Sharm el-Sheikh without assuring that Israeli citizens would be safe from *Fedayyin* attacks from Gaza and a guarantee of free passage through the Straits of Tiran. After a long negotiation process with the United States, and some input from France, Israel agreed to civil administration of Gaza by UN forces and complete withdrawal from Sharm el-Sheikh. In late January, Israel had wanted to make its withdrawal contingent on cessation of Egyptian belligerence and the beginning of a peace process. In the end, Israel withdrew from Gaza and Sharm el-Sheikh on March 11. Nasser agreed to installing UN forces in Gaza and at the Straits, and their stationing only on the Egyptian side of the international border. France convinced Israel to take the deal by offering military, economic, and diplomatic assistance, and most importantly, help with Israel's nuclear program. Michael Fry and Miles Hochstein, "The Forgotten Middle Eastern Crisis of 1957: Gaza and Sharm-El-Sheikh," *The International History Review* 15, 1 (1993), 46–83.
34. "Milestones: 1953–1960: The Eisenhower Doctrine, 1957," Office of the Historian, Bureau of Public Affairs, United States Department of State, http://history.state.gov/milestones/1953-1960/EisenhowerDoctrine.
35. Ray Takeyh, *The Origins of the Eisenhower Doctrine* (New York: St. Martin's, 2000), 152.
36. *Ibid.*
37. "Milestones: 1953–1960: The Baghdad Pact (1955) and the Central Treaty Organization (CENTO)," Office of the Historian, Bureau of Public Affairs, United States Department of State, http://history.state.gov/milestones/1953-1960/CENTO.

38. *Ibid.* In 1951, following Egypt's blockade of the Gulf of Aqaba, Israel had lodged a complaint at the UN, arguing that since the armistice agreement had effectively implemented a peace settlement, Israel (like all countries at peace with Egypt) had the right to pass freely through the Canal. The Security Council responded by passing a resolution proclaiming Egyptian interference with Israeli shipping as "an abuse of the exercise of the right of visit, search and seizure." But since the Resolution did not include an enforcement mechanism, Israeli ships continued (albeit sporadically) to be prevented from sailing freely through the Canal and the Straits of Tiran. See John Norton Moore, *The Arab–Israeli Conflict, Volume I: Readings* (Princeton: Princeton University Press, 1974), 707.
39. *Ibid.*, 708. See also Tessler, *A History of the Israeli–Palestinian Conflict*, 333–334 and 352.
40. Shlaim, *The Iron Wall*, 25.
41. As recounted in July 1953 by Mustafa Hafiz, Chief of Egyptian Intelligence in Gaza. See Yezid Sayigh, *Armed Struggle and the Search for State*, 62, quoting Egyptian documents published in Ehud Yaari, *Egypt and the Feda'iyyun, 1953–1956* (Givat Haviva, 1975), 35 [in Hebrew].
42. See also Benny Morris, *Israel's Border Wars, 1949–1956: Arab Infiltration, Israeli Retaliation, and the Countdown to the Suez War* (Oxford: Clarendon, 1993), 90.
43. Indeed, the *Bat Galim* incident was not the first time Israel and Egypt had sparred over the issue of free passage through the Suez Canal. Since the conclusion of the 1949 armistice agreement, Egypt had consistently argued that since it was still in a state of war with Israel – the armistice having only pertained to hostile acts on the part of the two countries' respective armed forces – it had every right to prevent passage of Israeli ships. An editorial in the *Egyptian Gazette* on March 7, 1957 summed up Egypt's legal argument well:

    > since the Armistice Agreement was signed in 1949 ships of all nationalities have used the Tiran Strait with no obstruction on the part of Egypt...Egypt has only insisted on stopping ships flying the Israeli flag because they do not belong to a "neutral" state, and, as such, cannot be considered as exercising the right of innocent passage...international law is divided into two sections – the Law of War and the Law of Peace...Egypt has officially announced that she is in a state of war with Israel, and by the mere fact of signing the Armistice Agreement, which ended the fighting, both sides admitted that the state of war exists...the agreement itself says that it is only a prelude to the conclusion of peace.

    March 7, 1957, 2, reprinted in Moore, *The Arab–Israeli Conflict, Volume I: Readings*, 705 fn. 31.
44. Tessler, *A History of the Israeli–Palestinian Conflict*, 333.
45. "UN Doc S/2157 Security Council resolution 93 of 18 May 1951," *United Nations Security Council*, May 18, 1951, http://www.un.org/documents/sc/res/1951/scres51.htm:

    > Noting the complaint with regard to the evacuation of Arab residents from the demilitarized zone: (a) Decides that Arab civilians who have been removed from the demilitarised zone by the Government of Israel should be permitted to return forthwith to their homes and that the Mixed Armistice Commission should supervise their return and rehabilitation in a manner to be determined by the Commission; (b) Holds that no action involving the transfer of persons across international frontiers, across armistice lines or within the demilitarised zone should be undertaken without prior decision of the Chairman.

46. Itzhak Bar-On, *Mitriya be-Yom Sagrir [An Umbrella on a Rainy Day]* (Israel: Effi Meltzer, 2010), 164 [In Hebrew].

47. Tessler, *A History of the Israeli–Palestinian Conflict,* 347; Maurice Vaisse, "France and the Suez Crisis," in Louis and Owen, *Suez 1956*, 131–143 and 137.
48. Escalation dominance is aimed at deterring adversaries from escalating violence by credibly convincing them of one's capacity to escalate further at every level of violence. Such superior capacity to escalate is intended to convince one's adversaries that there is no point in escalating violence since any such escalation will be more than matched. Escalation dominance was a key dimension of America's "flexible response" strategy during the Cold War. Robert Powell, *Nuclear Deterrence Theory: The Search for Credibility* (New York: Cambridge University Press, 1990), 24.
49. Michael Bar Zohar, "David Ben-Gurion," *Encyclopædia Britannica Online Academic Edition* (Encyclopædia Britannica Inc., 2011).
50. Ra'ouf Abbas, ed., *Suez War After 40 Years*, 42; Hani Raslan, ed., *The July Policies: The Revolution: Fifty Years After* (Cairo: Al Ahram Center for Political and Strategic Studies, 2002), 109–139; Nagla'a abo Ezz al Dein, *Nasser of the Arabs* (Cairo: Dar al Mostaqbal al Araby, Translated by Fareed abo Ezz al Dein, 1988), 181–182.
51. For more details on Palestinians in the 1950s, see Benny Morris, *Israel's Border Wars, 1949–1956*; Yezid Sayigh, *Armed Struggle and the Search for State*; Rashid Khalidi, *The Iron Cage: The Story of the Palestinian Struggle for Statehood* (Boston: Beacon Press, 2006); and Laurie A. Brand, *Palestinians in the Arab World: Institution Building and the Search for State* (New York: Columbia University Press, 1988).
52. Sayigh, *Armed Struggle and the Search for State*, 60–65.
53. Shlaim indicates that records of Egyptian intelligence show "that until the Gaza raid, the Egyptian military authorities had a consistent and firm policy of curbing infiltration … into Israel … and that it was only following the raid that a new policy was put in place, that of organizing the *Fedayyin* units and turning them into an official instrument of warfare against Israel." Shlaim, *The Iron Wall*, 128–129.
54. For the full text in Arabic, see: "The speech given by President Gamal Abdel Nasser after Friday prayers from Al Azhar Mosque during the Tripartite Agression 02/11/1956," http://nasser.bibalex.org/Speeches/browser.aspx?SID=524&lang=en.

4 The 1967 War: The Victory and the "Naksa"

This chapter covers the period extending from 1958 to 1968. It focuses on the dynamics that led to the 1967 War and its immediate outcomes: Israel's massive victory and the Arabs' defeat, the Arabs' adoption of the Khartoum Declaration, the initial Israeli construction of settlements in the West Bank and its de-facto annexation of East Jerusalem and areas beyond its municipal boundaries and the endorsement by Israel and the major Arab states of UN Security Council Resolution 242.

In large measure the developments of this period set the stage for the evolution of the Arab–Israeli conflict and the efforts to resolve it over the following four decades. It is during this period that the terms "occupied territories" and UNSC Resolution 242 entered the conflict's lexicon, and issues such as annexation and settlements became central features of the discourse about the conflict. Even more importantly, following the period covered in this chapter much of the conflict and the attempts to resolve it focused on efforts to undo the developments described here. For this reason, the analytical part of the chapter will attempt to answer two questions: What caused the 1967 War? and, What explains Israel's victory and the Arabs' defeat in the war?

The "Six Day War," as it was called in Israel, the "*Naksa,*" or setback, as it became known in Egypt and the rest of the Arab world, and the June 1967 War as it was termed by historians, was one of the main turning-points in the history of the Arab–Israeli conflict. It epitomized the intense Cold War that characterized the global order at the time, as well as its reflections on the Arab order. In addition, it ushered in the political resurrection of the Palestinians and their return to the forefront of a conflict that had been "Arabized" during the previous decade and a half. Finally, the road to war demonstrated that rivalries over natural resources, particularly water, would now be added to the long list of issues that divided Arabs and Israelis.

The June 1967 War was massive in its scale, swift in its execution and decisive in its outcome. In six days Israel was to defeat a combination of military forces that represented all types of Arab states: conservative and progressive, moderate and radical, traditional and revolutionary. The armies of Egypt, Syria, and Jordan were devastated. Nasser and Nasserism sustained a hit from which neither was ever able to recover. The area of land Israel occupied by the end of the war was more than three times larger than its pre-war territory. Israel's victory was to change the country in a variety of ways, most importantly its national security strategy. On the Arab states' agenda, the war was to launch an entirely new phase of the Arab–Israeli conflict – one dominated by the dynamics unleashed by Israel's 1967 conquest of Arab lands rather than by concerns about the issues related to the loss of Palestine in the 1948 War, which were placed on the back burner.

Developments in the Middle East during this period cannot be separated from the era's dramatic developments in the global arena: the major crises in Berlin (1961), the Bay of Pigs (1961), and the Cuban Missile Crisis (1962) – the most dangerous nuclear crisis of the Cold War. Despite the risks and costs entailed, the two superpowers, the United States and the USSR, continued their arms race and their competition for global influence. Thus, at the strategic level, Arab–Israeli dynamics during this period were informed by the Cold War, which projected itself into the region during the years leading to the 1967 War,[1] and by the Arab states' division between so-called radical, revolutionary, populist, and socialist regimes on the one hand and conservative, traditional, and reactionary regimes on the other. The radical camp was led by Egypt and supported by the Soviet Union, the conservative camp was led by Saudi Arabia and supported by the United States.

In the regional context, the mid-1960s are often described as the period of Arab summitry – an attempt to mitigate the effects of the region's anarchic nature through summit meetings of the Arab League. The purpose of these summits was to contain inter-Arab rivalries and to ease the tensions created by the war in Yemen, the Cold War and the Arab Cold War. The summits demonstrated Egyptian dominance in the Arab scene, exerted through the considerable influence it enjoyed in the Arab League.

On the Palestinian side, this period witnessed the birth of organized representation – the creation of the Palestinian Liberation Organization (PLO). The PLO's creation and the emergence of smaller guerrilla groups also manifested Palestinian frustrations with the limits and constraints imposed on them by the Arabization of the conflict.

Main Developments

The developments described in this section are those that led to the 1967 War, the various phases of the crisis, and its immediate aftermath. These involve the superpowers' fierce competition in the region following the 1956 Suez–Sinai War; the spread of radicalism inspired by the charismatic leadership of Egypt's President Nasser and its Ba'ath counterparts in Syria and Iraq; the external intervention to contain the threat that such radicalism posed to Lebanon's stability in 1958; the escalation of the conflict between the radicals and the monarchies to direct involvement in the civil war in Yemen in the mid-1960s; the growing violence between Israel and Syria over the sources of Israel's water supply; and the establishment of Fatah – the Movement for the Liberation of Palestine.

The Global Scene

The years between 1957 and 1968 witnessed the continuation of a development that had begun during the period covered in the previous chapter: the growing polarization in the Middle East between the superpowers. The Soviet Union attempted to maximize its presence in the region by supporting the Arab position on Israel and the Arab nationalist movement led by Egypt. Egypt's opposition to the Baghdad Pact and its anti-Western campaign after the Suez–Sinai War made it the cornerstone of Soviet foreign policy in the Middle East.[2] Thus, Egypt alone received 30.9 percent of all Soviet economic assistance to countries in the Middle East and North Africa as well as 49.1 percent of its military aid to those countries. When assistance to Syria and Iraq is included, these figures reached 53.1 and 80 percent respectively.[3]

The United States, on its part, through the Baghdad Pact and the Eisenhower Doctrine, was equally busy building an anti-Soviet semi-alliance which included Jordan, Saudi Arabia, Iran, Turkey and Israel. Together these countries received 98 percent of American military aid to the Middle East and North Africa and 59 percent of its economic aid to the region.[4]

In the cases of Egypt and Israel, where there had been an arms race, heavy conflict, and economic dependence on outside powers in place, arms transfers proved a useful great-power instrument for extracting additional increments of cooperation. Yet Egypt managed to retain a considerable measure of independence during this period, keeping a general non-aligned position in world affairs. It even managed to obtain substantial American assistance, thereby extracting maximum economic and political advantage from both poles of the bipolar world. As a result, Nasser's army was equipped with Soviet weapons while Egypt's population was fed by American wheat. Similarly, Eastern bloc countries advanced Egypt credit for the development of its infrastructure and industry, while American companies explored Egypt for new sources of oil.[5] Also noteworthy is that massive Soviet assistance did not prevent Nasser from banning the existence of a Communist party in Egypt and from opposing the creation of such parties in other Arab countries.

During this period, external involvement in the region assumed a nuclear dimension as well. In addition to the French decision to supply Israel with a 26-Megawatt nuclear reactor constructed near the southern town of Dimona, by 1958 the United States launched its "Atoms for Peace Program" in the framework of which it supplied states with small nuclear research reactors. Egypt located such a reactor in Inshass and Israel in Nachal Soreq.

The Spread of Radicalism

Another characteristic of the Middle East during this period was the spread of radicalism. One source of this was the success of the struggles by many Arab countries for independence from different colonial powers. In this context, Algeria's War of Independence proved particularly inspiring for an Arab region that considered itself humiliated by decades of Western domination.

Related to this, in the aftermath of the 1956 Sinai–Suez War, Nasser succeeded in raising Egypt's status in the Arab world and in bestowing the spirit of revolutionary defiance on Arab politics that characterized third-world politics during the late 1950s and most of the 1960s. In addition, Nasser's call for Arab nationalism was soon to spread among Arab masses, rekindling the old dreams of the Arab *Nahdha* [renaissance] of the 19th century and of the Arab kingdom of the early 20th century. Egyptian–Syrian unification during 1958–61 was seen as evidence that this dream could become a reality, and inspired others to attempt to emulate it. The rise of the Ba'ath party in both Syria and Iraq following bloody revolutions fueled further hopes for such a *Nahdha*.

Finally, the international environment was conducive to the rise of radical spirits in the region: the 1960s were an era of revolutionary fervor across the world. This was fueled by heroic struggles for independence, the opposition to the Vietnam War, radical thinking of the restless youth in the West, and the glamour of socialist ideas in search of renewal and justice.

The Rise of the Ba'ath

On February 22, 1958 a referendum was held in Egypt and Syria that led them to unify into a single state, the United Arab Republic (UAR).[6] Nasser became the president of the new republic and Cairo became its capital. Also in February, in response to the proposed creation of the UAR, the Hashemite Kingdoms of Iraq and Jordan formed the "Arab Federation of Iraq and Jordan." But on July 14, the waning of British influence in the region culminated in the Iraqi revolution, when units of the Iraqi army's 20th Brigade under the command of 'Abd al-Karim Qassim arrived in Baghdad and surrounded the Royal Palace, the home of the Premier, Nuri al-Sa'id, and the Baghdad radio station. King Faisal II (the grandson of Faisal I, whom the British had installed as King in 1921) and other members of the royal family were killed, and Nuri al-Sa'id, was later shot while attempting to leave the country. The founding of the Republic of Iraq was announced, and Qassim assumed the posts of premier, minister of defense and Commander in Chief of the Armed Forces.[7] One consequence of the coup was the dissolution of the short-lived Iraqi federation with Jordan.[8]

Two weeks after the coup in Iraq, a provisional constitution was promulgated, providing for an independent, Islamic Arab state in which executive authority was placed in the Council of Ministers.[9] Hundreds of members and supporters of the former regime were put on trial.[10] The Iraqi revolution of 1958 ushered in a period of instability in Baghdad, with four successive military regimes and several additional coup attempts. Qassim's government survived these until 1963, when the revolutionary regime collapsed, Qassim was executed, and a Ba'athist regime assumed power.[11]

The 1958 Crisis in Lebanon

In the mid-1950s, the Lebanese government was run by President Camille Chamoun, a Maronite Christian whose six-year term was set to expire in September 1958. Following the Suez crisis in 1956, Chamoun and his foreign minister, Charles Malik, drew harsh criticism from Syria, Egypt, and certain circles in Lebanon for refusing to sever ties with Britain and France.[12] Chamoun's popularity further plummeted when he indicated that he might move to revise Lebanon's constitution and seek a second term.[13]

The roots of the 1958 crisis can be traced to the sectarian divisions enshrined in Lebanon's National Pact (1943), which had promised the Sunni Muslim community greater political representation in exchange for protection of Christian interests. In return for the Christians not seeking French protection and accepting an Arab identity for Lebanon, the Muslims accepted Lebanon's independence within the borders set by the French Mandate, effectively renouncing aspirations for union with Syria.[14]

This tenuous political arrangement began to unravel with the rise of Nasser's influence in the aftermath of the 1956 War and the 1958 unification of Egypt and Syria. Lebanese Muslims now began to express growing support for the pan-Arab cause, and Egypt and Syria began funneling weapons to them in hopes of propping up opposition to Chamoun's administration.[15] Many Christian Lebanese now saw Muslim support for Nasser's pan-Arabism as threatening the country's independence.[16]

In May 1958 clashes erupted between Lebanese Muslim and Christian communities following the assassination of anti-regime Maronite journalist Nasib al-Matni, who had been critical of Chamoun's policies. By early July Chamoun announced that he would not be seeking reelection and the conflict appeared to dissipate. However, on July 14, when the coup in Baghdad took place, Chamoun invoked the Eisenhower Doctrine, requesting American military assistance on the grounds that he was threatened by the Iraqi coup. Eisenhower responded by sending troops into Lebanon to help maintain order. The American intervention was meant not only to help Chamoun's government against its political opponents but also to send a signal to the Soviet Union that the United States would act to protect its interests in the Middle East.[17]

In late September 1958 the commander of Lebanon's small army, General Fouad Chehab was elected President of Lebanon. A Christian, Chehab had nonetheless refused Chamoun's request to have the Lebanese army crush the Muslim and Druze opposition groups. By late October the United States had withdrawn its forces from Lebanon, hostilities had died down, and a new power-sharing agreement had been implemented.[18]

Turmoil in Syria

Meanwhile, after three years of attempted unity, the United Arab Republic was dissolved on September 28, 1961 when units of the Syrian armed forces led a national uprising against the union.[19] The army had felt that the union slighted Syria, giving too much power to Nasser and Egypt. While for the next two years the old conservative politicians ran Syria again, by 1963, following the coup in Baghdad that overthrew Qassim and brought the Iraqi Ba'athists to power, the Syrian Ba'athists launched a coup of their own, beginning a decades-long hold on the country.[20] When a group of Nasserist officers attempted a countercoup in July, the Ba'ath, led by Amin al-Hafiz, suppressed it aggressively, resulting in some 800 dead.[21]

In February 1966, the Syrian Ba'ath split, with Salah Jadid claiming power in yet another coup.[22] This new government brought Syria firmly into the Soviet camp, adopting ever more radical positions. Encouraged by the Soviets, on November 4, 1966 Egypt and Syria signed a mutual defense pact.[23]

Civil War in Yemen

The most extreme manifestation of the converging global and regional Cold War struggles was the civil war in Yemen that began in 1962. In this war, Saudi Arabia and Egypt supported militarily the two contending camps – the royalists and the republicans, respectively. The split that was now clear seemed to have resulted from both global and regional dynamics. One source was the rise of Nasser's Pan-Arabism, which implied an almost inevitable conflict with conservative Saudi Arabia. But the global Cold War further amplified this conflict and everything else that was already dysfunctional in the relations between the region's states.

The eight-year-long war began when, in September 1962, military officers in North Yemen attempted to assassinate their civilian leader, Imam Muhammad al-Badr. Although the attempt failed, on September 26 the officers declared the establishment of a republic and the end of the imamate, the traditional system of government that had prevailed in North Yemen since the withdrawal of Ottoman forces at the end of the First World War.

The civil war quickly became a proxy conflict between regional powers, with Saudi Arabia, Jordan, Morocco, and Iran backing supporters of the imamate (the royalists), and Egypt, Iraq and Algeria supporting the republicans. Saudi Arabia and Egypt became the most heavily invested in the war, and at one point, Egypt had as many as 70,000 troops deployed in Yemen, leading to the conflict being nicknamed "Nasser's Vietnam."[24] In August 1965 the parties convened in Jeddah, Saudi Arabia, and concluded the *Jeddah Agreement*, paving the way for Egypt's withdrawal from Yemen. However, the agreement was not implemented until after the 1967 War.

Conflict over Water

In the Arab–Israeli realm the focus of conflict shifted during this period to the use of water. Particularly contentious was the use of the waters of the Jordan River, which originates at the borders of Israel, Syria, and Jordan. In an earlier effort to reduce tensions in the region and resolve the conflict over these waters, in 1953 the United States introduced the Johnston Plan. This proposed dividing the use of the water between the major riparians, Israel and Jordan. Negotiations on implementing the plan continued through 1955 but were never concluded.

Water remained a contentious issue in the region, especially with Israel's construction of the National Water Carrier, which began in 1963. A major water diversion project, it was designed to take water from the Sea of Galilee into which the Jordan River flows, to replenish the water table along the Mediterranean coast and irrigate the Negev desert.

On the diplomatic front, water now became a central focus of Arab summits. Thus, one response to Israel's initiation of the National Water Carrier was the call to convene an Arab League summit, which met in Cairo on January 13–17, 1964. The summit produced a decision to end all Arab disagreements, emphasizing that the enemy was the State of Israel, which needed to be confronted with all necessary means, including military ones. The Arab leaders also established an Arab military command, led by an Egyptian, Lieutenant General Ali Amer. As for the Jordan River issue, the summit established an agency within the Arab League entrusted with planning and coordinating Arab projects for the utilization of the water of the river. The agency included representatives of the Jordanian, Egyptian, Syrian and Lebanese governments. A Committee for Implementation and Follow-Up was created with the purpose of ensuring that member states would execute these decisions. With the endorsement of the new agency, Syria began diverting the Banias River, one of the major sources of the Jordan.[25] In turn, Israel attempted to obstruct the Syrian work by targeting the heavy Syrian machinery assembled near its borders for the diversion project. Thus an escalation began that was further fueled by a threat made by IDF Chief of Staff, Lieutenant

General Yitzhak Rabin, to the effect that if violence were to continue Israel would move to overthrow the Syrian regime.[26]

Another Arab summit was held at Alexandria, Egypt on September 5–11, 1964. Its purpose was to agree on a general military plan to secure the implementation of all Arab projects on the Jordan River and promote the "liberation of Palestine."[27]

On the Palestinian and Jordanian Fronts

While the Arab summits were aimed at least in part to offer a pan-Arab approach to the resolution of the Palestinian question, some Palestinian youth had already reached the conclusion that the Arab countries were not prepared to commit themselves to a serious confrontation with Israel. As a result, they decided to work independently to achieve their goals. Although created in 1959, the Movement for the Liberation of Palestine – Fatah – was to lead the "armed struggle" with Israel beginning on January 1, 1965.

Fatah was soon to be followed by a variety of other Palestinian organizations, inspired by Algeria's War of Independence to seek victory in the face of extremely negative odds. The Vietnam War, where the Vietcong was seen as facing the greatest superpower of all times with valor and success, was another source of inspiration.

The January 1964 Arab League summit established the Palestinian Liberation Organization (PLO) to be funded by the member states' contributions to the League. The leaders convened also agreed to support the creation of a military arm for the PLO that would operate under the leadership of the Arab Command.[28] Egypt insisted on fully controlling the PLO: it was to be headquartered in Cairo and all weapons for Palestinian fighters were to be supplied through, if not by, Egypt. Cairo also picked Ahmad Shuqayri, a survivor of the old Palestine government, to preside over the organization. And, while Jordan now for the first time permitted expressions of Palestinian nationalism, it, too, monitored carefully every PLO move.

The Arab League summit held in Casablanca in September 1965 followed up the creation of the PLO and its military arm by forming a Palestinian legislature – the Palestinian National Council. It also issued the Arab Solidarity Declaration, calling upon all Arab states to work collectively for "the protection of the Arab nation and for the liberation of Palestine from Zionist occupation."[29]

Meanwhile in the Gaza Strip, in response to strong demands by Palestinians, Egypt took steps in the early 1960s to allow the establishment of a local legislative council and to write a Basic Law. These institution-building efforts reflected growing politicization of the refugees and their frustration with the lack of serious Arab efforts to "liberate Palestine."

Increasingly, Palestinians came to realize that Arabization did not mean that the Arab states were volunteering to solve the problem for them by mobilizing their resources to defeat Israel. Thus, not surprisingly, when Nasser met with Palestinian leaders in 1964, he told them that he had no plans to liberate Palestine – a statement he repeated in September 1965 publicly.[30] To the extent that his commitment to the Palestinian cause represented the Egyptian president's *Arab* dream, the Palestinians could understand from Nasser that this commitment would not be allowed to destroy his *Egyptian* dreams: to build a highly advanced industrial state.

Paradoxically, the Palestinians were to suffer simultaneously both from Nasser's Egyptian priorities and his regional dreams: his preoccupation with the war in Yemen also prevented him from focusing on Palestinian needs. In mid-1967, however, by becoming involved in an escalation with Israel over which he lost control, Nasser allowed the Arab–Israeli conflict to topple his Egyptian and regional dreams simultaneously.

Jordanian–Israeli relations in the years prior to the 1967 War reflected two separate realities. The first was the cycle of cross-border Palestinian attacks and Israeli retaliation raids. The second was the ongoing dialogue conducted by the two countries' leaders parallel to the violence taking place on the ground. In 1963 the two countries established a venue of direct communication in London. With Levi Eshkol as Israel's prime minister, the talks were aimed at exploring whether a settlement of the Arab–Israeli conflict was possible.[31] Building on these initial contacts, King Hussein met with Golda Meir, Israel's foreign minister, in Paris in 1965. The relationship continued to develop, despite the periodic attacks on Israel by Palestinian guerilla fighters launched from the Jordanian-ruled West Bank.[32]

This second reality was part of what made Jordan unique in the Arab world during this period: its general orientation was clearly Western – it received its arms from Western countries, mostly the United States and Britain. King Hussein was a welcomed visitor to the White House and London was his second home.

A Regional Arms Race

Heightened tensions in the region were also fueled by arms transfers. Despite growing arms shipments by the Soviet Union to the Arab states, and the adoption of the Eisenhower Doctrine, the United States did not provide Israel with significant military assistance until 1962, when it concluded a $23 million deal to equip Israel with Hawk anti-aircraft missiles. This new commitment was further cemented in 1965 with an agreement to deliver 210 M-48 tanks. During 1962–67 Britain also provided Israel with weapons, notably 300 Centurion tanks. It also supported Jordan, supplying it with Hunter aircraft and Saladin armored cars.[33]

In parallel, major Soviet arms supplies to the Middle East during the early 1960s included 163 MiG-21F fighter aircraft, 60 IS-3 tanks, and 18 SA-2 surface-to-air missile (SAM) systems to Egypt. The Soviets also provided 20 SA-2 SAM systems to Iraq and 100 P-15 anti-ship missiles to Syria.[34]

It was during this period that another dimension in weapons proliferation entered the Arab–Israeli arena: ballistic missiles and atomic weapons. First, with the revelation in December 1960 that Israel was constructing a French-supplied nuclear reactor near the town of Dimona, and later with news that Egypt had recruited German atomic scientists and missile engineers in an attempt to develop ballistic missiles for conventional or unconventional use. As previously noted, part of the incentive for Israel's participation in the Sinai–Suez War was to gain French help in building a reactor. When the news of the reactor broke in the international media and was confirmed by American officials, the Arab world, and Nasser especially, was horrified: it was considered to be a serious emerging threat. Yet it was not until the announcement of an Israeli space rocket in 1961 that the German scientists who had already been part of the military industry in Egypt were diverted to the development of ballistic missiles. However, by 1965, this project was slowing down owing to international pressure, internal strains, and a sustained Israeli campaign to kill and threaten the scientists.[35]

Winds of War

In the waning months of 1966, friction between Israel and its neighbors escalated. As Palestinian guerrillas launched attacks from the neighboring Arab states, Israel replied with growing force. On November 12, three Israeli soldiers were killed by a mine placed along the Jordanian border. Israel responded the following day against the Jordanian village of Samu, south of the West Bank town of Hebron. Twenty one Jordanian soldiers and civilians were killed and 37 were wounded in the attack, which took place on King Hussein's birthday.[36] The operation had serious consequences for Jordan, as radical Arab states now accused the Hashemite Kingdom of responding irresolutely to the Israeli attack, arguing that Jordan was trying to avoid a major clash with Israel.

The Israeli–Syrian border was equally tense: on April 7, 1967 an Israeli–Syrian air battle took place, resulting in six Syrian MiGs being shot down.[37] Despite their mutual defense pact, Egypt did not come to Syria's defense, leading to heavy criticism of Nasser in the Arab media.

The region moved closer to war on May 13, when the Soviets told the Egyptian government that Israel had begun a major troop buildup along the Syrian border. Despite the fact that Nasser was informed by both the UN Truce Supervision Organization (UNTSO) and by Egyptian officers stationed along the Syrian–Israeli border that the Soviet report was false, on May 14 he ordered Egyptian Army units into the Sinai Peninsula. On May 18, following Nasser's demand that UNEF forces in the Sinai be confined to their bases, UN Secretary General U Thant ordered their complete removal. On May 21 Nasser moved Egyptian troops into Sharm el-Sheikh.[38]

The final precursor to war came on May 23, when Nasser ordered the closure of the Straits of Tiran, blockading Israeli navigation to the port of Eilat. Israel had made clear since the 1956 War that any blockade of the Straits would be regarded as a declaration of war. The United States and Britain supported Israel's position, calling the act a violation of international law, and the American Sixth Fleet was ordered to deploy in the eastern Mediterranean. Backing Nasser, however, the Soviets now blocked attempts by the UN Security Council to condemn Egypt's actions.[39]

Figure 4.1. UN Secretary General U Thant (2nd from left) conversing with President Gamal Abdel Nasser, 24 May 1967. *Source*: United Nations Photo Library.

On May 30, 1967 the deteriorating situation on the Israeli–Syrian border and the growing tensions between Egypt and

Israel forced Jordan's King Hussein to travel to Cairo to restore his relationship with Nasser. There, he signed a defense pact with Egypt, subsequently handing over the command of his army to Egypt's General Abdel Monem Riyad as a further sign of unity with the Egyptian leadership.[40] Jordan also granted Iraq permission to deploy its troops in its territory, leading Israel to feel surrounded by large, hostile Arab military forces.[41]

Relations between the United States and Israel also experienced a number of important developments during the run-up to the war. The day after Nasser closed the Straits of Tiran, the Israeli government decided to send Foreign Minister Abba Eban to meet with President Lyndon Johnson and senior members of his administration.[42] Though Johnson thought the meetings would focus on the closure of the Straits of Tiran, by the time Eban landed in Washington he received instructions from Prime Minister Levi Eshkol to focus on what the Israeli government now perceived the threat of an imminent Egyptian attack on Israel. The president informed Eban that the United States would try to organize a multinational force to open the straits. Though Eban pressed him to declare that an attack on Israel would be considered an attack on the United States, Johnson instead focused on dissuading Israel from attacking Egypt, telling Eban that "Israel will not be alone unless it decides to go it alone."[43] Other senior American defense officials told Eban that the United States did not see an Egyptian attack as likely. He was also told of an American intelligence estimate that Israel would be able to fight a war on three fronts and win.[44]

Less than a week later, Meir Amit, the head of *Mossad* [Israeli intelligence] met with American officials in Washington. Amit's tasks were twofold: one was to establish whether Israel would be on its own if it acted preemptively; the second was to convince the Americans that if they did not act immediately, they would have to do so later, in order to "save what's left of the Middle East." Amit clarified that Israel was not seeking American military intervention on its behalf. Instead, it was requesting that the United States check Soviet intervention if that took place, support Israel in the UN, and expedite arms deliveries to Israel. As his interlocutors made clear that direct American military involvement to address Israel's predicament was not in the cards, Amit concluded that although the United States did not approve of an Israeli preemptive attack, it also did not forbid such a strike, thus providing Israel the "yellow light" it needed.[45]

Another dimension of the international environment on the eve of the war was the marked deterioration in French–Israeli relations – especially when compared to the two countries' close alliance during the 1956 Sinai-Suez War. Charles de Gaulle's return to power in 1958 and France's later withdrawal from Algeria began a process of gradual distancing from Israel. This reached a crisis point on May 24, 1967 when de Gaulle warned Eban unambiguously against an Israeli first strike.[46]

A final facet of the international scene was a last-ditch effort by the Soviets to prevent war. By contrast to their earlier contribution to the escalation of the crisis in mid-May, Soviet Premier Alexei Kosygin now attempted but failed to win support for a diplomatic resolution of the escalating tension between Israel and Syria, as he previously had done successfully between India and Pakistan. Despite Egypt's dependence on Soviet arms supplies, Nasser did not find it difficult to persuade Kosygin that the formula was not applicable to the Arab–Israeli conflict.[47]

The 1967 War

Following a long wait for a possible diplomatic resolution of the crisis, on June 1 Israel finally went into a war footing, forming a national unity government. On June 5, the war commenced with a massive Israeli air-strike against Egypt. The assault crippled the Egyptian air force, destroying 80 percent of Egypt's bomber fleet and 55 percent of its fighters, thus guaranteeing Israeli air superiority for the duration of the war.[48]

Israel informed Jordan that it would not be attacked if it opted to stay out of the war. King Hussein nevertheless decided to join in the Arab war effort, ordering his military to shell Jerusalem and bomb the coastal town of Netanya.[49] By the end of the fourth day of fighting, Israel had captured East Jerusalem and the West Bank from Jordan and the Gaza Strip and the Sinai Peninsula from Egypt. It then decided to move against the Syrian forces stationed on the Golan Heights, capturing that territory as well. On June 11, Israel agreed to a ceasefire with Syria, bringing the war to an end.[50]

The Immediate Aftermath

Following the 1967 War, several key resolutions and decisions came to shape the politics of the region: the Khartoum Resolution adopted by the Arab League, Israel's decision to greatly expand the boundaries of Jerusalem and to apply Israeli law to the newly occupied East Jerusalem, the UN's adoption of Security Council Resolution 242 and its acceptance by

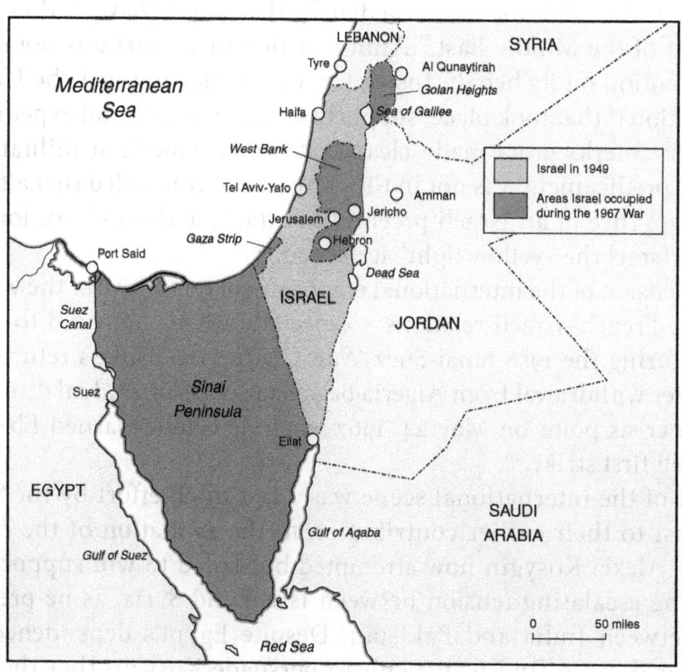

Figure 4.2. The territorial consequences of the 1967 War

a number of Arab states, and finally, Israel's decision to construct civilian settlements in a number of locations in the West Bank, East Jerusalem, Sinai, and the Golan Heights.

The Khartoum Resolution adopted by the Arab League on September 1, 1967 expressed Arab solidarity that brought together both sides of the Arab Cold War divide. The Arab states decided that the liberation of the territories occupied by Israel in the 1967 War was an all-Arab issue, requiring massive support for the defeated Arab countries. The leaders convened also decided to reject peace, recognition of, and negotiations with, Israel.

THE KHARTOUM RESOLUTION

Agreed to "consolidate all efforts to eliminate the effects of the aggression on the basis that the occupied lands are Arab lands and that the burden of regaining these lands falls on all the Arab States."

Outlined three Nos: "No peace with Israel, no recognition of Israel, no negotiations with it, and insistence on the rights of the Palestinian people in their own country."

Decided to "resume the pumping of oil, since oil is a positive Arab resource that can be used in the service of Arab goals."

"Set up an Arab Economic and Social Development Fund."[51]

Adopted unanimously on November 22, 1967, United Nations Security Council Resolution 242 included the following key lines as they appear in the English version of the resolution:

- "Emphasizing the inadmissibility of the acquisition of territory by war and the need to work for a just and lasting peace in which every State in the area can live in security."
- "Withdrawal of Israel armed forces from territories occupied in the recent conflict";[52]
- "Termination of all claims or states of belligerency and respect for and acknowledgement of the sovereignty, territorial integrity and political independence of every State in the area and their right to live in peace within secure and recognized boundaries free from threats or acts of force."
- "Achieving a just settlement of the refugee problem;"
- "Guaranteeing the territorial inviolability and political independence of every State in the area, through measures including the establishment of demilitarized zones."[53]

Differences between the French and English versions of the resolution opened a dispute as to whether the resolution required Israel to withdraw from "territories occupied" or "*the* territories occupied," and therefore whether it required a complete Israeli withdrawal or whether an Israeli withdrawal from some of the occupied territories would suffice. While Israel, Egypt, Jordan, and a number of other Arab countries accepted the resolution, Syria and the PLO rejected it when it was first adopted.[54]

Meanwhile Israel had taken a number of measures to change the situation on the ground, mainly, but not only, in and around Jerusalem. On June 27, just over two weeks after the war ended, the Israeli government voted to extend the jurisdiction of the Israeli municipality of Jerusalem to include East Jerusalem. Israeli law was imposed on the area and its Palestinian residents. Although the latter became permanent residents of the State of Israel, they were not forced to accept Israeli citizenship.

Israel also expanded the boundaries of East Jerusalem by adding some 28 West Bank villages, thus increasing its size from about 6 sq. km to 71 sq. km. The expanded city was now incorporated into the boundaries of the municipality of Jerusalem. Earlier, on June 26, 1967, a quick registration was done of the Palestinian population in the area to be added to the Israeli municipality.

In 1967–68, Israeli settlement construction began in Gush Etzion, the location of a former bloc of Jewish settlements from the 1920s that were destroyed during the 1948 War, and in the historically and religiously important city of Hebron. A settlement was also established in East Jerusalem, as were three in the Jordan Valley and along the Dead Sea. The settlement enterprise gained a significant boost when the Movement for the Whole Land of Israel was established almost immediately after the 1967 War ended. It articulated the demand that Jews should be allowed to settle in any part of "Greater Israel" in order to assert Israel's sovereignty. By September 1967, the Israeli government authorized the establishment of a settlement outpost in Al-Arish in the occupied Sinai. Six settlements were authorized in the Golan Heights.[55]

On November 23, 1967, a day after UN Resolution 242 was adopted, Secretary General U Thant designated a Swedish diplomat, Dr. Gunnar Jarring, to mediate its implementation – a mission that eventually extended through the following two years. The mission quickly exposed the very different approaches of the two sides to the sequence on which the post-1967 War diplomatic efforts needed to be pursued. The Israeli approach emphasized the primacy of direct negotiations, arguing that these should lead to the signing of a peace treaty which, in turn, would be followed by Israeli withdrawal to the boundaries agreed upon in the framework of the negotiated treaty. By contrast, Egypt and Jordan envisaged almost the opposite sequence, emphasizing the requirement for a total Israeli withdrawal to the pre-1967 lines, to be followed by indirect UN-sponsored negotiations which would result in a peace accord.

Parallel to Jarring's failed efforts to negotiate a compromise between these competing approaches, representatives of the United States and the Soviet Union met periodically ("the Two-Power talks") as did a larger group that also included representatives of Britain and France ("the Four-Power talks"). Yet these discussions could not break the stalemate, as the United States supported the Israeli view and the Soviet Union supported the Arab approach to the necessary sequence.

Narratives

The Israeli Narrative

In the late 1950s and through most of the 1960s Israelis continued to see themselves as extremely vulnerable, notwithstanding their military success in the 1956 Sinai–Suez War. This sense of vulnerability seemed to have had a number of dimensions. First, Israelis felt that Arab hostility remained high and showed no signs of dissipating. They saw no signs of willingness in the Arab world to accept Israel, even as an unfortunate but immutable fact. To the contrary, the Arab public discourse regarding Israel seemed as uncompromising as it had ever been.

Second, the anti-Israeli rhetoric of Nasser – the Arab world's most impressive leader at the time – frightened Israelis, who observed the resonance that Nasser's rhetoric had not only in the Egyptian street but among Arab publics at large. Thus, in eyes of Israelis, Nasser's charisma was no less important and no less threatening than other dimensions of Arab power – Israelis feared that with such charisma Nasser could transform latent sources of Arab power to real power.

The third dimension of Israeli concerns was a sense of encirclement fueled during this period by the declared unification between Egypt and Syria in the framework of the UAR. This rekindled memories of May 1948, when Arab armies invaded Palestine following Israel's declaration of independence.

The alliance between Syria and Egypt was associated with a fourth dimension of the Israelis' sense of vulnerability: the fact that the sources of the nation's water supplies were located in Syria and Lebanon, with Syria now seen as making every attempt to deny Israel these critically important supplies by diverting their sources. Indeed, Israelis sensed during this period that Syria – with Egypt's perceived tacit political support – was attempting to choke their state, thus achieving by focusing on a strategic resource what both states failed to accomplish militarily in 1948.

Another dimension of Israeli concerns was the sense of diplomatic isolation. While Arab countries led by Egypt were seen as a recipients of Soviet diplomatic support and military assistance, and Nasser was viewed as successful in placing himself and his country in the forefront of the Non-Aligned Movement (and as such as capable of mobilizing requisite majorities in the UN General Assembly) Israel viewed itself as alone – at most enjoying the support of a single ally: France. The gradual change in the United States' approach to Israel during this period – with the Kennedy and Johnson administrations beginning to supply Israel with arms – was not visible to the public. Rather, the Israeli public continued to be traumatized during this period by what it viewed as unjustified pressure exerted on Israel by the Eisenhower administration in late 1956 and early 1957 to withdraw from the Sinai and the Gaza Strip in the immediate aftermath of the Sinai–Suez war.

The Lead-Up to the 1967 War

This sense of extreme vulnerability dominated the Israeli narrative of the events that led to its decision to launch the 1967 War. The country's sense of encirclement was exacerbated by the signing in November 1966 of the Egypt–Syria Mutual Defense Treaty. When combined with Israel's narrow geographic confines – its narrow waistline and the resulting absence of strategic depth – this encirclement caused Israelis to feel trapped, with nowhere to go but the sea. By May 1967, Egypt's mobilization of forces, its remilitarization of the Sinai and its closure of the Straits of Tiran, seen in the context of the escalating conflict with Syria and the subsequent decision of Jordan to place its forces under the command of an Egyptian Army General, combined to further increase the Israelis' sense of extreme exposure.

Israelis also saw a dramatic asymmetry between the Soviet Union's clear siding with Egypt and Syria, and its own lack of external support. France, led by de Gaulle, had disassociated itself from Israel and the United States was seen as failing to abide by the commitments undertaken by the Eisenhower administration in the context of persuading Israel to withdraw from the Sinai and the Gaza Strip in 1957.[56] The comparison made Israel's sense of isolation even more extreme.

Another focus of Israeli perceptions was Egypt's decision to close the Straits of Tiran. This was viewed as a natural continuation of Syria's earlier efforts to divert the sources of Israel's water. Seen as an attempt to strangle Israel's maritime connection to Asia and Africa, the move was viewed as a clear attack on Israel's economy.

Finally, the escalation of Arab rhetoric beginning in mid-May 1967 when threats to "throw the Jews into the sea" were said to have been given repeated expression in Arab media, was viewed in Israel as preparing Arab publics for the final campaign to eradicate Israel. In the context of such rhetoric, Israelis viewed the remilitarization of the Sinai as demonstrating material preparedness and political readiness to strike, thus presenting them with a political as well as physical existential threat – the threat of physical extinction.

The cumulative effect of these perspectives was to persuade Israelis that their leaders' decision to attack Egypt on June 5, 1967 was a clear case of a preemptive strike – that if Israel did not attack first, it would have been attacked by the combined strength of its neighboring Arab states supported by the Soviet Union. Israelis believed that under such circumstances the so-called "international community" would have issued expressions of sorrow and condemnation but would have refrained from taking any effective action against the concerted Arab effort to undo the November 1947 UN decision to establish a Jewish state.

The War's Immediate Aftermath

In the immediate aftermath of the war, the pre-1967 horror was reinforced by Israeli perceptions of the post-war Arab summit in Khartoum. With the September summit seen as rejecting recognition, negotiations, and peace with Israel (the "three Nos"), Arab hostility toward the Jewish state seemed unmitigated, unqualified, and unreformed.

The acceptance of UN Resolution 242 by some of the key Arab states did not dent these Israeli perceptions. The fact that recognition of Israel was an integral part of the resolution was seen as beside the point. Israelis viewed this acceptance as resulting from pressures exerted by the international community on the Arab states. They believed that the true intentions of those states were reflected in the Khartoum Declaration. The ball, hence, was seen to be on the Arabs' side of the court: once the Arabs reversed Khartoum and accepted Israel's right to exist, Israel would be prepared to make a deal. In turn, such a reversal would require the Arabs to negotiate directly with Israel and to offer "real peace" in exchange for the territory returned. One version of this approach was suggested by Moshe Dayan, then Israel's minister of defense who reportedly said that Israel was "waiting for a phone-call from the Arabs."

The Palestinian Narrative

Pre-1967 Perspectives

Prior to the 1967 War, Palestinians continued to view Israel as a true menace to the entire Arab nation: an illegitimate entity, one that had dispossessed them of a homeland, destroyed their dreams of sovereign statehood, served as a tool of Western colonial powers, and proved to have an expansionist appetite. Israel was seen as unwilling to stop until it had occupied the rest of the Palestinian land and cleansed it of its rightful owners. Conflict with Israel was viewed as existential and zero-sum. Therefore, Palestinians strongly opposed any move towards a peaceful settlement of the conflict with Israel, and any recognition of its existence, seeing any such accommodation as denying them their legitimate and historic rights in Palestine.

Palestinians also opposed all efforts to resettle refugees in host countries, viewing such efforts as aiming to liquidate the Palestinian cause and to pave the way for Arab recognition of Israel. Defining their goals in terms of "liberation" and a "return to the homeland," Palestinians sought during this period to keep the refugee problem alive and to nurture refugees' hopes and dreams of returning to their homes and properties.

Models: Algeria and Vietnam

Algeria and Vietnam inspired Palestinian imagination about the way forward. The Algerian experience presented the Palestinians with a successful model to emulate on two counts: a resort to "revolutionary violence" or "armed struggle" as the means to liberate the homeland, and formation of a wide "national front" that would embrace various groups and individuals regardless of their political ideology, economic background or social beliefs (leading to the birth of Fatah's concept of "armed struggle"). The Palestinian experience of the 1930s and 1940s had created an aversion to political parties and leadership based on traditional elite families.

The war in Vietnam was seen by Palestinians as demonstrating that even a superpower could be successfully challenged by guerilla warfare. For Fatah and other mainstream nationalists this provided a vital inspiration, a motivation to confront the challenges posed by a much more powerful Israel. Leaders of the Marxist-leaning groups, who believed they could and should base their "national liberation" struggle on the model of Vietnam, saw themselves emulating the Vietcong, while the Arab states would provide close support, thus paralleling the role played by North Vietnam. However, mainstream nationalists, while viewing Nasser and the rise of Pan-Arabism positively, remained doubtful that the Arab states would be willing to sacrifice their particular and separate national interests for the sake of liberating Palestine.

Recognizing their own limitations, mainstream nationalists hoped to create conditions that would force the Arab states to fight Israel. Fatah, believing that the Arab states were not prepared to lend the magnitude and kind of support provided by North Vietnam to the Vietcong, advocated a strategy of *tawreet*, or forced entanglement, or "catalytic war": although the Arab states would prefer to avoid a serious confrontation with Israel, the Palestinians would initiate an escalatory process, thus embroiling the Arab states in such a confrontation irrespective of those states' preferences. Seeing the Palestinians as the weaker party and as unable to defeat Israel on their own, Fatah leaders proposed banking on their capacity to spur greater regional violence by carrying out acts that would provoke Israeli retaliation that Arab states would not be able to ignore. Thus, the Arab states would be propelled to weigh in against Israel by intervening directly in the conflict.

State-Building

The experiences of Vietnam and Algeria also highlighted the need for a friendly neighboring environment, one from which Palestinians could mobilize forces and launch attacks on Israel. Hence the emphasis placed by Palestinian nationalists on cultivating good relations with all four Arab countries bordering Israel. Accordingly, until 1967 the idea of establishing a Palestinian state was set aside in order to avoid poisoning relations with Jordan, which feared the rise of Palestinian nationalism, or complicating relations with Egypt, given its concerns about the possible destabilization of its northeastern front.

Still, with the Gaza Strip under Egyptian military rule, Palestinian nationalists counted on Nasser in the hope that he would allow the strip to become a center for Palestinian mobilization, institution-building, and preparation for armed conflict. In the early 1960s these efforts included the establishment of a legislative council and the enactment of a Basic Law. Moreover, Palestinians now believed that Nasser had accepted the idea of establishing a Palestinian liberation army as well as an organization that would represent all Palestinians, leading to the creation of the PLO in 1964. Although Palestinians fully recognized that these public institutions, their army and the PLO, were in fact subservient to Nasser and other Arab states, and that their interests were subject to the vagaries of Arab state politics and the Arab Cold War, they still saw an advantage in embroiling the Arab states in the conflict with Israel.

Post-War Perspectives

In the immediate aftermath of the 1967 War the Palestinian narrative emphasized that if in 1948 Israel had presented the Palestinians with a mortal danger, the 1967 War and its results proved conclusively that Israel's expansionist designs threatened all Arabs – not just the Palestinians. Soon, however, Palestinians came to discover that instead of unifying Arab forces and sharpening their determination to confront Israel, the 1967 War and the intensification of the Israeli threat had unforeseen consequences. With several Arab states, most notably Egypt and Jordan, accepting UN Resolution 242, Palestinians increasingly saw these states as unable to liberate Palestine and/or as unwilling to expend the costs entailed. The nationalist groups in particular now came to believe that Palestinians made a fatal error when they relinquished their cause to Arab states in 1948 and when they remained relatively passive in 1949–67. Now these same Arab states were seen as giving absolute priority to regaining the lands they lost in 1967 rather than trying to reverse the results of the 1948 War, namely the creation of Israel. Thus when a Palestinian delegation asked Nasser in the aftermath of the war about undoing the results of 1948, he was said to have responded: "First, 1967."

It was then that the Palestinian narrative swallowed a dose of realism as the limitations of their pre-1967 strategies became apparent. In particular, Palestinians now recognized that one important dimension of the pre-1967 narrative and strategy, the catalytic war, had to be abandoned under the weight of the Arab defeat. In turn, the defeat was seen as the Arab states' ultimate betrayal of the Palestinians and as a negligence of their cause. And, while the PLO may have had some role in the escalation that led to the war, the war itself proved a disaster, resulting in the resounding defeat of all of Israel's neighbors, save Lebanon who stayed out of the fighting. Given this outcome, any notion that catalytic war could be a viable option was now discarded and any hope that Arab states would liberate Palestine for the Palestinians was now abandoned.

The 1967 War and its immediate aftermath were, therefore, a source of great consternation for the Palestinians. They viewed the Arab defeat and the Arab states' acceptance, without consulting the Palestinians, of UN Resolution 242 and the Jarring Mission as an attempt by these states to de-Arabize the Palestinian–Israeli conflict. The Palestinians were threatened by the prospect that Resolution 242 might be used to resolve the refugee issue without including them in the conflict-resolution process and without allowing them to claim sovereignty over former Palestine.

An even more threatening process was now seen by Palestinians to be developing in the occupied territories. The annexation of Jerusalem, the confiscation of land and the post-1967 construction of Israeli settlements were seen as part of a single, unified Israeli strategy designed to squeeze out the Palestinians. The Palestinian narrative began to emphasize the need to take matters into their own hands and to build their own capacity to wage an "armed struggle" against Israel from any available location. The preferred location was Jordan, due to its proximity to the occupied territories. Having lost the West Bank to Israel in the 1967 War, Jordan had no moral case to make against the Palestinians' efforts to seek their liberation: indeed Palestinians now saw the hosting and supporting of the guerrilla groups as Jordan's duty.

During this timeframe the PLO and the guerrilla groups outside the occupied territories strongly opposed the establishment of a Palestinian entity in the West Bank and the Gaza Strip, believing that the idea was a Zionist ploy. They viewed it as intended to grant Israel legitimacy and to liquidate the Palestinian cause, ending-up with an Israeli-controlled entity, a mere "civil administration" working for its Israeli masters. In the West Bank, too, the idea was suspected as being aimed at creating a state that would benefit Israel by serving as a buffer between Israel and the Arab World.

For a short period in 1968 Fatah and leftist PLO factions declared support for the idea of a democratic state in all of Palestine, in which Jews and Arabs could live together as citizens enjoying equal rights. The message of the nationalists was clear: the Palestinians were not fighting Jews, with whom they have lived for centuries in peace and cooperation; instead, their conflict was with the Zionists who intended to cleanse Palestine of Palestinian Arabs and establish a racist entity, for Jews only. In the absence of positive international reaction and in light of its total rejection by Israel, the "one-state" idea was soon dropped. This rejection was seen by Palestinians as additional evidence of the racist nature of the Zionist entity and its ideology.

Arab Narratives

During the run-up to the June 1967 crisis and War the Arab narrative continued unchanged from the earlier periods of the 1948 War and the 1956 Suez–Sinai War. As Israel was considered the primary threat to all Arab states, Arabs saw an imperative for these states to unite and pool all their military, political, economic, and social resources under one Arab command to be directed against their sole enemy – "the so-called State of Israel." Thus the Arab narrative continued to view Israel as a band of gangsters and conspirators who were manipulated by the world imperial powers.[57]

Israel was also perceived as part of the neocolonial influence in the region and as attracting different patterns of support from the colonial powers. The United States was seen as providing Israel with advanced armaments, the requisite political support, and a guarantee of its territorial integrity. In addition, France and Britain were viewed as continuing to comfort Israel with necessary political and military assistance. It is against this challenge that the Arab League developed its plans to liberate Palestine, to overcome Arab states' disagreements, to establish the PLO and to create a unified Arab Command. The command was charged with leading the Arab armies and coordinating and executing their plans to end Israel's existence. The Arabs saw themselves as encircled by danger, challenges, and conspiracies; Israel and Zionism were viewed as merely parts of a larger colonial conspiracy against them.

Israeli policies confirmed Arab views of Israel as an expansionist state. Its National Water Carrier project and its conduct during the 1967 War were regarded as perfect evidence of its aggressive designs. Arab states viewed the water project as intended to enable greater immigration to Israel as well as the construction of additional settlements for these immigrants. They considered it a further threat to Arab rights – this time, the rights to the water of the Jordan River – and as part of a larger expansionist plot that threatened the security of the Arab states.[58] The 1967 War provided final confirmation, as Israel extended its borders on all fronts.

It was during this period that the nuclear issue entered the Arab narrative for the first time. In a series of articles published in 1962–65, Egyptian journalist Mohamed Heikal, editor in-chief of *Al-Ahram*, argued that the ambiguity with which Israel responded to inquiries about activities in Dimona were merely "noise" to cover Israeli development of nuclear weapons. Heikal, who was very close to President Nasser, declared that Egypt would not allow Israel superiority in either missiles or nuclear capability.[59] He later cited American sources who expressed fear that Israel might lose its nerve and use one of its nuclear bombs. Heikal estimated, however, that a variety of factors would constrain Israel from using the bomb except in a case of self-defense should Arab armies penetrate into Israel.[60]

Given the danger that Israel was seen to pose to all Arab states, the Arab narrative called for all-Arab efforts to support the Palestinian cause and to build capacity for the inevitable confrontation with Israel. Thus, all Arab summits of the 1960s showed consensus regarding the Palestinian cause – all called for confronting Israel's expansionist designs.[61]

Egypt and the Naksa

The Arab narrative regarding the 1967 War was more complex. On one hand there was an effort to avoid describing the war's outcome as a "defeat"; instead it was termed a *Naksa* or setback. Since Israel's war aims were perceived to have been the overthrow of the Arab revolutionary regimes, particularly in Egypt and Syria, the mere survival of these regimes was considered a victory. When millions of Egyptians marched to Cairo on June 9–10 asking Nasser not to resign, this comprised a vote of confidence and signaled a determination to continue the struggle. The narrative adopted was that patriotic regimes can face defeats in battle – they will eventually win the war. The initial British defeat on the European continent and the evacuation of its forces from Dunkirk during the Second World War was recalled to demonstrate the point.

At the same time a separate narrative developed to explain the causes of the defeat. Primarily it was attributed to Israel's technological superiority, particularly in the realm of air power, which enabled it to cripple the Arab armies at the opening stage of the war. Another part of this narrative, expressed by General Muhammad Fawzy, who served as Egypt's Armed Forces' Chief of the General Staff during the 1967 War, attributed Egypt's defeat to the priority it gave to its involvement in Yemen at the expense of the requirements of facing Israel. In his words, "the basic error, no doubt, was that our strategy lost its focus and looked south instead of north. This caused an imbalance in the focus of the military command responsible for national security."[62]

In addition, Egypt saw itself as having been misled by American diplomacy, resulting in its strategic surprise. Egyptians argued that the invitation to Egyptian Vice President Zakariya Muhie Eddin to travel to Washington on June 5 in an effort to resolve the conflict led their leaders to believe that an Israeli attack was not imminent. For Egypt, it was inconceivable that Israel would attack while diplomacy was being pursued. Hence the Israeli surprise attack was seen as evidence of an American collusion in Israeli aggression.

Diplomatic developments in the war's aftermath were seen by Egyptians as confirming their suspicions. As Israel was seen as the country that launched the war, Egyptians expected that Israel would be condemned as the aggressor and compelled to return to prewar lines. And yet, in Egyptian eyes, almost the opposite had happened: the West was complicit in protecting Israel by adopting the very dubious UN Resolution 242.

Realizing the enormity of Western involvement in supplying arms and providing diplomatic support for Israel, Egypt saw itself as having no choice but to mend fences with the conservative Arab regimes, particularly Saudi Arabia, which it had previously rejected as "reactionary." In addition, Cairo was determined to improve relations with those in the West who were critical of Israel – particularly France, which had condemned Israel's "aggression." At the same time, Egypt began preparing for another war, based on the premise articulated by President Nasser in his speech to the Egyptian Parliament on November 23, 1967, namely that "what was taken by force will not be returned except by force."[63]

Jordan's Perspective

For Jordan, Nasser's moves on the eve of the 1967 War were part of a bluff. Seeking to test Nasser's seriousness, the Jordanians raised the issue of the Straits of Tiran and UNEF's presence in the Sinai.[64] In King Hussein's view, once Nasser closed the straits and let UNEF go, he – Hussein – had no choice but to demonstrate his Pan-Arab credentials by going along and placing the Jordanian armed forces under the command of Egyptian General Abdel Monem Riyad. Once the war began, the king saw his options as very limited. He feared that if Jordan did not participate and the war ended with a victory for Nasser, his regime would be overthrown by triumphant nationalists; or, if Nasser lost, Jordan would be blamed for the defeat, again leading to the king's overthrow. A third option, the one chosen by the king, was to participate in the war, and lose alongside Nasser. In this case, Jordan would lose the West Bank, but the East Bank would remain intact and the king would remain in power.

Jordan's narrative of its defeat in 1967 was that it was attributable in large part to strategic errors made by General Riyad. These had to do, primarily, with the deployment of Jordanian armored forces in a way that exposed them to Israeli air force attacks, resulting in their destruction. Jordanians later argued that their army had little real-time information on the morning of June 6 regarding the immediate outcome of the Israeli strike against Egyptian airfields. The lack of information at that critical moment determined the outcome of the war.

Syria's Narrative

While joining the broader Arab narrative of this period, the Syrian narrative was more independent and radical, giving expression to the growing public resentment in the Arab world regarding the Arab leadership's pursuit of support and approval by the West.[65] The Syrian Ba'ath saw the region's other leaders as ineffectual and not fully committed to confronting Israel – it is through this prism that the Syrian narrative saw and heavily criticized Egypt and Jordan.

The Ba'ath saw the liberation of Palestine as an Arab mission. When it came to power in 1963, its revolutionary bent called for "armed struggle" against Israel through a People's Liberation War.[66] Moreover, as Ba'athists were growing in numbers beyond Syria's borders, more and more Syrians who previously looked to Nasser, began calling for Syrian nationalism as a substitute for pan-Arabism.[67] They placed the destruction of Israel at the forefront, contrasting their greater militancy with what was now seen as Nasser's more timid approach.

Syrians saw themselves as not only willing to stand against Israel but also as ready to engage in a people's war of liberation by sponsoring Palestinian guerrilla raids into Israel.[68] Yet they did not consider themselves capable of confronting Israel alone. By contrast, they viewed other Arab leaders as too focused on their particular self-interests.[69] Thus, they criticized Egypt's position, seeing it as unwilling to confront Israel.[70]

In November 1964, when Syria saw Israel begin construction near a natural spring by the Jordan River, it viewed the project as an "Israeli encroachment... but also as a threat to its interests as a riparian state." Viewing Israel as having ignored the United Nations Truce Supervision Organization (UNTSO), the Syrians argued that they could do the same, and fired on an Israeli military patrol in the area.[71] The Israelis were then seen as responding far too harshly when they launched a major assault into Syria, killing 50 Syrian soldiers.[72]

Israel was also viewed as taking advantage of Syrian instability and as pressuring the Syrian regime by conducting incursions into the demilitarized zones and sometimes even across the Syrian border, violating the terms of the 1949 armistice agreement. And when Syria resisted such measures, Israel acted aggressively to halt and defeat such resistance. But when border clashes continued, Israel launched its air force to strike targets deep inside Syria, including Damascus. The Syrian air force was said to have reacted defensively and it was only when such defensive action could not counter the superiority of the Israeli air force that Syria began using the Golan Heights with increased frequency to shell the Israeli settlements below, in what Syrians saw as part of a defensive strategy.

In 1966 the Syrian narrative took on an even more radical turn with the rise of Salah Jadid as leader of the Ba'ath party.[73] The new Ba'ath leadership began actively supporting guerrillas as fighters in a proxy war against Israel. Accordingly, Syrian sponsorship of Fatah was seen as aimed at reestablishing Syria's primacy in the Arab revolutionary struggle. By contrast, the Syrians saw Egypt and Jordan as restricting Palestinian action from fear of Israeli retaliation.[74]

By late 1966 the Syrians viewed themselves as having succeeded in imposing their brand of radicalism and narrative: Jadid declared his desire to liberate Palestine "in a revolutionary manner."[75] This opened the door to the signing on November 7, 1966 of the Egypt–Syria Mutual Defense Treaty.

In the immediate aftermath of the 1967 War Syria saw itself as continuing to be committed to the Palestinian cause, glorifying Palestinian guerrillas, affirming its commitment to a "people's war," and refusing to negotiate with Israel.[76] Yet, at this time some members of the Syrian public seem to have challenged the narrative of the government and Ba'ath party regarding the conflict with Israel. For example, while the Syrian media claimed that Israel had not achieved its war aims, since it had failed to topple the regime, public opinion is said to have remained unimpressed with this narrative.[77] Reportedly, there were voices holding the country's leaders – as well as those of the Ba'ath Party – responsible for the defeat in the 1967 War, charging that the best units had not been sent to the front because the party was more concerned with its own survival than with wartime performance.[78]

Hafez Assad, who later replaced Jadid as Syria's president, is said to have ascribed the defeat of 1967 to the fear of conspiracy that had brought about the repeated purges of the Syrian military in the years before the war, producing its inherent weakness. Thus, Assad saw the military as having been ill-prepared for the war: the purging of so-called "subversive officers" from the army was said to have left a highly fragmented, shaken fighting force. Assad's narrative was that the pathologies which brought about the defeat of 1967 convinced him of the need to remove all the clutter which had distracted and disorganized the party and decision-making, to move away from the class struggle that Jadid insisted upon, and to instead forge closer relations with the other Arab states.[79]

The Khartoum Declaration

In the immediate aftermath of the war, Nasser's statement that "what was taken by force will not be returned except by force" was reflected in the spirit of defiance expressed in the Khartoum

Declaration and its famous "Three Nos." The declaration was seen as signaling to Israel that Egypt was prepared to pay the price required for the liberation of its occupied territories and as signaling to the Egyptian people that regardless of the action taken at the diplomatic front, it was likely that Egypt would have to fight to restore what was lost.

Thus, Khartoum was a message to the world and to the Arab masses that Arab states would not reward aggression; that Israel would not be allowed to gain any benefit from launching an unjust war; and that the Arabs were determined to undo the consequences of the war, by force if necessary. Arabs seemed to have settled in their minds the apparent contradiction between the Khartoum Declaration and the spirit, if not the letter, of UN Security Council Resolution 242 by viewing their acceptance of 242 as their contribution to preventing further destabilization in the Middle East while upholding the principle of international legitimacy. In their eyes it was now up to the international community to ensure that violence and war would not pay and that Israel would not be allowed to "acquire" land by force. At the same time, Nasser explained to Palestinian leaders that his acceptance of Resolution 242 did not mean they would have to accept recognition of Israel, since Resolution 242 applied only to states and did not mean to resolve the Palestinian question.[80]

Analysis

The dramatic developments of the period addressed in this chapter demand that we answer two questions: What caused the June 1967 War? and, Why were the Arabs defeated in the war?

The Causes of the 1967 War

The International System

The *global-systemic level* created a permissive environment for the 1967 War. When the Egyptian–Israeli crisis erupted in May 1967, the anarchic nature of the international system, its effects on war and peace, and the failure of international institutions to mitigate the effects of anarchy, became apparent once more. Since the UN peacekeeping forces stationed in the Sinai following the 1956 War lacked enforcement capacity and had operated with Egypt's consent, once President Nasser ordered their confinement to their bases, they could not resist Egyptian orders. Frustrated, UN Secretary General U Thant ordered their complete evacuation, thus deepening the crisis by reinforcing Israel's premise that it was operating in a self-help system requiring it to take preventive if not preemptive measures.

A second factor at the global-systemic level was the reflection in the region of Cold War competition between the West and the East, between NATO and the Warsaw Pact, and between the United States and the Soviet Union. The most important ramification of this continuous conflict was the massive transfer of arms by these powers to their respective allies in the region. Thus, by the eve of the 1967 War, Israel and its Arab neighbors possessed formidable arsenals which, for the most part, comprised advanced weapons supplied by their patrons. These menacing-looking arsenals bred extreme insecurity among the region's states.

This sense of extreme insecurity was further exacerbated by the particular types of weapons which the patrons supplied to their clients in the Middle East. These weapons included state-of-the-art fighter aircraft, main battle tanks, armored personnel carriers and self-propelled artillery. The integration of these weapon systems allowed the region's states to create highly mobile, offensive-oriented military forces. In turn, the first-strike advantage associated with such forces created extreme fear – especially in Israel – of being attacked first.

A third contribution was the direct role that the Soviet Union played in triggering the spiral of escalation by conveying false information about an alleged Israeli mobilization of forces. While this communication may have merely reflected a Soviet interest in precipitating a crisis – not a war – it sparked a series of regional moves that locked Egypt into an escalation process that was difficult to reverse.

Equally important, once the regional states, first Egypt and Israel, and then Syria and Jordan, found themselves in an ever-deepening crisis, the two superpowers could not prevent the escalation from spiraling out of control. Thus, as noted earlier, Soviet Premier Alexei Kosygin failed to win support for a diplomatic resolution of the escalating tension between Israel and Syria, as he previously had done successfully between India and Pakistan. Despite Egypt's dependence on Soviet arms supplies, Nasser did not find it difficult to persuade Kosygin that the formula was not applicable to the Arab–Israeli conflict.[81]

Now, having contributed to the escalation process, the Soviets could not prevent the conflict from sliding into war. On the eve of the war, they reportedly pleaded with Egypt's Defense Minister Shams Badran to avoid further steps that might make war inevitable.[82] Possibly, by that time Moscow had estimated that Israel was likely to win the war and may have feared that this could topple the Syrian regime. But the Soviet pleas came too late.

The United States, while not providing an immediate trigger to the crisis, proved equally unable to prevent its escalation. Distracted by Vietnam, Washington failed to heed Israel's pleas that it acknowledge and abide by the commitments made by the Eisenhower administration in the framework of its efforts to persuade Israel to complete its evacuation of the Sinai in the aftermath of the 1956 War. Having failed to persuade the Johnson administration to fulfill the earlier American promise to guarantee freedom of navigation and safe passage to Israeli ports, the Israeli government felt it had no choice but to take self-help measures.

The Middle East Region

At the *regional-systemic level*, the outbreak of the war was induced by the regional arms race which provided the region's states with a perceived first-strike advantage. This, in turn, propelled Israel toward launching a first strike to decide the battle.

A related factor that contributed to Israel's decision to strike first was the set of structural asymmetries that its national security doctrine sought to address and which brought it to rely on an offensive first strike. The first of these structural problems was Israel's perceived geo-strategic vulnerability – the impact of its narrow confines: some 80 percent of its population was concentrated in a strip not more than 60 kilometers long and in some places no more than 13 kilometers wide. This meant the total absence of strategic depth:

the country was exposed to the danger of being cut in half by a military force invading it from the east.

The second Israeli vulnerability was demographic: with its small population, Israel could not afford a large standing army. Instead, it was forced to base its territorial defense on a reserve force which could be mobilized in an emergency. The drawback of this system, however, was that the same mobilized reservists also comprised the core of the Israeli economy's workforce. Hence, Israel could not keep its reserve fighting force mobilized for more than a few weeks without crippling its economy. This meant that the time it could give to the efforts to resolve a crisis diplomatically was very limited. With its neighbors' large standing armies mobilized and deployed close to the country's borders, and with its own forces facing considerable time constraints, in the absence of a non-military solution to the crisis Israel was bound to strike.

These two vulnerabilities made war almost inevitable once Egypt did not reverse the introduction of forces into the Sinai and the closing of the Straits of Tiran. Israel's military doctrine emphasizing preemptive and preventive strikes and operational offense meant that a hair-trigger situation developed in which, without Egypt backing down, war was unavoidable.

A third factor at the regional-systemic level was the scarcity of natural resources in the Middle East, water being the most important example. This made the Syrian–Israeli clash over Israel's Water Carrier project, and Syria's efforts to abort it by diverting the sources of the Banias, a sharp zero-sum conflict seen by both sides as involving their vital national interests. Finding it very difficult to back off, both sides were propelled to "up the ante."

A fourth factor was the Arab Cold War. The latter escalated the level of rhetoric in the Arab–Israeli arena, making it nearly impossible for the region's leaders to base their policies and the specific measures they took on rational strategic calculations. Nasser and the language of Nasserism and pan-Arabism raised Arab and Palestinian expectations to unparalleled heights. Thus, the conflict with Israel became an arena of intra-Arab competition, with the Arab states outbidding one another in belligerent language and in allegations of treachery.

Egypt's demand that the UN forces in the Sinai be withdrawn to their bases, its mobilization of its own military forces and their introduction into the Sinai, and, finally, its decision to close the Straits of Tiran to Israeli navigation, can all be attributed to the constant accusations voiced by the other Arab states to the effect that Egypt was not truly committed to opposing Israel. Thus Egypt was lured into an escalation process it did not intend – a considerable part of its military was deployed in Yemen and the rest was not prepared for the coming war.

Jordan was pushed to participate in the war by an array of factors that led King Hussein to conclude that if he did not enter the war, he would lose his kingdom. Rising tension in the Arab Cold War, Israeli reprisals, and the lack of Jordanian capacity to respond, as well as the growing tension in the West Bank against the regime, all contributed to a psychological environment that led the king to believe that, despite his inclination toward peace, if he did not enter the war he would be deposed.

Similar dynamics operated on the Syrian front. In the 1960s Syria's problematic relations with Israel revolved around three issues: water, the demilitarized zones, and the Palestinian guerrillas stationed in Syria. The conflict over the diversion of the sources of the Jordan led to cross-border military clashes. Similarly, Israeli attempts to cultivate the demilitarized zones during the same period led to Syrian artillery shelling.[83] The Syrians also encouraged Fatah guerrilla fighters to launch armed operations against Israel across the Syrian and Jordanian fronts: Syria used Palestinian guerrillas to fight Israel by proxy.

In this way the Palestinians also contributed to the creation of an unstable regional environment. Their guerrilla action destabilized border conditions in Jordan and Syria, inviting Israeli retaliation. This in turn resulted in Arab public anger about the lack of military responses to harsh Israeli reprisals, and demands for armed action. Thus, a Palestinian-centered process of forced entanglement of Arab states in armed conflict with Israel escalated.

Egypt's Domestic Scene

At the *unit level*, Egypt's domestic circumstances pressed Nasser into escalation as a means of diverting attention from the failures at home. His regime was not only involved in an expensive war in Yemen, its economic plans for progress and development faced growing difficulties. After a promising five-year development plan for 1960–65, the regime failed to produce another plan due to lack of resources. Soviet-style industrialization was soon to reach a dead end because of Egypt's inability to compete in world markets. The Egyptian success stories of nationalizing the Suez Canal in the 1950s and building the Aswan Dam in the first half of the 1960s were soon to be taken for granted and a growing population was asking for more. Although Nasser continued to be a hero for Egyptians and Arabs at large, his stardom was losing some of its luster as the United Arab Republic was broken and the war in Yemen dragged on. It did not help that the involvement of the military in running the country's political and economic life was marred by corruption and incompetence. Adding to these developments, lack of political freedoms and a rise in suppression and use of torture were now taking the country into a deep crisis.

By the mid-1960s, Nasser, realizing the risks of his political situation, began to change course. Internally, he began to look for measures to improve the performance of the Egyptian economy. The press was allowed to speak of the "fat cats" who gained wealth through corruption. The regime even contemplated the creation of a free trade area in Port Said. Externally, Nasser turned to Arab summitry in part to create an environment suitable for the extraction of Egyptian forces from Yemen. Yet, the dynamics of the Arab Cold war were still operating, whether because of global impacts or because of the different evolutionary processes of Arab countries. The pressure on Egypt to act under such domestic circumstances pushed the regime toward a highly risky military demonstration that was meant for domestic political consumption.

Syrian, Jordanian, and Palestinian Politics

Considerations of regime security meant that Syria could not avoid entanglement in the war. Power in the country changed hands many times throughout the 1960s, with successive regimes seeking to implement more extreme leftist and revolutionary ideas. The involvement of the military in these power struggles weakened both the country, which was deprived of stability, and the military, which could not but lose professionalism in such a struggle. The Ba'ath rhetoric of anti-Zionism and extreme Arab nationalism – particularly after the

December 1966 coup – opened a large gap between unlimited objectives and very limited human and material resources. Yet, the Syrian regime could not avoid participating in the war, as this would have meant losing whatever legitimacy and credibility it possessed.

At the domestic level in non-revolutionary Jordan, the situation was also severe. After the November 1966 Israeli raid on Samu, riots spread all over Jordan demanding a response to the Israeli attack. The army, the king's source of support, was criticized for its poor performance and poor readiness, and the king was criticized for his decision to ally with the United States, Israel's main strategic supporter. This differed very much from the case of Syria, whose Soviet ally was respected and feared.[84] King Hussein understood that he could not escape the pressures of Arab nationalism and that he therefore had no choice but to become part of the Arab collective effort in case of war, even if the Arab defeat was inevitable. [85]

Although the Palestinians did not have an independent military force deployed on Israeli borders and did not pose any serious military threat to Israel, violent attacks across the Israeli border by various Palestinian groups, most prominently *al-Asifa* (The Storm), the armed wing of Fatah, contributed to the escalation. Although many of these attacks were the outcome of Arab states' machinations to destabilize their opponents, there were also internal domestic factors at play. The competition between the traditional elite in control of the PLO and the newly emerging guerrilla groups led to escalation in rhetoric and violence against Israel.

The Israeli Internal Scene

On Israel's side the most important unit-level factor that propelled the war was the extreme sense of vulnerability of the country's population. This resulted in the "securitization" of Israeli internal discourse – the phenomenon of almost every important political, social and economic issue being viewed in security terms. While a model democracy in terms of civil–military relations at the formal level – placing the IDF completely under the control of Israel's civilian leaders – in reality, Israel's top generals had considerable influence over the affairs of state. As the month of May 1967 was about to end without a diplomatic resolution of the crisis in sight, members of the IDF's General Staff began to place the countries' civilian leaders under enormous pressure to allow the military to resolve the issue by striking preemptively.

The loss of trust by members of Israel's top military command in their civilian leaders paralleled a similar loss of faith by large segments of mainstream Israelis. Increasingly, they saw their government as uncertain and overly hesitant, a feeling exacerbated by an especially unfortunate radio speech delivered on May 28, 1967 by Prime Minister Eshkol during which he was heard stuttering. This led to huge public pressure to bring back the "Old Man" of Israeli politics – David Ben Gurion – and to further expand the political basis of Israel's governing coalition by including – for the first time in Israel's history – the right-wing Herut party, led by Menachem Begin.

While Eshkol resisted returning Ben Gurion to a position of power, he agreed to restore public confidence by handing the Defense Ministry to a former IDF Chief of Staff who had led Israel's military in the 1956 Sinai-Suez War, Moshe Dayan. Dayan's entry into the Defense

Ministry on June 1 made war inevitable, since he was one of the prime architects of Israel's offensive military doctrine.

The domestic dimension was especially at play in inducing Israel's decision to attack Syria on June 9. Once Egypt's military was destroyed and the West Bank was conquered in the first few days of the war, Israel perceived the threat it faced on the eve of the war as having been lifted. Until that point Dayan remained adamant that there was no strategic imperative to dislodge the Syrian forces from their strongholds on the Golan.

Sensing that the war might end with the Syrians keeping control of the Golan, representatives of Israeli towns and settlements in northern Israel who had been the victims of Syrian shelling and other violent clashes since the early 1950s now began to operate as an organized lobby, exerting huge pressure on Israel's civilian and military leaders to conquer the Golan. Despite his earlier reluctance to launch such an attack, on the early morning of June 9, Dayan saw satellite pictures of weakened and abandoned Syrian army camps near the border with Israel and read an intercepted cable from Nasser advising the Syrians to accept a ceasefire, all of which now convinced him that the Syrian army was weak. So, shortly after, he gave the green light to the IDF's northern command to launch a campaign of seizure.[86]

Nasser

At the *individual level* no single personality was more closely associated with the process of escalation to war, as well as with Egypt's defeat, than Nasser. Being seen to be the first Egyptian to actually rule Egypt for almost two millennia, his charismatic personality inspired Egyptians to dream of progress and development, and inspired Arabs to dream of unity.

Yet Nasser's personal contribution to the embroiling of his country in a war it was not prepared for is undeniable. It seems that by the mid-1960s Nasser's status as an unchallenged leader induced his belief in his own invincibility, resulting in cognitive blinders. Worse still, it discouraged those around him from providing reality checks by exposing him to unpleasant news.

Nasser replaced long-standing institutions, imposing in their stead an authoritarian system suffering from faulty decision-making and an inability to relate goals and objectives to capabilities and capacities. Unmistakable signals should have warned Nasser and his colleagues of the coming *Naksa*: the dismantling of the United Arab Republic, the failure in Yemen, and the paralysis of the Egyptian economy and society. But Nasser's stardom and eagerness to satisfy Arab masses enticed him to make decisions during the crisis that proved disastrous. Caught up in his own rhetoric, and pushed by other Arabs' propaganda machines that accused him of hiding behind the skirts of UN troops, he was trapped into demanding that UN observers in the Sinai be confined to their bases – leading to their departure – and eventually closing the Straits of Tiran.

Paradoxically what encouraged Nasser to take the steps that led to war in 1967 was his record of success in 1956 – turning a military defeat into a political triumph by mobilizing Arab public opinion and gaining sympathy and support in international forums, from the United Nations to the Non-Aligned Movement (NAM). Now overconfident and seemingly intoxicated by power, he deployed bellicose rhetoric, thus contributing to the escalation of the crisis. More importantly, his choice of advisors – surrounding himself with yes-men instead of courageous advisors who could provide him with reality checks – now resulted in his lack of awareness regarding the real state of readiness of Egypt's armed forces. Thus Nasser became a victim of his authoritarian personality as well as his failure to institutionalize Egypt's decision-making processes.[87]

Another factor at the individual level that contributed to the escalation of the crisis to war was the problematic personal dynamic between Nasser and the General Commander of the Egyptian armed forces, Marshall Abdel Hakim Amer. Although this was not made public, in Egypt's highest circles Amer was held responsible for the dysfunctional conduct of the Egyptian military in 1956 Sinai–Suez War as well as for the breakdown of the alliance with Syria (the UAR) in 1961. Now, when asked by Nasser whether the Egyptian army was prepared for war, Amer gave a positive response, vastly exaggerating the readiness of the Egyptian armed forces. Possibly, Amer sought a military confrontation the results of which would make up for his previous defeats.

The Arab Defeat

International and Regional Dimensions

One dimension of the *global-systemic level* that is widely asserted to have played an important role in causing the Arab defeat in the 1967 War was the technological superiority of Western arms supplied to Israel compared to the technology of Soviet weapons supplied to Egypt and Syria. Yet the extent to which this was indeed the case is far from clear. The IDF, prepared for war by then IDF Chief of Staff Rabin, had not yet received advanced arms from the United States. The only exception was the Hawk air-defense system. Instead, Israel's mainframe air force platforms were largely French and it is far from clear that these platforms – or Israel's French- and British-made main battle tanks – were superior to the Soviet-made equivalents that Egypt possessed.

Instead, the main causes of the Arab defeat seem to be located primarily at the *regional-systemic level*, namely the balance of power between Israel and its Arab neighbors. This balance included not only the quantity and quality of weapons which these states possessed but also, if not primarily, the qualitative factors that determined how these weapons would be utilized: quality and intensity of training, military doctrines, topographical conditions prevailing within the theater of operations, the advantage Israel enjoyed in its "internal lines," and the higher motivation of its fighting force.

Israel's small population compelled the IDF to meet its manpower requirements through a combination of total conscription and a reserve system, thus ensuring that the IDF was composed of a cross-section of Israel's skilled population. By contrast, the armed forces of Egypt and Syria during this period did not include many representatives of the better-educated and skilled sectors of their societies – especially university graduates. Moreover, the involvement of the Arab militaries in the political, economic, and managerial lives of their countries had led them to lose their military professionalism.

Fear of war obliged the IDF to implement a highly demanding training program that included military exercises at all levels. The IDF's qualitative superiority was particularly apparent in its air force. The IDF also seemed to prepare military plans for almost every contingency and to refresh these plans periodically. By contrast, the Egyptian military was underprepared for war with Israel, preoccupied as it was with its involvement in Yemen. Even less prepared for fighting were the Palestinian forces in Gaza.

Another problem confounding Egypt was the asymmetry between the Israeli and Egyptian military doctrines. Thus, General Muhammad Fawzy later testified that "El-Qaher, Egypt's defense plan, [which was] ratified in 1966, was conceived as the military dimension of the decision taken by the Arab Summit meeting in 1964, to prevent Israel from expanding into Arab territory. The Egyptian plan focused on defense and deterrence techniques, while the Israeli forces were trained in attacks and raids."[88]

One critically important dimension of the Arabs' lack of preparedness was that, despite the three weeks of constantly escalating crisis, the Egyptian military seems to have neglected to prepare for the possibility that war was coming. Certainly, its air force remained exposed on a small number of airfields, making it extremely vulnerable to Israel's surprise airstrike.

The theater of operations also provided Israel with significant advantages. The Sinai Peninsula was ideal terrain for the kind of offensive mobile warfare for which the IDF was configured and trained. Largely desert, it presented few obstacles to a rapid advance of the IDF's armored and mechanized formations. Moreover, the destruction of the Egyptian air force during the first few hours of the fighting, the absence of forests and other means of hiding Egypt's ground forces, and the near-perfect weather in the Sinai in early June, all combined to make Egypt's military formations completely transparent and exposed – easy prey for the Israeli air force.

Israel's second advantage was its ability to move military resources on internal lines. While the country's small size made it extremely vulnerable, once the war began the same factor turned into a great advantage for Israel. The combination of internal lines and short distances to the frontlines allowed Israel to shift forces quickly from front to front. Thus, the Israeli forces that defeated the Jordanian army in the northern part of the West Bank were then shifted to the southern part of the Golan Heights, where they forced the withdrawal of the Syrian forces fighting there.

By contrast, the haphazard way in which the Jordanians and Syrians engaged in the fighting – and the absence of a unified Arab command that could coordinate operations at all three fronts – allowed Israel to focus on one military force at a time, first destroying a large part of the Egyptian military, then taking Jordan out for the war, and finally focusing almost exclusively on dislodging the Syrian army from the Golan Heights.

At the tactical level the IDF seemed to be enjoying three significant advantages. The first had to do with the superiority of Western military doctrine, and especially the ethos of the British army, on the basis of which many of Israel's senior military officers were trained, which placed great emphasis on personal initiative by NCOs and junior officers. This was particularly well suited for the temperament of Israel's junior officers and for the rapid mobile warfare that required initiative and improvisation in the face of rapidly changing conditions. By contrast, Soviet doctrine on which the Egyptian military relied – which emphasized rigid implementation of set battle plans – proved less suitable to the demands of a rapidly evolving battlefield.

Second, the IDF had a huge advantage in military intelligence over its Egyptian counterpart. This was particularly the case with regard to target acquisition – accurate detailed data of the location of Egyptian weapons platforms, especially air assets – making Israel's surprise air-strike at the opening hours of the war all the more deadly and decisive. By contrast, Egypt's armed forces were thrown into the battlefield practically blinded by the lack of tactical and operational intelligence. In the words of Egyptian General Fawzy years later: "The Egyptian military command was handicapped by its lack of strategic reconnaissance facilities. Israel knew everything about us, while we knew nothing about its military might."[89]

The third advantage enjoyed by the Israeli military in the 1967 War was very high motivation. This was a consequence of the feeling – right or wrong – that Israel was facing an existential threat that had to be eliminated at all costs. This, in turn, translated to zero tolerance of any failure to implement commands or to fail to achieve the missions defined.

The Arab and Israeli Domestic Scenes

At the *unit level* the Arab militaries seemed to suffer from excessive politicization, the product of repeated coups in the case of Syria, and fear of coups in the case of Egypt and Jordan. The result was near-malignant civil–military relations, one dimension of which was the absence of any mechanism to correct Nasser's mistakes. A more important dimension was that these countries' leaders constantly feared that elements in the military might stage a coup against them.

The result was that, in building their military forces, Arab leaders had primarily internal security and regime security considerations in mind – not defense against external enemies or battlefields pitting large armored and mechanized formations against one another. Such fears induced declining professionalism within the ranks of the Arab armies' officer corps with a growing number among them becoming increasingly involved in domestic politics.

Another dimension of this phenomenon was the divorce between the political and the military leaderships in Egypt during the period preceding the war.[90] By contrast, Israel was led by civilian leaders who had no fears of being toppled. It enjoyed a single unified command structure, ready to execute a coherent national security strategy.

Concluding Notes

The period addressed in this chapter witnessed another dramatic surge in the Arabization of the conflict – that is, in the extent to which neighboring Arab states rather than the Palestinians became the principal and more consequential protagonists on the Arab side. With the 1967 War pitting Israel against Egypt, Jordan and Syria, the state-to-state dimension of the Arab–Israeli conflict now reached a new height, reminiscent of May 1948. The outcome of the 1967 War had entangled the Arab states in the conflict with Israel to an even greater degree than the war itself. Now, the sovereign territory and most vital national security interests of all three of Israel's principal Arab neighbors were affected by the conflict. Indeed, while the conflict could have been seen as existential from Israel's standpoint until 1967, now it was these Arab states that could regard the conflict as existential, with Israel's military forces stationed less than 40 kilometers from Damascus and just over 100 kilometers from Cairo. Such high stakes could only contribute to the conflict's resilience.

Other factors ushered in by the war contributed even more to making the conflict resistant to future efforts to resolve it. After 1967 Israel found itself controlling and governing a far larger Palestinian population. More consequential, however, was that on the Israeli side, a historical and religious narrative was now adopted, focusing on Israel's right to the Greater Land of Israel, to include a united Jerusalem under its sole sovereignty and the West Bank, using the biblical names of Judea and Samaria when referring to the area. A layer of *religion* was thus added to the already complicated conflict between two *national* movements. No longer limited to a pragmatic weighing of national security requirements, at least some Israelis now brought God into the already complicated discourse.

These factors translated to an Israeli project of settling the lands, with the first steps in the project rooted in history (Gush Etzion) and religion (Hebron). Now a still small but important Jewish constituency developed vested interests in maintaining control over the conquered territory. With this constituency adopting a narrative of "liberation," and with the population indigenous to the territory now developing a narrative of "occupation," it was hardly surprising that the conflict became even harder to resolve.

Interestingly and importantly, the 1967 *Naksa* had the opposite effect on the Arab side, and particularly on the neighboring Arab states, introducing the first signs of realism in their outlook and approaches to the conflict. Their shock in the face of the totality and lightning speed of the military defeat resulted initially in denial, expressed in the famous "Three Nos" of the Khartoum Summit. But only a short time later, most of the Arab states that were part of the consensus in Khartoum endorsed UN Security Council Resolution 242, which stipulated the terms for peace with Israel. Hence, its acceptance could not be interpreted other than as an acknowledgement that in some shape and size, Israel was here to stay. From Israel's standpoint, and from this point onwards, the conflict could no longer be considered existential.

Another dimension of this new realism was the fact that the extent of the Arab defeat in 1967 totally discredited the notion of Pan-Arabism. The particular interests of each Arab state now dominated their separate agendas – with each focusing on the requirements of restoring its sovereignty over the territories it had lost.

From the Palestinians' standpoint the dominant implication of these developments was the loss of any hope that the neighboring Arab states would "pull their chestnuts out of the fire." In some form or another, the new Palestinian sense of realism dictated self-reliance. Whether in the form of "armed struggle" or diplomacy or both, Palestinians now needed to find their own path to achieving the goals, even if only the minimum goals, of their national movement.

Readings

Bickerton, Ian and Carla Klausner, *A History of the Arab–Israeli Conflict* (Prentice Hall, 2010) 132–153.

Caplan, Neil, *The Israel–Palestine Conflict: Contested Histories* (Wiley, 2010) 143–148.

Dowty, Alan, *Israel/Palestine: Global Political Hotspots* (Polity, 2012) 113–125.
Lesch, David, *The Arab-Israeli Conflict* (Oxford University Press, 2008) 194–232.
Morris, Benny, *Righteous Victims: The History of the Zionist-Arab Conflict, 1881–2001* (Vintage, 2001) 302–346.
Oren, Michael B. *Six Days of War: June 1967 and the Making of the Modern Middle East.* (Oxford University Press, 2002).
Shlaim, Avi, *The Iron Wall: Israel and the Arab World* (W.W. Norton, 2001) 186–282.
Smith, Charles D., *Palestine and the Arab-Israeli Conflict* (Bedford/St.Martin's, 2007) 259–299.
Tessler, Mark, *A History of the Israeli-Palestinian Conflict* (Indiana University Press, 2009) 336–464.

Historical Documents

U.N. Security Council Resolution 242: Walter Laqueur and Barry Rubin, *The Israel-Arab Reader: A Documentary History of the Middle East Conflict* (Penguin Books), 116.
Lebanon National Pact
The Khartoum Resolution: available online at http://www.mideastweb.org/khartoum.htm.

Notes

1. Malcolm H. Kerr, *The Arab Cold War: Gamal Abdel Nasir and his Rivals, 1958–1970* (New York: Oxford University Press, 1971)
2. Ilana Kass, *Soviet Involvement in the Middle East: Policy Formulation, 1966–1973* (Boulder: Westview Press, 1978), 42–48; Galia Golan, "The Cold War and the Soviet Attitude Toward the Arab–Israeli Conflict," in Nigel J. Ashton (ed.) *The Cold War in the Middle East: Regional Conflict and the Superpowers, 1967–73*, (New York: Routledge, 2007), 59–73; and Galia Golan, *Soviet Policies in the Middle East: From World War Two to Gorbachev* (New York: Cambridge University Press, 1990), 44–57.
3. Taha Abdel Alim, "The Horizons of Arab–Soviet Economic Relations," *Al Mustaqbal Al Arabi*, 110, April 1992 [In Arabic]. Taha Abdel Alim, "USSR and Development in the Arab Homeland," *Al Fikr Al Istrategi Al Arabi*, 29, July 1992.
4. Lewis Weldon Snider, "Middle East Maelstrom: the Impact of Global and Regional Influences on the Arab Israeli Conflict, 1947–1973.", PhD Dissertation, University of Michigan, 1975, 32.
5. John Waterbury, "Egypt: the Wages of Dependency," in A. L. Udovitch (ed.) *The Middle East: Oil, Conflict and Hope* (Lexington: Lexington Books, 1976), 340.
6. During 1958–1961, the UAR was also part of the United Arab States, a loose confederation that also included North Yemen.
7. "Chronology July 1–September 15, 1958," *Middle East Journal*, 12, 14 (Autumn 1958), 418–477, 425; George Evans, "Witnessing Iraq's last revolution," *Contemporary Review*, 283, 1653 (October 2003), 211–218, 213. Qassim had led an infantry battalion in the 1948 War (for which he was later decorated for gallantry) but had no political experience prior to leading the Free Officers' coup.
8. Many observers at the time concluded that the Soviet Union and Egypt had instigated the Iraqi revolution. Indeed, the Iraqi Free Officers who carried out the coup under Qassim's leadership admitted that they had been inspired by Nasser's 1952 revolt. But recent scholarship has largely discredited the notion that the Soviet Union and Egypt were directly involved in the Iraqi revolution, highlighting instead the widespread opposition to the monarchy that had been building over decades.

See Rashid Khalidi, "Perceptions and Reality: The Arab World and the West," in Wm. Roger Louis and Roger Owen (eds.) *A Revolutionary Year: The Middle East in 1958* (London: IB Tauris, 2002), 181–208, 200. See also Elie Kedourie, *The Chatham House Version and Other Middle Eastern Studies* (Chicago: Ivan R. Dee, 1970), 236–285.

9. "Chronology," 427.
10. Evans, "Witnessing Iraq's last revolution," 214–215.
11. Fred Halliday, "The Gulf Between Two Revolutions: 1958–1979," MERIP (Middle East Research and Information Project), Report No. 85, (February 1980), 6–15.
12. Smith, *Palestine and the Arab-Israeli Conflict*, 269.
13. *Ibid.*; Michael C. Hudson, *The Precarious Republic: Political Modernization in Lebanon* (New York: Random House, 1968), 108.
14. Kamal Salibi, "Lebanon under Fuad Chehab 1958–1964," *Middle Eastern Studies*, 2, 3 (April 1966), 211–216, 212. For more on the National Pact, see "The National Pact," US Library of Congress, http://countrystudies.us/lebanon/77.htm.
15. Smith, *Palestine and the Arab-Israeli Conflict*, 269.
16. Salibi, "Lebanon under Fuad Chehab 1958–1964," 215.
17. See "Milestones: 1953–1960: The Eisenhower Doctrine, 1957," Office of the Historian, Bureau of Public Affairs, United States Department of State, http://history.state.gov/milestones/1953-1960/EisenhowerDoctrine. Irene L. Gendzier has argued that American intervention in Beirut in 1958 resulted from perceived threats to American oil interests in the region. See Irene L. Gendzier, "Oil, politics, and US intervention," in Louis and Owen, *A Revolutionary Year*, 101–142, 104.
18. Smith, *Palestine and the Arab-Israeli Conflict*, 269.
19. Egypt continued to use the name on its own until 1971.
20. Nasserism was an Arab nationalist ideology that espoused the ideas of, and revolved around, President Gamal Abdel Nasser, and dominated Arab politics during parts of the 1950s and 1960s. It combined the goals of creating one Arab nation, ending the dominance of Western powers over Arab states, confronting Zionism, solidarity with Third World countries, and building a modern secularist Arab political system. The Arab defeat in the 1967 war greatly weakened the appeal of Nasserism in Egypt and the Arab world.
    The Arab Ba'ath Movement was established by the Syrian Michel Aflaq in 1944 as a secular, socialist and pan-Arabist movement. It calls for the creation of one Arab state. Ba'athism means "rebirth" or "resurrection;" its motto calls for "unity, liberty, and socialism". It also calls for Arab enlightenment and the rebirth of Arab values and culture, and emphasizes the role of the party in the creation of the Arab state and in developing its society. With the rise and spread of Nasserism, the Ba'ath party for a time viewed itself as the vehicle to implement Nasser's goals.
    Peter Mansfield, "Nasser and Nasserism," *International Journal*, 28, 4 (Autumn, 1973), 670–688; P. J. Vatikiotis, *Nasser and His Generation* (New York: St. Martin's Press, 1978); Nissim Rejwan, *Nasserist Ideology: Its Exponents and Critics* (Transaction Publishers, 1974); John F. Devlin, "The Baath Party: Rise and Metamorphosis," *The American Historical Review*, 96, 5 (December, 1991), 1396–1407; David Roberts, *The Baath and the Creation of Modern Syria* (New York: St. Martin's Press, 1987); and Robert Springborg, "Baathism in Practice: Agriculture, Politics, and Political Culture in Syria and Iraq," *Middle Eastern Studies*, 17, 2 (April, 1981), 191–209.
21. Hopwood, *Syria 1945–1986*, 5.
22. Ibid., 47.
23. David W. Lesch, *The Arab-Israeli Conflict: A History* (Oxford: Oxford University Press, 2008), 204.

24. Manfred W. Wenner, *The Yemen Arab Republic: Development and Change in an Ancient Land* (Boulder: Westview Press, 1991), 134.
25. Mark Zeitoun, *Power and Water in the Middle East* (London: IB Tauris, 2008), 68; and Daniel Hillel, *Rivers of Eden: The Struggle for Water and the Quest for Peace on the Middle East* (New York: Oxford University Press, 1994), 162–163.
26. Shlaim, *The Iron Wall*, 228–229, 232–240, especially 236.
27. "Letter dated 6 October 1964 from the representatives of Algeria, Iraq, Jordan, Kuwait, Lebanon, Libya, Morocco, Saudi Arabia, Sudan, Syria, Tunisia, United Arab Republic and Yemen, addressed to the President of the Security Council," United Nations Security Council, DOCUMENT S/6003, October 8, 1964, http://unispal.un.org/UNISPAL.NSF/0/1D420331AB74CF90052564E500513FDC.
28. "Document 144: Declaration Issued by the Council of Kings and Heads of State of the Arab League at Its Second Session, September 5–11, 1964," in M. Cherif Bassiouni, (ed.) *Documents on the Arab-Israeli Conflict: Emergence of Conflict in Palestine and the Arab-Israeli Wars and Peace Process, vol. 1* (Ardsley, NY: Transnational Publishers, Inc., 2005), 544–546.
29. "Resolutions and Final Declaration of Arab Summit, Casablanca, 13–17 September 1965," League of Arab States, www.arableagueonline.org.
30. Khaldun S. al-Husry, "Through Shuqairy's Eyes," *Journal of Palestine Studies*, 3, 2 (Winter, 1974), 142–146, 144–145. See also Haykal, *Infijar 1967: Harb Thalatheen Aam* (*The Explosion of 1967– the Thirty-Year War*) (Cairo, 1990), 212 [In Arabic].
31. Shlaim, *The Iron Wall*, 226. The Jordanian–Israeli contacts continued to develop, gradually producing a degree of trust between the parties. Israel is said to have provided the king with intelligence regarding plots to overthrow him and assassination attempts on his life. With time this led to an Israeli assurance given to King Hussein to the effect that Jordan's stability and territorial integrity was a vital interest of the state of Israel. See also: Shlaim, *Collusion Across the Jordan*, 616–618.
32. Shlaim, *The Iron Wall*, 227–228.
33. Stockholm International Peace Research Institute (SIPRI) Arms Transfer Database, http://www.sipri.org/databases/armstransfers.
34. SIPRI Arms Transfer Database, http://www.sipri.org/databases/armstransfers.
35. Ariel E. Levité and Emily B. Landau, "Arab Perceptions of Israel's Nuclear Posture, 1960–1967", *Israel Studies*, 1, 1 (Spring, 1996), 34–59; Ephraim Kahana, "Covert Action: The Israeli Experience," in Loch K. Johnson (ed.) *Strategic Intelligence Volume 3: Covert Action, Behind the Veil of Secret Foreign Policy* (Santa Barbara: Praeger Security International, 2006), 61–82, 68. Owen L. Sirrs, *Nasser and the Missile Age in the Middle East* (London and New York: Routledge, 2006), 41–44.
36. Sadek al-Sharaa, *Horobana Maa' Israel 1947–1973*. [*Our War with Israel, 1947–1973*] (Amman: Dar Al Shourouk, 1997), 449. See also Lesch, *The Arab-Israeli Conflict*, 205; and Michael Brecher and Jonathan Wilkenfeld, *A Study of Crisis*. (Ann Arbor: University of Michigan Press, 2000, 280.
37. Brecher and Wilkenfeld, *A Study of Crisis*, 280.
38. Lesch, *The Arab-Israeli Conflict*, 206–207; Brecher and Wilkenfeld, *A Study of Crisis*, 281.
39. Lesch, *The Arab-Israeli Conflict*, 207–208; Brecher and Wilkenfeld, *A Study of Crisis*, 281.
40. Sadek al-Sharaa, *Horobana Maa' Israel 1947–1973*, 477–493.
41. Lesch, *The Arab-Israeli Conflict*, 210; Brecher and Wilkenfeld, *A Study of Crisis*, 281.
42. Michael Brecher and Benjamin Geist, *Decision in Crisis: Israel, 1967 and 1973* (Berkeley, CA: University of California Press, 1980), 117–122.

43. William B. Quandt, *Peace Process: American Diplomacy and the Arab-Israeli Conflict Since 1967* (Washington, DC: Brookings Institution Press, 2005), 31–35.
44. Michael B. Oren, *Six Days of War: June 1967 and the Making of the Modern Middle East* (New York: Presidio Press, 2003), 110.
45. *Ibid.*, 146–147.
46. *Ibid.*, 100–101.
47. Patrick Seale, *Asad of Syria: The Struggle for the Middle East* (Los Angeles: University of California Press, 1988), 144.
48. Lesch, *The Arab-Israeli Conflict*, 212; and Anton La Guardia, *War Without End: Israelis, Palestinians, and the Struggle for a Promised Land* (New York: Thomas Dunne Books, 2002), 124.
49. Brecher and Wilkenfeld, *A Study of Crisis*, 281; Shlaim, *The Iron Wall*, 244.
50. Lesch, *The Arab-Israeli Conflict*, 212; La Guardia, *War Without End*, 124; and Brecher and Wilkenfeld, *A Study of Crisis*, 281.
51. "League of Arab States Khartoum Resolution, 1 September 1967," UNISPAL, http://unispal.un.org/UNISPAL.NSF/0/1FF0BF3DDEB703A785257110007719E7.
52. In the French version, reference is to "withdrawal of Israel armed forces from *the* territories occupied in the recent conflict," emphasis added. Both, English and French are official languages of the UN. "Resolution 242 of 22 November 1967," United Nations Security Council Resolutions, http://www.un.org/documents/sc/res/1967/scres67.htm.
53. "Resolution 242 of 22 November 1967," United Nations Security Council Resolutions, http://www.un.org/documents/sc/res/1967/scres67.htm.
54. Syria and the PLO accepted UN resolution 242 in 1973 and in 1988, respectively.
55. For details on the early settlement activities, see Gershom Gorenberg, *The Accidental Empire: Israel and the Birth of the Settlements, 1967–1977* (New York: Times Books, 2006). See also, Meron Benvenisti, *The West Bank Data Project: A Survey of Israel's Policies* (Washington, DC: American Enterprise Institute for Public Policy Research, 1984). For an official Israeli list of all settlements, the dates of establishment, and population size, see, http://www.cbs.gov.il/population/localities/localbycode2004.xls. For a list prepared by the Foundation for Middle East Peace, see, http://www.fmep.org/settlement_info/settlement-info-and-tables/stats-data/comprehensive-settlement-population-1972-2006.
56. Oren, *Six Days of War*, 102.
57. Shlaim, *The Iron Wall*, 251.
58. "Resolutions and Final Declaration of First Arab Summit, Cairo, 13–17 January 1964." League of Arab States.
59. Mohamed Heikal, "The Arab Weapon," *Al Ahram*, July 20, 1962; Mohamed Heikal,"The Danger that Hovers over the Middle East," *Al Ahram*, August 20, 1965; and Mohamed Heikal, "The Changing Circumstances," *Al Ahram*, October 15, 1965.
60. Mohamed Heikal, "The Bomb," BeSraha [Frankly] Collection, *Al Ahram*, November 23, 1973.
61. *Ibid.*
62. "Interview with General Mohamed Fawzy," *Al-Ahram* Weekly On-Line, June 5–12, 1997, No. 328, Supplement, http://weekly.ahram.org.eg/archives/67-97/sup8.htm.
63. "Egypt Will Fight, Nasser Shouts," *Pittsburgh-Post Gazette*, November 24, 1967, Google News http://news.google.com/newspapers?nid=1129&dat=19671124&id=iy4NAAAAIBAJ&sjid=mmwDAAAAIBAJ&pg=7156,4781952. For the full text in Arabic, see: "The address by President Gamal Abdel Nasser at the opening of the 5th session of the National Assembly," Nasser.bibalex.org, http://nasser.bibalex.org/Speeches/browser.aspx?SID=1224&lang=en.

64. For more information on the Jordanian narrative of the entire period leading up to the 1967 war, see: Hussein Ibn Talal, *My "War" with Israel* (London: Peter Owen, 1969), 34–56; and Saad Juma'a, *al Mu'amara wa Ma'rakat al Maseer* [*Conspiracy and the Battle of Destiny*] (Beirut: Dar al Kateb an Arabi, 1968), 171 [In Arabic].
65. Smith, *Palestine and the Arab–Israeli Conflict*, 237.
66. Rabil, *Embattled Neighbors*, 16.
67. Itamar Rabinovich, *Syria Under the Ba'th, 1963–1966: The Army–Party Symbiosis* (Jerusalem: Israel Universities Press, 1972) 84–100
68. Rabil, *Embattled Neighbors*, 18.
69. In May 1965, at the Palestinian National Conference in Cairo, Syrian Ba'thists accused Nasser of hiding behind UNEF in Sinai since 1957. These same detractors additionally focused their attacks on Hussein; one of the goals of the Syrian decision to back Fatah was to stimulate opposition to Hussein; Smith, *Palestine and the Arab–Israeli Conflict*, 277–279.
70. Syrians are said to have attributed to Egypt the notion that "Palestinian nationalism could destabilize the ceasefire with Israel and jeopardize Egyptian security if left unchecked and uncontained." See Yezid Sayigh, "Escalation or Containment? Egypt and the Palestine Liberation Army, 1964–67," *International Journal of Middle East Studies*, 30, 1 (February 1998), 97–116, 99. [Rabil, *Embattled Neighbors*, quotes Sayigh on p. 17]
71. Seale, *Asad*, 120:

> Outgunned in the field, outvoted at the United Nations, the Syrian government began to trumpet a new if somewhat unrealistic doctrine: it would no longer waste time at the Security Council but would respond to every Israeli move by striking at targets inside that country. In addition, inspired by the examples of Algeria and Vietnam, it proclaimed its confidence in a "people's liberation war," as Damascus Radio put it: "Arab Damascus is no less heroic than Hanoi."

72. The UNSC and the UNTSO condemned this attack in UN Security Council Resolution 111, January 19, 1956.
73. Extraordinary Regional Congress of March 10–27, 1966, "We have to risk the destruction of all we have built up in order to eliminate Israel." Abraham Ben-Tzur (ed.), *The Syrian Baath Party and Israel: Documents from the Internal Party Publications* (Givat Haviva: Center for Arab and Afro-Asian Studies, 1968), 4.
74. Sayigh "Escalation or Containment?" 99, quoted in Rabil, *Embattled Neighbors*.
75. Smith, *Palestine and the Arab–Israeli Conflict*, 279 citing Robert Stephens, *Nasser, A Political Biography* (London: Penguin Series, Political Leaders of the Twentieth Century, 1973), 461.
76. "...whereas for Asad the war had proved that the Palestinians could not be allowed to freewheel as they pleased: their raids had played into the Israeli's hands, giving it pretext to threaten Syria and suck Egypt into the crisis." Seale, *Asad*, 144–145. Syria refused to attend the Khartoum Conference in September 1967 because even a diplomatic rejection of Israel was to legitimate diplomatic means of addressing Israel; the Syrian narrative maintained that the only solution was violent confrontation. It is for this exact reason that Syria rejected UNSC Resolution 242. See Rabil, *Embattled Neighbors*, 19.
77. *Ibid.*, 143.
78. Seale, *Asad*, 42–45.
79. Thus, Assad is said to have argued that the Syrian military "was a poorly trained, under-officered force...which had been equipped...with weapons being phased out of the Red Army...[Syria's]

greatest weakness lay in the fractured officer corps crippled by the great purge... in the wake of the military conspiracies of late 1966." *Ibid.*, 115–117.

80. Haykal, *Infijar 1967*, 212 [In Arabic]
81. Seale, *Asad*, 144.
82. Murad Ghalib, *Ma' 'Abdel Nasser wa-Al Sadat: Sanawat al-Intisar wa-Ayyam al-Mihan, Muthakirat Murad Ghalib [With Abdel Nasser and Sadat: the Years of Victory and the Days of Adversity, Memoirs of Murad Ghalib]* (Cairo: Markaz al-Ahram lil-Tarjamah wa-al-Nashr, 2001), 104–105 [In Arabic].
83. Shlaim, *The Iron Wall*, 228–229; Serge Schmemann, "General's Words Shed a New Light on the Golan," *New York Times*, May 11, 1997.
84. Shlaim, *The Iron Wall*, 233–237.
85. Samir A. Mutawi, *Jordan in the 1967 War* (Cambridge: Cambridge University Press, 2002). Army Commander-in-Chief General Sharif Zaid Ben Shaker warned in a press conference that "If Jordan does not join the war a civil war will erupt in Jordan," quoted in Mutawi, 102. Hussein's biographer Nigel Ashton argues that the King was confronted by the "choice between accepting the embrace of Arabism and accepting the embrace of Israel." Nigel Ashton, *King Hussein of Jordan: A Political Life* (New Haven: Yale University Press, 2008). Avi Shlaim notes that "Hussein went to war not because he was threatened by Israel but because he feared that he would be denounced as a traitor to the Arab cause if he did not." Avi Shlaim, *Lion of Jordan: The Life of King Hussein in War and Peace* (New York: Alfred A. Knopf, 2008).
86. Smith, *Palestine and the Arab–Israeli Conflict*, 284; Brecher and Geist, *Decision in Crisis*, 280–281; Michael Oren, *Six Days of War*, 278–279.
87. Abdel Magid Farid, *Nasser: The Final Years* (Ithaca, NY: Ithaca Press, 1996).
88. "The three-year war: Interview with General Mohamed Fawzi," *Al Ahram Weekly Online*, no. 1107, 19–25 July 2012, http://weekly.ahram.org.eg/2012/1107/sc3.htm
89. *Ibid.*
90. The later testimony of General Fawzy regarding this point is telling:

    At this point, I can assert, looking back 30 years after the battle took place, that we were doomed to lose before a single shot was fired. It was not the best time for Egypt to fight, and the situation was aggravated by the total discord between the political and military leaderships. The military leadership had separated itself from the constitutional organization of the state, a situation that could lead to nothing but failure. The proof is that the battle was fought by one side only: Israel. A staggering seventy five per cent of Egypt's ground forces did not even see the enemy, let alone engage in combat. The death toll among the Egyptian forces was only 10,000 men: 1,000 died in confrontations in Rafah and Gaza, and 9,000 were victims of the "wrong and arbitrary decision of one man." *Ibid.*

5 From Limited War to Limited Accommodation

This chapter spans some of the most violent struggles between Arabs and Israelis – from the 1969–70 War of Attrition, the October 1973 War, and the Palestinian–Israeli violence of the early 1970s – as well as intra-Arab violence in the form of Black September (1970) – to the beginning of accommodation between the Arab states and Israel: the signing of the disengagement agreements between Israel and Egypt and between Israel and Syria, and the beginning of the Palestinians' shift to pragmatism.

During this period the international environment was marked by the beginning of "détente" – a relaxation of Cold War tensions between the United States and the Soviet Union, the introduction of some forms of cooperation between the two, and, more generally, various efforts to prevent escalation of national and regional disputes to superpower confrontations.

At the same time, this period experienced a peak in Cold War tensions in the Middle East – tensions that were also manifested in the relations between the United States and the Soviet Union and their regional allies. During this period, key Arab countries, while remaining part of the Non-Aligned Movement, signed "treaties of friendship" with the Soviet Union. Similarly, this period witnessed the first steps in the eventual elevation of American–Israeli relations to the level of a strategic partnership.

The intensification of superpower rivalry in the Middle East was also manifested during this period in the regional arms race. Beginning in the late 1960s and certainly during the early 1970s, the United States and the Soviet Union began supplying their clients with ever-greater quantities of more advanced weapons. No less important, however, were the changes that had taken place during this period at the regional level. There, the most important development was the ending of the Arab Cold War. The civil war in Yemen – the most violent manifestation of this struggle – was brought to an end and, as a result of the resolutions adopted by the Arab summit in Khartoum, money began to flow from some of the oil-rich conservative states to Syria and Egypt.

In the Arab–Israeli arena, while the conflict witnessed some of the deadliest wars, it was now transformed from an existential to a non-existential one, as the focus of Arab efforts shifted from preventing the emergence of Israel or reversing its establishment to a dispute with the Jewish state about boundaries and future relations. This change was accompanied by a similar, although much more subtle strategic change among Palestinians.

Internally, within the region's main actors, this was also a period of dramatic change. In different states and in different ways, societies in the region now abandoned long-held beliefs which were increasingly regarded as illusions. Among Arab publics, revolutionary ideas were discredited as these countries' intellectual elites increasingly abandoned Marxist and socialist thought. In their stead, a number of trends emerged: state-centric forces that prioriotized the domestic economy and the social wellbeing of the population. This was clearly the case with Sadat's Egypt.

Another trend in the region, and especially in Egypt, during this period was the turn to Islam for solutions to the lingering social, economic, and political problems. Indeed, political Islam now seemed to be filling the gap created by the decline of the Pan-Arab and Nasserite ideologies, one of the most important socio-political effects of the Arab defeat in 1967.

The period addressed in this chapter ends with the implementation of the disengagement agreements which comprised the first step towards transforming the Arab–Israeli conflict from an existential conflict to a non-existential one. Moreover, it also marked a change in the approach towards diplomacy in the region: from the comprehensive approach expressed in UNSC Resolutions 242 and 338 to a step-by-step approach adopted by Henry Kissinger; and from diplomacy based on a collective approach to one based on dealing with each front separately. Finally, this period witnessed a shift from a Soviet Union–United States–UN-led multilateral approach to an American-dominated process.

Main Developments

The main developments addressed in this chapter span two international wars and a civil war in Jordan. Also experienced were the opening moves of what would later be called "the peace process." For the Palestinians this period was characterized not only by the bloodbath of September 1970 but also by the ascent of Fatah and, later, the first signs of pragmatism.

The War of Attrition

On November 23, 1967, a day after UN Resolution 242 was adopted, Secretary General U Thant nominated a Swedish diplomat, Dr. Gunnar Jarring, to mediate its implementation. However, as shown in the previous chapter, Jarring failed in his efforts to negotiate a compromise between the Israeli and Arab competing approaches to peace. The failure of diplomacy led to the second important development in Arab–Israeli relations during this period: the Egypt–Israel War of Attrition. Egyptian accounts see the war as having begun in September 1968,[1] whereas Israeli accounts refer to the months following September as characterized by sporadic fire and specify the war as having actually begun in March 1969.[2] The war ended in August 1970 when both parties accepted a ceasefire. It took a considerable toll on both sides: some 500 Israelis were killed and around 2,000 were wounded between 1967 and 1970.[3] Egyptian casualties were much higher: an estimated 10,000 civilians and military personnel were killed.[4]

From the outset, the war also had a civilian dimension: in response to Israel's attacks on civilian targets, particularly the Suez oil refineries, and in order to avoid even greater civilian casualties, Egypt evacuated the residents of the Canal cities – Port Said, Ismailiya, and Suez – to more sheltered locations, thus resulting in the displacement of between a million and a million and a half citizens.[5]

In July 1969 Israel took two measures: the first of these was the construction of a line of fortifications along the Suez Canal. These fortifications, which came to be known as the Bar-Lev Line – named after then IDF Chief of Staff, Lieutenant General Haim Bar-Lev – were designed to reduce the vulnerability of Israeli troops stationed on the Sinai side of the Suez Canal to Egyptian artillery fire.

Another Israeli measure, designed to compel Egypt to end the fighting, comprised the use of airpower in an attempt to take the war deep inside Egypt, by bombing the latter's industrial base and other infrastructure targets. The general policy of bombings was intended to establish "escalation dominance" – to demonstrate Israel's capacity to respond to any increased intensity of the war by escalating the fighting even further, thus extracting from Egypt higher costs.

Egypt responded to the IAF's capacity to penetrate its airspace by inviting the Soviets to play a more active role in the country's defense. This included the deployment of two types of Red Army units: first, air force fighter squadrons that immediately began patrolling Egypt's airspace, sometimes engaging IAF pilots in an attempt to dissuade Israel from continuing its deep penetration bombing. And second, the deployment of an air defense division equipped with an array of mobile anti-aircraft guns and missiles capable of shooting down Israeli combat aircraft.

Post-War Diplomacy

While diplomatic efforts to resolve the Arab–Israeli conflict prior to the War of Attrition had been led by the UN, the war ushered in an era of diplomacy led by the United States. These efforts began modestly with a proposal submitted to Egypt and Israel on June 25, 1970 by Secretary of State William Rogers. The Rogers Plan, a version of which was announced the previous December and immediately rejected by both the Soviet Union and Israel, called for the two adversaries to implement a three-month ceasefire, allowing the Suez Canal to be dredged and cleared of ships stuck there since June 1967. During the ceasefire, both sides were to adhere to a "standstill" by refraining from advancing forces and weapons in the Canal Zone. The dormant Jarring Mission was to be revived, and Israel was to commit to withdrawing from "occupied territories" in exchange for Egyptian and Jordanian commitments to live in peace with Israel.

On July 23, in a speech marking the 18th anniversary of the Revolution, President Nasser accepted the Rogers Plan. One reason for this may have been that the Egyptian army needed a breather to allow the completion of the air defense system which it was constructing along the Suez Canal.[6]

To obtain Israel's consent, the United States assured its government that: (a) It would not insist that Israel accept the Arab interpretation of Resolution 242, according to which Israel was required to relinquish *all* territories it conquered in the 1967 War; (b) Israel would not be forced to accept a settlement of the Palestinian refugee problem that would fundamentally alter the Jewish character of the state or jeopardize its security; and (c) Israel would not be asked to withdraw any of its troops "until a binding contractual peace agreement satisfactory to [Israel] has been achieved."[7] Following these assurances, a ceasefire between Egypt and Israel came into effect on August 8, 1970.

Fatah's Ascent and Black September

Meanwhile, against the background of the Arab defeat in 1967 and the acceptance by an increasing number of Arab states of UN Resolution 242 and the Jarring Mission, a major change in strategy took place on the Palestinian side. The Palestinians shifted from attempts to ignite a "catalytic war" – that is, action which would embroil the Arab states in a war against Israel – to a focus on consolidating their position in Jordan, in the hope of using it as a base for conducting a border war with Israel. This hope was inspired especially by the March 21, 1968 Battle of Karamah, during which Palestinian guerrilla forces and the Jordanian 1st Infantry Division deployed on the mountain ridge overlooking the Jordan Valley, succeeded in resisting the attacking IDF forces and in extracting from them substantial costs: 28 dead and 90 wounded.[8] As a result, thousands of Palestinians flocked to Fatah, the largest group taking part in the battle. Its leader, Yasser Arafat now achieved fame and emerged as a national hero, as Palestinians increasingly came to believe in the efficacy of violence and the relevance of guerrilla warfare.

Banking on this success, Fatah now moved to gain direct control over the PLO which, in the eyes of many Palestinians, had been discredited as a tool of the Arab regimes that lost the 1967 War. By February 1969 Fatah had overcome the resistance of the PLO's leadership, gaining a majority of the seats in the Palestinian National Council (PNC). Arafat, its leader, was now elected PLO Chairman.

While in 1969–70 Fatah gradually established its primacy within the PLO, its ability to control the Palestinian agenda was now challenged by another movement – the Popular Front for the Liberation of Palestine (PFLP). Moreover, the growth in the ranks of Palestinian guerrilla groups in the aftermath of the Battle of Karamah led some Palestinians to believe that they were becoming strong enough to challenge Jordan's King Hussein, that the Jordanian army would not be ordered to attack the guerrilla groups, and that it would refrain from doing so even if ordered to attack. Thus, a fragmented PLO found itself in conflict with its environment as the Palestinians, in attempting to use Jordan as a launching pad for war against Israel, now showed insensitivity to Jordan's priorities. As a result, the Hashemites now saw the Palestinians as threatening the survival of their kingdom.

In September 1970 the Jordanian army reacted to these developments – a turning-point that has since become known as Black September. Within the next ten months, the army destroyed all Palestinian guerrilla groups in Jordan.[9] Syria – led by President Salah Jadid – initially intervened to support the guerrillas and some of its units crossed its border with Jordan. However, following an explicit request of the Nixon administration, IDF units were deployed in the north, forcing Syria to abort its attack.

After their defeat and expulsion from Jordan, Palestinian guerrilla groups moved their political and military bases to Lebanon. Now, Fatah, too, entered the international terrorism fray. Elements within the organization established an underground group that came to be known as Black September to carry out terrorist attacks against Jordanian, Israeli and international targets. These attacks included the assassination of Jordan's Prime Minister Wasfi al-Tal in Cairo in late November 1970, the hijacking of aircraft (such as a Sabena passenger plane to Lod Airport in May 1972) and the attack on Israeli athletes at the Munich Olympics in September 1972. The Soviet Union now became the Palestinians' main external backer and some of the agencies of its satellite states, notably the East German security services, provided support and training to Palestinian guerrilla groups.

Following the PLO's expulsion, Jordan's King Hussein sought to reassert his country's authority over the West Bank. On March 15, 1972, he announced plans to create a United Arab Kingdom joining the East and West Banks of the Jordan River.[10] The two regions – to be known as Jordan and Palestine, respectively – would form a federation under the king's control. The PLO and most Arab countries rejected Hussein's plan.

Syria Changes Course

The abortion of Syria's September 1970 attack on Jordan was also propelled by the refusal of Hafez Assad, Syria's then defense minister, to provide the invading ground forces with close air support. The message implied by Assad's refusal was that President Salah Jadid could not lead Syria into war without the consent of the military. Not only did Assad point out that he alone could provide such consent, he soon used his influence to take control of the government. On November 13, 1970 he led a bloodless coup to oust Jadid.[11]

In turn, this led to a shift in Syrian Ba'athist policy away from a radical orientation and toward a pragmatic approach. Assad's government focused on two goals: gaining Arab unity and preparing for war with Israel by strengthening Syria's militarily through reviving its relations with the Soviet Union.[12]

Assad began focusing on national defense policies implemented by state institutions in cooperation with other Arab states. He now asserted Syria's control of Palestinian militant groups located in Syria and refused to allow the guerilla forces to use Syrian territory to launch attacks into Israel. Indeed he regarded these forces as a liability: their sporadic, small-scale attacks could not produce any significant gains but could draw costly Israeli retaliation against Syria.

Anwar Sadat Becomes President

President Nasser died of natural causes on September 28, 1970, and was succeeded by Anwar el-Sadat. In the following two years Egypt's new president took three important steps: in February 1971 he offered Israel a 30-day ceasefire during which Egypt would reopen the Suez Canal and Israel would conduct a partial withdrawal in the Sinai. Israel's right of passage through the Canal, however, would be linked to a settlement of the Palestinian question. While Israeli Prime Minister Golda Meir rejected the plan, both sides continued to abide by the ceasefire.

Sadat's second step, also in February 1971 was to endorse the Jarring mission.[13] The third and most spectacular of these steps was his move in July 1972 to expel 7,752 Soviet advisors and to close some of their military bases in Egypt.[14]

The 1973 War

The most dramatic development of this era was the 1973 October War. The war began at 2 p.m. on October 6, with a coordinated Egyptian–Syrian surprise attack against Israeli positions along the Suez Canal and a major armored and mechanized assault in the Golan Heights.

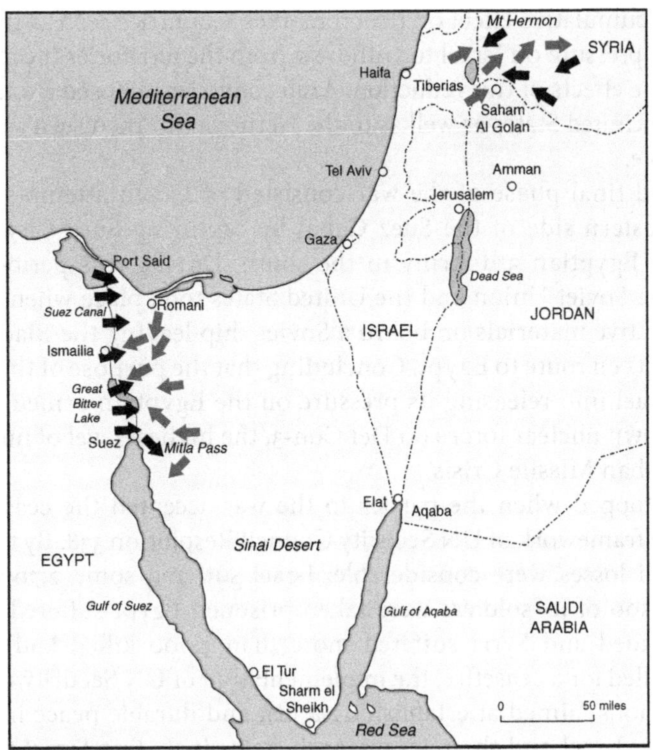

Figure 5.1. The 1973 War

Israel was caught off-guard by an attack that began on Yom Kippur, considered the Jewish religion's holiest holiday. In the first three days of fighting, the Israelis sustained major losses: the Egyptians captured the Bar-Lev Line east of the Suez Canal, and the Syrians pushed far into the Golan Heights, as deep as Nafah, the main IDF base on the Golan, and captured Mount Hermon.[15] On October 8, an Israeli counterattack in the south, conducted along a north–south axis parallel to the Suez Canal, failed.

During the second phase of the war Israel focused its efforts on the Syrian front. Beginning October 9 and continuing through the 14th, the IDF succeeded in pushing the Syrian army beyond the June 11, 1967 ceasefire lines, halting less than 30 miles from Damascus.

The war's third phase began on October 14, when the Egyptian army attempted a major assault into the Sinai, outside the envelope of its air defense system. The attack failed, resulting in Egyptian armor suffering heavy losses. The following day, the first IDF units crossed the Suez Canal and a major battle raged northeast of the crossing point.

It was during this third phase of the war that Arab states announced the imposition of an oil embargo, targeting Western countries which were seen as supporting Israel. On October 17, the oil ministers of the United Arab Emirates, Bahrain, Algeria, Saudi Arabia, Syria, Qatar, Kuwait, and Libya – members of OAPEC (Organization of Arab Petroleum Exporting Countries) – agreed to reduce their oil production by 5 percent each month, thus creating a robust cumulative effect on the oil market. Countries seen as supporting the Arab side or as putting pressure on Israel to withdraw from the territories it captured in 1967 were exempted from the effects of this reduction. Arab countries imposed a total boycott of direct oil exports to the United States as well as to the Netherlands, then seen as having adhered to a pro-Israeli stance.

The fourth and final phase of the war consisted of Israeli attempts to consolidate its hold over the western side of the Suez Canal by capturing Suez City in the north and surrounding the Egyptian 3rd Army in the south. During this period a major nuclear crisis between the Soviet Union and the United States took place when American sensors identified radioactive materials on board a Soviet ship leaving the Black Sea through the Dardanelles Straits en route to Egypt. Concluding that the purpose of the nuclear shipment was to coerce Israel into releasing its pressure on the Egyptian armed forces, the United States placed its own nuclear forces on Def Con-3, the highest level of nuclear alert applied since the 1962 Cuban Missile Crisis.

The fighting stopped when the parties to the war accepted the ceasefire proposed on October 22 in the framework of UN Security Council Resolution 338. By that time, Egyptian, Syrian and Israeli losses were considerable: Israel suffered some 2,700 killed and 8,800 wounded. Some 500 of its soldiers were taken prisoner. Egypt suffered some 5,000 killed and 12,000 wounded and Syria suffered more than 3,000 killed and 6,000 wounded.[16] Resolution 338 called for a ceasefire, the implementation of UN Security Council Resolution 242, and negotiations "aimed at establishing a just and durable peace in the Middle East." It was accepted by Israel and the relevant Arab states including Syria, which had rejected UNSC Resolution 242 when it was first adopted in 1967.

UNITED NATIONS SECURITY COUNCIL RESOLUTION 338

October 22, 1973
The Security Council,
Calls upon all parties to present fighting to cease all firing and terminate all military activity immediately, no later than 12 hours after the moment of the adoption of this decision, in the positions after the moment of the adoption of this decision, in the positions they now occupy;

Calls upon all parties concerned to start immediately after the ceasefire the implementation of Security Council Resolution 242 (1967) in all of its parts;

Decides that, immediately and concurrently with the ceasefire, negotiations start between the parties concerned under appropriate auspices aimed at establishing a just and durable peace in the Middle East.

The War's Aftermath

A number of developments in the immediate aftermath of the war later proved to have paved the road to an Arab–Israeli peace process: the first was the visit to the area of Secretary of State Henry Kissinger, beginning on November 6, 1973. The visit led to the launching of direct Israeli–Egyptian talks at km 101 on the Cairo–Suez Road. The talks were aimed at insuring that both sides respect the cease-fire and that Israel would allow non-military supplies to reach the surrounded city of Suez and the encircled Egyptian 3rd Army. Israel was also to withdraw its forces to the positions they held on October 22, when the ceasefire it accepted was declared.

A second development was the convening of the Geneva Conference for Peace in the Middle East on December 21, 1973. The purpose of the conference was to reach separation of forces agreements between Egypt and Israel and between Syria and Israel, as well as to negotiate the implementation of the UNSC Resolutions 242 and 338 calling for Arab–Israeli peace. The conference, attended by Egypt, Jordan, and Israel, but with Syria absent, failed to achieve any of its stated goals.

The third important development was the signing of the first Egyptian–Israeli disengagement agreement on January 18, 1974. The agreement stipulated the withdrawal of Israeli forces to a line a few kilometers east of the Suez Canal.

The 1973 War was also followed by an Israeli–Syrian mini-war of attrition that finally led Kissinger on April 30, 1974 to launch another round of shuttle diplomacy. His success resulted in the fourth development: a Syrian–Israeli disengagement agreement signed on May 30. In its framework, Israel ceded all Syrian territories captured in the 1973 War as well as areas just below the town of Qunaitra. In exchange, Syria privately agreed to prevent Palestinian militants from using Syrian territory to attack Israel. Another result of the agreement was the decision of OAPEC to lift the oil embargo.[17]

Finally, having stabilized the Syrian–Israeli front, in 1975 Kissinger shifted his efforts once again to Egypt. In February and March he embarked upon another set of shuttles. The difficult negotiations reached an impasse, leading Kissinger to threaten Israel with a reassessment of American policy in the Middle East. On June 5, 1975 Israel and Egypt reached a partial agreement under which Egypt opened the Suez Canal to international navigation, and Israel reduced the size of its forces positioned west of the Mitla and Gidi passes in the Sinai. This led Kissinger to resume his shuttles on August 20, resulting in the fifth important development of this period: the signing of the Second Disengagement Agreement on September 1, 1975. The agreement stipulated further Israeli withdrawals to the Sinai passes, the establishment of an early warning system, the deployment of a UN monitoring force, and the passage of non-military goods through the Suez Canal. The two countries also agreed that their dispute would be resolved solely by peaceful means and that both parties "consider the agreement an important step towards a permanent and just peace."

On the Palestinian Front

The 1973 War was followed by the decision of the Palestinian National Council (PNC) in June 1974 to adopt the Provisional Program – also known as the "10 point program" or the "Phases Program" – calling for the first time for the establishment of a National Authority on any territories vacated by Israel. Another important post-war development was the decision of the October 1974 Rabat Summit to recognize the PLO as "the sole representative of the Palestinian people."

Figure 5.2. Arafat addressing the UN General Assembly (13 November 1974). *Source*: United Nations Photo Library.

The adoption of the Provisional Program was motivated by the PLO's desire to join the political process and participate in the 1973 Geneva Conference. Secret contacts with the United States indicated that Washington viewed the question of who would represent the Palestinians – Jordan or the PLO – as an "inter-Arab concern." Under Arab pressure, Jordan, which had initially opposed the Arab summit resolution to recognize the PLO, went along.

The adoption of the Provisional Program prompted several major PLO factions, such as the PFLP, DFLP, and PFLP-General Command, to walk out and form the so-called "Rejectionist Front" or the "Front for the Palestinian Forces Rejecting Solutions of Surrender."[18] But on November 13 Arafat was invited to address the UN General Assembly, where the PLO received the status of an "observer." Within the next few weeks, the PLO won further recognition by the members of the Non-Aligned Movement, the Soviet bloc and other socialist countries.[19]

Soon after the 1967 War, Palestinian access to land and water resources was affected by measures taken by Israel. A series of military orders ensured Israeli control over all Palestinian water resources and restricted Palestinian ability to dig water wells without permission from the Israeli military government.[20] The military government issued very few permits during the 1960s and 1970s. Israel also monopolized the waters of the Jordan River by preventing Palestinians from physically reaching it, declaring it a closed military zone. It also destroyed all Palestinian pumps on the river, evicted farmers working in that area, and confiscated their cultivated land.

Similarly, confiscation of Palestinian land for security and other reasons and the construction of Israeli settlements and related infrastructure had a direct impact on Palestinian land and water resources, considerably reducing the areas available to Palestinian agriculture and to grazing for livestock. Israeli agricultural settlements in the Jordan Valley deprived Palestinians of their richest soil and wells. A similar situation developed in the Gaza Strip. While in 1967 Palestinians cultivated about 2,300 sq. km in the West Bank and the Gaza Strip, the figure dropped gradually to less than 2,000 sq. km by the mid-1980s. The contribution of agriculture to the Gross Domestic Product of the West Bank and Gaza Strip continued to decline. Employment in the agricultural sector continued to decline year after year, dropping from 43 percent of total employment to 24 percent by the mid-1980s.[21]

Israeli settlement activities in the West Bank during this period were guided by the Allon Plan. In line with this plan, Israeli Labor governments created about 20 settlements along the Jordan Valley and eastern slopes of the West Bank, an area not densely populated by Palestinians, and avoided construction on the mountain ridge where the majority of

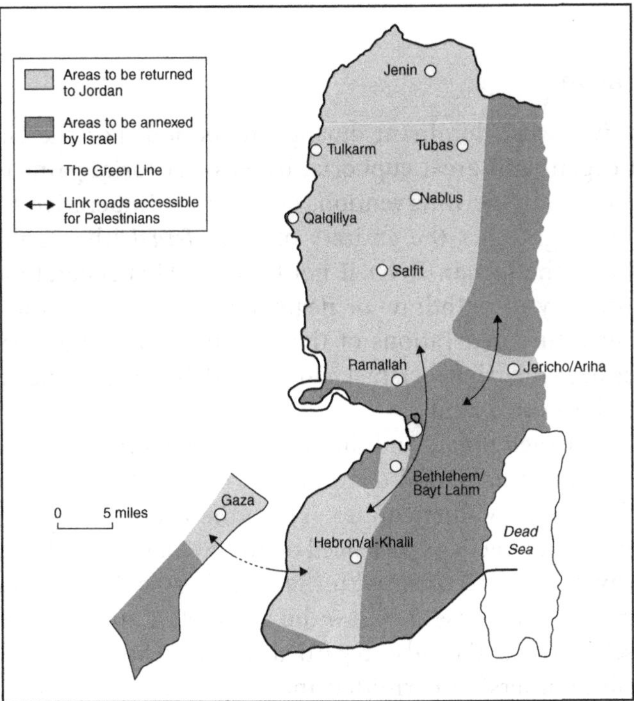

Figure 5.3. A map of the Allon Plan

Palestinians lived. The Allon Plan proposed that Israel would relinquish the main Arab-populated areas of the West Bank to Jordan while retaining the Jordan Valley under Israeli military control. The Plan also indicated that Israel needed to control the road connecting Jerusalem to the Dead Sea, as well as a widened Jerusalem corridor west of Ramallah, and stressed the importance of Greater Jerusalem. By 1976, there were 4,400 settlers in 20 settlements in the West Bank. Earlier, in 1973 the Israeli government established the settlement of Kfar Darom in an area of the Gaza Strip where a settlement of a similar name existed before 1948.

In 1973 the movement of *Gush Emunim* (Bloc of the Faithful), an ideological, religious–nationalist group originally associated with the National Religious Party (NRP), was formed. The movement's goal was to initiate settlement in areas exempted from such activity by the Allon Plan, such as the populated areas of the West Bank mountain ridge. In 1975 the first such settlement, Kadumim, was established to the north of one of the largest Palestinian cities, Nablus in the northern part of the West Bank. Ofra, near Ramallah, was also established by this group around the same time. Other religiously oriented settlements were established or expanded during this period, including Kiryat Arba adjacent to another large Palestinian city, Hebron in the southern West Bank. Several new Jewish neighborhoods were established during this period in East Jerusalem, including the French Hill, Ramot, Neve Yaakov, and Gilo. Settlements were also built in the Sinai, including the town of Yamit, and in the Golan Heights, where 14 new settlements were established by 1976.[22]

Narratives

The Israeli Narrative

Two Israeli narratives were dominant during this period. For the Israeli ideological and religious right, it began with great euphoria. Israel's territorial gains in the 1967 War were seen as resulting from divine intervention, creating an imperative to materialize Israel's biblical and historic right over the entirety of *Eretz Israel* [the Land of Israel]: from the Mediterranean Sea to the Jordan River if not beyond. This generation, it was said, lacked the right and legitimacy to withdraw or negotiate away parts of the Land of Israel since this would commit future generations of the Jewish people who currently had no say in such a momentous decision. Hence, Israel had a moral, historical, and religious obligation to maintain its control over this land.

For the bulk of the Israeli public and the center of its political spectrum, however, Israel's narrative during most of this period continued to be based not on the country's post-1967 strengths but rather on its vulnerabilities. Thus, the acute sense of danger – the fear of physical extinction – that Israelis experienced on the eve of the 1967 War, now propelled them to demand that any peace agreement with the neighboring Arab states provide Israel with "defensible borders." And because they saw the preemptive strike Israel launched on June 5, 1967 as a war of self-defense, they also regarded the acquisition of territory associated with obtaining "defensible borders" as permitted and fully legitimate under international law.

The top priority now ascribed to Israel's new security doctrine of "defensible borders" was reflected in a statement made by Defense Minister Dayan during this period. Referring to Egypt's closing of the Straits of Tiran in May 1967, thus blocking navigation to Israel's port of Eilat and thereby cutting-off its maritime connection to Asia, Dayan said that "it is better to have Sharm el-Sheik without peace than to have peace without Sharm el-Sheik."[23]

By contrast, the Allon Plan was never formally adopted by the Israeli government, although Israelis regarded it as expressing their country's quest for security. And since during this period the Israeli mainstream saw the justification of retaining territories acquired in the 1967 War exclusively in security terms, they also accepted a policy of constructing Israeli settlements in the West Bank and Gaza as justified only by the need to create "facts on the ground." Such "facts" were seen as designed to make it difficult to compel Israel to withdraw from these territories except in the context of a peace agreement which would provide Israel with "secure and recognized boundaries." For this reason, Israeli mainstream opinion during this period opposed the construction of settlements in heavily populated areas of the West Bank – that is, in areas the retention of which could not be justified on security grounds.

Israeli Views of the Palestinians

Interestingly, the Israeli narrative during this period did not ascribe hostility to the Palestinians, especially those residing in the territories Israel had acquired in the 1967 War: Gaza, the West Bank and East Jerusalem. by contrast, the PLO, seen as representing mostly the Palestinians in the Diaspora, was viewed as a murderous terrorist organization, uncompromising in its hatred and determined to destroy the Jewish state.

Not surprisingly, when in June 1974 the Palestinian National Council adopted the Provisional Program – declaring its willingness to establish a "national authority" on any territory that Israel would vacate, Israelis interpreted this as a tactical, rather than a strategic, change. In Israeli eyes, the change did not represent recognition of Israel's permanence. Instead, it represented acknowledgement that Israel's strength precluded its destruction in a single master-stroke, and that the destruction of the Jewish state could only be achieved piecemeal – that is, in a phased process, referred to by Israelis as "salami tactics."

Thus, the PLO's acceptance of independent statehood for parts of historic Palestine was not viewed by Israelis as implying increased pragmatism. Indeed, what characterized the Israeli narrative of this period was the almost wall-to-wall total rejection of independent Palestinian statehood. Sandwiched between Israel and Jordan, it was argued, a Palestinian state could not be made viable. Consequently, it would project irredentist pressures on Israel and Jordan, endangering both. Instead, during this period Israelis preferred the "Jordanian option" – some solution to the Palestinian issue to be reached in conjunction with Jordan.

By contrast to their view of the PLO, Israelis saw the Palestinians residing in Gaza, the West Bank and East Jerusalem as focused on improving their personal wellbeing. This, it was argued, also applied to Muslim religious groups who were seen as concentrating on providing social services and developing charities to provide these services as well as cultural activities aimed at self-improvement. It was the nationalist-secular forces, seeking to ignite a guerrilla war against Israel, who were seen as presenting a common challenge to the Jewish state as well as to the Palestinian offspring of the Muslim Brotherhood.

Accommodation with the Palestinians in the territories was viewed by Israelis during this period as possible – an assessment based on the assumption that these Palestinians would be happy to tie their economic future to Israel and to find their political expression in Jordan. This, mainstream Israelis believed, could be achieved either by the "Jordanian Option" or by sharing the different functions of governance with the Palestinians and Jordan (the "functional solution").

The War of Attrition and the 1973 War

The Israeli mainstream read neither the 1970 War of Attrition nor the 1973 War as "wars of choice." Quite the contrary, the War of Attrition was seen as an Egyptian attempt to undo the results of the 1967 War without addressing what Israelis saw as the causes of the war: Arab refusal to accept Israel and its right to secure and defensible borders. Since this hostility was assessed as constant, most Israelis viewed the War of Attrition with some relief: if Israel was condemned to fight the Arabs, the post-1967 territorial distribution at least enabled Israel to fight far away from the country's center core. Israelis felt that at least they no longer had to fear that their country would be sliced in two by an invading Arab force which would exploit its pre-1967 narrow waistline. Instead, they could now fight a war without their civilian population falling under mortal danger and without their economy being crippled. Only a minority in Israel regarded the territories captured in the 1967 War as a potential liability and questioned the justification for fighting along the Suez Canal, so far from home.

The two significant internal debates that did take place between the wars of 1970 and 1973 were whether Israel should accept Sadat's proposal requiring a limited Israeli withdrawal from the Suez Canal, and whether Israel should not opt for mobile defense in the depth of Sinai instead of static defense along the Suez Canal. However, these were confined to a small number of individuals at the top of Israel's defense community and political leadership. Most Israelis accepted the proposition that any withdrawal from the Canal other than in the context of a peace agreement would be interpreted by Israel's adversaries as a sign of weakness, thus undermining its future capacity to trade its newly-acquired territorial assets for peace.

For this reason, the Israeli narrative of the 1973 War did not focus on the justification for the war. It was seen as having been forced upon Israel, leaving it no choice but to defend itself, with whatever means were available. While the war was followed by a period of unprecedented questioning and self-criticism – expressed in the appearance of a mass protest movement – the focus of such questioning was not whether Israel's "all or nothing" approach in the aftermath of the 1967 War contributed to the 1973 debacle. Instead, it focused on the extent to which the total strategic surprise that Israel experienced when the war began – with Egypt's crossing of the Canal and Syria's breaking through Israeli defenses on the Golan – resulted from a "dereliction of duty" by Israel's top military and political leaders. The latter were now blamed for the hubris and euphoria that seemed to engulf nearly all members of the Israeli military and political elite in the aftermath of the 1967 triumph. It was this hubris that was said to explain why Israel's top brass underestimated their adversaries to the point of ruling out their capacity to attack. Thus the Israeli narrative focused on the complete strategic surprise suffered at the outset of the war and not on whether or not the war could have been avoided.

Relations with the United States

Israelis developed a narrative of being an increasingly important strategic ally for the United States, and indeed as being of considerable strategic utility – with many referring to it as a "strategic asset." The story comprised a number of elements: first, Soviet-made weapons which Israel captured during the wars of 1967 and 1973 were said to have been provided to the United States for study, thus allowing it to assess the technical properties of weapons with which Warsaw Pact forces were equipped. Second, Israel was said to have supported the American war effort in Vietnam by maintaining a military presence along the Suez Canal, thus closing it to navigation and so hindering the Soviets' capacity to supply the North Vietnamese. Confronting Soviet units deployed in Egypt during the War of Attrition contributed further to Israelis' perceptions that they were at the frontline of the struggle between the free world and the Soviet empire. Third, in September 1970, Israel deployed its forces to the north, thus forcing the Syrians to reduce the pressure they had been placing on the Jordanian Army. This was said to have been done at President Nixon's request – the first clear instance of Israel serving America's strategic interests in the region, in this case, the survival of the Hashemite Kingdom.

The Palestinian Narrative

During this period the Palestinians continued to emphasize the need for self-reliance. This emphasis informed the Palestinian narrative with regard to other key issues, especially the role of violence and the viability of diplomacy.

The Role of Violence

Once "catalytic war" had to be abandoned, seeking more independent decision-making meant that Palestinian violence would now be pursued not in order to spur Arab states into action or to embroil them in escalatory crises with Israel, but rather, to register Palestinian anger and frustration with Israeli policies in the occupied territories as well as with the complacency of the international community and its indifference to Palestinian suffering. This new ethos of violence achieved near-mythical dimensions in the March 1968 Battle of Karamah. The Palestinians' narrative of victory in the battle's aftermath aroused intense pride and gave them a chance to gain the attention of Arabs after decades of negligence.

Now, violence was seen as necessary to draw the attention of the international community to the Palestinian issue. In the eyes of some Palestinians – members of the PFLP and other leftist groups – gaining such attention required that emphasis be placed on what promised to produce the greatest televised dramas: passenger aircraft hijacking and hostage-taking, following the example of the hijacking of five airliners in September 1970. Later, this inspired Fatah to follow suit, most dramatically under the guise of the Black September Organization. On September 5–6, 1972 this group took hostage and eventually killed Israeli athletes taking part in the Munich Olympics.

Palestinian versus Arab Interests

In Palestinian eyes, a clear manifestation of the Arab states' tendency to give priority to their separate national interests over those of the Palestinians occurred in September 1970. Driven by what to most Palestinians seemed an exaggerated Jordanian fear of a Palestinian takeover, King Hussein's security services killed thousands of Palestinians, expelled the PLO leadership, and forced tens of thousands of Palestinians to relocate to Lebanon. Palestinians were dismayed that only a few Arab states condemned Jordan; not for the last time, they felt abandoned by their Arab brethren.

After the 1973 War, the Palestinians became concerned about Arab states' willingness to retake the diplomatic initiative in the light of the Egyptian–Israeli and Syrian–Israeli disengagement agreements, Syria's acceptance of UN Resolutions 242 and 338, and Jordan's reported interest in negotiating the future of the West Bank. These developments confirmed in the Palestinian mind that Arab states could not be relied upon to take care of their interests, and that therefore they – the Palestinians – had no choice but to take matters into their own hands. As Syria and Egypt opted to negotiate their disengagement agreements with Israel, it gradually became clear to Palestinians that they were on their own.

For the Palestinians, these resolutions and initiatives meant not only Arab recognition of Israel's permanence but also a willingness on the part of Arab countries to view their conflict with Israel as a border dispute, with Egypt focused on recovering the Sinai and Syria attempting to recover the Golan Heights. Jordan's position was viewed as even more threatening: it was seen not only as willing to recognize Israel but also as attempting to repossess the West Bank, at the Palestinians' expense. The resulting imperative was that the Palestinians were obliged to acquire what was now defined as "independence of decision" – a capacity to pursue a strategy independent of that of the neighboring Arab states.

Israeli Occupation

The Palestinian narrative regarding Israel underwent an important change during this period as the focus shifted from issues related to 1948 – liberation and return of refugees – and towards issues related to 1967 – Israeli occupation of and policies within the West Bank and Gaza Strip. Israel was seen as rejecting Palestinian nationhood and as wedded to the 1948 view that saw eviction and displacement as the only solution to the Palestinian problem. Annexation of more and more Palestinian land, and the building of more and more Jewish settlements in the newly occupied territories, were viewed as evidence of this mindset. Israel was also seen as continuing to believe that it could ignore Palestinian nationalism, instead dealing exclusively with Arab states, as evidenced by the recurring talk of "the Jordanian Option" and the declared position of Israeli Premier Golda Meir to the effect that there was no such thing as "Palestinians" or a Palestinian national identity.

The diplomatic outcome of the 1973 War – especially the limited Arab–Israeli accommodation that followed the war and the Geneva Conference – spurred another change in Palestinian perceptions and estimates. Now Palestinians came to the view that if the international community's support was to be obtained, drawing its attention would not be enough. Rather, coupled with attention-drawing events, the objectives of the Palestinians would have to be scaled back to what the international community might consider legitimate. Many Palestinians feared that if they did not moderate their positions and goals, the Arab states, including Jordan, would conclude separate peace agreements with Israel, without the involvement of the Palestinians.

The Fatah-led PLO began to consider the use of diplomatic tools in addition to "armed struggle" in the post-1973 period, without necessarily abandoning the goal of eventually establishing their state in all of Palestine. Its narrative implied that previous Palestinian insistence on not accepting anything short of the one-time gain of complete control over the entire land would have to be set aside in favor of a phased approach. Addressing its constituency, particularly in the Diaspora, the PLO asserted that the change did not imply historical concessions or recognition of Israel. Thus, the PLO emphasized that the establishment of the envisaged "national authority" was not the end of the struggle "to liberate Palestine" but that once established, the "national authority" would continue the struggle, using all means normally available to governments.

The change toward greater pragmatism outside the occupied territories coincided with an internal change among West Bank Palestinians: the decline of their traditional Hashemite-oriented elite. With the West Bank falling under Israeli control in 1967, many among the pro-Jordan elite moved to the East Bank or lost influence in the West Bank. The rise of guerrilla groups in Jordan, particularly in the aftermath of the Battle of Karamah, the Jordanian–Palestinian confrontations in 1970–71 and the opening of universities in the West Bank, mobilized public support for the national movement. For those nationalists in the West Bank and the Gaza Strip, the goal of ending occupation and building a sovereign independent state now gained greater support.

Arab Narratives

While Syria and Egypt cooperated during the run-up and the opening phases of the 1973 October War, through most of this period these countries developed competing narratives about their role, particularly regarding the Arab–Israeli conflict. Both countries agreed not only that Israel was the aggressor in the June 1967 War but also that the war was just another expression of Israel's aggressive and expansionist nature. In both countries' view, the results of the 1967 war could not be reversed except through the use of force and the reconstituting of the balance of power in the region which had become highly "unbalanced" as a result of the Arab defeat in the war.

The Egyptian Narrative

The Egyptian narrative during most of this period focused on one imperative: to regain and reassert its sovereignty over the Sinai Peninsula, lost to Israel in the 1967 War. In its thinking about how this could be achieved, Egypt now abandoned the idea of total war and replaced it with an approach that first emphasized limited war and was later supplemented with a willingness to accept limited accommodation.

Having explained its 1967 defeat by referring to the advanced weapons technology supplied to Israel by France and the United States, in contrast to the weapons it had received from the Soviet Union, Egypt saw itself as unable to compete with Israel technologically. Instead, it would now seek to confront Israel with superior will power. The War of Attrition launched in 1969 was thus seen as intended to demonstrate this superiority, illustrated by the willingness to sustain heavy losses and other costs, notably the relocation of over a million Egyptians away from the Canal cities, in order to execute the war.

The outcome of the War of Attrition was viewed in Egypt as a strategic turning-point – it was the first war with Israel that Egypt did not lose. At the same time, the Egyptian narrative acknowledged that this success would not be sufficient to end Israel's control of the Sinai Peninsula. Yet in weighing its options toward this desired outcome, Egyptian leaders saw themselves as seriously constrained by the United States and the Soviet Union. Egypt reasoned that the two superpowers did not wish to risk détente by allowing an all-out military confrontation in the Middle East. Although they came to Egypt's defense during the War of Attrition, the Soviets were now seen as denying Egypt the tools it needed to confront Israel.

Egypt now felt an absolute imperative to "break out of the box" into which it believed it had been placed by the superpowers' efforts to create a new world order. This new order was seen as manifested particularly in the Moscow Declaration of May 1972, which called for the relaxation of tensions in the Middle East. The declaration was viewed by Cairo as an act of American–Soviet collusion aimed at maintaining the status quo in the region, even if that entailed the continuation of Israeli occupation of Egyptian territories. Egypt concluded that, notwithstanding the enormous risks involved in going to war without superpower backing, the prerequisite for developing the ability to attack Israel in order to liberate Sinai was to release itself from Russia's hold.

From the outset, however, Egypt's leadership did not believe it would be capable of dislodging Israel from the Sinai by military means alone. Instead, it hoped the military confrontation would launch a diplomatic process aided by just enough Egyptian military success to convince Israel that the costs of trying to perpetuate its hold over the Sinai would be too high to sustain or tolerate. Egyptians now saw a need to place their interests first, which in turn generated another prerequisite: namely, that Egypt had to release itself from the hold of the more radical Arab states.

Egypt regarded the 1973 October War as an historical turning-point – this time not merely a war in which Egypt avoided defeat but rather the first war in which Egypt emerged victorious. All the more so since this victory was seen as having been achieved despite the Soviets' efforts to prevent Egypt from launching this heroic effort by denying it the means to do so. Thus, Egypt now prided itself on devising and implementing a military doctrine that compensated not only for Israeli superiority in armor and airpower but also for Soviet unwillingness to supply Egypt with the more advanced means at its disposal. As such, the war was viewed as not only liberating Egyptian territories but also as releasing Egypt's decisions from being hostage to Arab, Palestinian, or Soviet pressures that did not take the country's interests into account.

Adopting this Egypt-centered strategy, however, was not seen as depriving Cairo of significant international and Arab support for its positions. International diplomatic and political support was provided by the Non-Aligned Movement as well as by African and Islamic forums. Arab support, however, was viewed as much more meaningful, expressed in the form of the oil embargo and the participation of at least some Arab military forces in the war. While military participation by most Arab states was merely symbolic, Syrian participation was significant. However, Egypt saw itself as carrying the major burden of the war, as its forces were to fight along a 170-km front, cross a major barrier – the Suez Canal – defeat the IDF in the first three days of the war, and face not only the brunt of Israel's air superiority but also a massive Israeli counterattack. To Egypt's surprise, Syria's forces, which enjoyed a 6 to 1 numerical advantage over the IDF in the small area of the Golan, were not only to lose their earlier gains by October 8 but also to ask the Soviet Union to introduce a ceasefire resolution at the UN on the second day of the fighting, when it saw itself as having achieved its own objectives.

Egypt believed that it went out of its way, indeed against the judgment of its own military leaders, to assist Syria during the war by moving forces deeper into areas of the Sinai not protected by its mobile air defense systems, thereby reducing Israeli pressure on the Syrian front. Thus, while Egypt saw Syria as having been helpful in achieving the strategic surprise at the war's launching, it later regarded Damascus as having become a strategic liability. Syria's demands for Egyptian help were viewed as having robbed Egypt of its strategic victory because, until October 14, Egypt was well entrenched in the east bank of the Suez Canal with its major reserves intact on the Canal's west bank. These reserves were lost when Egypt attempted to relieve the pressure on Syria, while Syria failed to build on Egypt's goodwill by effectively improving the position of its armed forces.[24]

Despite Egypt's losses during the last week of the war, and even after the Israeli countercrossing, it regarded its limited war strategy as having proved successful. The war not only attracted the necessary international attention – particularly in the United States – required to launch a diplomatic process, it also demonstrated to Israel the limits of its power. At the same time, Egypt was well aware – in contrast to the views of Syria, other radical Arab states, and numerous Arab commentators – that it was impossible to expect limited wars to produce unlimited gains.

The Syrian Narrative

While by the end of this period Egypt's dominant narrative was that of victory, the Syrian narrative seemed to reflect a deep sense of betrayal. Hafiz al-Assad concluded that Israel could not be faced unless the Arab nations and their military forces were to aggregate and achieve full cooperation and coordination. Among the Arab states, Assad saw Egypt as the most formidable and reliable ally in the struggle against Israel,[25] the only realistic partner for a joint attack against Israel – it bordered on Israel, it was highly motivated to regain the territory it had lost, and it significantly rearmed immediately after the 1967 War. Conversely, Assad viewed the Palestinian concept of popular liberation as dangerous because it provided Israel with a pretext to retaliate in Arab lands. Most Syrians shared this dislike, identifying the concept of popular liberation with Assad's deposed predecessor, Salah Jadid.[26]

Syrians saw their relations with the Soviets as based on mutual interests, not on shared ideologies. Moreover, Assad assumed that any help from Moscow, or further development of Syria's relations with the Soviets, would come at a cost. For this reason, he refused in the early 1970s to sign a Treaty of Friendship with the Soviets, fearing that this would allow Moscow to assert greater control over Syrian policy and action, thus limiting its freedom of maneuver. In particular, he feared that the Soviets would attempt to prevent a Syrian attack on Israel.[27]

Syria saw itself as remaining an avid supporter of the Palestinians, sending its tanks across the border with Jordan in September 1970 to protect the Palestinians from an all-out massacre. However, it decided not to provide air cover to Palestinian Liberation Army forces entering Jordan. It justified this decision by its worry that the conflict would bring about the collapse of the Hashemite monarchy – an outcome it did not seek. Syria also refrained from committing its air force to battle, as Israel and the United States were seen as already making highly publicized military movements in the direction of Jordan. Syria at that time was not looking to get involved in an unequal battle with Israel, and perhaps the United States[28]

Viewing Israel as well organized, and the IDF as capable of repelling Arab attacks, Syria concluded that Israel could only be defeated and made to accept Arab priorities through a well-coordinated Arab offensive. The Syrian leadership was convinced that alone Syria could not launch a successful offensive, and that diplomacy was not a viable option. Thus, the main thrust of Syria's policy after Assad came to power was to prepare for a conventional war to retake the Golan.[29]

While initially trusting Egypt, Syrians became convinced in the aftermath of the 1973 War that Sadat had reneged on the commitments he had made. By delaying its military offensive towards the Sinai passes, Egypt was regarded as having left Syria to bear the full brunt of

Israel's counterattack. In Assad's words, the aim of the October War was "the retrieval of territory which Israel occupied in 1967... [i]t was agreed that Syria's aim was the recovery of the Golan while the Egyptian objective was to reach the Sinai passes in the first stage, before regrouping for the reconquest of the whole peninsula. This was what Sadat and I decided and it was on this principle that we went to war."[30]

The Syrian narrative posits that the Egyptians fed the Syrians false war plans throughout the war.[31] Sadat was said to have deceived Syria (and the Soviets) by allowing its leader to believe that Egypt's offensive would be wider in scope than he ever intended. In fact, Assad is said to have later discovered that Sadat planned only to cross the Suez Canal and capture a narrow strip of land on its eastern bank. Syria, by contrast, envisaged the capture of the entire Golan and Sinai, and the subsequent exertion of pressure on Israel to give up the occupied Palestinian territories.[32] The direct result was that Israel was able to take back all the land that Syria had gained, and then more – an outcome that Syria saw as resulting from an Egyptian betrayal.[33]

Not only reneging on the promise to conduct a coordinated two-front attack on Israel, Egypt was now held to have brokered its own peace with the United States and Israel, without Syria.[34] Assad's perception that this was the case came from the observation that UNSC Resolution 338 was brokered and signed without consulting him, leading to his decision to reject it. Once again, Sadat was seen as having deceived Assad and weakened Syria's position by covertly pursuing unilateral action. Egypt was now blamed for reducing Syria's leverage to strike a deal.[35]

Having earlier accused the Egyptians of betrayal, in 1975 Syria had to explain its decision to negotiate a disengagement agreement with Israel. It argued that while Syria's army was victorious during the earlier phases of the war, [36] Damascus had later come under direct threat, with Israel's forces advancing to a position only 20 miles from Syria's capital. As Syria had now lost additional territory – that is, beyond what it had lost in 1967 – Assad had no choice but to first accept a ceasefire as a means of stopping the Israeli advance and to later engage in American-brokered negotiations with Israel.[37] Moreover, he now replaced his previous trust in the Soviets' capacity to handle such negotiations by a new trust in American mediation.[38]

Jordan's Narrative

In justifying its crackdown on the Palestinian guerrilla groups and preserving its right to speak in the name of the Palestinians and oppose the PLO's attempts in the early 1970s to gain the status of the Palestinians' "sole legitimate representative," the Jordanian narrative of this period presents the Hashemite Kingdom as having proved its Arab national credentials by its participation in the 1967 War and its resulting loss of the West Bank. While Jordan saw its participation in the war as having given it the right to represent the Palestinians, it saw its loss of the West Bank as bestowing upon it the duty to do so.[39] Moreover, in its view, if the territory lost in 1967 was to be returned through international instruments like UNSC Resolution 242, this clearly could not be done except by the international community engaging with the Jordanian state, not with a revolutionary body like the PLO that was still widely regarded as a terror organization.

Indeed, since the late 1950s the Jordanian narrative had pointed to the Hashemite Kingdom's support for the Palestinian cause as evidence of the monarchy's allegiance to the broader pan-Arab cause. Now, many Jordanians felt they had sacrificed much in the name of Arab unity generally, and for Palestinian liberation specifically, in the country's various wars with Israel. Jordanians further emphasized that for a time after the 1967 War, King Hussein was willing to continue making such sacrifices, as when he committed Jordanian army units to fight alongside PLO forces in the battle of Karameh in March 1968. Jordanians also stressed that following the Israeli defeat in the battle, Hussein went so far as to proclaim that "We might soon reach a stage when we will all become *fedayeen*."[40]

However, the Hashemite Kingdom is said to have soon found itself facing an attempt by the PLO and other Palestinian fighting organizations to transform it into a kind of North Vietnam that would act as the backer of Palestinian resistance in the occupied territories. By the end of 1969, Fatah is said to have established an infrastructure of schools, clinics, and orphanages throughout Jordan, making the scenario of its becoming a "state within a state" seem very real. As King Hussein and Prime Minister Wasfi al-Tall explained, Jordan would never sacrifice its "stability, security and tranquility... for any kind of political, financial or economic consideration."[41] Hussein now became the recipient of growing support among Jordanians loyal to their monarch and intent on preserving a Jordanian identity that saw itself as threatened by competing Palestinian interests.

By September 1970 Jordanians believed that the clash between them and the Palestinians was inevitable. They saw the country as winning decisively twice: once on the battlefield, where the Jordanian army succeeded in dismantling Palestinian military bases, thus restoring the Kingdom's sovereignty, and second when Jordan's position was supported by the other Arab states in the September 1970 Cairo summit. Jordan regarded the summit as having endorsed the idea that support for the Palestinian resistance did not imply the surrendering of the right of every Arab country to exercise its national sovereignty over its own territory.[42]

Jordan presented its February 1972 proposal to establish the United Arab Kingdom as manifesting the unity of the Palestinian and Jordanian peoples in the West and East Banks – and as the only viable route to obtaining Israeli withdrawal and restoring Arab sovereignty over the occupied territories. Jordan's reasoning was that Israel was unlikely to return these territories except to a sovereign state, and that given Jordan's record of moderation, the West would argue that Israel could safely return these territories to the Hashemite Kingdom.

Following the negative reaction of Arab and Palestinian leaders to the United Arab Kingdom plan, Jordan saw itself increasingly isolated in the Arab world. Indeed in 1973 it was not even asked by either Egypt or Syria to join the war coalition. Even after the war had begun, President Sadat was said to have phoned King Hussein to request that Jordan refrain from participating in the war. The King was said to have been only too happy to oblige. Although Jordan's army had begun to modernize itself, thanks to a major arms deal with the United States, in the fall of 1973 its forces were still not ready to launch a major attack against Israel. Moreover, in Jordanian eyes, the risks of losing more territory to Israel and jeopardizing the monarchy's long-term goal of regaining the West Bank outweighed the potential benefits of joining a war whose outcome was far from certain.

Once the initial advantage of the Egyptian and Syrian surprise attack began to dissipate, however, Jordan decided to contribute forces to the battle by sending an armored brigade to assist the Syrians in the Golan Heights. Jordan saw this participation as meaningful and hoped to use it to acquire a say in post-war diplomacy. In the war's aftermath it stressed its right to represent the Palestinians and at the same time to gain a disengagement agreement with Israel similar to those concluded by Egypt and Syria, thus allowing it at least a limited liberation of territories. Soon, however, Jordan found itself let down on both counts when Kissinger failed to deliver a disengagement agreement on the Jordanian front.[43] Consequently, the 1974 Arab summit in Rabat declared the PLO as the sole legitimate representative of the Palestinian people. While at first expressing its opposition to the Rabat designation, Jordan later accepted the new development, viewing it as an expression of the consensus among the Arab states.

Analysis

This analytical section will address two sets of major developments: first, the move to limited war (the 1969–70 War of Attrition and the 1973 War) and the subsequent move toward limited accommodation (the adoption of UNSC Resolution 338 and the disengagement agreements) by Egypt and Syria as well as by Israel; and second, the move to pragmatism – the beginning of the move from unlimited to more limited goals (the Provisional Program) by the Palestinians. The two changes in approach by the Arab states will be dealt with simultaneously. This is because the two sets of developments seem to be interconnected, as both were informed by the same change of mindset: the realization that absolute goals are not achievable and\or that there are severe limits to what can be achieved by force. Many of the same factors that first caused the turn toward limited war turned out to have later caused the turn toward limited accommodation.

The 1973 War and the Disengagement Agreements

The International System

At the *global-systemic level*, the transition to limited war and limited accommodation was propelled by the application of détente in United States–Soviet relations to the Middle East. Focused on relaxing their bilateral relations as well as the relations between the two camps they led, NATO and the Warsaw Pact, the two superpowers wished to balance their interest in preserving their influence and protecting their investments in the Middle East with the need to avoid dangerous escalation and direct confrontation.

At first, balancing these competing pulls proved nearly impossible. Thus, at the beginning of this period, the War of Attrition brought about the highest-ever level of direct Soviet involvement in the Arab–Israeli conflict. However by 1972, the East–West summit held in Moscow called for "a military relaxation in [the] area."[44] Egypt's President Sadat interpreted this stipulation as a clear indication that the United States and the Soviet Union would not allow, let alone support, an effort to resolve the conflict solely by military means – that is, without a significant process of political accommodation. For Sadat, this conclusion also implied that Egypt's strategy for reversing the outcome of the 1967 War could not rely solely on the Soviet Union, since the assets it possessed were primarily relevant to the "military option." Instead, Egypt would have to improve its relations with Washington, now increasingly seen as the key to extracting from Israel the territories it had captured by June 11, 1967.

Sadat's resulting 1972 decision to order the departure of the Soviet advisors, when coupled with Egypt's anticipated efforts to regain the territories it lost in 1967, was broadly but wrongly interpreted by Israel and outside the region as implying a weakening of Egypt's position. Paradoxically, however, it was meant to achieve exactly the opposite: to increase Egypt's freedom of maneuver. Thus, it was precisely following the expulsion of the Soviet advisors that Sadat convened the Egyptian military's top commanders and instructed them to prepare for war with whatever limited resources were at their disposal. Not surprisingly, many among the gathering Egyptian generals were alarmed by the enormous risks associated with Sadat's directive.[45] Preparing to fight a war limited by restricted resources meant that Egypt would be exposed to a likely Israeli effort to counter such a strategy by escalating the fighting to a wider confrontation, as it had done only two years earlier when it reacted to the static attrition warfare along the Suez Canal by bombing Egypt's national infrastructure.

Cognizant of these risks, and successfully hedging against them, Sadat followed the expulsion of the Soviet advisors by sending a high-level delegation to Moscow. The delegation had clear instructions to strike a deal which would prevent any further rupture of relations between Moscow and Cairo, and would assure continued supply of Soviet weapons and munitions to Egypt. In exchange, Sadat agreed to allow the Soviets continued use of the naval facilities in Alexandria as well as the use of communication facilities in Egypt. The result of this maneuvering was paradoxical: the expulsion of the Soviet advisors actually led to an increase in the volume of arms transfers to Egypt and thus to improved Egyptian capacities to fight a limited war.

Moreover, the two superpowers' desire to protect détente by preventing potential international flashpoints from exploding also provided Egypt with a golden opportunity: it meant that a successful Egyptian attack would bring one or both superpowers to intervene sooner rather than later to end the fighting. If Egypt succeeded in achieving significant gains at the opening of hostilities, such superpower intervention would reflect these gains and restore a measure of equilibrium in Egyptian–Israeli power relations. As Mohamed Haykal noted, Sadat reasoned that if Egypt could win back "only 10 millimeters of ground on the Canal's east bank, this would immeasurably strengthen his negotiating hand."[46]

As noted earlier, to succeed in this maneuver, Egypt needed not only to end its near-total reliance on the Soviet Union but also to improve its relations with the United States. Accordingly, it began to open channels of communication with the United States through intelligence exchanges, messages to President Nixon, and finally in 1972 and 1973, by initiating two meetings between Egyptian National Security Advisor Hafez Ismail and American National Security Advisor (and later Secretary of State) Henry Kissinger.

Reciprocating the change in Egypt's grand strategy and its successful execution of the opening moves of the 1973 War, the United States stepped in to insure that the outcome of the war could become an opportunity for limited accommodation. For this, the war needed to end without the clear Israeli victory that would have prevented the restoration of Egypt's honor. Kissinger estimated that with their honor restored, Egypt and Syria would be amenable to engaging in post-war diplomatic "give and take" with Israel, unlike their refusal to do so following their humiliating defeat in 1967. He therefore delayed shipment of military supplies to Israel during the opening phases of the war and, later, exerted on the Israeli leadership enormous pressure to end the encirclement of Egypt's 3rd Army.

Once Israel stabilized the two fronts, the United States moved quickly to position itself as the sole broker of peace by convincing the Arab states that it could persuade Israel to concede captured land, and that it could do this largely without Soviet involvement. Such convincing was now possible as it became abundantly clear that to fight the war Israel was dependent on American supply and resupply of weapons and ammunition. Given such dependence, Israel was not in a position to resist Washington's demands for limited withdrawals in the framework of the Kissinger-engineered post-war disengagement agreements.

The Regional Security Dilemma

At the *regional-systemic level* in the aftermath of the 1967 War the main actors seemed to reverse their previous roles. If the period between the run-up to the 1948 War and its execution of the 1967 War manifested Israel's repeated successes at compensating for its weaknesses by materializing its potential sources of strength and by exploiting the weaknesses of its adversaries, the period addressed in this chapter was characterized by quite the opposite. It was now the Arab states' – and primarily Egypt's – turn to actualize their potential sources of strength and to exploit Israel's weaknesses.

In the study of international relations, the War of Attrition and the 1973 War were classical outcomes of what Robert Jervis calls "the security dilemma." In a nutshell, this refers to the likelihood that when one state attempts to maximize its security at the expense of its neighbors' security, the latter will take countervailing measures, ultimately resulting in reduced security for the maximizing state.[47]

In the aftermath of the 1967 War, Israel attempted to maximize its security and reduce the vulnerability of its metropolitan areas and industrial core by pushing its boundaries out, thus establishing what it had hoped would prove to be "defensible borders." Such "defense in depth" was to stabilize Israel's security by releasing it from its previous hair-trigger reliance on preventive and preemptive strikes.[48] Israel's new security strategy could not be seen, however, as anything but a challenge to its neighbors' own security. First, it entailed Israeli control of lands which its neighbors considered their sovereign territory. Second, Egypt and Syria now saw Israeli forces stationed dangerously close to their nations' capitals. Thus, Israel's quest for defensible borders was now making the capitals of Egypt and Syria highly vulnerable if not indefensible. Unwilling to tolerate either a serious breach of its sovereignty or a serious threat to its security, Egypt was determined to push the IDF away from the Suez Canal.

While Israel's post-1967 policy created an Egyptian imperative to defeat its designs, Israel's new defense doctrine made Egypt's success possible. Israel's pre-1967 doctrine allowed the IDF to maintain the initiative and to compensate for its numerical inferiority by exploiting its advantages in mobility and surprise. Its new doctrine, however, pegged its hopes on a static defense line. This allowed Egypt not only to take the initiative but also to exploit its most important asset: its larger numbers. Having been given the initiative, Egypt chose an attrition strategy that the numerically fewer Israelis would find difficult to sustain.

In addition, the post-1967 territorial distribution also changed the two parties' relative "national will." Until then, Israel had seen almost all security challenges as "existential." Consequently, it was willing to pay almost any price to see these threats removed. But now the roles were reversed: with IDF forces stationed just over 100 kilometers from Cairo, it was now Egypt that saw the Israeli threat as existential, and it was Egypt that was now willing to expend very high costs to see this threat removed. With larger numbers and a conviction that its nation's capital was threatened, Egypt was both better equipped for attrition warfare and more willing to sustain the costs entailed in the efforts to remove the threat.

Trapped in a policy of its own design, Israel attempted to respond to Egypt's successful prosecution of attrition warfare – using greater numbers, its superior static firepower and its greater willingness to sustain costs – by supplementing its static defense with aerial bombardment of Egypt's industrial base. The purpose of these "deep penetration bombings" which began on January 7, 1970 was to restore Israel's advantages in mobile offense by exploiting its air superiority to establish "escalation dominance." Thus, it was hoped that Israel's demonstrable ability to escalate at every level of warfare would persuade Egypt that continuing the fighting was futile.

What Israel failed to appreciate was that Egypt was now fully committed to the project of dislodging the IDF from the Sinai Peninsula. The price Egypt was willing to pay to achieve this now surpassed the casualties it sustained and the economic damage it experienced – it included a willingness to accept, at least temporarily, massive Soviet military presence in Egypt. Thus, to the Israeli move to match Egypt's advantage in attrition warfare by exploiting its air superiority, Egypt now moved to match this Israeli advantage by inviting the Soviets to defend Egypt's skies.

These moves and responses were a classic manifestation of *balance of power* theory: absent the capacity to balance Israel's power internally, Egypt sought and obtained external assistance by deepening its alliance with the Soviet Union. The result was a Soviet strategic move to change the balance of power by stationing air squadrons and an Air Defense division in Egypt.

The conclusion of the War of Attrition reflected the new Israeli–Egyptian balance of power: it ended in a draw. Both sides were exhausted and opted to accept a ceasefire proposed by the so-called "Rogers Plan." Egypt did not achieve Israel's withdrawal but nor was it permanently dissuaded from seeking this objective.

Now, however, the balance of power was serving only to maintain the status quo, the one thing Egypt sought to change. Therefore, with Israel refusing to budge, Egypt had no alternative but to wage war. But, as the case with the systemic level, the prevailing balance of forces made it imperative that Egypt limit its war goals. This meant that a number of preconditions had to be met. The most important of these was a major change in Egypt's approach to the utility of force. Instead of a military campaign that would aim at dislodging Israel from the Sinai by itself, it now adopted a war plan intimately linked to a negotiation strategy – it was designed to affect Israel's mindset and to bring it to the negotiation table. Thus, Egypt's ultimate objectives were not to be achieved by military means; instead, the violence unleashed was designed to spur a diplomatic process and to convince Israelis that their attempt to make their possession of the Sinai permanent would be far too costly. In turn, the negotiations spurred by the limited, but very violent, Egyptian attack were expected to result ultimately in the regaining and reassertion of Egypt's control and sovereignty over the Sinai.

Equally important, Egypt needed to take a series of steps to enhance its ability to wage a successful limited war. First, the quality of the soldiers and especially the officer corps of the Egyptian armed forces had to be dramatically increased. That was achieved by a near-total mobilization of university graduates into military service. Second, Israel's specific advantage in airpower and armor needed to be addressed. Israel expected Egypt to attempt this by acquiring better aircraft and more armor. But Egypt, accepting its inherent limitations in these realms, opted for another way of neutralizing Israel's advantages: mobile air defenses, even at the cost of limiting the theater of operations to the area covered by these defenses. The mobility acquired was designed to ensure that once Egypt's ground forces had crossed the Suez Canal, these forces would be accompanied by an umbrella of air-defense guns and missiles, protecting them from Israel's superior air force in a geographic area not exceeding several miles.

Similarly, Egypt addressed Israel's advantage in mobile armor not by building an equally robust tank force but by obtaining and deploying thousands of shoulder-carried anti-tank missiles, as well as similar missiles mounted on armored vehicles. It planned to spearhead the effort to reconquer a small slice of the Sinai by saturating the Israeli armor with thousands of infantrymen carrying such missiles, thus exploiting Egypt's numerical advantage. By deploying a preponderance of such weapons and by attacking IDF units across the Canal, the Egyptian military was to entice the IDF to pit its offensive forces against Egypt's well prepared defense in the newly "liberated" areas.

To sum up, Egypt's launching of the 1973 War was thus preceded by major changes in its military strategy for regaining the territories it lost in the 1967 War – from unlimited to limited war. While the roots of this change can be found in the earlier War of Attrition, the shift to a limited-war strategy now manifested itself at two levels: first, a reduction of operational objectives, making them more commensurate with Egypt's limited capabilities.[49] And second, by substituting the attempt to match Israel's superiority in offensive weapons by acquiring and deploying defensive weapons in an offensive mode.

Unlike Egypt, Syria did not launch a war of attrition against Israel in the aftermath of the 1967 War. The Syrian armed forces appeared too weak to maintain a fighting spirit against the Israelis. Their quick loss of the Golan humiliated Syria generally and its then defense minister, Hafez Assad, personally. Israel's control of the Golan now left Syria in an inferior position topographically and with its capital vulnerable. This situation could not be reversed without a fight, but there was a serious debate in Syria as to what type of fight should be pursued. The civil wing of the Ba'ath Party, and Syria's then leader (until 1970) Salah Jadid, pointed to these results as evidence of Syria's weakness in conventional war strategy, suggesting, instead, a popular war of "national liberation"[50] aimed at embroiling the Arabs in an all-out war against Israel.[51]

By contrast, Assad believed in waging a conventional war designed to retake the Golan Heights. Thus, while entering into an alliance with Egypt during the run-up to the 1973 War, he adhered to an approach to the use of force that was very different than Sadat's: war was not meant or designed to become a prelude to any negotiations for the return of land in exchange for peace.

Egypt's Domestic Scene

In the realm of domestic politics inside Egypt war was also intended to build the political capital required to engage Israel in a diplomatic process that would restore the country's sovereignty over the Sinai. Such engagement could not be launched without first healing the humiliation associated with the 1967 defeat. The War of Attrition and the 1973 War were both intended to restore Egyptians' sense of self-worth and self-confidence.

Equally important, the fighting was designed to restore the legitimacy of the governing regime – a legitimacy tarnished by the magnitude of the 1967 debacle. Given that the legitimacy of the Egyptian revolutionary regime of July 1952 was based on the military and its nationalist credentials earned by its liberation of Egyptian land from British colonial control and later, in 1956, from Israeli occupation of the Sinai, the 1967 defeat clearly undermined the regime. Indeed, the War of Attrition was launched much earlier than anyone anticipated, and the 1973 War could not await further rearmament efforts, precisely because the regime's legitimacy was increasingly questioned as a result of the Egyptian leadership's seeming indecision: its perceived acceptance of a no-war, no-peace situation.

The costs of this situation were deemed unacceptable: it was one thing to evacuate a million people from the Canal cities; it was quite another to accept such dislocation as an indefinite proposition. The difficulties entailed were further compounded by Nasser's death, which deprived the regime of his charismatic leadership, leaving his successor, Anwar Sadat, a huge legitimacy deficit and a dire need to prove himself by defending Egypt and defeating the Israelis.

The Israeli Domestic Scene

On the Israeli side, the post-1973 War disengagement agreements could not have been concluded and implemented if it were not for changes in the country's domestic scene spurred by the war. The most dramatic of these was the discrediting of the Labor leadership that had dominated Israeli politics since the state's establishment and the Yishuv since the mid-1930s. Indeed the war's aftermath comprised nothing short of the beginning of the end of this dominance.

Facing a public outcry about what many saw as a very poor performance by the country's leaders as well as that of the top echelons of the IDF on the eve of the war and during its opening phases, the Israeli government set up a national commission of inquiry headed by a Supreme Court judge – the Agranat Commission. The commission was charged with investigating the causes of the surprise, locating the responsibility for the lack of sufficient preparedness before the war, and examining the faulty decisions made on the eve of the war and during its first phases.

In the December 1973 elections, the Labor Party lost some five seats. More important, however, mass protests now developed, led by IDF reservists who demanded that Israel's political leaders be held accountable for the mistakes that led to the war. This included criticism of the paralysis that plagued Israeli diplomacy in the aftermath of 1967, which was now increasingly understood as having left Egypt no choice but war. When the Agranat Commission published its preliminary report on April 2, 1974 – finding the top ranks of the IDF responsible for many mistakes made but absolving the country's political leaders from responsibility – the protests escalated considerably, forcing Meir's resignation.[52]

The first Rabin-led government that began to serve in June 1974 was thus the outcome of the post-1973 War protests. Hence, it was hardly surprising that Rabin was willing to implement measures that were deemed inconceivable by Israel's pre-1973 governments – withdrawals in the Sinai and the Golan in exchange for commitments that fell far short of peace. Thus, the war's primary effect on Israel's domestic scene was to create an environment for replacing its pre-war "all or nothing" approach by a renewed pragmatism that accepted the logic of the disengagement agreements that Israel would now be negotiating on the Egyptian and Syrian fronts.

Leaders

At the *individual level* a number of personalities influenced the momentous developments in the Middle East during the timeframe discussed in this chapter. While almost any Egyptian leader could have been expected to make every attempt to dislodge Israel from its post-1967 hold over the Sinai, Nasser's responsibility for the debacle clearly gave him additional motivation to do everything to undo the results of the war. Thus, his personal role in the catastrophe of 1967 gave Egypt added motivation to launch the War of Attrition.

Yet relative to other factors, the personal input of President Anwar Sadat was much more important in determining the course of events during this period. In the first instance, Sadat was propelled to build his distinct image and establish his own imprint on Egypt's history and policy. Hence he was strongly motivated to break with his predecessor's Pan-Arabism and to implement a distinct "Egypt-First" approach. Specifically, Sadat reached the conclusion that Pan-Arabism placed Egyptian policy in a straitjacket. With the responsibility it gave Egypt as the purported leader of the Arab world, Egyptian policy became hostage to the priorities of every other player in the region – notably Syria and the Palestinians – ending up with the escalation that resulted in the 1967 debacle.

Second, uniquely for a leader of a non-democratic country, Sadat acquired an impressive capacity to understand how democratic systems work and, particularly, how public opinion in such systems could affect government policy. Thus, he initiated a war designed to begin a change in the Israeli domestic setting – cracking the post-1967 euphoria of the Israeli public and discrediting its leadership in an effort to produce the desired change in policy.

Finally, Sadat had a unique understanding of how force and diplomacy should be integrated to produce optimal results. Understanding the limitations of Egypt's power potential he concluded that his country would not be able to defeat Israel in the battlefield. But understanding the essence of Egypt's strength and of Israel's weaknesses, he devised a strategy based on these strengths and weaknesses – one that would produce for Egypt just enough of an advantage as to defrost the diplomatic process in a way that would, in the end, allow the restoration of its sovereignty over the Sinai.

On the Israeli side, no single individual contributed as much to the creation of conditions that led to Sadat's adoption of the limited war option, the 1973 War, as well as to the strategic surprise that Israel suffered at its launching, than Prime Minister Golda Meir. Being one of the "last standing" among the country's "founding fathers," and equipped with a unique voice intonation, she established herself as the unchallenged leader of her party and government soon after replacing her predecessor, Levi Eshkol. As of that point and until after the 1973 War, no one challenged her authority and no one rivaled her dominance over Israeli policy.

In many ways Golda Meir was the antithesis of Anwar Sadat. Terrified by what she considered threats to Israel's existence, convinced of the immutability of Arab hostility, self-righteous and completely convinced of the justice of Israel's cause and demands, and unable to empathize with the plights and dilemmas of Israel's neighbors, Meir led Israel's policy to a dead-end. Stuck with a dogmatic "all-or-nothing" and "take it or leave it" approach, she refused to contemplate any measure to ease the pressures experienced by Israel's neighbors. Instead, she insisted that Israel would not engage in any withdrawals except in exchange for "real peace" and that even in exchange for such peace Israel would not withdraw to the 1967 lines and would not accept minor improvements in these borders; rather, Israel would insist on significant modifications in these boundaries, making them "defensible."

The result was diplomatic paralysis: Israel waited for its neighbors to adjust their expectations to Israel's priorities. But Israel's neighbors would do nothing of the sort. In the absence of another alternative, Sadat had no choice but to unleash a deadly war to defrost what Meir sought to freeze.

From outside the region, Henry Kissinger – first as National Security Advisor (1969–72) and particularly as Secretary of State (1972–76) – played a pivotal role in masterfully engineering the set of agreements that paved the way to the first peace treaty between Israel and an Arab state. It was he who created a common vocabulary for crisis management during the 1973 War and the peace process in its aftermath. His political philosophy of seeking equilibrium, balance of power, and the understanding of moderate leaders in the region were instrumental in working out the first Arab–Israeli disengagement agreements.[53] Yet he could not have played this unique role were it not for his particular personality traits.

A political scientist by training, Kissinger's many years in academia had a strong influence on his subsequent career in government. Despite this training, however, Kissinger has noted that the actual practice of diplomacy still sometimes surprised him. During his first Middle East shuttle mission in January 1974 he commented that: "As a professor, I tended to think of history as run by impersonal forces. But when you see it in practice, you see the difference that personalities make."[54]

Kissinger's own "larger than life" personality clearly made a considerable impression on the Middle East during his years in the Nixon and Ford administrations. Of key importance was his "willingness to place himself in the middle, his opportunistic risk-taking, and his ability to put each agreement together by manipulating... a combination of factors."[55] Kissinger managed to become a trusted confidant to leaders on both sides of the

Arab–Israeli divide, and his personal gravitas allowed him to persuade these leaders to take steps towards peace that they may have otherwise avoided. He was not afraid, however, to pressure the same leaders when this was required, earning a reputation for toughness and resolve seldom matched by subsequent American officials.

Kissinger's single greatest strength may have been his ability to maintain strong relationships with all the key parties while also upholding a reputation for fairness. Seeking a balance between the sides, he developed a deep sensitivity to what each side required in order to get the other side to act. It was this grasp of "the mediator's challenge: making sure that your sensitivity to one side doesn't preclude being sensitive to the other, and producing what both require,"[56] that made Kissinger stand out from other mediators.

Kissinger was instrumental in affecting the politics of the Arab–Israeli conflict during this period; he initially neglected the Middle East conflict, concentrating instead on the global balance with the Soviet Union, China, and the Vietnam War. Only later did he turn his attention to the region in the aftermath of the October war. As the first Jewish Secretary of State in American history, Kissinger had been reluctant to get involved in the Middle East politics. His fascination with global politics made the region too small for his ambition to restore the world to stability. Hence, the Middle East was to be put on the back burner so that it did not disturb détente politics. To insure this, at the May 1972 summit meeting of the United States and the Soviet Union Kissinger negotiated an agreement to work for the relaxation of tensions in the Middle East.

Kissinger later reversed his procedures by engineering the new step-by-step approach in the Middle East. With President Nixon distracted by the Watergate scandal, it was Kissinger's hand that largely crafted the American response to the 1973 War. It was his recognition of the need to both minimize Soviet influence in the region and to ensure that the Arab armies did not suffer a humiliating defeat that helped pave the way for the post-war negotiations. Kissinger's strategic thinking during the war and his active engagement in the peace talks which followed allowed the region's leaders, who themselves were eager for a change, to turn that desire into reality.

After Kissinger manipulated the delay of the implementation of the ceasefire to Israel's advantage, enabling the encirclement of the Egyptian 3rd Army, he and Nixon, as a result of the nuclear crisis with the Soviet Union, put heavy pressure on Israel to end the fighting. Such Kissingerian behavior was aimed at preparing the Middle East environment for his preferred step-by-step approach to a diplomatic resolution of the conflict. Kissinger went from being minimally engaged in the Middle East to being a frequent visitor, taking eleven trips to the region between November 1973 and September 1975. These two years included periods of intense shuttle diplomacy such as that in the spring of 1974, when in the course of a month he made 16 stops in Damascus and 15 in Jerusalem.[57] The intense talks produced the 1974 disengagement agreement.

Kissinger was able to produce these dramatic results thanks to the complete backing he received from Presidents Nixon and Ford, allowing him to put the weight of the United States fully behind these negotiations, making clear to the parties that they were expected to find a way to work out their differences or face the consequences in terms of their relations with the United States. These threats, stated or implied, were viewed as credible precisely because Kissinger was seen as speaking for the President of the United States; the region's leaders understood that they had little room for maneuver as Kissinger skillfully made sure that there would be no distance between him and the president that others might exploit.

The Palestinian Provisional Program

Global-systemic, regional and domestic factors also affected the Palestinians' more modest moves during this period to limited accommodation. At the *global-systemic level*, Palestinian power deficits – in relation to Israel as well as in relation to Arab states who were threatened by the Palestinians – were to be compensated through closer association with the Soviet Union. Without support from the USSR the PLO would not have been able to gain the international attention it did.

At the *regional level*, the momentous developments culminating in the 1973 War and its immediate aftermath also shaped the regional environment of the Palestinians, as they could no longer rely on the Arab states' military power to liberate their country. Therefore, they, too, had no alternative but to move toward some sort of accommodation with Israel. While the immediate aftermath of the 1967 War, particularly after the Battle of Karamah, saw some Palestinian flirtation with the notion of "people's war," it soon became clear to them that at best violence could only help promote their case more forcefully and that like other Arabs they, too, would have to accommodate the new reality.

The PLO's expulsion from Jordan meant that the Hashemite Kingdom could no longer serve as a launching pad for the struggle against Israel. With Lebanon becoming a substitute only later on, the Palestinian groups, now much weaker and more fragmented, were left without a base from which guerrilla war could be pursued. In a sense, then, they faced a danger that the Battle of Karamah would not only be the first Palestinian victory, but also the last.

Deprived of such a land base, Palestinian groups – first the PFLP and later the Fatah-inspired Black September Organization – turned to international terrorism. Thus, Fatah's turn to terrorism reflected a growing desire for revenge for its defeat in Jordan, greater fragmentation and warlordism inside its top leadership, as well as a desire to upset the new emerging balance in Arab and international politics, which was perceived to be tilted decidedly against the Palestinians.

The Palestinian National Council's 1974 adoption of the Provisional Program seems to have been spurred at least in part by a combination of all these factors. At the regional level, the revival of Arab–Israeli diplomacy in the aftermath of the 1973 War resulted in Palestinian worries that Jordan might return as a player in the determination of the future of the West Bank, and that the Arab states might once again take the initiative away from the Palestinians. Palestinian fear of Jordan's ascribed intention to reassert its historical role in Palestinian affairs was further spurred by Kissinger's rumored intentions to follow-up the Israeli–Egyptian and Israeli–Syrian disengagement agreements with a somewhat similar Jordanian–Israeli deal. In the framework of this deal, Israel was to yield to Jordan a 10-km-wide strip in the Jordan Valley as a first step towards the latter's gradual return of the West Bank. To abort Jordan's perceived designs, the PLO needed to establish itself as the only Palestinian representative and the sole Arab decision-maker regarding Palestinian affairs. But to gain regional recognition for such a role in an environment of Arab–Israeli diplomacy the PLO needed to moderate its stance and limit its operational goals.

In addition, some Arab governments, wishing to prevent Jordan from reasserting itself in the West Bank and East Jerusalem, now advised the PLO leadership to adopt a more realistic program. In return, they were willing to recognize the PLO as the "sole legitimate representative of the Palestinian people." Hence, the recognition given to the PLO at the October 1974 Rabat Summit was tied to the PLO's earlier adoption of the Provisional Plan.

Furthermore, Palestinian armed attacks carried out in the early 1970s, and particularly the horrific acts of international terrorism, created an even greater imperative on the part of some of the Arab states to disassociate themselves from the Palestinians. Yet this was now to be turned to the Palestinians' advantage. Not interested in being associated with such acts, the Arab states were happy to grant the Palestinians the right to lead the struggle to secure their rights.

More broadly, Palestinian behavior was now affected by a sober assessment of the regional distribution of power, which raised doubts about whether in the future Arab states would be prepared to launch any kind of war against Israel. Thus the Palestinians had come to regard the October War as "the last Arab–Israeli war." Violence exercised in the aftermath of the 1973 War was aimed in part at spoiling any peace efforts that would have denied the Palestinians the right to statehood and self-determination. Hence, coupled with violence, the PLO witnessed during these years a shift in aims and programs as well as in its organizational structure: away from a "liberation strategy" and toward state-building.

At the *unit level*, the Palestinian National Council's adoption in 1974 of the Provisional Plan was partially also the result of competing priorities within the Palestinian camp. While the "insiders" – Palestinians who now found themselves under Israeli occupation of the West Bank and Gaza – were focused on undoing the results of the 1967 War, the "outside" Diaspora Palestinians were more attentive to the needs of the refugees and their demands that the results of the 1948 War be reversed.

The shift from liberation strategy to state-building required the PLO to focus much of its efforts on the West Bank and Gaza, with the aim of winning public support. With the PLO developing in exile, it was more attentive to the needs of Palestinians in host countries, almost all refugees. These refugees feared permanent exile, loss of their land and property, and denial of their Palestinian national identity. The PLO's slogan of "liberation of Palestinians and return to the homeland" served those needs and addressed those fears. Refugees in exile viewed the idea of a Palestinian state limited to the West Bank and the Gaza Strip with suspicion, as it implied possible recognition of Israel, an indefinite postponement of the "liberation" of their homeland, and even the possible denial of their "Right of Return."

Yet, as the PLO sought to build its base inside the occupied territories in the late 1960s and early 1970s, it needed to pay attention to the needs of Palestinians in the West Bank and the Gaza Strip, of whom only less than one-third were refugees. Israeli occupation contributed to accelerating the rise of Palestinian nationalism, particularly among the youth and the urban elite. The occupation's political economy deprived Palestinians of some of their water and land resources and forced farmers to become laborers in Israel. Greater restrictions on travel, applied particularly to youth, encouraged Palestinians to rely on locally created universities that became hotbeds of Palestinian nationalism.

For the nationalists inside the occupied territories, the immediate threat seemed therefore to emanate from two sources: (a) Israeli "creation of facts" on the ground: annexation of East Jerusalem, destruction of villages, settlement construction, land confiscation and deportation of hundreds of national leaders and activists; and (b) efforts by Jordan and Israel to share control of the West Bank and Israeli talk about the so-called "Jordan Option." In the eyes of the "insiders," asserting national identity in a sovereign territorial base was the immediate national objective: the idea of a Palestinian state in the West Bank and the Gaza Strip was born as a response to the immediate post-1967 short-term threats. Seeking to win hearts and minds in the West Bank and Gaza Strip, the PLO inside the territories could not ignore the demand for statehood. As the voice of those "insiders" gained strength, particularly in the aftermath of the expulsion of the PLO from Jordan, the drive toward statehood gained momentum. The PLO's acceptance of the phased approach in the framework of the 1974 Provisional Program was, in part, aimed at creating harmony between the goals of Palestinian "insiders" and those of the "outsiders."

At the *individual level*, it was Yasser Arafat who led the process of the de-Arabization of the conflict, bringing it back to its Palestinian–Israeli core. Acutely aware of the legacy of the Mufti and the flaws of that leadership, Arafat, a fierce Palestinian nationalist and a man of charisma, initiative and great communication skills, sought during the period under examination to minimize the role of Arab countries in Palestinian decision making, to insure the inclusive nature of the national movement under his leadership, and to move the Palestinians to more realistic goals. Aware of the disastrous consequences of rejecting compromise, Arafat's leadership was highly pragmatic, leading to the adoption of the PLO's Provisional Program. Similarly, aware of the disparity in the power relationship, Arafat viewed violence as means to realistic political ends.

While these qualities had their rewards, they were not without their own faults. On the one hand, pragmatism paid off in 1974–75, as the PLO gained greater Arab and international endorsement. Yet, Arafat's attempt in the early 1970s to accommodate leftist groups such as the PFLP contributed to the war in Jordan and to greater international condemnation of Palestinian terrorism.

The combination of all these qualities now helped Arafat to begin to move the Palestinian–Israeli conflict away from its existential mode to one addressing identity and statehood. Thus, Arafat's most important roles during this period were: (a) to foster one Palestinian voice by controlling the PLO and obtaining the Arab states' acceptance of its role as "the sole legitimate representative of the Palestinian people"; (b) to begin shifting the PLO's emphasis away from total violence and toward state-building; and finally, (c) to shift the PLO's strategy away from its "all-or-nothing" character and toward a phased approach that spelt eventual moderation and the adoption of the "two-state solution."

Concluding Notes

Spanning only five years, the period addressed in this chapter witnesses some of the most fascinating dramas of the Arab–Israeli conflict and the beginnings of serious efforts to resolve it: the sharpest and most extreme acts of violence – most notably the October 1973 War – to the first stages of what would later become known as "the peace process," with the signing of the Israel–Egypt and Israel–Syria Disengagement Agreements. With these agreements the conflict was transformed from an existential to a non-existential one, as key Arab states now abandoned the Khartoum Summit's "three Nos" in favor of first steps toward eventual accommodation with Israel.

The timeframe of this chapter witnessed periodic conflict and sharp disagreements among the region's important Arab players. In September 1970 ("Black September") one Arab state – Syria – had taken initial steps toward invading another – the Hashemite Kingdom of Jordan. Three years later, an act of intimately close cooperation – Egypt and Syria joining forces to spring an effective surprise attack against Israel in October 1973 – only exposed the two countries' very different approaches to the conflict and the efforts to resolve it. Thus, their different understanding of the interplay between force and diplomacy in 1973 anticipated the complete rupture of their relations in the late 1970s, when Egypt opted for peace with Israel.

Not surprisingly, during the period addressed here not only did the narratives of Israel, the Palestinians and the Arabs diverge – equally sharp was the difference between the narratives of the key Arab states about the main developments experienced during this era. Thus, the understanding of Syria and Jordan, and even more so, that of the Palestinians and Jordan, regarding the developments of September 1970 and about the circumstances that led to "Black September" could not have been more different. The same was true for the different narratives of Egypt and Syria about one another's conduct during the 1973 War and its aftermath.

As this chapter shows clearly, the dramatic developments of this period cannot be explained without reference to all three levels of analysis. The global-systemic level had enormous influence over the parties' conduct. Thus, Soviet force deployments in Egypt during the 1971 War of Attrition set clear limits to Israel's capacity to decide the war in its favor. Also, without the structural weaknesses that Soviet involvement in the Middle East had suffered in the mid-1970s, the United States would not have been able to propel Israel, Egypt and Syria to accept the terms of the three disengagement agreements they signed in 1974–75.

No less important was the role of unit-level factors, from Israel's odd mix of anxieties and hubris originating in its pre-1967 War trauma and its subsequent victory, to the complexities of Jordan's domestic scene. Absent an appreciation of these factors it is impossible to understand the roots of Israel's diplomatic paralysis in 1970–73 and the launching in Jordan of Black September in 1970.

Yet no other period of the Arab–Israeli conflict has provided more convincing evidence of the critically important contribution of individual leaders to the shaping of policy and history. Without the pivotal role of Egypt's President Sadat and that of Secretary of State Kissinger, it is difficult to imagine how the conflict could have been moved from its existential to a new, non-existential phase, or "From limited War to Limited Accommodation" – the title of this chapter. Especially important in that regard was President Sadat. Without his unique understanding of the interplay between force and diplomacy, it would have been impossible to explain what shaped the logic and the parameters of the 1973 War and the post-war Egypt–Israel disengagement agreements.

For the Palestinians this period is replete with paradoxes. Most importantly, just as the Arabization of the conflict reached a peak in the 1973 War, the war's immediate aftermath witnessed a dramatic shift to de-Arabization, with the Rabat conference designating the PLO as "the sole representative of the Palestinian people." This process was accelerated by the gradual defeat of the pro-Jordanian political figures in the West Bank. Finally, the end of the period described here witnessed a clear Palestinian shift in favor of state-building as they began to build a "state-within-a state" in southern Lebanon.

In Israel the most important development experienced during this period was the discrediting of the Labor party – a political and social movement that led Israel throughout the struggle for statehood which included the waging of five wars. While the political defeat of Labor did not become apparent before the 1977 elections, all the seeds of this defeat were planted in the early 1970s. Secondly, another outcome of the two wars of this period – 1970 and 1973 – and the enormous stocks of weapons and ammunition required to wage these wars, was Israel's increased dependence on the United States. This affected the outcome of post-1973 diplomatic efforts – the steps depicted here as "limited accommodation" which would, in turn, become the precursors to a future "peace process" – because it provided the United States leverage which it later used to extract the Israeli concessions necessary for these efforts to succeed.

What future developments did this period anticipate? What would be the result of the three disengagement agreements signed by Israel, Egypt, and Syria? Would it lead to a peace agreement with one of the two Arab states but not with the other? And what would the PLO do with the de-Arabization of the conflict and with its new standing crowned in Rabat? Would it propel it towards political pragmatism? Or military defeats? Or both? These are the questions that the next chapters will address.

Readings

Bickerton, Ian and Carla Klausner, *A History of the Arab–Israeli Conflict* (Prentice Hall, 2010) 154–176.

Caplan, Neil, *The Israel–Palestine Conflict: Contested Histories* (Wiley, 2010) 148–177.

Dowty, Alan, *Israel/Palestine: Global Political Hotspots* (Polity, 2012) 125–137.

Gelvin, James, *The Israel–Palestine Conflict: One Hundred Years of War* (Cambridge University Press, 2007) 208–209.

Jamal, Amal, *The Palestinian National Movement: Politics of Contention 1967–2005*. (Bloomington: Indiana University Press, 2005).

Lesch, David, *The Arab–Israeli Conflict* (Oxford University Press, 2008) 233–258.

Morris, Benny, *Righteous Victims: The History of the Zionist–Arab Conflict, 1881–2001* (Vintage, 2001) 347–443.

Sahliyeh, Emile F., *In Search of Leadership: West Bank Politics since 1967* (Washington, DC: Brookings Institution, 1988).

Shlaim, Avi, *The Iron Wall: Israel and the Arab World* (W.W. Norton, 2001) 283–324.
Smith, Charles D., *Palestine and the Arab–Israeli Conflict* (Bedford/St.Martin's, 2007) 300–344.
Tessler, Mark, *A History of the Israeli–Palestinian Conflict* (Indiana University Press, 2009) 465–532.

Historical Documents

U.N. Security Council Resolution 242: Walter Laqueur and Barry Rubin, *The Israel–Arab Reader: A Documentary History of the Middle East Conflict* (Penguin Books, 2008), 116.
U.N. Security Council Resolution 338: Laqueur and Rubin, *The Israel–Arab Reader*, 152.
Palestine National Council Resolutions (10 Point program): Laqueur and Rubin, *The Israel–Arab Reader*, 162–163.
Egyptian–Israeli Accord on the Sinai: Laqueur and Rubin, *The Israel–Arab Reader*, 194–200.
The Rogers Plan.
The Allon Plan: map available in Tessler, *A History of the Israeli–Palestinian Conflict*, 501.
United Arab Kingdom Plan.

Notes

1. Lieutenant-General Sa'd El Shazly, *The Crossing of the Suez* (San Francisco: American Mideast Research, 1980), 18.
2. Ya'acov Bar-Simon-Tov, *Israeli–Egyptian war of Attrition, 1969–1970: A Case Study in Limited War* (New York: Columbia University Press, 1980).
3. According to Bar-Simon Tov, between March 1969 and July 1970 the number killed was 792, ibid. 97 and 171. According to Herzog, the number of dead was 500 between 1967 and 1970. Chaim Herzog, *The Arab–Israeli Wars: War and Peace in the Middle East* (New York: Random House, 1982), 220.
4. Morris, *Righteous Victims*, 362.
5. Mohammad Fawzy, *The Three Years War: 1967–1970* (Cairo: Dar al-Mostaqbal al-Arabi, Arabic Edition, 1984), 225.
6. General Taha Al-Magdoob, *Years of Preparation and Days of Victory, June 1966–October 1973* (Cairo, Al-Ahram Center for Translation and Publishing, first edition, 1999), 43; Ahmed Hamroush, "William Rogers and First US Initiative to Solve the Middle East Problem," *Al-Sharq Al-Awsat*, London, January 16, 2001; Heikel, "The Road to October, Roger's Initiative and Project," *M'a Heikel* [*With Heikel*] *Show*, *al-Jazeera* News Channel, July 14, 2010.
7. Quandt, *Peace Process: American Diplomacy and the Arab–Israeli Conflict Since 1967*. (Washington, DC: Brookings Institution Press, 2005), 74.
8. Yezid Sayigh, *Armed Struggle and the Search for State*, 178. According to Sayigh the IDF also lost some four tanks, five other vehicles and aircraft; the Jordanian army lost 61 dead, 108 wounded, 20 tanks damaged and 13 destroyed, and 39 other vehicles disabled; the Palestinian guerrilla forces lost 116 dead, 100 wounded and 40–66 prisoners.
9. According to Sayigh, in the end, up to 5,000 people were killed in the fighting. The Jordanian army lost over 600 men, along with 5,000–7,000 defectors to the Palestinian side. Roughly 950 Palestinian militants were killed, of whom over 400 belonged to Fatah. Of the remaining dead,

up to 3,500 were civilians. In the meantime, the Jordanians had rounded up 16,000–20,000 Palestinians and imprisoned several hundred more in the al-Jafr desert camp. Sayigh, *Armed Struggle and the Search for the State*, 267.

10. Figure cited in Jillian Becker, *The PLO: The Rise and Fall of the Palestine Liberation Organization* (London: Weidenfeld and Nicolson, 1984), 62–63.
11. Robert Rabil, *Embattled Neighbors*, 21–22; Moshe Ma'oz, *Asad: The Sphinx of Damascus: A Political Biography* (New York: Weidenfeld and Nicholson, 1988), 86.
12. Rabil, *Embattled Neighbors*, 22.
13. See, Bernhard Reich, "The Jarring Mission and the Search for Peace in the Middle East" in *Wiener Library Bulletin* [Great Britain], no 26, 1972. For the Israeli response, see "The Jarring Initiative and the Response, 8 February 1971," http://www.mfa.gov.il/MFA/Foreign%20Relations/Israels%20Foreign%20Relations%20since%201947/1947-1974/28%20The%20Jarring%20initiative%20and%20the%20response-%208%20Febr .
14. El Shazly, *The Crossing of the Suez*, 191.
15. Tessler, *A History of the Israeli–Palestinian Conflict*, 476.
16. George W. Gawrych, *The Albatross of Decisive Victory: War and Policy Between Egypt and Israel in the 1967 and 1973 Arab–Israeli Wars* (Westport, CT: Greenwood Press, 2000), 243–244. Some Egyptian sources estimate the losses on the Arab side to be between 8,528 and 15,000 killed, and between 19,540 and 35,000 wounded, and on the Israeli side 2,656 killed and 7,250 wounded. See, Mohamd abdel-ghany al-Gamasy, *Al-Gamasy Biography October War 1973* (Cairo: General Egyptian Book Organization, Arabic Edition, Second Edition, 1998).
17. Rabil, *Embattled Neighbors*, 32.
18. PFLP: the Popular Front for the Liberation of Palestine, a Marxist group established by George Habash, a Palestinian Christian, in the immediate aftermath of the 1967 war. It joined the PLO in 1968 and was considered the second-largest Palestinian guerrilla group after Fatah. When the PLO adopted in 1974 its Provisional Program the group withdrew from the Executive Committee of that organization to join the Rejectionist Front. PFLP-GC: Popular Front for the Liberation of Palestine-General Command, under the leadership of Ahmad Jibril, broke away from the PFLP in 1968. DFLP: Democratic Front for the Liberation of Palestine, under the leader of Naif Hawatmeh, broke away from the PFLP in 1969.
19. Sayigh, *Armed Struggle and the Search for the State*, 329–357; Avraham Sela and Moshe Ma'oz, eds., *The PLO and Israel: From Armed Conflict to Political Solution, 1964–1994* (New York: St. Martin's Press, 1997).
20. With Military Order 92 (15 August, 1967), Israel transferred full authority over all matters concerning water resources in the West Bank and Gaza Strip from the various governors, municipalities and village councils to a single person, an Israeli official appointed by the area military commander. Military Order 291 (19 December, 1968) declared all water resources to be Israeli State property and stated that all prior and existing settlements of water disputes were invalid. Between 1967 and 1969 Israel also limited Palestinian access to surface water sources by declaring irrigated farmland along the Jordan River to be a closed military area. With Military Order (MO) 92 (15 Aug. 1967) Israel transferred the authority over WBGS water resources to the area military commander; private owners and communities lost control. MO 158 (19 Nov. 1967) forbade the unlicensed construction of new water infrastructures, and MO 291 (19 Dec. 1968) confiscated all water resources, declaring them state property. For the full text of MO 92, see, http://www.israellawresourcecenter.org/

israelmilitaryorders/fulltext/m00092.htm .For other MOs, see http://www.israellawresourcecenter.org/israelmilitaryorders/israelimilitaryorders.htm.

21. For further details of Israeli policies affecting water and land cultivations, see World Bank September 1993 study "Developing the Occupied Territories—An Investment in Peace." For an Israeli source, see, B'Tselem, "Disputed Waters: Israel's Responsibility for the Water Shortage in the Occupied Territories," Information Sheet, Jerusalem: B'Tselem, September 1998. For Palestinian sources, see, Sharif Elmusa, *Water Conflict: Economics, Politics, Law and Palestinian-Israeli Water Resources* (Washington, DC: Institute for Palestine Studies, 1998); LAW, "An Overview of the consequences of Israeli Occupation on the environment in the West Bank and Gaza," 2000; Passia, http://www.passia.org/palestine_facts/pdf/ Water%20&%20Environment.pdf; PASSIA, "Water: Blue Gold," 2002. For a joint Israeli–Palestinian source, see, Hillel I. Shuval, Hassan Dwiek, eds, *Water Resources in the Middle East: The Israeli-Palestinian Water Issues - From Conflict to Cooperation* (New York: Springer, 2007).
22. For further details, see Gorenberg, *The Accidental Empire*, Benvenisti, *The West Bank Data Project*, ICBS, and FMEP (see Chapter 4, note 54, above). See also, Ann M. Lesch, "Israeli Settlements in the Occupied Territories," *Journal of Palestine Studies*, 8, 1 (Autumn, 1978), 100–119; Idith Zertal and Akiva Eldar, *Lords of the Land: The War over Israel's Settlements in the Occupied Territories, 1967–2007* (New York: Nation Books, 2007); Ian Lustick, *For the Land and the Lord: Jewish fundamentalism in Israel* (New York: Council on Foreign Relations, 1988); Robert I. Friedman, *Zealots for Zion: inside Israel's West Bank Settlement Movement* (New York: Random House, 1992); William W. Harris, *Taking Root: Israeli Settlement in the West Bank, the Golan, and Gaza-Sinai, 1967–1980* (New York: Research Studies Press, 1980).
23. Dayan stated this in the early 1970s, and reiterated it during the period of Camp David negotiations, from September 1978 until November 15, 1978. Edwin G. Corr, Joseph Ginat, Shaul M. Gabbay, eds., *The Search for Israeli-Arab Peace: Learning from the Past and Building Trust* (Portland: Sussex Academic Press, 2007), 55. This statement was mentioned by Boutros Ghali, a member of the Egyptian team at the Camp David negotiations, when he was interviewed by al-Jazeera Satellite Channel. "Shahed ala al-Asr (Witness of an Era)," Part No.6, Feb.13, 2005, al-Jazeera, http://www.aljazeera.net/NR/exeres/042208BE-D6D2-4D38-B8E6-6589C70670B5
24. El-Shazly, *The Crossing of the Suez*, 248–253.
25. Patrick Seale, *Asad of Syria*, 190. "Egypt was Syria's only choice as war partner: a two-front strategy with Egypt was in fact the bedrock of the secret planning which Asad and Anwar al-Sadat began early in 1971. Asad had full confidence in his Egyptian ally."
26. Seale, *Asad*, 186. See also Rabil, *Embattled Neighbors*, 21. Rabil explains, "[Asad] advocated a nationalist policy that gave priority to strengthening the Syrian Defense establishment..., Asad had reservations about the role the Palestinian guerillas could play in [the struggle against Israel]. He believed that irregulars could do little to change the outcome of a battle and were in fact a military liability, for they provided Israel with a pretext to strike against Syrian positions. So he wanted the guerillas placed under strict army control."
27. Seale, *Asad*, 190–192.
28. *Ibid.*, 156–162.
29. Raymond Hinnebusch, *Syria: Revolution from Above* (New York: Routledge, 2001), 153.
30. Seale, *Asad*, 197.
31. *Ibid.*, 197.
32. Ma'oz, *Asad: The Sphinx of Damascus: A Political Biography*, 120.

33. Seale, *Asad*, 198.
34. *Ibid.*, 214: "Sadat's deception of Asad went beyond the sabotage of their two-front strategy...it extended to the peace diplomacy which he secretly conducted throughout the conflict."
35. *Ibid.*, 215: "Sadat dumped Asad in favor of the U.S."
36. Rabil, *Embattled Neighbors*, 34.
37. *Ibid.*,, 25–6:

> Syria had no other option than to accept U.S. mediation with Israel in order to recover its newly occupied territory...Inasmuch as it needed the withdrawal of Israel, it could not settle only for the restoration of the October 6 (prewar line). It needed a symbolic gain of land...to safeguard the legitimacy of the regime, to rationalize domestically the negotiations with Israel, to keep pace with Egypt..., and to justify the October War itself.

38. *Ibid.*, 216.
39. For more on the Jordanian narrative, see Adnan Abu-Odeh, *Jordanians, Palestinians and the Hashemite Kingdom in the Middle East Peace Process* (Washington, DC: US Institute of Peace Press, 1999); Michael N. Barnett, *Dialogues in Arab Politics; Negotiations in Regional Order* (New York: Columbia University Press, 1998); Aaron David Miller, *The Arab States and the Palestine Question: Between Ideology and Self-Interest* (New York: Praeger, 1986); Philip Robins, *A History of Jordan* (Cambridge: Cambridge University Press, 2004); Kamal Salibi, *The Modern History of Jordan* (London: IB Tauris, 1993); Asher Susser, *On Both Banks of the Jordan: A Political Biography of Wasfi al-Tall* (Essex: Frank Cass, 1994).
40. Daily Report, Middle East & North Africa. Washington, DC: Foreign Broadcast Information Service (FBIS), 1968–1974, March 25, 1968: D8. Hussein's remarks are also reprinted in William B. Quandt, Fuad Jabber, and Ann Mosely Lesch, *The Politics of Palestinian Nationalism* (Berkeley, CA: University of California Press, 1973), 195.
41. Quoted in Susser, *On Both Banks of the Jordan*, 155.
42. Sulaymān al-Mūsá, *Tarikh al Urdun al Siyasi al Mu'asir: Huzairan 1967–1995* (*Current Political History of Jordan: June 1967–1995*) (Amman: Da'irat al Maktabah al Wataniyyah: 1998), 95–107.
43. In the middle of 1974, Kissinger started thinking of delivering a disengagement agreement on the Jordanian front. See: Quandt, *Peace Process*, 157–159.
44. "Joint Communiqué, Moscow 1972," *Washington Post*, http://www.washingtonpost.com/wp-srv/inatl/longterm/summit/archive/com1972-1.htm (Accessed Jun 13, 2011).
45. Tessler, *A History of the Israeli–Palestinian Conflict*, 479; Shlaim, *The Iron Wall*, 313–314.
46. Mohamed Haykal, *The Road to Ramadan* (New York: Ballantine Books, 1976), 180.
47. Robert Jervis, "Cooperation Under the Security Dilemma," *World Politics*, 30, 4 (January 1978), 167–214.
48. Yigal Allon, "Israel: The Case for Defensible Borders," *Foreign Affairs*, 55, 1 (October, 1976), 38-53.
49. El-Shazly, *The Crossing of the Suez*, 36.
50. Rabil, *Embattled Neighbors*, 31. "In central disagreement with Jadid, Asad advocated a strategy of cooperation with Arab countries in the interest of confronting Israel." Asad saw Israel as an expansionist extension of colonialism, that posed an existential threat to Syria as well as the Arab World.
51. Seale, *Asad*, 186: "Syrians were outraged by [Israel's] wartime expansion and believed that what had been taken by force could only be regained by force."
52. Morris, *Righteous Victims*, 442–443.

53. Abdel Monem Said Aly, "The United States and The October 1973 Middle East Crisis," PhD Dissertation, Northern Illinois University, 1982, 235–260; and Henry Kissinger, *Years of Upheaval* (Boston: Little, Brown, 1982).
54. Walter Isaacson, *Kissinger* (New York: Simon and Schuster, 1996), 13, as quoted in Aaron David Miller, *The Much Too Promised Land* (New York: Bantam Books, 2008), 140.
55. Miller, *The Much Too Promised Land*, 140.
56. *Ibid.*, 144.
57. *Ibid.*, 139 and 155.

6 Camp David and the Lebanon War

The period addressed in this chapter, spanning from 1975 to 1986, witnessed the first major breakthrough in state-to-state Arab–Israeli peacemaking: the surprise visit of Egypt's President Sadat to Israel in November 1977, the 1978 summit at Camp David, and the signing of the two countries' peace treaty in March 1979, leading to Egypt's isolation in the Arab world. These developments were not only a sharp departure from long-standing patterns of regional behavior – they also defied the region's broader international environment, occurring when East–West relations were at their worst. The Cold War now came back, overcoming détente politics, and its temperature now rose again: in late 1979 the Soviets invaded Afghanistan, and Soviet–United States competition increased over Central America and the Horn of Africa.

In the Middle East at-large, this period was characterized by a number of important developments: first, the 1979 revolution in Iran, which fueled the politicization of Palestinian Islamists during the early 1980s. The Iranian revolution also inspired some members of the Palestinian Muslim Brotherhood to create a new group – Islamic Jihad – fully supported by Iran.

The second significant, although more gradual, development in the region beginning in 1979 was the consolidation of Saddam Hussein's power in Iraq. This resulted in greater tensions between Syria and Iraq, with each country's Ba'ath government assisting the opponents of the other. Saddam's fierce opposition to Israel also led him to attempt to rally support against Egypt. But his simultaneous launching of the war against Iran in 1980 placed him in a new position: as gatekeeper of the Arab world against the revolutionary regime in Persia.[1]

Saddam's ascendance was associated with another development: the reintroduction of the nuclear issue into the Arab–Israeli conflict with the Israeli bombing of the Osiraq nuclear research reactor in Iraq in June 1981.

With dramatically higher prices of oil, this era could have belonged to the oil producers, primarily Saudi Arabia, and in some ways it did. This was certainly reflected in the beginning of Saudi investments in the media sector, often with regional reach, such as *Al-Hayat* and *A-Sharq al-Awsat* newspapers (although a far cry from the much later phenomena of Al-Jazeera and Al-Arabia television stations). But building military capabilities to deter Iran and participating in an array of activities designed to contain it – most notably by supporting Iraq – as well as helping roll-back the Soviets in Afghanistan, all required substantial investments by Saudi Arabia and other Arab oil producers.

Another dramatic development in the Middle East during this period was Israel's 1982 invasion of Lebanon. With its southern flank secured by its peace treaty with Egypt, Israel felt it had the requisite freedom to pursue more ambitious plans: transforming Lebanon and restructuring the region.

In the West Bank this period was characterized by Israeli efforts to decapitate the local PLO-leaning leadership, while in Gaza the Israelis sought to promote Islamists as a counterbalance to the PLO. Meanwhile the PLO turned to strengthen its hold in Lebanon, especially in the southern parts of the country, which would eventually place it at the "receiving end" of the 1982 War.

If the first half of the period covered in this chapter, from the mid-1970s until the early 1980s, was marked by sharp disagreements in the Arab world, the second half, from the early 1980s until the outbreak of the First Palestinian Intifada in 1987, witnessed a compromise of sorts and a bridging of the gap between these camps. Some among those who were previously uncompromising in their rejection of Sadat's peace initiative now moved a step or two closer to Egypt.

Main Developments

The events that shook the Middle East during this period made up the clearest manifestation of the change in character of the Arab–Israeli conflict from an existential to a non-existential conflict. This was reflected particularly in Egypt's decision to pursue peace with Israel. Because Egypt was and remains the most important, largest and most populous of the Arab states, its decision to reach an accommodation with Israel was transformative and affected the entire region. In turn, Israel adopted a multi-faceted policy: making all the concessions required to reach a peace agreement with Egypt while pursuing an aggressive policy with regard to Iraq's nuclear program and the PLO's presence in Lebanon. The broader region also witnessed dramatic developments: the revolution in Iran, the Soviet invasion of Afghanistan, and the eight-year Iraq–Iran War.

East–West Détente and Revolution in Iran

The period covered by this chapter witnessed dramatic developments in the international system as well as in the Middle East. It began with détente that rapidly became a Second Cold War. In the beginning of this period, members of the Western and Soviet blocs worked out the first broad understanding regarding their international and even internal behavior – the 1974 Helsinki Final Act. Signed by the United States, Canada, and 33 European states, it dealt with various issues, including disarmament and security arrangements; human rights and humanitarian principles; trade and economic rules; and scientific and environmental cooperation.[2] By 1977, the two superpowers also agreed on a common approach to the Middle East conflict – the Soviet–American Communiqué. The document called for a comprehensive peace settlement between Israel and the Arabs, including the Palestinians, with negotiations to begin by December 1977 in the framework of the Geneva Peace Conference.[3] At the end of this period, the two blocs concluded the most detailed agreement on security and confidence-building: the 1986 Stockholm Accords. The agreement anticipated the end of Cold War by stipulating a degree of transparency between rivals unprecedented in international behavior.

Between 1974 and 1986, however, the international system experienced the Second Cold War, featuring one of the most dangerous and violent developments of the post-war era: the 1979 Soviet invasion of Afghanistan. Closely associated was the election of President Ronald Reagan, who regarded the Soviet Union as an "evil empire." Together with some of its Middle Eastern allies, notably Saudi Arabia, the Reagan administration mounted a major effort to contain the Soviets in Afghanistan by arming their Muslim opponents – the various Islamic *Muja'hadin* groups. In parallel, the administration launched a new arms race at almost every level: from the construction of America's largest-ever fleet of naval vessels to the further expansion of the American arsenal of nuclear weapons and delivery systems. The Reagan administration also launched the Strategic Defense Initiative (SDI): an ambitious effort to substitute the post-war deterrence system based on the capacity for mutual assured destruction (MAD) by defense against nuclear-armed ballistic missiles.

The developments experienced in the Middle East at large during this timeframe were no less tumultuous. The first of these took place in the Persian Gulf area: the February 1979 revolution in Iran which replaced the Pahlavi dynasty by an Islamic state. This introduced Islam for the first time as a major factor in regional politics and regional security. A number of aspects characterizing Iran determined the regional ramifications of this development: it is an important, large country located at the eastern edge of the Middle East; it is Islamic revolutionary of the Shi'a persuasion; and, it is Persian and thus non-Arab. Yet the Iranian revolution resonated well among Middle East publics, the new regime declaring its support for Palestinian rights in land "occupied in the 1948 War."[4]

In a broader sense, the Iranian Revolution, closely followed by the prolonged hostage crisis – where 52 officials and members of the United States embassy in Tehran were held hostage for 444 days – left a legacy and spread a sense of empowerment as a demonstration of the ability to remove a tyrant and an ally of Israel and to defy the all-powerful United States of America. In the latter context, the decision of Iran's Supreme Leader, Ayatollah Khomeini, to hand over the Israeli Embassy in Tehran to the PLO resonated well among Arab publics.

Another development that followed the Iranian Revolution, which eventually turned out to be one of the bloodiest episodes in the region's history, was Iraq's launching of a war against Iran. The war witnessed the deployment of chemical weapons and the extensive use of ballistic missiles against Tehran and Baghdad. It is estimated to have resulted in the deaths of some 150,000 Iranians in battle, with another 40,000 listed as missing in action, and 2,000 civilians killed. Iraq lost 60,000 men in battle with another 6,000 Iraqi Kurdish civilians killed by their own government.[5] In an unprecedented leap from the Arab–Israeli side of the region to the conflict in the Gulf, in June 1981 Israel sent aircraft a distance of 965 kilometers to destroy Osiraq, Iraq's nuclear research reactor in Tuwaitha, near Baghdad. As a result of these developments, ballistic missile technologies and weapons of mass destruction now became for the first time an integral part of the discourse on Middle East security.

Egyptian–Israeli Peace and Discord

In the realm of Arab–Israeli peacemaking, the period addressed in this chapter manifested two extremes: the most dramatic breakthrough in Arab willingness to make peace with Israel and, at the same time, signs of continued hostility toward the Jewish state. The first of the two trends witnessed the stunning visit of Egypt's President Anwar Sadat to Israel in November 1977, a first-ever by an Arab leader to the State of Israel; the Camp David Accords – the agreement produced by the Egyptian–Israeli negotiations at Camp David in mid-1978; and the signing of a peace treaty between the two countries in March 1979.

Sadat's trip to Israel was preceded by a number of important but less dramatic positive developments in Egyptian–Israeli relations, mostly noted in the previous chapter. The first was the Disengagement Agreement signed by the two countries on January 18, 1974. The Second Egyptian–Israeli Disengagement Agreement signed on September 1, 1975 allowed for further Israeli withdrawals.

Less than two years later, efforts by the Carter administration to reconvene the Geneva Conference led to tension with the new Israeli Likud-led government, elected in mid-1977 and headed by Prime Minister Menachem Begin. On July 19–21, Begin and Carter conferred in Washington and reached agreement on the reconvening of the Geneva Conference in the fall of 1977 – an agreement confirmed by Begin in a speech to the Knesset on July 27.[6]

On August 2, Sadat and Secretary of State Cyrus Vance agreed to hold a conference of Middle Eastern Foreign Ministers prior to a full scale Geneva Conference. But Syrian President Hafez Assad demanded an advance formulation of substantive issues for discussion at a reconvened Geneva Conference, and in talks with Vance he rejected the idea of holding a Foreign Ministers' meeting. Israel, in turn, rejected any kind of participation of the PLO in Geneva.[7]

Sadat's Visit to Jerusalem

To break the deadlock, on November 9 Sadat stunned the Egyptian parliament by stating that he would to go "to the end of the universe to end the conflict and save the sons of Egypt" and that he was prepared to travel to Jerusalem to address the Israeli Knesset. Two days later Begin responded by inviting Sadat to hold peace talks in Jerusalem. On November 16, Sadat conferred with Assad in a failed attempt to persuade him to join the trip.

Earlier that month, Egypt and Israel engaged in direct secret talks held under the auspices of King Hassan of Morocco. Hassan Al Tuhami, a special emissary, represented Sadat and Foreign Minister Dayan represented Begin.[8] Precisely what if any understandings were reached in these talks remains uncertain, as does their impact on subsequent developments.

On November 19, Sadat traveled to Jerusalem, thus becoming the first Arab leader to pay an official visit to Israel. The next day, after praying at the al-Aqsa Mosque and visiting the Holocaust memorial Yad Vashem, he addressed the Israeli Knesset, calling for the establishment of comprehensive peace predicated on Israel's withdrawal from the territories

Figure 6.1. Egyptian president Anwar Sadat in the Knesset, with Golda Meir and Shimon Peres.
© Yaacov Saar/epa/CORBIS

it occupied in the 1967 War and the establishment of a Palestinian state, stating that "there can be no peace without the Palestinians."[9]

While historical and transformative, it took a while for Sadat's visit to Jerusalem to be translated to a significant change on the ground. Meanwhile the reaction of other Arab states to Sadat's overture was viral: in early December Syria, Iraq, Libya, Algeria and South Yemen suspended relations with Egypt to protest Sadat's initiative.

Reciprocating Sadat's visit, on December 25 Begin traveled to Egypt and met with its president in Ismailiya. The two failed to bridge the gap between their positions, particularly on dealing with the Palestinian issue. Instead, they agreed to create joint political and military committees. While the Palestinian issue continued to prevent agreement in the political committee – where Israel's settlement policy was the subject of continuous friction – the military committee made greater headway in addressing the security dimensions of future Egyptian–Israeli relations. On January 4, 1978 Presidents Carter and Sadat met in Aswan and issued the Aswan Proclamation calling for the recognition of the legitimate rights of the Palestinian people and their participation in the determination of their future.[10]

The Run-up to Camp David

January 1978 witnessed a flurry of diplomatic activities between Egypt and Israel. The Israel–Egypt military committee began talks in Cairo. Meeting Israeli Defense Minister Ezer Weizmann in Aswan, Sadat demanded total Israeli withdrawal from the Sinai. Begin countered by stating that "peace cannot be established should Israel restore or agree to restore the fragile, breakable, aggression-provoking and bloodshed-causing lines preceding the 5th of June 1967."[11]

Recurring diplomatic failures led President Carter to make a daring move. On August 17 he formally invited Sadat and Begin to a summit at Camp David, the president's country residence. On August 27, the Israeli Government authorized the Israeli delegation to Camp David to present an autonomy plan for the West Bank and Gaza as the basis for a settlement of the Israeli–Palestinian conflict. The summit, held on September 6–17 produced two agreements signed at the White House lawn: the first provided the principles for an Israel–Egypt peace treaty and the return of Sinai to Egypt while the second established a

Figure 6.2. Anwar Sadat and Menachem Begin after signing the Camp David Accords. *Source*: Library of Congress, LC-DIG-ppmsca-09792.

format for negotiating a 5-year autonomy regime in the West Bank and the Gaza regions.[12]

The Road to the Peace Treaty

Despite the success of the Camp David Summit, the road to signing the Egypt–Israel peace treaty was not easy. When the two sides resumed discussions in the summit's aftermath, this time at Blair House on October 12, the talks ran into difficulties over the linkage between the proposed bilateral treaty and the issue of establishing autonomy for the Palestinians, as well as some aspects of the bilateral deal – notably the issue of oil supply for Israel and Egypt's demand for early Israeli withdrawal.

On March 10–13, Carter visited Egypt and Israel to iron out the remaining differences. On March 19, the Israeli Government approved the text of the peace treaty and on March 22, the Knesset approved it by a margin of 95 to 18 with five abstaining or absent. The Egyptian parliament unanimously approved the peace treaty with Israel on March 21, and on March 26 the treaty was signed at the White House.[13]

As an important part of implementing its obligations under the peace treaty, in 1982 Israel evacuated its settlements in the Sinai. Eighteen settlements consisting of about 7,000 settlers were evacuated. Just prior to transferring the Sinai Peninsula to Egypt in April 1982, Yamit, the largest settlement with 3,000 inhabitants, was evacuated after resistance by many of its settlers.

The Arab Reaction: From Opposition to Accommodation

The initial reaction in the Arab world to Sadat's peace initiative was sharp and negative, as many Arab states opposed a separate peace with Israel and others remained wedded to continued confrontation. Egypt was ostracized, boycotted and sanctioned in the Arab world – it was expelled from the League of Arab States and the League's headquarters were relocated from Cairo to Tunis.[14] Egypt's membership in the Organization of Islamic States was also suspended and it was threatened with expulsion from the Non-Aligned Movement.

Some of the most negative immediate reactions to Egypt's change of course took place within Egypt itself. There was broad opposition to the move, even within Sadat's own government – leading to the resignation of Foreign Minister Ismail Fahmy, and, after the

Figure 6.3. Forced evacuation of Yamit, 1982. © David Rubinger/CORBIS

meetings in Camp David, Foreign Minister Ibrahim Kamel. But the opposition outside the governing circles – from secular Nasserites to the Muslim Brotherhood and violent radical Islamists – was much stronger and more violent, ultimately resulting in the October 1981 assassination of President Sadat.[15]

Sadat's successor as President of Egypt, Hosni Mubarak, remained committed to the strategic decision to end the conflict with Israel. Moreover, even before Sadat's assassination important elements in the Arab world had begun to shift their position in Egypt's direction and to accept the logic of Sadat's move. The first to support Egypt's actions were Morocco, Oman and Sudan, countries which shared Sadat's assessment that a military solution to the Arab–Israeli conflict was impossible and a political settlement of the conflict was inevitable.

More importantly, on August 7, 1981, Saudi Crown Prince Fahd Bin Abdul Aziz proposed an eight-point peace plan for the Arab–Israeli conflict, henceforth referred to as the Fahd Plan. It called on Israel to withdraw from all the territories it conquered in June 1967 and to dismantle the settlements it constructed in these territories, including those in East Jerusalem. The plan also proposed that the West Bank and the Gaza Strip be held under UN supervision for a transitional period that would not exceed a couple of months. It also called for the establishment of a Palestinian state with East Jerusalem as its capital and it affirmed the Palestinians' Right of Return in addition to guaranteeing the right of worship for all religions in the Holy Places. Israel was not mentioned by name; instead the plan affirmed "the right of all countries in the region to live in peace."[16] It was adopted by the Twelfth Arab Summit held in Fez on September 9, 1982, where it won the endorsement of the Arab League.[17]

Figure 6.4. Hosni Mubarak. © Bettmann/CORBIS

THE FAHD–FEZ PLAN

1. Israeli withdrawal from all Arab territories occupied in 1967, including Arab Jerusalem. 2. Removal of the settlements established by Israel in the Arab territories after 1967. 3. Guaranteeing the freedom of worship and religious practices for all religions in the Holy Places. 4. Asserting the right of the Palestinian people to return to their homes and compensation for those who do not wish to return. 5. Placing the West Bank and Gaza Strip under the auspices of the United Nations for a transitional period not exceeding several months. 6. Establishing an independent Palestinian state with Jerusalem as its capital. 7. Affirming the right of all states in the region to live in peace. 8. Guaranteeing the implementation of these principles by the United Nations or some of its member states.[18]

The March to War in Lebanon

In Lebanon, meanwhile, this period begins in the mid-1970s with the eruption of the Lebanese Civil War, the subsequent Syrian intervention in that country – effectively seizing direct or indirect control of the country's key assets – and the 1976 "red lines" agreement between Syria and Israel, which set the boundaries to the deployment of Syria's military forces in Lebanon and stipulated rules of engagement between the two countries in the Lebanese arena.[19]

The Palestinians' earlier expulsion from Jordan and the deterioration of central authority in Lebanon as a result of the civil war set the stage for the Palestinians to establish a strategic base in the country's south, from which the struggle against Israel could continue. During the second half of the 1970s, this led to violent clashes between Palestinian groups, who launched Katyusha rockets against Israel, and the IDF, which took measures to suppress the fire. By March of 1978 these clashes escalated into Israel's first large-scale invasion of

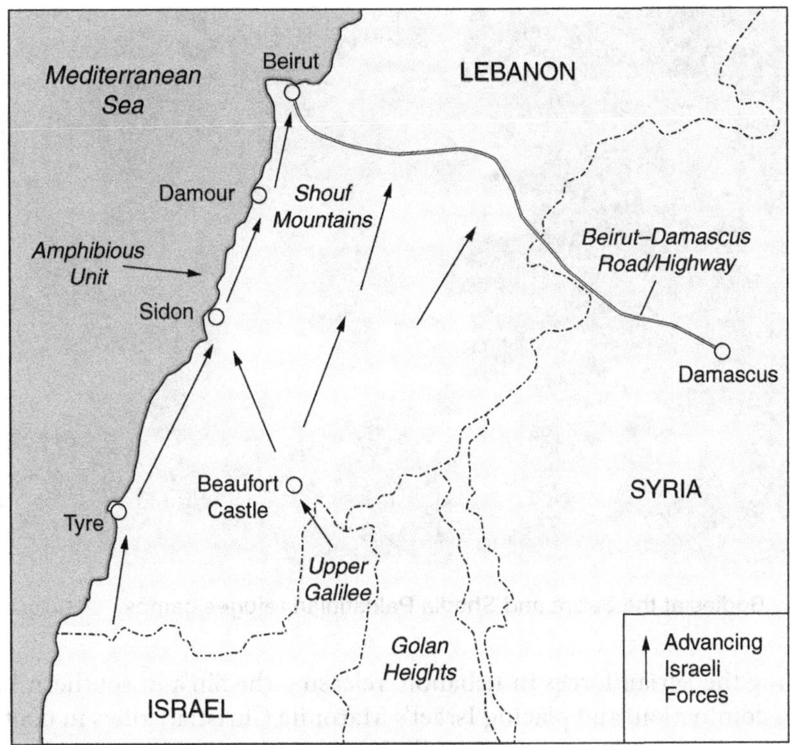

Figure 6.5. The Israeli Invasion of Lebanon, 1982

Lebanon – the Litani Operation. It consisted of a 36-hour advance by the IDF to the Litani River and the subsequent clearing of PLO, mostly Fatah, fighters and weapons from villages between the river and the international border. Israel then attempted to transform the area into a "security zone" by creating a local militia comprised mostly of Shi'a and Christians, headed by a former Lebanese military officer, Major Sa'ad Haddad.[20]

The Israeli-supported South Lebanese militia had a mixed track record.[21] While effective in preventing Palestinian infiltration, it could not prevent the PLO from rebuilding its positions north of the zone and from acquiring and positioning Katyusha rocket launchers of somewhat longer ranges, allowing them to reach Israel. By 1981, this resulted in a long, violent exchange between the Israeli air force and PLO Katyusha launchers. While causing considerable damage, the IAF failed to suppress the PLO fire. The result was a ceasefire between Israel and the PLO.[22]

In June 1982 Israel launched an ambitious effort to destroy the PLO's presence in Lebanon altogether. Some in the Israeli government that launched the war – possibly including Begin – believed it was aimed merely at clearing a 45-kilometer strip north of the Israel–Lebanon border of all Palestinian fighters and weapons.[23] But the war's architects, Defense Minister Ariel Sharon and IDF Chief of Staff Lieutenant General Raphael Eitan, set out to dislodge the Palestinian groups from Lebanon altogether by conquering Beirut, defeating

Figure 6.6. Bodies at the Sabra and Shatila Palestinian refugee camps. © Reuters/CORBIS

and expelling the Syrian forces in Lebanon, releasing the Shi'a in southern Lebanon from Palestinian domination, and placing Israel's Maronite Christian allies in control.[24]

Syria proved far more resistant to Israel's designs in Lebanon than had been anticipated. Israel's Maronite allies proved far too few and crude to control an entity as complex as Lebanon.[25] Syria's robust covert capacities allowed it to dispose of Israel's principal Christian ally, Bashir Jumail, through assassination. In their reaction, the Maronite forces proved unruly, conducting a massacre of civilians of all ages and genders in the Palestinian camps of Sabra and Shatila. The regional and international outcry that followed the massacre forced Israel to begin withdrawing from Beirut, with foreign troops – including a contingent of US Marines – sent to Lebanon to secure the safe departure of the Palestinians.[26]

Once the IDF began its retreat and foreign forces were injected into the scene, Israel had lost the ability to control the agenda in Lebanon. Now others initiated and Israel reacted. Strategically, the injection of American forces into an area where the IDF was still deployed resulted in unprecedented tension between American diplomats and military officers and their Israeli counterparts.[27] More enduring, however, were the effects of these developments on the Lebanese domestic scene. In one sense the Israeli project succeeded: PLO fighters were transferred away from Lebanon to other destinations including Tunisia, to which the PLO headquarters was now relocated. On the other hand the weakening of the Palestinians and the Christian Maronites resulted in the beginning of a Shi'a era: for the first time in Lebanon's history this large minority had the opportunity to assert itself.

On the Palestinian and Jordanian Fronts

Seeking to undermine the influence of the PLO, Israel began to encourage the emergence of an anti-nationalist force in the West Bank and Gaza. In this context, Israel hoped to see a strong pro-Jordanian elite emerge in the West Bank and a traditional Islamist elite in the Gaza Strip as a means of combating the PLO and leftist groups. While nationalist guerrilla groups engaged the IDF almost immediately after these territories were conquered in June 1967, Islamist groups, operating mainly under the banner of the Muslim Brotherhood, did not join the fight. Instead, they focused on building mosques, charities, schools, and other social services and institutions. These religious forces viewed the nationalists as secularists and labeled leftist forces as "atheists" in Friday sermons.[28]

Given this rivalry, and believing that the Islamists did not pose an immediate threat to its control of Gaza, the West Bank and East Jerusalem, Israel tolerated the activities of the Muslim Brotherhood, including their large-scale efforts at institution-building. Thus, in 1979, the Israeli military authorities in the Gaza Strip allowed Sheikh Ahmad Yassin, later the founder of Hamas, to officially register one of the largest Islamic institutions in the territories - *al-Mujama al-Islami* [the Islamic Compound]. For almost a decade thereafter the institution served as the political headquarters of the Muslim Brotherhood and became a symbol of the Islamists' growing power.[29] From an Israeli perspective the Islamists' goal of an Islamic state in all of Palestine seemed far-fetched and irrelevant. As long as the Muslim Brotherhood continued to oppose the secular nationalists and leftist forces, Israel was willing to tolerate, and indeed encourage, it.[30]

In the West Bank, Israel decided in 1976 to organize local elections. The brainchild of Defense Minister Shimon Peres, the elections were meant to provide legitimacy to the pro-Jordanian elite and weaken the nationalists. Peres hoped that the elected leaders would accept his idea of Palestinian self-rule. This was part of Peres' concept of a functional arrangement with Jordan – a kind of federation or confederation and a version of the "Jordan Option" whereby Israel would retain security control while Jordan would have control over civil administrative matters.[31]

His efforts backfired, however, producing the opposite of what they intended. The majority of those who won the municipal elections were nationalists. The new mayors were younger and better educated than the pro-Jordanian ones. Even in traditional communities like Hebron, a nationalist Fahd Qawasmeh, an agronomist, replaced Sheikh Jaabari, a strong pro-Jordanian. Similarly, in Nablus, Bassam Shak'a, a Ba'athist, won and replaced Mazouz al-Masri, a strong pro-Hashemite. This result ushered in a new chapter in the development of the "inside" Palestinian nationalist movement. The new elite reflected hard-line views, identified fully with the PLO and the desire of Palestinians for independence.[32] The new mayors, along with other members of the West Bank urban nationalist elite, created the National Guidance Committee (NGC), a forum that spoke in the name of West Bank Palestinians.[33]

These results were undermined a few years later when, in 1979, Israel sought to decapitate the emerging local nationalist leadership and to replace it with a rural-based traditional elite. It banned the NGC, deported to Jordan ten elected mayors for their pro-PLO activities, and created the so-called Village Leagues. Moreover, on June 2, 1980, two mayors were severely wounded by bombs placed in their cars by a Jewish terrorist group. For a short period, until the expulsion of the PLO from Lebanon, the decapitation of the local leadership only strengthened the influence of the "outside" PLO leadership.[34]

Another development on the Israeli–Palestinian front that took place during this timeframe was the passage by the Israeli Knesset on July 30, 1980 of the "Basic Law: Jerusalem, Capital of

Israel." The new legislation stated that "Jerusalem, complete and united, is the capital of Israel." It did not specify the exact jurisdictional boundaries of the city nor did it change the status of Palestinians living in East Jerusalem who remained "permanent residents" rather than Israeli citizens. Nevertheless, it was interpreted as providing the basis for an Israeli official annexation of East Jerusalem to Israel, although the word "annexation" is not mentioned in the law. On August 20 the UN Security Council reacted to the new law by adopting Resolution 478, declaring that it was a violation of international law, that it was "null and void," and that it "must be rescinded."

With Likud coming to power following the 1977 elections, Israel's new government embarked in 1978 on a new phase of settlement construction in the West Bank, the Gaza Strip, and the Golan Heights. Dozens more settlements were established, this time, guided by "Greater Israel" ideology, close to populated Palestinian areas. Settlement budgets also increased, growing from $3.4 million in 1976 under Labor to $34 million in 1983. By 1985, the number of settlements in the West Bank increased from 20, under Labor, to 102, under Likud. The largest settlements of the West Bank, Ma'aleh Adumim, Modi'in Illit, Beitar Illit, and Ariel, and large settlements like Beit El and Giv'at Ze'ev, near Ramallah, and Efrat, near Bethlehem, were established during this period. The number of settlers increased from 4,400 to 42,000.[35] Jewish neighborhoods in East Jerusalem were expanded and new ones, such as Pisgat Zeev, were created. In the Golan Heights, 11 new settlements were established. In 1981, Israel extended the application of its law to the Golan Heights, passing the "Golan Heights Law," which granted permanent residency, ID cards, and Israeli citizenship to the residents, but did not formally annex the territory.[36]

The outcome of the Lebanon war weakened the PLO considerably – a weakness exacerbated by a mutiny within Fatah in Lebanon. Supported and perhaps instigated by the Syrians, the mutiny aimed at replacing Arafat with a more pro-Syrian figure or forcing him to abandon his efforts to reach out to Egypt and Jordan.[37] By contrast, it became clear that Israel's attempt to weaken the nationalists in the West Bank through the encouragement of rural elites had failed. But the Israeli efforts – and, just as important, the outcome of the Lebanon war – did succeed in significantly weakening the more hard-line nationalist elite in the West Bank. Now, a more pragmatic nationalist leadership gained prominence. Indeed, even the pro-Jordanian elite now witnessed some resurgence. Pragmatic nationalists such as Faisal al-Husseini and Sari Nusseibah from East Jerusalem and Zafir al-Masri from Nablus, and pro-Jordanians such as Elias Freij from Bethlehem and Rashad al-Shawwa from Gaza, gained prominence.[38]

The PLO–Jordan dialogue in 1984–86, described below, facilitated cooperation between the pragmatic nationalists and the pro-Jordanians. By contrast, the differences between hard-liners and pragmatists within the Palestinian camp now sharpened. The hard-liners wanted a continued PLO–Syrian alliance and opposed the PLO–Jordan dialogue. They also supported strong PLO relations with the Soviet Union and opposed Arafat's attempts to engage the West, particularly the United States. They worked toward the establishment of a Palestinian state and opposed a confederation with Jordan.[39]

In September 1982, the United States announced the Reagan Plan – calling for negotiations between Israel and a joint Jordanian–Palestinian delegation regarding the establishment of a Palestinian self-rule entity within a Jordanian–Palestinian federation. The plan also called for a freeze in settlement construction activities.[40] Israel rejected the proposal furiously and immediately.[41] Jordan's King Hussein, who had been consulted before the Reagan announcement, was tempted by the plan and the incentives President Reagan offered him to accept the initiative. However, after talks with the PLO over several months, Hussein failed to gain support for a Jordanian delegation representative of the Palestinians as well. He therefore officially announced Jordan's rejection of the Reagan Plan.[42] The plan's possible implementation was aborted by the Sabra and Shatila massacres which took place shortly after it was announced, and the bombing of the US Marine barracks in Lebanon in October 1983 in which over 200 marines were killed, leading to the eventual American withdrawal from Lebanon. The hasty withdrawal was a blow to the prestige of the United States in the region, affecting negatively its ability to implement any kind of Middle East peace plan.

As indicated above, by the mid-1980s, a major attempt was being made to end the rift between Jordan and the PLO – a rift that had reached its violent peak more than a decade earlier, during Black September of 1970. Now the veterans of Palestinian–Jordanian fighting tried to come together around a program. Following Egyptian mediation, Jordan and the PLO were able to reach an understanding: the Amman Accord. Signed on February 11, 1985 its core was an agreement to reach a settlement with Israel based on an Israeli withdrawal from all territories occupied in the 1967 War. It stipulated that Jordan and the PLO would work together toward a peaceful resolution of the conflict with Israel. The signatories also promised to establish a confederation between Jordan and the West Bank and Gaza and that the Palestinian refugee problem would be dealt with "in accordance with the relevant U.N resolutions."[43]

Yet the Jordanian–Palestinian rapprochement proved short-lived: a year after the Amman Accords were signed, Jordanian–PLO disagreements resurfaced. Given its similarity to the Reagan Initiative, King Hussein hoped to use the Amman Accord as a trigger for an international diplomatic initiative under American leadership. For that to work, however, he needed PLO willingness to accept UN Resolutions 242 and 338.[44] When Arafat and the PLO contradicted the Jordanian position and refused to endorse the two UN resolutions, the king felt betrayed.

On the Palestinian side, while the Accord was supported by mainstream nationalists and pro-Jordanian elements in the West Bank, leftist forces supported by Syria strongly opposed it. Suspicion about Jordanian motives grew as Jordanian activities in the West Bank increased dramatically during this period.[45] In turn, the PLO suspected Jordan of intending to reach an agreement with Israel while the Labor Party was still in an influential position, albeit within a National Unity Government – an agreement Jordan knew it would not be able to reach with a Likud-dominated government.[46]

At that point the king felt he could no longer wait for the PLO to adopt a realistic position, one that would allow a joint Palestinian–Jordanian approach to peace with Israel. In 1986, he opened direct but secret bilateral negotiations with Israel, aimed at concluding a peace agreement between the two countries. The resulting London Agreement, reached in April 1987, called for the Palestinian issue to be addressed by negotiations between Israel and Jordan based on UN Resolutions 242 and 338. It required that all participating parties denounce terrorism and violence, implying that the PLO would not take part in the negotiations.[47]

The London Agreement subsequently fell victim to its mishandling in Jerusalem and Washington, partly as a result of the faulty logic of the two-headed Israeli government of national unity: with Prime Minister Shamir effectively derailing every significant initiative of Foreign Minister Peres.

As Peres presented the agreement to Secretary of State George Shultz, so that the United States could promote it, Shamir sent emissaries to Washington to clarify that he was not a party to the agreement, thus torpedoing the idea. Not surprisingly, Israel's national unity cabinet declined to adopt the London Agreement.[48]

Narratives

The Israeli Narrative

The Israeli narrative of this period spans all three dramatic developments: the breakthrough in the relations with Egypt, the bombing of Osiraq, and the invasion of Lebanon. The narrative with regard to the breakthrough with Egypt focused on explaining why Israel accepted all of Egypt's demands, returned the entire Sinai Peninsula to Egyptian sovereignty, and dismantled all Israeli settlements constructed in the northern Sinai during the 1970s. The thrust of this narrative was intended to demonstrate that when offered genuine peace, Israel responds.

Peace with Egypt

The Israeli narrative regarding its relations with Egypt rested on a number of elements: the first was an appreciation of the historical importance of Sadat's gesture. Egypt was seen as the most important of the Arab states. Therefore, reaching peace with Egypt was viewed as a transformative event – a development promising a revolutionary change in Israel's standing in the region, thus justifying far-reaching concessions.

In turn, this assessment was based on a number of expectations and judgments. One was that given Egypt's leadership role, other Arab states would eventually follow, thus opening Israel's path to the Arab world at large. Another was that Egypt was essential to any Arab war coalition against Israel – that is, that given Egypt's pivotal role, the Arab states could not launch a war against the Jewish state without Egypt's participation. This assessment placed enormous value on taking Egypt out of any potential Arab war coalition.

Also, by visiting Israel and delivering the speech he gave to the Israeli Knesset, President Sadat was seen as appreciating that Israel had real security concerns that must and deserved to be addressed. As such, he was viewed as deviating from the earlier and broader Arab narrative that interpreted Israeli behavior as driven solely by aggressive impulses. Instead, Sadat was now regarded as associating himself with the Israelis' very different understanding of their conduct: namely, that even their more aggressive acts were driven by a deep sense of insecurity, steeped in the Jewish peoples' difficult history. Accordingly, Egypt's president was seen as appreciating that in order to tame Israeli behavior and extract requisite concessions, the Israeli public must be reassured rather than sanctioned. And, that in the framework of

Israel's democratic political system such reassurances would also help the Israeli government to persuade its public that Egypt deserved to be accommodated.

Additionally, while hoping that peace with Egypt would eventually lead to broader Arab–Israeli accommodation, Israelis tended to interpret Sadat's move as a "separate peace" - that is, as an expression of a grand-strategic decision to "place Egypt first" in determining his country's priorities. Hence they viewed Sadat's overture as signaling a willingness to settle Egypt's dispute with Israel independently of developments in the Israeli–Palestinian sphere. Accordingly, Israelis chose to ignore the Egyptian president's insistence - stated clearly in his speech to the Knesset - that peace with Israel must be comprehensive. Instead, they chose to see the Egyptians' Palestinian-focused demands at Camp David and their emphasis on the importance of the Israeli–Palestinian Autonomy talks in the aftermath of the 1979 Peace Treaty, as Egyptian "lip service" to the Palestinian cause.

This narrative had considerable consequences for Israel's interpretation of later developments. On one hand, the view that Egypt had made a strategic decision to place its interests first and to give priority to settling its dispute with Israel was seen as having been confirmed by the fact that the two countries' peace treaty survived over decades, despite recurring pressures of conflict and war on Israel's other fronts. Conversely, many Israelis were disappointed when it became increasingly clear that it would be impossible to immunize Egyptian–Israeli relations completely from such dramatic developments as Israel's 1981 bombing of the Osiraq reactor and the 1982 invasion of Lebanon. That is, for as long as conflict, violence and war continue to characterize Israel's relations with its other Arab neighbors, Egyptian–Israeli relations could not evolve and develop beyond the boundaries of a "cold peace."

The Bombing of Osiraq and the Invasion of Lebanon

The Israeli narrative with regard to the June 1981 bombing of the Osiraq reactor was Holocaust-driven. Iraqi President Saddam Hussein was seen as committed to the acquisition of nuclear weapons and Osiraq was judged to be potentially capable of producing the requisite fissile material. Lacking confidence in Saddam's rationality, Israelis did not see it as likely that a stable deterrence relationship could be established with Iraq. Consequently, they viewed Saddam's acquisition of nuclear arms as negating the very purpose of Zionism - to provide the Jewish people with a safe haven - and as raising the specter of another Holocaust. Thus they saw the bombing of Iraq's reactor as a natural consequence of the Zionist commitment to the concept of "never again."

Israel's 1982 invasion of Lebanon - referred to as Operation Peace for Galilee - was seen through a very different prism. The initial dominant Israeli narrative - soon to be challenged primarily from within the Israeli elite - viewed the invasion as a clear case of "preventive war." The roots of this war were seen as embedded in the developments that followed Black September of 1970. In its aftermath, the PLO, having relocated its headquarters from Jordan to Lebanon, was seen as using the southern parts of the Lebanese state as a launching board for terrorizing the population of northern Israel.

By the late 1970s, growing PLO presence in Lebanon was viewed as presenting Israel with two challenges - one tactical and operational, the other grand-strategic. The tactical-operational

Israeli concern focused on the PLO's use of South Lebanon to launch Katyusha rockets against northern Israel. Secured by their complete control of the south, the PLO could use what Israelis now called "Fatahland" as protected turf from which such rockets could be launched.

Israel's grand-strategic fears were that the PLO had transformed southern Lebanon into a "state within a state." Since, at that time, Israelis viewed the prospects of an independent Palestinian state in the West Bank and Gaza as a mortal danger, they feared that the Palestinians would develop all the machinations of an independent state in southern Lebanon and would later transport these institutions to the West Bank.

When in June 1982 Israel launched "Operation Peace for Galilee," most of its citizens believed it to be a limited operation designed to free Israel's northern towns and settlements from the threat of the PLO's Katyusha attacks. Addressing the Israeli Knesset a few days after the war began, Prime Minister Menachem Begin presented it as an operation of limited scope and duration. The operation, said Begin, was merely designed to push the PLO some 45 kilometers north of the border, placing the Galilee beyond the range of the PLO's 22–24 km-range Katyusha rockets. Once this happened, promised the prime minister, Israel's goals would have been achieved and all fighting would cease.

Two narratives later evolved to explain why Israel's forces continued their thrust northward, eventually reaching Beirut and the Beirut–Damascus highway. The dominant narrative blamed Defense Minister Sharon for conceiving the ambitious "Oranim" plan – to dislodge the PLO from Lebanon and to place the Maronites at its helm – while deceiving the Israeli Cabinet into believing that the operation it approved was designed to achieve a far more modest goal: to push the PLO away from the border. Thus, when Begin addressed the Knesset and presented the latter as the operation's objective, he is said to have believed that this was indeed the case. According to this narrative, Sharon, knowing that most of the Israeli Cabinet members were opposed to a major incursion into Lebanon, sought their approval for much more modest objectives, only to then interpret these approvals expansively. At the same time, Israel's Defense Minister was said to have withheld from the Cabinet knowledge that the IDF's operational plans were never downsized from the ambitious "Oranim" plan that it had refused to authorize.

Consistent with this narrative, an Israeli National Commission of Inquiry later found Sharon culpable in the Maronites' massacre of Palestinian refugees in the Shabra and Shatila camps. While not accusing Sharon of responsibility for the massacre, he was found responsible for creating the conditions that allowed the massacre to take place and for failing to take steps that could have prevented it. Sharon's competing narrative was that he deceived neither the Cabinet nor the prime minister. Rather, while wishing to avoid responsibility for the possible negative repercussions associated with the attempt to implement "Oranim," the Israeli Cabinet approved every significant move by the IDF in Lebanon.

The Palestinian Narrative

The Palestinians viewed the developments that led to the Egyptian–Israeli Peace Treaty as a succession of acts of defection and betrayal. In this context what was seen by Israelis as a clear gain – justifying far-reaching concessions – was viewed by the Palestinians as a clear loss. Not only did Egypt defect from any potential future war coalition, the Palestinians understood that this defection meant the end of any option to resolve the Arab–Israeli conflict by force. While this process had begun earlier, with the Egyptian–Israeli and Syrian–Israeli disengagement agreements in the aftermath of the October 1973 War, the Palestinians regarded the 1977–79 Egyptian–Israeli peace breakthroughs as the "final nail in the coffin" of the broader Arab–Israeli "armed struggle".

Egyptian–Israeli Peace and Israel's Invasion of Lebanon

Like some Israelis, Palestinians believed that in accommodating Egypt, Israel made a grand bargain with its neighbor to the south: the return of the Sinai to Egypt in exchange for tacit Egyptian acceptance of continued Israeli control over the West Bank and Gaza. By offering these areas autonomy in the framework of the Camp David Accords, Israel was seen by the Palestinians as intending to continue its occupation while avoiding the stigma of an occupying power.

Another component of the Palestinian narrative was that these Egyptian–Israeli developments propelled the PLO's closer association with Syria and Iraq during the period of 1977–82. With Egypt viewed as having abandoned its role as the leader of the Arab nationalist camp, the Palestinians saw no choice but to seek alternative allies. Thus, in Palestinian eyes, it was Egypt's betrayal that pushed them into the arms of Hafez Assad and Saddam Hussein.

Not surprisingly, the Palestinians' narrative of the 1982 War was a derivative of their interpretation of these earlier developments. They saw Israel's invasion as materializing their worst expectations regarding the likely consequences of Egypt's defection from the Arab war coalition. With its southern flank secured by a peace treaty, Israel was said to have felt free to direct its aggression against the Palestinians: first in decapitating the Palestinian leadership in the West Bank and Gaza, and later in invading Lebanon. In this context, the Palestinians viewed Israel as directly responsible for the massacre of Palestinian civilians in the Sabra and Shatila refugee camps. Indeed, the 1982 War was seen as designed to squash if not actually exterminate Palestinian national identity: first by denying such identity and then by rejecting the PLO as the sole representative of the Palestinian people.

The Reagan Plan and the Shift to Moderation

While the Palestinians expressed concern about the Reagan Plan, which was proposed right after the PLO's withdrawal from Beirut, their narrative at the time attempted to explain why they were concerned about the plan but also why they did not reject it. The core of their concern was that the initiative called for Palestinian self-rule, not independence, in the West Bank and the Gaza Strip. Worse still, such self-rule was to be in association with Jordan. Therefore, the initiative was perceived as an attempt to capitalize on the PLO's weakness after its defeat in Lebanon and to deny Palestinian self-determination. Palestinians were particularly unhappy that the initiative called for Jordan to negotiate on their behalf, as the Egyptians had in the Egyptian–Israeli autonomy talks.

The Palestinians' growing anxieties about Jordan's possible role in future negotiations was further enhanced by King Hussein's positive response to the Reagan Plan. Indeed, Palestinians suspected that Jordan was involved in the plan's design. Nevertheless, the initiative was not rejected by the PLO despite internal pressure from the leftist forces in the PLO to do so. The mainstream Palestinian narrative argued that Palestinian options after the Lebanon war were limited, particularly in the aftermath of an internal mutiny within Fatah – the largest PLO faction – that was perceived to have been orchestrated by Syria.

Now the Palestinian narrative began to focus on the cup half full. They took comfort in the fact that the Israeli Likud government categorically rejected the Reagan Plan. They also credited the plan for expressing American opposition to permanent Israeli control or annexation of the occupied territories and to the construction of new Israeli settlements. Palestinians also argued that PLO rejection of the plan would have resulted in Jordan negotiating on their behalf. The need to maintain its status as the sole representative of the Palestinian people was presented by the PLO as a vital national goal, justifying not only the non-rejection of the initiative, but also the opening of a dialogue with Jordan based on the Reagan Plan.

The PLO narrative tolerated Arafat's visit to Egypt in 1983 as the only possible move to maintain the Palestinians' "independence of decision." The reason this was not self-evident was that having been evicted from Lebanon Arafat chose to make his first stop at the only Arab country that had signed a peace treaty with Israel. Arafat, it was said, left Tripoli (in Lebanon) after the Syrians orchestrated the mutiny against him. Therefore, going to Egypt was a Palestinian imperative. In any case, by then Mubarak's Egypt had already been highly critical of the Israeli invasion of Lebanon, and hopes were high that Egypt's new president would bring his country back into the Arab fold, particularly now that Egypt had regained the whole of Sinai. The Palestinian narrative emphasized the need to balance the shift in the Syrian position by bringing Egypt back into the equation of Arab politics.

Another change in the Palestinian narrative occurred in the aftermath of the withdrawal from Lebanon, further justifying the imperative of working closely with Jordan. The narrative now focused on the need to pay attention to "the inside" – the West Bank and the Gaza Strip – emphasizing the importance of keeping links with "the inside" to prevent the Israelis from dominating the scene, as they already had begun to do. But to achieve this, the PLO had no choice but to partner with Jordan – the only available access to the occupied territories – even if that meant accepting the notion of a Jordanian–Palestinian delegation to any future negotiations and de-emphasizing Palestinian statehood by endorsing the goal of a Jordanian–Palestinian confederation. Still, the PLO emphasized that it kept its options open by refusing to accept UN Resolution 242 – a demand the Jordanians, echoing American demands, kept reiterating.

The Palestinians argued that the failure to coordinate with Jordan was not their fault, and that their efforts to establish closer relations with Jordan were genuine. They pointed to the fact that the PLO held its 17th PNC meeting in Amman in 1984 under the banner of the "independence of decision," and that Palestinian–Jordanian coordination led in fact to the signing of the Amman Accord in February 1985, an agreement that was seen as meeting most of the Jordanian demands while helping the Palestinians achieve two goals: insuring that they would be part of any negotiations over the future of the occupied territories and opening a gateway to the West Bank.

The Palestinians' narrative of this period also emphasized the shift in their position regarding the conflict with Israel, moving away from the Provisional Program to a gradual endorsement of the two-state solution. This shift was not seen as a matter of choice: Egyptian–Israeli peace eliminated any serious Arab war option, and the Lebanon war placed the PLO on the defensive, with Arab states either ignoring the PLO or trying to control it, as was the case with Syria. As a result, Palestinians now saw the political gains they made in the 1970s threatened. They responded to this danger by changing their position significantly: the goal of a Palestinian state in the West Bank and the Gaza Strip with East Jerusalem as its capital now replaced the talk of establishing a "national authority" as part of a phased program; the Reagan Plan's goal of self-rule was not rejected and the Fahd (or Fez) peace plan was endorsed as part of "Arab legitimacy." While these steps were presented as indicating moderation, Palestinians continued to insist that Israel's rejection of their aspirations for independence and statehood justified their refusal to recognize it.

By working closely with Egypt and Jordan, the PLO saw itself on the road to a political settlement. The PLO pointed to its new focus on institution-building in the West Bank and the Gaza Strip as evidence of the shift in its position, a process that was initially spurred by Israeli efforts to decapitate the nationalist leadership in the occupied territories and was greatly facilitated by Jordanian–Palestinian coordination, particularly in 1984–86. Palestinians attributed the eventual failure of this coordination to Jordan's dependence on the United States and its resulting vulnerability to American pressure, and to Israeli and American refusal to reciprocate by endorsing the Palestinian goal of self-determination or agreeing to talk to the PLO or accept the Fahd plan.

The Arab Narrative

The Arab narrative underwent drastic transformations in the period 1975–86. In fact, there were two main Arab narratives during this period: one stressed negotiations and diplomacy as the most promising path toward a resolution of the Arab–Israeli conflict while the second advocated the continuation of the "armed struggle" against Israel. Egypt saw the 1973 War as having restored Arab honor and as having demonstrated to Israel that continued occupation of Arab lands would be associated with heavy costs. Additionally, in the aftermath of the October 1973 War, Sadat concluded that the United States was the only power capable of resolving the Arab–Israeli conflict. In his words, the United States possessed 99 percent of the cards.[49] By contrast, the Soviet Union, supportive of the Arab radical camp, could not be considered part of the solution. Instead, it was now seen as part of the problem.

In the view of the second Arab camp, Egypt's peaceful approach was disastrous in concept and in reality. In concept, Egypt was seen as pursuing peace with an enemy - Israel - that was propelled by a fanatic and expansionist Zionist ideology and hence not ready for peace. The election of the Likud government in 1977 was regarded as additional and conclusive evidence for this assessment. Accepting that Israel was an American ally that held important cards in the game was tantamount to either political foolishness or simply treason.

In reality, the Arab world was angry that Egypt had opted for peace and in doing so further weakened the Arab coalition. Arab states also argued that by securing Israel's southern front, Egypt was allowing Israel to increase its reach if not actually expand its empire north and east. For these states, Israel's 1982 invasion of Lebanon provided conclusive affirmation that they were right to fear the effects of what to them was seen as Egypt's betrayal.

Egypt's Narrative

On their part, Egyptians now saw peace as a necessary condition for returning to normal life. After decades of wars and suffering for "Arab causes," Egypt was now ready to give its own wellbeing a higher priority and to pursue prosperity through improved relations with the West and, especially, the United States. Thus, Egypt was no longer willing to allow radical Arabs to set the agenda – Arabs who were now seen as willing to continue fighting Israel at the expense of the last Egyptian soldier. Now Egyptians considered it no longer acceptable that they would remain in a state of poverty but committed to "Arab causes" while other Arabs were "getting rich" by the ever-higher price of oil, which was seen as secured by Egyptian blood. Instead, Egyptians now sought to resume development of their country's potential, which had been held hostage for far too long by a conflict that some Arab parties made a career of not resolving.

The Egyptian narrative regarding the 1974–75 Disengagement Agreements with Israel was that they comprised the beginning of the country's break from the collective pattern of the Arab–Israeli conflict. Egypt had reached a stage in which it was more concerned with its own national interests and in restoring its sovereign territory through the peaceful resolution of its conflict with Israel.[50]

Yet in Egyptian eyes, Sadat's move was never intended to be a "separate peace" with Israel but, instead, the cornerstone of a broader and comprehensive regional deal. Accordingly, the Egyptian narrative emphasized that the two parts of the Camp David Accords – the Israeli–Egyptian deal and the agreement on Palestinian Autonomy – should be seen as inseparable and as having equal weight.

Moreover, the deal made with Israel was seen by Egyptians as an "honorable peace" – well-earned by Egyptians' sacrifice and bravery in the difficult and costly battles of the October 1973 War. If it were not for the war, Egypt's dignity could have been restored and Israel could not have been forced to accept Egypt's territorial demands. Egypt's bravery thus set limits to Israeli power, forcing the Jewish state to negotiate and concede.

In Egyptian eyes, accusing their country of having defected from the Arab consensus by reaching a separate deal with Israel was nothing short of hyperbole. The accusations were expressed by countries that pretended that the Arabs had a realistic military option against Israel but who themselves had never invested nearly as much as Egypt had in opposing Israel's designs. Moreover, Arab leaders who had propagated notions of Egypt's defection were seen as knowing full well that in reality the Arab side lacked a military option against Israel. Instead, such accusations were seen as an effort by Arab leaders suffering a legitimacy deficit to solidify their own domestic support.

While deviating sharply from the Israeli and Palestinian interpretations of the Egyptian–Israeli peace treaty, Egypt shared some of the broader Arab frustrations with the regional consequences of the deal. Thus, Israel's bombing of the Osiraq reactor, immediately after a highly publicized meeting between Begin and Sadat, was viewed as painting Egypt as an accomplice to Israel's regional designs. Similarly, only three years after the signing of the peace treaty, pictures of destruction in Lebanon during the 1982 War portrayed Israel to the Egyptian street as an aggressor. Yet the negative ramifications of these developments in Egyptian opinion were at first limited: the departure of Moshe Dayan and Ezer Weizmann, Israel's foreign minister and defense minister respectively, from the Begin government, and the mass demonstrations in Israel against the war in Lebanon, allowed Egyptians to differentiate between their more benign if not generous assessments of Israeli intentions and their sharp criticism of the Begin government's policies. Thus, the Egyptian narrative of the early 1980s differentiated between "good Israelis" and "bad Israelis."

The Jordanian Narrative

Jordan viewed the Camp David accords and the Egyptian–Israeli peace treaty as a "separate peace." It came to believe that in order to regain control over its lost territories Egypt was forced after the 1973 War to seek American support and to negotiate directly with Israel. It viewed its initial response to Sadat's visit to Israel as balanced: it denounced the step but asked Arab countries to deal with it in a wise manner that would not widen Arab differences. Accordingly, the king viewed the visit as a "daring step."[51]

Nevertheless, in the aftermath of the Camp David Summit, Jordan saw Egypt as having weakened the Arab collective position and as seeking instead to pursue its own separate national interests. This difference, however, was mitigated by the eruption of the Iraq–Iran war. Egypt now provided Iraq – a friend and ally of Jordan – with military hardware and spare parts, resulting in an improvement in Iraqi–Egyptian relations and, hence, also in Jordanian–Egyptian relations. King Hussein met President Mubarak in April 1984, leading to the resumption of diplomatic relations between the two countries. Jordan viewed the resumption of these relations as an indication of its commitment to peace with Israel.

At the same time, Jordan saw the more or less simultaneous improvement of its relations with the PLO as a reflection of common interest in opposing the Camp David grand bargain. Yet it also knew that this rapprochement would not last long, owing to the PLO's dependency on Syria.

Nevertheless, when Israel invaded Lebanon, Jordan sympathized with the plight of the PLO and offered help. After the 1983 split in Fatah and the associated worsening of relations between the PLO and Syria, Jordan hosted the 1984 PNC meeting in Amman. The Jordanians believed that the PLO sought Jordan's help out of necessity as other Arab countries were unwilling to host the meeting because of Syrian opposition. Jordan's goal was to secure the PLO's consent to a joint Jordanian–Palestinian move that would respond positively to the Reagan Plan while at the same time meeting the requirements of the Fahd Plan. Jordan further believed that such a joint move must be based on a commitment to UN Resolution 242. But it also assessed that the PLO was not ready to make such a commitment, so therefore sought to take the lead in negotiations and to include some independent Palestinians – nominated by the PLO – in its delegation.

Jordan viewed the February 1985 Amman Agreement with the PLO as meeting Jordan's vital interest in opening negotiations with Israel within the context of an international conference. But American insistence on an explicit PLO acceptance of UN Resolution 242 impeded Jordanian efforts to launch such negotiations.

Continuing to press the PLO to accept UN Resolution 242, Jordan believed by the end of 1985 that Arafat had yielded, indicating his willingness to do so. King Hussein conveyed the message to President Reagan in person, leading the latter to express his willingness for the United States to convene an international conference. Soon enough, however, Jordan was shocked and dismayed when Arafat refused to accept Resolution 242, instead insisting that such recognition would only be granted in the context of an American endorsement of Palestinian self-determination. King Hussein viewed Arafat's behavior as deceitful and in February 1986 he took immediate steps to sever links with the PLO and close its offices in Amman. The King believed that by conducting himself in such a manner Arafat had turned down a historic opportunity to end Israeli occupation of Arab land.

While terminating contacts with the PLO, Jordan sought to unilaterally help Palestinians in the occupied territories through an ambitious program of economic development. It hoped that such efforts would ultimately convince West Bankers to shift loyalty to Jordan, thus weakening the PLO's standing and\or forcing Arafat to moderate his position.

Analysis

This section will attempt to address two questions: first, What led to the breakthrough in Egyptian–Israeli relations resulting in the signing of the first Arab–Israeli peace treaty? In turn, this issue entails three sub-questions: What propelled Egypt to seek peace with Israel? What induced Israel to make the concessions necessary for a peace agreement to be concluded? and What led a warm peace to quickly turn cold? Second, What were the causes of Israel's invasion of Lebanon in June 1982?

Egyptian–Israeli Peacemaking

The International System

At the *global-systemic level*, the breakthrough in Egyptian–Israeli relations seems to have been propelled by a number of developments. First, by the mid-1970s Sadat became convinced that the global balance of power was shifting away from the Soviet Union and that, at any rate, Moscow could not help Egypt meet its basic needs. Hence a complete reorientation of Egyptian policy was required, away from the Soviet Union and towards the United States. When, by late 1977, President Carter proposed the reconvening of the Geneva Middle East Peace Conference – with the United States and the Soviet Union as co-sponsors – Sadat, worried about a potential stalemate, set out to abort the move by talking directly to his Israeli adversaries.

This added to Egypt's assessment that the Soviet Union was not totally supportive of its objectives. This assessment was not new: it had already led to the departure of the Soviet military advisors in 1971, to the contraction of "socialist" projects in Egypt in the early and mid-1970s, and to growing criticism in Egypt of the Nasser era, seen as characterized by close Egyptian–Soviet ties. Some of this criticism was intended to prod the Soviets to provide Egypt with greater assistance, indeed it spurred them to sign and implement two huge arms deals in 1973. Egypt also continued to provide the Soviet Union with access to bases during this period. But none of this could help Egypt address its problems in the aftermath of the 1973 War: how to restore its sovereignty over the Sinai and rebuild its economy.

By contrast, America's primacy in the economic realm placed it in a superior position to offer Israel as well as Egypt considerable side-payments as rewards for the concessions they were asked to make. Indeed for decades later American military and economic assistance to the two countries continued to be presented – especially when seeking Congressional approval – in the context of the Camp David grand bargain. In Egypt's estimation, the United States was now also strongly motivated to help resolve the Arab–Israeli conflict, spurred by the unrest in Iran. Since Washington thought it could no longer rely on Iran to act as "regional policeman" in the case of a Middle East emergency, Carter was now looking to Egypt (and Israel) to be his new pro-Western "anchors of Middle East stability."[52]

Another dimension of the global-systemic level was the growing importance and increasing price of oil during the 1970s. The huge revenues generated by these developments reduced the relative importance of radical Arab regimes in favor of conservative oil-producing countries. In this competition, some in Egypt saw their country handicapped while oil producing competitors for regional influence were gaining ground. This motivated Egypt to make a deal with Israel before its standing in the region was further eroded.

The Middle East Region

At the *systemic-regional level*, Egypt's decision to pursue peace, and Israel's decision to accept nearly all of Egypt's territorial demands were a direct outcome of the two countries' reading of the Middle East balance of power. Egypt appreciated that the restoration of its sovereignty over the Sinai could only be achieved in the framework of a peace treaty. Thus its reading was that its strategic success in the October War, while restoring its pride and dignity, was not enough to return the Sinai to Egyptian hands. It further understood that regardless of the narrative of victory it would write, operationally the war ended with the IDF on the western side of the Suez Canal, surrounding Egypt's 3rd Army and positioning itself just over a hundred kilometers from Cairo. Reflecting on the balance of power between the two countries, Egypt could not hope to induce Israel to surrender the territories it acquired in 1967 solely by military means. Thus, to gain the return of the Sinai, direct engagement with Israel could not be avoided.

The same war, however, had an equally sobering effect on the Israeli side. Israel's conclusion from the October War was that Egypt (and Syria) were able to make war very costly to Israel. The combination of these countries' capabilities and determination negated Dayan's assumption in the aftermath of the 1967 War that the Arabs would "get used" to

Israeli control of their lands. This had set clear limits to Israeli power: while unable to defeat Israel, Egypt and Syria succeeded in annulling Israel's post-1967 defense concept that called for Israel to base its national security on "defensible borders." Instead, Israel now understood that since defensible borders could only be obtained at its neighbors' expense, the latter were capable and determined to demonstrate – at considerable costs to themselves but also to Israel – that the security provided by such borders was illusory.

Developments at the regional level in 1981 and certainly by the second half of 1982, however, soon led to the deterioration of what had started as a warm peace into a cold one. Paramount among these were the stalled Palestinian autonomy talks, Israel's bombing of Osiraq, and its invasion of Lebanon. This did not signify an Egyptian retreat from the strategic choice it made in 1977–79 to avoid any further wars with Israel. But it did limit the peace to the realm of government-to-government interactions and prevented its trickling down to the "people-to-people" level.

At the systemic-regional level, an important factor affecting the precise nature of the evolving Egyptian–Israeli relationship was the heavy price Egypt paid for what most Arab states regarded as its defection from the Arab consensus. As already noted, Egyptians associated with Sadat's peace initiative were sanctioned, boycotted and ostracized by most Arab governments, including many who had previously regarded Egypt unquestioningly as the leader of the Arab world. Now, Egyptian politicians, diplomats, business leaders, scholars and artists felt unwelcome in these same Arab states. This heavy price made Egypt vulnerable to the pressures that relations with Israel imposed almost from the very beginning.

The first of these pressures was Israel's June 1981 bombing of Osiraq – Iraq's nuclear reactor. What irked Egyptians most was that the attack took place just two days after a summit meeting between Begin and Sadat. And what bothered the Egyptians was not that Begin did not warn Sadat of the drama to come but of quite the opposite: that the proximity between the two events created an impression in the Arab world that Egypt was partner to – or at least complicit in – a conspiracy to attack a fellow Arab country.

Also damaging to the two countries' relations was Israel's decision to refuse to withdraw from Taba –a tiny area along its border with Egypt where a single hotel and some minor tourist attractions were located. This soured the two countries' relations and left Egyptians convinced that Israel was trying to escape its obligations.

Much more significant were two other developments that affected Egypt's vulnerabilities in the Arab world. The first of these was a non-event: the absence of any serious progress in the talks on Palestinian autonomy stipulated in the Camp David accords. Lack of any progress toward resolving the Palestinian issue exposed Egypt to the continuing accusations leveled against it in many Arab quarters that it had concluded a "separate peace" with Israel by neglecting all other dimensions of the Arab–Israeli conflict, particularly the plight of the Palestinians. That Israel was responsible for this lack of progress was seen in Egypt as indisputable: after all, both Foreign Minister Dayan and Defense Minister Weizmann had quit the Begin government over what they perceived as Begin's refusal to allow these talks to succeed.

Probably even more devastating was Israel's June 1982 invasion of Lebanon. The invasion exposed Egypt to another accusation which its detractors in the Arab world were only too happy to reiterate: that by concluding peace, Egypt had enabled Israel to attack Lebanon without fear that this might ignite its southern front. Once again, and this time with far greater consequences, Egypt's government was portrayed as having become complicit in a deadly Israeli design against a fellow Arab state.

Thus, while the Camp David accords might have contributed to creating the conditions allowing the war in Lebanon, the war also set limits to the peace that the accords meant to establish. Indeed, the two dynamics were connected: Egypt's feeling that Israel had exploited the peace agreement to pursue other, less benign regional designs led Cairo to begin a process of cooling its relations with Israel even before Israel's withdrawal from Sinai had been completed. In 1982 Egypt recalled its ambassador from Tel Aviv, not to be reinstated until the bilateral dispute over Taba was resolved through legal arbitration.

Domestic Politics

At the *unit level*, Egyptian–Israeli peace seems to have been propelled by a different set of factors. On the broader Egyptian scene, there seems to have developed a new willingness to reexamine all policies associated with the Nasser era. An important component of this was a growing sensitivity to the ever-increasing costs of the continued state of war. For a decade, between the 1967 War and Sadat's trip to Israel, this required the dedication of every available resource to the fight against Israel. Inevitably, these costs were at the expense of Egypt's social and economic needs. Bread riots had erupted in January 1977, eleven months before Sadat's dramatic trip to Jerusalem. Clearly, these social-economic challenges could not be addressed without reallocating resources away from military spending and into social services. Moreover, external economic aid could not be obtained – especially not from the United States – except in the context of a complete reorientation of Egypt's policies: away from reliance on the Soviets for the means of confrontation and war and towards Washington.

Israel's domestic scene was also conducive to a grand bargain with Egypt. With Labor's demise, Golda Meir, who had propagated the concept of "defensible borders," ended her political life. Ideologically still committed to the Greater Land of Israel, the new Likud leaders saw in a peace agreement with Egypt an opportunity to achieve two things simultaneously: first, to prove that Likud was capable of succeeding where Labor had failed – reaching peace with the most important of the Arab states. And second, to gain time and quiet on the Palestinian front by placating and pacifying Israel's southern neighbor. Thus, the shift from Labor's security-centered approach which emphasized the strategic significance of the Sinai, to an ideological approach focused on the West Bank, facilitated the deal with Egypt.

Prime Minister Begin also knew that, as a social-democratic movement, Labor could not but support a peace treaty with Egypt, regardless of a price-tag that was far higher than the one Labor leaders had been willing to contemplate prior to the 1973 War. Thus, when half of the Likud's section in the Knesset refused to support their prime minister in the critical vote on the Camp David accords, Labor Members of Knesset came to his rescue, providing Begin with the requisite majority.

Yet, while the idea of peace with Israel was initially very popular in the so-called "Egyptian street," despite the Muslim Brotherhood's objections, such enthusiasm soon evaporated under the effect of regional developments, making it difficult for the country's rulers to expand relations with Israel beyond the limits of a "cold peace." These developments included the Arab states' very negative reaction to Egypt's peace overture, the bombing of Osiraq, the continued squabble over Taba, and the invasion of Lebanon. Armed by these developments to support their arguments, opponents of peace among the Muslim Brotherhood and the syndicates pressed their case for cooling down relations, if not altogether cancelling the treaty, with Israel. For its part, Egypt's government refrained from making a serious attempt to overcome the various boycotts declared against interactions with Israel by almost all Egyptian professional syndicates. In the aftermath of Sadat's assassination, this was the reality that his successor inherited.

This difficult challenge was compounded by the dire state of the Egyptian economy, which experienced recession and stagnation throughout the 1980s. Egyptian infrastructure was collapsing and the value of its currency was deteriorating. In such circumstances many Egyptians flocked to the Gulf region, and their government had no choice but return to the Arab fold. At the same time, the Egyptian leadership had very little to show on the Palestinian front – an issue that continued to be of great interest to the Egyptian public. Mubarak's response to this situation was an effort to restore balance to Egypt's foreign policy. Accordingly, he asked the Egyptian media to stop attacking other Arab governments and made a concerted effort to restore Egyptian–Soviet relations to their previous warmth.

Begin, Carter and Sadat

At the *individual level*, peace between Egypt and Israel could not have been achieved without the personal role of three individuals: Anwar Sadat, Menachem Begin, and Jimmy Carter. Other Israeli and Egyptian leaders and senior officials played important roles in forging the breakthrough, pushing or at least helping their leaders along. In years past Begin's defense minister, Ezer Weizmann, was known to be a super-hawk – once reportedly going so far as to suggest that Israel conquer Arab capitals to coerce its neighbors to accept peace – not a likely candidate for urging the concessions required for peace. But, during the 1970–71 War of Attrition Weizmann's son was near-fatally shot by an Egyptian sniper, leaving him seriously and permanently damaged. These injuries seem to have driven home the costs of war. As bellicose as he was in years past, Weizmann was now determined to do everything possible to end the conflict. Similarly, Dayan may have pushed for peace to compensate for his role in the 1973 catastrophe and to ensure that it did not comprise the last page in his contribution to his country's history.

Yet no Israeli leader during this period could match Begin's role in forging the country's policy and no-one enjoyed anything remotely resembling his unique authority – authority that allowed him to make the far reaching territorial concessions that peace with Egypt required. Therefore, Begin was critically important to the success of the process launched by Sadat's trip. For Sadat's project to succeed there needed to be an Israeli leader who could rise to the challenge that the Egyptian leader's grand gesture presented. And this is where Begin's propensity for theatrical grand gestures of his own became an important contribution to the play. Although at times legalistic and argumentative to an extreme, Begin was also a "big picture man" who loved to engage in gestures and theatrics. As such, it would have been unlike him to pass the opportunity for the historical breakthrough offered by Sadat's overture.

These characteristics of Begin's also help explain why, despite his resistance to the specific terms of the Camp David accords, he would become a party to the grand bargain entailed. Thinking "big," and ideologically committed to the Greater Land of Israel, Begin could convince himself that the risks entailed in a complete withdrawal from the Sinai were well worth the potential gains: Israel's continued control of the West Bank, Gaza and East Jerusalem, while granting some sort of autonomy to the Arabs residing in these territories. Begin's assessment was based on his personal reading of Sadat – namely, that the latter's insistence on the Palestinians' rights did not express a genuine and deep commitment to the Palestinian cause but rather the minimum "lip service" required to limit criticism of Egypt's dramatic move in the Arab world. A more cautious and conservative leader than Begin, who would have been more comfortable with a "tit for tat" approach to international negotiations, would not have subscribed to the grand historical gesture offered at Camp David.

Given his earlier role as the grand strategist of the 1973 October War and now as the architect and CEO of Egypt's overture to Israel, Sadat was indispensible to all aspects and dimensions of the peace breakthrough. At the personal level, Sadat's reorientation of Egyptian policy toward the United States was inspired by a long visit – lasting a number of weeks – which he paid to that country in 1966. Thus, he was inclined to review the Soviets' legacy in Egypt long before the 1973 War.

In addition to the traits that were essential to his earlier role in the 1973 War, Sadat's overture was informed by his remarkable and thorough understanding of Israel's democratic system and its implications for meeting Egypt's objectives. As a man of grand gestures and political drama himself, Sadat saw that Begin could be brought to becoming a willing partner to his project. Moreover, Sadat seems to have realized – or at least was willing to bank on the proposition – that while Israel's governing coalition structure was cumbersome, the Israeli public would lend massive support to making peace with the largest and most populous Arab state. The conclusion Sadat drew from this premise is that he had to find a way to go "over the heads" of Israel's divided political leadership and appeal directly to the Israeli public. By traveling to Israel in November 1977, communicating to Israelis directly and demonstrating sensitivity to Israeli security concerns, Sadat did exactly that: molding Israel's public opinion and domestic scene in a manner that made it nearly impossible for Begin's government not to respond.

Yet, other aspects of Sadat's personality played a negative role in affecting the regional ramifications of his peace initiative. Particularly damaging was his reaction to Saudi and moderate Gulf countries' expressions of concerns about his decision. This was particularly unfortunate given that there was considerable sympathy in these countries for breaking the deadlock of the Arab–Israeli conflict. Instead of finding a way to placate and reassure the Saudis without retreating from his initiative, Sadat alienated them completely. While this served to signal to Washington that he was America's only reliable address in the Arab world, it resulted in deep Saudi and Gulf hostility.

Nor was Sadat in any mood to use his diplomatic and political skills to expand the space of peace supporters or at least those who might have tolerated his daring initiative, such as

Sudan and Oman. Of no less importance, and despite his great ability to persuade Western and Israeli audiences, he did not apply his talents to the Egyptian public. He neglected his domestic base, and instead tried to appease Islamic fundamentalists, who finally assassinated him.

The difficulties involved in actually forging Egyptian–Israeli agreements, from the Camp David Accords to the Peace Treaty, could not have been overcome without the tenacity of Jimmy Carter. His willingness to invest in Egyptian–Israeli peace was partly tied to his appreciation – similar to Kissinger's before him – of Egypt's importance and the resulting need to lure it further away from the Soviet camp. But in contrast to Kissinger, Carter's motivation seems to have had a religious dimension as well: his commitment to bring "peace to the Holy Land" was deep and captivating. This conviction was supplemented by the president's domestic political consideration: if the previous Nixon–Kissinger Republican administration adopted a "step-by-step" approach to resolving the Arab–Israeli dispute, Carter would distinguish his administration by adopting a comprehensive approach: peace treaties resolving the warring parties' relations in all their aspects.

Two additional aspects of Carter's character that allowed him to play his historic role in Camp David were his supreme patience and command of details. Consequently, Carter could engage the negotiators in detailed conversation about alternative formulations that could bridge the gap between their positions on dozens of issues. His conviction that the opportunity created by Sadat's trip to Israel should not be wasted led him to take an unprecedented and very risky step: to devote nearly two weeks of presidential time and energy to helping the Israelis and Egyptians iron out, if not resolve, their differences.

While the personalities of Sadat, Begin and Carter played a key role in the breakthrough that resulted in the conclusion of the Egyptian–Israeli peace, Hosni Mubarak was critical to Egypt's decision to adhere to the treaty but also to keeping the peace "cold" during the subsequent three decades. Mubarak, who had been sitting close to Sadat when assassins sprayed the presidential group with gunfire, did not have to be persuaded that the costs of "going it alone" could be prohibitive. Yet like his predecessor, he believed that Egypt should put its own interests first. Hence, he refused to change the central tenets of Egypt's policy: its new close ties with the United States and its commitment to peace with Israel as a strategic choice. This continuity demonstrates the long-term effect of the systemic determinants – international as well as regional – and the domestic factors that propelled Egypt to adopt these policies.

At the same time, Mubarak was far more sensitive than Sadat had been to the importance of Egypt's standing in the region. This impelled him to use Israel's invasion of Lebanon as the perfect reason for cooling relations with Israel. While Sadat had been prepared to accept the consequences that warm relations with Israel would initially entail – cool to icy relations with Egypt's Arab neighbors – Mubarak was not. Instead, he sought to keep all of Egypt's options open.

Generally, Mubarak was much more cautious and careful than Sadat. Thus, whereas Sadat seemed to relish confrontations with Arab leaders for whom he did not have much respect, Mubarak seemed uncomfortable with Egypt's isolation. If the price of returning to the Arab fold was a cooling of Egypt's relations with Israel, Mubarak would pay this price. What increasingly seemed to Mubarak as repeated instances of Israeli insensitivity to Egypt's predicament made it easy for him to limit the two countries' interactions to a "cold peace."

Israel's Invasion of Lebanon

Regional Realities

At the *regional-systemic level*, the effects of the Egyptian–Israeli peace agreement on the distribution of power in the Middle East created a more permissive environment for an Israeli attack on Lebanon. In addition to Egypt's exiting from any potential Arab war coalition, the distribution of power now favored Israel, owing to Syria's strategic isolation. Although still enjoying Soviet support, Syria was in no position to check Israeli designs in Lebanon. Its relations with Jordan remained cold, unrepaired since Syria's 1970 attempt to invade the Hashemite Kingdom; the relations between Syria's Ba'ath regime and that of Saddam Hussein's Iraq remained equally tense. And Syria's relations with Turkey were bad, resulting in and from Syria's assistance to Turkey's Kurdish militant insurgents, the PKK.

Another development that tilted the regional balance in Israel's favor was Iraq's invasion of Iran. By 1982 the two countries had already been embroiled for some two years in deadly and bloody violence. As a result, neither was in a position to come to the assistance of any of Israel's more proximate adversaries.

With Egypt out of the equation, Syria isolated, and Iraq consumed by its war with Iran, Israel was constraint-free to pursue its national security objectives. More specifically, it could now hope to end the PLO Katyusha attacks against Israel from South Lebanon, and expel the PLO from Lebanon altogether. The ramifications of the regional distribution of power were that Israelis advancing the idea of a military incursion into Lebanon could argue that even if this would bring about a clash with Syria – and such a clash with Syrian forces in Lebanon was inevitable – the risks entailed would be limited, as none of Syria's neighbors were likely to come to her assistance. Moreover, Israel hoped to change this regional distribution of power by building an alliance with the Maronites in Lebanon, one that might eventually lead to a peace treaty with that country.

Domestic Politics

On the Israeli side, the most important domestic development that affected the odds of a war in Lebanon was the change in the composition of the Israeli cabinet following the 1981 elections. As noted earlier, Begin's first cabinet (1977–81) included two members – Dayan and Weizmann – who played a moderating role overall, and who actively encouraged Begin to respond positively to Sadat's overture and to accept the compromises necessary for reaching an agreement at Camp David. But by 1981 both had left the government, discouraged by what they viewed as Begin's unwillingness to abide by his commitment under the Camp David accords to engage in serious Palestinian autonomy talks. In Begin's new government, they were replaced by two hard-liners: Yitzhak Shamir as foreign minister and Ariel Sharon as minister of defense. This placed Sharon in a position to pursue his plan to redesign Lebanon as elaborated below.

Domestic developments in Lebanon meanwhile contributed to the conditions allowing Israel's incursion. The PLO had made a mess of its presence in Lebanon. It was perceived as playing Lebanese politics and as wasting most of its energies on inter-Lebanese feuds. Moreover the PLO seemed to have learned little from its experience in Jordan – experience that led to its earlier expulsion from that country. As in Jordan, the PLO now manifested insensitivity to Lebanese demographic concerns and flaunted its military capacity – siding with one religious sect – in a manner that reminded Lebanon's Christians and the then still passive but growing minority of Shi'a "who is the boss." Of particular distaste to most Lebanese was the PLO's building of a "state within a state" in the southern part of the country. Consequently, Israel's Defense Minister Sharon could hope to find willing allies within the Lebanese mosaic for his grand design.

The unique role played by Sharon in the decision to invade Lebanon in June 1982 is an excellent example of the role of *individuals* in making the history of the Arab–Israeli conflict. Designed by Sharon, the war reflected his preference for large changes – moves that promise to change the region's strategic landscape. Indeed, no other leader than Sharon could have moved Israel to the kind of war it launched in mid-1982.

What made Sharon so unique was a combination of three characteristics: first, he was a grand strategist who was determined to implement his grand design; second, he was unable to read domestic politics and appreciate their implications; and finally, he was manipulative to an extraordinary extent. The combination of these three characteristics helps explain not only Israel's decision to launch the war but also why the project was doomed to failure.

Sharon's "big" thinking was evidenced by his grand design that was meant to ensure Israel's indefinite control of the West Bank by initiating a chain reaction that would result in the Palestinians' national aspirations being expressed east of the Jordan River. The plan included crowning the Maronites over Lebanon, expelling the Syrians and spurring Palestinian pressures on Jordan that would have transformed that country into an "alternative homeland." For this, the dormant historical convergence of interests between Israel and Lebanon's Maronites would have to be resurrected and transformed into a fully fledged alliance. Clearly, implementing such a grand design required a willingness to undertake considerable risk because meeting the goals of the design required that the desired developments would take place sequentially, with one leading to the other.

Sharon proved unable to read the domestic politics of Lebanon and Israel. In the case of Lebanon, he wildly overestimated the Maronites' willingness to take risks, as well as their ability to dominate Lebanon, even with the help of the IDF. Sharon failed to understand how the internal balance of power in Lebanon had shifted in the 1970s as a result of the changes in the country's demography. By 1982 the Christians were a minority in retreat and were limited in the extent to which their greater mobilization, superior access to resources and the charismatic leadership of Bashir Jumayyil, would continue to allow them to assert themselves in a manner that far exceeded their relative standing in Lebanon's population. His grand design was doomed to failure when it became clear that the Maronites would not be willing or able (or both) to fulfill the role ascribed to them in Sharon's design.

Equally, Sharon completely misjudged the implications of the opposition his design elicited at every level of the Israeli scene: from the general public to the cabinet. Specifically, what he did not understand were the hazards of entering a war without sufficient domestic support and the extent to which the opposition to the war would come to haunt him the minute his grand design faced serious turbulence.

Finally, without his unique talent for manipulation, Sharon could not have garnered the minimal consent he required to implement his plan. Encountering consistent opposition within his government to his grand design, Sharon gradually downsized the war plans he presented to the Israeli cabinet. But from the beginning this entailed a major element of manipulation, if not deception, because the IDF, which continued to plan for war under Sharon's supervision, was not instructed to adjust its operational planning to the more limited dimensions presented to the cabinet. Thus, Sharon seems to have planned to exploit the cabinet's eventual approval of a very limited plan to enter Lebanon to a depth of 40 kilometers to implement his original grand military plan for a full-scale invasion of Lebanon.

The deception, while brilliant in allowing Sharon to initially overcome the opposition to his design, also doomed his plan to failure for three reasons: first, in the long run, he could not overcome the problems of fighting a war in the absence of a supporting national consensus; second, as cabinet members increasingly realized the extent of Sharon's deception, they turned against him; and finally, when the war turned sour – especially with the massacre in the Sabra and Shatila Palestinian refugee camps – few among his colleagues were there to defend him. Feeling deceived, they left him alone to face the national inquiry that followed the catastrophe.

Concluding Notes

The period addressed in this chapter was replete with paradoxes and strategic surprises. For the first time in Israel's history, the right wing succeeded in ending the 40-year dominance of the Labor movement at the helm of the Zionist project. Thus, with the 1977 elections Labor leaders whose ancestors won the leadership of the Zionist movement in the mid-1930s were now ejected from power and replaced by those of Likud. Yet it was a Likud leader, Begin, who responded to Sadat's peace initiative and made the concession that no Labor leader would have contemplated after the 1967 War: returning to Egypt every square inch of conquered Sinai.

This is a period when systemic factors prove very important in determining outcomes, particularly in that these factors also affected the behavior of the system's units. Thus, without the 1973 War changing the balance of power – indeed the entire gamut of strategic relations – between Egypt and Israel, it was inconceivable that Sadat would have been able to take the initiative that ultimately resulted in a peace treaty. Similarly, without changes in the regional balance of power favoring Israel – from the peace treaty with Egypt that took the largest and most populous Arab state out of any potential war coalition, to the Iraq–Iran War which preoccupied Iraq and ruled it out as a potential threat to Israel – it is difficult to see how Israel could have invaded Lebanon in 1982.

But domestic politics were also of critical importance in determining outcomes during this period. Without the changes in Israeli public attitudes affected by the 1973 War, Israel would not have abandoned its post 1967 rigidity and tried another path. And without Sadat reaching out to the Israeli public and acknowledging that it had legitimate security concerns, Israelis would not have felt that an opportunity for peace had been presented and should not be missed. Similarly, without the changes in Israeli leadership in late 1981, with the peacemakers of Camp David – Dayan and Wiezmann – now leaving the scene to be replaced by Shamir and Sharon, Israel would not have had the leadership that took it into Lebanon in 1982.

The importance of personalities was particularly apparent in understanding the breakthrough in Egyptian–Israeli relations. Simply, no one other than Sadat could have pulled off such a feat. Without Sadat's unique intuitive notions of combining force and diplomacy – and using force to create diplomatic breakthroughs – there would have been no summit at Camp David and no Egyptian–Israeli peace treaty. Also, without Jimmy Carter's sense of mission, personal commitment to doing everything in his power to bring peace to the Holy Land, and ability to command the details of the various issues that were at dispute between Egypt and Israel, the negotiations that followed Sadat's visit to Jerusalem would not have been brought to a successful conclusion. And without Sharon's grand-strategic, even if deeply flawed, thinking, tenacity, and willingness to bend every rule in order to reshape the region, Israel would not have found itself in 1982 entering the Lebanese quagmire from which it would not extract itself for some 18 years.

For Israel this period offered a number of mutually reinforcing strategic developments that firmed up its permanence in the region. Most important was the departure of Egypt from any potential war coalition. This was complemented by the departure of Iraq from any such coalition as it became embroiled in a series of strategic disasters that condemned it to irrelevance in the Arab–Israeli context. Finally, Israel's bombing of Osiraq allowed it to maintain its nuclear monopoly in the region for years to come.

For Egypt this period crystallizes the drawbacks of being ahead of the curve. Yet, while Egypt continued to be ostracized for some time, soon enough – in the Fez Plan adopted by the Arab League in 1982 – the same Arab states that condemned Sadat's initiative would tacitly accept its strategic logic.

The Palestinians experienced a dramatic change of fortunes, which would have far-reaching consequences in later years. Exiled to Tunis, the PLO was now completely deprived of any credible option to continue the "armed struggle" against Israel.

The Lebanon war had a number of surprising outcomes, illustrating once again that, in the words of Kenneth Waltz, "international politics is the realm of unintended consequences." First, it changed the balance of power among the Palestinians from the "outsiders," who were now deprived of options for effective action against Israel, to the "insiders" of the West Bank and Gaza. As we shall see in the next chapter, this ultimately resulted in the "insiders" coming to the conclusion that they had no choice but to take matters into their own hands – hence the First Intifada, launched in December 1987. Second, the PLO's departure from "the rejectionist front" was accelerated, resulting in two pragmatic moves that were now inevitable if the organization was to remain politically relevant: the 1988 Declaration of Independence and the simultaneous de-facto adoption of the "two-state solution" to the conflict, which opened the way to the United States–PLO dialogue. Finally, the war, the PLO's expulsion, and the simultaneous defeat of the efforts to impose Maronite supremacy over Lebanon, opened the road to *Hezbollah* – the more militant and menacing among the Shi'a movements – to gain dominance over the country. This would have far reaching consequences, rocking the Lebanese scene well into the 21st century.

Readings

Bickerton, Ian and Carla Klausner, *A History of the Arab-Israeli Conflict* (Prentice Hall, 2010) 177–218.

Caplan, Neil, *The Israel-Palestine Conflict: Contested Histories* (Wiley, 2010) 178–194.

Dowty, Alan, *Israel/Palestine: Global Political Hotspots* (Polity, 2012) 137–141.

Eisenberg, Laura Zittrain and Neil Caplan, *Negotiating Arab-Israeli Peace: Patterns, Problems, Possibilities* (Indiana University Press, 2010) 35–72.

Gelvin, James, *The Israel-Palestine Conflict: One Hundred Years of War* (Cambridge University Press, 2007) 222, 235, 242–243.

Lesch, David, *The Arab-Israeli Conflict* (Oxford University Press, 2008) 259–300.

Morris, Benny, *Righteous Victims: The History of the Zionist-Arab Conflict, 1881–2001* (Vintage, 2001) 444–560.

Schiff, Ze'ev and Ehud Ya'ari, *Israel's Lebanon War* (London, Unwin, 1986).

Shlaim, Avi, *The Iron Wall: Israel and the Arab World* (W.W. Norton, 2001) 325–450.

Smith, Charles D., *Palestine and the Arab-Israeli Conflict* (Bedford/St.Martin's, 2007) 345–393.

Tessler, Mark, *A History of the Israeli-Palestinian Conflict* (Indiana University Press, 2009) 533–676.

Historical Documents

Camp David Summit Meeting: Walter Laqueur and Barry Rubin, *The Israel-Arab Reader: A Documentary History of the Middle East Conflict* (Penguin Books, 2008), 222–227.

Egyptian–Israeli Peace Treaty: Laqueur and Rubin, *The Israel-Arab Reader*, 227–228.

The Fahd Plan: Laqueur and Rubin, *The Israel-Arab Reader*, 234–235.

Jordan–PLO Joint Communique (Amman Accord): Laqueur and Rubin, *The Israel-Arab Reader*, 298–299.

Lebanon and Israel Truce Agreement: Laqueur and Rubin, *The Israel-Arab Reader*, 287–290.

The Reagan Plan: Laqueur and Rubin, *The Israel-Arab Reader*, 257–263.

U.N. Security Council Resolution 242: Laqueur and Rubin, *The Israel-Arab Reader*, 116.

U.N. Security Council Resolution 425, on Lebanon: Laqueur and Rubin, *The Israel-Arab Reader*, 221–222.

Notes

1. Indeed, Saddam Hussein declared himself and his country "the guardian of the Eastern gate of the Arab homeland." Jerrold M. Post and Amatzia Baram, *Saddam Is Iraq: Iraq Is Saddam* (Maxwell Airforce Base, Alabama: Air University, 2003), 17.
2. Margaret E. Galey, "Congress, Foreign Policy and Human Rights Ten Years after Helsinki," *Human Rights Quarterly* 7, 3 (1985), 334 n. 1.
3. "U.S., U.S.S.R. Issue Statement on the Middle East," Department of State Bulletin, vol. 77 (November 7, 1977), 639–40.
4. Mohamed Heikal, *Secret Channels*, 326–341.
5. Efraim Karsh, "Iran–Iraq War (1980–1988)," *Encyclopedia of the Modern Middle East and North Africa*, Vol. 2. ed. Philip Mattar, 2nd ed. (New York: Macmillan Reference USA, 2004) 1127–29.

6. William B. Quandt, *Peace Process*, 183–184; for Begin's speech to the Knesset, see Laqueur and Rubin, *The Israel–Arab Reader*, 218–219.
7. Quandt, *Peace Process*, 185–187.
8. Mohamed Heikal, *Secret Channels*, 225; Quandt, *Peace Process*, 188.
9. M. Cherif Bassiouni, ed., *Documents on the Arab–Israeli Conflict: Emergence of Conflict in Palestine and the Arab–Israeli Wars and Peace Process*, vol. 1, 862–863.
10. President Jimmy Carter, "Statement on Palestinian Rights," in Laqueur and Rubin, eds. *The Israel–Arab Reader*, 220–221.
11. Menachem Begin, "Speeches at Gala Dinner in the Knesset on the occasion of the opening of the talks of the Political Committee," in Meron Medzini (ed.), *Israel's Foreign Relations: Selected Documents*, Vol. 4–5: 1977–1979 (Jerusalem: Israel's Ministry of Foreign Affairs, 1981); Quandt, *Peace Process*, 200–201.
12. "Camp David Summit Meeting: Frameworks for Peace," in Laqueur and Rubin, *The Israel–Arab Reader*, 222–227.
13. Medzini, *Israel's Foreign Relations*, Vols. 4–5: 1977–1979; Quandt, *Peace Process*, 228–235.
14. Heikal, *Secret Channels*, 267–289.
15. Tessler, *A History of the Israeli–Palestinian Conflict*, 554–557. The assassins seem to have been propelled by two issues: corruption, and peace with Israel. By contrast, socioeconomic issues did not figure in any of the assassins' writings. In his letter to his mother prior to assassinating Sadat, Khalid Al Eslamboli wrote: "We are determined to kill the Pharaoh of Egypt; so God may save us from wilderness in the friendship with Zionists and the corruption of soul and conscience." See Adel Hammouda, *Assassinating a President: Documenting the Secrets of the Assassination of President Sadat* (Cairo: Iqra House, 1985), 211.
16. Phil Baum, "The Fez declaration; an analysis and commentary," *Political Communication and Persuasion*, 2, 4 (1984), 333–344, 336.
17. "Between Fez and Beirut, two Saudi initiatives for peace," *Al Jazeera*, March 25, 2002; "Document 531; Excerpts from the Final Declaration of the Twelfth Arab Summit Conference, Fez (Fez Arab Peace Plan), September 9, 1982," in *Documents on the Arab–Israeli Conflict: The Palestinians and the Israeli–Palestinian Peace Process*, vol. 2, ed. M. Cherif Bassiouni, 863–864.
18. *Ibid.*
19. Yair Evron, *War and Intervention in Lebanon* (Beckenham, Kent: Croom Helm, 1987), 71–74.
20. Robert Rabil, *Embattled Neighbors*, 58–59.
21. Evron, *War and Intervention in Lebanon*, 69–73.
22. David K. Shipler, "Cease-Fire in Border Fighting Declared by Israel and P.L.O," *New York Times*, July 25, 1981, http://www.nytimes.com/1981/07/25/world/cease-fire-border-fighting-declared-israel-plo-us-sees-hope-for-wider-peace.html (accessed November 28, 2012).
23. Evron, *War and Intervention in Lebanon*, 148–149.
24. *Ibid*, 142; Shai Feldman and Heda Rechnitz-Kijner, *Deception, Consensus, and War: Israel in Lebanon* (Tel Aviv: Jaffee Center for Strategic Studies, Paper no. 27, October, 1984); Zeev Schiff and Ehud Yaari, *Israel's Lebanon War* (New York: Simon and Schuster, 1985).
25. Evron, *War and Intervention in Lebanon*, 167.
26. Rabil, *Embattled Neighbors*, 70–72.
27. John Boykin, *Cursed Is the Peacemaker: The American Diplomat Versus the Israeli General, Beirut 1982* (Belmont, CA: Applegate Press, 2002).
28. Yezid Sayigh, *Armed Struggle and the Search for State*, 627–628.
29. *Ibid.*, 628–629. The Islamic Compound was started in 1973, but was only registered officially by the military administration six years later, in 1979.

30. David Shipler, a former *New York Times* reporter, later recounted that he was told by the military governor of the Gaza Strip at that time, Brigadier General Yitzhak Segev, that the Israeli government had financed the Islamic movement to counteract the PLO and the communists. David Shipler, *Arab and Jew: Wounded Spirits in a Promised Land* (New York: Times Books, 1986), 177. According to Sayigh "Israeli authorities were initially content to let the Islamic challenge to the PLO grow, and turned a blind eye to attacks by Islamist militants on known PLO supporters in the early 1980s." See Sayigh, *Armed Struggle and the Search for State*, 629.
31. Amal Jamal, *The Palestinian National Movement: Politics of Contention, 1967–2005* (Bloomington: Indiana University Press, 2005), 48.
32. *Ibid*, 48–49.
33. Emile Sahliyeh, *In Search of Leadership: West Bank Politics since 1967* (Washington, DC: The Brookings Institution, 1988), 71–72.
34. *Ibid.*, 82–85.
35. For settlement statistics, see The Foundation for Middle East Peace http://www.fmep.org/settlement_info.
36. Tessler, *A History of the Israeli–Palestinian Conflict*, 558–560.
37. Sayigh, *Armed Struggle and the Search for a State*, 574–606.
38. Sahliyeh, *In Search of Leadership*, 163–178; Sayigh, *Armed Struggle and the Search for a State*, 596–601.
39. Emile Sahliyeh, "The West Bank Pragmatic Elite: the Uncertain Future," *Journal of Palestine Studies*, 15, 4 (Summer, 1986), 34–45; Emile Sahliyeh, *In Search of Leadership: West Bank Politics Since 1967*; Emile Sahliyeh, "Jordan and the Palestinians," in William Quandt (ed.), *The Middle East: Ten Years After Camp David* (Washington, DC: The Brookings Institution, 1988), 279–318.
40. From "President Ronald Reagan's Speech and Talking Points, September 1, 1982," in Quandt, *The Middle East: Ten Years after Camp David*, ed. Quandt, 461–470: The Reagan Plan suggests two ideas regarding settlement construction. The first is a settlement freeze during the first five years of the plan's implementation; these are to make up a transitional period where power over the West Bank and Gaza is handed over to a Palestinian authority from Israel (pp. 465–466). In addition, the Plan endorses UNSCR 242 and calls for Israeli withdrawal in return for peace whereby the extent of the withdrawal is parallel to the "extent and nature of the peace and security arrangements offered in return" (p. 469). The plan also says that "Further settlement activity is in no way necessary for the security of Israel and only diminishes the confidence of the Arabs that a final outcome can be freely and fairly negotiated" (p. 466).
41. Samuel W. Lewis, "The United States and Israel: Constancy and Change," in Quandt, ed., *The Middle East: Ten Years After Camp David*, 217–257, 246.
42. William B. Quandt, "U.S. Policy toward the Arab–Israeli Conflict," in *The Middle East: Ten Years After Camp David*, ed, Quandt, 357–386, 367.
43. Yehuda Lukacs, *Israel, Jordan, and the Peace Process* (Syracuse NY: Syracuse University Press, 1999), 163–64; Quandt, *Peace Process*, 261–63.
44. For more details, see Avi Shlaim, *Lion of Jordan: The Life of King Hussein in War and Peace*, 428–445.
45. Kamal S. Salibi, *The Modern History of Jordan*, 265–66.
46. *Arab Strategic Report 1986*, Al Sayed Yassin, Editor In Chief (Cairo: Al Ahram Center for Political and Strategic Studies, 1987), 112.
47. Salibi, *The Modern History of Jordan*, 265–66.

48. David Makovsky, *Making Peace with the PLO: The Rabin Government's Road to the Oslo Accord* (Boulder: Westview Press, 1995).
49. "Man of the Year: Anwar Sadat: Architect of a New Mideast," *Time*, January 2, 1978.
50. Heikal, *Secret Channels*, 233.
51. Sulaymān al-Mūsá, *Tarikh al Urdun al Siyasi al Mu'asir: Huzairan 1967–1995*, 145–147 [In Arabic].
52. Heikal, *Secret Channels*, 273. For the term "regional policeman" as it applied to the Middle East in general and the Persian Gulf in particular, see Shahram Chubin, "Iran: Between the Arab West and the Asian East," *Survival* (July–August 1974), 173–82; Mark J. Gasiorowski, *U.S. Foreign Policy and the Shah: Building a Client State in Iran* (Ithaca: Cornell University Press, 1991).

7 From the First Intifada to Madrid and Oslo

This chapter spans the period 1987–94, from the First Intifada to the launching of the Madrid process and the signing of the Oslo Accords, as well as of the Jordanian–Israeli Peace Treaty. From the global level to the realm of bilateral Israeli–Palestinian relations, this period witnessed momentous changes: the end of the Cold War and the dissolution of the Soviet Union, the 1991 Gulf War and the subsequent convening of the first truly multilateral Arab–Israeli peace conference.

At the global level, the waning of the Soviet Union and the subsequent end of the Cold War resulted in a shift from a bipolar to a unipolar international system. Also associated with this era were the effects of the advent of globalization, a generally more conciliatory international environment, and the end of the Cold-War-induced arms race in the Middle East. For the United States – the only remaining superpower – not all this news was good, as regional balancing was now increasingly replaced by direct American intervention.

In the region at large, the major development during this period was Iraq's invasion of Kuwait and the resulting First Gulf War. Among Arab countries, the invasion created for a very short period a very dramatic split, similar to the Arab "Cold War" of the 1950s and early 1960s.

This period now also became an "Egyptian–Saudi moment" in the region. Iran was seriously weakened by its eight years of war with Iraq; the Soviet Union was driven out of Afghanistan by forces supported by America and Saudi Arabia; and Iraq emerged weakened and bankrupted by its long war with Iran and its later defeat in the First Gulf War by an American-led coalition that included Egypt and Syria. However, Syria's participation in the anti-Iraq winning coalition did not prevent it from being significantly weakened by the loss of its Soviet patron, much like the PLO, which did not side with the Americans.

In the Arab–Israeli arena this period began with a dramatic development in the context of the Palestinian–Israeli conflict – the First Intifada, which broke out in early December 1987. The period closed with the signing of the Israeli–PLO Oslo Accords and the Israeli–Jordanian Peace Treaty. In between, the convening of the Madrid peace conference, an equally historical development in the broader dimension of the Arab–Israeli dispute, launched a complex set of negotiations: bilateral negotiations between Israel and Syria as well as between Israel and a joint Jordanian–Palestinian delegation, and multilateral negotiations between Israel, the Palestinians, and thirteen Arab states, aimed at addressing the region-wide problems of the Middle East.

The Madrid process was a direct outcome of the 1991 Gulf War. Doubts about whether the United States could manage another such expensive and logistically demanding enterprise motivated the Bush administration to launch an impressive attempt to settle the region's conflicts – an effort designed to reduce the probability that such direct American-led intervention would be needed again. While Madrid failed to produce an Israeli–Syrian accord or sustainable breakthroughs in its multilateral track, it opened the door to another dramatic development – the Oslo Accords signed between Israel and the PLO in September 1993.

Main Developments

On the international and regional scenes, the most important developments addressed in this section involve the end of the Cold War, the winding down of the eight-year war between Iraq and Iran, Iraq's 1990 invasion of Kuwait and the resulting 1991 Gulf War, and finally the post-war Madrid Peace Conference. In the Palestinian–Israeli arena the most significant development during this period was the eruption of the First Palestinian Intifada and the resulting increased Islamization of the Palestinian scene. Together, the Intifada, the Gulf War, and the Madrid Conference seemed to pave the way to the 1993 Israel–PLO Oslo Accords and the 1994 Israel–Jordan Peace Treaty.

The Global and Regional Scenes

In the world at-large, this era witnessed one of the most dramatic developments of the 20th century: the end of the Cold War and the ensuing dissolution of the Soviet Union. This was symbolized by the fall of the Berlin Wall on November 9, 1989 and the unification of Germany a year later. These developments were preceded by two changes in Soviet policy in the mid to late 1980s: *Glasnost* and *Perestroika*. The first called for economic liberalization, while the latter stipulated greater political freedom and the easing of the Soviet Union's foreign relations. Both were conceived as a desperate response to the USSR's deteriorating economy. These developments had an immediate, direct effect on Israel: beginning in 1989 the Soviet Union's gates were opened to over a million Jews to emigrate, many of them choosing Israel as their destination. This resulted in a dramatic change in Israel's demography. In turn, the funds required to absorb these immigrants created an Israeli imperative to obtain $ 10 billion in United States loan guarantees.

In the Middle East, this period witnessed the end of the Iran–Iraq War. The war, which began in September 1980, finally ended when a ceasefire was announced on August 20, 1988 after Iran accepted UN Security Council Resolution 598. By that time, some 150,000 Iranians had been killed in battle, with another 40,000 listed as missing in action and 2,000 civilians killed. Iraq lost 60,000 men in battle with another 6,000 Iraqi Kurdish civilians killed by their own government.[1]

The end of the war enabled the two countries to reenter the oil market. The psychological effects of a more stable Gulf region and the restoration of high oil production levels in Iraq and Iran led to a sharp decline in oil prices. The resulting decline in oil revenues made it more difficult for Iraq to pay the costs of post-war reconstruction and to return the loans

Figure 7.1. The fall of the Berlin Wall. © Regis Bossu/Sygma/CORBIS

it received during the war. In the broader region it diminished the capacity of Arab governments who presided over rentier economies to continue funding the basic needs of their population. This reduction of government subsidies ignited the April 1989 "food riots" in Jordan and gave added ammunition to those arguing that the Hashemite Kingdom should focus on the East Bank and leave it to others to worry about the Palestinians in the West Bank, Gaza and East Jerusalem.

The Intifada

The Arab Summit held in Amman in November 1987 was often viewed, especially by the Palestinians, as a further indication that the Arab world had turned its back on the Palestinian cause. Indeed, the conference focused primarily on the Iran–Iraq War and the thawing of relations with Egypt.[2] Six months earlier, on April 26, 1987, during the 18th PNC Conference, Arafat conceded to the PFLP and the DFLP by abrogating the Amman agreement he made with King Hussein in February 1985. The accord stipulated the formation of a joint Palestinian–Jordanian delegation and the formation of a Jordanian–Palestinian confederation in a future peace agreement.

A month after the November 1987 Summit, the First Palestinian Intifada broke out. The term Intifada is used in Arabic to mean an "uprising." Different from insurgency, guerrilla warfare, or armed resistance, it refers to collective action taken by masses to demonstrate their rejection of the status quo. In the Palestinian case, the term meant spontaneous action, at least at its beginnings, triggered by one or more major events that pushed the Palestinians to declare that they could not take the pressures of occupation any more. As a political statement designed to mobilize world public opinion it involved the massive use of rock-throwing children and youth.

A series of events in December 1987 brought the simmering tensions between Israel and the Palestinians to a head. On December 6, an Israeli settler was stabbed to death in Gaza City by a member of Islamic Jihad. Two days later, an Israeli truck struck a group of Palestinians from the Jabaliya refugee camp, killing four of them. Rumors quickly spread amongst the Palestinians that the deaths were a deliberate response to the murder of the settler. Hence, Palestinians took to the streets of Jabaliya in mass demonstrations. Throughout Gaza many soon followed, later

Figure 7.2. Palestinian protest march during the First Intifada. © David H. Wells/ CORBIS

joined by the Palestinians in the West Bank. Thus the First Palestinian Intifada was under way.[3]

While the First Intifada began as a series of non-violent protests, it gradually became more violent. Thus, by the end of its third year, in December 1990, as it wound down when attention in the region shifted to Iraq's invasion of Kuwait, the Intifada resulted in 160 Israeli and some 2,000 Palestinian dead. However, the latter figure includes some 800 Palestinians killed by other Palestinians on suspicion of collaboration with Israel. Also significant was the damage Israel's reputation suffered, as the international and new regional media broadcast scenes of harsh measures taken by the IDF to suppress the rebellion.

Even more significantly, two constituencies that bore the brunt of the struggle during the First Intifada now rose to the forefront of Palestinian ranks: the nationalist young guard of Fatah, who now gained greater influence at the expense of the "outside" PLO; and the Islamists of Hamas, who now gained greater independence from their parent movements – the Egyptian and Jordanian Muslim Brotherhood.

Three national figures, Faisal Husseini, Hanan Ashrawi, and Sa'eb Erekat, clearly left their mark on the manner in which the Intifada evolved and, even more so, on the international echo it created. Together, they represented a new breed of Palestinian nationalists who were familiar with Western and Israeli politics.

In turn, the rise in the relative power of the Islamists, the broader radicalization of the population in the West Bank and Gaza, and the shifting of the emphasis of Palestinian politics from the Diaspora to these territories, resulted in deep concern among PLO leaders in the Diaspora that they might be losing control. Later, this concern was exacerbated by the convening of the 1991 Madrid Conference, as the Palestinians were forced to accept that their representation in the conference and the subsequent talks would be confined to residents of the West Bank and Gaza within the framework of a Jordan–Palestinian joint delegation.

On the ground, Israel continued to build and expand settlements during the Intifada years. About half a dozen new settlements, such as Talmon, northwest of Ramallah, and Shvut

FACES OF THE FIRST INTIFADA

Faisal Husseini was the dean of the Oriental House in Jerusalem – one of the most important symbols of Palestinian nationalism. In the aftermath of the Gulf War he represented the new face of Palestinian politics. As a soft-spoken, lucid, and graceful individual, he was well acquainted with the ways of the world media.

Figure 7.3. Sa'eb Erekat © KHALED ELFIQI/epa/Corbis

Figure 7.4. Hannan Ashrawi and Faisal Husseini (with Nabil Shaath, far right). *Source*: Barry Iverson/Time Life Pictures/Getty Images

Sa'eb Erekat, a Professor of Political Science at An-Najah National University in Nablus, used the local media to call upon Palestinians to "endure, reject and resist Israeli military rule, withdrawing their cooperation from all the trappings of the Occupation." In May 1988, he was one of three Palestinian leaders, along with Haidar Abdel Shafi and Hanan Ashrawi, to participate in *ABC Nightline's* Town Hall meeting from Jerusalem – the first time ever that Palestinians and Israelis had addressed American TV audiences together.

Hanan Ashrawi, an extraordinarily articulate professor of English literature, became the voice of the Intifada.

Rachel, near Shilo on the main road linking Nablus to Ramallah, were established. By mid-1992, the Jewish population of East Jerusalem and the West Bank reached 135,000 and 110,000 respectively. By 1993, the number of settlers in the Golan Heights reached 12,600.[4]

The Rise of Hamas

The eruption of the First Intifada was accompanied by a significant development in domestic Palestinian politics. Islamists, who had been gaining in strength since the late 1970s, and by the mid-1980s had become deeply involved in the socio-economic and political life in the West Bank and the Gaza Strip, decided to join the activities targeting Israeli forces. In the early and mid-1970s, they had risen to prominence, in part due to their focus on promoting traditional and religious values and in part to the well-organized social service network that provided services and charitable programs to Palestinians. The 1979 Iranian Revolution and the rise of Hezbollah in South Lebanon in the early 1980s inspired Palestinian Islamists. In December 1987, a few days after the eruption of the Intifada, the Muslim Brotherhood, now the largest Islamist organization in the Palestinian areas, changed its name to Hamas.[5]

The establishment of Hamas indicated a shift to a new balance of power in Palestinian domestic politics. While nationalists were consolidating gains against the pro-Jordanian forces in Palestinian society, Islamists now came to gradually challenge the nationalists. Joining the resistance efforts gave the Islamists a certificate of credibility and legitimacy they lacked in the 1970s and early 1980s. But while the struggle of nationalists had by now focused on ending occupation and building a Palestinian state, Hamas aimed at establishing an Islamic state on all of historic Palestine. Hence, it rejected the two-state solution, embodied in the PLO 1988 Declaration of Independence; its founding charter committed the group to the destruction of the State of Israel. With the rise of Hamas, the monopoly of the nationalists over Palestinian politics came to an end.

Jordan Disengages

The outbreak of the Intifada and the ensuing surge in the popularity of the PLO throughout the West Bank led to another major development. On July 31, 1988, Jordan's King Hussein declared his intention to sever Jordan's legal and administrative ties to the West Bank. Two days earlier, Jordan's Council of Ministers had announced the cancellation of a $1.5 billion development plan for the occupied territories which the king had announced in 1986. Jordan explained the move as permitting "the PLO to shoulder its full responsibility as the sole legitimate representative of the Palestinian people."[6]

On August 4, 1988, the Hashemite government decided to retire almost all the Jordanian civil servants employed in the West Bank, a decision that affected some 18,000 teachers, health workers, and municipal employees (most of whom were also receiving salaries from Israel). The only ones to be exempted from the consequences of Jordan's disengagement were the nearly 3,000 employees of the *Awqaf* [Ministry of Religious Endowment and Religious Affairs], which included the Islamic religious court system.

On August 20, Jordan's prime minister issued new regulations according to which all Jordanian citizens residing in the West Bank before July 31, 1988 would no longer be considered Jordanian citizens, but rather Palestinians. Residents of the West Bank could obtain temporary Jordanian passports, to be used solely as travel documents.[7] As a result of these developments, the general elections held in Jordan in November 1989 produced the first Parliament since 1950 that did not include representatives from the West Bank.[8]

Palestinians Declare Independence

The next important development to follow Jordan's decision to disengage from the West Bank was the announcement made by PLO Chairman Arafat on November 15, 1988: the

Figure 7.5. Palestinian Declaration of Independence Source: Patrick AVENTURIER/Gamma-Rapho via Getty Images

Palestinian Declaration of Independence. The declaration, made at the closing session of the 19th Palestine National Council, established the State of Palestine on the West Bank and Gaza Strip, with Jerusalem as its capital and affirmed the rights of the Palestinian people to their land and to their political self-determination. It also acknowledged the legitimacy of "the Resolutions of the United Nations Organization since 1947." Since Israel was not mentioned by name, there was some question as to whether the declaration should be interpreted as binding the envisaged new Palestinian state to peaceful coexistence with Israel.[9]

Arafat's November 15 statement was followed by intense United States–Palestinian back-channel talks that aimed to address an American–Israeli understanding reached in 1975 that committed the United States to refrain from dealing with the PLO until the latter endorsed UN Resolution 242, renounced terrorism, and recognized Israel's right to exist. As the Reagan administration considered the PLO's November declaration insufficient to warrant direct talks with the PLO, two informal channels of communication were opened to focus on finding a formula that would enable the United States to begin such talks. One back-channel was conducted by a number of members of the American Jewish community, along with Swedish Foreign Minister Sten Andersson and PLO representatives. The other was conducted by economist and author Mohamed Rabie, a Palestinian-American, who approached former National Security Council staff member William B. Quandt for his State Department and NSC contacts. Rabie was in contact with the PLO leadership in Tunis and was convinced the PLO would eventually accept the American conditions for dialogue.[10]

The result of these talks was a clarification issued by Arafat on December 14 affirming "the right of all parties concerned in the Middle East conflict to exist in peace and security, and, as I have mentioned, including the state of Palestine, Israel, and other neighbors, according to the Resolutions 242 and 338…we totally and absolutely renounce all forms of terrorism, including individual, group and state terrorism."[11] In response, Secretary of State George Shultz announced that the American conditions were met. Consequently a United States–PLO dialogue was launched in Tunis. By late January 1989, 84 countries officially recognized the State of Palestine and an additional 20 countries extended qualified recognition. As a result, the PLO gained the right to address the Security Council.[12]

The Gulf War and Madrid

On August 2, 1990, following Iraq's failed attempts to settle the debts it accumulated as a result of its eight-year war with Iran, Saddam Hussein ordered his forces into Kuwait. A few days later, these forces were sent to southern Kuwait and were positioned along the Kuwaiti–Saudi border, north of Saudi Arabia's vast oil fields.

Iraq's invasion of Kuwait led to one of the most impressive logistical operations in modern military history as the United States moved nearly half a million troops and their equipment to the Persian Gulf in a span of four months. At the same time, the Bush administration executed an impressive diplomatic feat as it assembled a broad coalition to thwart Saddam's move. Particularly important was that the coalition included key Arab states, primarily Saudi Arabia, Egypt and Syria. Jordan, Yemen and the PLO refused to join the American-led coalition.[13] On January 17, following the failure to compel Saddam to withdraw his forces from Kuwait, the coalition began major combat operations against Iraq.

The First Gulf War lasted 42 days. It began with a week-long aerial bombardment of Iraqi forces in Kuwait, followed by an American-led ground assault against these forces as well as a major flanking move launched from the territory of Saudi Arabia into southeastern Iraq. The move succeeded in forcing Iraq to withdraw its remaining forces from Kuwait in order to protect Baghdad. The war also saw a major Iraqi attempt to involve Israel in the war by launching 41 extended-range Scud missiles against Israeli population centers as well as the vicinity of Dimona, the location of Israel's nuclear reactor. Anticipating this possibility, the United States stationed US Army Ballistic Missile Defense units in Israel – the first time ever that the United States deployed troops in Israel's defense. Heeding the requests of the Bush administration, Israel refrained from taking retaliatory measures in response to the Iraqi Scud attacks.

The success of the American-led coalition, forcing Saddam to end the occupation of Kuwait, led the Bush administration to launch a major effort to resolve the Arab–Israeli conflict and to address the region's major challenges. On October 30, 1991, Israel, Syria, Lebanon, and a joint Jordanian–Palestinian delegation attended the historic Madrid Peace Conference under the dual sponsorship of the United States and the ailing Soviet Union. This was quickly followed by the launching in Moscow of multilateral talks between Israel, the Palestinians and thirteen Arab countries aimed at dealing with the region-wide problems of the Middle East: economic development, water and other natural resources, the environment, refugees, and arms control and regional security (ACRS).

Figure 7.6. Leaders attending the Madrid Peace Conference. © Pascal le Segretain/Sygma/CORBIS

The convening of the Madrid Conference was preceded by intense American diplomacy, orchestrated by Secretary of State James Baker, focused on ensuring the participation of Syria and Israel. It was also associated with considerable tension in American–Israeli relations, as the Bush administration clashed with the Likud-led government led by Itzhak Shamir. The clash centered on Washington's attempt to persuade Israel to halt the construction of and within settlements in the West Bank and Gaza. For the first time since the mid-1970s, the United States exerted overt pressure on Israel, threatening to deny it the $10 billion in United States government loan guarantees that Israel sought in order to fund the absorption of Jewish immigrants from the Soviet Union.

The Road to Oslo

In January 1993, Arafat authorized a number of senior PLO officials and PLO-affiliated non-officials to engage a number of Israeli non-officials in a Track-II attempt to negotiate a set of principles on which a process to resolve the Israeli–Palestinian conflict would be based. Two Palestinian leaders were among the architects of the Oslo Accords that resulted from these talks: Mahmoud Abbas (Abu Mazen) and Ahmed Qurie (Abu Ala'). Abbas's Israeli counterpart was Deputy Foreign Minister Yossi Beilin and Qurie's Israeli interlocutors were two independent scholars: Yair Hirschfeld and Ron Pundak. Following the understanding reached on the first draft of the proposed Declaration of Principles (DOP), the Israeli unofficial participants were joined and later largely replaced by senior government officials: Uri Savir, Director General of the Foreign Ministry and Joel Singer, a former military advocate, who was now recruited from private practice to become the Legal Advisor to the Foreign Ministry.[14]

THE THREE ARCHITECTS OF OSLO

Mahmoud Abbas (Abu Mazen) was, together with Yasser Arafat, a founding member of Fatah. Beginning in 1980, he led the PLO's department for national and international relations. By 1991, after top Fatah leaders such as Salah Khalaf (Abu Iyad) and Khalil al-Wazir (Abu Jihad) had been assassinated, he became second in command in the Fatah leadership and a member of the PLO Executive Committee.

Also known as Abu Ala', Ahmed Qurie was the chief Palestinian negotiator in the Oslo talks. A banker by profession, he joined Fatah in the late 1960s and helped manage PLO financial and economic operations from the 1970s onwards. He later rose to the position of the director of the PLO's foreign investment branch and director-general of the PLO's economic branch.

Deputy Foreign Minister Yossi Beilin was the Israeli mentor of the Oslo talks. Having served during the previous fifteen years as the closest aide to the then Foreign Minister Peres, he enjoyed complete access to Peres and, to a somewhat lesser extent, to Rabin. The latter respected Beilin's tenacity and creativity despite earlier clashes over Beilin's staunch opposition to Israel's defense relations with South Africa. By late 1992 Beilin had become frustrated by what seemed to him to be the total futility of the post-Madrid Track-I negotiations being conducted in Washington. He believed that the window for diplomacy was rapidly closing and that if a creative approach were not adopted, the opportunity created by the PLO's predicament in the aftermath of the Gulf War would be missed.

By September 1993, these talks produced an agreed DOP for resolving the Palestinian–Israeli conflict. The DOP, better known as the Oslo Accords, comprised a grand bargain that entailed significant concessions from both sides and raised equally great expectations. Widely regarded as a historical breakthrough, it won its principal signatories – Prime Minister Itzhak Rabin, Foreign Minister Shimon Peres, and Chairman Yasser Arafat – the Nobel Prize for Peace.

The Oslo Accords included:

1. An agreement on interim self-government arrangements to last not more than five years during which Israel would transfer to the Palestinians jurisdiction over the West Bank and the Gaza Strip, seen as one territorial unit, excepting issues of permanent status.
2. A stipulation to the effect that the interim period would begin with Israeli withdrawal from the Gaza Strip and the Jericho area, to be followed by additional withdrawals from West Bank areas and cities.
3. Permanent status negotiations to commence as soon as possible, but not later than the beginning of the third year of the interim period. By the end of the interim period, these negotiations were to resolve all outstanding issues: refugees, Jerusalem, settlements, borders, security arrangements, and others.
4. Palestinians would hold free elections, establish a council of government, and govern themselves democratically.
5. In order to guarantee public order and internal security, the Palestinian Authority would establish a strong police force, while Israel would continue to carry the responsibility for

Figure 7.7. Israeli Prime Minister Yitzak Rabin, Israeli Foreign Minister Shimon Peres, and Palestinian leader Yasser Arafat, the joint Nobel Peace Prize winners for 1994, Oslo, Norway.
Source: Getty Images.

defending against external threats, as well as the responsibility for overall security of Israelis.

6. During the interim period, Israel was to remain in control of areas not transferred to Palestinians' jurisdiction and was to remain responsible for the overall security of Israelis in the West Bank and Gaza and of Israeli settlements.

On September 9, 1993, a few days before the signing of the DOP, Arafat and Israeli Prime Minister Rabin exchanged letters covering issues related to mutual recognition, violence, and the PLO charter. Arafat's letter affirmed PLO recognition of Israel, accepted UNSC Resolution 242 and 338, committed the PLO to resolve the outstanding issues through negotiations, and renounced the use of terrorism and violence. It further committed the PLO to change its Charter by removing articles that deny Israel's right to exist. Rabin's letter to Arafat stated that "Israel has decided to recognize the PLO as the representative of the Palestinian people and commence negotiations with the PLO within the Middle East peace process."[15]

The Jordan–Israel Peace Treaty

The next significant development in the history of the conflict during this period took place roughly a year after Oslo. On October 26, 1994 in Wadi Arava along the Jordanian–Israeli border, King Hussein and Prime Minister Rabin signed the second peace agreement between Israel and an Arab state. The agreement culminated two years of negotiations that began in Madrid but were soon largely replaced by direct bilateral talks between personal representatives of the Israeli prime minister and the Hashemite king.

Figure 7.8. Signing of the Israeli-Jordanian Peace Treaty. *Source*: Cynthia Johnson//Time Life Pictures/Getty Images

In addition to establishing peace between the two countries, including full diplomatic relations, the main elements of the treaty were:

1. An agreement on the international borders, settling territorial disputes between the two states which included (a) an exchange of territories, about 11.5 square miles, and (b) a lease of two small areas, about 700 acres in the Arava and near the Sea of Galilee.
2. An agreement on water whereby Israel agreed to make 50 million cubic meters, or 13.2 billion gallons, available to Jordan each year, mostly by diverting flows from the Jordan River.
3. A pledge that neither side would permit its territory to be used as a staging area by third countries for military strikes against the other.
4. An Israeli commitment that the Hashemite Kingdom's claims to Islamic sites in Jerusalem would be given "high priority" when Israel and the Palestinians would eventually negotiate Jerusalem's fate.
5. A commitment to resolve the problem of the refugees in Jordan "in accordance with international law" and in the meantime to cooperate in order to relieve the suffering of those refugees and to resolve the problem of displaced persons residing in Jordan.
6. A commitment by the two sides to broad cooperation in tourism, water, energy, transportation, environmental protection, agriculture and economic development.[16]

Unlike the Egyptian–Israeli treaty, the Israeli–Jordanian accord did not include arms-limitations measures or the stationing of monitors on the borders. Yet as indicated above, it did include reference to one of the most important issues of the permanent settlement between Palestinians and Israelis: Jerusalem. The Jordanian–Israeli treaty also included reference to another problem that has stirred serious Jordanian fears for a long time, the "transfer" of Palestinians from the West Bank to Jordan. The treaty stipulated that "involuntary movement of persons in such a way as to adversely prejudice the security of either Party should not be permitted."

Narratives

The Israeli Narrative

The First Intifada

The initial Israeli interpretation of the First Intifada was that it comprised a clever Palestinian ploy to battle Israel within rules of engagement that were much more acceptable to world public opinion than violence. These rules had the added advantage of presenting images of weak but determined sling-shooting Palestinian youth challenging heavily armed and well-equipped Israeli soldiers – thus conclusively reversing the image planted in world opinion up to and during the 1967 War of "Israel as David" and the "Arabs as Goliath." Now, television pictures of the confrontations were projected to all corners of the earth, portraying the Palestinians as David and the Israelis as Goliath.

Israelis saw this new perception as a distortion of reality and viewed the means used by the rebelling Palestinians as more violent by far than was widely understood and appreciated. Indeed, Israelis viewed such Palestinian activities as putting Israeli lives in mortal danger and thus as justifying what to others seemed a disproportionate or excessive use of force in an attempt to quell the protests.

At the same time, Israelis at the center of the political map – those whose swing vote would enable the Labor party's return to power in 1992 – now understood the Intifada as a wakeup call: a warning against the notion that Israel could continue to occupy the West Bank and Gaza and control the Palestinians residing in these territories indefinitely and at tolerable costs. By 1991 many among these Israelis saw the PLO's decision to accept the two-state solution and to allow negotiations to begin in Madrid under the façade of a joint Jordanian–Palestinian delegation as the first real signs of Palestinian pragmatism: a willingness to abandon what was seen as their long-held "all or nothing" approach and to adopt instead a willingness to accept what is possible.[17]

Relations with the United States

A second important dimension of the Israeli narrative of this period was that American support of Israel was now associated with a clear price tag. During the Gulf War, the United States was seen as having elevated its support of Israel to a qualitatively new level: in the face of fear of, and the later actual launching of Iraqi Scud missiles against Israel's population centers and its nuclear reactor in Dimona, the United States for the first time in the history of the two countries' relations had sent troops – US Army Patriot Air-Defense Battalions – to Israel's defense. Notwithstanding the limited effectiveness of the Patriots – a subject of considerable debate in Israel as well as in the United States in the war's aftermath – the symbolic dimension of the American move was clear to Israelis during and after the war. Similarly, Israel appreciated the broader role that the United States had played in assembling the coalition that battled Saddam Hussein and seriously weakened Iraq – then viewed as a staunch enemy of Israel.

During the same time period, Israel faced the monumental task of absorbing more than a million immigrants from Russia. To be able to do this it saw an imperative to obtain American government guarantees for loans totaling some $10 billion. Under these circumstances, maintaining close ties with the United States seemed to many Israelis an absolute imperative. Consequently, once Secretary of State James Baker had obtained Syria's agreement to attend Madrid and join the ensuing process, Israelis understood they could not be absent from the conference. Moreover, with the Bush administration taking strong exception to continued Israeli settlement activity in the West Bank and Gaza – viewing it as prejudging the outcome of negotiations and as detrimental to American peacemaking efforts – Israelis saw no alternative but to comply, even if this ultimately required a change in the composition of their government.

The Oslo Breakthrough

The Israeli narrative regarding Oslo was that it was made possible by three changes in the Palestinians' situation and positions. The first was that the Intifada had shifted the Palestinians' center of gravity from the diaspora to the West Bank and Gaza, and that this, in turn, forced Arafat to respond to the requirements of the population residing in these areas. The imperative of ending Israeli occupation thus received priority. Appreciation of this was viewed as having resulted in the PLO's 1988 decision to adopt the two-state solution. By doing so the Palestinians were seen as signaling for the first time the option of fulfilling their aspirations in a way that would not necessarily jeopardize Israel's survival. This was viewed as being in sharp contrast to the PLO's historical position, reflected in its Covenant, the letter and spirit of which was understood to stipulate that the Palestinian problem could not be resolved except through Israel's destruction.

The Israeli understanding was that the second and third changes in the Palestinian position resulted from Arafat's colossal strategic error of siding with Saddam Hussein during the Gulf Crisis and war. Arafat's decision was assessed as having resulted in huge anger directed against the PLO by Saudi Arabia and the smaller Gulf States. Yet these states – those most directly affected by Saddam's aggression – also happened to have been the most important financial backers of the Palestinians. The anger led to the drying up of the PLO financial resources, placing the Palestinian project in unprecedented jeopardy. In order to remain relevant, the PLO was seen as having no choice but to compromise its traditional position, thus allowing a historical breakthrough in its relations with Israel.

What were these compromises? First, the Palestinians were understood to have committed themselves to end the "armed struggle" before a deal covering all aspects of the conflict was concluded. Israelis understood this Palestinian commitment as having clear ramifications in the domestic realm: namely, that as the "sole representative of the Palestinian people" the PLO's commitment to end the "armed struggle" implied a promise to impose an end to violence on all Palestinian factions.

Second, the PLO was seen as having accepted an open-ended process. That is, that in contrast to their long-standing insistence that no steps be taken to ease the conflict unless their historical demands were met – from the refugees' Right of Return to Arab sovereignty over al-Haram al-Sharif (also known as The Noble Sanctuary) – the Palestinians now agreed to implement interim steps without a firm Israeli promise regarding the end-state of the process.

Israelis viewed the breakthrough in Oslo as comprising a Palestinian–Israeli grand bargain. In that framework, Israel saw itself as having agreed to a gradual transfer of control to the Palestinians over parts of the Land of Israel – the first time in history that the Palestinians were to gain such control. A second component of the bargain was seen as Israel's willingness to accept the PLO as its sole Palestinian negotiations partner – in sharp contrast to the long-held Israeli view of the PLO as a terrorist organization and to Israel's resulting refusal to talk to PLO members.

Peace with Jordan

The Israelis' narrative with regard to the peace treaty signed with Jordan in November 1994 was that it was not surprising. Over the years, Israelis became aware that a state of de-facto peace if not an alliance had increasingly characterized the relations between the two countries. Israelis also believed that this tacit alliance was based on the shared interests that the two countries had developed in maintaining stability in the region. Both were seen as viewing the Palestinians as potentially posing a threat to their interests. But Israelis fully understood that Jordan could not dare make peace with Israel before Syria or the Palestinians. With the signing of the Oslo agreement, Israelis believed that it was only a matter of time before Jordan and Israel would sign a peace treaty.

In Israeli eyes there were significant potential advantages to the peace agreement concluded with Jordan and far fewer downsides. Israelis hoped that the second peace treaty signed with an Arab state would secure the first one – signed years earlier with Egypt – by making the latter less exceptional. Second, although not unaware of the post-Gulf War tensions between Jordan and the Gulf Cooperation Council (GCC) states, Israelis hoped that Jordan might serve as a bridge between their country and the wealthy GCC states, especially in the economic realm. That is, they hoped to be able to market Israeli products in the Gulf through Jordanian intermediaries. At the same time, the conclusion of peace with Jordan appeared not to require any significant costs; Israelis believed that Jordan's disengagement from the West Bank in 1988 eliminated any serious territorial dispute with Israel. Hence, peace with Jordan did not require any territorial concessions.

The Palestinian Narrative

In Palestinian eyes by 1987 Israel was enjoying a relatively cost-free occupation of the West Bank and Gaza Strip. In fact, in the Palestinians' estimate, occupation was highly profitable for Israelis: settlements with cheap housing were being built on confiscated Palestinian land; precious water resources were diverted for Israeli use while Palestinians were denied their fair share of their own water; the attraction of the Jerusalem and Bethlehem Holy Places resulted in a significant increase in Israeli tourism revenues; Israel exploited Palestinian laborers who were skilled and cheap; and all Palestinians were forced to pay taxes and other fees for various types of permits now required by the Israeli occupation authorities.

The First Intifada

Palestinians concluded that they needed to send a message to the Israelis that the status quo was untenable. They assessed that without making occupation costly, and indeed painful, the Israelis would not consider ending it. But they also calculated that the balance of power precluded any use of force against the mighty Israeli army. The confrontation, therefore, had to be non-violent. Non-violence promised to neutralize Israel's military superiority as tanks and fighter aircraft were no match for the scenes of stone-throwing children. Since the Intifada methods posed no existential threat to Israel, it was believed that Israel's cost–benefit calculation would compel it to sit at the negotiating table and, ultimately, cede the occupied territories.

The Intifada was said to have achieved many of its goals because the Israelis came gradually to realize that they needed to come to terms with Palestinian nationalism. As evidence, Palestinians noted that only a few years after the Intifada was launched, Israel began negotiations with the PLO, first indirectly through the Madrid process and later directly, leading to the signing of the Oslo Accords and to the beginning of the end of occupation.

The Intifada came also as a response to the belief of Palestinians under occupation that they needed to take matters into their own hands. Palestinians believed that the agenda of the last Arab summit before the Intifada neglected to address the Palestine issue – a first in the history of Arab summits – leading to a Palestinian sense of Arab abandonment. Moreover, Arab disregard for Palestinian interests reminded Gazans and West Bankers of the evolving PLO weakness. Since 1982, when the PLO was forced into exile as a result of Israel's invasion of Lebanon, the frequency of armed confrontations with Israel had diminished year after year. Palestinian institution-building shifted from the Diaspora to the "inside." Many Palestinian state-like institutions, in the areas of education, health, and housing, came into existence with the aim of gradually displacing those of the Israeli occupation and of preparing for the day when a Palestinian state would be established.

While the PLO was paralyzed, unable to take any bold military or political initiative, beginning in 1985 Jordan was seen as flirting with various plans aimed at restoring its standing in the West Bank. This rekindled Palestinian fears of a return of the "Jordanian Option." The Intifada, therefore, also sent a message to Jordan to the effect that Palestinian nationalism "is here to stay" and that Jordan had no place in the occupied territories. Accordingly, Palestinians were happy with Jordan's decision in 1988 to "disengage" from the West Bank and sever all legal and administrative links with it. The Jordanian step was viewed as one of the Intifada's great achievements, as it put an end once and for all to Jordan's ambitions and laid to rest the Israeli illusion of a future Jordanian role in governing Palestinians.

Endorsing the Two-State Solution

The PLO's acceptance in 1988 of UN Resolutions 181 and 242 and its issuing of a Palestinian Declaration of Independence to apply to the West Bank and the Gaza Strip only, were viewed by Palestinians as concessions that were enabled by, and associated with, a sense of victory, and as expressions of pragmatism rather than signs of defeat and despair. Thus, the acceptance of the "two-state solution" as enshrined in "international legitimacy and UN resolutions," was seen as a culmination of a process of moderation and realism that began among Palestinian ranks in the mid-1970s with the PLO's adoption of the Provisional Program. While that program signaled recognition that the goal of Arab liberation of Palestine had become unrealistic after

1973, the added realism of the late 1980s was seen as the outcome of the Egyptian–Israeli peace.

With the PLO unable to manage the daily conduct of the Intifada from exile, the nationalists inside the territories were now thrilled to take charge of Palestinian politics. Nonetheless they continued to look to Arafat's Tunis-based leadership for guidance, inspiration and financial support. The same nationalists were also happy to see Islamists from Hamas and Islamic Jihad taking part in the Intifada, but they were displeased with the rising popularity of the Islamists and particularly with the Islamists' efforts to create their own separate, parallel public institutions and militias, and to apply their own rules of engagement in the pursuance of the Intifada. As the nationalists were seeking to create one single unified command for the Intifada, they were unhappy that the Islamists created their own separate command.

Madrid and Oslo

The Palestinians were displeased with the Madrid process. Particularly objectionable was that it avoided direct PLO involvement and made no mention of the goal of Palestinian statehood. Clearly, they regarded the definition of the goal of negotiations as the establishment of Palestinian "self-rule" as inadequate. The joint Palestinian–Jordanian delegation within which the Palestinians were forced to operate at Madrid also brought back Jordan as a player in Palestinian–Israeli relations – a state of affairs that Palestinians had repeatedly rejected. At the same time, the Madrid formula for Palestinian representation – denying the PLO direct participation – was seen by young nationalist Palestinians in the West Bank and Gaza as strengthening their hand.

Palestinians recognized that the defects of the Madrid process reflected the PLO's weaknesses within Arab and international circles, particularly given Arafat's perceived decision to side with Saddam Hussein in his invasion of Kuwait. It is true that the Palestinians viewed Saddam's role in the Arab–Israeli front – particularly the use of rockets against Israel during the subsequent war – as highly positive. Nonetheless, they did not view his invasion of Kuwait as serving Palestinian or Arab interests.

The majority of Palestinians in the West Bank and the Gaza Strip welcomed the Oslo Accords, believing that the agreement began a process of ending occupation. But most were unhappy with many aspects of the agreement: the prevailing perception was that it was not the best deal possible, given the Intifada's successes. Most objectionable was that the agreement fell short of declaring that the goal was to build a Palestinian state, and that it did not explicitly and unconditionally end all settlement activities. Another source of unhappiness was that the agreement left East Jerusalem and its Palestinian population outside the mandate of the Palestinian Authority. Oslo was also seen as giving the Israelis upfront all they wanted, including recognition and end of violence, while the most important of the Palestinians' grievances and vital needs were seen as having been left to future negotiations.

Yet unlike Jordan and Syria, Palestinians did not regard the Oslo Accords as a "separate peace." Instead, they viewed it as an interim measure and as a part of an open-ended process similar to the disengagement agreements that Egypt and Syria signed with Israel in 1974–75, and thus in contrast to a permanent agreement such as the Egypt–Israel peace treaty. Accordingly, when Jordan signed its peace agreement with Israel in 1994,

Palestinians were not very happy. Not only did they feel that they should have been consulted, they were troubled by the fact that the agreement did not address the refugee problem. They also regarded the reference in the treaty to the Holy Places as representing Jordanian intervention in Palestinian internal affairs as well as in ongoing Palestinian–Israeli negotiations.

Arab Narratives

The Arab world saw itself as supporting the First Intifada as a mode of resistance and resurrection of the Palestinian cause in the aftermath of what seemed to have been failures – failure of Egypt's efforts to advance that cause in the framework of the Autonomy Talks of the early 1980s, failure of the Fahd and Reagan plans, and failure of the PLO to leverage its 1988 acceptance of the two-state solution – the latter having taken place well after the Intifada was already under way. The Gulf War was later seen as having created an Arab moderate coalition that was ready to make peace with Israel, and was willing to regard it as having been threatened during the war by Iraqi Scud missiles in much the same way as had been Saudi Arabia. Accordingly, the convening of the Madrid Conference was welcomed by the majority of Arab governments, allowing Israel for the first time since its establishment to negotiate with them.

Similarly, the general Arab narrative of the Jordanian–Israeli peace treaty was positive. Arab governments welcomed the agreement, regarding it as a positive outcome of the Madrid process. To the Arab side it seemed clear that the signing of the Oslo Accords and the associated mutual recognition of Israel and the PLO would open the door for Jordan to be the second Arab country to sign a peace treaty with Israel. Some concern, however, was expressed regarding the possibility that the signing of an Israeli–Jordanian treaty might make Israel less inclined to offer the concessions necessary to reach an agreement with Syria, or to end its conflict with the Palestinians. Yet, in general the Madrid process was seen as moving matters forward, and the parties were viewed as engaged in serious negotiations.

Egypt's Narrative

The Egyptian narrative of the mid- and late-1980s emphasized Cairo's efforts to get the parties to the conflict to agree on holding an international conference to resolve their dispute. In November 1987 Egypt was readmitted as a full member of the Arab League, thus reentering its regional environment. Accordingly, a resolution adopted by the United Nations in December 1987 calling for the convening of a Middle East peace conference was received very positively in Cairo. Four years before Madrid, Egypt's approach to the proposed conference largely anticipated the structure of the Madrid process. It argued that to be effective the conference should be held under the auspices of the United Nations, that it should be based on UN Resolutions 242 and 338, and that it should quickly break up into sets of direct bilateral negotiations between the conflicting parties. Through meetings with Foreign Minister Shimon Peres in February and July 1987, President Mubarak urged Israel to agree to the convening of the proposed conference.[18]

After the eruption of the Intifada in December 1987, Egypt sought to revitalize its leadership position in the Arab world by declaring its support for the Intifada as an expression of national resistance. At the same time, Cairo called for a halt to all acts of violence in the occupied territories as well, and to all Israeli settlement activities, for a period of six months. In addition, Israel was asked to respect the natural rights of Palestinians under occupation and their requirements of personal safety. Finally, the international community was urged to begin working on the convening of the aforementioned international conference to establish Arab–Israeli peace.

In parallel, Egypt saw the approach it took in the late 1970s – an approach which was rejected at the time by the Palestinians – as now being affirmed by reports of a Palestinian initiative launched by Yasser Arafat to hold direct talks with Israeli leaders Shimon Peres and Yitzhak Shamir.[19] Yet Egypt also stood firmly against the PLO's National Council declarations that continued to reject the 1978 Egypt–Israel Camp David Accords.[20]

During this period, Egypt believed it necessary to coordinate even more closely with the PLO, especially after Jordan's July 1988 decision to disengage from the West Bank. While Egypt was hesitant regarding the PLO's decision to declare the establishment of an independent Palestinian state, it did express its support for the declared state and by November 1988 it provided full recognition.[21]

Egypt's policy regarding these issues remained unchanged until Iraq's invasion of Kuwait in August 1990. Egypt saw the invasion as signaling the collapse of the Arab regional system, and it viewed the results of the subsequent war as manifesting the decline of the revolutionary forces in the region. As a leading partner in the international effort to liberate Kuwait, Egypt now attempted to seize the opportunity presented by the unique political circumstances to find a collective solution to the Arab–Israeli conflict. For this purpose, the Egyptian government recruited a committee of experts to examine all aspects of the Arab–Israeli conflict. At the same time, Egyptian diplomatic efforts were directed at establishing an Arab collective position similar to the Fez Initiative but one that integrated the principles of its own peace initiative of the late 1970s.[22]

Egypt regarded its efforts as having culminated in the convening of the Madrid Conference – a development in which Egypt invested considerable diplomatic resources, especially in helping to find a compromise formula for the Palestinian representation at the conference. Having already signed a peace agreement with Israel more than a decade earlier, Egypt viewed Madrid as comprising a setting that uniquely placed its leaders at the same level as the conference sponsors: the United States and the Soviet Union. Not surprisingly, Egypt saw the conference as endorsing its decision to sign the Camp David Accords and as demonstrating the wisdom of its position, namely that peace with Israel did not imply surrender of Arab rights. Cairo also viewed Madrid as an opportunity to emphasize once more its commitment to peace based on the principal of "land for peace," and to again call upon Israel to withdraw from all lands occupied in 1967 in accordance with Egypt's interpretation of UN Resolutions 242 and 338.

Thus, the Egyptian narrative of this period is that of vindication: the Arab countries that had viciously criticized President Anwar Sadat in the late 1970s for having taken the road to peace were now seen as having come around to adopting Egypt's approach. Moreover, those who had sided with the alternative revolutionary, militant, and belligerent approach, notably Iraq's President Saddam Hussein, were now seen as having condemned their population to a monumental disaster. Thus, in Egyptian eyes, the experience of the Gulf War had shown the Arab world, the United States, and even Israel how critically important Egypt's role was, not only in establishing peace but also in standing firm against the region's radical and destabilizing forces.

The PLO's adoption of the two-state solution, its decision to accept the format of Palestinian representation in Madrid in the framework of a joint Jordanian–Palestinian delegation, and finally its signing of the Oslo Accords, were taken together as clear evidence that the Palestinians had also adopted Egypt's earlier pragmatic approach to Israel. To Egyptians, the Palestinians now seemed to be following Egypt's footsteps with precision: first, the Intifada as a move designed to clarify to Israel the costs of continued occupation, similar to Egypt's launching of the 1973 October War. Then, follow-up diplomatic moves culminating in the Oslo Accords – moves that were intended to cash in on the violence to achieve political gains.

As such, Egypt regarded the series of steps taken by the Palestinians as the ultimate vindication and definitive response to the accusation that by adopting this approach in the late 1970s Egypt had betrayed the Palestinian cause. Now Egyptians could feel perfectly comfortable with their policy: Egypt's peace with Israel and achieving a solution to the Palestinian issue no longer seemed to be contradicting one another. Moreover, Egypt now began to see the new circumstances as providing it an opportunity to act not only to broaden its peace with Israel to the entire Middle East but also to advance the prospects of a regional security system that would be more consistent with Egypt's own national security interests, particularly in the nuclear realm.

The Jordanian Narrative

Jordan's narrative regarding the Palestinian Intifada evolved over time. Anxious that the outbreak of hostilities would lead to a resurgence of support for the PLO, Jordan at first tried to portray the Intifada as a spontaneous expression of Palestinian discontent with the Arab states and the PLO. When the PLO circulated a petition calling upon West Bank members of the Jordanian Parliament to resign, and when King Hussein learned that several Palestinian members of parliament residing in the *East* Bank were actually contemplating such a move, the Jordanian narrative shifted to one recognizing that the Palestinians had chosen the PLO to be their main representative. In light of such recognition, Jordan now identified the Intifada as allowing it to wash its hands clean of "any more burdens."[23] It is precisely in those terms that Jordan could explain its decision in 1988 to disengage from the West Bank.

Jordan's narrative regarding the Madrid peace talks reflected its own geopolitical concerns following the Gulf War of 1990–91. Having refrained from joining the alliance against Saddam Hussein, Jordan at the same time denied vigorously that it had sided with Saddam. It emerged from the war with two strategic options: to forge stronger ties with

Iraq, or to pursue the Israeli–Arab peace process, thereby turning away from Iraq and restoring its relations with the West, particularly the United States.[24] Faced with serious economic instability, the Hashemite Kingdom saw the Madrid process as an opportunity to regain American favor (and with it, financial and military assistance) by seeking a peaceful settlement with Israel.[25]

The Madrid process engendered an atmosphere of increasing trust between Israel and Jordan, but King Hussein was stunned and angered by the signing of the Oslo Accords between Israel and the PLO in September 1993.[26] The Jordanians interpreted the Oslo agreement as a deliberate attempt to undermine Hashemite influence in the West Bank. Feeling marginalized and excluded by the Oslo process, Jordan worried that the accords would compromise the economic ties between the West and East Banks.[27] As one scholar noted, "the Jordanians were obviously concerned that the Oslo Accords were the harbinger of a Palestine-centric process whereby Jordan would gradually lose its geopolitical value to Israel and to other key players in the international community."[28]

While the signing of the Oslo Accords upset the Hashemite monarchy, the event also provided something of a green light to pursue the regime's own peace accord with Israel. The monarchy's narrative regarding peace with Israel justified the agreement on two grounds. First, since Jordan and Israel had not been at war in decades, the time had come to formalize peaceful relations between the two. Second, concluding peace with Israel would enable a badly needed economic revival to the kingdom by restoring Jordan's relations with wealthy Western powers.[29]

Analysis

What enabled the momentous events of this period to take place? What explains the Palestinians' First Intifada? Why did the PLO decide to adopt the goal of independent statehood in 1988? Why did Israel and the Arab states agree to take part in the Madrid Conference and the ensuing process – the first time ever that the Palestinians and thirteen Arab states agreed not only to solve some of their bilateral conflicts with Israel but also to join Israel in addressing some of the most difficult regional issues: from economic development to regional security and arms control? and finally, What explains the first tangible results of this process: the signing of the Oslo Accords and of the peace treaty between Israel and Jordan in late 1994?

The following analysis will address these questions, but not in chronological order: instead, an attempt will be made to explain these developments in two categories. The first includes the milestones in the Palestinian–Israeli realm experienced during this period: the *First Intifada*, the PLO's 1988 *Declaration of Independence* and its acceptance of American conditions for a United States–PLO dialogue, and the *1993 Oslo Accords*. The second involves two important developments experienced during this period in the relations between Israel and its neighboring states: the *1991 Madrid Conference*, and the *1994 Jordan–Israel Peace Treaty*.

The Evolution of Palestinian–Israeli Relations

Systemic Factors

At the *global-systemic level*, the First Palestinian Intifada seems to have been propelled by the indifference to a Palestinian cause that had sunk very low in the hierarchy of international and regional priorities during the second half of the 1980s. Relocated to Tunis in the aftermath of Israel's 1982 invasion of Lebanon, the PLO had been deprived of a territorial base from which it could continue the "armed struggle" against Israel. Thus, the Palestinians' sole representative was no longer in a position to threaten regional stability in a manner that might affect the interests of the international community. Instead, the community now shifted its attention to the Gulf region, where dramatic developments appeared more urgent and significant. If the international community was not woken up it very likely would slip into permanent indifference if not amnesia regarding all matters Palestinian.

What was true for the international community was also true at the *systemic-regional level*, on which the danger that the Palestinian–Israeli conflict would escalate in a manner threatening the Arab states' interests appeared remote. These states were now much more concerned about containing the increasing influence and growing threat to regional stability of non-Arab fundamentalist Iran, the ramifications of the Iran–Iraq War, and the dire social and economic consequences of the collapsing oil prices. The November 1987 Arab Summit reflected these realities when it readmitted Egypt to the Arab fold - de-facto accepting the Egyptian–Israeli peace treaty - but failed to even address the plight of the Palestinians.

The danger that these global and regional changes could result in the Palestinian plight being forgotten - and the perception that the PLO, now relocated far from the West Bank and Gaza could not prevent this development - led Palestinians residing in the territories to take matters into their own hands by protesting against this sad reality.

The PLO's 1988 *Declaration of Independence* and endorsement of the two-state solution was also a reaction to developments in the international and regional scenes. With the Soviet Union gradually losing its superpower status and the United States emerging as the only remaining superpower, opening a dialogue with Washington became critically important to the PLO. But without a fundamental shift in the PLO's formal position, the Reagan administration was prevented, politically by the American government's 1975 commitment to Israel, and legally by existing legislation, from engaging it officially. Thus, to reassert its international relevance, the PLO now had no choice but to meet America's preconditions for dialogue.

With Jordan's July 1988 disengagement from the West Bank, the PLO saw a unique opportunity to assert its full ownership of the Israeli–Palestinian conflict and peacemaking. It spotted a vacuum and was determined to fill it as quickly as possible. The November Declaration of Independence was the PLO's response, seeking to replace Jordan as the legitimate aspiring sovereign in the West Bank, Gaza, and East Jerusalem. But the PLO also recognized that without American endorsement of its move, it was unlikely to be accepted by the international community. The PLO therefore concluded that it had no choice but to accept the American conditions for reopening their bilateral dialogue.

At both the *global-* and *regional-systemic levels*, the earlier launching of the Madrid process opened the door to *Oslo*. On the positive side, Madrid created an environment conducive to a peace breakthrough by conveying to Middle East publics images of their representatives engaging in serious negotiations with Israel in an effort to resolve their different disputes and to address their region-wide problems.

Yet the Oslo breakthrough was no less the product of a number of factors that had hampered the ability of the United States to produce a breakthrough within the Madrid framework. The most important of these may have been the gradual waning of the dramatic impressions left by the Gulf War: America's spectacular success in the diplomatic front as well as in the battlefield. In retrospect it seems clear that while strong enough to allow the historical breakthrough in the convening of the Madrid Conference, and while Madrid was critically important in setting the stage for the subsequent developments, these forces did not remain robust enough to produce further breakthroughs within the Madrid framework itself.

Specifically, by 1992–93, the environmental factors that allowed the convening of Madrid were no longer strong enough to overcome the structural limitations of the Madrid framework. This was particularly the case in the Israeli–Palestinian context. While the formula invented for the Palestinian representation in the Madrid process was necessary to persuade the Likud-led, Shamir-headed Israeli government to attend, America's influence could not help overcome the limitations embedded in the composition of the Palestinian delegation and the fact that it was formally only part of a Jordanian–Palestinian delegation. Therefore, it was essential that a bypass to Madrid be found if a major breakthrough was to be achieved.

Soon after the Madrid process was launched, the Bush administration, which deserved enormous credit for its convening, was voted out of office. At least initially, this required a new "learning curve," thus hampering the extent to which the new American administration could provide the local players with adequate "adult supervision." This, as well as the other aforementioned factors that limited the effectiveness of American diplomacy, now created a vacuum. As a result, Norway could step in to offer its good offices, thus facilitating a breakthrough in Palestinian–Israeli relations.

Domestic Settings

At the *unit level*, the First Palestinian Intifada was in large part a product of the social changes that the Palestinians in the West Bank and Gaza experienced in the late 1980s. Palestinians who were born after the occupation of these territories in 1967 now came of age. More or less gainfully employed, this youth was less financially dependent than previous generations of Palestinians on the elderly and had greater freedom to assert themselves and to defy their society's traditional leaders. To the taste of the young nationalists and their leaders, the elders in the Palestinian territories were overly acquiescent with the occupation while the PLO leadership was far away, detached, and enjoying the good life in the Diaspora. It was this young nationalist leadership on the inside that, while loyal to the PLO on the outside, felt the need for the insiders to take the initiative using new means of non-violent resistance to challenge the Israeli occupation. With the support and coordination of more established leaders like Husseini, Ashrawi and Erekat, these young nationalists comprised the backbone of the Intifada leadership.

The PLO's political near-absence from the scene created another form of vulnerability. The increasing irrelevance of the exiled traditional secular-nationalist leadership to the problems affecting the Palestinians residing in the West Bank and Gaza set the stage for a leadership challenge from yet another direction: political Islam. In the early 1980s, Islamic Jihad, a group that had split from the Palestinian Muslim Brotherhood, gave the first signs of an attack on the hegemony of the nationalists. It criticized the Brotherhood for its lack of interest in confronting the Israeli occupation and urged Islamists to take up arms against "the occupiers."

Partly in response to this challenge, the Muslim Brotherhood in Gaza, which until this point had been primarily a religious and social movement, now became increasingly political. It asserted its independence from its parent movement – the Muslim Brotherhood in Egypt – and later, during the early period of the Intifada, reinvented itself as Hamas. Thus the backbone of the Intifada developed to consist of two elements: young rebels from the secular-nationalist camp and their counterparts in Hamas and Islamic Jihad, the latter two together comprising for the first time an indigenous political Islamist movement.

Finally, at the domestic level, Israel seems to have contributed to the Intifada through the accelerated construction of settlements in the West Bank and Gaza during the 1980s. This activity gave Palestinian youth in the territories a sense of urgency – a feeling that given the neglect of the Palestinian issue by the international community and the Arab states, if existing trends in settlement construction were not turned around, Israel's occupation of the lands would become irreversible.

The First Intifada then became the domestic setting for the next milestone in the evolution of the Palestinian position: the 1988 Declaration of Independence. This was because the Intifada created an imperative for the PLO to reassert its relevance. It was not difficult to read the uprising as a rebellion against the PLO for having failed to help alleviate the Palestinians' plight or advance the Palestinian cause. Without changing course in a manner that might make it once again relevant to addressing what concerned Palestinians most – Israel's occupation of the West Bank, Gaza, and East Jerusalem – the PLO was in danger of being replaced by three sets of challengers: the so-called PLO "insiders" – the secular nationalist leaders who were indigenous to the West Bank and Gaza, notably Faisal Husseini; the youth, who were now defying the traditional leaders of the territories; and the Islamists, who now began to gain prominence.

The domestic setting also provides powerful explanations for the Oslo breakthrough. Within Israel, the change to a more moderate Labor-led leadership that promised to negotiate autonomy for the Palestinians was propelled by the premise that the United States was too important for Israel to tolerate a Likud-led coalition government which was repeatedly injecting tensions into Israeli–American relations. The Labor Party's return to power in 1992 had a number of consequences which later informed the decision to pursue the Olso option. First, Israel's new prime minister, Itzhak Rabin, found himself torn between his commitment to reach an agreement granting autonomy to the Palestinians within nine months, and the impossibility of reaching such an agreement through the Madrid process with a Jordanian–Palestinian delegation that maintained the façade of independence from the PLO while actually being its subordinate. Gradually, Rabin seems to have reached the conclusion that Arafat was not likely to permit a breakthrough from which he was not in a position to reap any political benefits.

Second, Rabin judged that the aftermath of the Gulf War presented Israel with a golden opportunity: Arafat had made a fatal strategic mistake that placed him at a disadvantage – his siding with Saddam Hussein following the invasion of Kuwait left his backers in the Persian Gulf feeling betrayed. As a result, financial assistance to the PLO was frozen, threatening the organization and its leadership in Tunis with bankruptcy. Arafat was now in a very weak position, raising the possibility that he might make concessions that the Palestinians had always resisted, such as a willingness to enter into an open-ended process.

In turn, the dramatic change in Rabin's approach was enabled by growing support among the Israeli mainstream for more dovish views and for negotiating with the PLO. The change in public attitudes was generated by the First Palestinian Intifada, which led to most Israelis beginning to question the viability of the status quo. The Intifada highlighted the burden of continued occupation, leading to greater willingness to compromise: a larger proportion of Israelis than ever supported return of the occupied territories and the establishment of Palestinian self-rule or even statehood.[30]

The PLO, in turn, was propelled to make historical concessions by a different set of domestic considerations. The willingness of Arab states to go along with a compromise regarding Palestinian representation in Madrid was a stark reminder of the PLO's weakness: Arab governments seemed to be willing to participate in a process that might determine the fate of the Palestinians without the PLO's direct participation. Second, Arafat and the PLO "outside" leadership were now threatened by Palestinian leaders on the "inside," who were perceived as an expression of the willingness of Palestinians in the West Bank and Gaza to make a deal that would address their plight, even at the expense of the Palestinian Diaspora – the PLO's primary constituency.

While the Oslo breakthrough required historical concessions, it addressed the two PLO domestic predicaments. First, it placed the PLO once again at the forefront of the Palestinian cause as the only address for negotiating the future of Palestine. Thus, in contrast to the Palestinian delegation to Madrid and to the later talks in Washington, which was not formally answerable to the PLO, Oslo would be run by people directly under Arafat's command. Second, a breakthrough at Oslo would allow the PLO leaders in Tunis to abort the rise of the "insiders" and to reassert themselves as those on whom the population of the West Bank and Gaza could rely to deliver "salvation."

As the PLO was well aware, a deal negotiated by the "insiders" would have led to immediate elections of a local leadership from the West Bank and the Gaza Strip. State-building would have been carried out by the "insiders" while the PLO, outside, lost influence by the day. Instead, Arafat wanted a deal that would require the PLO, with him at the pinnacle, to implement the agreement – a deal that would give him an immediate foothold in the West Bank and Gaza and allow the PLO to return to the occupied territories where they could build institutions and organize elections if they so wished. All this, however, required that the PLO and not the "insiders" negotiate the deal. Finally, Arafat also knew that while the "insiders" negotiating in Washington were loyal to him, he could not control them. Since he needed greater room for maneuver in negotiating a deal that would be acceptable to Israel, he could only operate through a mechanism that involved people who were completely subservient to him. Keeping the talks secret also shielded Arafat from criticism by the "inside" leadership that was now gaining ground.

Leaders

While the first Palestinian Intifada seemed to have broken out spontaneously – no single individual was responsible for its eruption – Yasser Arafat appears central to the next milestone in the evolution of the Palestinian position: the 1988 Declaration of Independence and especially meeting the Americans' conditions for a dialogue with the PLO. Indeed, in many respects this was Arafat's moment as his pragmatism became evident. As indicated in Chapter 5, Arafat began this process in 1974 with the Provisional Program. Now he saw an opportunity in the Jordanian disengagement – one created by the Intifada, in which the Palestinians had taken the initiative. Only in this unique context was it possible for Arafat to make the requisite concessions, including the acceptance of UN Resolution 242. In doing so, he was assisted by the realism demonstrated by "inside" leaders like Hussieni, Ashrawi, and Erekat, who were willing to lend immediate support to his move.

Individual leaders were no less central to Oslo. On the Palestinian side the breakthrough was affected in no small measure by the fact that the talks were supervised by Mahmoud Abbas, Arafat's most trusted advisor, who never challenged his leadership and who was among the most moderate of the PLO leadership in Tunis. Equally, the Oslo Accords would probably not have come about if it were not for the daring of the ultimate Israeli mentor of the talks, Prime Minister Rabin.

Abbas was one of only a few Palestinians to have formally studied Israeli history and politics, always displaying immense curiosity about Israeli domestic debates and events. In the 1970s he worked in secret with pacifist movements in Israel, leading talks that resulted in January 1977 in the announcement of "principles of peace" based on a two-state-solution – a position rejected by the PLO at that time. Distancing himself at times from PLO violent operations, Abbas's contacts with Israelis throughout the years gave him a reputation as a PLO dove. But perhaps as important in preparing him for the task in Oslo, Abbas preferred to keep a low profile and to conduct secret negotiations behind the scenes, thus posing no threat to Arafat's leadership. Arafat trusted him, making him one of his closest aides.[31]

On the Israeli side, the key to the Oslo breakthrough was Prime Minister Itzhak Rabin. Indeed, there was no one other than Rabin on the Israeli domestic scene who could garner the requisite acceptance for the Oslo deal. That such acceptance would be forthcoming was far from self-evident given that up to that point the Palestinian party to the talks – the PLO – was viewed by Israelis as an arch-enemy and a terror organization. Rabin could not have succeeded if it were not for the defense credentials he had accumulated over decades and his reputation and credibility as an individual who would not compromise Israel's security. Moreover, Rabin's long years of combativeness toward the PLO, his earlier skepticism if not hostility towards suggestions that Israel reach an agreement with Arafat, and the hard line he took in managing Israel's military response to the Palestinian Intifada, now served him well. With such a track-record, Rabin could credibly argue that if he reached the conclusion that the proposed agreement would not jeopardize Israelis' safety and security, it merited public support.

Yet Rabin was not the one to invent the Oslo grand bargain. Rather he was supported in this endeavor by a unique policy entrepreneur, Deputy Foreign Minister Yossi Beilin. Convinced that settling Israel's conflict with the Palestinians was an absolute imperative, and certain that the official post-Madrid negotiations being conducted in Washington between Israel and the Palestinians in the framework of a joint Jordanian–Palestinian delegation were going to fail, Beilin was willing to break with diplomatic orthodoxy. Utilizing his unique creativity and imagination, he authorized two Israeli academics to engage in talks with officials of the PLO, reasoning that only in the framework of unofficial and secret settings that allow political leaders total deniability would it be possible to explore seriously whether an agreement could be reached.

Beilin also proved politically savvy; once the unofficial talks yielded a first draft of a Declaration of Principles, he used his close relations with his immediate superior, Foreign Minister Shimon Peres, and his open channel of communications with Rabin, to persuade them to assume ownership over the process by instructing their trusted aides to take over the negotiations.

The Madrid Conference and the Jordan–Israel Peace Treaty

The Global and Regional Systems

At the *global-systemic level*, Madrid was enabled by the decline of the Soviet Union and the victory of the American-led coalition against Iraq. These developments made this period America's moment in the Middle East in almost every respect. Perceived as having won the Cold War and as having successfully rolled back Saddam's invasion of Kuwait, the influence of the United States in the region now peaked, allowing it to impose its terms on the Middle East.

The building blocks of this American moment were the following: first, the United States had just proven its enormous power, applying superior military technology and executing a very impressive achievement in military logistics. Second, the Bush administration had demonstrated its first-rate diplomatic skills by putting together a very broad coalition that contributed forces to the campaign – even if in some instances such participation was more symbolic than real. And indeed, the United States was able to skillfully form and maintain an even broader coalition that supported the campaign, diplomatically and financially. As a result, this very ambitious and expensive undertaking involved no net financial burden to American taxpayers.

Amazingly, the coalition created by the United States included Arab states that a decade earlier quarreled bitterly with Egypt – another member of the coalition and a founder of the Arab League. It also included Syria – a socialist secular revolutionary arch-enemy of Israel and the United States, whose forces were now on the front line, defending ultra-conservative Saudi Arabia.

Also, during the Gulf War, the United States for the first time translated its commitment to Israel's security and defense to sending US Army units to protect the Jewish state. Thus, ironically, US Army Patriot missiles were now protecting both Jerusalem and Riyadh. With such assets accumulated by the Americans, it became nearly impossible for local players to oppose their designs. Hence, when Secretary of State James Baker impressed upon the Israeli government the need to attend the Madrid Conference, even a very skeptical hard-liner like Shamir could not refuse the invitation.

An additional factor at the global level affecting Israel's decision to go to Madrid was that the complete collapse of the Soviet Union was resulting in the immigration to Israel of a million Jews with an associated need for $10 billion in American loan guarantees. Obtaining the latter, however, was contingent on a more accommodating Israeli behavior toward the Palestinians, including a freeze on settlement construction in the West Bank and Gaza. It is precisely because the Shamir government had rejected the American demand for such a freeze that it felt it had no choice but to accommodate the Bush administration regarding participation in Madrid.[32]

At the *regional-systemic level*, Madrid was made possible through the credit that some Arab governments had accumulated as a result of their joining the anti-Iraq coalition. Thus, Egypt, Syria, and Saudi Arabia were in a position in the war's aftermath to impress upon the United States the need to balance its aggressive reaction to the misdeeds of an Arab state – Iraq – by taking positive steps to resolve the Arab–Israeli conflict.

The PLO, by contrast, more closely reflected Arab public opinion, which asked why the liberation of Kuwait was so urgent while Palestinian and Syrian territories remained occupied for decades. It was obvious during the crisis and the war that the Palestinian question was one of the most effective political weapons utilized by Saddam Hussein against Arab governments participating in the international coalition. Thus, if the United States wished to protect its regional allies who were exposed to such attacks, it needed to move effectively toward a resolution of the Arab–Israeli conflict.

Conversely, Jordan's behavior during the Gulf Crisis, which was interpreted in Washington and elsewhere as siding with Saddam Hussein, now forced it to accept an invitation to Madrid in the framework of a joint Jordanian–Palestinian delegation.[33] At least on the surface, such a partnership seemed to contradict King Hussein's announced decision in 1988 to divorce his kingdom from responsibility for Palestinian affairs. But Jordan's acceptance of the proposed representation formula was not entirely surprising – at that point King Hussein did not completely abandon his long-standing ambition to restore Jordan's influence in the West Bank. Moreover, Jordan saw having a joint delegation with Palestinian leaders from the West Bank and the Gaza Strip as an opportunity to diminish the role of Arafat and the PLO.

In turn, Yasser Arafat's decision to side with Saddam Hussein during the Gulf Crisis and subsequent war earned the PLO such opprobrium that it was obliged to accept that the Palestinians be represented in Madrid in the framework of a joint Palestinian–Jordanian delegation which would have no official ties to the PLO.

These changes also affected Israel's perceptions of its regional environment. For the first time, the country no longer viewed its Middle East neighborhood solely in zero-sum terms.

Indeed, during the 1990–91 Gulf Crisis and War, Israel found itself on the same side as Egypt and Syria. In a way, Israel now became a tacit member of one Arab coalition facing another. As a result, Israelis had reason to hope that the new regional environment might present their country with new opportunities to crack the remaining walls of hostility with which it was surrounded and that, therefore, they needed a new leadership and a different orientation that would place Israel in a better position to exploit these opportunities.

Second, for the first time since it came to Jordan's rescue twenty years earlier, Israel found Arab states, especially those in the more distant Persian Gulf, more worried about the threat posed by another Arab state – Iraq – than about Israel. This seemed to be especially the case for Saudi Arabia and some of the smaller Gulf States who remained concerned, even after the Gulf War, that Saddam would provide another demonstration of his expansionist impulses. This induced these states to accommodate Washington in its quest for a new global and regional order, as reflected in the Madrid process. Finally, again for the first time since September 1970, Israelis saw that important Arab states were as exasperated by the behavior of Yasser Arafat as they were.

The net effect of these changes was that Israel could no longer regard the Arab world as a homogeneous entity: namely, as an environment that, with the exception of Egypt, was unified in its uncompromising hostility to Israel. Consequently, Israel's national threat assessment needed to be revised. Most importantly, the new divisions in the Arab world and the considerable weakening of Iraq now eliminated any danger that Israel might have to face a threat on an eastern front. This meant that not only could Israel now be generally more relaxed about its regional environment but also that it could begin to reexamine the positions it had taken that had been previously informed by its traditional threat perception.

Global-systemic level factors also played an important role in bringing about the signing of the Jordan–Israel Peace Treaty. In the aftermath of the Gulf War, Jordan had an urgent need to repair its relations with the United States. Throughout the previous decade, Jordan remained close to Iraq and to the United States simultaneously – not so difficult at the time since the United States clearly sided with Iraq during its eight-year war with Iran. During these war years, Jordan was a critically important lifeline for Iraq through which much of the material Iraq needed from abroad to prosecute the war could be delivered. Since the United States and many of its Arab allies saw Iraq as the frontline against the Islamic Republic, by playing this role Jordan had served America's broadest strategic interests in the region.

But the Gulf Crisis and War changed all that, and Jordan's continued close ties with Iraq angered not only the first Bush administration but – no less importantly – many key members of the United States Congress. As a result, American economic and military assistance to Jordan was suspended during the crisis, and now were in urgent need of being restored. Yet Congress, as the Clinton administration argued effectively after Madrid, would not cooperate in repairing these ties if Jordan did not take dramatic steps to restore its previous positive image in Washington as a reliable ally, sensitive to America's interests and priorities in the region. There would be no better way to demonstrate such sensitivity than the successful negotiation of peace with Israel.

Regional-systemic factors also played an important role in bringing about the Jordan–Israel Peace Treaty. The most important of these was that by the early 1990s Syria was no longer in a position to derail Jordan's decision to negotiate and sign a peace agreement with Israel. In the immediate aftermath of the Gulf War, Syria's spirits were temporarily lifted by the defeat of its Iraqi Ba'ath rival and by the rewards it received, primarily from Saudi Arabia, in exchange for its participation in the coalition against Iraq. However, these temporary gains could not overcome the structural weaknesses that Syria suffered as a result of the loss of its Soviet patron.

Moreover, having banked on the Madrid process in late 1991, the Syrians found themselves in 1992–94 in the midst of American-brokered negotiations with Israel. Threatening Jordan in order to dissuade it from signing a peace agreement with Israel would have been difficult to explain and would have clouded these negotiations with considerable bad faith, possibly inducing the United States or Israel, or both, to pull out of the talks. Thus, Jordan could now count not only on Syria's weakness but also on the constraints within which Damascus was operating to give it confidence that it could pursue peace with impunity.

Another very important development at the regional level affecting Jordan's calculations was the mid-September 1993 signing of the Israel–Palestine Oslo Accords. While the Palestinians never exercised a veto-power over Jordan's decisions regarding Israel, refraining from signing a peace agreement with Israel after the PLO had already signed the Oslo Accords would have required that King Hussein be "more Palestinian than Arafat." Thus, the PLO's earlier signing of the Oslo Accords paved the way for Jordan to conclude a peace agreement with Israel by making such a move legitimate: Jordan could not be accused of signing such an agreement behind the Palestinians' back or at their expense.

Another effect that Oslo had in propelling Jordan toward peace with Israel is that not only was it impossible after Oslo to frame Jordanian–Israeli peace as at the Palestinians' expense, the opposite had taken place: Jordan was surprised by the breakthrough at Oslo and feared that if it did not take preventive measures, Palestinian–Israeli peace might come at *its own* expense. This was particularly the case insofar as Jerusalem was concerned, where Jordan saw itself as having real interests. Granting Palestinians rights in Jerusalem without taking Jordanian sensitivities into account was deemed truly dangerous in Amman. In this situation, Hussein and his government could at least hope that through the stipulations of a peace treaty it could oblige Israel to attend to Jordan's interests in Jerusalem.

Israel's regional interest in peace with the Hashemite Kingdom of Jordan was self-explanatory. Not only did such peace expand the process of stabilizing Israel's relations with its immediate neighbors, it had the potential of providing Israel with a buffer between itself and then hostile Iraq. Equally important, there were no insurmountable issues involved.

Domestic Settings

Developments at the *unit level* were no less important in understanding what brought the regional players to Madrid. In Israel, Shamir's small, extreme right-wing coalition partners, such as the Moledet and Tehiya parties, opposed the Madrid process, particularly the direct Israeli negotiations with the joint Jordanian–Palestinian delegation. However, Shamir easily overcame potential sources of opposition within his own Likud party and he could be confident that such a move could not be opposed by the Labor party. Equally important, Israeli public opinion supported Shamir's decision to accept the invitation to attend the Madrid Conference.

Domestic politics also played a role in allowing the conclusion of Israeli–Jordanian peace. Most importantly, in Israel there was no important opposition to a deal with Jordan. Once Jordan ceded responsibility over the West Bank to the Palestinians in 1988, the remaining territorial disputes between Jordan and Israel – mostly having to do with small pieces of land in the Arava over which Israel gradually asserted control after 1948 – were relatively insignificant. Ceding these lands was unlikely to be painful to the Jewish state. Water was likely to become a more complicated issue, but it involved mostly economics, free of sacred values, historical disputes, or religious fervor. For this reason, no domestic Israeli constituency had opposed the deal with Jordan.

Moreover, over the years Israeli leaders had held frequent meetings with Jordan's leaders, and the Israeli public was largely convinced that King Hussein had tried to warn the Israeli leadership of the pending attack on the eve of the 1973 War. In addition, the heads of Israel's defense community had numerous interactions with their Jordanian counterparts and had come to admire their professionalism. Indeed, channels of communication between the two defense communities were kept open even during times of tension in the region. Moreover, Jordan's security services more than once provided a conduit for communications between Israel and other Arab countries. Thus, for Israel to make peace with Jordan in 1994 was a "no-brainer."

In Syria, participation in the Madrid Conference also met no significant domestic opposition. But the regime needed to prepare the public for a change in policy. In what seemed to be a justification for Syrian participation in the Madrid Conference and an attempt to prepare the public for possible change in policy regarding negotiations with Israel, the Assad regime began to use a term not used in the past – "land for peace" – and President Assad was now presented as "the hero of war and peace."[34]

In Egypt, there was no opposition to Madrid, as it was seen as vindicating Egypt's strategic choice to conclude peace with Israel more than twelve years earlier. This was important given the doubts raised within Egypt as to whether its choice was the right one – doubts exacerbated by Sadat's assassination and the failure of the Egyptian-sponsored Israeli–Palestinian autonomy talks as well as by the earlier boycotting of Egypt by the members of the Arab League and the Organization of Islamic States.

Yet much more significant in motivating Egypt to participate in the coalition facing Iraq in the Gulf War, as well as to cooperate in convening Madrid, was the country's economic situation. Egypt's economy was hard-hit by the sharp drop in oil prices in the 1980s, affecting revenues from the Suez Canal and remittances from the Gulf countries, all combining to increase Egypt's external debt, which reached $50 billion, constituting 200 percent of GDP and 343 percent of exports by the late 1980s.[35] By 1987 this caused Egypt's Central Security Forces to protest their low wages – reminiscent of the 1977 food riots. One reaction was to join the coalition confronting Saddam Hussein and the other was to help convene the

Madrid Conference – steps for which Egypt was rewarded by having half of its external debt forgiven.

The most important unit level factor on the Jordanian side seems to have been the effect of the Oslo Accords concluded a year earlier. Once the PLO entered direct negotiations and a historical agreement with Israel, no one within Jordan could accuse the king of betraying the Palestinian cause by signing a peace agreement with the Jewish state. Moreover, Jordan's earlier disengagement from the West Bank – a move that was also affirmed by the Palestinians' later assertion of responsibilities by signing the Oslo Accords – tilted the balance in Jordan in favor of the "East Bankers." Thus, the constituency for the "Jordan First" approach – convinced that Jordan needed to take care of its own interests and requirements – had gained ground. The signing of a peace treaty with Israel was consistent with this approach.

Another domestic impetus to Jordan's decision was the state of its economy. The decline in the oil revenues of its backers in the Arab world during the 1980s resulted in a major recession in Jordan. This was exacerbated by Jordan's population growing at a much faster rate than its GDP, resulting in higher unemployment and a lower standard of living. By the mid 1980s, budget deficits skyrocketed, and by 1989 the cost of servicing debt reached 45 percent of exports and 20 percent of GDP. That year, the value of the Jordanian Dinar dropped from $3.3 to $1.3.[36] These dire economic circumstances created a strong incentive for Jordan to take steps – from agreeing to a joint Jordanian–Palestinian delegation at Madrid to the signing of a peace treaty with Israel – that would find favor in Washington.

For the Palestinians, going to Madrid as part of a joint delegation with the Jordanians was associated with two concessions: to allow Palestinians from the "inside," not the PLO on the "outside," to represent the Palestinians; and to accept a status less than equal to that of Israel. The first of these concessions was forced on Arafat in part by domestic imperatives: Arafat's pro-Saddam policy not only weakened the PLO at the regional level, but also placed the PLO in Tunis in an inferior position to the nationalist leadership in the West Bank and Gaza. Second, the change in the PLO's regional standing came about at a time when the nationalist leadership on the "inside" became stronger than ever due to its leadership of the Intifada and the salience it gained in international and Arab media. Third, the change in the relative strength of the "inside" versus the "outside" leaderships began after the PLO was expelled from Lebanon. The center of gravity of Palestinian politics shifted further from the "outside" to the "inside" with significant institution-building that took place in the West Bank and the Gaza Strip during that period. This institution-building process allowed the "inside" leadership to gain grassroots legitimacy that the PLO leadership on the "outside" did not possess.

Leaders

At the *individual level,* one person was the key to the convening of Madrid and to the process it launched: Secretary of State James Baker. With the ending of the Cold War and in the aftermath of the Gulf War, Baker had a realist's vision and the capacity to seize the moment to create a change in world history and to extend this opportunity to the Middle East. Having demonstrated the requisite patience, resolve, stamina, and resilience, as well as the necessary diplomatic skills, to build the international coalition required to liberate Kuwait, including the gaining of the Soviet Union's consent, Baker, between March and September 1991, conducted eight rounds of negotiations to assemble the Madrid Conference. In both efforts, he was able to build trust and confidence among Middle East leaders regarding America's ability to deliver security for Israelis and to help Arabs step back from the abyss of past occupation and the Gulf Crisis that had divided their ranks only a short time before. Thus, Baker turned out to be the right person at the right moment for the reshaping of world order as well as that of the Middle East arena.

Belonging to the Realist school of international relations, Baker was quick to seize on the fundamental change that had occurred in the global balance of power which established America's clear supremacy. It was this dramatic change that also allowed him to persuade the Soviet Union to accept no more than a minor role in Madrid. He also understood that separately, Arabs and Israelis were now both indebted to the United States not only for liberating Kuwait but also for protecting Israel and Saudi Arabia. Provided the right formula was found, all the parties were ready to accept America's leadership. Baker had the skill of a lawyer, the forcefulness of a politician, and the candor of a diplomat to walk through the Middle East maze and bring all the parties to Madrid.

While Baker's role in shaping the international environment and the post-Gulf War Middle East demonstrates the importance of *individual* leaders in affecting the Arab–Israeli conflict, Israeli Prime Minister Itzhak Shamir illustrates the opposite point. Namely, that in the face of strong global- and regional-systemic forces as well as important unit-level factors, even a strong personality cannot resist the forces of change.

Shamir was not a leader comfortable in a fast-changing environment. Convinced that the moment was exceptional and transitory, his instincts were that Israel should remain steadfast and resist any change that might harm its long-term interests. By his own testimony, he was prepared to negotiate with the Palestinians without significant results for the next ten years, all the while building up settlements in the territories.[37] His traditional views of uncompromising meetings between Zionism and Palestinian nationalism could have been the great obstacle for the Madrid Conference. Yet, the tide of the political and strategic environment was much stronger than the individual. The Middle East, as well as Israel, was ready for the change that he was not capable of accepting. Recognizing this, the Israeli electorate sent him home in 1992. As a result, the process moved from the Madrid ceremony to Oslo and the Jordanian–Israeli Peace Treaty, the obstacles and objections raised by Shamir and his followers notwithstanding.

By contrast, the conclusion of the Jordanian–Israeli Peace Treaty was clearly the moment of a different individual: Jordan's King Hussein. A descendant of the noble Hashemite family, Hussein was the king of a poor country that came to being only as a byproduct of the politics of the First World War. Indeed, the ever-vulnerable monarch was always constrained by the geopolitics of Jordan's location and the relative power and the demographics of his country. Yet he played his cards remarkably well in the service of his country's survival in a tough Arab and regional political environment.

Hussein's grandfather was one of the pillars of Arab politics during the first half of the 20th century, competing with the Aloutes (the Muhammad Ali dynasty) in Egypt, the Saudis in Saudi Arabia, and the Hashemites in Iraq. Hussein, on the other hand, had to struggle to stay alive in the face of threats to his throne and the different wars and frequent crises of the Middle East, most recently the Kuwait crisis and Gulf War. With a deep sense of Jordan's diplomatic, economic and military vulnerability relative to a much stronger Israel on one hand and to the fast-changing Arab revolutionary and nationalist movements on the other, Hussein, unlike his grandfather, who decades earlier had extended his hand to the Zionist leaders, was compelled until Madrid and Oslo to accept the constraints of the Arab order. Weakened by his linkage to Saddam Hussein, Jordan's king saw in Madrid and the peace treaty with Israel an opportunity to restore his standing with the West as well as with the Arab states who opposed Saddam Hussein.

Concluding Notes

The period addressed in this chapter was characterized by two historic turning-points. One was the de-Arabization of the conflict as the Palestinians, by launching the First Intifada in December 1987, now spearheaded the opposition to Israel for the first time since the eve of the 1948 War. Thus, they created a new front line in the confrontation with Israel.

Another important feature was the Palestinians' formal Declaration of Independence and, separately, acceptance of the two-state solution and a number of associated stances, making them eligible for a dialogue with the United States. Finally, in following-up the Intifada by later agreeing to participate in the Madrid Conference – and, even more dramatically, by later signing the Oslo Accords – the Palestinians implicitly accepted the logic of Sadat's 1977–79 peace initiative: namely, that violent action followed by diplomatic initiatives enables the translation of such violence into political gains.

The change in the Palestinians' approach was tied to a broader dramatic change experienced during this period: the clear break from violence and war to peacemaking. Now, Arab states that fourteen years earlier had rejected Sadat's peace initiative as treasonous came to Madrid to engage Israel in bilateral peace negotiations. Arguably even more importantly, most Arab states now accepted Israel as a potential partner in addressing the region-wide problems plaguing the Middle East.

A number of developments at the global- and regional-systemic levels proved to be decisive in causing this dramatic change. The dissolution of the Soviet Union and the associated end of the Cold War, and the Bush administration's successful execution of the Gulf War, militarily and diplomatically, combined to create a unipolar moment for the United States in the Middle East. Without such primacy it is doubtful that its administration could have convened the Madrid Conference.

The disappearance of the Soviet Union as an important player, and Iraq's defeat in the Gulf War, tilted the regional balance away from the rejectionists and in favor of more pragmatic forces in the Middle East. Thus, winning favor with the United States by accepting its invitation to come to Madrid became the only insurance policy available to Syria. And once Assad said yes, even hard-line Shamir could not say no.

Unit level changes proved no less consequential in determining the most important developments during this era. The shift in the internal balance of power among the Palestinians ushered in by the Intifada meant that the PLO could not remain relevant without a game-changer that would thrust it back to center-stage. This explains at least in part the PLO's willingness to accept the historical concessions that were required to conclude the Oslo grand bargain.

A parallel change occurred on the Israeli side. The combined effect of the Palestinian Intifada and the increasing influence of the United States on the Israeli electorate resulted in the ousting of Likud and the return of Labor to power. Without this change, an Oslo-type deal would have remained inconceivable.

The same set of developments later both compelled and allowed Jordan to sign a peace treaty with Israel. Jordan's behavior during the Gulf Crisis and War, causing Washington to see it as siding with Saddam Hussein, created a post-war Jordanian imperative to mend fences with the United States by coming to terms with Israel. At the same time, the PLO's signing of the Oslo Accords legitimized the Israeli–Jordanian Peace Treaty.

No leader had an effect on the historical developments described here to match Egypt's President Anwar Sadat or Israel's Defense Minister Ariel Sharon during the period addressed in the previous chapter. Yet the characteristics of the leaders who orchestrated Madrid or who signed the Oslo Accords were not inconsequential. Thus, it is far from self-evident that a secretary of state who lacked James Baker's skills and savvy use of American leverage could have successfully cajoled and corralled Syria's Assad and Israel's Shamir to Madrid. Similarly, it is doubtful if an Israeli prime minister who did not enjoy the defense credentials of Itzhak Rabin and a Palestinian leader who did not have the aura of Yasser Arafat as the founding father of modern Palestinian nationalism, could have combined to make the far-reaching concessions required of both sides to reach Oslo.

Readings

Abbas, Mahmoud (Abu Mazen), *Through Secret Channels: The Road to Oslo* (Garnet Publishing, 1995)

Beilin, Yossi. *Touching Peace: From the Oslo Accord to a Final Agreement* (Weidenfeld & Nicolson, 1999).

Bickerton, Ian and Carla Klausner, *A History of the Arab-Israeli Conflict* (Prentice Hall, 2010) 218–265.

Caplan, Neil, *The Israel–Palestine Conflict: Contested Histories* (Wiley, 2010) 195–201.

Dowty, Alan, *Israel/Palestine: Global Political Hotspots* (Polity, 2012) 142–163.

Eisenberg, Laura Zittrain and Neil Caplan, *Negotiating Arab–Israeli Peace: Patterns, Problems, Possibilities* (Indiana University Press, 2010) 73–94, 116–134.

Gelvin, James, *The Israel–Palestine Conflict: One Hundred Years of War* (Cambridge University Press, 2007) 178, 179, 212–240.

Lesch, David, *The Arab-Israeli Conflict* (Oxford University Press, 2008) 94–161.

Morris, Benny, *Righteous Victims: The History of the Zionist–Arab Conflict, 1881–2001* (Vintage, 2001) 561–610.

Said, Edward. *The End of the Peace Process: Oslo and After* (Pantheon, 2000).
Shlaim, Avi, *The Iron Wall: Israel and the Arab World* (W.W. Norton, 2001) 450–546.
Smith, Charles D., *Palestine and the Arab–Israeli Conflict* (Bedford/St.Martin's, 2007) 165–221.
Tessler, Mark, *A History of the Israeli–Palestinian Conflict* (Indiana University Press, 2009) 677–752.

Historical Documents

Hamas Charter: Walter Laqueur and Barry Rubin, *The Israel–Arab Reader: A Documentary History of the Middle East Conflict* (Penguin Books, 2008), 116.
Israel and Jordan Peace Treaty: Laqueur and Rubin, *The Israel–Arab Reader*, 477–486.
Israel and PLO, The Oslo Agreement: Laqueur and Rubin, *The Israel–Arab Reader*, 413–422.
Israeli Prime Minister Yitzhak Shamir and Palestinian Delegation Leader Haydar Abd al-Shafi, Speeches at the Madrid Peace Conference: Laqueur and Rubin, *The Israel–Arab Reader*, 388–400.
King Hussein of Jordan, Disengagement from the West Bank: Laqueur and Rubin, *The Israel–Arab Reader*, 341–349.
Palestine National Council Declaration of Independence: Laqueur and Rubin, *The Israel–Arab Reader*, 354–358.
PLO Executive Committee Statement on the Intifada: Laqueur and Rubin, *The Israel–Arab Reader*, 323–326.
PLO Executive Committee, on the Intifada: Laqueur and Rubin, *The Israel–Arab Reader*, 314–317.
U.N. Security Council Resolution 242: Laqueur and Rubin, *The Israel–Arab Reader*, 116.

Notes

1. Efraim Karsh, "Iran–Iraq War (1980–1988)," in *Encyclopedia of the Modern Middle East and North Africa*, ed. Philip Mattar, 2nd ed. Vol. 2 (New York: Macmillan Reference USA, 2004), 1127–29.
2. "Excerpts From Meeting In Jordan," The Associated Press (as published in the *New York Times*), November 12, 1987 Available at http://query.nytimes.com/gst/fullpage.html?res=9B0DE7DD153EF931A25752C1A961948260&sec=&spon=&pagewanted=all
3. Ze'ev Schiff and Ehud Ya'ari, *Intifada: The Palestinian Uprising – Israel's Third Front* (New York: Simon and Schuster, 1990), 17–18; Don Peretz, *Intifada: The Palestinian Uprising* (Boulder, CO: Westview Press, 1990), 39.
4. For an official Israeli list of all settlements, the dates of establishment, and population size, see, http://www.cbs.gov.il/population/localities/localbycode2004.xls. For a list prepared by the Foundation for Middle East Peace, see, http://www.fmep.org/settlement_info/settlement-info-and-tables/stats-data/comprehensive-settlement-population-1972-2006.
5. Hamas took its name from the Arabic initials for the Islamic Resistance Movement (or Harakat al-muqawama al-Islamiya). For more on the establishment of Hamas, see Khaled Hroub's *Hamas: Political Thought and Practice* (Washington, DC: Institute for Palestine Studies, 2000), and Yonah Alexander's *Palestinian Religious Terrorism: Hamas and Islamic Jihad* (Ardsley, NY: Transnational Publishers, 2002). Yezid Sayigh, *Armed Struggle and the Search for a State*, 607–637.
6. Tessler, *A History of the Israeli–Palestinian Conflict*, 715.
7. Asher Susser, "Jordan, the PLO and the Palestine Question," in Joseph Nevo and Ilan Pappé, eds, *Jordan in the Middle East 1948–1988: The Making of a Pivotal State* (Portland, OR: Frank Cass, 1994), 218.

8. *Ibid.*, 221.
9. The Declaration states that the State of Palestine would be "a peace-loving State, in adherence to the principles of peaceful co-existence. It will join with all states and peoples in order to assure a permanent peace... The State of Palestine herewith declares that it believes in the settlement of regional and international disputes by peaceful means, in accordance with the U.N. Charter and resolutions... rejects the threat or use of force, violence and terrorism against its territorial integrity or political independence, as it also rejects their use against territorial integrity of other states." For the full text of the Declaration of Independence, see "Document 462: Declaration of Palestinian Independence Issued by the Palestine Liberation Organization, November 15, 1988," in M. Cherif Bassiouni, ed., *Documents on the Arab–Israeli Conflict: The Palestinians and the Israeli–Palestinian Peace Process*, vol. 2, 590–591.
10. The group of American Jewish personalities included Rita Hauser, a New York attorney; Stanley Sheinbaum, a Los Angeles economist and publisher; Menachem Rosensaft, a Holocaust survivor; Drora Kass, from the American branch of the Israeli International Center for Peace in the Middle East; and A. L. Udovitch, a professor of Middle Eastern history (p. 482). Quandt, *Peace Process: American Diplomacy and the Arab–Israeli Conflict since 1967*, 278–285, 482–486.
11. Sayigh, *Armed Struggle and the Search for State*, 624, citing *Middle East International*, 341, January 6, 1989.
12. Sayigh, *Armed Struggle and the Search for State*, 624.
13. While almost all Arab countries condemned, or at least criticized, the Iraqi action, the PLO was seen as being soft on the Iraqis. PLO–Iraqi relations were at their best at that time as Arafat came to gradually rely heavily on Saddam Hussein's political support. Moreover, Arafat had been disappointed with the American termination of the United States–PLO dialogue only two months before the Iraqi invasion of Kuwait. Given Palestinian public support for Saddam, Arafat could not allow King Hussein to become more popular than him among the Palestinians.
14. Hussein Agha *et al.*, *Track-II Diplomacy: Lessons from the Middle East* (Cambridge, MA: MIT Press, 2003), 37–44.
15. "Israel–PLO Recognition – Exchange of Letters between PM Rabin and Chairman Arafat – Sept 9– 1993," http://www.mfa.gov.il/MFA/Peace+Process/Guide+to+the+Peace+Process/Israel-PLO+Recognition+-+Exchange+of+Letters+betwe.htm (accessed October 2, 2011).
16. The Associated Press, "The Jordan–Israel Accord: The Agreement: Establishing Principles for a Lasting Peace," *New York Times*, October 27, 1994.
17. Morris, *Righteous Victims*, 605–607.
18. *Ibid.*, 396–398.
19. Al Sayed Yassin, ed., *The Arab Strategic Report 1987* (Cairo: Al Ahram Center for Political and Strategic Studies, 1988), 123–133.
20. *Ibid.*, 387.
21. Al Sayed Yassin, ed., *The Arab Strategic Report 1988* (Cairo: Al Ahram Center for Political and Strategic Studies, 1989), 648–652.
22. Al Sayed Yassin, ed, *The Arab Strategic Report 1991* (Cairo: Al Ahram Center for Political and Strategic Studies, 1992), 498.
23. Asher Susser, "Jordan, the PLO and the Palestine Question," 216–217 (citing Radio Amman, August 4, 1988 and Jordan News Agency, May 10, 1988).
24. Asher Susser, "Jordan: Case Study of A Pivotal State," Washington Institute for Near East Policy (Policy Paper No. 53), 74.
25. *Ibid.*, 76.

26. Philip Robins, *A History of Jordan*, 185.
27. Susser, "Jordan: Case Study," 78–79.
28. *Ibid.*, 80.
29. Curtis R. Ryan, *Jordan in Transition: From Hussein to Abdallah* (Boulder, CO: Lynne Rienner Publishers, 2002), 78–79.
30. Jacob Shamir and Michal Shamir, *The Anatomy of Public Opinion* (Ann Arbor: University of Michigan Press, 2000), 191. See also Asher Arian, Michal Shamir, and Raphael Ventura, "Public Opinion and Political Change: Israel and the Intifada," *Comparative Politics*, 24, 3 (April, 1992), 317–334.
31. Abbas provides his narrative of the Oslo negotiations in Mahmoud Abbas, *Through Secret Channels*.
32. These American loans were not granted until the new Rabin government agreed in July 19, 1992 to impose a partial construction freeze and to refrain from using American funds beyond Israel's pre-1967 borders.
33. For more on the Madrid conference, see James A. Baker, III, *The Politics of Diplomacy Revolution, War & Peace, 1989–1992* (New York: G.P. Putnam's Sons, 1995).
34. Eyal Zisser, "Asad Inches toward Peace," *Middle East Quarterly*, 1, 3 (September 1994).
35. See Muna Kasim, *Economic Reform in Egypt* (Cairo: Maktabat Al Osra, 1998), 23–24; Frag Abdel Fatah, *Al Ahali*, May 18, 2011; Amani Fawzi Furure, "Visions for the Egyptian Economy," *Democracy*, October, 2011.
36. www.arab-hdr.org/publications/other/escwa/eco-socialdev-08a.pdf, *69, 78, 21.*
37. Avi Shlaim, "Prelude to the Accord: Likud, Labor, and the Palestinians," *Journal of Palestine Studies*, 23, 2 (1994), 10.

8 Failures of Implementation of the Madrid Conference

This chapter centers on the period 1992–2000 and the two great failures to fulfill the promises for Arab–Israeli peace kindled by the 1991 Madrid Peace Conference: the unsuccessful conclusion to the bilateral peace negotiations between Israel and Syria; and the breakdown of the multilateral efforts launched by Israel, the Palestinians and thirteen Arab countries in 1993–95 in an effort to address the region-wide problems of the Middle East.

At the global level, this was the first post-Cold War era. It was characterized by unipolarity: the United States was the only remaining superpower. It asserted its new power by orchestrating NATO's expansion to the East and by projecting its capabilities in the Balkans, all the while ignoring Russia's objections to these moves. This was also a period of considerable expansion of American capabilities in terms of its economy, technology and innovation.

During this period, important features of globalization asserted themselves: international institutions, such as the European Union, the United Nations, the International Monetary Fund, and the World Trade Organization, gained more influence and an expanded reach. In the realm of global disarmament and arms control, the indefinite extension of the 1968 Nuclear Nonproliferation Treaty (NPT) in 1995 was an important milestone.

The influence of global forces on the Middle East was more limited during this period, since in the aftermath of the Cold War, Russia's influence in the Middle East reached its lowest ebb. Conversely, with economics assuming greater importance, the European states found themselves playing a greater role in the region, at least in the diplomatic realm.

In the Middle East, the coalition of Egypt, Syria, and Saudi Arabia created to contain and then roll-back Iraq's August 1990 invasion of Kuwait, continued to enjoy closer ties. At a different level, the relations between Egypt and Jordan improved, while Saudi Arabia and the smaller Gulf States took their time in mending relations with Jordan following the rupture associated with the latter's perceived siding with Saddam Hussein during the Gulf War.

Separately, this period also witnessed the development of much closer ties between two non-Arab players in the Middle East: Turkey and Israel. While these ties were manifested mostly in the defense–industrial realm, they had broader diplomatic and economic implications. At times, Jordan joined this improved relationship, with the three countries contemplating a number of joint projects.

The 1990s also witnessed a sharp rise in political Islam and Islamic terrorism in the Middle East. In large part, this resulted from the Islamists' earlier success in defeating the Soviets in Afghanistan. Now, a large number of daring and experienced Islamist fighters who were well trained in the use of weapons and explosives became unemployed and hence available for recruitment to new missions. From the June 1996 demolition of the Khobar Towers in Saudi Arabia, to the November 1997 massacre of tourists in Luxor, Egypt, to the August 1998 bombings of United States embassies in Africa, and, finally, the October 2000 attack on the USS *Cole* – an American naval vessel docked in Yemen – the trajectory of Islamist terrorism, mostly inspired, if not orchestrated, by al-Qaida, was already on the rise some years before September 11, 2001.

Main Developments

The main developments addressed in this chapter concern the failures to solve key issues in the Middle East through Israeli–Syrian peace negotiations as well as through region-wide multilateral talks. Four different Israeli governments – headed by Prime Ministers Rabin, Peres, Netanyahu, and Barak – were involved in peace negotiations with Syria during this period. These serious negotiations were preceded by a brief period of talks held by the government of Itzhak Shamir in the immediate aftermath of the Madrid Conference. The second set of talks discussed here – multilateral talks to address the region's different problems – were launched in Moscow in January 1992 as a consequence of the Madrid Conference.

Israeli–Syrian Negotiations under Rabin

The first rounds of Israeli–Syrian negotiations took place promptly after the Madrid Conference. On the Israeli side, these talks were still held under the Likud-led government headed by Itzhak Shamir. Lacking any intention to pay the price for reaching an agreement with Syria – an Israeli withdrawal from the Golan – the Israeli delegation to these talks, headed by Shamir's close associate, Yossi Ben Aharon, did everything possible to avoid serious negotiations. Instead, Israel provoked the Syrians by repeatedly accusing the Assad regime of anti-Israeli and anti-Semitic incitement in school textbooks and the media.[1]

Israeli elections were held on June 23, 1992, five months ahead of schedule. They resulted in a Labor Party victory, allowing its leader, Yitzhak Rabin, to form the 25th government of Israel. Shortly thereafter, Rabin opened an indirect line of communication to Syrian President Hafez Assad through American facilitation. The direct talks between the two parties began at the ambassadorial level, led by Syrian Ambassador to the United States, Walid al-Moualem, and Israel's Ambassador to the United States, Itamar Rabinovich. As the negotiations began to progress, the Syrians and Israelis agreed that they should focus on "three core issues that had to be resolved... peace, territory, and security."[2]

By the summer of 1992, however, American efforts to advance Arab–Israeli negotiations were placed on the back-burner, as President Bush's reelection efforts seemed in deep trouble, causing a last minute reconfiguration of his administration. Secretary James Baker, the key American architect of the Madrid Conference, now left the State Department to join the

Bush reelection team. Meanwhile, trouble on Israel's Palestinian front escalated, resulting in Hamas's killing of three Israeli soldiers and a border policeman in Gaza in December 1992. In response, Rabin ordered the expulsion from the West Bank and Gaza of more than 400 suspected Hamas and Islamic Jihad activists.[3]

The expulsion brought Israeli–Syrian talks to a halt. They resumed in April 1993, but floundered. Distrust between the two parties continued to saturate the atmosphere, fed by the continued violent conflict between Israel and the Syrian-supported Hezbollah. Violence escalated again in July 1993, with Hezbollah attacks leading Israel to launch a major offensive into Lebanon, "Operation Accountability."[4]

In all the initial talks, the Syrians consistently asserted that in order for serious negotiations to begin, Israel must first promise a full withdrawal from the Golan Heights – that is, from all territories it conquered from Syria during the 1967 War. On its part, Israel stressed that it needed to know exactly what kind of peace Syria had in mind before it could commit itself to the precise dimensions of its eventual withdrawal. A Syrian formula made public in April 1993 offering "full peace for full withdrawal" also failed to create a breakthrough, as the Syrians refused to specify what they meant by "full peace."[5]

In order to break the deadlock, in August 1993 Rabin conveyed to the new Secretary of State, Warren Christopher, a "hypothetical, conditional willingness to withdraw from the Golan as part of a peace settlement between Israel and Syrian on terms acceptable to Israel."[6] Rabin reportedly emphasized to Christopher that this hypothetical willingness to withdraw was to remain secret and was to be kept in America's "pocket" – that is, not to be placed on the table.[7] However, Secretary Christopher apparently conveyed to Assad that if Israel's expectations for peace and security were met, Rabin was prepared to have Israel implement a "full withdrawal" from the Golan.[8] On his part, Rabin was dissatisfied with Christopher's message from Syria regarding what comprised peace and the security arrangements they were prepared to accept. Hence, he gave the green light to Israel's negotiators at Oslo to conclude a grand bargain with the PLO – an agreement which took the Syrian leadership by surprise.[9]

The months following the Oslo agreement saw the Israeli leadership giving priority to its implementation. Nevertheless, in a meeting held on January 16, 1994, in Geneva, President Clinton conveyed to President Assad America's interest in seeing the Israeli–Syrian talks brought to a successful conclusion. Yet these talks continued to falter as a result of tragedies on both sides: President Assad lost his eldest son, Bassel – widely viewed as his most likely successor – to a traffic accident, and a Jewish-Israeli extremist Baruch Goldstein killed 29 Palestinians in Hebron.

Nevertheless, between April and July 1994, the United States undertook a series of extended shuttles between Jerusalem and Damascus in an effort to narrow the differences between the parties' positions. By late July this is said to have led to an important breakthrough when Prime Minister Rabin is said to have authorized Secretary Christopher to tell Assad that, at the very least, it was Christopher's "impression" that the "full withdrawal" referred to in Rabin's August 1993 "deposit" meant a commitment to withdraw to 1967 lines.[10]

Meanwhile, however, Israel brought its negotiations with Jordan to a successful conclusion at the signing ceremony held on October 26, 1994, at Wadi Arava, with President Clinton presiding. By contrast, Rabin introduced another complication in the talks with Syria by promising that any agreement reached would be brought to a national referendum.[11] Nevertheless, on his way back from Wadi Arava, Clinton stopped in Damascus to assure Syria's leader that the United States remained committed to reaching a Syrian–Israeli agreement and that Rabin remained committed to the basic equation expressed in the so-called "deposit" of August 1993.

Supported by these American assurances, a first meeting between Syrian and Israeli military chiefs of staff – Syria's General Hikmat Shihabi and Israel's General Ehud Barak – took place on December 21, 1994. By May of 1995, the talks produced a draft agreement referred to as a "Non-Paper on the Aims and Principles of Security Arrangements" to be implemented following Israel's expected withdrawal.[12] Syrian Foreign Minister Shar'a traveled to the United States in early May to provide important input to the drafting of the document, and two weeks later Rabin came to Washington as well, finally approving the document on May 22.[13]

On June 27–29, 1995 a second set of talks was held at Fort McNair in Washington, DC, between Syrian and Israeli military officials headed by Syrian General Shihabi and the new IDF Chief of Staff, General Amnon Shahak.[14] General Zvi Shtauber of the IDF's Planning Branch presented the Syrians with the security arrangements Israel would require in the framework of a comprehensive Israeli–Syrian security regime. Soon thereafter, a 17-page document which is said to have been Shtauber's talking points (the so-called "Shtauber Document") was publicized by the then Leader of the Opposition, Benjamin Netanyahu to chastise the Rabin Government.

In July, further talks were held without reaching any agreement. The Israeli side then became absorbed by a number of developments: increased opposition within Rabin's Labor government to conceding the Golan Heights to Syria, the accelerated Israel–PLO negotiations of the Oslo-II implementation agreement, and acts of Palestinian violence.[15] Then, on November 4, 1995, after speaking at a Tel Aviv pro-peace rally, Rabin was assassinated by Yigal Amir – a right-wing Israeli opponent of the peace process.[16]

Talks under Peres

On the day of Rabin's funeral, President Clinton is said to have asked Shimon Peres – Rabin's successor as prime minister – whether he intended to abide by the "commitments" made by Rabin on the Syrian front, referring to the so-called "deposit." Peres reportedly told Clinton that he would fulfill whatever commitments Rabin had made.[17] Soon thereafter, in early December, Peres also sent a letter to President Assad, affirming his commitment to Rabin's pursuit of comprehensive peace with Syria.[18] He reiterated the same message publicly in a speech presenting his new cabinet to the Knesset.[19]

After a series of volleyed positive messages between Peres and Assad, Dennis Ross (President Clinton's special Middle East coordinator) and his team organized meetings between the two sides, held at Wye River Conference Center, near Washington, DC. The first of the sessions at Wye took place on December 27–29, 1995 and on January 3–5, 1996. After the sessions Secretary Christopher traveled to Jerusalem and Damascus.[20]

The second round of the Wye negotiations was held on January 24–26 and January 29–31, 1996. With senior military officers now joining the diplomats in both teams, this round focused on post-withdrawal security arrangements. It seemed to have ended in a stalemate around two key points: the first of these was Syria's insistence and Israel's refusal to accept equally deep buffer zones on the two sides of the border, with international forces deployed on both Israeli and Syrian territory;[21] the other was Israel's demand that Syria deploy its forces inside Syria in a manner that would reduce the likelihood of a surprise attack against Israel – a demand that Syria rejected.[22]

Another focus of the negotiations at Wye was the water issue – a subject of critical importance to Israel given its reliance on sources in Syria and Lebanon for its water supply. The Syrian position seems to have been that once it had solved its conflict with Turkey, there would be no problem guaranteeing Israel a supply of water from Syria.[23] In February 1996, however, in between the second and third round of the meetings at Wye River, Israel signed a defense cooperation agreement with Turkey – a move Syria interpreted as threatening, given the history of tense Syrian–Turkish relations.[24]

The third round of the talks at Wye was held on February 28–March 4, 1996. When Syria refused to condemn two suicide attacks, in Jerusalem on March 3 and in Tel Aviv on March 4, Peres instructed the Israeli team to suspend its participation in the Wye talks.[25] The suspension was followed by an anti-terrorism conference convened by Clinton and by Egypt's President Mubarak on March 13–14 in Sharm el-Sheikh. Syria refrained from taking part in the meeting.[26] Meanwhile, Peres decided to call for early elections, to be held on May 30.[27]

Continuous rocket attacks by Hezbollah from southern Lebanon against targets in Israel's north led to the latter's decision on April 2, 1996, to launch Operation Grapes of Wrath – a major Israeli military incursion into southern Lebanon.[28] On April 18, the UN Security Council adopted Resolution 1052 calling for an immediate ceasefire. That same day, however, Israeli artillery shelled a UN base near Qana – a village in southern Lebanon. Over 100 Lebanese civilians who had taken refuge in the base were killed, with many others injured. Despite Israeli claims that the bombing was in error, international opinion swung decidedly against Israel, and on April 26, 1996, an Israeli–Lebanese Ceasefire Understanding (also known as "The Grapes of Wrath Understandings," as well as the "April Understanding") was concluded. The agreement included two novel aspects: the establishment of a monitoring system to supervise the implementation of the ceasefire and a role for France in that system as demanded by Syria. [29] Regardless, the operation led to the closing of this chapter in Israeli–Syrian negotiations.

Indirect Negotiations under Netanyahu

Having changed its election laws, on May 29, 1996, Israel held its first-ever direct prime ministerial election while at the same time also holding elections to its parliament – the Knesset. In the prime ministerial vote, Peres, the incumbent, was defeated by Likud leader Benjamin Netanyahu, who formed Israel's 27th government on June 18.[30] Almost immediately thereafter, the Syrian and Israeli governments both took steps related to the talks held during the tenure of Rabin and Peres. While Syria sought an affirmation of the "deposit," as well as of the May 1995 Non-Paper, Netanyahu asked that Secretary Christopher confirm that the United States did not regard the Non-Paper as binding. Other than such positioning, there seem to have been no significant Israeli–Syrian interactions during the first two years of Netanyahu's government. However, in the fall of 1998, Netanyahu reportedly asked an American Jewish leader and businessman, Ronald Lauder, former United States Ambassador to Austria, to approach Syria's President Assad. The talks were to be kept secret, even from President Clinton.[31] Indeed, among the various chapters of Israeli–Syrian talks, this one seems to be the most shrouded in secrecy and the most subject to conflicting accounts. According to one account, Lauder eventually reported the results of his negotiations to Clinton, telling him that Assad would accept an Israeli withdrawal to the internationally recognized borders – a position less severe than Assad's previous long-standing demand that Israel withdraw to the pre-1967 lines. Exactly what transpired in these talks remains unclear, as Lauder later admitted "that his previous briefing of the President had outlined some points 'that were never accepted by the Syrians.'"[32] The Lauder talks reportedly ended when Netanyahu refused to provide a map indicating Israel's line of withdrawal.[33]

However, at least one account, provided by the former IDF Director of Military Intelligence, Major General (reserve) Uri Sagie, gives considerably more credit to the Lauder Mission. According to Sagie's account, Netanyahu's foreign policy advisor, Dr. Uzi Arad, participated directly in some of the talks in which all the core issues were discussed, including the possibility of an Israeli withdrawal to a line based on both the international border and the June 1967 lines. The Syrians were presented with an Israeli document defining the principles for an Israeli–Syrian agreement, probably drafted by Arad. However, the Syrians later denied an Israeli account according to which they were prepared to accept the document as a basis for negotiations. Nevertheless, according to Sagie, the talks "reached a very advanced stage and were more far-reaching than the talks previously held [with the Syrians]."[34]

Negotiations during Barak's Tenure

In the elections held on May 17, 1999, Netanyahu was defeated by Labor leader and former IDF Chief of Staff, Ehud Barak. An important feature of Barak's election campaign was his promise to withdraw the IDF from southern Lebanon, preferably in the framework of an agreement with Syria. Not long after his assumption of the premiership, Barak sent General Sagie to hold secret preparatory talks with the Syrians, as a prelude to full-fledged negotiations. Sagie's Syrian counterpart in the talks was Riyad Dawudi, a former Legal Advisor to the Foreign Ministry.[35]

On December 8, 1999, President Clinton formally announced that Barak and Assad agreed to resume Israeli–Syrian peace negotiations from the point reached in January 1996. The first round of the new talks was held at Blair House in Washington, DC, on December 15 as a Clinton-convened summit with Barak and Syrian foreign minister Farouk Shar'a.[36]

Beginning on January 3, 2000, a more lengthy second round of talks between Barak, Shar'a and their negotiation teams was held in Shepherdstown, West Virginia.[37] On the second day of negotiations the two sides agreed to create four committees to work simultaneously on borders/withdrawal, water, normalization of relations, and security arrangements. While the

Figure 8.1. Presidents Assad and Clinton. © Wally McNamee/CORBIS

normalization and security committees met immediately, only informal talks were held on the ideas of demilitarized zones and early warning stations that would remain on the Golan following Israel's expected withdrawal. Syria then complained that Israel prevented the other two committees (water and borders) from meeting, and that informal meetings on those subjects would not suffice. They therefore suspended their participation in the normalization and security committees until the other two committees were convened. Attempts by President Clinton to break this impasse failed. Before the negotiators left, the United States presented them with a draft Israeli–Syrian core agreement.

Another effort to conclude an Israeli–Syrian deal took place at a meeting between Presidents Clinton and Assad in Geneva on March 26, 2000. The President told Assad he would meet with him secretly and present a detailed map of Barak's offer of withdrawal and that if this was acceptable to Assad they would call Barak to join them and sign an agreement. The Barak map was based on the June 4, 1967 line, with some adjustments such as a change in the northeastern section of the Sea of Galilee. The proposed new line was to be drawn some 500 meters from the shoreline, allowing Israel to build a road around the lake. This is an area where five Syrian fishing villages were located prior to the 1967 War. In return, Barak reportedly drew the line around the southeastern section of the lake, 500 meters west of the June 4, 1967 line.[38]

When Clinton met with Assad in Geneva, however, he was interrupted numerous times by the Syrian President and barely got through the beginning part of his presentation before Assad declared that Barak's request of a strip of land around the northeastern shore of the Sea of Galilee meant that he, Barak, did not want peace. It was clear to Clinton that

Assad was not prepared to conclude a deal that included Israeli possession of a strip of land around the lake and that Barak would not conclude a deal without this. The meeting thus ended in failure.[39]

Arab–Israeli Multilateral Talks

In addition to the sets of bilateral Israeli–Syrian and Israeli–Palestinian/Jordanian negotiations, the 1991 Madrid peace process also included an attempt to address the issues plaguing the Middle East region at large. Talks for this purpose began at a meeting in Moscow in late January 1992, with 35 states participating, including 13 Arab states, Israel and the Palestinians. Neither Iraq nor Iran were invited to take part in the talks while Syria and Lebanon announced that they would not participate until serious progress has been made in their bilateral negotiations with Israel. The participants in the Moscow Conference agreed to form five multilateral working groups to discuss the region's five challenges: water, refugees, economic cooperation, the environment, and arms control and regional security.[40] The discussions were also intended to complement the bilateral talks launched in Madrid by improving the climate for resolving the core issues negotiated in these bilateral frameworks.

Arms Control and Regional Security Working Group (ACRS)

The Arms Control and Regional Security (ACRS) working group was entrusted with reducing the likelihood and consequences of violence and war in the Middle East.[41] The initial round of discussions, held in Washington in May 1992, was plagued by fundamental disagreements, primarily between Israel and Egypt. Egypt gave the highest priority to arresting nuclear proliferation in the Middle East, focusing on Israel's alleged nuclear weapons capability. Conversely, Israel stressed the importance of dealing first with the deep distrust prevailing in the region as well as with the stockpiles of conventional weapons possessed by the region's states.

The second ACRS working group meeting, convening in Moscow in September 1992, attempted to settle these conflicting agendas by adopting an American–Russian proposed compromise that incorporated both priorities. It called for the parties to define long-term objectives ("a vision") for the process but stipulated that progress toward the realization of these goals must be built "brick by brick" through the gradual growth of mutual confidence.[42]

Between September 1992 and May 1993, Israel and Jordan launched internal efforts to define ultimate purposes for a regional arms control process. Egypt already possessed such a definition in the form of the 1990 Mubarak Initiative which called for the transformation of the Middle East into a Weapons of Mass Destruction Free Zone (WMDFZ). In a speech delivered in Paris on January 13, 1993 by then Foreign Minister Shimon Peres, Israel presented its approach that viewed the establishment of a WMDFZ in the Middle East as requiring the prior achievement of a stable and durable peace and the application of mutual verification measures.

In the ACRS plenary held in Washington in May 1993, the participating parties decided to hold intersessional meetings with external sponsors to escort the parties through the complexities of their tasks. Thus, the United States and Russia co-sponsored the effort to define the ultimate purposes of a Middle East arms control process; Canada was asked to sponsor an examination of possible maritime Confidence and Security Building Measures (CSBMs); Turkey was nominated to guide the exploration of methods for exchanging military information and providing pre-notification of large-scale military movements; and the Netherlands agreed to guide the efforts to explore the utility of creating a regional communication network.

The next meeting of the ACRS plenary was held in Moscow in early November 1993. It resulted in a decision to divide the working group's efforts into two "baskets": a "conceptual basket" and an "operational basket." The first of these was intended to explore the possibility of agreeing on principles to guide the future relations of the region's states and on the ultimate objectives of arms control in the Middle East. The operational basket was to suggest various practical mechanisms to increase transparency and reduce the danger of unintended escalation.

Participants in a meeting of the conceptual basket held in Paris in mid-October 1994 reached agreement on all subjects except the nuclear issue. Given the approaching 1995 NPT Review and Extension Conference, Egypt insisted that the statement must include a clear stipulation that "all the parties in the region" should "adhere to the NPT in the near future." By contrast, Israel insisted that the document confine itself to a commitment to transform the Middle East into a "mutually verifiable" zone free of weapons of mass destruction. Compromise language proposed by United States delegates failed to bridge this gap.

In April 1994 in Turkey, in May in Qatar, and in November in Amman, considerable progress was made on a number of issues related to the operational basket of the ACRS process. These concerned maritime CSBMs, regional communications, exchange of military information and pre-notification of military movement and exercises. At the ACRS plenary in Tunis in early December 1994, the Israeli and Egyptian delegations made some effort to accommodate one another's priorities on the NPT issue but failed to agree on any formulation that might allow the adoption of the proposed statement. At the same time, further progress was made in Tunis on issues related to the operational basket, especially concerning the establishment of a regional communication network, the creation of a Regional Security Center, the implementation of maritime CSBMs, and the exchange of military information.[43]

The December 1994 plenary meeting in Tunis turned out to be the last of its kind. Unable to bridge the gap between the Israeli and the Egyptian competing priorities for the ACRS process, the parties failed to agree on a formula that would allow them to continue meeting. Thus, the United States canceled a plenary session scheduled to convene in Amman in September 1995. The meeting was to have provided final approval for a wide array of regional CSBMs.

The Economic Working Group

The deliberations of the Regional Economic Development Working Group (REDWG) began with a two-day conference held in Paris on October 29–30, 1992. At the meeting, the World Bank suggested establishing a Middle East Reconstruction Bank.[44] This was followed by two meetings of the working group that focused on regional economic cooperation.[45]

These meetings led to the first Middle East/North Africa (MENA) Economic Summit, hosted by Morocco's King Hassan II in Casablanca on October 30–November 1, 1994. The summit endorsed the decision of the Gulf Cooperation Council (GCC) countries to forgo the secondary and tertiary aspects of the Arab boycott of Israel, as well as a move to end the primary boycott. In addition, the summit produced an agreement to establish four regional centers of economic activity: a Middle East and North Africa Development Bank, a Tourist Board to facilitate regional cooperation in tourism, a regional Chamber of Commerce and a Business Council to facilitate intra-regional trade relations.[46]

In the next meetings of REDWG participants agreed to form three regional councils to strengthen regional cooperation. These were to focus on finance, trade, and tourism.[47] On May 16, 1995, a smaller REDWG task force invited draft proposals for a Middle East Development Bank.[48] And in June 1995, REDWG met in Jordan and recommended approval of regional transport projects, mainly rail, road and port, as well as coordination on civil aviation.[49] A second MENA Economic Summit was held in Amman on October 29–31, 1995. The summit yielded an agreement on the establishment of a Bank for Economic Cooperation and Development in the Middle East and North Africa to be headquartered in Cairo; a Middle East-Mediterranean Travel and Tourism Association (MEMTTA); and a Regional Business Council to promote cooperation and trade among the private sectors of the countries of the region.[50]

A smaller MENA economic meeting was held on November 16–18, 1997, in Doha, Qatar, but with only six Arab states attending.[51] The most important of the meeting's outcomes was an agreement reached by Israel and Jordan to establish a free trade zone in Irbid, Jordan.[52]

Environmental and Water Working Groups

Chaired by Japan, the Environmental Working Group (EWG) was created to coordinate "activities on maritime pollution, wastewater treatment, environmental management, and desertification."[53] The EWG's discussions were launched in May 1993, and over the following year a number of proposals for dealing with pollution were approved. Most importantly, on October 25, 1994, in a meeting in Bahrain, the EWG unanimously adopted the Bahrain Environmental Code of Conduct for the Middle East. The meeting agreed that: (a) natural resources of the region must be preserved and all activities that would have an adverse effect on these resources must be avoided; (b) comprehensive peace in the region and environment protection are interdependent, and the regional parties would cooperate on environmental issues; (c) the parties would facilitate and encourage public awareness of these issues and participation in addressing them by training and education; and (d) the regional parties would join forces for environmental protection and conservation and would begin working in the following fields: water, marine and coastal environment, air, waste management, and desertification.[54]

In the EWG's seventh meeting, which took place in June 1995 in Amman, an agreement was reached to merge with the Water Resources Working Group (WRWG), thus forming the Multilateral Working Group on Water Resources (MWGWR). Prior to this merger, the WRWG had successfully established a regional effort to invest in desalination. In February

1996, Jordan, Israel, and the Palestinian Authority approved a DOP for Cooperation among the Core Parties on Water-Related Matters and New and Additional Water Resources.

However, it gradually became clear that it was politically impossible to separate the discussions of the MWGWR from the difficulties experienced in the ACRS working group. One example of this took place in September 1995 when the head of the Egyptian Atomic Energy Authority, Dr. Muhammad Izat Abdul Aziz, argued that nuclear waste from Israel was harming the region's environment.[55]

Refugee Working Group (RWG)

The Refugee Working Group (RWG) began its meetings in Ottawa, Canada, in May 1992. By the end of this first session, a number of "themes" were decided upon that would make up the RWG's agenda. These were: human resource development, job creation and vocational training, public health, child welfare, economic and social infrastructure, databases, and family reunification. Israel took particular issue with the last "theme," regarding it as connected to the Palestinian demand for the "right of return."[56]

In the fourth round of talks, held in Tunis in October 1993, participants agreed that, in accordance with the terms of the Israel–PLO DOP and the Israel–Jordan Common Agenda signed in September 1993, the issue of the 1948 Palestinian refugees was to be discussed solely in the framework of permanent status negotiations between Israel and the Palestinians. At the same time, Israel and the Palestinians agreed to set up a four-member group, to include Jordan and Egypt, to address the issues of persons displaced by the 1967 War.[57]

Six months later, at a RWG meeting held in Cairo in May 1994, agreement was reached on a set of activities designed to promote economic and human development. Israel, the United States, and various European states would offer refugees skills and career training in varied fields, Sweden agreed to help with $2 million in aid for child welfare programs, and the United States and Israel were to provide social and economic infrastructure for refugees in Syria/Lebanon and the West Bank, respectively.[58] On December 3–4, 1997, the RWG met in Aqaba to discuss the conditions of refugees in Jordan.[59]

The RWG activities then began to wind down, with substantive issues rarely being addressed. On April 19–21, 1998, the Coordination Committee of the RWG met in Canada and discussed developments in databases on refugee statistics. The RWG's next action was a mission to observe refugee living conditions in the West Bank and Gaza.[60] In mid-March, 1999, the RWG held an intersessional meeting and two unofficial discussions in Paris that focused on family reunification.[61] The last action of the RWG was a mission to refugee camps in Jordan on June 13–17, 1999, to assess ways of improving living conditions.[62]

Narratives

The Israeli Narrative

Going to Madrid

Israelis saw this period in the history of the Arab–Israeli conflict as determined by America's dominance of the region following the end of the Cold War and the different regional ramifications of the Gulf War. They attached considerable importance to the Madrid Conference, viewing it as the first effort to convene Israel and its neighbors for peace talks since the 1974 Geneva Conference.

Indeed, this time around, the international gathering was to launch the most extensive set of bilateral and multilateral negotiations between Israel and its neighbors since the state's establishment. As such, it was viewed by Israelis as very different from the kind of international conference they traditionally feared – one comprising a session in which a large number of Arab states would "gang up" on Israel, forcing it to accept what it regarded as impossible concessions.

In contrast to the "territories for peace" approach embedded in UNSC Resolution 242, the Shamir government seemed to anchor its policy and negotiations position on an approach that can be described as "peace for peace." Shamir articulated this approach by saying: "I just don't believe in trading land for peace. I mean I don't believe in it."[63] Thus, in response to Syria's insistence that for peace to be concluded Israel was required to first agree to a full withdrawal from the Golan Heights as decreed by UNSC Resolution 242, the Shamir government insisted that, in any case, UNSC Resolution 242 called for Israel's withdrawal from territories (and not from *the* territories) conquered by Israel in the 1967 War. And since Israel withdrew from the bulk of conquered territories by withdrawing from the Sinai in the framework of the Egypt–Israel Peace Treaty, Israel was not under any international obligation to offer additional territorial concessions.[64]

After Madrid, Israel also saw itself as having risen to the new occasion by adjusting its policy in response to the opportunities that the new international and regional environment offered. Thus, by 1992 the Israeli public took credit for ousting the Likud-led government headed by Itzhak Shamir, replacing it with a Labor-led coalition headed by Itzhak Rabin – a former IDF Chief of Staff, a former Ambassador to the United States, and a former prime minister – who promised to grant autonomy to the Palestinians residing in Gaza and the West Bank.

Land for Peace

The Israeli narrative changed with Rabin's return to power. Rabin accepted that the principle of "territories for peace" enshrined in UNSC Resolution 242 applied to all fronts, including the Golan Heights.[65] Indeed, in the eyes of the Israeli electorate, the victory it gave Rabin signaled the country's commitment to peace and its assessment that the existence of Arab partners provides an opportunity for peace.[66]

At the same time, the Israeli narrative stipulated that in order to commit itself to withdrawal, Israel needed to know what kind of peace it could hope to gain in return. In a radio interview Rabin stressed this point:

> We said that in return for contractual peace or, in other words, a peace treaty that guarantees the termination of the state of war, open borders between Syria and Israel, diplomatic relations and exchanges of ambassadors and normalization, Israel will be ready to implement resolutions 242 and 338...This implies, of course, a certain readiness for some kind of territorial compromise. Until Syria declares that it is ready

to reach such a peace, we have not and will not enter any territorial discussions or draw up any maps.[67]

Or, in the words of Ambassador Itamar Rabinovich, then head of Israel's delegation for talks with Syria: "Israel understood that in order to conclude this negotiation, very painful concessions on its part would be required, but Israel would not deal with the extent of withdrawal before it had a clear indication of Syria's concept of peace and its willingness to make a real political investment in obtaining it."[68]

Thus while Rabin was willing to consider a deeper Israeli withdrawal than any Israeli leader had previously contemplated, his position was that Israel should do so only in exchange for "real peace" – that is, the establishment of peaceful relations that go beyond an agreement between governments to include facets of "people to people" exchanges that would be less reversible than an agreement that would be limited to stipulations for future "government-to-government" interactions. In turn, this principle bred an important negotiations guideline: namely, that "the depth of [Israel's] withdrawal will reflect the depth of peace [which Syria will be prepared to offer Israel]."[69] As Israelis saw themselves being asked to relinquish tangible real-estate in exchange for intangible promises of peace, they reasoned that they should at least insure that such peace would manifest various forms of people-to-people interactions rather than be limited to a government-to-government arrangement which they regarded as easy to reverse.

Talks with Syria under Rabin

The Israeli narrative of this period emphasized the priority that Rabin gave to achieving peace with Syria. Indeed, for many reasons, Rabin is said to have preferred a deal with Syria over a grand bargain with the Palestinians. Accordingly, he is said to have given his "green light" to finalize the negotiations with the PLO in Oslo only after he concluded that it would not be possible to reach an acceptable compromise with Syria.

The priority given to a deal with Syria and, at the same time, the insistence that a firm commitment to withdrawal would only make sense once it was clear what kind of peace Israel could hope to gain in return, informed Israel's narrative regarding the "deposit" provided by Rabin: namely, that the "deposit" was only to be translated into an Israeli commitment after the Syrians committed themselves to the kind of peace that Israel had in mind.[70]

This "real time" narrative highlighted the Israeli formal approach to the sequencing of the issues under negotiation – emphasizing that the Syrians would first need to clarify what kind of peace they intended to establish before Israel could commit itself to specific dimensions of withdrawal. However, Israel's later narrative of the talks stressed that it was Rabin's commitment to peace that led him to go farther than any previous Israeli government, including the one he headed in 1974–77, in exploring the possibility of reaching a deal with the Syrians. The "deposit" he provided Secretary Christopher was designed to find out what kind of peace Syria was willing to offer Israel in exchange for the latter's withdrawal from the Golan.[71]

The Israeli narrative placed the responsibility for the failure to conclude a deal with Syria during this period entirely on the Syrian side. Two facets of Assad's approach to peace during

Rabin's premiership were said to have caused the failure: the first was Assad's refusal to promise that in exchange for Israel's withdrawal from the Golan, Syria would be prepared to establish "real peace," which, in Israeli eyes, entailed relations that would exceed a commitment to non-belligerence, the establishment of diplomatic relations, and the reciprocal opening of embassies in one another's country. The second was Assad's refusal to engage in meaningful public diplomacy – that is, to communicate to the Israeli public his intention to establish real peace with the Jewish state in any way remotely resembling President Sadat's November 1977 trip to Israel.

Given the history of the Israeli–Syrian dispute and the deep distrust bred by many years of conflict, the Israeli public needed some assurances that Syria meant peace. Moreover, to make the required concessions, Israeli leaders needed Assad's help in persuading the Israeli public that its government could safely make those concessions. For this, it was argued, Assad would need to abandon his passive and distant mode and appeal directly to the Israeli people, as Sadat had done. Yet all effort to persuade Assad to engage in meaningful forms of public diplomacy failed.

Talks with Syria under Peres

The Israeli narrative with regard to the talks held by Rabin's successor, Shimon Peres, was that the Israeli side had made an honest effort to conclude a deal with Syria. First, Peres assured President Clinton that he would abide by the "deposit" that Rabin had provided two years earlier. Thus, under Peres the "deposit" had now become a "commitment" of sorts.[72] Moreover, Peres is said to have taken pains to convey the essence of this commitment to Assad. In his letter, Peres also made clear that he was interested in moving quickly to conclude an agreement with Syria's leader.

Second, Peres clearly gave priority to the attempts to achieving a breakthrough with Syria. This was reflected in his decision, shortly after succeeding the fallen Rabin, not to pursue a possible breakthrough in Israeli–Palestinian negotiations based on the so-called Beilin–Abu Mazen agreement of which he had been informed immediately after taking office. Instead, he instructed his negotiators to explore the possibility of coming to terms with Damascus.[73]

Third, Peres is said to have improved upon Rabin's negotiation strategy by attempting to change Syria's incentive structure for a deal with Israel. Primarily this was done by demonstrating to Syria the possible economic benefits of peace. This was propelled by Peres' belief that the more economically developed Syria became, the less danger it would pose to Israel.[74]

The priority Peres gave to reaching peace with Syria is said to have rested on his estimate that this was the key to comprehensive peace in the Middle East. Achieving such an agreement was expected to also stabilize the peace accords Israel had already concluded with Egypt and Jordan as well as giving a green light to other Arab states in the Persian Gulf and North Africa to establish peaceful relations with the Jewish state. Peace with Syria was seen by Peres as a stepping-stone to comprehensive peace with Israel's other Arab neighbors. In addition, such a deal was expected to increase the likelihood of achieving a breakthrough in Israel's talks with the Palestinians as it would have made it untenable for Palestinian opposition groups headquartered in Damascus to continue to play a destructive role in Palestinian politics.

The Israeli narrative portrays Syria as responsible for the failure of the talks during the Peres premiership as well. Most importantly, Syria continued to refrain from contributing anything to improving the environment for negotiations by engaging in some productive form of public diplomacy. The clearest example of this was Syria's lukewarm reaction to Rabin's assassination.[75]

Peres could, therefore, have no hope that Assad would go along with his preferred modus operandi: direct negotiations by the two leaders held intermittently in Jerusalem and Damascus. In Peres' view, such direct talks would have signaled to the Israeli public a complete break with Syria's past behavior, thus increasing confidence in the durability of the agreement reached and, as a result, diminishing internal Israeli opposition to a withdrawal from the Golan.[76]

Assad also refrained from taking steps to curb terror attacks from Lebanon against Israel. Not only did this failure have a confidence-destroying effect on the Israeli public – allowing Israeli opponents of a withdrawal from the Golan to argue that this revealed Assad's real intentions to continue to undermine Israeli security – it was said to have forced the Israeli government to take countermeasures that made it impossible to continue negotiations with Syria. The most destructive of these measures, which doomed Israeli–Syrian talks, was the launching of Operation Grapes of Wrath.[77]

Finally, the positions regarding the security issue that Syria presented at Wye could not be acceptable to Israel. Specifically, the idea that the security arrangements implemented following Israel's withdrawal would be applied not only reciprocally but also symmetrically – that is, that both sides would need to apply them in equal measure, were seen by Israelis as unreasonable given Israel's lack of strategic depth. Accordingly, Israel saw its demand that Syria deploy its forces away from Israel's border as the only way to be sure that Israel's withdrawal would not be exploited by a surprise attack against the Jewish state.[78]

At the same time, it is noteworthy that the Israeli side did not regard the talks at Wye as having failed. Although many issues required considerable more work in the meetings' aftermath, the negotiations did end positively with a mutual agreement on an agenda for a trip by the American secretary of state to the region.[79]

Talks with Syria under Barak

The Israeli narrative about the Syrian–Israeli talks during Barak's premiership emphasizes the seriousness with which the Israeli side took the talks, as evidenced by the meticulous preparations it made, with working groups preparing every aspect of a possible deal: borders, water, security arrangements and normal relations.[80] Even more indicative of the seriousness is that Barak created a secret planning authority to prepare the relocation of Israeli settlers residing on the Golan Heights.[81] The Israeli narrative also noted that considerable progress was made in these talks. Especially important was an Israeli account of the Syrians acknowledging – while insisting on complete Israeli withdrawal to the 1967 lines – that there was some dispute about the precise location of these lines, thus opening the door to some Syrian flexibility on this issue.[82]

The Israeli narrative about the failure of these talks – especially at Shepherdstown – was that the tough positions presented by Barak resulted from his need to show the Israeli public that he had bargained as strongly as he could, and that he was insisting on Israel's needs before making any territorial concessions. Barak is said to have calculated that in order to avoid being seen by the Israeli public as too hasty, he needed to refrain from agreeing to a deal at Shepherdstown and to, instead, save his final compromise for a subsequent round of talks.[83]

The Israeli side noted that the Syrians not only continued to refrain from public diplomacy steps that would have made it easier for Barak to garner support for the obvious costs entailed in a deal with Syria – they did exactly the opposite. Most noteworthy was an extremely belligerent speech which Foreign Minister Shar'a delivered at the opening of the pre-Shepherdstown talks at Blair House and in addition, the refusal of the members of the Syrian delegation to shake the hands of their Israeli counterparts – a matter that received much attention from the Israeli media.[84]

Finally, the Israeli side regarded the failure of the talks at Shepherdstown as merely a tactical setback. Thus, in the aftermath of this failure, Barak is said to have continued a process of detailed preparations regarding all aspects of a future deal with the Syrians. This included talks with, and messages delivered through, senior members of the Clinton administration.[85]

The Multilateral Talks

Israelis blamed Egypt – the first Arab country to have signed a peace treaty with Israel – for the failure of the multilateral track talks. In Israeli eyes, most Arab states preferred to continue the post-Madrid multilateral talks. However, Egypt put huge pressure on these states to discontinue the discussions in the various multilateral frameworks as long as Israel refused to meet Egypt's demands in the ACRS talks – namely, that Israel commit itself to signing the NPT, thus dismantling its nuclear deterrent. Consequently, Israelis viewed Egypt as holding the entire multilateral track "hostage to the nuclear issue."

By the time these talks came to a complete halt in early 1995, Israelis had become convinced that two considerations propelled Egypt to prevent these talks from continuing. The first was that if the other multilateral talks addressed the region's problems successfully, this would have provided Arab states a permissive environment to open the doors to Israel's integration in the region. Egypt was understood to fear that such Israeli engagement would have allowed it to utilize its advantage in "soft power," and particularly its robust economic performance, making it very difficult for Egypt – a country seriously lacking in this realm – to compete. In Israeli eyes these Egyptian anxieties were particularly galvanized by the perceived eagerness of other Arab states – especially the smaller but wealthy Gulf States – to "do business" with Israel without necessarily waiting for a resolution of all outstanding issues in the Arab–Israeli sphere. Indeed, Israelis noted that some of the states of the Persian Gulf and North Africa had already begun to normalize relations with Israel following the November 1994 signing of the Jordan–Israel Peace Treaty.[86]

Egypt's failure to persuade Israelis to roll back their nuclear program was seen as the second Egyptian motivation to end the multilateral talks. Here Israelis seemed truly incredulous: they expected Egypt to celebrate the multilateral talks as manifesting the Arab world's de-facto acknowledgement that Sadat's dramatic move in November 1977 was the right one and that engaging Israel made much better sense than confronting it. Instead,

Cairo now seemed interested in the multilateral talks only if they would result in "cutting Israel down to its natural size." In no realm was this seen as more relevant than that of nuclear weapons.

Israelis were surprised because they viewed the peace process as asymmetric in the sense that Israel was being asked to relinquish real assets – territories – in exchange for "soft" and reversible promises of peace. Such surrendering of land, they assessed, would require a complete transformation of Israel's national security doctrine, de-emphasizing territorial defense and hence placing a far greater reliance on deterrence. How, Israelis asked, could they be expected to accede to Egypt's demand to sign the NPT, thus relinquishing Israel's nuclear posture – the most important component of their strategic deterrence?

The Palestinian Narrative

The Palestinians were uneasy about the Israeli–Syrian negotiations conducted during this period as well as about the post-Madrid multilateral talks. Indeed, Palestinians regarded a possible Israeli–Syrian deal with apprehension, if not alarm. They saw the negotiations with Syria as an Israeli attempt to shift attention away from the need to resolve the conflict with them. Moreover, they attributed to Israel a specific intent, especially after the signing of the Israel–Jordan Peace Treaty, to leave the Palestinian issue as the last unresolved dimension of the Arab–Israeli conflict. This, the Palestinians feared, would place them under enormous pressures to make concessions that they would not otherwise agree to make.

The post-Madrid multilateral talks were viewed by the Palestinians as a form of normalization granted by the Arab states to Israel before the latter proved its willingness to meet the basic aspirations of the Palestinian people – a down-payment made before it was clear that a deal could be finalized. The Palestinians saw themselves as the party in greatest need of normalization with Israel, and they opposed the idea that Arab states, for whom normalization with Israel was far less important, should provide Israel with such a sweetener at Madrid and in the subsequent multilateral talks before it became clear that Israel deserved to be rewarded. Thus, though for entirely different reasons, the Palestinians found themselves echoing Egypt's criticism of other Arab states as "rushing to normalize" relations with Israel.

The aforementioned concerns notwithstanding, the Palestinians held a nuanced view of the multilateral talks. While they would have liked these talks to move in tandem with the bilateral negotiations and not ahead of them, Palestinians were interested in using the multilaterals to advance their regional interests, especially in the realm of refugee resettlement. Although they viewed the latter as requiring an agreement with Israel in the framework of permanent status talks, they appreciated that a regional discussion of this issue might help expedite its resolution. Similarly, they viewed the multilateral talks focusing on water and natural resources as providing an opportunity to mobilize broader Arab support for their claims.

Arab Narratives

Different Arab states had developed diverse, competing and often conflicting narratives about this phase of the Arab–Israeli conflict. Particularly divergent were Egypt's views regarding the multilateral track of the Madrid process and those of Jordan, Saudi Arabia, and some of the smaller Gulf States regarding the same developments.

Egypt

From Egypt's perspective, the decade of the 1990s held great opportunities for integrating Israel peacefully into the Middle East. Not only was Israel engaged in bilateral direct negotiations with all its neighboring former foes, it was also involved in a process of regional development through the post-Madrid multilateral talks, the Barcelona Process, and the MENA Economic Summits.[87] In Egypt's view, its bilateral relations with Israel turned from cold to warm after the Madrid Conference – a change manifested in many different realms: trade, investment, tourism, agricultural cooperation, air flights between the two countries, and individual visits.

Egyptians further pointed out that at one point during this period – in 1996 – Israel was Egypt's second largest trading partner in the Middle East (after Saudi Arabia). Similarly, Israeli tourists were ranked fourth in the number of tourists to Egypt and more Egyptians traveled to Israel for reasons other than work or pilgrimage than to any other country in the region. In addition to Cairo being chosen at the 1995 MENA Economic Summit in Amman to house the Bank for Economic Cooperation and Development, in 1996 Egypt proudly hosted the third MENA Economic Summit and participated positively in all the multilateral negotiations.

Egyptians emphasized that in the framework of the Arms Control and Regional Security (ACRS) talks, their government had accepted the Israeli position that confidence-building measures and the control of conventional weapons in the region should be discussed before the nuclear issue. Egyptians argued that they showed even greater flexibility in accepting that nuclear weapons should not be singled out and that, instead, a comprehensive approach that would tackle all weapons of mass destruction – nuclear, chemical, and biological – should be adopted. As the NPT Review Conference was approaching in 1995, Egypt could not ignore the opportunity to raise the issue of the Israeli nuclear capability at the conference. This capability was seen in Cairo not as a deterrent weapon but rather as an instrument of coercion, allowing Israel to maintain its occupation of Arab territories, which were taken by Israeli brute force. Cairo also argued that in light of Israeli superiority in conventional weapons, it had no need for nuclear weapons.

Egypt's perspective was that its sense of uneasiness and discomfort regarding Israel's behavior had developed only gradually. In Egyptian eyes, instead of using the opportunity of the changed mindset of the Arab world, Israel proved to be a slow and reluctant partner to the process. To Cairo, Israel did not seem to be in any hurry to conclude the peace that it said it longed for. Thus, the question that Golda Meir posed to Anwar Sadat during his historic visit to Jerusalem – "why did it take you so long?" – seemed applicable to Israel in the post-Madrid and post-Oslo period.

Moreover, in Egyptian eyes, the attitude of a number of the region's states was not conducive to improved Egyptian–Israeli ties. As these states seemed to be willing to improve relations with Israel unconditionally, Egypt felt not only that its relative importance was diminishing but also that Israel was attaching less importance to its relations with Egypt. Indeed, Egypt heard with alarm voices in Israel as well as the United States to the effect that its role in the region was declining. Similarly, it felt threatened by calls for the formation of a "golden triangle" – Israel, Jordan and Palestine – which were interpreted in Cairo as intended to establish a new regional alliance at Egypt's doorstep.

During the first half of the 1990s, Egypt's alarm was further raised by calls for regional economic cooperation – suggestions which, to Egyptian ears, sounded like preparing the ground for an Israeli regional hegemonic role. Accordingly, the call of then Israeli foreign minister Shimon Peres at the October 30–November 1, 1994 Casablanca Conference for the creation of a Middle East Security Regime was viewed by Cairo not only as premature, given the realities of the region and the state of the peace process, but also as an indication of an Israeli ambition to achieve regional dominance. Finally, Israel's refusal throughout the ACRS multilateral talks to place the subject of its nuclear weapons on the table only confirmed Egyptian beliefs that Israel wanted peace only on its own terms, and that it sought to achieve such peace from a position of regional hegemony.

Thus, Egyptians, who viewed themselves as having inaugurated the Arab–Israeli peace process a decade and a half earlier, now saw Israeli policy as aimed at manipulating the process in order to solidify its dominance in the region. This was true for Egypt's perception of Israel's bilateral negotiations with Jordan, Syria, and the Palestinians, and it was even more the case with regard to its perception of Israel's involvement in the multilateral talks. While Israel was seen as refusing to make serious concessions in the various bilateral negotiations, it was viewed as continuing to construct settlements in the occupied territories, thus undermining the peace process. Accordingly, Egypt's media accused Israel during this period of attempting to establish economic hegemony in the region, thus "achieving economically what it failed to achieve militarily."

In other multilateral negotiations – and especially in the talks focusing on economic development – Israel was seen as basing its approach on a call to add "Gulf Money to Egyptian Labor to the Israeli Mind" – in the words attributed to then Foreign Minister Peres. This theory was not only insulting to Egyptians, it was seen as reflecting a mistaken perception that money, labor, and minds were not available to all the parties concerned.

Moreover, in Egypt's eyes, Israel was attempting to gain its integration in the Middle East without accepting the regional norms and "rules of the game." This was particularly the case with regard to Israel's nuclear arsenal. Having accepted the Israeli demand that confidence-building measures and conventional weapons should be discussed first, Egypt nevertheless regarded nuclear weapons as the deadliest threat and hence as requiring urgent attention. It viewed Israel's refusal to discuss its nuclear arsenal as an attempt to gain exemption from regional and international non-proliferation norms. In Egypt's eyes, while Arab states were expected to enter a multilateral process of security- and confidence-building with Israel and to sign on to the indefinite extension of the NPT, Israel was asking to be exempted from the stipulations of these international instruments. Granting such an exception, Egyptians believed, would mean acceptance of Israel's right to enjoy all the fruits of peace and integration with its neighbors while maintaining its nuclear monopoly.

Egypt also saw Israel's refusal to negotiate away its nuclear advantage as duplicitous. Israel had complained that its peace with Egypt had remained "cold," and it worried that other Arab states would also refrain from providing it "real peace." In Egypt's eyes Israeli expectations of "people-to-people peace" were unrealistic, given its insistence on continuing to base its security on nuclear deterrence. Since deterrence was based on the injection of fear, Egyptians asked, how could Israelis expect "that we would love them and fear them at the same time."[88]

Jordan and the Gulf States

Egypt's narrative with regard to the multilateral dimension of the Madrid Process was not shared by all Arab states. Jordan and especially some of the smaller Gulf States suspected that Egypt's approach was driven less by regional concerns and more by calculations of the Egypt–Israel bilateral strategic balance. In their view, it was Egypt's worry about the bilateral implications of Israel's nuclear monopoly that informed its approach – not concern about the impact of Israeli policy on regional norms. What these states took most exception to was not Egypt's worries about Israel's nuclear arsenal, but rather its willingness to hold the entire multilateral track hostage to the resolution of this issue.

Jordan and the smaller Gulf States saw themselves as potentially benefitting from normalized relations with Israel as well as from the effort to address an array of regional problems in the framework of the multilateral talks. For them, the nuclear issue was important but not all that important – they did not see Israel's nuclear monopoly as affecting them in any meaningful way. Therefore, they could not understand why the ability to address more urgent regional issues should be made contingent on first resolving the nuclear stalemate.

Syria

The Syrian approach to the multilateral track differed sharply from that of Jordan and the smaller Gulf States and was similar to that of the Palestinians: in Assad's view, bilateral negotiations should have received priority, and the efforts to address regional issues should have taken place only after a breakthrough in the bilateral talks. In Syrian eyes, the multilaterals provided Israel with an opportunity to gain normalization without first paying the price entailed in a resolution of its bilateral disputes. But in contrast to the Palestinians, who had strong reservations about the multilateral discussions while taking part in them, Syria's objections led it to boycott these talks altogether.

Syria's narrative regarding its negotiations with Israel deviated significantly from Israel's story. Its main thrust was that President Hafez Assad made "a strategic choice for peace" – a message he also conveyed specifically to President Clinton when they met in Geneva on January 16, 1994 – and that Israel's conduct in the negotiations prevented such an agreement from being reached.[89]

The Syrians recounted that, beginning with Rabin's "deposit," successive Israeli leaders had committed their country to full withdrawal from the Golan.[90] Indeed, this narrative claimed that by mid-1994 all aspects of Israel's withdrawal were negotiated, allowing the parties to move on to other issues involved, including normalization, security arrangements, and the timetable for implementation.[91] However, the Syrians also claimed that Israeli demands for inequitable and asymmetric security arrangements comprised unacceptable infringements on Syrian sovereignty, thus subtracting from the real meaning of Israel's commitment to full withdrawal.[92]

More broadly, the Syrians argued that Israel's demands in the realm of security arrangements were exaggerated, given Israel's military superiority. Hence, they suspected that hidden behind these demands were some sinister intentions. In the words of Syrian negotiator Walid al-Moualem: "...we kept asking ourselves what was behind this exaggeration?"[93]

Further, Syrians stressed that regardless of Israeli leaders' acceptance of full withdrawal the very same leaders who communicated this commitment all balked at making the deal.[94] In Syrian eyes, this began with Rabin's "deposit"; two weeks after delivering the "deposit" through Warren Christopher, Rabin is said to have abandoned the Syrian track in favor of concluding a deal with the Palestinians in Oslo.[95] The Syrian narrative was that Israel then diverted its attention to negotiating a peace agreement with Jordan and stalled the Syrian talks, arguing that it could not move on the Palestinian, Jordanian, and Syrian tracks simultaneously. To the Israeli message that the "circuit was overloaded" and that Israel needed time to "digest" the agreements with the Palestinians and with Jordan before it could consider the Golan, Assad reportedly asked: "What is the problem with Israel's digestion?"[96]

Thus, Syrians saw Israel as giving priority to the Palestinian track and argued that Israel returned to the Syrian track only after it concluded the Oslo-II agreement with the Palestinians in September 1995.[97] The Syrians believed that they had been deceived – that what earlier appeared to be a serious Israeli attempt to reach a deal with them was simply intended to serve as leverage in Israel's negotiations with the Palestinians.

The Syrians also argued that following Rabin's assassination, his successor, Shimon Peres, reiterated Israel's commitment to the "deposit." However, they saw this commitment as having been negated by Peres' decision to launch Operation Grapes of Wrath.[98]

Syrians also argued that while they were not insensitive or incurious about the intricacies of Israeli domestic politics, marketing a deal to the Israeli public was not their responsibility.[99] Hence, it was not their role to help their Israeli counterparts sell an agreement by engaging in public diplomacy directly with the Israeli people. Similarly, they rejected the suggestions made by Peres that he and Assad meet to resolve the conflict. The Syrian position was that such a meeting would be premature if it were not preceded by considerable preparatory work to narrow the differences in the two parties' positions.[100]

Even more pointed was the Syrians' response to Israeli uncertainty with regard to the type or "content" of the peace being offered. The Syrian narrative about "normalization" was twofold: first, that, since the Golan was sovereign Syrian territory, Israel was obligated to return it unconditionally. Precisely what form the ensuing Syrian–Israeli peace would take following such withdrawal was to be a result of decisions that the Syrian government would be fully sovereign to take regardless of Israel's withdrawal.[101] Second, Syrians rejected the notion that normalization could be implemented overnight. Thus Moualem argued:

> Israel believed that you can push a button to make peace warm, to direct Syrian popular attitudes from a state of war to a state of peace. This is not logical, especially that you cannot find a household in Syria that has not lost someone on the battlefield.... An agreement, which is signed by the leadership, tells what is required from our side, but we cannot be obliged to make the peace warm.[102]

Third, Syrians regarded the term "normalization" that Israelis used to describe the peace they were seeking as a misnomer. Israel's analogy as to the content of the desired peaceful relations was the post-Second World War relations between Germany and France. Syrians, however, pointed out repeatedly that what is considered "normal" in Europe is far from normal in the Middle East, where inter-state relations are tightly controlled. This was especially the case with their own country, whose relations with its neighbors at the time these negotiations took place ranged from cool to hostile. Syria, they pointed out, never had European-type relations with Turkey, Jordan or Iraq. Why, they asked, would they be obligated to develop closer ties with Israel than with their Arab or Muslim neighbors?[103]

Indeed, it was during this period that the Assad regime viewed with suspicion, if not apprehension, the close relations that Israel had developed with some of Syria's neighbors: Jordan and Turkey. Given the history of tense relations between Syria and Turkey, it was only natural that Damascus would view such growing ties with alarm.[104]

As noted earlier, an important aspect of Syria's narrative of the negotiations with Israel concerned the security dimension of these talks. While willing to discuss Israel's security concerns and alternative ways of addressing them, Syria's approach was that these should be addressed without infringing on Syria's sovereignty; that Israel's security requirements could not become an excuse for continued occupation of parts of the Golan; and, even more broadly, that the security arrangements to be implemented should not allow Israel a strategic advantage that would serve its ascribed ambition to establish "long-term dominance" and become "a regional hegemon" in the Middle East.[105]

Second, Syria is said to have acknowledged Israel's concerns that Syria's permanently mobilized standing force – which provided it an option of starting a war without mobilizing reserves – exposed Israel to the danger of surprise attack. However, Syria's narrative was that it could not address this issue by transforming many of its regular army units to reserve units as Israel was demanding. Syrians argued that with communication and mobilization systems far less modern and efficient than Israel's, it would not be able to mobilize its reserves at a speed to match the IDF. For this reason, Syrians argued, if both countries adopted the same reserves-based military force-structure, Israel would enjoy a clear advantage.

Likewise, Syrians argued that Israel's fears of surprise attack could not be addressed by asking them to reposition their forces deep inside the country. They pointed out that the proximity of Damascus to the Golan meant that such suggested redeployment would leave their capital unprotected.[106] More broadly, Syria regarded as unacceptable, if not insulting, that its ability to deploy its forces on parts of its sovereign territory would be limited by some treaty obligation.[107]

Syrians were also adamant that there was no justification for asking them to accept limitations that Israel would not apply in equal measure. Hence, they argued that any limitations on force deployments must be applied not only reciprocally but also symmetrically – that is, to the same depth as Syria was required. Syrians stressed that Israel's refusal to accept this principle – instead demanding "preferential treatment" – made it impossible to reach an agreement.

The Syrian narrative was that considerable progress was made in their negotiations with Israel during the premiership of Shimon Peres, especially at Wye River in 1996. They faulted

Peres, however, for the failure of the efforts on three counts: first, because they saw him as in a hurry to achieve quickly what his predecessor failed to build over time; thus, the Syrians were not persuaded that one could "fly high and fast" in the peacemaking realm as Peres preferred. Second, they interpreted Peres' ambition to build peace through a web of economic interactions – thus establishing "A New Middle East" – as an attempt to establish economic dominance in the region. Thus Assad suspected that "the true aim of Peres' 'Middle Easternism' was to eliminate the concept of Arabism, and by extension the Arabs... our inner feeling of being a nation, and our national and social identity." Finally, the Syrians saw Peres as having derailed the negotiations by first calling for early elections and then launching Operation Grapes of Wrath in Lebanon.[108]

Similarly, the Syrian narrative placed the blame for the failure of the talks at Shepherdstown entirely in the hands of Prime Minister Barak. The Syrians emphasized that Assad had made a strategic decision to make peace with Israel and that the differences with regard to all the main issues dividing the parties were narrowed significantly in the preparatory talks before and during the meeting at Blair House on December 15, 1999. The Syrians also stressed that, based on this narrowing of the differences, it was agreed that the details of the general understandings reached would be worked out at Shepherdstown and that this would be done by experts who would address all four baskets *simultaneously*: border demarcation, water, normalization of relations and security arrangements. In the Syrians' view, Barak had reneged on this understanding by preventing any serious discussion of two of these issues: water and border demarcation, thus condemning the talks to complete failure.

Analysis

The analytical section of this chapter seeks to address two questions: Why did Israel and Syria fail to bring the different rounds of negotiations to a successful conclusion? and, Why did the post-Madrid multilateral talks collapse?

The Failure of Israeli–Syrian Negotiations

The International System

In the aftermath of the 1991 Gulf War, important dimensions of the *global-systemic level* seem to have provided a strong incentive for Syria to engage in peace negotiations with Israel. Yet other aspects of the same environment set even greater limits on what could be achieved in these talks. Having lost their Soviet superpower protector, and lacking sufficient military resources, Syria must have feared that it would not be able to defend itself against an Israeli military threat.[109] Under those circumstances, earning positive marks in the United States may have been viewed as the only possible "insurance policy" against such a threat. Syria began to earn such points in early 1991 by joining the American-led coalition against Iraq.[110] Responding positively to Secretary of State James Baker's invitation to attend the Madrid Conference and to participate in the resulting process was a natural extension of Syria's earlier strategic choice and its reading of the global and regional distribution of power.

Yet, lacking a history of supporting Syria, the United States now found itself with very limited influence and leverage over Syrian policy. The assets that the United States now had, while sufficient to lure Syria into taking part in the talks, were not enough to help extract from Assad the concessions required for making an Israeli–Syrian deal possible.

Moreover, the troubled history of American–Syrian relations made Syrians continuously nervous about the American role in Israeli–Syrian negotiations. Their view of the United States as closely tied to Israel made Syrian leaders permanently suspicious about Washington's true intentions. Thus, for example, in 1996, they viewed the United States as having permitted Israel to launch Operation Grapes of Wrath – thus derailing the negotiations with Syria. For Syrian leaders it was inconceivable that Israel could launch such an undertaking at that sensitive moment without a green light from Washington.[111]

Neither was the distribution of power in the international arena and in the Middle East conducive to extracting from Israel the concessions it needed to make for an agreement with Syria to be reached. With its superpower protector and mentor now finding itself unchallenged, and with the Arab world displaying unprecedented disunity and fragmentation, Israel apparently felt that it was relatively immune to consequences flowing from a failure of the talks.

Another impediment to Israel reaching a deal with the Syrians concerned limitations on American influence imposed by some domestic forces in the United States. While both the Bush and Clinton administrations would have liked to have brokered an Israeli–Syrian deal, there was considerable opposition to such a deal from some members of the United States Congress, resulting, at least in part, from an effective campaign waged by right-wing political organizations. The focus of the campaign was the anticipated costs and risks associated with such a deal to American servicemen and taxpayers. A specific target was the possibility that the United States would be asked to station troops in the Golan and to man early-warning and other facilities there, following Israel's withdrawal. A scare campaign replete with horror stories was waged to convince elected officials that such presence would place American servicemen and servicewomen in harms' way.[112]

This American domestic factor could not but affect Syria's calculus. Notwithstanding its interest in a deal, Washington could not provide the Israeli and Syrian governments with side-payments and other incentives without the approval of the United States Congress. But such approval was uncertain at best, given the magnitude of the pressures against an agreement with Syria to which members of congress were now increasingly subjected.

Regional Realities

The *regional-systemic level* also provided both incentives and constraints to a possible Syrian–Israeli deal. On the one hand, Israeli assessments that a deal with Syria would open the door to improved relations with other Arab countries – particularly in the Gulf and the Maghreb – motivated Israeli leaders to explore seriously the prospects of reaching such an agreement. In addition, by the time negotiations with Syria began, Israel had been occupying parts of southern Lebanon for over 11 years. An agreement with Syria was seen as allowing Israel to withdraw from Lebanon in an orderly, negotiated framework, which would include a Lebanese commitment to prevent Hezbollah from attacking Israel following the withdrawal.

On the other hand, other opportunities that the region provided – concluding a deal with the PLO in Oslo in September 1993 and negotiating a peace treaty with Jordan concluded in November 1994 – kept distracting Israel from reaching a deal with Damascus and gave Syrian leaders the impression that achieving peace with them was not an Israeli priority.[113]

Domestic Factors

At the *unit level*, an array of different considerations encouraged both Syria and Israel to seek a peace agreement. On the Syrian side, President Assad appeared to wish to close the file on the Golan before succession took place: to make the minimum concessions required to gain the Golan's return to Syrian sovereignty before leaving the scene.

Moreover, while economic considerations did not appear to be a deciding factor for Syria in the short run,

> in the long run both regime and bourgeoisie realize that with the collapse of the socialist bloc, sustained economic prosperity requires further incorporation into the world capitalist economy. This depends on a peace settlement, since a "no-war-no-peace" situation, isolating Syria from an Arab world at peace with Israel, does not provide a favorable investment climate.[114]

Israeli leaders were equally motivated to reach an agreement with Syria. By comparison to the Palestinian issue, a resolution of the conflict with Syria seemed simpler by far. Absent the emotional, historical, and religious dimensions of the Israeli–Palestinian conflict, the potential grand bargain with Syria seemed quite simple: territory in exchange for peace and security.

Moreover, while Israelis were distrustful of the Palestinian leaders' intentions and capacity to deliver on any promises of peace, by the early 1990s the Syrian leadership had earned a reputation in Israel for having never violated the 1974 Disengagement Agreement. Finally and most importantly, Israeli leaders believed that Syria was the key to achieving comprehensive peace. That is, that leaders ranging from Jordan's King Hussein to those of the smaller Gulf States would not dare to defy Syria by making peace with Israel before Syria's dispute with Israel was resolved. "No war without Egypt and no peace without Syria" became a central tenet of many Israelis' strategic outlook.

Another Israeli consideration was particularly important during Barak's premiership: an agreement with Syria would have allowed Barak to fulfill his promise to withdraw the IDF from Lebanon in the context of an agreement with Syria, and thus in an orderly way, limiting possible damage to Israeli deterrence.

Israeli and Syrian Politics Interact

Yet an array of domestic factors in Syria and Israel made reaching an agreement between the two countries anything but easy. The Syrian government appeared fragile, relying on Ba'ath ideology to gain legitimacy for a regime that rested on an Alawite minority comprising only 11 percent of the country's population. A major component of this ideology concerned Syria's responsibility for the Arab world at large: as a bastion of Arab nationalism, it was extremely difficult for Syria to abandon its "Palestinian brothers" by making a separate deal with Israel.[115]

Even less believable was the possibility that Syria would make peace with Israel under terms inferior, or even merely equal, to those gained by Egypt more than a decade earlier. For this reason, the Syrians seemed to have conducted the negotiations with Israel with an eye constantly focused on the danger that concessions would be interpreted as a willingness to accept infringements of Syria's sovereignty.

In Israel, as well, matters turned out much more complicated than they initially appeared. First, as this period was characterized by a parallel effort to reach an agreement with the Palestinians, it was not clear to Israeli negotiators what would happen if an agreement with the Palestinians were reached and the Israeli public was confronted by two deals almost simultaneously. Since the two agreements were likely to be opposed by somewhat different constituencies, attempting to gain approval for both could unify and solidify these opponents into one large and effective mass protest movement.

Second, Israeli leaders found it difficult, if not impossible, to garner support for an agreement with Syria, particularly with Assad unwilling to engage in public diplomacy. The lengths to which the opposition in Israel would go to derail such an agreement were made apparent when the then Leader of the Opposition, Benjamin Netanyahu, chastised the Rabin government by publicizing the so-called Shtauber Document.[116]

Finally, for Labor leaders Rabin, Peres, and Barak, the affiliation of many among the Israeli settlers of the Golan presented a unique problem. Not only were all settlements in the Golan regarded as completely legal, many among their residents originated from the Labor movement. Thus a deal with the Syrians would have forced these leaders to preside over the evacuation of settlers who were members of their own camp.

These difficulties were also clear to the then head of Israel's delegation to the talks with the Syrians, Ambassador Itamar Rabinovich:

> It is hardly necessary to spell out the difficulties involved in Israeli acceptance of the notion of full withdrawal from the Golan Heights. It is true that... Israel had not disputed Syrian sovereignty over the Golan Heights and that having withdrawn from the Sinai in return for a satisfactory peace agreement Israel could ill afford to deny the application of the same principle to her peacemaking with Syria. And yet any Israeli political leader, Yitzhak Rabin more than many others, would grapple first and foremost with himself before he made the decision: what is the value of a written agreement as against holding on to this dominant terrain? Would Assad and would his successors respect their commitments? And what about the settlements and the settlers? There were by now more than 12,000 Israeli settlers in the Golan Heights. The trauma of dismantling the settlements after nearly thirty years of living in the Golan with a sense of mission would be, if it came to that, unbearable.[117]

Rabin and Barak

At the *individual level*, the personal role of Rabin and Barak as the ultimate deciders in the negotiations with Syria was an important factor in the talks' failure. On the one hand, no one was better endowed with the requisite defense credentials to reach an agreement with Syria than these two individuals. And since, in contrast to the Palestinian sphere, an agreement with Syria was bound to center on security issues, Rabin and Barak, whose defense credentials were impeccable, would have been better able to garner the requisite support to market such a deal, domestically than anyone else.

The downside was that both Rabin and Barak were extremely cautious, suspicious leaders who did not view themselves as capable of leading public opinion toward an Israeli–Syrian deal. Neither would make significant concessions without being certain of what the other side was prepared to provide in return. Thus, for example, Rabin would not address the most significant aspect of the negotiations from Syria's standpoint – the dimensions of Israel's eventual withdrawal – except as a "hypothetical." This caused great consternation in Damascus, since Assad could not understand how restoring Syrian sovereignty over its territory could be considered a "hypothetical."

Equally, both Rabin and Barak seemed to be personally torn as to what priority they should give to reaching a deal with Syria. That is, as to what should be primary: negotiating peace with Syria or attempting to end the conflict with the Palestinians. Both leaders seemed to be attracted by the relative simplicity of reaching an agreement with Syria in comparison with the complexities entailed in resolving the history-filled and religion-laden conflict with the Palestinians. And both seemed to initially hope that an agreement with Syria would pave the way to an agreement with the Palestinians, at the very least by neutralizing the Damascus-based Palestinian rejectionist groups and by depriving Iran its most important ally and a critically important corridor through which it supported the opponents of peace. For these and other reasons Rabin and Barak both adopted a Syria-first approach.

Yet in the end both Rabin and Barak balked at reaching a deal with Syria, unsure that they would be able to overcome domestic opposition. Both attributed greater importance to resolving the conflict with the Palestinians, both felt too weak to garner support for a deal without Assad helping out with public diplomacy aimed at alleviating the Israeli public's concerns, and both feared that an internal battle over a deal with Syria would deplete their political capital, leaving them without sufficient clout to pursue peace with the Palestinians.

Assad

Yet Assad's even greater caution and suspicion elicited equal distrust in Israel. The Syrian leader's apparent unwillingness to specify the various dimensions of the proposed peace, and his insistence that the precise forms of normalization would be decisions that Syria would be sovereign to make after peace was established and Israel's withdrawal completed, was interpreted by Israelis to imply that he had no intention of allowing the two countries' relations to exceed a type of armistice.

Assad's personality played an even greater role in his reluctance to engage in the kind of public diplomacy that might have made it easier for the cautious Rabin and Barak to sell a deal with Syria to the Israeli public. Simply, Assad lacked both the penchant for the kind of dramatic gestures which were almost second nature to Egypt's President Sadat, and the human sensitivity that endeared Jordan's King Hussein to the Israeli public.

Moreover, Assad's diplomacy was curtailed by a number of factors. Belonging to the small Alawite sect in Syrian society, he was highly sensitive to any concession. Also, having criticized Sadat for making concessions to the Israelis that were unnecessary and, indeed, bordered on treason, he could hardly refrain from making sure that at the conclusion of any deal he would look much better than Sadat did and so not be exposed to the same kind of criticism.

The Madrid Multilaterals

The International System

At the *global-systemic level*, many of the successes and failures of post-Gulf War Middle East diplomacy seem to have resulted from the fact that there was a *Pax Americana* – activity that was largely engineered by the United States, the only remaining superpower. This was especially the case with regard to the multilateral talks that followed Madrid. As policy-makers driven by a problem-solving approach, American leaders assumed that post-Second World War European integration could serve as a model for the Middle East. Sharing this disposition were Europeans, who were not only convinced of the validity of their model but also had a direct interest in the successful tackling of Middle East regional problems. Improving conditions in the Middle East, they reasoned, would lessen the pressures of immigration from the region to Europe.

Yet the forces undermining the multilateral negotiations proved more robust. At the *global systemic level*, despite it being "the American moment" the external sponsors of the talks seemed too weak or simply unfocused to overcome the resistance to the process at the regional level. Specifically, the United States, whose moment it was, placed far greater emphasis on the bilateral Arab–Israeli negotiations than on the multilateral tracks. In addition, the disintegration of Yugoslavia and the resulting deteriorating situation in the Balkans took much of America's attention away from the Middle East.

Moreover, from the outset, the multilateral process was plagued by disagreements between its American and European promoters. Specifically, the Europeans resented what in their view was Washington's insistence on reserving for itself the role of pilot for the important issues, while the Europeans were relegated to involvement in issues the resolution of which would require them to write large checks to fund the ambitious projects suggested.

Another impediment at the global level to the multilateral talks was the unfortunate fact that the Nuclear Nonproliferation Treaty (NPT) stipulated that its indefinite extension must be approved in mid-1995, 25 years after its entry into force. This affected Egypt's calculus, since it now saw this deadline as the last opportunity to press Israel into ceding its nuclear monopoly – or at least committing itself to do so in the future – by joining the NPT framework. And since, by coincidence, the NPT's indefinite extension needed to be determined just as the ACRS talks were progressing, Egypt could not refrain from attempting to leverage these discussions as well as the broader multilateral talks in an attempt to extract an Israeli commitment to the NPT.

Regional Factors

At the *regional-systemic level*, there were also a number of factors pushing for the success of the multilateral track. Just when the global-level players had adjusted themselves to the

"American moment," Arab states were struggling to overcome the trauma caused by the Gulf War, which had provoked the sharpest divisions in the Arab world. The multilateral talks provided a framework in which Arab states could reunify.

A second regional consideration favoring the talks was that, given the distribution of power in the Middle East which in the aftermath of Iraq's defeat favored Israel dramatically, forms of regional integration discussed in the multilateral talks could serve to tame Israeli behavior. Thus, by normalizing Israel's presence and integrating it into the region, Arab states could hope to induce it to abide by acceptable norms of behavior.

Ultimately, however, the integrative forces at the regional-systemic level favoring the multilateral discussions were no match for the fragmentation of the Arab world, primarily between those who still viewed matters almost exclusively through a geopolitical prism – seeing the arena in zero-sum terms and focusing on relative rather than absolute gains – and those who were prepared to approach the Middle East in geoeconomic non-zero-sum terms, emphasizing absolute gains and paying less attention to how these gains would be distributed.

Yet within this split, those emphasizing geopolitics seemed to hold the upper hand. In their determination to continue viewing the region in zero-sum terms they were boosted by the failures of the bilateral Arab–Israeli discussions, which injected repeated measures of distrust into the multilateral venues, condemning them to failure.

In turn, the failure of geoeconomics was partly the result of the structures of the region's economies, which were ill-suited to the application of regional integration: most economies in the region were statist, whereas interdependence makes more sense under conditions of free-market economies. Also, most of the larger Arab economies, such as those of Egypt, Iraq and Syria, were during the 1990s "basket cases" – weak and incompatible. This was another reason why it was difficult to see what they could gain from integration under regional frameworks.

Also at the regional-systemic level, Israel and Egypt continued to see themselves as hampered geostrategically by the security dilemma: especially in the nuclear realm, neither could advance its security without making the other insecure.

A final cause of failure at the regional level was the role played by the Pan-Arab and new region-wide media. These outlets were continuously critical of the multilateral talks, as they were universally opposed to any form of normalization with Israel. This had considerable influence on Arab public opinion: decision-makers in Arab states were not insensitive to such opinion.

Domestic Politics

At the *unit level*, the forces rooting for the success of the multilateral track were relatively weak. In Israel, the business community was hoping that the talks on economic development would lead to the opening of new markets. This was mirrored to some extent by business interests in the Persian Gulf who wished to benefit from what Israel had to offer economically and, more important, technologically. Other domestic constituencies in the Gulf saw some connection between supporting the multilateral talks and gaining America's goodwill and thus Washington's backing for post-Gulf War reconstruction. In some corners of the

Maghreb, especially Morocco, support for the multilaterals was motivated by the desire to gain American assistance.

These small islands of support notwithstanding, the most important domestic factor dooming the multilateral process was the absence of any significant domestic constituency in any of the region's states backing the multilateral talks enthusiastically. If anything, significant domestic constituencies in most of these states were strongly opposed to the normalization of relations with Israel that the formation of the envisaged regional frameworks implied. This was particularly true for Islamists such as the Muslim Brothers, especially in Egypt and Jordan, who worried that normalization would result in outsiders influencing Arab societies.

Such domestic opposition was often exacerbated by periodic escalation of tensions in Israeli–Palestinian relations. For example, in 1996, the REDWG talks were paralyzed by the tunnel crisis under Netanyahu's government (discussed in Chapter 9), in which the Israeli government began an archaeological dig in places that the Palestinians and Arabs at large felt undermined Islamic holy sites.[118]

Yet this was also the case in Israel – a long-standing proponent of normalization – where the realization that normalization is a two-way street began to develop. This realization, in turn, raised concern that under conditions of normalization it would be very difficult to control immigration and maintain the demographic composition of the Jewish state. Thus, while seeking Jordanian willingness to engage in various forms of "people-to-people" peace, Israelis feared that Palestinians carrying Jordanian passports would exploit such arrangements to move permanently to Israel. Equally, Israeli farmers feared the competition of high-quality but cheaper Jordanian produce.

A more robust domestic opponent in Israel to meeting Arab – particularly Egyptian – demands and so making the multilateral discussions succeed, was Israel's defense community, particularly its nuclear establishment. Some members of the community saw clearly the ways Israeli security could be enhanced by the web of security and confidence-building measures discussed in the framework of the ACRS talks. However, many powerful members of Israel's defense establishment were reluctant, if not unequivocally opposed, to accepting any limitations – or even promising to apply such limitations in the future – on Israel's nuclear potential. Thus, suggestions by Egypt that Israel should at least be willing to discuss this issue, elicited strong opposition on grounds of a "slippery slope" – the fear that once Israel agreed to participate in such discussions, it would be difficult to prevent the formation of real regional and international pressures on Israel to roll-back its nuclear project. This was particularly true for the Israeli Atomic Energy Agency – the gatekeeper of Israel's strategic deterrent.

Concluding Notes

This chapter is about high hopes and great disappointments. It describes genuine efforts by two Middle East adversaries – Israel and Syria – to settle their disputes. These efforts spanned almost an entire decade: from the 1991 Madrid Conference to the Clinton–Assad summit in April 2000. During this period Syria's Assad negotiated with four Israeli prime ministers:

Rabin, Peres, Netanyahu, and Barak. Regional circumstances changed during this period, and the personalities and domestic constraints of Assad's four Israeli interlocutors were somewhat different, but the result was the same: a failure to bridge the gap between the two parties' differences and to bring their negotiations to a successful conclusion.

If anything, the convening of the post-Madrid multilateral negotiations was even more miraculous. Here were the Arab states, who up to the immediate aftermath of the 1967 debacle rejected Israel altogether, now engaging with it in wide-ranging and detailed talks about rescuing the Middle East from the problems that had been plaguing it for decades. Unfortunately, by 1996 these talks also reached a dead end, when discussions of economic development, refugee resettlement, water and the environment all fell victim to the inability of Egypt and Israel to bridge their differences regarding the nuclear issue in the ACRS talks.

The hopes that the relevant parties attached to both sets of talks seem to be related to an all-encompassing global-systemic factor: this was a unipolar moment, allowing the United States to corral Israel and Syria to the multilateral conference in Madrid and to post-Madrid bilateral talks, as well as to launch, preside over, and orchestrate the most important of the regional multilateral negotiations. Why did these two sets of discussions fail?

On the surface, the Israeli–Syrian talks appeared truly promising. In retrospect, however, it seems that for both parties the costs of the deal seemed higher than the costs of no deal. The Israelis seemed happy enough with the status quo, enjoying quiet on the Golan and believing that the system of mutual deterrence established with Syria following the signing of the 1975 Disengagement Agreement was sufficiently stable. Assad was surely interested in a deal, but not one that, in his view, gave Israel strategic advantages or constituted an infringement of Syrian sovereignty. And while Israelis seemed to believe that their Syrian foes were rational, Syrians seemed to be captive to a rhetoric which had demonized Israel for decades.

Similarly, the multilateral negotiations became a victim to the triumph of traditional geopolitics over geoeconomics. Expectations that the opposite might take place proved illusory: in a highly conflictual and therefore securitized region the major players were unable to subordinate their zero-sum security concerns to the higher goals embodied in the efforts to resolve their region-wide problems.

Finally, by the mid-1990s a number of global- and regional-systemic factors became less favorable to both tracks. As the Serbs, the Croats, and the Bosnians reopened their feuds, the United States became embroiled in the efforts to contain the flames. Similarly, in the Middle East the United States was now unable to help overcome regional constraints that the negotiating interlocutors were facing: Syria could not be brought to ignore the opposition of Iran and Hezbollah to a deal with Israel.

Readings

Caplan, Neil, *The Israel–Palestine Conflict: Contested Histories* (Wiley, 2010) 202–206.

Dowty, Alan, *Israel/Palestine: Global Political Hotspots* (Polity, 2012) 163–176.

Eisenberg, Laura Zittrain and Neil Caplan, *Negotiating Arab–Israeli Peace: Patterns, Problems, Possibilities* (Indiana University Press, 2010) 95–115, 135–164.

Morris, Benny, *Righteous Victims: The History of the Zionist–Arab Conflict, 1881–2001* (Vintage, 2001) 611–651.

Shlaim, Avi, *The Iron Wall: Israel and the Arab World* (W.W. Norton, 2001) 484–546.

Historical Documents

Israel and Palestinian Authority, The Wye River Memorandum: Walter Laqueur and Barry Rubin, *The Israel–Arab Reader: A Documentary History of the Middle East Conflict* (Penguin Books, 2008), 529–534.

Israeli Prime Minister Yitzhak Shamir and Palestinian Delegation Leader Haydar Abd al-Shafi, Speeches at the Madrid Peace Conference: Laqueur and Rubin, *The Israel–Arab Reader*, 388–400.

Syrian President Hafiz al-Asad and U.S. President Bill Clinton Statement on their Meeting: Laqueur and Rubin, *The Israel–Arab Reader*, 440–442.

U.N. Security Council Resolution 242: Laqueur and Rubin, *The Israel–Arab Reader*, 116.

Notes

1. Urit Galili, interview with Yossi Olmert, *Ha'aretz*, August 7 and 28, 1992; cited by Avi Shlaim, *The Iron Wall: Israel and the Arab World since 1948* (New York: W.W. Norton, 1999), 470; and by Helena Cobban, *The Israeli–Syrian Peace Talks: 1991–96 and Beyond* (Washington, DC: US Institute of Peace, 1999), 41.
2. Itamar Rabinovich, *The Brink of Peace: The Israeli–Syrian Negotiations* (Princeton, NJ: Princeton University Press, 1998), 95.
3. Cobban, *The Israeli–Syrian Peace Talks*, 47.
4. *Ibid.*, 82.
5. *Ibid.*, 48. See also Raymond A. Hinnebusch, "Does Syria Want Peace? Syrian Policy in the Syrian–Israeli Peace Negotiations," *Journal of Palestine Studies*, 26, 1 (Autumn 1996), 42–57, 52.
6. Itamar Rabinovich, *The View from Damascus: State, Political Community and Foreign Relations in Twentieth-Century Syria* (London: Vallentine Mitchell, 2008), 255–256; see also Patrick Seale, "The Syria–Israel Negotiations: Who is Telling the Truth?" *Journal of Palestine Studies*, 29, 2 (Winter 2000): 65–77, 66–71. According to Seale the precise message conveyed by Christopher to Assad was: "Prime Minister Rabin has asked me to tell you that Israel is ready for full withdrawal from the Golan provided its requirements on security and normalization are met" (p. 66).
7. *Ibid.* See also Bill Clinton, *My Life* (New York: A. A. Knopf, 2004), 893.
8. Accordingly, at President Assad's later suggestion that both parties deposit their positions with the United States, President Clinton replied that Israel had already "deposited its position with the United States and now it was Syria's turn to do the same." Rabinovich, *The Brink of Peace*, 97.
9. Cobban, *The Israeli–Syrian Peace Talks*, 60; Seale, "The Syria–Israel Negotiations," 67.
10. Seale, "The Syria–Israel Negotiations," 70.
11. Hinnebusch, "Does Syria Want Peace?" 53.
12. Walid al-Moualem, "Fresh Light on the Syrian–Israeli Peace Negotiations. An interview with Walid al-Moualem," *Journal of Palestine Studies*, 26, 2 (Winter 1997), 81–94, 91.
13. Cobban, *The Israeli–Syrian Peace Talks*, 67.
14. Rabinovich, *The Brink of Peace*, 180; Reportedly, the meeting was preceded by the following message conveyed by President Clinton to President Assad through Dennis Ross: "As I told you in

Damascus, and as I assured your Foreign Minister, I have a commitment in my pocket from Prime Minister Rabin for full Israeli withdrawal to the June 4, 1967 line…" Seale, "The Syria–Israel Negotiations," 74.

15. Cobban, *The Israeli–Syrian Peace Talks*, 100–101.
16. *Ibid.*, 103.
17. Rabinovich, *The View from Damascus*, 257–258. See also Cobban, *The Israeli–Syrian Peace Talks*, 109–110. According to the Syrians – as conveyed by Patrick Seale – Christopher told them that Peres told Clinton: "I will stand by the commitment which Rabin put in your pocket." See Cobban, 120; see also Seale, "The Syria–Israel Negotiations," 75.
18. Dennis Ross, *The Missing Peace: The Inside Story of the Fight for Middle East Peace* (New York: Farrar, Straus and Giroux, 2004), 229–230.
19. Cobban, *The Israeli–Syrian Peace Talks*, 111–112.
20. *Ibid.*, 133.
21. Hinnebusch, "Does Syria Want Peace?" 54; Interestingly, this disagreement seems to have persisted despite an earlier agreement reached during the Rabin era, in the framework of the Non-Paper on the Aims and Principles of Security Arrangements, to the effect that "Security arrangements should be equal, mutual, and reciprocal on both sides." See Seale, "The Syria–Israel Negotiations," 73.
22. Walid al-Moualem, "Fresh Light on the Syrian–Israeli Peace Negotiations," 86.
23. Rabinovich, *The Brink of Peace*, 219.
24. Cobban, *The Israeli–Syrian Peace Talks*, 146, 158.
25. Rabinovich, *The Brink of Peace*, 225–229; Cobban, *The Israeli–Syrian Peace Talks*, 145, 147.
26. Rabinovich, *The Brink of Peace*, 229; Cobban, *The Israeli–Syrian Peace Talks*, 153.
27. Cobban, *The Israeli–Syrian Peace Talks*, 165.
28. Rabinovich, *The Brink of Peace*, 232.
29. Simon Murden, "Understanding Israel's Long Conflict in Lebanon: The Search for an Alternative Approach to Security during the Peace Process," *British Journal of Middle Eastern Studies*, 27, 1 (May 2000), 25–47, 36–38. See also Cobban, *The Israeli–Syrian Peace Talks*, 159–165; David Hirst, "South Lebanon: The War That Never Ends?" *Journal of Palestine Studies*, 28, 3 (Spring 1999), 5–18, 8; Tom Masland and Mark Dennis, "Crossfire," *Newsweek*, 127, 18 (April 29, 1996), 20.Text of April Understanding: http://www.mfa.gov.il/MFA/Peace+Process/Guide+to+the+Peace+Process/Israel-Lebanon+Ceasefire+Understanding.htm
30. Don Peretz and Gideon Doron, "Israel's 1996 Elections: A Second Political Earthquake?" *Middle East Journal*, 50, 4 (Autumn 1996), 529–546.
31. Rabinovich, *The View From Damascus*, 327.
32. Martin Indyk, *Innocent Abroad: An Intimate Account of American Peace Diplomacy in the Middle East* (New York: Simon and Schuster, 2009), 250; See also Dore Gold, Shimon Shapira, Richard N. Haass and Martin Indyk, "Defending the Golan Heights," *Foreign Affairs*, March/April, 2009.
33. Rabinovich, *The View From Damascus*, 316; See also Dore Gold *et al.*, "Defending the Golan Heights."
34. Uri Sagie, *The Frozen Hand* (Tel Aviv: Yediot Ahronot Books, 2011), 33, 43 [in Hebrew].
35. *Ibid.*, 37–55.
36. http://clinton6.nara.gov/1999/12/1999-12-15-remarks-by-president-pm-barak-and-foreign-minister-al-shara.html . See also Sagie, *The Frozen Hand*, 69.
37. Ross, *The Missing Peace*, 549.
38. Indyk, *Innocent Abroad*, 271–273, 275.

39. *Ibid.*, 276–277.
40. Abdel Monem Said Aly and Shai Feldman, "Ecopolitics: The Regional Dimension of Palestinian–Israeli Peacemaking," (Cambridge, MA: Belfer Center for Science and International Affairs, Harvard University, 2003), 16–56.
41. Bruce Jentleson, "The Middle East Multilateral Arms Control and Regional Security (ACRS) Talks: Progress, Problems, and Prospects," IGCC Policy Paper 26, http://igcc.ucsd.edu/assets/001/501219.pdf, 4.
42. Shai Feldman, *Nuclear Weapons and Arms Control in the Middle East* (Cambridge, MA: MIT Press, 1996), 7–15.
43. *Ibid.*, 7–15.
44. "Chronology: 16 August–15 November 1992," *Journal of Palestine Studies*, 22, 2 (Winter 1993), 169–186, 182.
45. "Chronology: 16 February–15 May 1993," *Journal of Palestine Studies*, 22, 4 (Summer 1993), 162–179, 177; "Chronology: 16 August–15 November 1993," *Journal of Palestine Studies*, 23, 2 (Winter 1994), 160–179, 177; "Chronology, 16 May–15 August 1994," *Journal of Palestine Studies*, 24, 1 (Autumn 1994), 152–174, 159.
46. Israel Ministry of Foreign Affairs, "Regional Economic Development Working Group," http://www.mfa.gov.il/MFA/Peace%20Process/Guide%20to%20the%20Peace%20Process/Regional%20Economic%20Development%20Working%20Group (accessed September 16, 2011).
47. "Peace Monitor: 16 November 1994–15 February 1995," *Journal of Palestine Studies*, 24, 3 (Spring 1995), 116–121, 118.
48. "Peace Monitor: 16 May–15 August 1995," *Journal of Palestine Studies*, 25, 1 (Autumn 1995), 122–130, 129.
49. *Ibid.*, 127.
50. Etel Solingen, "The Multilateral Arab–Israeli Negotiations: Genesis, Institutionalization, Pause, Future," *Journal of Peace Research*, 37, 2 (2000), 167–187, 174–176.
51. "Peace Monitor: 16 November 1997–15 February 1998," *Journal of Palestine Studies*, 27, 3 (Spring 1998), 123–134, 132.
52. *Ibid.*, 129.
53. Solingen, "The Multilateral Arab–Israeli Negotiations," 176.
54. "Environment Working Group," Israel Ministry of Foreign Affairs, January 28, 1999, http://www.mfa.gov.il/MFA/Peace%20Process/Guide%20to%20the%20Peace%20Process/Environment%20Working%20Group. As part of the same code of conduct, parties also agreed to a number of other steps including: enacting effective environmental legislation, developing environmental risk-management tools and notifying others of region-impacting environmental risks, coordinating and facilitating environmental policy and technology transfer between countries, and resolving all environmental disputes peacefully. See also Solingen, "The Multilateral Arab–Israeli Negotiations," 176–177.
55. Salameh Ahmed Salameh, "Up Close," *Al Ahram* (reported by Gai B'chor, Ha'aretz, January 3, 1996: B2).
56. Rex Brynen, "Much Ado About Nothing? The Refugee Working Group and the Perils of Multilateral Quasi-Negotiation," *International Negotiation*, 2, 2 (November 1997): 279–302, 282–283.
57. Solingen, "The Multilateral Arab–Israeli Negotiations," 181.
58. Refugee Working Group, Israel Ministry of Foreign Affairs, May 1, 2000, http://www.mfa.gov.il/MFA/Peace%20Process/Guide%20to%20the%20Peace%20Process/Refugee%20Working%20Group.

59. "Peace Monitor: 16 November 1997–15 February 1998," *Journal of Palestine Studies*, 27, 3 (Spring 1998), 123–134, 129–130.
60. "Peace Monitor: 16 August 1998–15 November 1998," *Journal of Palestine Studies*, 28, 2 (Winter 1999), 114–127, 122.
61. "Peace Monitor: 16 February–15 May 1999," *Journal of Palestine Studies*, 28, 4 (Summer 1999), 121–134, 128.
62. Michele L. Kjorlien, "Peace Monitor: 16 May–15 August 1999," *Journal of Palestine Studies*, 29, 1 (Autumn 1999), 106–119, 114.
63. Michael Kramer, "The Political Interest Nobody Does Nothing Better Than Shamir," *Time*, September 30, 1991, http://www.time.com/time/magazine/article/0,9171,973944-1,00.html#ixzzorjgkzEpd.
64. Rabinovich, *The Brink of Peace*, 41. For an Israeli narrative of the negotiations with Syria conducted during the Shamir premiership, see Yossi Ben-Aharon, "Negotiating with Syria: A First Hand Account," *MERIA Journal*, 4, 2 (June 2000).
65. Ross, *The Missing Peace*, 100.
66. This understanding seems to have been shared by the American side. Thus, describing these circumstances American negotiator Dennis Ross later wrote:

    > [W]hen the Israeli public believe they have a partner for peace, they want a government that is capable of negotiating peace. By the same token, if the public feels there is no partner, if the public feels security is the paramount issue, if anger and fear are the dominant concerns, the Israelis vote for those who will show the Arabs the consequences of not being a partner—and will vote against those they deem too "soft" toward Israel's neighbors... In 1992, the Israeli public, post-Madrid, believed that there was an opportunity for peace and they wanted a government capable of pursuing it. A Rabin-led government certainly seemed to promise this. Ross, *The Missing Peace*, 84–85.

67. Rabinovich, *The Brink of Peace*, 82.
68. *Ibid*, 81.
69. *Ibid.*, 83.
70. Rabinovich, *The View From Damascus* 257; See also Sagie, *The Frozen Hand*, 44–45.
71. Sagie, *The Frozen Hand*, 46; see also Ross, *The Missing Peace*, p. 100.
72. Rabinovich, *View From Damascus*, 257–258.
73. Rabinovich, *The Brink of Peace*, 200–201.
74. In meetings with Dennis Ross, Peres presented additions to previous Israeli offers. The salient feature of this new offer consisted of: "a definitive solution of the water problem, cessation of terrorism, and public diplomacy." *Ibid.*, 204.
75. *Ibid.*, 208. While, in the absence of a peace treaty with Israel, and given Israel's continued control of the Golan, it was improbable that Assad would follow the lead of Egypt's President Mubarak and Jordan's King Hussein by attending Rabin's funeral, there were other possibilities for Assad to provide some sign of empathy that could have endeared him to the Israeli public. Yet Syria's president refrained from any such gestures.
76. *Ibid.*, 203.
77. Rabinovich, *The Brink of Peace* 232 and 234.
78. *Ibid.*, 220–222.
79. *Ibid*, 215–216.
80. Sagie, *The Frozen Hand*, 70–76.

81. *Ibid.*, 109.
82. *Ibid.*, 63.
83. Indyk, *Innocent Abroad*, 258. According to then United States Ambassador to Israel, Barak wanted to "create the impression at home that he was negotiating Israel's concerns on security and peace before discussing Syria's demand for full withdrawal" (p. 256).
84. Sagie, *The Frozen Hand*, 113–114.
85. *Ibid.*, 124.
86. Rabinovich, *Waging Peace*, 224–226.
87. The Barcelona Process was launched in November 1995 by the ministers of foreign affairs of the then, 15 EU members and 14 Mediterranean partners, as the framework to manage both bilateral and regional relations. It formed the basis of the Euro-Mediterranean Partnership which has expanded and evolved into the Union for the Mediterranean.
88. This narrative was conveyed by Egyptians to their Israeli counterparts in various Track-II meetings held in the 1990s and attended by the authors.
89. Seale, "The Syria–Israel Negotiations," 69.
90. Walid al-Moualem, "Fresh Light on the Syrian–Israeli Peace Negotiations," 81–94, 93.
91. *Ibid.*, 81.
92. *Ibid.*, 87.
93. *Ibid.*, 86.
94. *Ibid.*, 83; see also Patrick Seale and Linda Butler, "Assad's Regional Strategy and the Challenge from Netanyahu," *Journal of Palestine Studies*, 26, 1 (Autumn 1996):, 27–41, 36.
95. Assuming Patrick Seale reflected the Syrian narrative, Assad saw three deficiencies in the manner in which the "deposit" was delivered: it was delivered indirectly, orally, and in secrecy. Further, it was conditional on Syria's meeting Israeli requirements which Assad judged as exaggerated. Seale further argues that the "deposit" was nothing but a ruse; Rabin gave priority to striking a deal with the Palestinians in Oslo and "Rabin's offer was, therefore, tailored to engage Asad just enough to blunt his attack on Oslo..." See Seale, "The Syria–Israel Negotiations," 67–68.
96. Seale, "The Syria–Israel Negotiations," 69.
97. Walid al-Moualem, "Fresh Light on the Syrian–Israeli Peace Negotiations." 85.
98. *Ibid.*, 82.
99. *Ibid.*, 87. In Moualem's words:

    > We always felt that the Israelis wanted Syria to do the work for them. They wanted us to convince their public that peace was in their interests.... [T]hey wanted us to speak in the Israeli media to prepare Israeli public opinion. They wanted us to allow Israelis to visit Syria. We considered such insistence a negative sign: When you do not prepare your own public for peace with your neighbor, this means you do not really have the intention to make peace.

100. *Ibid.*, 81.
101. Thus Syrian negotiator Muwaffak al-Allaf reportedly insisted that Syria was not legally obligated under UN Resolutions 242 or 338 to accept open borders and free trade; those can only be the result, not the precondition of peace. See Hinnebusch, "Does Syria Want Peace?" 51.
102. Walid al-Moualem, "Fresh Light on the Syrian–Israeli Peace Negotiations," 86.
103. *Ibid.*, 86. In Moualem's words: "They wanted open borders, open markets for their goods, and so on....Our economic regulations are not against them; we do not open our markets to any country."

104. *Ibid.*, 88; Rabinovich, *The Brink of Peace*, 223–224.
105. Seale, "The Syria-Israel Negotiations," 71–72.
106. In the words of Syrian negotiator Moualem: "... [Israel] insisted that the demilitarized zone reach just south of Damascus. This means you open the capital to them." Walid al-Moualem, "Fresh Light on the Syrian–Israeli Peace Negotiations," 86.
107. Rabinovich, The Brink of Peace, 220–222; see also Seale, "*The Syria-Israel Negotiations*," 72.
108. Walid al-Moualem, "Fresh Light on the Syrian–Israeli Peace Negotiations." 81, 87; see also Seale, "The Syria–Israel Negotiations," 76; Seal and Butler, "Assad's Regional Strategy," 36.
109. Hinnebusch, "Does Syria Want Peace?" 43, 48; see also Seal and Butler, "Assad's Regional Strategy," 32.
110. Hinnebusch, "Does Syria Want Peace?" 44; see also Seale and Butler, "Assad's Regional Strategy," 33.
111. Seale and Butler, "Assad's Regional Strategy," 29.
112. Douglas Feith, General John Foss, Frank Gaffney, and Admiral Carl Trost, "Mission Impossible: The Case Against Deploying U.S. Forces on the Golan Heights" (Washington, DC: Center for Security Policy, October 12, 1994).See also Thomas Moore and James Phillips, "Beware of Deploying U.S. Peacekeepers on the Golan Heights," The Heritage Foundation, February 1, 1996.
113. Walid al-Moualem, "Fresh Light on the Syrian–Israeli Peace Negotiations," 89; see also Hinnebusch, "Does Syria Want Peace?" 43, 50.
114. Hinnebusch, "Does Syria Want Peace?" 46.
115. *Ibid.*, 47, 49–50.
116. Rabinovich, *The Brink of Peace*, 180–182. See also Cobban, *The Israeli–Syrian Peace Talks*, 88–91.
117. Rabinovich, *The Brink of Peace*, 72–73.
118. Solingen, "The Multilateral Arab–Israeli Negotiations," 176.

9 Oslo's State-building and Peacemaking

This chapter focuses on the unfulfilled promises of the Oslo process: shattered Israeli hopes for peace and security and shattered Palestinian expectations for state-building and an end to occupation. It begins in 1994 with two important Oslo implementation agreements: the May 1994 Gaza and Jericho First Agreement – which led to Israel's withdrawal from most of the Gaza Strip and from the city of Jericho in the West Bank, and to the creation of the Palestinian Authority (PA) in those areas – and the September 1995 Oslo-II Interim Agreement. It ends in 1999 with the launching of the efforts to conclude an Israeli–Palestinian permanent status agreement.

The progress made during this period toward Palestinian state-building and the peaceful resolution of the Israeli–Palestinian conflict was impressive. First, the initial period surveyed in this chapter witnessed a partial end of Israeli military occupation of Palestinian areas, including an Israeli withdrawal from Palestinian cities (with the exception of Arab East Jerusalem and Hebron). Second, the establishment of the PA in 1994 and the process of state-building that gained momentum after the January 1996 Palestinian elections led to the creation of state-like institutions and security services.

Yet this was also a period of considerable disappointment for the Palestinians. The Israeli "end of occupation" had occurred at a far slower pace than the Palestinians had expected in the immediate aftermath of Oslo, with their civil control extending to less than 50 percent of the land they had expected to receive during the interim period and with security jurisdiction extending to less than a quarter. Even more worrisome from the Palestinians' standpoint was that Israeli settlement activity had continued in the West Bank and Gaza throughout this period. Neither were they happy with the pace and manner with which their own leaders – especially those who had now returned to Gaza and the West Bank from many years of exile – were pursuing the task of state-building in these territories.

For Israelis, this period is noted for the impressive gains their country made, both economically and diplomatically, which were partly, but not entirely, the outcome of the Oslo breakthrough. Diplomatically, Israel made a huge leap forward, with dozens of countries renewing if not forging for the first time diplomatic relations. Equally, for Israel this was a period of huge economic gains.

But at the same time, this was also a period of great disappointment for Israelis as they paid the price of continued Palestinian violence and terrorism. In turn, this continued violence contributed to the success of Likud – opponents of the Oslo process – in the 1996 elections.

Thus, the entire logic of the Oslo process was undermined. The basic premise guiding Oslo was that since the gap between the parties regarding the permanent status issues dividing them was too wide, a confidence-building process should be initiated, comprised of gradual Israeli withdrawals and Palestinian institution-building, and that with confidence built over time, the parties would eventually be able to resolve their core issues.

But what was expected to build confidence over time now turned out to have exactly the opposite effect. With Israelis viewing Palestinians as unwilling or unable to end the violence, and the Palestinians viewing Israelis as unwilling or unable to part with the occupation if not the colonization of Palestinian lands, the level of mutual mistrust between the parties increased instead of diminishing.

Main Developments

The main developments in Israeli–Palestinian peacemaking and in Palestinian state-building during this period traced a number of different, sometimes conflicting, trajectories. These included continued Palestinian–Israeli negotiations on the steps needed to implement the Oslo Accords; horrific acts of violence and terrorism aimed at derailing the peace process; major steps taken by Palestinians to build their state; and political change in Israel: the brief premiership of Shimon Peres, the 1996 electoral victory of Benjamin Netanyahu and the resulting Likud-led government, and finally, Ehud Barak's victory in the 1999 elections.

The Negotiation Process

After the signing of the Oslo Declaration of Principles (DOP), the Rabin government and the PLO turned to the difficult task of implementing the new framework. The DOP had laid out a rough skeleton for how to proceed, but was deliberately vague in regards to how to accomplish its goals. Even seemingly straightforward elements such as the stipulation that "the two sides will conclude and sign within two months from the date of entry into force of this Declaration of Principles, an agreement on the withdrawal of Israeli military forces from the Gaza Strip and Jericho area," proved difficult to implement in practice, as specified dates and goals continued to slip.[1]

Negotiations regarding the aforementioned pullout, one of the first tangible changes outlined under the Oslo DOP, began in early October 1993. This took place via two committees, a ministerial-level committee headed by Shimon Peres and Mahmoud Abbas, which was to meet in Cairo every two or three weeks, and a committee of experts, headed by Nabil Sha'ath and Major General Amnon Lipkin-Shahak, which was to meet two or three days each week in the Egyptian resort town of Taba.[2] The talks dragged on for much longer than the two months stipulated under the DOP.

Rabin and Arafat finally met in Cairo on May 4, 1994 to sign the "Agreement on the Gaza Strip and the Jericho Area" under the auspices of Egypt, the United States and Russia.[3] The agreement was the first to formally transfer control of land to the newly created Palestinian National Authority (PNA, better known as the Palestinian Authority (PA)). Following the

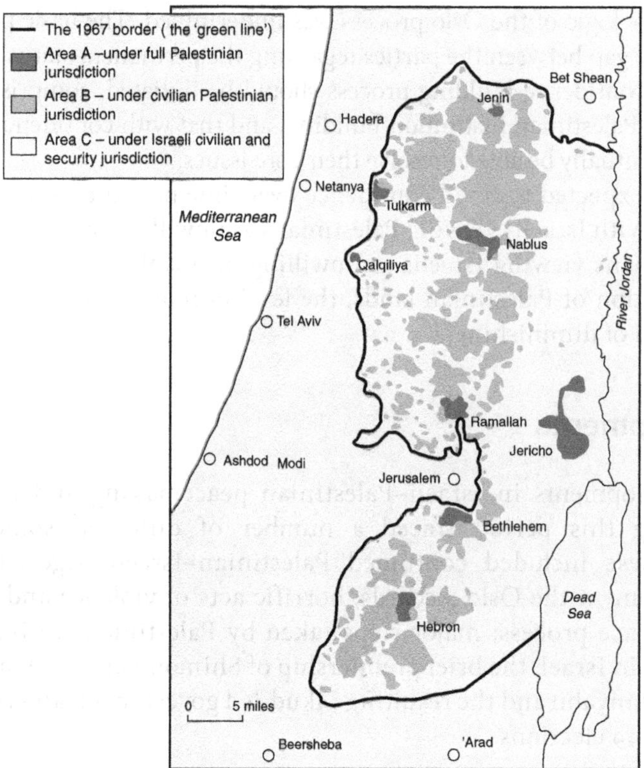

Figure 9.1. The Oslo II Map

signing, Israeli forces withdrew from Jericho on May 13 and from most of the Gaza Strip on May 18–19, leaving the Palestinians in control of the internal affairs of both areas.[4]

On September 28, 1995, another round of negotiations culminated in the signing of the Israeli–Palestinian Interim Agreement on the West Bank and the Gaza Strip, better known as Oslo II. This agreement, negotiated with the key mediation of Egypt's President Hosni Mubarak in Taba, created a new division of the West Bank along differing levels of Palestinian and Israeli control.[5] Regions classified as Area A were transferred from Israel to full Palestinian control, while Area B lands entailed initial Palestinian civilian control coupled with Israeli security control, and area C was territory that remained under almost full Israeli control. The agreement also called for additional territories to be transferred to Palestinian control in "three further redeployments" in the West Bank and it granted Palestinians "safe passage" between the West Bank and the Gaza Strip. Article XXXI of the agreement stipulated that "nothing in this Agreement shall prejudice or preempt the outcome of the negotiations on the permanent status" and that "neither side shall initiate or take any step that will change the status of the West Bank and the Gaza Strip pending the outcome of the permanent status negotiations," commitments that Palestinians interpreted as implying a freezing of

Israeli settlement construction during the interim period. The agreement also stipulated the holding of elections for a head of the Executive Authority and for a Council which would have legislative authority.[6]

By contrast, during Shimon Peres' brief tenure as Israel's prime minister no significant progress was registered in the Palestinian–Israeli negotiations realm. This was largely the result of Peres' decision not to pursue the so-called Beilin–Abu Mazen agreement, but instead focus on Syria. The document, detailing the principles for an Israeli–Palestinian permanent status agreement, was negotiated by two Israeli and two Palestinian non-officials during 1994–95. These private individuals reported to, and were guided by, two senior leaders: Deputy Foreign Minister and later Minister of Planning Yossi Beilin and PLO Secretary General, Mahmoud Abbas.[7]

During Netanyahu's tenure (1996–99), two additional Oslo implementation agreements were negotiated and signed: the Hebron Agreement on the terms of Israel's withdrawal from that city, signed on January 17, 1997, and the Wye River Memorandum, stipulating Israel's withdrawal from 13.1 percent of the West Bank, signed on October 23, 1998.[8] While the Wye agreement did not commit Israel to withdraw immediately from more than a small part of the West Bank – and in the end even that agreement was only partly implemented – it was a very significant development in the Israeli domestic scene. For the first time, a leader of the camp championing Israel's historical right to the entire Land of Israel – from the Sea to the River – now signed off on the transfer of territory located within these boundaries to Palestinian control.

In addition to providing for Israeli territorial withdrawals, the Wye River Memorandum included a number of additional understandings, ranging from preventing and punishing incitement to violence and terrorism to the opening of a Palestinian airport in Gaza. On the economic front, the memorandum also called for an opening of an industrial park on the Gaza–Israel border. Addressing Israeli concerns that the Palestinians were still not fully committed to a final peace process that included a recognition of Israel's right to exist, Arafat agreed to convene a joint meeting of the Palestine National Council, the Palestinian Central Council, and Palestinian heads of ministries, so that the assembled Palestinian leadership could formally nullify the provisions of the Palestinian National Charter that contradicted key elements of the Oslo process. Lastly, the two parties agreed to "immediately" turn to permanent status negotiations in order to achieve a final settlement by May 4, 1999.[9] In mid-November 1998, the Israeli Knesset approved the agreement, and shortly thereafter Israel withdrew from some small areas of the West Bank, primarily in the Jenin area.[10]

As a result of these developments, Palestinian civil and territorial control was extended to about 42 percent of the occupied territories by 1999, of which less than half also came under Palestinian security control. At the same time, there was a major reduction in the frequency of Palestinian violence against Israeli targets. Decades of terrorism and violence were now replaced by cooperation in the security realm: joint patrols, information sharing, and other forms of cooperation, all designed to prevent the opponents of the peace process from derailing its course.

Violence and Terrorism

Parallel to the negotiations process, some of those opposed to the accords on both sides took steps to derail the process. On February 25, 1994, an Israeli settler, Baruch Goldstein, opened fire on Muslim worshipers at a Hebron holy site, killing 29 and injuring dozens before he was bludgeoned to death by survivors of the attack.[11] The massacre was followed by riots in the West Bank and Gaza, leading to the death of some 30 Palestinians, with hundreds of others wounded by IDF fire.[12] In April, Hamas carried out two bus bombings, killing 13 Israelis.[13]

On November 4, 1995, the peace process experienced another major violent setback when Prime Minister Itzhak Rabin was assassinated at the end of a pro-peace rally in Tel Aviv. The role of prime minister was temporarily transferred to Shimon Peres. In February and March of 1996, soon after the beginning of his tenure, Islamist Palestinian opponents of the process launched a wave of suicide bombings inside Israel, killing 62 and wounding scores of Israelis.[14] Peres reacted to Israel's attackers from the north by launching an IDF offensive in South Lebanon on April 11, 1996 – Operation Grapes of Wrath.

Palestinian State-building

On July 1, 1994, accompanied by Egypt's President Mubarak to the Rafah Crossing, Yasser Arafat arrived in Gaza – the first time he had set foot in the territories since the 1967 War. Tens of thousands of Gazans came out to greet him and to hear his speech marking the occasion.[15] The Palestinian leader was followed by much of the PLO bureaucracy and thousands of troops that had been built up over the years of exile. Thus the PLO moved its offices, bureaucracy, and armed forces into Palestinian areas under PA control. As a result, almost 100,000 Palestinians linked to the PLO returned from the Diaspora to live in PA areas. Negotiations continued in the following months as the Palestinians began constructing the elements of a proto-state, as stipulated in the Oslo framework.

On January 20, 1996, Palestinians held their first general elections for President and for the Palestinian Legislative Council (the PLC). The elections were held in accordance with Article III of the Oslo Accords and the subsequent Palestinian Elections Law of 1995.[16] Some 672 candidates – among them some 25 women, of whom five actually won seats – competed in this contest. Three-quarters of the Palestinians living in the West Bank and the Gaza Strip, of whom 43 percent were women, participated in the elections. Arafat was elected President with 88.2 percent of the votes cast, and the 88 seats of the Council were filled by candidates from across the West Bank and Gaza, mostly members of Fatah.[17] Hamas boycotted the vote, arguing that elections were part of the Oslo process, which they considered to be illegitimate.[18]

On November 24, 1998 another symbolic step in state-building took place: the Gaza international airport was finally opened, more than a year after construction had been completed. The opening was important for both economic and symbolic reasons. Though Israel still retained control over security, flight schedules and routes at the new airport, its presence there was less obvious than at other crossing points into the West Bank or Gaza.

The symbolic importance of the airport opening was underscored by President Bill Clinton's visit to Gaza in December. He arrived via helicopter and was greeted with all of the pomp and circumstance of a state visit as he officially opened the airport with a ribbon cutting.

Table 9.1 Major socio-economic indicators in the West Bank and the Gaza Strip 1994–2000[a]

	1994	1995	1996	1997	1998	1999	2000[a]
Population (in millions)	2.3	2.5	2.6	2.8	2.9	3.0	3.2
GDP (US $ million)	3,283	3,587	3,791	4,290	4,821	5,095	4,939
Growth Rate		6%	2%	12%	12%	9%	-5%
Poverty			27%	25%	23%	21%	32%
Unemployment			23%	20%	15%	12%	15%

[a] Negative results in 2000 were mostly due to the eruption of the Second Intifada in the third quarter of that year.

Source: various reports issued by the Palestinian Central Bureau of Statistics, the Palestinian Economic Policy Research Institute, IMF, and the World Bank.

Later that day he attended a joint meeting of the Palestinian National Council and other Palestinian bodies that, as the Wye River Memorandum had stipulated, had formally voted to strike down the provisions of the Palestinian Charter that called for Israel's destruction.[19]

In the economic realm, by October 1993, only two weeks after the signing of the Oslo Accords, donors had pledged $2.4 billion over a period of five years to assist Palestinian socio-economic development. The resulting international financial support, averaging about $0.5 billion per year between 1995 and 2000, helped establish the Palestinian Authority, covering a significant portion of start-up and running costs for both the civil service and the Palestinian police force. It also helped the Palestinians begin a process of independent economic development and the rebuilding of Palestinian infrastructure. Meanwhile, the financial sector was also strengthened and major investors, mostly Palestinians living in the Diaspora, returned to Palestine. The PA was able to initiate trade links to several external markets, and some progress was made in economic growth and poverty reduction.

In some respects the PA's achievements were impressive. International financial support contributed to significant growth, particularly in 1997–99. Poverty declined from 27 percent in 1996 to 21 percent in 1999, and unemployment fell from 23 percent to 12 percent during the same period (see Table 9.1). In 1997, the PLC approved a Basic Law providing for a parliamentary democracy based on rule of law and separation of powers. The executive established ministries and security services, appointed local councils, improved service delivery in areas of health and education, and maintained security and law and order. The judiciary reopened various levels of courts which had been closed during the period of Israeli military control. In January 1996, national legislative and presidential elections were successfully organized.

Yet other aspects of the Palestinians' state-building efforts proved less effective. Primarily, they failed to build effective and democratic governance either at the national or local levels. Indeed, not long after its establishment, the PA showed signs of inefficiency, corruption and authoritarianism. All this began to be exposed in 1997 when an official report issued by the Palestinian General Controller's Office (GCO) found that $326 million, approximately half of the authority's 1997 budget, had been lost through negligence, corruption, and financial mismanagement. Following the issuing of the report, the PLC Monitoring Committee conducted an investigation and in July of that year it reported its findings. The committee confirmed the PA's financial mismanagement and cited many examples of corruption,

Figure 9.2. Israeli Prime Minister Benjamin Netanyahu. © Ricki Rosen/CORBIS SABA

cronyism, nepotism, and monopolies. It recommended that the PA President dissolve the cabinet and form a new one made up of competent technocrats, and that several ministers be brought to trial.

Reports issued in 1999 and 2000 by various PLC committees and local and international NGOs that examined the status of governance and institution building accused the PA of over-concentration of presidential power, rule by decree, selective use of legal codes, and disregard for democratic process. These and other measures weakened the ability of the executive to manage a growing and increasingly complex system of public administration and finance. The reports found the judiciary in a state of disrepair. Public administration was still weak in several areas. These included duplication of functions and redundancy of institutions, competing chains of command, and insufficient delegation of authority. The PA was also found to have a significantly inflated payroll, and its domestic revenues and expenditures were seen as lacking transparency.

The performance of the court system was also seen as weak. There were serious shortages of courts, judges, bailiffs, clerks, and equipment. The decisions of the courts were ignored in most security and political cases. Judges who issued such decisions were sometimes dismissed. Security services resorted to intimidation of judges in order to prevent them examining security cases. The PA executive, without any basis in law, significantly curtailed the jurisdiction of the attorney general's office in order to keep security prisoners in PA jails, and the executive routinely ignored the High Court's decisions dealing with these security detainees.[20]

Israeli Gains

Coinciding with the effects of the end of the Cold War, in Oslo's aftermath Israel became fully integrated in the international community. It forged closer ties with the countries of Eastern Europe and the former Soviet Republics as well as with African countries and the Asian giants – China, Japan and India. It was also during this time that Israel established relations of sorts with the largest Muslim country in the Far East: Indonesia.

Now, the renewed legitimacy it received in world markets coincided with a revolution in Israeli exports led by its high-tech sector and supported by the macro-economic gains of an economic policy that emphasized fiscal restraint, privatization and reduced government intervention. As a result of these measures Israel enjoyed an average growth rate of about 5.5 percent during the 1990s.[21]

The Return of Israel's Right

The Peres-led Labor Party lost the May 1996 elections and was replaced by the Likud. Benjamin Netanyahu, the new prime minister, campaigned vigorously against the Oslo Accords and vowed not to deal with PLO Chairman Arafat, whom he considered a terrorist.

The beginning of Netanyahu's tenure was rocky: a decision he took to open an entrance to a tunnel alongside the walls of the Temple Mount (also known as al-Haram al-Sharif) on September 25 led to violent Palestinian protests. To end the riots he reversed his earlier decision and engaged Arafat, first indirectly and then directly. Moreover, having opposed the Oslo process, Israel's new prime minister now formally accepted the obligations undertaken by the previous Israeli governments of Rabin and Peres and committed his own government to operate within the Oslo framework.

In 1992, the year Labor regained control, there were 100,000 settlers in the West Bank and Gaza. By the end of the decade their number had reached 198,000. The Rabin government undertook to establish no new settlements in the West Bank, except in the Jordan Valley and the "greater Jerusalem area."[22] It did, however, expand existing settlements in the framework of what was termed "the natural growth of the settler population." While the Rabin government slowed down the number of new settlements that were created, it was unable to slow the growth of existing settlements.

The return of Likud ensured the further expansion of all settlements. Several settlement outposts were established during this period. (Outposts were distinguished from settlements by the fact that they did not receive official government authorization and in some cases, such as Amona (established in 1997) and Migron (established in 1999), they were built illegally on private Palestinian land.[23])

Despite tangible gains made in Palestinian wellbeing in the territories during this period, the peace negotiations did not proceed further before the strain on Netanyahu's coalition proved to be too much. In December 1998 he dissolved the government and called for new elections. The peace process was now put on the back burner as the campaign season unfolded.

Narratives

The Israeli Narrative

Palestinian Failure to End Violence

The Israeli narrative of this period was that it was plagued by the Palestinian side's violations of the commitments it undertook at Oslo. The Israeli understanding was that the Oslo grand bargain obligated the Palestinians to end the violence in exchange for Israel's commitment to gradually end its control over them and transfer to their control parts of the West Bank and Gaza. Yet Palestinian terror continued during this period.

Israelis placed the responsibility for this failure squarely on the shoulders of Arafat. Israelis observed that instead of establishing a monopoly of force and enforcing an end to hostilities consistent with the PLO's commitment under Oslo, Arafat preferred to avoid a confrontation with the opponents of peace. In making this point, Israelis drew a sharp contrast between

Arafat and the founding father of their state, David Ben Gurion. During what they saw as the parallel phase of Israel's state-building, Ben Gurion decided to disarm militias and establish the state's monopoly of force even at the cost of sinking the *Altalena* – a ship bringing badly needed weapons to *Etzel*, a Zionist armed group – during the first phase of the 1948 War.[24] Israelis argued that a consequence of Arafat's unwillingness to take similar steps was that any number of armed groups or individuals could hijack the peace process by launching terrorist attacks against Israelis, inviting Israeli reprisals.

To those Israelis who opposed the process in the first place, this was no surprise. For them, Arafat was a terrorist before Oslo and remained a terrorist afterwards. A slightly more generous Israeli interpretation saw Arafat as never having made the strategic decision to fully abandon violence. Thus, he was seen as having kept all of his options open while attempting to play a two-level game: continuing to appeal to his domestic constituents as a revolutionary leader while presenting himself to the United States and Israel as having converted from a revolutionary to a state-builder. In this context Israelis paid special attention to gaps between Arafat's statements in English and more generally to foreign audiences, versus the rhetoric he used when addressing Arab publics in Arabic. On the latter occasions, Israelis noted, Arafat never abandoned the language of the revolution, at times invoking the call for continuing Jihad. Palestinian claims that Jihad could take different forms, many non-violent, did not convince the Israelis.

An even more generous Israeli interpretation viewed Arafat as a revolutionary leader who was simply not built for the tedious tasks involved in nation-building. Thus, he was seen as more comfortable with continued conflict, especially if conducted at lower levels of violence which he did not expect to derail the process of Israeli withdrawals. This perception was reinforced by the observation that Arafat had largely refrained from preparing his public for a different relationship with Israel – one characterized by peaceful co-existence rather than violent conflict. This, Israelis pointed out, was reflected in the refusal to revise school textbooks and avoid incitement in television broadcasts.

Israeli Implementation of Oslo

Israelis explained their own failure to meet the Palestinians' expectations regarding withdrawals as a legitimate and perfectly understandable precautionary response to the Palestinians' failure to end the violence. With terrorism continuing, Israelis were wary of relinquishing control of the Palestinian population which inevitably involved the ceding of important intelligence assets – assets that could not be maintained without the IDF's physical presence in the territories.

Moreover, through the middle of this period Israelis became convinced that Palestinians' failure to abide by their commitments to end the violence was the result of a lack of will and not the result of a deficit in capacities. This conclusion was based on the observation that when Arafat finally decided – after the wave of suicide bombings in early 1996 – that the continuation of the violence was undermining his interests and the Palestinians' cause, he moved quickly and effectively against Hamas and Islamic Jihad.

These developments led Israelis to conclude that for the Oslo process to be viable, it must be based on the principle of reciprocity. In the words of Prime Minister Netanyahu: "...you will get something if you give something." And "If they give, they will receive."[25] Moreover, Israelis rejected the notion that settlement construction in the West Bank and Gaza comprised a violation of the Oslo Accords. They repeatedly pointed out that the Accords did not prohibit such activities and that Israeli settlements did not undermine a two-state solution to the conflict. Such a solution, argued Israelis, should not preclude Israelis from remaining in the West Bank and Gaza under Palestinian rule, just as 1.2 million Arabs would continue to reside in Israel.

The Palestinian Narrative

Palestinians blamed Israel for the failure of Oslo as a peacemaking process. They questioned Israel's commitment to end its occupation of Palestinian land and pointed out that its behavior showed that it was seeking to use Oslo to consolidate its occupation and give it a stamp of legitimacy rather than end it. The fact that the Israeli settler community doubled between 1993 and 2000 was viewed by Palestinians as confirming their suspicions: in their view, settlement construction was a violation of Oslo, contradicting Israel's commitment not to take any steps that would prejudice the final outcome of negotiations. Palestinians wondered: if Israel really intended to end its occupation, why did it continue to build in precisely those areas from which it was eventually to withdraw?

Fighting Violence

The Palestinians' failure to bring violence to a complete end was explained as a result of factors that were not entirely under their control. In their view, in the first few years after Oslo this failure resulted primarily from limited capacity and jurisdiction and not from any shortage of will: PA forces needed time and expanded jurisdiction if they were to contain and then reduce violence. Thus, Palestinians pointed out that only when the PA finally took control of West Bank cities at the end of 1995 were they able to take effective measures against those committing the violence.

Indeed, Palestinians rejected the comparison that Israelis made in arguing that Arafat lacked the will to end violence – comparing Arafat's conduct with the behavior of Ben Gurion during what they saw as the parallel phase of Israel's state-building.[26] Palestinians argued that Arafat did not possess the instruments and institutions of statehood that were available to Ben Gurion when he moved to establish a monopoly of force in 1947–48. Without such instruments the limited forces available to Arafat could not be expected to end violence more effectively than had the Israeli security forces when they had been in full control of the Palestinian territories.

Palestinians also argued that to fight violence, the PA needed public legitimacy, but that such legitimacy could not be obtained before and without the January 1996 parliamentary elections. Accordingly, in Palestinian eyes it was not increased motivation that propelled Arafat to move in mid-1996 against Hamas and Islamic Jihad. Rather, it was the greater capacity placed at his disposal by the September 1995 Oslo-II agreement – greater autonomy and greater jurisdiction – as well as the increased legitimacy provided by the elections that made the difference.

But once negotiations stalled and Israel refrained from implementing its core commitments under Oslo, as the Netanyahu government had done, Palestinians saw their ability to deliver security to Israelis as also linked to progress in the peace process. Israeli settlement construction, a freeze in implementing the transfer of control over land, and the failure to make progress in permanent status talks that began in 1996, were all said to have contributed to diminishing Palestinian political will to fight violence.[27]

Palestinian Expectations and Israeli Violations

In Palestinian eyes, Israeli violations of the Olso understandings were indisputable. Israeli withdrawals were seen as having been implemented late and grudgingly – exemplified in the statement made by Israeli Prime Minister Rabin to the effect that "no dates are sacred."[28]

For the Palestinians, the most important dimension of the Oslo grand bargain was Israel's commitment to end its occupation of Palestinian land. In this context, the Palestinians' understanding was that the three withdrawals ("redeployments") that Israel was obligated to conduct under the Oslo framework would result in their assertion of control over 90 percent of the West Bank. Yet reality fell far short of this expectation: only 42 percent of the West bank was eventually transferred to Palestinian control (areas "A" and "B") of which slightly less than half (18 percent) was transferred to full Palestinian control (area "A").[29]

Another important Palestinian expectation regarding the end of occupation was that the Oslo process would result in greater freedom of movement. In their view, however, what had happened was almost the exact opposite: with more checkpoints and roadblocks in the West Bank than when the Oslo process began, Palestinians found their movement facing more restrictions, not fewer. Moreover, Palestinians pointed out that their treatment by Israeli security forces at checkpoints and roadblocks demonstrated that Israelis had not abandoned the mentality of an occupier.

While this was the case with regard to movement within the West Bank and within Gaza, it was seen as even more pronounced with regard to movement between the two areas. In Palestinian eyes none of the promises of "safe passage" or "free passage" between the two parts of their future state had materialized. This was viewed as impacting not only their quality of life but also their prospects of efficient state-building, since the separation between the West Bank and Gaza required that two sets of institutions be built: one for each of these areas.

Finally, Palestinians saw Israel as responsible for the failure to complete the Oslo process within the agreed timeframe: that is, to conclude a final status agreement within five years.[30] In their eyes while "going through the motions" Israel never engaged in these talks seriously. Following Rabin's assassination, Shimon Peres, his successor, was seen as giving far higher priority to reaching an agreement with Syria; and Netanyahu was viewed as lacking any intention to conclude a permanent status agreement and permit the establishment of an independent Palestinian state.

Nearly mirror-imaging Israeli complaints that PLO Chairman Arafat was not confronting Palestinian opponents of peace in a manner that would insure the end of violence against Israelis, Palestinians saw similar Israeli government complacency toward Israeli right wing opponents of the process, especially among the settler community. And just as Israelis viewed the Palestinian failure to act as permitting the process to be derailed by suicide bombings and other forms of violence, Palestinians saw similar Israeli deficits in resolve as having led to Rabin's assassination, with catastrophic consequences for the process.

While Palestinians continued throughout this period to view resistance to occupation as a legitimate tool guaranteed to them by international law, they nonetheless saw themselves as supporting diplomacy and opposing violence, as evidenced by public opinion polls conducted at the time. Palestinians viewed themselves as giving diplomacy a chance. But once they concluded that Israel had no intention of ending occupation, it was natural, they believed, that they would seek alternative means to end occupation, including violence.

State-Building Failure

Palestinians measured success in Israeli–Palestinian peace-building in terms of developments in two processes that were, in their mind, tightly linked: state-to-state peacemaking and intra-state dynamics of state-building. They argued that any meaningful assessment of state-building or peacemaking must take account of the interplay between the two processes. For example, they understood that they needed to deliver security for the Israelis if they were to be allowed to engage in any meaningful process of state-building, such as building a strong, effective and accountable police force. But they emphasized that to be able to deliver security for Israelis, they first needed to have a strong police force – a force that not only had sufficient capacity but also a clear state-building mission, and not merely an Israeli-protection mission. At a time when Israel was unwilling to transfer security jurisdiction to the PA, let alone accept Palestinian statehood, such state building mission was impossible. To deliver security for the Israelis under such conditions, Palestinians argued, would be tantamount to collaboration with the occupiers.

On the issue of state-building, however, two Palestinian narratives evolved during this period, one articulated by Fatah's old guard and the other by its young guard. For the former, there was nothing wrong in the manner in which the PA went about the task of state-building. Thus, the authoritarian tendencies of the system were denied or viewed as dictated by the requirements of the peace process (see below). By contrast, for the young guard, the PA's failure to translate the 1993 Oslo agreement into actual measures to "end occupation" greatly reduced the legitimacy of the PA and the agreement it signed. Members of the nationalist young guard believed that having lost the legitimacy it had acquired from the signing of the peace agreement with Israel in 1993, the old guard leadership of the PLO increasingly relied on force to maintain control, leading to the creation of an authoritarian regime. In their view this resulted in an exclusionist political system that marginalized them and the Islamist forces.

Palestinians blamed Israel directly for many of their state-building failures. From the outset, they felt that Oslo was unfair because it front-loaded benefits for the Israelis (for example, a permanent end to Palestinian violence) while back-loading benefits to Palestinians – postponing the resolution of all the major issues of the conflict, including that of Palestinian independence and statehood. But, meanwhile, Israel continued to build settlements in the occupied Palestinian territories in direct violation of the Interim Agreement. Unable to compel Israel to cease settlement construction, as the weaker party, the PLO saw itself as forced to accept these conditions even if they were unpopular. To confront dissent at home, the PLO elite had no choice but to crack down on those opposed to it if it wanted to remain in power and protect the peace process.[31]

Thus, the Palestinian narrative of this issue is that the Oslo context for Palestinian governance was simply not conducive to success in promoting good governance: the failure of state-building to deliver democracy and clean government served Israel's interest because Israel believed it would be easier to make a deal with an authoritarian leader like Arafat.

Palestinians also held Israel at least partially responsible for the corruption plaguing their own higher ranks – itself a cause of their failure in state-building. In their view, Israel "spoiled" Palestinian leaders by tolerating their corruption and engaging them in practices that resulted in their accumulation of private wealth. Accordingly, Israel was said to have had no interest in promoting honest Palestinian leaders, encouraging democratic practices, and supporting good governance, since it found it easier to deal with Palestinian leaders who, Israelis assessed, "can deliver."

Finally, Palestinians put some blame for state-building failures on the international community. The latter's tendency to focus on what Palestinians regarded as short-term needs, such as security for Israelis, rather than on long-term imperatives, such as the Palestinian desire to enjoy good governance and to see a complete end of occupation, was viewed as resulting from the disparity in power favored and sustained by the United States.

The Arab Narrative

The broader Arab narrative regarding Palestinian–Israeli bilateral relations during this period was similar to that of the Palestinians. Israeli arguments were understood as transparent attempts to justify the continuation of the occupation. The results of the 1996 Israeli elections, returning a right-wing coalition to power, were read in different Arab capitals as exposing Israel's "true face." Arabs saw the fact that these elections followed Operation Grapes of Wrath and the "Qana Massacre" (as described in Chapter 8) as conclusive evidence that there was not much difference between moderates and conservatives in Israeli politics. The Palestinians were not blamed for their failure in state-building as they were still under occupation, suffering the ills characteristic of all developing countries in the decolonization process.

Yet, this perspective was still seen by Arab countries as enabling them to push for further accommodation between the Palestinians and Israelis, and to rescue the peace process when necessary. Indeed, it is in this context that Egypt saw its role as making the Palestinians feel more secure within a power relationship that was definitely in Israel's favor. It was therefore understandable that the Gaza–Jericho Agreement was signed on May 4, 1994 in Cairo and that the interim agreement was signed in September 24, 1995 in Taba, the Egyptian resort adjacent to the Israeli town of Eilat.[32] Similarly, the Egyptian resort town of Sharm el-Sheikh was soon to become the location of a number of summits and meetings aimed at resurrecting a peace process that now experienced one crisis after another. Saudi Arabia and the other GCC countries also prided themselves on providing some help to the newly established Palestinian National Authority. However, such assistance was limited by lingering anger with Arafat, particularly in the Gulf, due to his siding with Saddam Hussein during the 1991 Gulf Crisis and War.

At the same time the Arab states' narrative during this period was that they need *not* get involved in the detailed implementation of Oslo because the Palestinians were now finally representing their own interests and managing their own affairs with a variety of international actors. Thus, Jordan, which was completely surprised by the signing of the Oslo accords, stressed that the PLO, like Egypt in the late 1970s, had now embarked on its own path without consultation with other Arab countries, Jordan included.[33]

However, as the implementation of Oslo and that of the Jordanian–Israeli peace treaty began to take shape, there was also a sense of relief in Amman that the prospects of a Palestinian state in the West Bank and Gaza would finally take the so-called "Jordan is Palestine" or the "Alternative Homeland" – which made Jordan itself a candidate for becoming a Palestinian state – off the table. And, as was the case with Egypt in the aftermath of the Egyptian–Israeli peace treaty, the Oslo implementation process now bred a "Jordan-First" atmosphere in Amman. This was in sharp contrast to previously held pan-Arab notions that considered the Palestinian question as central to all Arab countries.

Paradoxically, these "we are first" attitudes toward the Palestinian issue took hold at the expense of traditional Pan-Arab notions, just as an important unrelated development had exactly the opposite effect: the birth and spread during the second half of the 1990s of pan-Arab media, especially satellite TV stations. For a variety of reasons, Al-Jazeera and other similar but smaller stations now opened their doors to Arab intellectuals of the 1960s vintage who regarded Israel as a mere remnant of the colonial past. The lack of progress in the peace process gave ample opportunities for the opponents of the process to question its premises, its value, and its future. In their eyes the peace process was lopsided, reflecting the imbalance of power between the negotiating parties. As Israel enjoyed a preponderance of power and held almost all the assets, it was viewed and presented in the media as seeking to remain the sole determinant of the talks' outcome and, consequently, as able to claim that any concession it made was "generous."

In the eyes of these opponents of peace, this imbalance was further exacerbated by the key role played by the United States as the pre-eminent facilitator and mediator. The very close ties between the United States and Israel resulted in deep suspicion among many on the Arab side that Washington's conduct was not impartial.[34]

Analysis

There were two dimensions to Oslo: the promise of peace-building and the promise of state-building. Oslo failed to deliver on both, for related but not identical reasons. Nevertheless, as the following analysis illustrates, these two dimensions of Oslo were highly interdependent, with the failure of one negatively affecting the other. The reasons for these failures were many and at every level of analysis.

The International System

The United States' contribution to the failure of Oslo peace-building seemed to flow from its preoccupation during much of this period with other aspects of the Arab–Israeli conflict:

primarily, its efforts to broker a deal with Syria. During both the first and second terms of the Clinton administration, Secretaries of State Warren Christopher and Madeline Albright devoted considerable time and energy to Israeli–Syrian negotiations.[35] In addition, these administrations were busy with other activities in the Middle East, such as the continuous need to monitor and contain Saddam Hussein's Iraq following the first Gulf War.

A second dimension of America's contribution to the failure of Oslo was its reluctance to play a more intrusive and yet also a more dispassionate role by monitoring the parties' compliance with the agreements reached at Oslo and thereafter. Thus, the United States refrained from using its leverage to compel Arafat to comply with his promise to end the "armed struggle." Similarly, it would not utilize its close relations with Israel to press it to stop its violations of the spirit if not the letter of Oslo by adding more settlements and more housing units in existing settlements. This contributed to Israel and the Palestinians both concluding that the Oslo Accords could be violated without penalty.

At least as important was the failure of the United States and of other important members of the international community to support the institution-building dimension of Palestinian state-building. While the United States and other countries funded significant components of PA activities, they did not always focus on providing assistance in the transition to democratic governance and sound economic development. The message from the United States and other members of the donor community was a clear priority for peacemaking over Palestinian state-building and "good governance."

The difficult dilemma confronting the donor community was: how could international assistance promote good governance without weakening the powerful and authoritarian Palestinian elite whose success was essential to peacemaking efforts? Thus, when conflict between these two goals developed, the donor-driven development agenda gave priority to ending violence even if this came at the expense of long-term good governance. Donors' peace-promoting policies often led to the entrenchment of authoritarianism and to the toleration of corruption.

The Regional System

Important states in the region acted as spoilers of the peace process by sponsoring violent groups and movements who were opposed to the Oslo process and made every effort to undermine it. This was particularly true for Syria and Iran, who supported Hezbollah and Islamic Jihad. And, in the era preceding September 11 2001, "private" foundations in Saudi Arabia played such a role as well, especially in aiding Hamas. These groups battled the PLO under Arafat and worked to undermine him and the peace process with which he was now associated and identified, repeatedly stressing that Arafat's negotiations brought no benefit to the Palestinians.[36]

Other states in the region, while not active spoilers, refrained from lending the process meaningful support. Jordan was pivotal in that regard, but it could hardly be expected to support Arafat and the PLO. The latter were viewed by Jordan as having signed a "separate peace" with Israel without any consultation or coordination and without regard to Jordan's interests (and despite the fact that the Palestinians went to the Madrid Conference as part of a Jordanian–Palestinian delegation). Under such circumstances and to hedge their bets, the Jordanians were now happy to allow Hamas to relocate its headquarters to Amman. This at a time when the Islamist group was strongly opposed to the Oslo Accords and sought to derail the peace process altogether through violence and suicide attacks against Israelis. Once Jordan signed its own peace agreement with Israel, the presence of Hamas served another useful purpose – to help pay off Jordanian Islamists so that they would not derail Jordan's agreement with Israel. For the Gulf countries, who never forgave Arafat for siding with Saddam Hussein after Iraq's invasion of Kuwait, helping the PLO in any meaningful way was simply out of the question.

Neither was the regional environment conducive to supporting Palestinian institution-building. Rarely enjoying good governance themselves and always vulnerable to demands for greater freedom and accountability, the region's states did not prioritize the imposition of such norms on Palestinian state-building. Quite the contrary, these states feared that a democratic Palestine would quickly become a model to emulate, leading to demands that the norms of good governance be applied to their own countries.

The Unit Level

On the peace-building front, neither the Israeli nor the Palestinian side seems to have been equipped to deal with the extremists who were determined to undermine the peace process. The Israeli security apparatus – despite its fame as a world-class organization – failed to intercept and apprehend Israeli opponents of the process and abort their designs, from the February 25, 1994 massacre in Hebron conducted by Baruch Goldstein to Yigal Amir's assassination of Prime Minister Rabin.[37] By comparison, the failure of the Palestinian services to deal with opponents of the process is much easier to explain: as security services, these organizations were still in their infancy, they did not have the resources and expertise, and they did not enjoy the backing of an existing fully sovereign state and its institutions.

Another feature of the Israeli domestic setting that contributed to the failure of peacemaking during this period was the inability of successive Israeli governments to end the construction of settlements in the West Bank and Gaza. While Oslo was broadly understood by the Israeli public to be a process intended to end Israel's occupation of these lands, the right wing in Israel was determined to thwart this design. Arguing that the settlements issue had been left for permanent status negotiations, the various post-Oslo Israeli governments avoided confronting the settlers and their supporters. The ability of pro-settler forces to make this point was assisted by the disappointment of many in the center of Israel's political map with Oslo's failure to deliver an end to Palestinian violence. As a result, Israelis' support for the Oslo process dropped to less than 50 percent by early 1995.[38]

In turn, continued Israeli settlement activity only bolstered Palestinians' grave suspicions of the open-ended nature of the Oslo process, a process that was expected to lead to independent statehood but did not *guarantee* that it would, and even less so that it would lead to such statehood under terms that would be acceptable to the Palestinians. Without such guarantees, Fatah, like other factions, believed that Palestinians had to keep all options open for exerting pressure on Israel.[39] This included mobilizing for violence, notwithstanding the PLO's commitment in Oslo to abandon the "armed struggle." Thus the PA refused to change the curriculum in Palestinian schools or to delegitimize Hamas and Islamic Jihad in a manner indicating a strategic decision to abandon violence permanently.

Continued Israeli settlement construction during the Oslo years confused the Palestinians: if Oslo was about ending Israel's occupation, why were new settlements being created under different guises, and why were many new housing units being added to existing ones? With control over these areas being ceded gradually and grudgingly, and Israeli settlement construction continuing, it was difficult to persuade Palestinians that their minimum aspirations to achieve sovereign statehood in the West Bank and Gaza were about to be fulfilled.[40]

Furthermore, in the face of continuous Palestinian violence, and fearing more to come, Israel, having ceded control over some of the large Palestinian metropolitan areas, now took measures outside these towns and cities to restrict Palestinians' access and movement. The result was that what at the national level could have been considered a historical breakthrough now proved to have actually diminished the quality of daily life for the average Palestinian in these territories.

Further, the restrictions had extremely detrimental effects on the Palestinian economy. Four decades of Israeli occupation had isolated Palestine from the rest of the world and made the Palestinian economy dependent on Israel. In fact, Israel had become the Palestinians' sole trading partner, and a large proportion of the Palestinian labor force was employed inside Israel. The territories constituted an Israeli captive market: in simple terms, Palestine was a captive economy. The PA's trade deficit with Israel remained very substantial and increases in foreign aid went mainly to finance this deficit. The PA's budget was dependent on external financial support and even Palestinian customs and taxes were collected on the PA's behalf by Israel. Movement of people and goods, particularly between the West Bank and the Gaza Strip, was restricted, and Israel continued to control Palestinian borders and international crossing points.[41] Indeed, the PA lacked undisputed control over key resources such as land, water, and contiguous territory. It did not have exclusive jurisdiction over the legal and administrative systems that served its population, nor did it have unfettered access to external markets.

The failure to garner internal support for peacemaking was linked to, and motivated, Palestinians' failure to implement good governance and institution-building. The PLO elite sought to confront dissent at home, needing to crack down on those opposed to it if it wanted to protect the peace process and remain in power. The post-Oslo context for Palestinian governance, therefore, was not conducive to success in promoting good governance. The primacy of security in this initial phase of the process further marginalized the embryonic judiciary, as security considerations took precedence over the requirements of institution-building, respect for human rights, and the rule of law.

Another unit-level determinant of the failure of institution-building concerned the nature of Palestinian governance at this early stage of reconstruction. The PA achieved legitimacy once a Palestinian parliament was elected, in January 1996.[42] Seventy-five percent of eligible voters participated in the election, despite opposition groups' call for a boycott. Soon, however, the PA turned into an authoritarian regime and began to lose public confidence. In addition to the reasons outlined above, this turn was a consequence of the requirements of national reconstruction in the early stages of the peace process – requirements which led to a focus on strengthening the capacity of the central government and its security forces. Little attention was given to the impact of such policies on the rational allocation of resources and transition to democracy.

Moreover, the transitional nature of the Oslo process, with its limits on Palestinian independence and emphasis on security for Israelis, constrained Palestinian governance and the PA's ability to perform the normal functions of a sovereign authority. Another internal constraint on Palestinian institution-building and good governance concerned the fact that the agreement with Israel that authorized the creation of the PA and conferred legitimacy upon it was signed by the PLO. The legitimacy conferred on the PLO implied that the PA would be required to govern not only along lines delineated in the peace agreements and existing constitutional and legal bases, but also in ways that would not represent a fundamental departure from PLO norms and practices. The tension between the imperatives of the two sources of legitimacy – the PLO and the peace agreements – remained a source of irritation and discord among Palestinians as they embarked on their process of national reconstruction.

Thus, while the PLO's continued role was essential for the peace process, it led to a PLO–PA duality that impacted negatively on the process of creating effective and viable public institutions. Continued PLO existence provided the Palestinians with a fallback mechanism to maintain their institutional national existence even if the peace process collapsed or failed to reach its desired destination – the establishment of a Palestinian state in the West Bank and the Gaza Strip. But for this fallback to be maintained, the PA and PLO institutions had to both operate in the same territory. This hampered the process of institution-building by fostering rivalries between similar PA and PLO governing bodies with similar mandates.

Even more important, the resulting constitutional and legal ambiguity made it very difficult to define the boundaries between the mandates of the PA and the PLO. This gave rise to problems in major areas of governance, such as accountability, rule of law, and constitutionalism, as non-PA institutions such as the PLO made decisions that had significant impact on Palestinians in the West Bank and Gaza without being subject to political accountability or due process of law.

The open-ended nature of the Oslo framework also affected Palestinian priorities, placing continued emphasis on the national political agenda of ending occupation and the need for economic progress, and paying less attention to public pressure regarding governance issues like democracy and clean government. Thus, the need for a stronger and more consolidated process of institution-building seemed to lack urgency as long as Israeli military occupation still dominated Palestinian life.[43] Grass-root demands for the building of stronger institutions and a swift transition to democracy remained weak and hesitant.

While failure at peacemaking negatively affected institution-building, the reverse causal relationship also took place, with failed institution-building negatively affecting the prospects for peace. Thus, the lack of strong public institutions and a democratic political system weakened the PA's capacity to deliver on the commitments it made – including on the peace-building front – resulting in considerable disillusionment among both Palestinians and Israelis. Low public confidence in the PA's institutions affected its ability to win legitimacy from many Palestinians, particularly those who rejected the Oslo accords and supported

Hamas. The latter was seen as doing a better job than the PA in delivering services to the Palestinian population.

Similarly, many Israelis had developed growing doubts about the success of Oslo as they saw how inept and corrupt the PA had become. The weakness and ineffectiveness of the PA, many Palestinians and Israelis rightly argued, had adversely affected its ability to negotiate with Israel.[44] Israel's confidence in the PA's ability to implement agreements had similarly declined. In turn, and partly in reaction to these deficiencies, the Israelis slowed the implementation of their commitment to redeploy their forces and continued the construction of settlements.

Good governance and strong public institutions were therefore seen as a critical condition for the success of the peace process. Many Palestinians were willing to endorse Oslo not because they saw it as fair or effective in ending Israeli occupation, but because they saw it as promising a democratic state. This group, estimated at roughly 15–20 percent of the population of the West Bank and Gaza, turned against Oslo once it concluded that its own leaders were not committed to insuring that the resulting state would be democratic.[45]

The peace process also created a political system that marginalized Fatah's young guards and the Islamists. The new system relied almost exclusively on PLO's old guard nationalists, who had signed the peace agreement with Israel: the founding fathers of the national movement, who had lived most of their life in the Diaspora. The old guard derived legitimacy from the PLO legacy as well as the Oslo agreement and its outcome. Its power was also based on its control of the financial resources of the PLO and the PA and of the main bodies and institutions of the PLO and the PA, including the bureaucracy and the security services, as well as on the diplomatic recognition accorded it by the international community.

While the old and the young guards shared common views regarding the basic components of the peace process – for example, that it should be based on a two-state solution – they deeply disagreed over issues of governance.[46] As the leaders of the old guard had been socialized in the Diaspora, and thus in the Arab political culture of the 1950s and 1960s that endorsed authoritarianism, they proved to be anything but democrats. Not surprisingly, therefore, when Palestinians were placed in charge of state-building through the Oslo implementation agreements, they followed an authoritarian model rather than adhering to democratic or "good governance" norms. In addition, the secretive nature of the Palestinian armed groups prior to the inception of the peace process did not encourage openness, transparency, or respect for the rule of law.

As a result of this lack of democracy, the young guard nationalists who had led the First Palestinian Intifada felt deprived of the fruits of their victory as they were quietly marginalized by the new, authoritarian political system. They regarded the old guard leaders as seeking not only to exclude them from senior PA positions but also to deliberately weaken civil society organizations and marginalize local government, the two primary homes of the young guard.

The failure to create a more inclusive political system created strong internal polarization among Palestinians, with young guard nationalists and Islamists gradually establishing common ground against the old guard. For most members of the young guard, who had never felt they had a stake in the success of Oslo, the formation of armed militias and violence against

Israelis was supported as a way of embarrassing the old guard. Such actions undermined the short-term stability of the peace process.

The First Intifada intensified Palestinian grass-root and civil society efforts to deal with societal needs in the face of a harsher Israeli military occupation. A large number of NGOs established in the 1980s gave the young guard the means to rely on decentralized and pluralistic networks that sought to encourage self-help and deliver services while encouraging Palestinians to disengage from Israeli military institutions. After the establishment of the PA, these NGOs fought, with limited success, to defend freedom of expression, freedom of association, political pluralism, and decentralization of authority.

Now, however, members of the old guard, empowered by the peace process, sought to undermine the same civil society organizations. Many of these NGOs were incorporated into, or lost their best staff to, the PA. Under the urging of the old guard, international donors who previously supported NGOs now diverted their resources to the PA, forcing many NGOs to scale down their activities or close down.

The failure to integrate Islamists into the political system early in the process, when the PA enjoyed its greatest legitimacy, also prevented supporters of Oslo from forcing Islamists to abandon violence and follow the rules of a democratic political system. Integration, particularly the competition it allows for public support, could have helped to moderate the positions of the Islamists regarding peace with Israel. The twin failure of the nationalists to deliver peace on the one hand and good governance on the other led to the eventual rise of the Islamists.

The decision to exclude Islamists also hampered Palestinian institution-building, and particularly the ability of the PA's institutions to acquire legitimacy. One way that Islamists were excluded was to link the 1996 Palestinian national elections to the peace process and to adopt a majoritarian electoral system, rather than the more widely supported proportional representation. A majority system serves the interests of a party with a majority, or even a mere plurality, of the votes, leaving others with no significant representation. Polls among Palestinians at that time showed a majority support for Fatah, while support for Hamas stood at no more than 20 percent.

While excluding the Islamists was understandable, given their opposition to the Oslo process, they did have the support of almost one-third of Palestinians, and a broad network of social, economic and political organizations and activities. While Islamists rejected the legitimacy of Oslo and never accepted the commitment to cease violence against Israelis, failure to integrate them only confirmed them in their opinion that the process was illegitimate.

For its part, Israel shared the view of many in the international community, including the United States, that priority should be given to peacemaking over good governance. Thus, it contributed to the cultivation of Palestinian bad practices by transferring funds to Arafat's personal bank accounts instead of to the accounts of the emerging Palestinian proto-government ministries. In the same spirit, Israel permitted senior Palestinian government officials to benefit personally from transactions with the emerging Palestinian Authority – by receiving certain percentage of either the volume of the transaction or the revenues involved.

Equally detrimental, Israel permitted some of its former security officials – notably Yossi Ginosar, a former high-ranking official with Shabak, its General Security Service, to carry out business dealings with senior PA security officials who were still in office. This had a particularly corrupting effect, since he simultaneously advised Israeli leaders on negotiating with the Palestinians. Such constant mixing of roles between the private and public domains contradicted every principle of good governance.

Moreover, politically and security-motivated Israeli policies greatly constrained the process of Palestinian institution-building. Such policies as the partial severing of links between the West Bank and Gaza, occasional closures of cities and towns, the denial of access to certain areas in the West Bank, and other restrictions on the movement of Palestinians, had a direct impact on the performance of PA institutions and greatly hampered their efficiency.

The partial cutting of geographic links between the West Bank and Gaza, for instance, led to a monumental waste of resources and lack of coordination. It forced PA institutions to create duplicate offices and hire more staff than needed. Ministries opened main offices in the two areas and faced the daunting task of coordination between them. Likewise, Israeli policy of denying PA access to areas still under full Israeli control ("C" areas), prevented effective implementation of infrastructure and other development projects.

Leaders

At the *individual level*, Arafat's contribution to the failures in state-building and peace-building was in his insistence on keeping all the options open. Despite favoring the option of negotiations as the means to end occupation and build a Palestinian state, Arafat nonetheless continued to believe in the efficacy of violence. He believed that Israel's willingness to implement its commitments under the Oslo agreement was contingent on its belief that if it did not do so, it risked a Palestinian return to violence. In order to insure that the option of return to violence was viable, he kept its infrastructure in place. For this reason he refrained from cracking down on the armed wings of Hamas or Fatah, allowing both to operate, albeit in a low-profile manner. In his view, if Israel reneged on its commitment he needed to fall back on that option. In doing so, however, he raised concerns about his ultimate goals, prompting Israeli leaders to slow down or postpone the implementation of elements of the Oslo agreements.

Arafat's personal characteristics and priorities also contributed to the Palestinian failure in the institution-building dimension of state-building. Arafat rose to power as an authoritarian leader. In earlier years he could be quite unforgiving when sensing competition. He was suspicious almost to the point of paranoia, preferring personal loyalty to institutional responsibility. To fortify his position and gain his lieutenants' loyalty he was willing to tolerate their corruption. This had a devastating effect on the modus operandi of the emerging state.

As president of the PA, Arafat concentrated almost all power in his own hands and excluded those who had significant differences with him. He ruled by decree, a selective use of the legal code and blatant disregard for democratic processes. He did his best to frustrate PLC's attempts to issue a Basic Law and other primary legislation. He then delayed promulgation of important laws passed by the PLC including the Basic Law. He controlled and micromanaged

PA finances and security services, and made all senior civil service, security, and judicial appointments.

On the Israeli side, as explained in Chapter 8, when succeeding Rabin, Shimon Peres made a personal choice of refraining from charging ahead with Palestinian–Israeli peace, instead choosing to concentrate on attempting to reach an agreement with Syria. Throughout this period, it seems that in addition to the systemic- and unit-level factors, some Israeli moves that had a detrimental effect on the process resulted from Peres' perceived need to compensate for his lack of defense credentials enjoyed by Rabin. The killing of Yahia Ayash, a high ranking Hamas militant, on January 5, 1996 led to a wave of suicide bombings. Peres' launching of Operations Grapes of Wrath led Israeli Arab Labor voters to stay home during the 1996 elections, paving the way for Likud's electoral success.

Concluding Notes

The drama associated with the signing of the 1993 Oslo Accords led to sky-high expectations: Palestinians expected that the Israeli occupation would end, even if gradually, that they would be building a state based on a commitment to democratic government, and that economic prosperity would follow. Likewise, Israelis expected that violence and terror would cease. None of this materialized, at least not to an extent that came anywhere close to the parties' expectations. The Palestinians established a National Authority (the PA), began to build proto-state institutions and received massive foreign assistance. However, these institutions were soon plagued by inefficiencies, if not incompetence, and corruption. And by the mid-1990s Israelis experienced the first large-scale Hamas-orchestrated suicide bombings.

What went wrong? Why have Israeli and Palestinian dreams remained unfulfilled? Three basic characteristics of the Oslo process seem to have doomed it to failure: the first was the step-by-step yet open-ended nature of the Oslo process. The process was intended to help the parties build trust and confidence in one another, thus improving the environment for the envisaged negotiations on permanent status. The consequence of this process was the opposite of that intended: a confidence-destruction process. This is because the phasing-out process gave the parties ample time and a strong incentive to cheat in order to improve their bargaining positions in the anticipated permanent status negotiations. The patron of the process, the United States, made such cheating possible by failing to monitor the parties' compliance with the agreements they signed and by not punishing them for their failures to do so.

A second aspect of the Oslo process, Israel's decision that the PLO would be its primary negotiation partner, had its own drawback: the organization came with much baggage which, in turn, caused it to mishandle its state-building mission. Indeed, three deficiencies made it difficult for the PLO to succeed: the first was that its leadership comprised *revolutionaries* – not state-builders – who now returned from the Diaspora. Importantly, many among these "outsiders" had spent many years in exile, mostly in countries governed by authoritarian and corrupt regimes. Lacking experience of democratic government, they predictably mishandled the task of state-building. Second, given this background, it is not surprising that the Israelis were not convinced that the PLO would be able to fulfill their promises. In turn, this caused Israelis to avoid taking what they saw as excessive risks. Third, feeling that they were corralled into signing a bad deal at Oslo, the leaders of the PLO were tempted to cheat to "improve" the terms they had agreed to.

The final factor plaguing the Oslo process was that there was a strong connection - if not tight interdependence - between its peacemaking and state-building facets. While the priority given to security matters - because of their critical importance to the peacemaking mission - caused Israel and the United States to ignore corruption and deficiencies of top Palestinian officials, this ultimately discredited the peace process itself.

Readings

Bickerton, Ian and Carla Klausner, *A History of the Arab-Israeli Conflict* (Prentice Hall, 2010) 266–297.

Caplan, Neil, *The Israel-Palestine Conflict: Contested Histories* (Wiley, 2010) 202–206.

Eisenberg, Laura Zittrain and Neil Caplan, *Negotiating Arab-Israeli Peace: Patterns, Problems, Possibilities* (Indiana University Press, 2010) 165–221.

Lesch, David, *The Arab-Israeli Conflict* (Oxford University Press, 2008) 330–364.

Shlaim, Avi, *The Iron Wall: Israel and the Arab World* (W.W. Norton, 2001) 546–595.

Tessler, Mark, *A History of the Israeli-Palestinian Conflict* (Indiana University Press, 2009) 770–818.

Historical Documents

Israel and Palestinian Authority Interim Agreement on the West Bank and Gaza Strip (Oslo II): Walter Laqueur and Barry Rubin, *The Israel-Arab Reader: A Documentary History of the Middle East Conflict* (Penguin Books, 2008), 502–521.

Israel and Palestinian Authority, The Wye River Memorandum: Laqueur and Rubin, *The Israel-Arab Reader*, 529–534.

U.S. President Bill Clinton Speech to the Palestinian Leadership: Laqueur and Rubin, *The Israel-Arab Reader*, 535–541.

Notes

1. DOP Annex II (Available at http://www.mfa.gov.il/MFA/Peace%20Process/Guide%20to%20the%20Peace%20Process/Declaration%20of%20Principles#annexii)
2. Shlaim, *The Iron Wall*, 523.
3. "The Agreement on the Gaza Strip and the Jericho Area," available at: http://www.mfa.gov.il/MFA/Peace+Process/Guide+to+the+Peace+Process/Agreement+on+Gaza+Strip+and+Jericho+Area.htm
4. Morris, *Righteous Victims*, 624–625; and Shlaim, *The Iron Wall*, 525–527.
5. Lesch, *The Arab-Israeli Conflict: A History*, 335; and CQ Press, *The Middle East*, 11th ed. (Thousand Oaks, CA: CQ Press), 86.

6. Morris, *Righteous Victims*, 627–628; and Shlaim, *The Iron Wall*, 527–528. The full text of Oslo II, or the Interim Agreement, can be found at: http://www.mfa.gov.il/MFA/Peace+Process/Guide+to+the+Peace+Process/THE+ISRAELI-PALESTINIAN+INTERIM+AGREEMENT.htm.
7. See Hussein Agha *et al., Track-II Diplomacy: Lessons from the Middle East*, 71–90.
8. As part of the Hebron Agreement instruments, Netanyahu and Arafat asked Dennis Ross, the United States Special Middle East coordinator, to prepare a "Note for the Record" in which he summarized what had been agreed to at their meeting on January 15, 1997. It noted that, "the two leaders reaffirmed their commitment to implement the Interim Agreement on the basis of reciprocity." The note listed all outstanding Oslo issues to be implemented or negotiated. Full text is in http://www.mfa.gov.il/MFA/Peace%20Process/Guide%20to%20the%20Peace%20Process/Note%20for%20the%20Record
9. Morris, *Righteous Victims*, 647.
10. *Ibid.*, 648.
11. Morris, *Righteous Victims*, 624; Shlaim, *The Iron Wall*, 524.
12. *Ibid.*
13. Israel MFA, "Suicide and Other Bombing Attacks in Israel Since the Declaration of Principles (Sept 1993)," available at http://www.mfa.gov.il/MFA/Terrorism-+Obstacle+to+Peace/Palestinian+terror+since+2000/Suicide+and+Other+Bombing+Attacks+in+Israel+Since.htm
14. *Ibid.*
15. Sosebee, Stephen J., "Yasser Arafat's Return: New Beginning for Palestine," *Washington Report on Middle East Affairs*, September/October 1994; Shlaim, *The Iron Wall*, 527.
16. http://www.elections.ps/admin/pdf/Results_election_1996.pdf
17. *Ibid.*
18. "Palestinians turn out for historic vote," CNN, January 20, 1996 (http://www.cnn.com/WORLD/9601/palestine_elex/)
19. Morris, *Righteous Victims*, 648–649; Shlaim, *The Iron Wall*, 605; Susan Page and Jack Kelley, "'Great Moment' for Peace, Though Distrust Simmers," *USA Today*, December 15, 1998.
20. Examinations of the performance of local councils, international and local organizations concluded that the PA also marginalized local government by central government control over local councils and municipalities, their finances and decision-making. Local councils, all appointed by the PA, were unable to meet local public demands as they not only lacked the capacity to provide the needed services, but also continued to suffer from a centralized system of local government and lack of public legitimacy. See Yezid Sayigh and Khalil Shikaki, *Strengthening Palestinian Public Institutions* (New York: Council on Foreign Relations, 1999); *After the Crisis: Structural Changes in Palestinian Political Life and Work Horizons*, proceedings of the Fourth Annual Conference of the Muwatin Foundation, Ramallah, Palestine, September 22–23, 1998 (Ramallah, Palestine: Muwatin, 1999); Nathan J. Brown, "Requiem for Palestinian Reform: Clear Lessons from a Troubled Record," *Carnegie Papers*, February 2007; Nathan J. Brown, "Evaluating Palestinian Reform" *Carnegie Papers*, June 2005; PLC Special Committee Report (The Corruption Report) May 1997, at http://www.jmcc.org/politics/pna/plc/plccorup.htm .
21. "GDP Growth (annual %) for Israel," http://data.worldbank.org/indicator/NY.GDP.MKTP.KD.ZG/countries/IL?display=graph.
22. In July 1992, the Labor Party platform promised that "new settlements will not be established and existing settlements will not be thickened, except for those in Greater Jerusalem and the Jordan Valley." Rabin objected to what he termed "political settlements" as opposed to "security settlements." He asserted during his election campaign that the purpose of political settlements

"is to block any option of launching a meaningful political process, such as autonomy, and their existence will later limit the range of options for the permanent arrangement." IDF Radio, February 23, 1992 Quoted in Foundation for Middle East Peace, *Report on Israeli Settlement in the Occupied Territories*, 2, 3 (May 1992), 10. For details on settlement expansion during this period, see "Land Grab: Israel's Settlement Policy in the West Bank," *Be'Tselem*, May 2002.

23. See "Summary of the Opinion Concerning Unauthorized Outposts - Talya Sason, Adv. 10 Mar 2005," Israeli Ministry of Foreign Affairs. http://www.mfa.gov.il/MFA/Government/Law/Legal+Issues+and+Rulings/Summary+of+Opinion+Concerning+Unauthorized+Outposts+-+Talya+Sason+Adv.htm. See also, Gideon Alon, "Gov't okays Sasson report, panel set up to implement it," *Haaretz*, March 14, 2005.
24. Morris, *Righteous Victims*, 236–237.
25. http://www.pbs.org/wgbh/pages/frontline/shows/oslo/interviews/netanyahu.html.
26. Avi Shlaim, *Israel and Palestine* (London: Verso, 2009), 207.
27. Shlaim, *The Iron Wall*, 527–530.
28. Clyde Haberman, "Israel Sees New Delays to Palestinian Self-Rule," New York Times, Dec 14, 1993 http://www.nytimes.com/1993/12/14/world/israel-sees-new-delays-to-palestinian-self-rule.html?pagewanted=all&src=pm (accessed December 8, 2011).
29. Morris, *Righteous Victims*, 643.
30. *Ibid.*, 645.
31. *Ibid.*, 625, 628.
32. *Ibid.*, 624; Lesch, *The Arab–Israeli Conflict*, 331–333.
33. Shlaim, *The Iron Wall*, 538.
34. Shlaim, *Israel and Palestine*, 208–209.
35. Morris, *Righteous Victims*, 619.
36. *Ibid.*, 615.
37. *Ibid.*, 634–640.
38. "Peace Index 1995," The Tami Steinmetz Center for Peace Research, Tel Aviv University, http://www.tau.ac.il/peace/.
39. Lesch, *The Arab–Israeli Conflict*, 383.
40. Edward Said cited in Shlaim, *Israel and Palestine*, 351–352.
41. Lesch, *The Arab–Israeli Conflict*, 378–379.
42. Morris, *Righteous Victims*, 636.
43. Shlaim, *The Iron Wall*, 601.
44. *Ibid.*, 601–603.
45. For more details on Palestinian public opinion, see Khalil Shikaki, *Willing to Compromise: Palestinian Public Opinion and the Peace Process* (Washington, DC: United States Institute of Peace, January 2006). See also, Khalil Shikaki, "Peace Now or Hamas Later," *Foreign Affairs* (July–August 1998), and www.pcpsr.org.
46. Morris, *Righteous Victims*, 606.

10 The Failure of Permanent Status Negotiations

This chapter is devoted to the heroic effort made by Israel and the Palestinians during the year 2000 and the first weeks of 2001 to resolve their conflict. It encompasses the secret talks conducted by Israel and the Palestinians in Stockholm during the first half of 2000, the efforts of the Clinton administration to broker an agreement between the two sides in the Camp David Summit of July 2000, the talks at Bolling Air Force Base in December which led to the formulation of the Clinton Parameters, and finally the negotiations held at Taba at the twilight of the Barak government in late January 2001. While by no means ignoring the historical achievements in peacemaking made during this period, this chapter will focus on attempting to explain why the process ultimately failed despite the enormous investment made.

The period surveyed in this chapter cannot be described as anything other than a great opportunity lost. The United States – despite, and maybe at least in part due to, its new status as the only remaining superpower – faced a number of serious challenges in the mid-1990s, from the conflicts in the Balkans to the Asian financial crisis. By late 1999, however, it seemed to be "out of the woods" on most of these fronts, and hence in a position to focus on Middle East peacemaking.

President Clinton was committed to utilizing this "unipolar moment" to advance Israeli–Palestinian accommodation. The result was unprecedented American involvement; the time and energy invested by the President in this effort was nothing short of staggering. In doing so, his administration did not face serious regional opposition. Another important enabler was the Israeli electorate's 1999 decision to replace the Likud-led coalition government headed by Benjamin Netanyahu by a Labor-led government headed by Ehud Barak. Thus, an Israeli leader who appeared to be dragging his feet on peace issues and to be generating tension in American–Israeli relations was now replaced by a leader who seemed committed to breakthroughs.

Hence it is also not surprising that the gains made in Israeli–Palestinian peacemaking during this period were considerable. Beginning with the Camp David talks and culminating with the Clinton Parameters, the gaps between the parties' positions on some of the more important dimensions of the conflict narrowed significantly as long-standing taboos were successively broken: from progress toward the demarcation of a border between Israel and the future Palestinian state to the placing of the hypersensitive issue of Jerusalem on the negotiation table. These were achievements of historic proportions: by serving as points of departure for any future discussions of Palestinian–Israeli permanent status core issues, these breakthroughs were to affect the two parties' discourse for years to come.

Tragically, however, this huge investment of resources was insufficient to produce a peace agreement, let alone one that would announce a historic end to the conflict. While motivated to reach an agreement, neither Barak nor Arafat seemed to possess enough energy to leap over the remaining gaps in their positions. Both were too skeptical about the process, incapable of overcoming their previous contributions to the souring of relations, and unwilling to go all the way and confront the domestic opponents of the talks – Hamas on the Palestinian side; Likud and the settler community on the Israeli side.

Main Developments

This section begins by providing an international, regional and domestic context for the various elements of the permanent status negotiations. It also describes the negotiations leading to the conclusion of the last instrument of the interim agreement: the Sharm el Sheikh Memorandum. Finally, it describes the main components comprising the permanent status negotiations.

The International and Regional Scenes

At the *global level* 1999 was characterized by success in overcoming the financial crises and currency crashes experienced in various markets, notably in Asia, Russia and Mexico. Once again the robust American economy had been the key stabilizer of the international financial system, proving its resilience. Globally, the success in curbing and then reversing the downslide introduced a measure of optimism into world stock markets on the eve of the new millennium. Increasingly, elites in various corners of the earth looked to China and India as the next vehicles of world economic growth and expected globalization to spread democracy and progress.

America's confidence in its capacity to bring about a breakthrough in Arab–Israeli affairs by transforming and translating the "unipolar moment" into peacemaking gains now rested on a track record of recent United States successes in the Balkans. Thus, the Clinton administration's successful brokering of the November 1995 Dayton Accords for the settlement of the Bosnia war seems to have endowed it with optimism that similar success in the Middle East was possible and should now be attempted.[1]

Another dimension of America's unipolar moment was its confidence that it would be able to successfully manage the predictable negative Russian reactions to the eastward expansion of the EU and NATO. More or less at the same time, Russia experienced the end of the Yeltsin era and the ushering-in of a new leader – Vladimir Putin. While the United States and its allies in the West applauded what was widely viewed as Putin's determination to end the corruption that corroded almost every echelon of the Russian governmental system, they viewed with dismay the signs of resurgence of Russian nationalism and Moscow's determination to defy the West's repeated post-Cold War humiliation of Russia.

In the Middle East at large, the period addressed in this chapter was characterized by an odd mix of positive and disquieting developments. In Iran this was a period of some hope as a reformist, Mohammad Khatami, president during the years 1997–2005, was seen as representing the most enlightened Iranian leadership since the 1979 revolution. Many observers regarded Khatami's offer to open a new page in Iran's relations with the West as genuine. Coupled with previous attempts by then president Rafsanjani to rebuild the Iranian economy and his ascribed understanding that this required an opening to the West, this period held the greatest hopes that Iran might yet play a positive role in the region.

In the broader Arab–Israeli arena this was a period of improved Egyptian–Israeli relations, as the two countries attempted to overcome the bitter taste left by their 1995 disagreement over the nuclear issue as well as the Egyptians' distrust of Israel's intentions, fueled by their earlier interactions with Prime Minister Benjamin Netanyahu. At the level of the two societies, 1999–2000 witnessed the most frequent and positive Egyptian–Israeli interactions since the period immediately after the 1979 peace treaty. Cooperation between the two countries in a variety of areas, especially trade and tourism, was resumed. The peak of such cooperation was the commencement of negotiations to supply Israel with Egyptian natural gas. On January 26, 2001, East Mediterranean Gas (EMG), an Egyptian–Israeli consortium, signed a deal worth US$3 billion to supply the Israel Electric Corporation with 56 percent of its gas needs for the following ten years, beating Israeli and Palestinian rival bids.[2]

Another positive aspect of this period was that two of the leaders who had often derailed positive developments in the region were now too busy to engage in such behavior. Libya's leader Muammar Qhaddafi was embroiled in the aftershocks of his government's involvement in the bombing and crashing of a Pan Am airliner over Lockerbie, Scotland. In Syria, President Hafez Assad was ailing and thus preoccupied with issues of succession. The transition from Hafez Assad to his son, Bashar was remarkably smooth, as was the succession in Jordan from King Hussein to his son, Abdullah.

Much more worrisome, however, were the signs of a new nexus of Islamic militancy and violence, exemplified by al-Qaida. This new nexus was first evidenced by the simultaneous bombing of two American embassies in Africa on August 8, 1998 and by the attack on the destroyer USS *Cole* in Yemen on October 12, 2000.

In Israel: The Return of Labor

In Israel, meanwhile, this period was characterized by the election of a Labor-led government headed by Ehud Barak. Barak's victory generated sky-high expectations propelled by three factors: first, broad discontent with the lack of significant progress in the peace process during Netanyahu's tenure and the perception that he mismanaged Israel's critically important relations with the United States; second, Barak's promise that he would end Israel's military presence in Lebanon and negotiate an end to Israel's conflict with the Palestinians; and third, the belief that, as the most decorated soldier in Israel's history, Barak enjoyed the requisite credibility, and the resulting ability to convince skeptical Israelis that their country could safely assume the risks associated with the concessions that would be required for an agreement with Syria and the Palestinians to be reached.[3]

Figure 10.1. Barak, Clinton, and Arafat at Camp David, 2000 (see p. 336). © Cynthia Johnson/Time Life Pictures/Getty Images

That the stakes involved in Barak's electoral victory were enormous was clear to outsiders as well. President Bill Clinton was indirectly involved as some of his political consultants, including James Carville and Stanley Greenberg, were recruited by Barak to advise his election campaign. In different ways moderate Arab states were also involved, as their official and unofficial representatives encouraged Israeli Arab voters to participate in the elections. They were urged not to deprive the Labor Party of victory by staying at home as they had done three years earlier, when they contributed to Shimon Peres' 1996 electoral defeat. In the aftermath of the 1999 election, Egypt signaled its positive expectations by welcoming Barak to Cairo, thus inaugurating a period of intensely positive Egyptian–Israeli interactions, official and unofficial, which lasted until the outbreak of the Second Palestinian Intifada.[4]

Palestinian–Israeli Interactions

On the internal Palestinian scene, the first half of 1999 witnessed discussions of the advantages and disadvantages of a possible unilateral declaration of statehood. Those favoring such a declaration argued that since the interim period defined in the Oslo Accords was to expire on May 4, 1999, serious questions would be raised regarding the implications of the deadline for the continued legitimacy of the PA and its institutions in light of the failure of the Oslo process to "end occupation" and the widespread public discontent with the performance of PA institutions. Thus, unilateral declaration of statehood gained support among the ruling Fatah faction and among the public at large as a way to maintain and reinforce the PA's legitimacy. However, Israeli, and particularly American, warnings about the implications of such a step for the future of the peace process and for continued American assistance dampened the enthusiasm of most Palestinian leaders for such a declaration. Moreover, since the Palestinian threat to make this move was being used by Netanyahu to rally support for his reelection, Arafat feared that it might harm Barak, the Israeli peace camp's candidate in the May 1999 elections. Hoping that Barak would win and that negotiations would consequently resume, Arafat and Fatah opted to refrain from such a declaration and to await the outcome of the Israeli election.

In the realm of Palestinian–Israeli interactions, the Israeli election led, quite surprisingly, to immediate tension. Barak's first demand on the Palestinians was to modify the 1998 Wye River Accord signed by the previous Israeli government. Arguing that it made more sense to

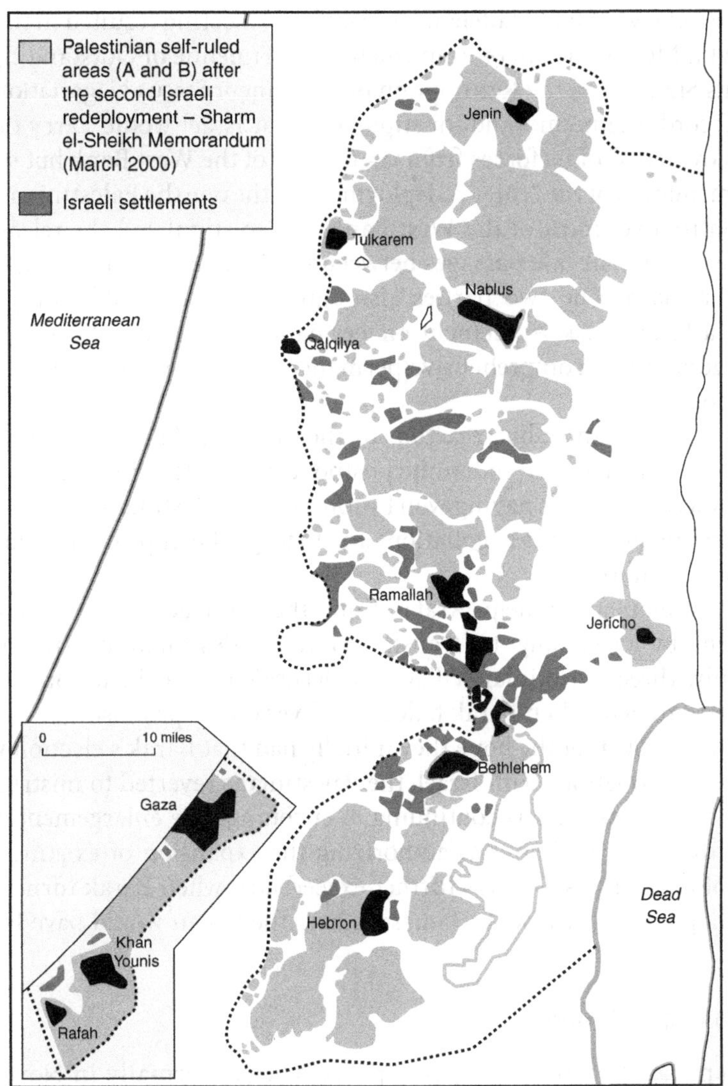

Figure 10.2. West Bank and the Gaza Strip after the Redeployments of Sharm el-Sheikh, 2000

go directly to permanent status negotiations, Barak now sought to forgo the implementation of Israel's commitments under the accord, particularly regarding the IDF's redeployments and the transfer of territorial and jurisdictional control. While willing to accept some delays in the implementation of Israel's commitments, the Palestinian side rejected the essence of Barak's demand and insisted on the full implementation of Israel's obligations and its commitments to negotiate a permanent status agreement.[5]

To help Israel and the Palestinians overcome their differences, Egypt hosted a summit in Sharm el-Sheikh in September 1999. Attended by Barak, Arafat, Mubarak, King Abdullah of

Jordan, and Secretary of State Madeleine Albright, the meeting resulted in the signing of "The Sharm el Sheikh Memorandum on Implementation Timeline of Outstanding Commitments of Agreements Signed and the Resumption of Permanent Status Negotiations." Revising the Wye River Accord, the memorandum stipulated that Israel would carry out the "first and second redeployments" of its forces from 11.3 percent of the West Bank but set no date for the Israeli implementation of the "third redeployment" – the one the Palestinians expected would give them control over most of the West Bank. It also stipulated the release of Palestinian prisoners, the opening of safe passages between the West Bank and Gaza, and the building of a seaport in Gaza. The two parties also agreed on a timetable for permanent status negotiations: a Framework Agreement on Permanent Status (FAPS) was to be concluded by February 2000 and a comprehensive permanent status agreement was to be reached by September 2000.[6]

Predictably, Palestinian public reaction to the Sharm el-Sheikh Summit was uniformly negative. Having negotiated an indefinite postponement of the third redeployment of Israeli forces, Barak was now seen as having won by forcing the Palestinians to accept his demand to go directly to permanent status negotiations and to forgo the implementation of Israel's "third redeployment" commitment.

Barak first attempted to help Arafat limit the damage entailed in this Palestinian disappointment by promising to transfer to full Palestinian control, unilaterally and unconditionally, three Palestinian villages in Jerusalem's outskirts. But this attempt only exacerbated the problem when Barak failed to deliver on his promise.

Having now lost much of the hope they initially had that Barak's election would usher in a new era in their negotiations with Israel, the Palestinians reverted to mistrust. This mistrust intensified as Barak was seen as continuing to encourage the enlargement of the settlement enterprise in the West Bank and as authorizing the expansion of existing settlements and the building of new outposts. It was further exacerbated when Barak turned his attention to Syria, in the hope that a deal with Damascus over the Golan would pave Israel's way out of Lebanon.

The Road to Camp David

The pre-Camp David preparatory peace process began formally in November 1999 with the opening of negotiations led by teams of professionals headed by a veteran Israeli diplomat, Ambassador Oded Eran, and by Palestinian negotiator Yasser Abed Rabbo. The talks, held in Israel and the West Bank, encompassed all permanent status issues but without the direct involvement of the two sides' top leaders. Reportedly, these talks began with a "low" Israeli offer. Thus on the territorial issue the Israeli team was instructed to open the negotiations by offering what the Palestinians understood to be 60–70 percent of the West Bank.

In May 2000, while the Eran–Abed Rabbo talks continued, Barak and Arafat opened a secret channel for negotiating permanent status issues. The talks, held in Stockholm, Sweden, were conducted on the Israeli side by Foreign Minister Shlomo Ben Ami and the prime minister's policy coordinator Gilead Sher, and on the Palestinian side by Ahmed Qurie, Speaker of the Palestinian Legislative Council and a senior member of Fatah's Central

Committee. Other Palestinian negotiators, including Mahmoud Abbas, then head of the PLO's Negotiations Department, were kept in the dark regarding the Stockholm channel. The Clinton administration was not represented in all the meetings but was briefed by the participants, and senior American diplomats attended the second round of the talks.[7]

Leaked to the press by a source inside the official Palestinian negotiating team, the fact that secret talks were taking place in Stockholm became public knowledge in June, bringing them to an abrupt and complete halt before closure was reached on any of the issues discussed. The leak also damaged the relationship between Abbas and Qurie as well as the relations between Arafat and his two top lieutenants.[8] While not closing the gaps between the two sides' positions, and while a serious discussion of the Jerusalem issues was not even attempted, the Stockholm talks did seem to narrow these gaps somewhat, especially regarding borders and refugees.

As elaborated in Chapter 8, a critically important development which took place in parallel to the pre-Camp David preparatory talks was the failure to resolve the Syrian–Israeli conflict. On March 5, 2000, while still hoping to reach an agreement with Syria, the Israeli cabinet approved a withdrawal from Lebanon by July. With talks failing to produce an agreement, Israel withdrew unilaterally on May 24. Hezbollah responded by taking control of the evacuated Israeli strongholds and by disarming the remnants of the South Lebanon Army – Israel's Lebanese allies in the security zone. In the broader region, Israel's unilateral withdrawal was viewed as a victory for Hezbollah.[9]

Camp David and its Aftermath

On the Palestinian–Israeli track, the 2000 Camp David permanent status negotiations process spanned five important developments:

1. The July Summit at Camp David.
2. President Bill Clinton's July 25, 2000 press conference in which he indirectly blamed Arafat for the failure to achieve a breakthrough at Camp David.
3. The numerous Israeli–Palestinian talks conducted in August and most of September in various locations and through different channels in an effort to salvage Camp David. These included an Egyptian attempt at mediation, conducted by Osama al-Baz, a senior advisor to President Mubarak, and Arafat's visit to Barak's home in Kochav Yair in early September.
4. The December Israeli–Palestinian negotiations held in Bolling Air Force Base outside Washington, DC and the resulting presentation of the Clinton Parameters.
5. Finally, the talks held at Taba in January 2001.

The 13-day summit at Camp David began on July 11, 2000. Hosted by President Clinton, it was attended by the two lead protagonists, Arafat and Barak, and their teams of negotiators and advisors. The talks addressed all core permanent status issues – borders, security, Jerusalem, and refugees – although the latter was not discussed in great detail, possibly as a result of the failure to reach a breakthrough regarding the other, less intractable dimensions of the conflict. One permanent status issue – water – was not discussed at all.

What the parties neglected to do at Camp David – document their agreements and identify their disagreements – was a task left to senior Palestinian and Israeli negotiators, Sa'eb Erekat and Gilad Sher, respectively, after the summit. In August–September 2000 they held some three dozen sessions on an outline and contents of a permanent status deal based on the Camp David talks. Reportedly, Erekat and Sher even began to draft some of the chapters of a possible agreement. While the product was impressive, it was not complete, leaving significant gaps for further negotiations. However, the eruption of the Second Intifada on September 28 brought the effort to a halt.[10]

It was in this environment – when Palestinian frustration with the lack of progress in the efforts to resolve the conflict was growing stronger by the day – that the leader of the Israeli parliamentary opposition, Ariel Sharon, decided to visit Temple Mount or al-Haram al-Sharif. His stated objective was to assert Israeli control over the holy place in response to Barak's ascribed willingness to divide Jerusalem.[11] Violence ensued, and the Second Palestinian Intifada was under way – a development elaborated in the next chapter.

Despite the ongoing violence, the parties returned to official negotiations in late December 2000 at Bolling Air Force Base, near Washington, DC. Unlike the Camp David Summit, this meeting was not attended by the two sides' top leaders. The Israeli delegation was headed by Foreign Minister Shlomo Ben Ami and the Palestinian side by veteran negotiator Sa'eb Erekat. With both sides unable or unwilling to take bold steps needed to reach an agreement, the United States decided, instead, to use these talks – and the parties' positions as they evolved by the end of the meeting – as the basis for articulating possible parameters for resolving the conflict. Hence, President Clinton invited the two delegations to the White House, and on December 23 read to them what has since become known as the "Clinton Parameters," letting them know that he expected a response in five days. Barak's response on December 28, 2000 was positive, accepting the President's parameters as a basis for negotiation of a final status agreement, with some reservations. Arafat's response was less decisive, finally giving a conditional approval on January 2, 2001.[12]

On January 21, 2001, a few weeks after the White House meeting, Israeli and Palestinian negotiators met at the Egyptian resort of Taba, just south of the Israeli town of Eilat. The Israeli delegation was headed by Foreign Minister Ben Ami and the Palestinian team by senior negotiator Ahmed Qurie. The odds of a breakthrough were slim; the two negotiating teams were not authorized to make a historical compromise and both were cognizant of the Israeli elections scheduled to be held only a few weeks later. The Palestinians had doubts about Barak's chances of retaining office against his opponent on the right, Ariel Sharon. Most Israelis, polls showed, viewed the Taba talks with suspicion, believing that it was not legitimate for Barak to engage in last-minute diplomacy of this nature. This perception was buttressed by the Legal Advisor to the Government, Elyakim Rubinstein, who questioned the morality of conducting such negotiations so close to election day.[13]

The meeting lasted some seven days and, as expected, failed to produce an accord. Yet the talks seemed to have further narrowed the differences between the two parties' positions on most issues, including territory, security, and refugees. Accordingly, the concluding joint communiqué noted the unprecedented progress made at Taba: "The sides declare that they have never been closer to reaching an agreement and it is thus our shared belief that the remaining gaps could be bridged with the resumption of negotiations following the Israeli elections."[14]

The electoral victory of the Sharon-led Likud party in Israel's January 2001 elections brought to a close this chapter of Israeli–Palestinian diplomatic efforts to resolve the conflict through permanent status negotiations, not to be resumed until November 2007. With the two sides increasingly engulfed by the Second Intifada, Israel's new prime minister declared that his government would not return to the negotiation table as long as violence continued.[15]

Narratives

The Israeli Narrative

The Israeli mainstream was unanimous in holding the Palestinian side responsible for the failure of the permanent status talks. It was also unanimous in seeing Arafat as holding the prime responsibility for this failure. But even some Israeli mainstream participants and observers of the process assigned some blame for the failure to Barak.[16]

Interim versus Permanent

In light of the break of trust between Israelis and Palestinians experienced during Israel's previous government, some Israelis questioned the wisdom of Barak opening a new page in the relationship with the Palestinians by asking to renegotiate the terms of implementation of the Wye River Memorandum. To these Israeli observers, depriving the Palestinians of the further withdrawals promised in the memorandum – the only achievement the Palestinians could boast of during Netanyahu's tenure – did not seem wise.

However, most Israelis supporting Barak were sympathetic to two arguments advanced to justify his quest to skip the third redeployment and instead move directly to negotiating a permanent status agreement. The first was that given the past experience of the length of time it took to iron-out the details entailed in such withdrawals, attempting a historic compromise on all permanent status issues would prove a far better use of the limited time and energy available to the government. The second was that further redeployments would leave Israel controlling a smaller part of the West Bank, thus depriving it of the most important bargaining chip required for a permanent status grand bargain to be reached. Thus, statements to the effect that: "We give and give; what will we have left to bargain with when we come to negotiating permanent status?" resonated well with the Israeli public.

Camp David

The significance of these opening acts notwithstanding, the Israeli mainstream narrative of the important developments of this period focused instead on Israel's pre-Camp David negotiating positions, on the Israeli conduct at the Camp David Summit, on Israel's positions at the end of Camp David, and on its response, as well as that of the Palestinians, to the Clinton Parameters. Israel's "low" opening positions – at the Eran–Abed Rabbo preparatory talks as well as at Camp David – was justified by a number of considerations: first, the desire to leave Israeli negotiators sufficient room for compromise in forthcoming talks. Second, the need to avoid discussing conciliatory opening positions during the run-up to Camp David due to the chronically "leaky" nature of the Israeli decision-making system, assuring that these discussions would have been exposed immediately. In turn, such exposure would have allowed the Palestinians to "pocket" these concessions as gains even before the talks began.

Israelis believed that by the time the talks at Camp David ended, their side had put on the table the most generous offer ever made to the Palestinians. The latter, it is said, were offered independent statehood for the first time in their history. The Palestinian independent state was to encompass over 90 percent of the West Bank and all of the Gaza Strip.[17] To allow such statehood, Barak was said to have broken every Israeli taboo, including the willingness to redivide Jerusalem by attaching most of its Arab neighborhoods to the proposed Palestinian state and to withdraw all Israeli settlements located beyond the envisaged boundaries. Israel's position was said to have addressed the Palestinians' two most important imperatives: ending Israel's occupation and establishing an independent Palestinian state with its capital in Jerusalem at large.

It return, Barak was said to have demanded only one thing: that with these far-reaching concessions the Palestinian–Israeli conflict would end, the file of the conflict would be closed, and all grievances addressed. From a legal standpoint this demand meant that following the implementation of this deal, the Palestinians would have no further recourse to Israel – that is, no excuses would be acceptable as justifying a "reopening of the file." Barak's insistence on an "end of conflict" declaration was understood to have emanated from three sources: first, his desire to leave a legacy as the Israeli leader that brought a historical breakthrough – closing a chapter in Jewish history that began with Ben Gurion's bold move to declare Israel's independence; second, a desire to ensure that the permanent status agreement would not become another "interim" – that is, that the closing of the chapter would indeed be final and receive broad recognition as such; and finally, a political judgment to the effect that the Israeli public would not accept the far-reaching concessions that Barak was prepared to make unless they were made in the context of an agreement that ended the conflict.

Arafat's Role

Given these concessions, Israelis believed that the responsibility for failing to reach an agreement during this period lay squarely on the Palestinian side. In plain terms, Israelis emerged from Camp David convinced that Arafat was simply not prepared for the historical compromise required. Some believed the problem lay in Arafat's reluctance to face his constituency – particularly Palestinians in the Diaspora – and to explain, as Ben Gurion had done during the debates on partition in 1937 and in 1947, as well as in connection to Israel's withdrawal from the Sinai in early 1957, that not all Palestinian aspirations could be met.

Other Israelis ascribed Arafat's failure to another dimension of his character: namely, a reluctance to change roles from that of a revolutionary leader to a state-builder. This interpretation, supported by what Israelis believed they heard from some of their Palestinian interlocutors, saw Arafat as unwilling to trade the heroics of the defiant fighter for the mundane task of state institution-building. Among some Israelis this was seen as associated with what to them appeared to be Arafat's emotional attachment to, and possibly envy of, the younger generation of Fatah leaders as the revolutionaries of the day. This narrative was reinforced by Arafat's ascribed later endorsement of the violence of the Intifada.

This, in turn, is connected to another dimension of the responsibility ascribed by Israelis to Arafat: namely, the failure to prepare Palestinian public opinion to accept the concessions that would have to be made. To many Israelis, the domestic constraints that Arafat faced when going to Camp David appeared to be self-made. Had Arafat prepared the public by talking peace rather than offering the rhetoric of continuous Jihad, he would have had the broad support needed to reach agreement.

Israelis also argued that Arafat further contributed to the failure at Camp David by violating what they understood to be the pre-Camp David tacit understanding regarding the purpose of the exercise. Israelis assumed that the agreed purpose of the negotiations was to undo the results of the 1967 War. This required a deal over such issues as the future of Jerusalem, border demarcation, the removal of settlements, security arrangements and the division of water rights. Israelis assessed that notwithstanding the enormous difficulties entailed, it was not impossible to bridge the gap between the parties' positions on what some have referred to as "1967 issues." By contrast, Israelis assumed that it was impossible to undo the results of the 1948 War, since these involved the very existence of the State of Israel and its unique character as a Jewish state: therefore, any attempt to negotiate "1948 issues" was doomed to failure. Thus, they faulted Arafat for raising at Camp David the refugees' Right of Return, a non-starter from their standpoint.

While admiring Barak's boldness, some Israelis questioned his insistence that the negotiations with the Palestinians must result in an "end of conflict" declaration. While these Israelis were sympathetic to Barak's ascribed assumption that the Israeli public was not likely to support the far reaching concessions Israel was asked to make regarding the "1967 issues" except in the context of ending the conflict, they warned that the Palestinians were not likely to accept an "end of conflict" declaration without a resolution of the unbridgeable "1948 issues." This, these Israelis warned, would require that the two sides confront their most basic narrative about the 100-year-old conflict, something neither was prepared to do.

Another aspect of the Israeli narrative regarding Camp David was that the neighboring Arab states made an Israeli–Palestinian deal more difficult, instead of helping broker a compromise. This was viewed as particularly the case with regard to Jerusalem. The Palestinians were seen as requiring these neighbors' support for any concessions they would be prepared to make over this hypersensitive issue. In Israel's view what Palestinians were told during and after the talks at Camp David – namely, that Jerusalem was an issue for all Arabs and all Muslims and that they were not authorized to make concessions over the city's future – made them less disposed to compromise.

As noted earlier, while Israelis were unified in faulting Arafat for the failure at Camp David, some Israeli participants in the process stressed that the Israeli side also contributed somewhat to the failure. In particular they argued that within an attempt to resolve a conflict that carried huge emotional baggage, Barak should have shown more emotional empathy to the Palestinians, who saw themselves as the chronic victims and who sought some recognition of their suffering. Within this context they pointed out that throughout the talks, Barak, while deeply engaged intellectually in the negotiations, remained aloof and unengaged emotionally, thus contributing his share to the near-absence of direct personal talks between the two sides' leaders.[18]

The Clinton Parameters

Consistent with their quest for a historical compromise, Israelis welcomed the Clinton Parameters as a fair and balanced peace proposal. While aware that their government had expressed a large number of reservations regarding the details of the proposal, Israelis were impressed by the offer's sensibilities, especially as a basis for further talks. Yet by the time a version of the proposal was made public, most Israelis were no longer focused on the ongoing diplomatic efforts. Instead, they had increasingly turned their attention to their personal safety in the face of the growing violence of the Second Palestinian Intifada.

At the same time, members of the Israeli elite who continued to follow diplomatic developments were astonished by what they judged to be Arafat's huge blunder – his failure to respond enthusiastically to the Clinton Parameters. The weeks that elapsed between the issuing of the parameters and Arafat's response – with the many reservations attached – were seen by these Israelis as a historic failure and as evidence of Arafat's continuous attachment to the Palestinians' traditional "all or nothing" approach. The parameters were seen by Israelis as comprising the most important act of international recognition of the Palestinians' national aspirations – more concrete, meaningful and detailed than the Balfour Declaration on the basis of which the Zionist movement had constructed its state-building project. That Arafat failed to grab this historical opportunity was seen as an unforgivable error – together with the violence of the Intifada that followed – which cast huge doubt in the minds of most Israelis about Arafat's true intentions.

By the time the parties had convened at Taba in January 2001 for what proved to be the final act in this saga of negotiations, Israeli views had hardened considerably. By that time they had experienced more than three months of intense Palestinian violence. As these negotiations took place on the eve of the scheduled Israeli elections, they were seen by many Israelis as an illegitimate and "last ditch" effort by Barak to avoid almost certain electoral defeat. Finally, Israelis' perceptions of the Taba talks were marred by uncertainty as to what actually transpired in these discussions. Even months, if not years, later it still seemed that no two Israelis who took part in the talks could agree on what happened at Taba. As no record of the talks was kept, and as the Israeli side in the negotiations did not appear to have been coordinated in any fashion, Israelis tended to dismiss the entire affair as a futile if not pathetic exercise.

The Palestinian Narrative

The Palestinian narrative is that, by the year 2000, Israel was not ready for a historic compromise and that the United States, by coordinating and siding with Israel throughout the permanent status negotiations, was as responsible as Israel for the failure of the talks. Moreover, the efforts to conclude a permanent status agreement during this period were seen as doomed from the start due to the manner in which Israel behaved during the preceding post-Oslo years. Instead of seeking accommodation, Israel was seen as continuing to seek maximum gains by conceding few assets while creating "facts on the ground." The result was that between the signing of the Oslo Accords in 1993 and the Camp David talks in July 2000, the Jewish settlement enterprise had doubled in size, while only 42 percent of the territory of the West Bank had been transferred to full or partial Palestinian control.

Syrian–Israeli Negotiations

This general disappointment with the Oslo process was now coupled with specific Palestinian pre-Camp David frustrations with Israel's Labor-led government headed by Barak. Early on, the Palestinians were uneasy about Barak's clear preference for an agreement with Syria. This preference was assessed as serious because of Barak's pre-election promise to withdraw from Lebanon, preferably by agreement. Palestinians feared that if these efforts were to succeed and an Israeli–Syrian agreement were reached, they would be at a serious disadvantage, as Israel might feel less pressure to resolve the last unresolved dimension of the Arab–Israeli conflict.

Palestinians also judged Syria as more important to Israel than their own issues, and they were convinced that Israel would avoid making concessions on two fronts simultaneously. If Israel obtained an agreement with Syria, they argued, it would surely freeze any further diplomatic efforts on the Palestinian front.

Paradoxically, however, Palestinians were not relieved by the later failure of Israeli–Syrian negotiations. When this occurred, their previous fear was replaced by concern that this failure had left the Israeli government too weak to conclude an agreement with them. Moreover, the failure of Israeli–Syrian talks made Palestinians even more skeptical about the ability to reach a breakthrough in their talks with Israel, given that the issues dividing the Israelis and the Syrians seemed much less complicated than those at dispute between Israel and the Palestinians.

Suspicion of Barak

Palestinians were also suspicious of Barak's early efforts to forgo the implementation of the Wye River Memorandum. His argument that a permanent status agreement would supersede any interim accord and would make such an accord redundant seemed to them a potential trap: should the permanent status talks fail, they were at the risk of being left with nothing.

The Palestinians saw the idea of convening a summit at Camp David as Barak's, and they suspected his intentions. They feared that the talks there might become an even bigger Israeli–American trap designed to force concessions from their leader – Arafat – or to blame him for the failure if the summit were to end without agreement. They also feared that Barak planned to use the summit's likely failure as the means to avoid further implementation of Israel's commitments under the interim agreements, particularly regarding the transfer of territory and jurisdiction. They insisted on receiving an American guarantee that Israel would implement its interim commitments regardless of the outcome of the planned summit. And, they saw themselves as having been forced to come to Camp David despite their failure to obtain such assurances.

Camp David

In light of these circumstances and considerations, Arafat was said to have gone to Camp David under what many Palestinians saw as extremely negative circumstances. He was said to have bowed to enormous pressures from the Clinton administration and to have participated despite the fact that he had made his reservations clear. The Palestinian leadership is also said to have pointed out to American officials that the progress made in the secret pre-Camp David preparatory talks was insufficient and hence did not warrant the convening of a summit. They argued that with the gap between the parties' positions remaining so wide, such a summit could not possibly succeed. They further noted that the Jerusalem issue, including sovereignty over Muslim Holy Places, remained largely untouched in the secret talks held earlier in Stockholm. The territorial issue was also very problematic, with Israeli offers still falling short of the 90 percent mark and with the Barak government not yet accepting the principle of equal territorial swaps. Finally, the principle of the Right of Return, while critical for the Palestinians, remained a non-starter for the Israelis.

Palestinians saw the talks at Camp David as confirming their worst suspicions. In their eyes Israeli offers were never generous and failed to come to terms with the Palestinian reference point: the territories they had lost in 1948. Barak's reference point was seen as the 2000 status quo. As the Palestinians viewed themselves as having already conceded 78 percent of their historic homeland to the Jewish state in 1948, Israel's ambition to hold on to some 10 percent of the remaining land appeared anything but generous.

Palestinians also questioned the proposition that a clear Israeli offer was proffered at Camp David. They stressed that nothing was ever put in writing and there was never a full offer made. Ideas were floated but were never tied together in a cohesive, unified package. Indeed, the consensus among Palestinians was that the failure of the talks exposed Israel's unwillingness to accept all or most of the following Palestinian minimum demands from Israel: that it be willing to return to the 1967 borders; to accept *equal* land swaps; to allow Palestinian sovereignty over al-Haram al-Sharif and the Arab neighborhoods of Jerusalem; that it accept a truly sovereign Palestinian state with full control over its skies, land, water resources, and territorial waters; and that it recognize the Palestinian refugees' Right of Return. In exchange for the latter, Palestinians were willing to show flexibility in accepting modalities for Palestinian refugees' resettlement and compensation that would meet Israel's vital demographic requirements.

Accordingly, Palestinians viewed the Clinton administration as having made the decision to go to Camp David under Israeli pressure and despite its awareness of the substantive gaps in positions and its knowledge that the issue of Jerusalem remained untouched in previous talks. In the Palestinians' opinion, the Clinton administration did not consider the cost of failure of such talks, including Barak's clear intention, in case of failure, to abandon Israel's interim commitments. From the Palestinians' standpoint, the implementation of these commitments was essential to providing them a cushion in case the permanent status talks failed.

The Palestinians took very strong exception to the tendency of Israel and the United States to present Camp David as a one-shot deal upon which the success or failure of the entire Palestinian–Israeli peacemaking effort rested. In their eyes, they should not have been made to accept a perspective that resulted from the special circumstances of Clinton and Barak in the summer of 2000, with Clinton about to leave office and Barak having by now lost his domestic constituency. These circumstances, Palestinians feared, would doom the negotiations structurally and would preclude their continuation after the summit. Thus Palestinians saw the timing of the Camp David summit as highly problematic. Why, Palestinians asked, should their fate be dictated by the American electoral cycle, forcing the search for peace to end in 2000 or in January 2001?

With regard to the manner in which the talks at Camp David eventually evolved, the Palestinian view was that Barak's insistence on an agreement that would "end the conflict" left Arafat no choice but to insist that the refugees issue – clearly a "1948 issue" – be resolved in its entirety. While recognizing the need to compromise on some issues, such as security arrangements, practical refugee-return modalities, and Jewish settlements and Holy Places, Palestinians insisted that these compromises must be linked to the resolution of other issues. Thus, they were reluctant to negotiate security arrangements before the border issue was clarified. Similarly, they were unwilling to negotiate practical modalities for refugee absorption before Israel was willing to accept the principle of refugee rights. And Palestinian concessions on Jerusalem settlements and Jewish Holy Places in the old city were viewed as possible only in return for an Israeli acknowledgment of Palestinian sovereignty over Arab East Jerusalem and over Muslim and Christian Holy Places in the city. Summing up, Palestinians pointed out that they could not accept the Israeli demand for an agreement that would end the conflict except within a context of a comprehensive agreement – a deal which would leave no issue unresolved.

Members of the Palestinian elite with inside knowledge of the details of the negotiations rejected the depiction of Arafat as responsible for the failure of Camp David. Specifically, they rejected the accusation that Arafat made no counteroffers at Camp David, arguing that in fact he did make such proposals. The most important of these was said to allow Israel to annex certain settlements in exchange for equal amounts of territory. This offer was said to have been put in writing and to have been submitted together with a detailed map during the discussions with Clinton administration officials – a map the Americans later showed their Israeli colleagues. In Palestinian eyes this clearly proves that the Palestinians were fully engaged in the process of "give and take."

In the immediate aftermath of Camp David the Palestinian leadership avoided publicizing these concessions, especially to the Palestinian public, and remained silent on what positions they had taken at the summit and beyond. Yet Palestinian leaders claimed that American and Israeli officials at Camp David were fully aware of their content. For example, ideas were said to have been presented with the aim of reconciling Palestinian demand for the Right of Return with Israel's demographic concerns. In addition, several proposed security arrangements, very close to what the Israeli side demanded, were accepted. More importantly, Palestinians pointed out that their ideas, in contrast to those offered by Barak, were not presented as a single package that the Israelis were required to either accept or reject.

The Palestinian narrative denied responsibility for the failure of the permanent status talks and depicted Israel and the United States as responsible for this failure. Another dimension of the narrative also denied that the talks ended in failure. Thus Palestinians pointed out that significant progress was made and that negotiations were moving in the right direction, allowing further progress to be made over time.[19] Indeed it is through this prism that Palestinians later assessed the Taba talks. Citing the meeting's closing statement, Palestinians stressed that the two sides had become closer on most issues, including territory, security, and refugees. Thus, the discussions proved it was possible to reach a comprehensive permanent status agreement as most of the remaining problems from Camp David had been resolved. In their view, it was only a matter of time – not major disagreements – that prevented the parties from concluding an agreement at Taba.

In Palestinian eyes, failure to meet American and Israeli *artificial* deadlines did not constitute a strategic impasse; instead, it affirmed the need to revive negotiations at the earliest possible date. The continuous progress achieved over the period of negotiations in 2000–2001 dispelled the notion that failure was inevitable.

Beyond a firm rejection of the perception that the Camp David summit failed, Palestinian leaders regarded Clinton's decision to point to Arafat as responsible for the failure as a clear violation of the understandings that led to their consent to attend the summit in the first place. Their decision to attend, they pointed out, was affected by the promise given to them by the Clinton administration to refrain from "finger pointing" in the event that the summit ended in failure. Instead, they stressed, Clinton not only violated the commitment made to Arafat, but in what the Palestinians saw as a transparent bid to help Barak's reelection, he praised the latter for the courage he had shown at Camp David.

The Clinton Parameters

The Palestinian narrative also dismissed the notion that their side rejected the Clinton Parameters. Instead, it viewed their response as similar to Israel's: acceptance but with some reservations. Arafat was said to have simply taken longer than Israel to respond. He was then said to have told Clinton that he accepted the parameters but with even greater reservations than Barak's.

As evidence of their eventual acceptance of the Clinton Parameters, Palestinians cite their active participation in the Taba talks, and present the latter as having been based on the parameters. Palestinians further cite the significant progress made in these talks toward resolving all permanent status issues as evidence that they had played a constructive role in the search for a solution to the conflict.

That the ascribed progress was made at Taba despite the earlier eruption of the Second Intifada was taken by Palestinians as further evidence that their conflict with Israel could be resolved. This also demonstrated that the failure to reach a permanent status agreement was not the result of the violence that had erupted earlier but rather because Israel terminated the negotiations after the election of Ariel Sharon. In their view, it was this event that "killed" the two sides' ability to capitalize on the achievements made up to that point.

The Role of the United States

The Palestinian narrative is that the Clinton administration bears a considerable measure of responsibility for the failure of the Camp David talks. Believing that Israel's dependence on the United States for diplomatic, financial, and military support means that the United States is the only power with the ability to pressure Israel, Palestinians viewed direct American involvement in the negotiations as an absolute prerequisite to their success. But in their view the Americans confined themselves to conveying Israeli ideas, never making a contribution or presenting ideas of their own. Palestinians held some Jewish-American officials deeply involved in the negotiations as particularly guilty of serving as "Israel's lawyers."

Palestinians are said to have expected that despite great domestic constraints, particularly during times of elections, the United States, due to its international and regional interests and outlook, would prove to be a potential ally against Israeli extreme right-wing leaders. The Clinton administration's experience with the 1996–99 Netanyahu government during the negotiations of the Hebron Agreement and the Wye River Memorandum demonstrated to Palestinians that it was easier for them to induce American pressure on Israel when the latter was ruled by a right-wing coalition. Indeed, once Barak's Labor-led government came into office in 1999, the Clinton administration was seen as willing to show far greater understanding of its constraints. As a result, Palestinians perceived American pressure on Israel to have vanished.

Palestinians also believed that American officials at Camp David coordinated every step with their Israeli counterparts. Thus, they believed that what was presented at Camp David as American "bridging proposals" were in fact initiated by Israel. They believed this because those "American" proposals were said to have been presented informally to Palestinians earlier by some of their Israeli interlocutors.

The Arab Narrative

The Camp David Summit

The Arab world observed closely the convening of the Camp David summit. However, key Arab states, such as Egypt, Jordan, and Saudi Arabia, complained that they were kept in the dark regarding the various aspects and dimensions of the permanent status negotiations. They pointed out that it was only during the later part of the summit that they were contacted by the United States, mostly to ask that they assure Arafat of their support for a possible deal on Jerusalem.

Reportedly, on July 21, 2000, Barak contacted Mubarak to brief him on the negotiations. An intensive series of consultations is said to have then taken place among Egypt, Jordan, Saudi Arabia, and Syria.[20] Yet the Arab countries refrained from endorsing the pressures exerted on Arafat. Instead, Cairo declared that the Palestinians were not free to make concessions on Jerusalem since the matter involved broader Arab, Islamic, and Christian interests – issues that were not within the Palestinians' purview. Other Arab countries adopted a similar approach, arguing that since they were kept in the dark during the run-up and preparation for the summit, they could not be asked at that late stage to support a compromise on Jerusalem.

Second, Arab governments whose support was now requested argued that even at this late stage the precise nature of the deal over Jerusalem was never made clear to them. Consequently, they could not know whether the compromise discussed was attractive enough to rally sufficient public support for the deal, especially given the tight time constraints. Clearly, for example, any hint that such a deal would include Israeli sovereignty over the Islamic al-Haram al-Sharif was unacceptable to the Arab states.[21] Moreover, even when they were finally asked for help with the issue of Jerusalem, they saw themselves as still being kept in the dark regarding the details of the broader parameters of the proposed Israeli–Palestinian deal.

Third, Egypt in particular could not eagerly help to market a breakthrough at Camp David given that its relations with Israel remained quite tense over different facets of Israeli policy, including Israel's earlier repeated bombardments of Lebanon, and Egypt's earlier depiction of Hezbollah activities as "resistance." At the time, Israel's relations with Jordan, Oman and Qatar experienced similar cooling.

Finally, the earlier failure of Syrian–Israeli negotiations made it difficult for Arab countries to support a peace breakthrough elsewhere. Specifically, it was not clear how such Arab support could be provided without it appearing as if these Arab states were neglecting the Syrian issue.

Despite these reservations, Arab countries – and especially Egypt – viewed the Camp David talks as having achieved considerable progress. In the summit's aftermath, and following further communications with Washington and Jerusalem, Cairo was prepared to help in closing the remaining gaps in the parties' positions. Meetings with Israeli and Palestinian officials were conducted in Cairo during the month of September. These meetings were said to have sharpened and clarified the positions presented at Camp David.[22]

The Role of Violence

From the Arab states' standpoint, however, the eruption of the Second Intifada in late September 2000 was a major setback for the efforts to capitalize on the progress made at Camp David. Moreover, in the Arab world the Intifada led to an immediate shift in priorities: from dealing with a possible Israeli–Palestinian agreement to containing the potentially negative ramifications of the Intifada on the Arab street.

To salvage the process, Egypt saw itself as playing a positive role when on October 17, 2000, in coordination with President Clinton, it convened the Middle East Peace Summit at Sharm el-Sheikh in an attempt to put the process back on track. The summit produced an agreement on the creation of the so-called Mitchell Commission, led by former United States Senator George Mitchell, to recommend ways for ending the violence and restoring the negotiation process. While failing to end the violence, the meeting was seen as having paved the road to the subsequent talks at Bolling Air Force Base – which produced the Clinton Parameters – and at Taba. Yet both were viewed by the Arab states as having come too late. With the militarization of the Intifada and the election of Ariel Sharon as Israel's new prime minister, these developments were seen as opening a new and more deadly chapter of the Israeli–Palestinian conflict.

Analysis

The progress made during the period explored in this chapter toward reaching a permanent resolution of the Palestinian–Israeli conflict, and the eventual failure to reach such an agreement, were affected by a large number of factors. Some are to be found in the international and regional environments of the two negotiating parties, yet others in their domestic scenes. Finally, the individuals involved – Israelis, Palestinians, and Americans – played an important role in providing the greatest hope ever that a resolution of the conflict might be reached and, in the end, in contributing to the effort's failure.

The International System

On the *global-systemic level*, this phase of the peace process was affected by the fact that it was launched during an "American moment" – that is, in a period of United States supremacy. Moreover, within this unipolar period, by early 2000 the United States had overcome many of the transitional problems it faced in the late 1990s.

Armed with this unique capacity, the administration was now in a position to sponsor some of the most dramatic achievements in this realm. It brought the parties to a serious and painful exploration of the most hypersensitive issues during thirteen days of tough negotiations at Camp David, in the framework of which both sides seemed willing to break long-standing taboos. The United States later articulated, for the first time ever, a set of parameters within which a permanent status deal could be concluded. In that, it succeeded in channeling the parties to more precise and narrow confines within which any future Palestinian–Israeli talks about resolving their conflict would be held.

Yet the United States failed to translate all this into an agreement reached by the parties to settle their dispute peacefully if not to end their conflict entirely. First, there seems to have been great reluctance on the part of senior American officials to translate their country's latent power into actual power, and to exercise the leverage it possessed by exerting its influence over both parties to extract the concessions needed for an agreement to be reached. This may have been more a matter of style than of substance but it certainly seemed to contrast sharply with the uninhibited Bush–Baker administration a decade earlier that pressed the parties to go to Madrid. Also, by the time the summit at Camp David was convened, the Clinton administration's days were numbered, with only six months left of a two-term presidency. Domestic political considerations and the decades-long "special relationship" with Israel also made it difficult to exert pressure on Israel for more concessions. Finally, the reluctance of Arab states to support the United States weakened Washington's position by robbing it of the power to argue that a deal with the Palestinians was bound to open the gates for Israel to the region at large.

International meets the Regional

At the intersection between the *systemic-global* and the *systemic-regional* levels, the Clinton administration also seems to have refrained from a serious effort to shape the Middle East environment in a manner conducive to reaching a grand bargain at Camp David. This was especially surprising given that the regional environment for such a deal was not entirely negative – at least not in comparison to previous eras. On the one hand, the Arab world was still grappling with the intensification of globalization, the decline in oil prices, and the growing levels of Islamic fundamentalism and terror. Gradually, every one of the region's states had also come to experience a sense of diplomatic fatigue with the Arab–Israeli conflict.

Nevertheless, with Syria having lost its Soviet patron, and Saddam's Iraq trying to withstand the cumulative weight of its 1991 defeat and the UN sanctions and monitoring regime to which it was subjected thereafter, the balance of power in the region shifted in favor of the moderate Arab states: Egypt, Jordan, and Saudi Arabia. Yet the Clinton administration failed to solicit the assistance of these recently empowered moderate states. Whereas in negotiating the Wye River Memorandum President Clinton sought the help of Jordan's King Hussein in preparing for Camp David, his administration seemed to have largely ignored its regional allies. Thus Egypt, Jordan, and Saudi Arabia were never seriously mobilized to support the process – especially not during the run-up to Camp David – neither through persuasion nor by offering them significant side-payments.

Another negative dimension of the regional scene was Israel's May 2000 unilateral withdrawal from Lebanon. The perception that Hezbollah succeeded where the Palestinians and even established Arab governments like Syria had failed – to coerce Israel out of occupation – placed moderates on the defensive in every Arab country as well as among the Palestinians.

Moreover, the continued rise of the new pan-Arab media made it more difficult for an Israeli–Palestinian agreement to be reached. Nor was any significant attempt made to shape the message delivered through the new Middle East media. This media, which now hosted Islamist and hypernationalist opponents to any United States-led effort to reach accommodation with "the Zionists" was never pressed to provide an alternative voice, nor was it offered one. Thus, the atmosphere in the Arab street regarding the Camp David effort ranged from indifference to scathing critique.

In these realms Israel and the Palestinians did no better. Neither was proactive in soliciting support among the region's states. Israel made no particular effort to see if it could remove sources of tension in its relations with Egypt and Jordan so that they might play a more supportive role in Camp David and beyond. In turn, the Palestinians feared that coordination and exposure would limit their freedom of action or expose them to accusations that they made too many concessions or, worse, that they betrayed the Arab cause. They therefore refrained from soliciting the support of Arab governments and from trying to have the Arab media give expression to voices of reason and peace.

Back at the global-systemic level, the failure of the Clinton administration to persuade Israel and the Palestinians to fully embrace the parameters it offered in December 2000 was probably tied to the fact that by the time this took place the administration was at its twilight and hence not in a position to offer the parties meaningful inducements or side-payments. Any significant side-payments would have required congressional approval, but with only a few weeks left for the administration to complete its second term there was little chance that such approval would be forthcoming.

By the time the talks at Taba took place, the global-systemic level was nowhere to be found. With the Clinton administration having left office and the Bush presidency having barely begun, the international dimension was absent from the talks. Thus, just as the process was running out of steam, the parties directly involved – Israel and the Palestinians – proved they could engage in productive dialogue without American participation. At the same time, the absence of any international presence may have made it even more difficult for the two sides to conclude a permanent status deal.

American Politics

Turning to the *unit level*, the obstacles to peace at the regional level, and the failure of the parties involved to exploit the favorable factors at the international and regional levels, were joined by many factors in the American, Israeli and Palestinian domestic scenes - some conducive to a breakthrough in Arab–Israeli peacemaking while others had the opposite effect. In the United States, the Clinton administration was highly motivated to write a legacy that would not leave the Monica Lewinsky affair and its ensuing congressional investigations as the Clinton presidency's contribution to American history. In Israel, a Labor-led government headed by Barak had come to power only a year earlier, motivated to resolve the conflict. And on the Palestinian side, Fatah's rule of the PLO and the PA, and Arafat's standing as the Palestinian nation-builder and his often repeated commitment to conclude "the peace of the brave," made him a natural partner to the effort.

Yet the domestic scenes of all three parties threw up many more obstacles than incentives, ultimately condemning the heroic effort to failure. For the United States, the many other earlier crises, from the Balkans to Iraq, and the Lewinsky Affair, meant that the Clinton administration could not refocus on Arab–Israeli peacemaking until the second half of its second term. Moreover, the Lewinski Affair left the Clinton administration weak and exposed and limited its capacity to take risks. Having barely survived the media obsession with the affair and the associated congressional investigation and impeachment process, President Clinton could hardly afford to antagonize important constituencies by taking steps that could have been interpreted as pressing Israel to accept concessions it was not prepared to make. Hence, exercising leverage and utilizing tactics like those used by Secretary of State James Baker in the early 1990s to extract a freeze on Israeli settlement activities were not in the realm of the possible.

When the Clinton administration finally refocused on Arab–Israeli peacemaking, the decision it took, together with the Barak government, to first attempt a diplomatic breakthrough on the Syrian front - and then the failure of this effort - had three negative implications for the subsequent attempt with the Palestinians: first, it delayed the launching of the effort to conclude an Israeli–Palestinian permanent status agreement until the second half of the last year of Clinton's two-term presidency. Second, the failure of the Syrian effort meant that the attempt on the Palestinian front could not ride the tide of a recent diplomatic success. And finally, it meant that Israel would have to withdraw from Lebanon unilaterally - rather than in the context of a deal with Syria - sending an unintended message to the Palestinians that violence could obtain better results than diplomacy.

The Palestinians

The Israeli and Palestinian domestic scenes were even more complicated and inhibiting. By the time he arrived at Camp David, Arafat had lost a significant degree of legitimacy. Accused of tolerating and even encouraging rampant corruption, his popularity had sunk. In addition, even a year earlier, when the interim period ended in May 1999, the Palestinian leadership had faced demands that it issue a unilateral declaration of statehood in the West Bank and the Gaza Strip. Some viewed the declaration as a potentially useful tool for providing legitimacy to the PA and credibility to the peace process. Others in the leadership, however, feared that – given that Israelis viewed such a unilateral Palestinian step as undermining the peace process – such a declaration might harm the chances for a Barak-led Israeli Labor party victory at the polls.

There was also concern that with the most important Oslo deadline passing without any observable progress on permanent status negotiations, disillusion with diplomacy and negotiations might set in, leading to broad public support for violence. This was reinforced by evidence of fascination in the Palestinian street with Hezbollah that, only months before Camp David, under the cumulative effect of its violence, had succeeded in compelling Israel to withdraw unilaterally from Lebanon.

A third issue involved the end of the terms of the PA's President as well as that of the Palestinian Legislative Council in January 2000, four years after being elected. Without electoral legitimacy, it was feared that other sources of legitimacy, such as Islamist (capitalizing on religious sentiments) or the pre-Oslo PLO revolutionary legitimacies (capitalizing on nationalist and anti-colonial sentiments) might reassert themselves. Without a state, PA legitimacy or strong public support for diplomacy, the Palestinian leadership was now more willing to follow than to lead the street.

Israeli Politics

The Israeli domestic scene was at least as complicated. Wishing to protect himself against the accusation that the process of interim agreements would leave Israel without assets when permanent status came to be negotiated, Barak sought to abort this process and to leap directly to permanent status talks. In doing so he began to lose Arafat's trust. When Barak tried to address the potential negative ramifications of such a change by promising to transfer to Palestinian control three towns located in the outskirts of Jerusalem, he experienced even stronger Palestinian distrust when he failed to deliver on his promise.

Barak's failure resulted from the fact that by the time his promise came to be implemented he had been politically wounded by three developments: first, increasing Palestinian violence exposed him to criticism that in contrast to Netanyahu's perceived adherence to a policy of reciprocity which linked Israeli concessions tightly to Palestinians refraining from violence, his policy was encouraging Palestinians to press Israel through violence. Second, the talks with the Syrians were domestically costly, since the Barak government was exposed as willing to return the Golan to Syria, almost to the shores of Lake Tiberias. This earned it the wrath of the relatively small but very vocal and effective constituency opposed to ceding this territory. Finally, but importantly, by the time of Camp David, Barak had lost a number of his key coalition partners, reducing the size of his parliamentary grouping to a mere plurality in the Knesset, far too small to drive through the ratification of a historical compromise with the Palestinians. This loss resulted from Barak's initiation of a "civic agenda," dubbed by the press a "secular revolution," a program intended to usher in an era of secular reforms, which antagonized the religious party, Shas – a critically important member of his coalition. Designed to implement a greatly increased degree of separation between religion and state, the initiative placed the Barak government in the position of attempting two monumental changes simultaneously: a reform on the domestic front that had eluded all previous Israeli governments, and an ultimate grand bargain with the Palestinians.

Palestinians and Israelis

Now the domestic ills of both sides began to interact to the process's detriment. Initially Arafat saw Barak's promise of withdrawal in Jerusalem's outskirts as an opportunity to establish a presence closer to the Holy Places in East Jerusalem. Accordingly, in Abu Dis, one of the three towns, construction of a parliament building with an office for Arafat overlooking al-Haram al-Sharif had now begun. For this reason, Barak's failure to deliver on this promise dealt another blow to Arafat's legitimacy and to his confidence in Barak's intentions. Combined with Arafat's failure to gain the release of a larger number of Palestinian prisoners, Israel's failure to deliver on Barak's promise accelerated the loss of the PA's legitimacy and a decline in the credibility of its leaders.

Other important causes for the loss of the PA's credibility and legitimacy concerned the nature and level of competence of Arafat's regime. As noted in the previous chapter, by the end of 1999 the PA had accumulated a record of bad governance, corruption, and incompetence, and had become increasingly authoritarian.

In addition, by the eve of Camp David, Arafat's constituency had already begun to fragment. Fatah ranks were increasingly divided between the old guard and the young guard, with the young guard – impatient with the slow pace of the peace process and envious of Hezbollah's victory in southern Lebanon – gaining influence. And in Fatah's higher ranks and Arafat's inner circle, a competition over his eventual succession had already begun, with Speaker of the Legislative Council, Ahmed Qurie, and Fatah's number two, Mahmoud Abbas, as the prime contenders.

Israel's decision in May 2000 to unilaterally withdraw from southern Lebanon, under military pressure from Hezbollah and without a peace agreement with Syria or Lebanon, contributed to a change in the discourse among Palestinians. It encouraged many Islamists and young guard nationalist leaders to conclude that Israel could be forced out of the West Bank and the Gaza Strip through the use of force. A Palestinian poll at the time showed 63 percent of the public agreeing with this proposition.[23] This attitude, and the concern that Barak might refrain from implementing Israel's commitments under agreements previously negotiated with the Palestinians, completely undermined Arafat in the eyes of Palestinian critics of the process. By the eve of the Camp David summit it had created an environment of ill-will in higher Palestinian circles.

In addition to these features of domestic weaknesses, if not endemic fragmentation, both sides' leaderships seem to have failed to do anything significant to prepare their respective publics for the concessions that would need to be made if a permanent status agreement were to be achieved. Thus, while the Palestinian media continued to exhort its public to join a long struggle, Barak failed to address the Israeli public to redefine Israel's national aspirations, or reassure them with regard to the security risks entailed in necessary Israeli concessions in a way that would make the costs entailed in a deal better understood and hence more acceptable.

Much more important, however, was the failure on both sides to deal effectively with their respective opponents of peace. The Israeli government and the Palestinian leadership faced different, though similar, challenges to the efforts they were making. Hamas, committed to the establishment of an Islamic state in all of historic Palestine, was opposed to every aspect of the Oslo process. So was the Israeli right wing, including many Shas and Likud voters, most followers of the National Religious Party and parties to its right, and almost all Israeli settlers in Gaza and the West Bank. Particularly dangerous on the Palestinian side were members of the armed wing of Hamas, who were willing to go to any length to derail the process, and on the Israeli side some of the extreme elements within the Israeli settler community, from whose ranks the assassin of Prime Minister Rabin had come less than five years earlier.

Arafat and Barak faced two options with regard to the opponents of peace. They could have made every effort to suppress and delegitimize them, as Rabin had done just before his assassination and as Arafat had done during a short period in 1996. Or, they could have attempted to co-opt these opponents by adopting an "inclusive" approach aimed at taming them by making them partners to the process.

Both options had serious drawbacks. Delegitimizing the opposition would have left it with no option other than to make every effort to derail the process through violence. In the mid-1990s this had led Palestinian opponents of the process to launch a wave of suicide bombings against Israeli civilians and encouraged an Israeli extremist to assassinate the country's prime minister. Strategically, the two acts of violence succeeded, since their combined result was the 1996 electoral victory of Likud, which in turn led to a considerable slowdown of the process.

But the success of the alternative – following an inclusive approach – was far from assured. In the Israeli case the attempt to include proponents and opponents of peace under one umbrella in the form of the 1980s national unity governments did not result in any "taming of shrews." Instead, it subjected any attempts at peacemaking, such as the 1987 London Agreement, to death by paralysis.

As a result of these dilemmas, during most of the post-Oslo years both leaderships had taken a middle-ground approach to the opponents of peace, arguably pursuing the worst of all options. Thus, Arafat neither fully suppressed Palestinian opponents of the process nor allowed Hamas to become part of it. As a result, Hamas had no real stake in the success of the process but, at the same time, was not wholeheartedly confronted to make sure it did not derail the effort.

On the Israeli side, while some attempts were made by Rabin and Barak to delegitimize the opponents of peace, both leaders allowed settlement construction to continue – if not by building new settlements then by permitting significant further construction in existing ones – apparently in a futile attempt to placate the opposition. The most important consequence of this "middle option" was that it led to a crisis of confidence and loss of trust in the process on both sides. Israel interpreted Arafat's reluctance to suppress Palestinian opponents of peace as a desire to keep open all options – including the option to completely violate Oslo by returning to "armed struggle" either directly or by outsourcing such a move to Hamas. On their part, Palestinians interpreted continued Israeli settlement activities as indicating that Israel was not serious about its Oslo commitment to end its occupation of Palestinian lands.

At the domestic level there is little doubt that the failure to embrace the Clinton Parameters in December and to conclude a deal at Taba in January were affected by the Second Intifada that erupted in late September. Four months into the violence – with many Israelis convinced that Arafat had initiated it and was now orchestrating it, and with many Palestinians complaining of Israeli disproportionate response – the parties' mutual trust had completely eroded. While the Intifada itself is the subject of the next chapter, its effects on the diplomatic efforts of late 2000 and early 2001 were clearly negative. On the Palestinian side the eruption was exploited by Fatah's young guard activists demanding a shift in Palestinian strategy. What Palestinians considered as Israeli excessive use of force against civilian demonstrators now further constrained the PA's ability to confront the young guard and put an end to the ensuing violence. More broadly, the net outcome of the violence was to reduce Arafat's room for maneuver, making it more difficult for him to agree to further Palestinian concessions.

Palestinian violence had a similar effect on the Israeli political scene. By the time the Clinton Parameters were presented to the two parties, the Intifada had been raging for some three months. As a result, the Israeli body politic had turned its attention and support from diplomacy to the perceived imperative of suppressing the violence. Accordingly, the Israeli public was preparing to replace its negotiator, Ehud Barak, with Ariel Sharon, a retired general with decades of experience combating terrorism, who could now be counted on to act as the "town sheriff," restoring order in the violent streets. With such a background, neither the Clinton parameters nor the talks at Taba seemed relevant to a domestic scene preoccupied by the need to cope with the unexpected surge of violence.

There was also a mutually reinforcing effect between the surge of violence and the post-Oslo Israeli narrative about the failure of the talks. The Israeli narrative that there was no Palestinian partner for peace, and that Camp David had served to "unmask" Arafat's true intentions, produced two outcomes: a broad Israeli consensus that there was no point in continuing the negotiations, and an emerging Palestinian consensus that saw violence as the only remaining alternative to end occupation.

One final complication on the Israeli side was that with the election only weeks away from the Clinton Parameters, and only days ahead of the Taba talks, it was unclear whether the Israeli government had the legitimacy required to negotiate any significant transaction. This was particularly the case since every public opinion survey had indicated that the Barak-led Labor party was likely to be defeated at the polls.

Arafat

At the *individual level*, the process was also replete with management failures by the two leaders involved. Arafat wanted a comprehensive agreement or no agreement at all – an "all or nothing" approach, and he refrained from considering various "hypothetical" fallback positions and interim understandings – anything short of a comprehensive permanent status agreement. Furthermore, having developed an internal consensus on the parameters of permanent status, the Palestinian leader preferred to wait for a serious Israeli proposal before making any counteroffer. This left the impression that he was not interested in any positive conclusion of the talks.

Historically, Arafat rarely took the initiative in the peace process. Even when others negotiated on his behalf, he found ways to avoid taking responsibility for the positions presented during negotiations until a deal was concluded. Instead, he remained constant to his declared positions. He relied on his senior advisors, particularly Abbas and Qurie, to propose deals and to explore the extent to which Israel was willing to compromise. This dynamic gave these two individuals considerable power over the negotiation process, but it also gave Arafat the opportunity to avoid and, if necessary, to deny responsibility for any concessions made.

Ehud Barak

On the Israeli side, no individual was more consequential to the failure of peacemaking during this period than Barak. He would consider nothing less than a complete end to the conflict. But resolving every aspect of the conflict meant that "1948 issues" could not be excluded, since it was inconceivable that the Palestinians would accept an end to the conflict without addressing the consequences of the *Nakba*. Thus the "all or nothing" approach adopted by both leaders made reaching an agreement impossible.

An equally negative aspect of Barak's negotiating style was his apparent belief that opening negotiations with a "low offer" would make it more likely that the compromise ultimately reached would be closer to what he could market to his constituency. This raised questions as to his seriousness and true intentions for the talks, contributing to the Palestinian side's mistrust of him. And when the Palestinians dismissed the proposal out of hand, Barak permitted the Israeli team to offer more territory. This had a disastrous effect on the substantive talks, as Arafat drew the conclusion from the pre-Camp David meetings that he should always await a better deal.

A final facet of Barak's personality which may have played a role in the failure of the Camp David talks was his deficit in emotional intelligence. Often ridiculing the idea that nations' histories can be affected by the chemistry of their leaders, Barak consciously and consistently rejected the idea that he should express sympathy for Arafat's predicament and empathy with his plights. Remaining emotionally aloof, Barak contributed his share to the failure to build the minimal trust required between leaders, especially when the mission is ending a historic conflict.[24]

Leaders Interact

Beyond negotiating styles, Barak and Arafat both tolerated a high degree of discord inside their own negotiating teams. On the Palestinian side, the most damaging problem seems to have been the personal rivalry between Arafat's two senior negotiators, Abbas and Qurie, after the Stockholm secret negotiations. Thus, during Camp David he did not have the confidence of his two most senior advisors, seriously damaging his capacity to manage the process.

Individual-level factors also contributed their share to the particular failure of the Clinton Parameters and the Taba talks. On the Palestinian side, Arafat's lukewarm reaction to the Clinton Parameters may have been at least partly the result of his anger at President Clinton for singling him out publically as the prime culprit responsible for the failure of the Camp David talks. In addition, by the time of the Taba talks, Arafat may have been relying on an erroneous expectation – based on the Arabs' positive experience with the administration of George H. W. Bush – that the Palestinians might get a better deal from the incoming George W. Bush administration. On the Israeli side, Barak's awkwardness about attempting to negotiate an agreement on the eve of his leaving office caused him to distance himself from the talks he authorized, almost as if they were held at the Track-II level. Hence his post-Taba denials that serious negotiations had ever taken place there.

Concluding Notes

The failure of Israeli–Palestinian permanent status negotiations in 2000 and early 2001 demonstrates the significance of all three levels of analysis when attempting to understand critically important developments in the history of the Arab–Israeli conflict. At the global systemic level it was the supremacy of the United States that allowed it to convene the summit at Camp David and the talks at Bolling Air Force Base. Another testimony to the same effect is that the Clinton Parameters articulated at the conclusion of the Bolling talks remained a reference point for future Palestinian–Israeli discourses for years to come. By the time of this writing it has become a semi-common wisdom that ultimately no permanent status agreement will likely deviate much from these parameters.

However, the outcome of the negotiations was also affected by United States failures. Most important among these was the failure to persuade key Arab states not to make it difficult for the Palestinians to offer the concessions required for an agreement to be reached – notably, on the sensitive issue of Jerusalem – let alone to persuade them to play a positive role in providing the Palestinians and the Israelis with incentives to compromise.

At the *regional-systemic level* Israeli–Palestinian relations during the period addressed here were affected by Israel's unilateral withdrawal from Lebanon in May 2000. By forcing this withdrawal, Hezbollah presented Palestinian nationalists with a yardstick for measuring their relative gains.

There is also little doubt that domestic factors played an important role in making the negotiations possible but also in limiting the negotiators' room for maneuver. Despite the fact that the governments in 1999–2000 – Labor-led in Israel and Fatah-led on the Palestinian side – were committed to reaching a peace agreement, this was also a period that demonstrated the strength of domestic constraints. By the time Barak made Israel's most generous offer at Camp David he had already lost his parliamentary majority and by the time the Palestinians came closest to reciprocating, at Taba, the Second Intifada had already limited their leadership's room for maneuver.

Even more unfortunate is that the talks' failure was not the most important outcome of the period surveyed here. Rather it was the huge despair caused by this failure, first and foremost among the Palestinians in the West Bank and Gaza – despair that led to the eruption of the Second Intifada. In turn, this new wave of violence further affected the attitudes of the general publics involved, reducing and ultimately closing the leaders' room for maneuver in the negotiations process. On the Israeli side this change had immediate political consequences as the election early in 2001 resulted in the demise of the Labor-led coalition and the return to power of Likud, now led by Ariel Sharon.

Another dimension of the failure – fanning the conflict's flames – was the blame game, or the "no partner" narrative, that ensued following the failure of discussions. The contribution of narratives to the resilience of the conflict was now illustrated clearly: the discourse of "no partner" now dominated the Israeli viewpoint of the Palestinians and was not questioned until the November 2007 Annapolis Peace Conference.

Readings

Bickerton, Ian and Carla Klausner, *A History of the Arab-Israeli Conflict* (Prentice Hall, 2010) 298–332.

Enderlin, Charles, *Shattered Dreams: The Failure of the Peace Process in the Middle East, 1995–2002* (Other Press, 2003).

Gelvin, James, *The Israel-Palestine Conflict: One Hundred Years of War* (Cambridge University Press, 2007) 240–241.

Klieman, Aharon, *Compromising Palestine: A Guide to Final Status Negotiations* (Columbia University Press, 2000).

Lesch, David, *The Arab-Israeli Conflict* (Oxford University Press, 2008) 365–382.

Morris, Benny, *Righteous Victims: The History of the Zionist-Arab Conflict, 1881–2001* (Vintage, 2001) 651–673.

Smith, Charles D., *Palestine and the Arab-Israeli Conflict* (Bedford/St.Martin's, 2007) 499–512.

Tessler, Mark, *A History of the Israeli-Palestinian Conflict* (Indiana University Press, 2009) 818–827.

Historical Documents

Israel and Palestinian Authority, The Wye River Memorandum: Walter Laqueur and Barry Rubin, *The Israel-Arab Reader: A Documentary History of the Middle East Conflict* (Penguin Books), 529–534.

Israeli Prime Minister Ehud Barak Statement after the Camp David Talks: Laqueur and Rubin, *The Israel-Arab Reader*, 554–556.

The Clinton Plan: Laqueur and Rubin, *The Israel-Arab Reader*, 562–565.

U.S President Bill Clinton Statement after the Camp David Talks: Laqueur and Rubin, *The Israel-Arab Reader*, 551–554.

U.S. President Bill Clinton Summarizing his Experience with the Peace Process: Laqueur and Rubin, *The Israel-Arab Reader*, 573–580.

Notes

1. The General Framework Agreement for Peace in Bosnia and Herzegovina, also known as the Dayton Accords, is the peace agreement brokered by a multinational team led by Americans Warren Christopher, Secretary of State at the time, and negotiator Richard C. Holbrooke to resolve the war in Bosnia and Herzegovina. The Accords, reached in November 21, 1995, were negotiated over a two-week period when all parties were sequestered in the Wright-Patterson Air Force Base near Dayton, Ohio. For more information about the brokering of the Dayton Accords, see Richard Holbrooke, To End a War (New York: Random House, 1998).
2. Tal Musacal, "IEC Chooses Egyptian Natural Gas," *The Jerusalem Post*, January 26, 2001;"Israel Electric Goes for Egyptian Gas Deal," *Ha'aretz*, January 26, 2001.
3. Don Peretz and Gideon Doron, "Sectarian Politics and the Peace Process: The 1999 Israel Elections," *Middle East Journal*, 54, 2 (Spring 2000), 259–273.
4. "Barak Arrives in Egypt on First Foreign Visit as Prime Minister," *Deutsche-Presse Agenteur*, July 9, 1999.
5. Smith, *Palestine and the Arab–Israeli Conflict*, 500.
6. "Document 566, Sharm el-Sheikh Memorandum, September 4, 1999," in M. Cherif Bassiouni, ed., *Documents on the Arab–Israeli Conflict: The Palestinians and the Israeli–Palestinian Peace Process, vol.* 2, 1149–1152.
7. Tessler, *A History of the Israeli–Palestinian Conflict*, 799–800.
8. Ahmed Qurie, *Beyond Oslo, the Struggle for Palestine: Inside the Middle East Peace Process from Rabin's Death to Camp David* (London: IB Tauris, 2008), 108–160.
9. T.P. Najem, "Palestinian–Israeli Conflict and South Lebanon," *Economic and Political Weekly*, 35.46 (November 11–17, 2000), 4006–4009; Augustus Richard Norton, "Hizballah and the Israeli Withdrawal from Southern Lebanon," *Journal of Palestine Studies*, 30, 1 (Autumn 2000), 22–35.
10. Gilead Sher, *Just Beyond Reach: The Israeli–Palestinian Peace Negotiations 1999–2001* (Tel Aviv: Miskal-Yedioth Ahronot Books, 2001), 234–267.
11. Smith, *Palestine and the Arab–Israeli Conflict*, 512; "Likud Leader Ends Visit to Temple Mount; Protests Reported," Voice of Israel Radio, BBC Summary of Word Broadcasts, Jerusalem, September 29, 2000; Etgar Lefkovits, Herb Keinon, and Lamia Lahoud, "Reacting to PM's Remarks to the 'Post' Sharon Vows to Fight Division of Jerusalem," *The Jerusalem Post*, September 29, 2000.
12. Dennis Ross, *The Missing Peace: The Inside Story of the Fight for Middle East Peace*, 753–756; Gilead Sher, *Just Beyond Reach: The Israeli–Palestinian Peace Negotiations 1999–2001*, 188–209.
13. *American Jewish Yearbook, 2002* (New York: American Jewish Committee, 2002), 520–521.
14. "The Taba Negotiations (January 2001)," *Journal of Palestine Studies*, 31, 3 (Spring 2002), 79–89; "Israeli–Palestinian Joint Statement, 27 January 2001," Israeli Ministry of Foreign Affairs, http://www.mfa.gov.il/MFA/MFAArchive/2000_2009/2001/1/Israeli-Palestinian%20Joint%20 Statement%20-%2027-Jan-2001. From those same talks at Taba, another document produced was the non-paper prepared by the EU Special Representative for the Middle East Peace Process, Ambassador Miguel Moratinos, which claimed to represent the results of the Taba talks, as well. The Moratinos Document was viewed by the Palestinians as accuratelyreflecting the discussions at Taba, while the Israeli side did not share this assessment. "Non-paper by EU Special Representative for the Middle East Peace Process," Division of Palestinian Rights: Developments Related to the Middle East Peace Process, Issue 16 (January 2000-December 2001). The document can be accessed at: http://unispal.un.org/UNISPAL.NSF/0/D3D719A10F2E7AA8852571170 050765F.]

15. "Israel's Sharon Reacts to Jerusalem Car Bomb: Talks Only After Terrorism Ends," IDF Radio, Tel Aviv, BBC Monitoring Middle East, February 8, 2001.
16. One such critic was Oslo Accords negotiator Ron Pundak. See Ron Pundak, "From Oslo to Taba: What Went Wrong?" *Survival*, 43, 3 (Autumn 2001), 31–46. Shlomo Ben-Ami, minister of internal security and then acting minister of foreign affairs under Barak, also commented on this in his book; see Shlomo Ben-Ami, *Scars of War, Wounds of Peace: The Israeli-Arab Tragedy* (New York: Oxford University Press, 2006), 250–252.
17. Ben-Ami, *Scars of War*, 260.
18. Pundak, "From Oslo to Taba: What Went Wrong?" 37–38.
19. In an op-ed in the *Washington Post*, Palestinian negotiator Saeb Erekat wrote, "We made real progress at Camp David, and the imperative now is to build on that progress and keep the momentum going." Saeb Erekat, "Camp David: A Story of Success," *Washington Post*, August 5, 2000.
20. *Al Ahram*, July 22, 2000, 1.
21. *The Arab Strategic Report 2000* (Cairo: Al Ahram Center for Political & Strategic Studies, 2001), 282.
22. Ross, *The Missing Peace*, 717. For some specific meetings, see Sher, *Just Beyond Reach*, 204–207.
23. The poll was conducted in July 2000 by the Palestinian Center for Policy and Survey Research in Ramallah (posted at: http://www.pcpsr.org/survey/polls/2000/p1a.html). Indeed, shortly before Camp David, in a late-May 2000 meeting, Arafat told Israeli Minister of Environment Dalia Itzik that Israel's withdrawal decision increased pressure on him from young Fatah leaders, thereby limiting his room for maneuver. By then Arafat had already seen his authority challenged by Fatah young guards in March 2000 when one of his most senior guests, French Prime Minister Lionel Jospan was attacked at Birzeit University. Later in May, the same young guards organized anti-Israeli violent protests in the West Bank over the issue of Palestinian prisoner release. Arafat's message to Minister Itzik was meant to warn Israel that without rapid and significant progress in the peace process he would soon lose internal control. During his meeting with Itzik, Arafat said: "You have to understand what sort of pressure is being placed on me by the public. My public perceives Hezbollah to be heroes who succeeded in getting the Israel Defense Forces out of Lebanon and believe that that is the route we should take as well." See Ross Dunn, "Arafat Pressed to Abandon Peace and Resume Warfare," *Sydney Morning Herald*, June 1, 2000.
24. Ben Ami, *Scars of War*, 253–256; Pundak, "From Oslo to Taba: What Went Wrong?" 36–44.

11 The Second Intifada

This chapter centers on the Second Palestinian Intifada that began on September 28, 2000 and on Israel's efforts to suppress it. The period addressed here is characterized by international and regional events that transformed the Middle East, including the inauguration of the George W. Bush administration, al-Qaida's horrific terrorist attacks on September 11, 2001, and the invasion of Afghanistan and subsequently Iraq. One result of these invasions was a growing perception in the Middle East and beyond that the United States had declared war on Islam. To others, the combination of the September 11 attacks and the wars in Afghanistan and Iraq appeared as violent confirmations of Samuel Huntington's prediction of a coming "Clash of Civilizations."[1]

In the aftermath of the collapse of the diplomatic efforts to resolve the Palestinian–Israeli conflict in late 2000, the Intifada represented a total breakdown of trust in the efficacy of diplomacy among Palestinians and Israelis alike. In a broader sense Palestinian–Israeli relations were now transformed from what could be described as "limited cooperation" to open hostility. Yasser Arafat, previously seen by some Israeli leaders as their partner, was now viewed as anything but that.

Israel's response to the new circumstances was the resumption of full security control of the West Bank, the isolation of Arafat in his Ramallah headquarters (the Muqata'a), the reoccupation of Palestinian towns and cities in mid-2002, an array of counterinsurgency operations, the erection of hundreds of checkpoints and the separation barrier and, finally, in the summer of 2005, the disengagement from Gaza.

In Israel, as well as among the Palestinians, this period is also characterized by the collapse of pro-peace communities, the weakening of the center of the political map and the parallel rise of the secular and religious right wing.

Some regard the end of the Intifada as having occurred when Arafat died in November 2004, while others see it as having taken place when Arafat's successor, Mahmoud Abbas, negotiated a ceasefire with Hamas in March 2005. Thus, this chapter ends at the close of 2005, after Israel disengaged from Gaza.

Main Developments

The most dramatic developments during this period were the eruption, escalation and eventual abatement of the Second Palestinian Intifada. In addition to Palestinian actions that largely determined the agenda of the Arab–Israeli conflict during this period, also of great significance were the Israeli, regional and international reactions to the Intifada. Particularly important among the regional reactions was the Arab League's adoption of the Arab Peace Initiative, and especially significant among the international reactions was the "road map for Middle East peace" suggested by a quartet composed of the United States, the UN, the EU and Russia. Final milestones of this period were the most concrete outcomes of the Intifada: Israel's construction of a separation barrier and its unilateral withdrawal from Gaza.

The Eruption and Escalation of the Intifada

On September 28, 2000, Israeli opposition leader Ariel Sharon paid a visit to the Temple Mount – al-Haram al-Sharif (also known as The Noble Sanctuary) in Jerusalem. Palestinians reacted by demonstrating against the visit, and Israeli security agencies moved to suppress the protests. In the days that followed, these exchanges resulted in a score of Palestinian dead and some 200 wounded, as well as a number of Israeli police officers injured.[2] Arab citizens of Israel soon joined the demonstrations, resulting in violent clashes between protestors and the Israeli police. Within the next ten days (October 1–10, 2000), 13 Israeli Arabs lost their lives and hundreds were wounded.[3]

The confrontations of September–October 2000 launched more than five years of Palestinian–Israeli deadly violence. Palestinians labeled this period "The Second Intifada" – a term later adopted by Israelis as well.

The Intifada had four main characteristics. First, Palestinians resorted to suicide attacks and other forms of violence, carried out mostly by Hamas and supported by most Palestinians, who viewed the violence as legitimate. In turn, there were equally high levels of Israeli public support for harsh measures to suppress the violence.

Second, the Intifada represented a transformation of the relations between the Palestinian Authority and Israel. By mid-2002, Israel had reoccupied all the cities and towns in the West Bank, resuming full security control over the area. Israel then placed Arafat under siege in his headquarters in Ramallah, refusing to negotiate any agreements with him.

Third, the Intifada weakened the Palestinian Authority (PA) as a central government. In part this reflected Arafat's decision to step aside and abdicate his responsibility to maintain calm. He justified this abdication by arguing that the Israelis had abandoned their own Oslo obligations. Equally, such weakening also resulted from Israeli measures targeting PA security services, based on Israeli assessments that members of these services were taking part in the violence.

Fourth, during the Second Intifada the nationalist young guard rose, as discussed in Chapter 9. The young guard originated from the ranks of the *Tanzim*, an organized militia that represented Fatah's cadre in the West Bank and the Gaza Strip. During the First Intifada the group developed its own armed "strike force" and carried out violent attacks against Israeli targets in the occupied territories. During the early years of the Oslo process the Tanzim was essentially unarmed. But immediately after the eruption of the Second Intifada, the Tanzim provided the leadership and most fighters of Fatah's militia – the al-Aqsa Brigades.[4]

The deadly attacks and efforts to suppress them reached a peak in 2002, resulting in some 7,000 casualties: 1,068 dead and 3,296 wounded Palestinians and 452 dead and 2,309 wounded Israelis.[5] By the end of 2005, the violence resulted in a total of more than 38,000 casualties:

Figure 11.1. The aftermath of a suicide attack (Haifa bus bombing) 2001. © Alex Rozkovsky/Getty Images

about 1,000 dead and over 5,000 wounded Israelis, and about 4,000 dead and over 25,000 wounded Palestinians.[6]

While Palestinians' suicide bombing during the Second Intifada was not the first time this human weapon was used, this period is marked by the first large-scale use of the method in the context of the Israeli–Palestinian conflict.[7] By the end of 2005, Palestinians had carried out 147 such attacks.[8] Another 450 attempted suicide bombings were aborted at the final phase of implementation.[9] While these attacks constituted a small part of the overall number of violent incidents during the Second Intifada, they accounted for a majority of Israeli casualties: approximately 50 percent of Israeli dead during this period were the result of suicide bombings.[10]

The Palestinian public supported most of the suicide attacks carried out against the Israelis during this period. The perceived failure of diplomacy in the aftermath of the Camp David summit led to a dramatic increase in public demand for violence, including suicide attacks. By contrast, the death of Arafat in 2004 and the election of Abbas to replace him as president of the Palestinian Authority increased public optimism about the peace process and reduced public support for violence. Polling data show that while three-quarters of the Palestinian public supported suicide attacks during the 2002–04 period, support for such attacks dropped considerably in 2005. A suicide attack in Tel Aviv in March 2005 was supported by only 29 percent of respondents; 67 percent opposed such attacks.[11]

Another relatively novel aspect of the Second Intifada was the extensive reporting and coverage of its developments by the international media and, particularly, the new region-wide Middle East media. The latter was spearheaded by the relatively new Qatar-based Al-Jazeera Television – a very well-endowed outlet, able to position television crews in many locations throughout the West Bank and Gaza. As a result, almost every important development in the violent confrontation was televised to millions of homes in the region and beyond. These reports included pictures of tragedies, from a Palestinian father and his son, Mohammed Dura, finding themselves in crossfire between Israeli soldiers and Palestinian militants, ending with the child's death, to the lynching of two IDF reservists by a crowd in Ramallah that included some members of the Palestinian security services.

Israeli Reactions

The violence led to an almost immediate suspension of the post-Oslo Palestinian–Israeli security cooperation, including the joint patrols conducted in accordance with the Oslo implementation agreements. The operation of various military and civilian Israeli–Palestinian coordination committees was also terminated. With exports from Gaza and the West Bank to Israel also gradually brought to a halt, the Palestinians could no longer benefit from the customs union previously agreed upon with Israel.

Following the onset of the violence, Israel also moved to reassert control over parts of the West Bank from which it had previously withdrawn. In April 2002, in response to a particularly deadly suicide bombing in the Israeli coastal city of Netanya – killing 30 and wounding 140 Israelis who had gathered at a hotel to celebrate the eve of the Passover holiday – the IDF launched Operation Defensive Shield, its most extensive incursion into the West Bank, reoccupying the large Palestinian metropolitan areas. According to a UN report, this resulted in 497 Palestinians being killed and 1,447 wounded during the actual operation.[12] The fighting was particularly fierce in the city of Jenin, where armed Palestinians ambushed an Israeli patrol, killing 13 and wounding seven Israeli soldiers.[13] The damage to infrastructure was also substantial: dozens of buildings in Jenin were demolished or seriously damaged.[14]

The Second Intifada also witnessed widespread Israeli use of airpower in counter-insurgency operations. The IAF used attack helicopters and F-16 fighters, mostly but not exclusively as platforms for precision-guided munitions, particularly to kill Palestinian militants. These operations were referred to in Israel as "focused prevention" (in Hebrew *Sikul Memukad*), by the Palestinians as extra-judicial assassinations (in Arabic *Ightialat*) and elsewhere as "targeted killings."

Some two and a half years into the Second Intifada, Israeli offensive measures (reoccupation, use of airpower, targeted killings) were supplemented by its government's decision to construct a separation barrier in the West Bank (see map on page 460). A similar barrier had been constructed along the border between Israel and the Gaza Strip in the early 1990s. The new barrier constituted a system of fences and sensors along most of its route and a high concrete wall in urban areas, notably in and around Jerusalem. The decision represented a major change in Israeli national security policy: from a counterinsurgency strategy that relied almost exclusively on offensive measures to an added dimension of passive defense.

The Arab Reaction

In the broader regional environment the Second Intifada elicited much sympathy for the Palestinians, in the Arab street as well as among intellectual circles who were affected by the regional media's reporting of the violence. Demonstrations and declarations of support were widespread in different Arab capitals.

Accordingly, an extraordinary Arab Summit was called for in Cairo in October 21–23, 2000. The Summit "confirmed its complete solidarity with the Palestinian People in their struggle to restore their legitimate rights." After denouncing Israeli actions and stating that "a just and comprehensive peace will not be achieved without the establishment of the Palestinian State with the 'Honorable *Quds*' as its capital," the summit called for the formation of an international commission under UN auspices to investigate "Israeli crimes." It also proposed the establishment of an international criminal court to put "Israeli war criminals" on trial.[15]

Arab governments also expressed their sympathy by pledging financial support for the Palestinians. Thus, the Cairo Summit agreed to establish "The Quds Intifada Fund," with $200 million to help the victims of the Intifada, as well as the "Al-Aqsa Fund," with $800 million to help the Palestinians withstand Israeli economic pressures. Arab countries were urged to help the Palestinians' economy by importing Palestinian goods without quantitative or qualitative restrictions and to exempt such goods from customs. The summit also urged that a complaint be registered with the World Trade Organization against economic measures Israel had taken against the Palestinians. In reality, however, Arab governments' subsequent support for the Palestinian Intifada fell short of their pledges.[16]

Another important development took place in January 2002, when the Israeli Navy captured *Karine A* – a ship carrying weapons and ammunition to the Palestinians from Iran. Seen as evidence of Iranian assistance to the PA, the incident contributed to a further deterioration in relations between the United States and the PA. It also added to growing frustration in Arab governmental circles with Arafat. In Egypt and Jordan in particular, there was already anger at Arafat's unwillingness and/or inability to fulfill the promises he made in late October 2000 at Sharm el-Sheikh (see below), and on later occasions, to help de-escalate the violence. Now these Arab governments also blamed Arafat for "bringing Iran in" – a development they regarded as extremely unwelcome in light of its potential impact on their own Islamic movements.

By mid-2002 a number of Arab states attempted to revive the dormant Palestinian–Israeli peace process by proposing a new, comprehensive Arab–Israeli grand bargain. The first to suggest this was Saudi Arabia's then Crown Prince Abdullah in an interview he gave on February 17, 2002 to *New York Times* columnist Tom Friedman.[17] Abdullah proposed that in exchange for Israeli withdrawal to the 1967 lines the Arab states would enter into normal peace relations with Israel.

A somewhat lengthier and more complicated version of the proposal was adopted by the Arab League Summit which convened in Beirut two weeks later.[18] The Arab Peace Initiative (API) that the summit endorsed differed from the simple formulation suggested earlier by the Saudis primarily by adding a resolution of the Palestinian refugee issue to the original "package." This elicited a negative Israeli reaction. With the aforementioned suicide bombing attack in Netanya occurring only a few days later – leading Israel to launch Operation Defensive Shield – the API went into hibernation.

The Global Reaction

In the broader international context, the Second Intifada began with the Clinton administration attempting two final initiatives: first, a conference held in the Egyptian resort town of Sharm el-Sheik in October 2000 in an attempt to halt the Intifada. The conference set up an international commission, headed by former United States Senator George Mitchell, which was tasked to explore the reasons for the eruption of violence and to suggest ways of ending it. Second, a meeting of Palestinian and Israeli negotiators at Bolling Air Force Base outside Washington, DC, resulting in the so-called Clinton Parameters for resolving the Palestinian–Israeli dispute (see Chapter 10).

Navigated by President George W. Bush, American policy during most of the Second Intifada was characterized by an approach that differed sharply from that of its predecessor. Initially, the new administration's most important driving force seems to have been the desire to avoid the heavy investments made by the Clinton team in its unsuccessful bid to resolve the Palestinian–Israeli conflict. Thus, during its first nine months in office the Bush administration pursued what some have referred to as a "hands off" policy – refraining from involvement in mediation between the two parties unless and until they demonstrated the will to reach a comprehensive peace agreement.

While the Bush team did not wash its hands entirely of the conflict, it pursued modest objectives, focusing almost exclusively on trying to stem the violence. In this framework it took two steps. First, it endorsed the recommendations of the aforementioned Mitchell Commission, submitted on April 30, 2001. These focused on an Israeli freeze on settlement construction, the dismantlement of outposts and an end to Palestinian violence coupled with a reform of the PA's security sector.

Second, the administration launched a number of additional stabilization efforts intended to implement the recommendation of the Mitchell Report: first, it sent CIA Director George Tenet in June 2001 to try to arrange a ceasefire between the warring parties and to start the implementation of the Mitchell Plan; later, United States Marine General Tony Zinni, a former commander of the American Central Command, was dispatched to the area with a similar mission. These two failed efforts were later followed by the successive stationing "on the ground" of senior American military officers, from William E. Ward to Keith Dayton. Their missions, however, were initially limited to help stabilize the situation by assisting the Palestinians in implementing security sector reform.

Following the horrendous al-Qaida attacks on New York and Washington, DC on September 11, 2001, the Bush administration's approach to the Middle East completely changed: it now regarded the region almost exclusively through the prism of its newly announced "War on Terror." This led President Bush to embrace sharply differing opinions of the Israeli and Palestinian leaders: great sympathy for Israeli Prime Minister Ariel Sharon's lifelong track-record as an anti-terror warrior, but growing anger at Arafat for his perceived unwillingness and/or inability to end the violence. Increasingly, as Palestinian violence escalated, American policy manifested greater understanding for Israel. Thus, while the PA was accused of failing, Israeli responses were viewed as legitimate. This was accompanied by rhetoric that equated Palestinian terrorism with that of Bin Laden and that regarded Arafat and his circle as another Taliban.

Yet the September 11 attacks also drove the Bush administration back into Middle East diplomatic activity. Its reinvolvement in the conflict began in the framework of the attempts to build a coalition of moderate Muslim states to fight al-Qaida terror. It became even more pronounced once the American military campaign against the Taliban succeeded. American strategy in the region then shifted the focus of the War on Terror from Afghanistan to Iraq, a change that required even greater measures of support by America's Arab allies. For this to be achieved, it was deemed, the Palestinian–Israeli peace process had to be reignited.

Diplomatic Outcomes

The first step in this new direction was President Bush's announcement at the UN General Assembly on June 24, 2002 of his support for the establishment of an independent Palestinian state and of his vision for a two-state solution to the Palestinian–Israeli conflict. The solution to the conflict, said Bush, must be based on the creation of two states, residing "side by side in peace and security." The announcement – made at the urging of Saudi Arabia[19] – was also intended to provide the Palestinians with an incentive to end the violence. With this, for the first time, the creation of an independent Palestinian state became American policy. But Bush coupled this support with a call for regime change in the Palestinian camp. Consistent with his administration's general neoconservative approach, Bush now challenged the Palestinians to elect a leadership "not compromised by terror and corruption."[20]

In this new international environment, Bush now came to see Arafat as part of the problem rather than part of the solution. This perception became particularly dominant in his mind following the January 3, 2002 interception of the *Karine A*. Having decided that Arafat had deceived him when he assured him that he had no knowledge of the transaction, Bush now lost all confidence in the PLO leader.[21]

EXCERPTS FROM PRESIDENT BUSH'S SPEECH OF JUNE 24, 2002

- "It is untenable for Palestinians to live in squalor and occupation... My vision is two states, living side by side in peace and security."
- "Today, Palestinian authorities are encouraging, not opposing, terrorism. This is unacceptable... If Palestinians embrace democracy, confront corruption and firmly reject terror, they can count on American support for the creation of a provisional state of Palestine."
- "I call on the Palestinian people to elect new leaders, leaders not compromised by terror. I call upon them to build a practicing democracy, based on tolerance and liberty."
- "I can understand the deep anger and despair of the Palestinian people... You deserve a life of hope for your children. An end to occupation and a peaceful democratic Palestinian state may seem distant, but America and our partners throughout the world stand ready to help, help you make them possible as soon as possible."

Palestinian responses to these pressures, for example by establishing a position of a prime minister similar to that in parliamentary democracies, fell short of America's expectations. Thus, the United States observed that Arafat, while establishing the requested post, refused to provide Mahmoud Abbas, the new prime minister, with the authority needed to direct the Palestinian security agencies – agencies that the Bush administration regarded as requiring reform if they were to fight terror.

In April 2003, immediately following its invasion of Iraq, the United States cooperated with the EU, Russia and the UN, together comprising the "Quartet," to formulate and announce a road map to a permanent two-state solution to the Israeli–Palestinian conflict. The plan included three-phases: a stabilization phase, focusing on a complete cessation of Palestinian violence and a total ban on settlement construction; a state-building phase, leading to an option of establishing a Palestinian state with provisional borders; and finally, negotiations of a permanent resolution of the Israeli–Palestinian conflict.

KEY PROVISIONS OF THE QUARTET'S ROAD MAP TO A PERMANENT TWO-STATE SOLUTION APRIL 30, 2003

- "In Phase I, the Palestinians immediately undertake an unconditional cessation of violence ...Palestinians undertake comprehensive political reform in preparation for statehood, including drafting a Palestinian constitution, and free, fair and open elections upon the basis of those measures. Israel takes all necessary steps to help normalize Palestinian life. Israel withdraws from Palestinian areas occupied from September 28, 2000 and the two sides restore the status quo that existed at that time, as security performance and cooperation progress. Israel also freezes all settlement activity, consistent with the Mitchell report."
- "Phase II starts after Palestinian elections and ends with possible creation of an independent Palestinian state with provisional borders in 2003. Its primary goals are continued comprehensive security performance and effective security cooperation, continued normalization of Palestinian life and institution-building, further building on and sustaining of the goals outlined in Phase I, ratification of a democratic Palestinian constitution, formal establishment of office of prime minister, consolidation of political reform, and the creation of a Palestinian state with provisional borders...Creation of an independent Palestinian state...through a process of Israeli–Palestinian engagement...As part of this process, implementation of prior agreements, to enhance maximum territorial contiguity, including further action on settlements in conjunction with the establishment of a Palestinian state with provisional borders."
- "Phase III objectives are consolidation of reform and stabilization of Palestinian institutions, sustained, effective Palestinian security performance, and Israeli–Palestinian negotiations aimed at a permanent status agreement in 2005."

The Bush administration continued to make its deeper involvement in the efforts to resolve the conflict conditional on PA action to halt violence and terror. The PA was also urged to dismantle the infrastructure of all armed militias in the Palestinian territories and to reform itself by applying practices of good governance. When Sharon announced Israel's unilateral disengagement from the Gaza Strip in late 2004, the Bush administration praised his act as a step in the right direction.

While the launching of the road map in 2003 signaled that the United States was at least minimally sensitive to Europe's priorities, for the Europeans the Second Intifada was a period of growing frustration with Palestinian–Israeli affairs. The European street and much of its media and intellectual elites seemed to sympathize with the hardships endured by the Palestinians, but governmental circles were utterly disappointed to see their post-Oslo investments in the PA collapse. Largely blaming Arafat for the slide toward violence, European governments were no longer willing to ignore the corruption and mismanagement plaguing his regime. Instead, they now attempted direct involvement in the Palestinian reform process, demanding that the PA exercise transparency and accountability, particularly in all matters financial.

Israeli Disengagement and Arafat's Death

With a reputation as a right-wing super-hawk, rooted in his role in Israel's 1982 invasion of Lebanon, Sharon, at this point, evolved into a pragmatist, orchestrating Israel's disengagement from the Gaza Strip: the complete evacuation of all settlers and IDF forces. This disengagement was conducted unilaterally – that is, not in the framework of an agreement with the Palestinians. In addition, Sharon's move included the dismantling of four small settlements in the northern West Bank. By August 23, 2005, some 8,500 settlers were evacuated and some 21 settlements were dismantled in Gaza, and some 680 settlers were evacuated from the four dismantled settlements in the West Bank. Homes in the settlements were demolished. While also withdrawing its military forces from the Rafah area along the Gaza border with Egypt, the so-called Philadelphi Corridor, Israel continued to control Gaza's coastline and airspace. The total cost of the evacuation at that time, including compensation to settlers, was $2.2 billion.[22]

With that, Sharon became the first Israeli leader to dismantle settlements in areas regarded by Israelis as parts of the Land of Israel. By November 21, 2005, he had continued this metamorphosis by leaving the right-wing Likud party, which he had previously led twice to electoral victories, and formed a new centrist party, Kadima ("Forward"). The new party was broadly understood to be calling for continued disengagement, now in the West Bank. However, on January 4, 2006, Sharon suffered a massive stroke from which he has not recovered, consequently leaving the political scene.

Arafat's personal evolution during this period was no less dramatic. Having led the Palestinian national movement on its journey from uncompromising rejection of Israel through the acceptance of a two-state solution in 1988 and the later adoption of the Oslo framework, the PA's president now absolved himself of responsibilities. Not only did he now preside over a complete deterioration in Palestinian–Israeli and Palestinian-American relations, he also made no attempt to mitigate the competition between Fatah and its radical Islamist rivals – Hamas and Islamic Jihad – or the conflict between the old guard and the young guard within his own Fatah movement.

After decades during which Arafat was the region's most avid jetsetter, he was now confined by Israel to the small governmental compound (the Muqata'a) in Ramallah. This surreal existence appeared to cause him to become increasingly detached from developments in the region as well as among his own Palestinian constituency.

The final chapter in Arafat's personal slide was the sharp deterioration in his health beginning in late October 2004, leading to his departure for emergency medical treatment in France and subsequent death on November 11, 2004. Following a brief interim leadership, on January 9, 2005 Arafat was replaced as PLO Chairman and as PA President by Mahmoud Abbas. This followed PA presidential elections that Abbas won with 62 percent of the vote. While Hamas did not field a candidate, preferring instead to boycott these elections, turnout was over 65 percent. Six other candidates contested the election, with the independent Mustafa Barghouti coming second with almost 20 percent of the vote. During the election campaign, Abbas declared his opposition to what he called the "militarization of the Intifada," arguing that violence had been destructive to Palestinian national interests.[23]

Abbas's victory helped to create a more open Palestinian political system, as four local election rounds were held during 2005. Hamas performed extremely well in these rounds, particularly in December when it won most of the contests in the large cities. Abbas's victory also led to the resumption of a serious dialogue between Fatah and Hamas; Abbas and Fatah sought a ceasefire with Israel while Hamas sought a formal role in the Palestinian political system. With Egypt hosting the dialogue, an agreement was reached on March 17, 2005. Thirteen Palestinian factions signed the Cairo Declaration, which included: (1) affirmation of the goal of Palestinian statehood; (2) a commitment to a ceasefire with Israel; (3) an agreement on the need for political reforms, the holding of elections, and the main elements of a new electoral system; (4) an agreement on reforming the PLO and integrating Hamas and Islamic Jihad into its institutions; and (5) a commitment to refrain from any use of violence in internal Palestinian disputes.[24]

Narratives

Israeli Narratives

The dominant Israeli narrative describing this period is that the Second Intifada comprised a Palestinian return to terrorism and thus a violation of the Oslo grand bargain in the framework of which the Palestinians had committed themselves to abandon the "armed struggle." For the Israeli right-wing, who argued that the Palestinians' recognition of Israel and promise to refrain from violence in Oslo were mere tactical ploys aimed at gaining Israeli concessions, the outbreak of the Second Intifada was simply an affirmation of long-held beliefs.

Arafat's Responsibility

An important dimension of the Israeli narrative was that the Second Intifada was "made by Arafat." Some Israelis viewed the Palestinian leader as having planned and orchestrated the violence. But even those who were not sure that Arafat was the architect – or, for that matter, that the Intifada had any architect at all – held him responsible for allowing the violence to escalate. In this, Arafat's conduct was contrasted with his ability to bring a complete halt to the violence in previous clashes.

No less important, Israelis held Arafat responsible for creating the conditions that allowed the violence to occur and escalate. This responsibility was seen as threefold: first, his rejection of Israeli offers presented at Camp David was viewed as signaling a move away from the efforts to reach a peaceful resolution of the conflict; second, his failure to revise Palestinian textbooks and to ban anti-Israeli incitement in the Palestinian media was seen as part of a continued cultivation of "a culture of violence"; finally, at the practical-operational level, Arafat was viewed as able but unwilling to order a halt to the violence by instructing his security services to enforce peace.

This narrative seemed to be supported by what some senior Israelis said they were told by some of Arafat's closest aides: namely, that they were prepared to take steps to stem the violence but that Arafat was unwilling to give them the required commands. Worse still, Israelis observed that "under Arafat's watch" members of the Palestinian security services were taking part in the violence against Israelis. An often cited example of this was the participation of Palestinian security forces in the lynching of Israeli reservists in Ramallah on October 12, 2000.

At the broader strategic level, the Israeli narrative now stipulated that despite Arafat's Oslo promise, he never abandoned the "armed struggle," instead keeping it as an option to which the Palestinians would revert if the circumstances so required. His post-Oslo refusals to confront the Islamic opposition to the accords and to cleanse the Palestinian media of anti-Israeli and anti-Jewish diatribes were now regarded as mere preludes to the Second Intifada.

On the topic of the immediate circumstances explaining the Intifada, Israelis believed Arafat's decision to allow the violence to escalate was a reaction to the public relations debacle that he suffered in the immediate aftermath of the Camp David Summit: namely, when President Clinton and key European leaders identified him as responsible for the summit's failure. The clashes in late September and early October 2000 generated "David and Goliath" images favorable to the Palestinians. The broadcasting of pictures of protesting youth confronted by heavily armed Israeli soldiers resulted in considerable international sympathy for the Palestinians, thus alleviating the Camp David public relations disaster. Noticing and approving of this outcome, Arafat now saw only benefits to allowing the violence to continue and escalate.

"No Partner"

With Arafat seen as having "returned to his terrorist ways," Israelis now concluded that they no longer had a Palestinian partner for a negotiated resolution of the conflict. And, in the absence of such a partner, they now saw themselves as having no choice but to launch an array of unilateral measures designed to address the security threats posed by the Intifada, including a redeployment of IDF forces in areas of the West Bank and Gaza from which they had previously withdrawn, and the launch of a program of preemptive and preventive killings of Palestinian terrorist operatives and commanders.

In this context Israelis also saw themselves as obliged to battle members of the Palestinian security services with whom they previously cooperated. These security personnel were now regarded as believing that Arafat supported continuation of the violence, leading them to take part in the attacks. Thus, Arafat's later claims that he was unable to stem the violence because Israel had destroyed the Palestinians' security institutions were regarded as merely another example of his duplicity. Had members of these services not taken part in the violence, Israelis argued, there would have been no reason to fight them.

The Security Fence

A related aspect of the Israeli narrative was that the proposed security fence between Israel and the West Bank should be viewed as an inescapable and fully justified measure to prevent suicide bombers reaching Israel's large metropolitan areas. Israelis pointed out that during the 23 years that lapsed between the conquest of the West Bank in 1967 and the outbreak of the Second Intifada in late 2000, no one had proposed fencing the area. They further stressed that it was precisely because the Gaza Strip had been similarly fenced beginning in the early 1990s that not a single suicide bomber managed to penetrate Israel from Gaza during the Second Intifada.

At the same time, Israelis emphasized that because it was a temporary measure to combat terrorism, the security fence's positioning should not be taken to indicate their "bottom line" with regard to Israel's permanent boundaries. Their insistence that in some areas this demarcation should clearly deviate from the pre-1967 borders was said to be motivated not only by the desire to protect Israelis residing in the small number of large settlement blocks located beyond the 1967 lines but also by the perceived need to emphasize that final boundaries would need to be negotiated, so that the positioning of the fence should not be taken to indicate agreement to withdraw to any particular line.

At the same time, the Israeli right wing, and especially the settler community, developed an entirely different narrative about the security fence. In their eyes the decision to erect the fence was not only a violation of Israeli national security doctrine – substituting active offense by passive defense – it also manifested a loss of national will to fight terrorism by offensive means. Much more important, however, was that in their eyes the barrier implied a willingness to partition the Land of Israel unilaterally. As such, it sent a wrong message, namely that Israeli settlers residing "on the other side of the fence" were less worthy of effective defense than Israeli assets and population inside the 1967 lines. The latter were now to benefit from protection provided by the security fence.

The API, the Road Map and Disengagement

When the Arab Peace Initiative was announced at the 2002 Arab League Summit in Beirut, it was greeted with skepticism, if not rejection, by Israelis. For them, what at first appeared a very positive grand bargain – with the Arab states seen as offering to embrace Israel and integrate it into the region in exchange for withdrawal to the 1967 lines – was in reality highly deficient. First, by tying Israel's integration into the region to its complete withdrawal on all fronts, the incentives for Israel to reach an agreement with the Palestinians were held hostage to a resolution of the Syrian–Israeli conflict. In other words, it gave Assad de-facto veto power over any agreement to end the Palestinian–Israeli conflict.

Second, by expanding the dimensions of the proposed grand bargain to include a resolution of the Palestinian refugee issue, and by tying this to UN Resolution 194, the API was seen as reintroducing through the back door the hypersensitive issue of the Palestinians' Right of Return. As Israelis regard this ascribed right as threatening their future as a Jewish and democratic state, they viewed the API as a major challenge rather than as a historic opportunity.

By contrast, Israelis viewed the road map offered by the Quartet in 2003 more positively. They regarded the proposal as realistic because it was based on an appreciation that, given the violence that had been raging for more than two years, meaningful steps toward resolving the Palestinian–Israeli dispute could only be considered after a radical change in the environment – a complete halt to the violence. Thus, Israelis emphasized the plan's preamble, which presented it as "performance based" – a term interpreted by Israelis to imply that movement toward implementing the more advanced phases of the road map would be contingent on the prior implementation of stipulations of the earlier phases. Israelis insisted that there was good reason for the plan to have three phases. Thus, when Palestinians indicated acceptance of the road map while insisting on jumping straight to renewed permanent status negotiations – the third phase – Israelis saw this as an attempt to undermine the very logic of the whole plan.

Far from seeing themselves as having withdrawn from Gaza in the summer of 2005 "under fire," mainstream Israelis viewed their disengagement from the area as a consequence of their success in abating the Intifada and, at the same time, their growing recognition of the limits of force. For them, by 2005 Israel was threatened not by violence but rather by demographic trends in the population residing between the Mediterranean Sea and the Jordan River: changes in the relative size of population groups that now appeared to pose an enormous challenge to Israel's future as a Jewish and democratic state. Since Jews were about to lose their majority status in the area, it became clear that Israel's continued control of Gaza, the West Bank and East Jerusalem posed the following dilemma: either grant the Arab population in these areas full participatory rights, in which case Israel would lose its character as a Jewish state, or continue to deny them such rights, in which case Israel could no longer be considered a democracy.

Thus, in Israeli eyes, the success of their counterinsurgency strategy, the need to end the occupation, and the absence of a negotiation partner, together combined to create a need for an Israeli initiative: to disengage from Gaza and a part of the West Bank. The dismantling of the four settlements in the West Bank was deliberate and important for the Israelis. It was designed to send a clear message internally and externally that Israel's disengagement was not "Gaza first and last" but quite the opposite: that disengagement from Gaza was to be followed by a similar significant move in the West Bank. Once Israel brought to an end its control of the Palestinians residing in these areas, it was reasoned, its character as a Jewish and democratic state would be restored.

Palestinian Narratives

The Palestinians regarded the Second Intifada as a spontaneous, popular response to the failed peacemaking efforts. While the clashes were said to have been ignited by Sharon's visit to al-Haram al-Sharif (the Temple Mount), the protests were presented as an expression of

Palestinian post-Camp David frustrations with what they regarded as an untenable status quo. Since the effort to achieve a permanent status agreement at Camp David was seen as replacing the flawed Oslo step-by-step approach, the summit's failure now meant the absence of any diplomatic drive to "end occupation." The blame placed on Arafat for the failure of the talks, particularly by Clinton, further exacerbated the situation. Clinton's behavior was seen as further evidence of the United States siding with Israel, thus raising questions about the viability of diplomacy.

The Role of Violence

The mindset guiding Palestinian conduct in the Second Intifada was that the only language Israelis understand is that of force. This was the main lesson to be drawn from Oslo: Israeli concessions were seen as reactions to the Palestinians' earlier successful resistance during the First Intifada. This lesson was later reinforced by Israel's unilateral withdrawal from Lebanon in May 2000, which was interpreted as Israel being chased out of that country "under Hezbollah's fire." Moreover, while the less violent First Intifada was viewed as having a relatively modest objective of changing the status quo, the violence of the Second Intifada was now justified by its less limited aim: to force an end to Israeli occupation. Israel's summer 2005 *unilateral* disengagement from Gaza was seen as an affirmation of this goal.

In Palestinian eyes the *escalation* of violence during the Second Intifada resulted primarily from Israel's excessive use of force. The Palestinians argued that to ensure their own security they had no choice but to create a "balance of fear" that would offset Israel's military preponderance. In this context the use of suicide bombers against Israeli civilians was considered justified on two grounds: first, Israelis, it was claimed, did not discriminate in their attacks on Palestinians; Israel was said to be indifferent to the fact that its attacks on Palestinian militants resulted in heavy casualties among innocent civilians. Second, Palestinians saw the distinction between Israeli military and civilians as artificial, as they regarded every Israeli citizen as also serving as an IDF reservist.

The absence of a diplomatic alternative and the demonstrated utility of force was also viewed as the foundation of Hamas's rise to power. Since Fatah was identified with the Oslo negotiations process, the dead-end reached at Camp David made Fatah less relevant. Instead, Palestinians were now willing to explore a Hezbollah-type option, with which Hamas was associated and identified. Moreover, a majority of Palestinians now viewed Hamas as a legitimate political actor – a clean and trustworthy player siding with the poor. While Hamas continued to be seen as deficient for peacemaking, in the absence of an active peace process this was no longer deemed significant.

The Young Guard

For members of Fatah's young guard, the two processes of state-building and peacemaking pursued in the framework of the Oslo process were flawed. In their eyes, the process of state-building merely led to the creation of another typical Arab regime – authoritarian and backward. Instead of ending Israeli occupation, the process of state-building was seen as having consolidated it. Responsibility for this state of affairs was placed squarely with the old guard and Yasser Arafat's leadership. They were accused of excluding the young guard from leadership positions, of building weak public institutions that were based on loyalty instead of merit, and of making deals with Israelis that enriched and empowered members of the old guard at the expense of the public good. The old guard was also seen as having abandoned the armed resistance to Israeli occupation, thus removing any incentive for the Israelis to fulfill their obligations in the peace process.

To change this miserable reality, young guardsmen believed that the old guard had to be removed from power, by democratic means if possible. They favored reforms and elections within Fatah, but were also willing to forcibly challenge the formal institutions of the PA, thereby making it impossible for them to function or enforce law and order. Moreover, believing that Arafat and the old guard would never confront Israel militarily, the young guard sought to carry out their own attacks against Israelis. Indeed, their resort to arms and the formation of their own militia – the al-Aqsa Brigades – were often presented as the means to make the old guard pay attention to their concerns, as well as to force the Israelis to reassess their policies in the occupied territories. Their alliance with the Islamists was justified in similar terms.[25]

The Wall and the Arab Peace Initiative

Israel's construction of what the Palestinians called "the Apartheid Wall" was viewed as lacking any security rationale. If security were the objective, Palestinians argued, the barrier would have been constructed along pre-1967 lines – making it shorter and faster to erect. Instead, the Israelis decided to construct it well inside the West Bank. As a result, Palestinians viewed the barrier as merely another Israeli unilateral attempt to create "facts on the ground" and to grab more Palestinian land.

The Palestinians viewed the 2002 Arab Peace Initiative as an expression of the ongoing Arab and Palestinian aspiration for peace. By contrast, Israel's rejection of the offer was seen as indicative of Israeli intransigence and opposition to "a fair deal."

Frustration with the United States

Palestinians now felt great frustration with the United States. Palestinians who had viewed positively America's role in peacemaking during most of the 1990s and who had become critical of the Clinton administration in 2000 for siding with Israel, now viewed the Bush administration's labeling of Israeli use of force as self-defense, while Palestinian violence was depicted as acts of terror, as further evidence of a total American bias in Israel's favor.

In turn, this bias was viewed as reflecting the Jewish Lobby's control of the administration and Congress. While many Palestinians welcomed the Bush administration's call for PA reform and democratization, America's framing of its calls in "regime change language" led Palestinians to suspect the administration's motives and to doubt its sincerity. Palestinians concluded that the United States was seeking to remove Arafat from power not because he was not a democrat, but rather because he resisted Israeli and American pressures to sign a peace deal that did not meet Palestinian minimum demands.

The Road Map

Finally, the Palestinians viewed the road map proposed by the Quartet in 2003 as a positive development, but unrealistic, given that it required improvements in Palestinian governance and security control which Arafat was unable to implement. Palestinians pointed out that since Israel had seriously damaged, if not destroyed, their security services, they could not fulfill their obligations under the first phase of the road map. Hence, it was said, the capacity of these services had to be rebuilt before they could be expected to perform the requested functions.

In Palestinian eyes the second phase of the road map was no more promising. While they interpreted the creation of a state with provisional borders as "an option," they were reluctant to invest so much merely to achieve yet another interim arrangement. Having seen what happened during Oslo's phased process, with Israel greatly expanding its settlements, they now believed that another "interim" agreement would only be used by Israel to create even more "facts on the ground." These facts, Palestinians believed, tended to have a life of their own, making it impossible to undo them. Thus, the Palestinian narrative came to view interim arrangements with Israel as easily becoming permanent; they feared that the road map's suggested "provisional state" would become permanent, resulting in failure to address their remaining grievances.

The Arab Narrative

The broader Arab world's narrative regarding the Second Intifada was not very different from that subscribed to by the Palestinians. The Arab publics viewed Sharon's visit to al-Haram al-Sharif as a blatant insult to Muslim shrines, thus justifying the Palestinian reaction. Following Sharon's ascent to power in early 2001 the Arab street regarded the Israeli prime minister as responsible for the escalation of the Intifada – an assessment based on Sharon's image in Arab countries as a warmonger and a bloodthirsty leader. Accordingly, the Intifada was seen as revealing "the true face of Sharon," leading to a litany of Arab complaints about his leadership as well as about "the real face of Israel" as basically an aggressive state.

Public Support and Regimes Concerns

For Arab publics, the earlier failure of the peace process made the Palestinians' violent reaction to Sharon's visit to al-Haram al-Sharif all the more natural – they were seen as having nothing to lose and as having a natural right to resist occupation. Hence, Arafat was viewed as the defender of the Palestinian cause; his conduct was seen as legitimate and justified.

As violence escalated, and as Israeli efforts to suppress the violence seemed increasingly harsh, the Arab narrative became more complex. Arab publics and much of the media viewed Israeli actions in the aftermath of the September 11 attacks as part of a broader American and Western attack on Arabs and Muslims. At the same time, Arab governments now came to view the escalation of Palestinian–Israeli violence with increasing alarm, for two reasons: first, because the Intifada was seen as a form of "people empowerment" denied to their own populations and thus as embarrassing to their regimes. Demands for such empowerment, they feared, could be emulated at home. Second, because Islamists' participation in the Intifada earned them respect among Arab publics, who increasingly viewed suicide bombings as legitimate. Yet, the ambivalence felt about the rise of fundamentalism and the increased frequency of religiously inspired suicide attacks fueled a debate among Arab elites: should suicide bombing be regarded as a legitimate form of resistance and thus as "martyrdom operations" or as an illegitimate tool that hurt many innocent non-combatants?

Clash with the West

As the neoconservative and "Clash of Civilization" rhetoric became the language of the day in the United States in the aftermath of the September 11 attacks, and as the American-led coalitions invaded Afghanistan and Iraq, Arab publics and elites began to see the Palestinian Intifada as part of a much larger confrontation with the forces determined to suppress all Palestinians, Arabs and Muslims. In this context, Palestinian suicide bombings were viewed as simply another form of resistance in a theater of operations that happened to be located in Palestine. Moreover, these bombings seemed the only course of action open to anyone seeking to correct the imbalance of power between Arabs and the West.

However, as suicide operations began to devastate Iraq and terrorize a number of Arab and Muslim countries as well, Arab elites became increasingly divided regarding the religious and ethical legitimacy of these operations. While Palestinian suicide bombings were exempted for some time from this developing debate, and continued to be accepted as a legitimate form of resistance, it was soon realized that differentiating legitimate resistance from terror is a very daunting task. Consequently, in different Arab capitals it became increasingly obvious that the continuation of the Intifada was highly problematic not only because it could be seen as a form of "people empowerment" but also because such violence was now seen as having become a vehicle for increased Iranian influence all over the Middle East. To address this challenge, Arab governments now searched for peace through the Arab Peace Initiative and the Quartet's road map.

Among the general Arab public, support for the Intifada lasted much longer. This was aided by the new pan-Arab media, which found in the Intifada a long-lost heroic cause of defiance against the much stronger West. Indeed, the Intifada was now portrayed as a defensive shield against the massive Western onslaught against Islam. The trio of resistance in Iraq, Lebanon, and Palestine was viewed as carrying jointly the torch of confrontation, whereas Arab governments were viewed as corrupt and incompetent, and as failing to provide necessary help to the noble fighters.

However, these perceptions did not endure for long. With a growing number of horror stories from Iraq appearing in Arab national and region-wide media, with linkages between Hezbollah and Iran increasingly seen in the context of the Sunni–Shi'a divide, and with the split between Fatah and Hamas over the spoils of a non-existent Palestinian state becoming increasingly apparent, sympathy for the Intifada and for the Palestinians more broadly began to wane.

Analysis

This section addresses two questions: What caused the Second Intifada to erupt? and, What caused the eventual abatement of the violence? The seeds of the Intifada's abatement appeared very soon after its eruption, resulting in a significant degree of overlap between the two processes. They will therefore be treated together in this section: at each level of our analysis we will explore what factors played a role in causing the eruption of the violence and what factors worked to abate it.

The International System

At the *global-systemic level*, the most important factor associated with the eruption of the Second Intifada seems to have been the failure of the Clinton administration to achieve a breakthrough at Camp David, which may have led Palestinians to believe that they were unlikely to attain their aspirations through diplomacy. Yet the suggestion of a direct causal relationship between the failure of Camp David and the eruption of the Intifada requires some caution. This is because Israeli–Palestinian negotiations continued after Camp David and even after the Second Intifada broke out. Indeed, the failed summit was followed almost immediately by an important and fairly productive effort of Israeli and Palestinian negotiators to articulate and formalize the limited understandings that were reached at Camp David. However, it is noteworthy that most of the post-summit talks were held far from public view and therefore did not diminish the popular frustration about the failure, which provided the background to the violence sparked later by Sharon's visit to Temple Mount.

It is easier to establish the effect of the failure at Camp David in persuading the incoming Bush administration to avoid similar investments. This effectively ruled out any significant effort on its part to achieve a political resolution of the conflict, at least until 2007.

This predisposition was reinforced by the effects of al-Qaida's September 11, 2001 attacks, which created a strong tendency in Washington to view the Intifada almost exclusively through the prism of the new "War on Terror." The imperative was now to combat terrorism and avoid steps that could be interpreted as rewarding terrorist acts. Thus, the administration felt sympathy toward Israel's own unyielding stance against terror, and inclined to give it a free hand to escalate its response to Palestinian violence.

Moreover, having adopted very tough measures in the framework of its own War on Terror – including the Patriot Act, unlimited detention in Guantanamo Bay, the "rendering" of terrorism suspects and their "export" to countries where they could be interrogated by "unconventional methods" – the Bush administration would not criticize Israel for pursuing aggressive counterterror and counterinsurgency tactics such as "targeted killings." In effect, the systemic level gave Israel a free hand to take whatever measures it deemed necessary to suppress the Intifada.

The September 11 attacks also inclined the Bush administration to focus less on the broader context of the Palestinian–Israeli conflict and more on the violent aspects of the confrontation. Thus, the emissaries it sent to the region – from George Tenet to Keith Dayton – all focused on trying to stabilize the situation, not on addressing the underlying causes of the violence.

Another consequence of the September 11 attacks was the growing influence of neoconservative thinking on the Bush administration's foreign policy. This included a unilateral approach – a willingness to go it alone – as well as a predisposition to use military means to achieve political objectives. It also included unwavering support of Israel, fueled in part by the affinity to Zionism among America's Christian right. These increasingly influential neoconservatives perceived the Arab–Israeli dispute as a protracted conflict that would not yield itself to resolution through diplomacy. They also placed responsibility for the conflict's resilience solely on the Arab side.

Neoconservatives also saw Israel as a major and reliable strategic ally of the United States. They viewed the two countries as sharing the same democratic traditions as well as religious roots. Often referred to as the Judeo-Christian heritage, this now served as a basis for the further consolidation of the two countries' strategic ties, especially after Sharon became Israel's prime minister. As a result, the Bush administration made very few attempts to limit the means used by Israel in what was now perceived to be its own "War on Terror."

The effect of these developments on the Israeli–Palestinian realm was twofold: they contributed to the escalation of the violence by permitting Israel to respond to Palestinian violence with ever greater doses of countermeasures. And by giving Israel a relatively free hand to suppress the violence as it saw fit, these factors also contributed to the abatement of the Intifada by demonstrating to the Palestinians its ever-increasing costs.

Furthermore, the global environment after the September 11 attacks was not hospitable to Palestinian violence, particularly suicide attacks, leading to a significant loss of international sympathy. While the Palestinians did achieve considerable international acknowledgement of their right to demand an "end to occupation," suicide bombings of Israeli civilians were generally seen as a microcosm of the gruesome attacks on New York and Washington, DC.

The September 11 attacks also led to the formation of an international coalition against terror. In order to sustain this coalition the Bush administration responded to the demands of some of its important members that the United States lead efforts to develop a political horizon for the Palestinians. This resulted in Washington's unprecedented support for the establishment of a Palestinian state and the Quartet's development of the road map for Middle East peace. In turn, a reduction in Palestinians' demand for violence – and increased demand for a ceasefire at the popular level – were induced in part by the gradual emergence of an alternative: a political horizon provided by the road map.

By that time, much of the international community, and especially the United States, also accepted that certain new realities "on the ground" – specifically the large Israeli settlement blocks in the West Bank – would not be reversed, and that the demarcation of both the newly-built barrier and Israel's final borders would need to take these realities into account. These developments signaled to the Palestinian leadership and elite that Israel had a free hand in dealing with the Intifada and that Israeli reoccupation of the West Bank could continue unhindered. In turn, such assessments affected Palestinian cost–benefit calculations regarding the continuation of the Intifada, leading to increased demands for a ceasefire.

The Second Intifada had a very negative impact on American–Palestinian relations and led to deep American disillusionment with the Palestinian leadership. This was illustrated by President Bush's refusal to meet with Arafat, or even to shake his hand in the corridors of the United Nations. After September 11, when the Bush administration began to define itself by its conduct of the War on Terror, the rupture with Arafat became complete. On June 24, 2002, President Bush made his support for independent Palestinian statehood conditional on the Palestinians electing a new leadership "not compromised by terror." This signaled to the Palestinians that if they wanted America's support for Palestinian statehood, they had to cooperate in the abatement of the Intifada.

Yet the effects of the international environment after September 11 on America's willingness to invest in resolving the Palestinian–Israeli conflict were not straightforward. On the one hand, direct American intervention in the region – first in Afghanistan and later in Iraq – absorbed the Bush administration's energies and resources. Under such circumstances, neither the president nor his secretary of state would have the time and energy to launch a major diplomatic initiative in the Arab–Israeli context. Yet retention of the support of at least one important external ally – Britain's Prime Minister Tony Blair – required that his political needs, domestically in Britain and in Europe at large, be minimally satisfied. Hence the Quartet's adoption of the road map. But the attention that Iraq required also set a limit to this initiative: Washington refrained from pressing the parties to meet their obligations under the plan. The result was that while the development of a political horizon had a positive impact by reducing the demand for violence among the Palestinian masses and the elite, lack of implementation meant that this particular impact was unsustainable.

At the same time, direct American intervention in the Middle East also meant that Washington could not completely ignore the sentiments of the Arab street. This was because these sentiments were seen as constraining Arab leaders' ability to cooperate – even if only tacitly – with Washington's designs. And since the Arab street saw Israel and the United States as one and the same, some limits to Israeli freedom of action would need to be imposed. The implication of this was that while Israel would be able to gradually and partially defeat the Intifada, it would not be allowed to crush the Palestinians. In mid-2002 American pressure on Israel to terminate Operation Defensive Shield illustrated this point.

In turn, such American pressures affected Israel's strategic calculations, inducing it to adopt measures other than military ones. These measures included the Israeli endorsement of the two-state solution as articulated by President Bush in his June 2002 speech; a reserved acceptance of the road map; and disengagement from Gaza and a more symbolic disengagement in the West Bank. In turn, these Israeli non-military responses provided the Palestinians with an alternative to violence, leading them eventually to favor an abatement of the Intifada.

Moreover, the Intifada itself had by now left its mark on the international community. As an insurgency, the Second Intifada registered a number of impressive gains: at the global level, the Palestinians succeeded in persuading key elites and opinion-makers that the struggle they were waging was legitimate resistance aimed solely at ending Israeli occupation of their lands. Moreover, the widespread use of suicide bombing had a reinforcing effect on the new emerging consensus regarding the purpose of the Palestinians' struggle. What was interpreted as a willingness to die for the cause of ending Israeli occupation could not have left the publics of Western Europe indifferent. Thus the Palestinians gained appreciation for the depth of their grievance: if they were willing to die – so thought an increasing number of their sympathizers, especially in Europe – the status quo or at least important dimensions thereof must be seriously flawed. In turn, as the search for a political horizon seemed to gain momentum, an increasing number of Palestinians concluded that they had succeeded in making their point and that there was little to be gained by further stressing it. Instead, it was time to seek an alternative to violence.

Another element of the international environment indirectly contributing to the abatement of the Intifada was the Bush administration's evolving observation that corruption and tyranny were the breeding ground for terrorism and that, hence, terrorism would not be defeated without the spread of democracy and good governance. This view, a central tenet of the American neoconservative philosophy, led the administration to press Arab governments to liberalize, to allow free and fair electoral processes, and to adopt transparency and other good governance measures. Consistent with such demands, the international community's interference in Palestinian domestic affairs increased significantly during this period, pressing for political and financial reforms and isolating Arafat. International financial support shifted from development to humanitarian aid and to direct budget support.

The Palestinians' response to these pressures was to balance these various demands. Violence was not completely ended, but it was reduced. Moreover, some of the reform measures adopted tended to reduce the violence. For example, improved financial transparency reduced Arafat's ability to finance some of Fatah's armed groups. The appointment as prime minister of Abbas – a strong opponent of the so-called "militarization of the Intifada" – further encouraged anti-violence voices.

But American pressures on Arab regimes to democratize had other, more negative consequences for Arab–Israeli peacemaking. In almost all cases where more inclusive elections were held due to American pressure – from Egypt to Lebanon – Islamists made considerable electoral gains. This in turn produced a less moderate regional context for Palestinian–Israeli interactions. In the Palestinian case the pressure to democratize led to the inclusion of Hamas in the Palestinian political system and to the holding of local and legislative elections, a development that contributed to the revival of the Islamist movement's motivation to continue the violence.

Regional Politics

At the *regional-systemic level*, the most important development driving the Palestinians to try a more violent course was Israel's May 2000 withdrawal from South Lebanon "under fire." Hezbollah then used every regional media outlet at its disposal to chastise the Palestinian leadership for the meager results of its efforts to attain its goals through diplomacy, in contrast to the success of the Lebanese "resistance" in obtaining its objectives by force. This communication campaign pressured the Palestinians to attempt to emulate Hezbollah's methods.

During this period, Hezbollah established itself as the de-facto sovereign in South Lebanon, Hamas gained strength in the West Bank and Gaza, and the Muslim Brotherhood did better than ever in Egypt's parliamentary elections. While the precise effects of the broader resurgence of Islamic forces in the Middle East on the Second Intifada's escalation are difficult to estimate, it must have emboldened Hamas and Islamic Jihad.

Yet, other developments in the regional environment worked to abate the violence associated with the Second Intifada. Feeling American pressure, conservative Arab regimes attempted to placate the United States by abandoning their traditional passivity in the peacemaking realm. By the spring of 2002, partly in response to these pressures and partly to offset criticism of Saudi Arabia in the United States due to the participation of a large number of Saudi nationals in the September 11 attacks, Crown Prince Abdullah launched what later became the API. In turn, the launching of the API created an impression of movement and impending progress in the peace process, thus increasing optimism and reducing demands for violence among Palestinians.

The API was propelled by two additional regional considerations: the first required that the violence of the Intifada be ended and the second that the Arab states substitute for the Palestinians' leadership deficit. The first of these considerations, subscribed to by a number of conservative Arab governments, was that as a form of "people empowerment" the Second Intifada might be emulated within their countries, thus threatening the stability of their regimes. The conclusion was that an alternative to the Intifada must be found before this happened. The second was the observation that the Palestinian leadership had abrogated its responsibilities and could no longer be relied upon to alleviate the Palestinians' plight. The conclusion was that responsible Arab governments had to step in to substitute, or at least compensate, for the Palestinian leaders' weakness. One specific manifestation of this development was Egypt's growing role in convincing Arafat to adopt domestic financial and constitutional reforms and to bring about a rapprochement between Fatah and Hamas. The renewal of friendly relations between the two organizations reduced the potential for civil war and, as will be shown, brought about a ceasefire between Palestinians and Israelis.

Different regional-systemic factors played a role in allowing Israel to make a move that contributed to the abatement of the Intifada: its unilateral disengagement from Gaza. Most important among these was the change in Israel's strategic environment in the aftermath of the Western allies' occupation of Iraq. With its military power weakened by the cumulative effects of its 1980–88 war with Iran, the 1990–91 Gulf War and the sanctions imposed in its aftermath, Iraq saw its armed forces completely crushed in the 2003 Iraq War. Adding to the effect of the Syrians' loss of their Soviet patrons in the late 1980s, resulting in a severe weakening of the Syrian armed forces, the war in Iraq completed a dramatic transformation of Israel's strategic environment. This improvement enabled Israel to shift its attention to other threats, most notably the demographic one. The result was increased demand for political separation from the Palestinians.

The Palestinian Domestic Scene

In the domestic realm the Second Intifada seems to have been fueled by a number of important developments in Palestinian society. At the *elite level*, as we have seen, the most important of these was the growing frustration of Fatah's young guard during the second half of the 1990s with the performance of the movement's old guard.

The young guard not only formed their own independent armed wing but also found common ground, and thus a basis for an alliance, with Hamas and Palestinian Islamic Jihad

(PIJ). This alliance was spearheaded by two leaders: Marwan Barghouti, head of Fatah's Tanzim and Khaled Mashaal of Hamas. The creation of this new coalition then intensified the violence as it manifested growing Islamist influence. At first, Fatah's young guard was able to "outsource" suicide bombing to Hamas and the PIJ. However, following the January 14, 2002 killing of Ra'ad Karami, commander of the al-Aqsa Brigades in Tulkarem, the Brigades participated directly in such attacks.

Meanwhile, Fatah's old guard leadership was almost totally split and hence unable to face the young guard. It was also unable to deliver any kind of security agreement with Israel. PA security forces, which began to deteriorate soon after the Second Intifada began, could no longer match the power of the various militias that now ruled the Palestinian street. The ability of the PA leadership to control developments further diminished as its security services became riddled in rivalries. This fragmentation became all the more acute as members of the Tanzim penetrated the PA's security services.

By late 2001 the security services completely collapsed under threefold pressure: Israel embarked upon a preventive and preemptive strategy to insure that the PA forces would not be able to attack it; Arafat ordered them to abandon their security enforcement role; and the young guard's leadership urged all members of Tanzim to defect to the al-Aqsa Brigades. The result of these developments was complete anarchy. The PA government lost all ability to perform as a central government and the Palestinian street was now ruled by semi-independent militias.

At the *mass level*, the most important domestic development that fueled the Intifada was a growing frustration with the peace process, as we have seen. Palestinians were also suspicious of the Israeli public as a whole, not just its leadership. By the time the Second Intifada broke out, most Palestinians interacted with Israelis only at gunpoint – of Israeli soldiers and armed settlers. Lack of normal personal interaction encouraged misperception and the inclination to portray the other side in negative terms. When asked in June 2003 what they believed was the attitude of Israelis to a two-state solution only 37 percent of Palestinians responded that they believed that most Israelis supported such a solution. A survey conducted among Israelis at the same time showed that actually 65 percent of them supported a two-state solution. Misperceiving the views of Israelis as hard-line made Palestinians more disposed to blame them for the failure to reach a peace agreement.[26]

A related important domestic determinant of the Second Intifada was increased Palestinian public support for violence, based in part on the judgment that violence pays. While such beliefs declined in the aftermath of the Oslo agreement, the perceived stagnation of the process during the Netanyahu government (1996–99) led to a gradual increase in support for violence. By July 2000, after the failure of Camp David but before the eruption of the Second Intifada, 52 percent of Palestinians polled already approved of the use of violence; a year later, that figure reached the unprecedented level of 86 percent.[27]

The increase in support for violence during the Second Intifada was correlated with Palestinian perception of increased threat. Such threat perceptions were associated with: Israeli use of military force, including tanks, helicopter gunships and F-16s against Palestinians in densely populated areas; the imposition of collective punishment measures (such as closures, checkpoints, and other restrictions on movement); and the continued buildup of Jewish settlements in the occupied territories. The anger generated by these measures led Palestinians to demand revenge and to support violence against Israelis.

Perhaps more than any other factor, however, the rise of Hamas was responsible for the escalation of the violence of the Second Intifada. The same failures of the PA which account for Fatah's young guard breaking ranks and adopting violence also led the Palestinian public to gradually shift loyalty to the Islamists who opposed the peace process and believed in "armed struggle." Having suffered a severe blow when the Oslo process was launched, now, with the collapse of the process and the failure of the Camp David summit in 2000, the Islamist Hamas reemerged as a credible alternative to the nationalist Fatah movement.

Capitalizing on Palestinians' growing fear and thirst for revenge, Islamist groups – both Hamas and the PIJ – won public favor with suicide bombings and other violent attacks against Israelis. Israeli restrictions and retaliatory measures against the PA security services and institutions further weakened the PA's ability to deliver security and social services at a time of extreme need. The Islamists proved much more effective in providing such services.

Finally, public support for the nationalists and the Islamists was affected by different perceptions of the two movements' leaders. While Arafat was now seen as having abdicated responsibility, Hamas leader Sheikh Ahmad Yasin was regarded as a pious man, a spiritual and a political leader, a man of integrity and a defender of the national interests who could be trusted. These contrasting images of the two leaders made the rise of Hamas possible.

At more or less the same time, other developments in the Palestinian realm were no less important in the abatement of the Intifada, determining its course and consequences. These developments – the death of Arafat, the election of Abbas, public demand for law and order, and support for a cessation of violence coupled with the integration of Hamas into the formal political process – created opportunities and incentives for reducing violence.

For the Palestinians, while the Intifada had its successes, it also resulted in heavy losses. In dead and wounded, the Palestinians' toll was at least four times higher than Israel's. Further, while for Palestinian opponents of accommodation with Israel the Intifada successfully aborted such a deal at least for some years, for Palestinians striving for statehood the Intifada was a dramatic setback. Negotiations over a permanent status agreement that would provide for an independent Palestinian state were frozen for at least seven years. Finally, the violence of the Intifada and of Israel's tough measures to suppress it resulted in serious damage to many proto-state institutions that the Palestinians had begun to build after the 1993 Oslo Accords, indeed sometimes their complete destruction. By 2006, the process of Palestinian institution-building had been set back to a point not far from where it began some thirteen years earlier.

Public anger with the collapse of law and order and the PA's inability to deliver services, Israeli countermeasures, and Palestinian fatigue after several years of violence led to the gradual dying down of the Intifada. Although the belief that the "militarized" Intifada had helped Palestinians achieve national rights remained very strong during 2003 and 2004, a growing number called for a mutual cessation of violence. Gradually, Palestinians became aware of the limits of force. When asked in a poll about the lessons learned from the 2006 Lebanon War and their implications for the Palestinian–Israeli situation, three-quarters responded that Palestinians could not depend on armed action alone and had to reach a political settlement with Israel. A similar percentage also expressed a belief that Palestinians could not count on themselves alone and that they needed the help and understanding of the international community.[28]

In addition, the September 11 attacks led to Western demands for democratization in Arab countries and in the Palestinian Authority, as a means of "drying the swamp in which terrorists grow." The PA responded to this demand by indicating a willingness to integrate Islamist political parties and groups into the political process, thus providing them with an alternative to violence. Moreover, the further opening of the political system following Arafat's death allowed the integration of Hamas into the formal political process. With Arafat out of the picture, Hamas capitalized on the opportunity to translate its street popularity into formal political power by agreeing to participate in local and national elections and to be integrated into the PLO.

Hamas's decision to seek formal integration into the political process came in the middle of Israeli preparations for unilateral disengagement from the Gaza Strip. Widespread public belief that Israeli disengagement from Gaza was a victory for violence served Hamas's interests well, since the public gave it credit for forcing the Israelis out of Gaza "under fire." Polls indicated that between December 2004 and December 2005 Hamas's popularity increased by almost 50 percent, leading to its electoral victory in January 2006. Hamas coined the phrase "partners in blood, partners in decision-making," indicating an eagerness to share formal power with Fatah. For this, it was willing to pay a price: reducing the flames of the Intifada.[29]

All this took place in the context of the March 2005 Cairo Declaration. In its framework, Hamas accepted a bargain: its integration into the political process – elections and its inclusion into the PLO – in return for a ceasefire. Once it accepted the tradeoff, it needed to stop the violence in order to allow the unfolding of a process that would ultimately lead to elections in which it believed it would do well—capitalizing on its popularity and the unilateral nature of Israeli disengagement. Continuing violence at this stage would have been a violation of Hamas's commitment in the declaration and might have led to postponement or cancellation of elections. Moreover, local and parliamentary elections – which Hamas was now interested in facilitating – could not take place in an environment of violent confrontations. Consequently, between March 2005 and January 2006 Hamas did not carry out violent attacks on Israelis; self-interest dictated at least a temporary halt. For these reasons, Israel's disengagement did not spur any fighting, despite the fact that Palestinians interpreted Israel's disengagement as evidence that violence paid.

At the *popular level*, support for Arafat, which, according to a poll conducted in the West Bank and Gaza stood at 46 percent in July 2000, just before the eruption of the Intifada, declined to 35 percent by September 2004.[30] Not surprisingly Arafat's subsequent death was greeted by a rise in optimism, reflected in public opinion polls as well as in a dramatic surge in the stock market.[31] The public expected the peace process to be renewed and violence to drop. Public willingness to compromise, and support for cessation of violence, increased considerably around the end of 2004 and early 2005. In his January 2006 election campaign, Abbas, who was a long-standing opponent of the "militarization of the intifada," repeated his opposition publicly, capitalizing successfully on the same pubic demand for a ceasefire that led to the March 2005 agreement with Hamas. For its part, Hamas did not alter its belief that violence pays and that it was the only means of ending occupation. Refraining from violence in order to allow elections to take place did not mean abandoning the strategy: Hamas did not dismantle its militia or change its own views about the role of violence.

The Israeli Domestic Scene

Within Israel, the failure of Camp David and the outbreak of the violence in late September 2000 also had profound effects, including the "unmasking" of Arafat, the perception of his culpability for the turn to deadly violence and the subsequent discrediting of the Israeli peace camp. Key Labor leaders like Barak and Ben Ami now joined Likud's narrative about the futility of efforts to reach an agreement with Arafat, so there was no significant opposition to the proposition that very tough measures should be employed to suppress the Intifada.

Much like many Palestinians, Israelis now regarded the negotiations option as irrelevant, if not dead. And if diplomacy was not an option, the challenge of violence evoked the need for a sheriff, not a negotiator. Hence, Sharon's victory in the February 2001 elections, some four months into the Second Intifada, was a logical outcome of the ensuing violence.

Yet these developments were only a prelude to Israel's own contribution to the subsequent escalation. With Palestinian suicide bombings producing gruesome pictures projected on television screens in every Israeli home, Israelis now experienced unprecedentedly high levels of anxiety about sending their children to shopping malls, cinemas and coffee shops. The result was a very broad demand for the restoration of personal safety and security at all costs. Hence, while not withdrawing their support for compromises that would ultimately enable an agreement with the Palestinians, Israelis now regarded such compromises as merely theoretical. Instead, this willingness was now accompanied by more immediate support for the harshest preventive, preemptive and punitive measures to stem the violence.

The continued escalating violence in 2001–02 reinforced the propensity to view relations with the Palestinians through the prism of the need to restore safety and security. Within the Israeli decision-making system, this led to a shift in the delicate civil–military balance, away from diplomacy and toward the military and civilian security services. This often meant that long-term strategic interests lost out to short-term security considerations. As priority was given to the prevention and interdiction of terrorist attacks, the effects of the resulting measures on Palestinians' motivation to join violent groups were viewed as secondary. Focusing on such possible effects was now seen as a luxury that Israel could not afford.

Yet, other developments on the Israeli side contributed to the eventual abatement of the violence. Successful integration of superb tactical intelligence with offensive and defensive measures resulted in a dramatic reduction in Israeli casualty numbers. Between 2001–2 and 2005–6, casualties fell by some 90 percent. While some of this reduction was the direct result of Palestinian organizations' decision to douse the fire, the decision of these organizations was affected by Israel's successful counterinsurgency warfare.

By 2004, as a result of reduced casualties from Palestinian violence, Israelis began to feel some return to normalcy in daily life. Yet the effectiveness of the offensive measures on the one hand and the fact that they sometimes entailed casualties among innocent Palestinians on the other, raised for the first time the specter of internal criticism from the center of the Israeli consensus. Such criticism focused primarily on what some Israelis regarded as the excessive use of airpower. When, on July 22, 2002, a large bomb dropped by an F-16 to kill Saleh Shehada, a Hamas militant leader, in Gaza resulted in the death of 14 civilians, including children in an adjacent building, the incident and its poor handling by then Commander of the Israeli Air Force, Major General Dan Halutz, led to protests by some of the IAF's elite reserve combat pilots. On September 24, 2003 these reservists sent a petition to General Halutz specifically protesting the use of "targeted killings."[32]

Moreover, the violence of the Intifada, particularly Palestinians' willingness to sacrifice their lives, as demonstrated by the suicide attacks, left a strong impression on the Israeli body politic. Many Israelis now concluded that the Palestinians would never accept Israeli occupation as an indefinite proposition, and that if violence was to end, a way had to be found to end Israel's control of the Palestinians.

The process of abatement was induced by both sides' cost–benefit calculations. For the Israelis, suicide bombers were a menace they could not easily or quickly neutralize. Yet by provoking broad Israeli public support for harsh measures on the one hand and demands for separation on the other, this development also added further costs to the Palestinian calculus, reducing their motivation to continue the violence.

Within Israel there was growing recognition that the combination of Palestinian motivation and the constraints imposed by the international and regional environment on Israel's ability to respond to violence implied that it would not be able to crush the Intifada solely by offensive means. The result was an increase in calls for Israel's offensive strategy to be augmented by a strong defensive component, primarily the erection of a barrier system designed to prevent car bombs and suicide bombers reaching Israel's metropolitan areas.

Finally, the success of Israel's counterinsurgency efforts coupled with a greater recognition of the limits of force led to a different type of internal challenge: What was Israel to do with this success given the perceived absence of a negotiation partner with whom this success could be translated to enduring political gains? As long as the Israeli government remained passive on the diplomatic front, others were bound to initiate. This was demonstrated in October 2003, when Track-II talks between a group of Israelis and a group of Palestinians, acting in an unofficial capacity, produced a draft permanent status agreement, called the Geneva Document.[33] This development placed the Israeli government on the diplomatic defensive: it had to explain why the Geneva Document was not acceptable without offering something in its stead. This coincided with another important development: with Syria's loss of its Soviet patron in the late 1980s and Iraq's military power crushed in the 2003 Iraq War, Israel no longer faced a significant "Eastern Front" threat. This led Israelis to reevaluate the importance of retaining control of the Jordan Valley to their national defense.[34]

Growing Israeli recognition of the limits of force and the need to end the occupation, perception of the absence of a negotiation partner, and the vacuum created by the success of Israel's counterinsurgency strategy – a vacuum into which the signatories to the Geneva Document had entered – together combined to create a need for an Israeli initiative. Israel's greatly improved threat environment after the Iraq War enabled such an initiative to be taken. These developments combined to persuade the Israeli government to adopt Prime Minister

Sharon's proposal: namely, that Israel should disengage from Gaza and a part of the West Bank.

In turn, offensive Israeli measures such as the reoccupation of the West Bank and defensive measures such as the building of the separation barrier and withdrawal from the Gaza Strip combined to reduce Palestinian violence. Thus, the increased costs of the Second Intifada for both sides – for the Israelis, the increased deadliness of Palestinian suicide attacks and for the Palestinians, Israel's return to direct occupation of the West Bank – led a majority of Israelis to support unilateral separation from the Palestinians, and the Palestinians to support a ceasefire.[35] These developments, and the anticipation of an Israeli withdrawal from the Gaza Strip as well as from a number of settlements in the northern West Bank, contributed to a further decline in Palestinian support for violence and increased demand for negotiating, or at least coordinating, Israel's withdrawal from Gaza.

Leaders

At the *individual level*, the Second Intifada cannot be explained without reference to the role played by Arafat and Sharon. However, this period was also notable for the rise of another leader, whose influence gradually unfolded: Marwan Barghouti, head of Fatah's Tanzim.

Arafat's role was to permit the Intifada to escalate. He continued during this period to believe in the efficacy of violence, seeing it as the means to press for progress in negotiations. Whereas in May 2000, when serious Palestinian–Israeli negotiations seemed promising, he believed he had much to lose if violence escalated, driving him to move quickly to stem it, he now, after the failure of the Camp David Summit, assessed that there was little to be gained by reining-in the protests. At first, Arafat seemed interested in examining whether the violence could improve the Palestinians' bargaining power in negotiations with Israel. But he soon decided to abrogate responsibility as, in his view, non-violent options for advancing the Palestinians' interests appeared to be absent. As his security forces were increasingly decimated in the confrontation with Israel, he saw no benefit in responding to what he regarded as efforts to compel him to end the violence. Instead, he turned to appease Fatah's young guard, providing its members with moral, political and financial support.

Another dimension of Arafat's personal input to the escalation was his decision not to check Hamas's ascent. Indeed, Arafat seems to have seen some benefits in tolerating Hamas's violence. Like most Palestinians, he believed the Israelis understood the language of force and would be more willing to make concessions under fire. In unleashing Hamas's, rather than Fatah's, violence during 2001–02, Arafat seems to have underestimated Hamas's long-term threat to Fatah's leadership. It seemed that his view was that if he succeeded in navigating the Intifada the Palestinian people would not support Hamas; whereas if his efforts were to fail and Israeli occupation continued, Hamas would be a problem for Israel, not for him.

Arafat's personal attributes also played a role in the abatement of the Intifada. This period was characterized by a dramatic slide in his personal fortunes. Isolated by Israel in the Muqata'a – the small governmental compound in Ramallah – and too weak to mediate the split within his former old guard colleagues, Arafat now yielded to international demands for reform – signing the Basic Law that curtailed his power significantly. He transferred important tools of control to the office of the prime minister held by Mahmoud Abbas. Most importantly, he surrendered to the international demand that principles of accountability and transparency be applied to the Palestinian government budget. With this, he lost his decades-long capacity for control through patronage and hence the ability to fuel the young guard's violence.

On the Palestinian side, the evolution of the Second Intifada cannot be explained without reference to the rising stock of Fatah's Tanzim leader, Marwan Barghouti – a West Banker who shared Arafat's views on the role and efficacy of violence. Barghouti was an insider and one of the leaders of the First Intifada, and, unlike Arafat, had been educated in a pluralistic environment, working very closely with Hamas. Furthermore, his disillusionment with the performance of the nationalist old guard, and his anger at the exclusion of the young guard from the political process, led him to rise against what he viewed as a corrupt and inept leadership.

During this period, Barghouti played a major role in three developments which contributed to the escalation of the violence: first, he proved to be the architect of the use of force, inspiring the young warriors to confront Israel; second, he engineered the Fatah–Hamas alliance, the first real coalition between secular and religious Palestinians; and finally, he fostered the notion that the Palestinians must get rid of the corrupt and ineffective Fatah old guard. But because the old guard was more conservative and cautious, its decline meant fewer stops on the slide toward greater violence.

Yet, this period also revealed some of Barghouti's shortcomings. Most pronounced was his failure to instill discipline and unify the ranks of his own young guard followers. Equally ominous was his inability to establish a clear chain of command in the al-Aqsa Brigades. As a result, this militia became highly fragmented, adding to the difficulty of containing the violence.

On the Israeli side, no individual played a more decisive role in affecting the turn of events during this period than Ariel Sharon. A number of aspects of Sharon's personal history and evolution seemed to have played a major role in charting the course of the Second Intifada. The first was his formative and formidable military experience, beginning with his service as a Special Forces IDF commander in the early 1950s, through his rise to be commander of the IDF's Southern Command, and ending with his key role in orchestrating the crossing of the Suez Canal during the 1973 War. What characterized these experiences, and Sharon's entire military career, was the strong conviction that given Israel's threat environment the only viable defense was aggressive offense – that is, that the less numerous Israelis could not afford to remain in defensive modes, since this would allow their more numerous adversaries to exploit the initiative.

For this reason, Sharon's initial instinct when becoming prime minister in early 2001 was to establish "escalation dominance" – to pursue Israel's detractors aggressively, demonstrating that Israel's reaction would always be considerably more painful than the attacks. Expressions of this predisposition reached their peak in April 2002 when, following the suicide bombing of the Park Hotel in Netanya, Sharon ordered the IDF to launch Operation Defensive Shield.

And yet Sharon's offensive-aggressive instincts were tamed during this period by two other dimensions of his personal history. The first of these was his earlier role as the architect of

Israel's 1982 invasion of Lebanon and his association with the September 1982 massacre of Palestinians in the Sabra and Shatila refugee camps at the hands of Israel's Maronite Christian allies. The Israeli Commission of Inquiry headed by then Supreme Court Judge Kahan found Sharon indirectly responsible for the massacre and recommended that he be removed from office as defense minister.[36]

It took Sharon some 16 years following the Kahan Commission Report to regain his standing as a legitimate political leader. By the time of the Second Intifada, rehabilitating his tarnished image and rewriting his legacy may have become an important motivation. At any rate, Sharon now seemed determined to avoid similar disasters. This allowed his close aides to talk him out of aggressive designs whenever his rage, usually following a gruesome suicide bombing, led him in that direction.

The second factor mitigating Sharon's aggressive instincts was the special relationship he developed with President George W. Bush following the September 11 attacks. The importance of this relationship cannot be understood without reference, again, to the early 1980s. In the aftermath of the Lebanon War, Israel's then defense minister was treated by Washington as persona non grata. He was seen as an extremely belligerent former general, insensitive to America's priorities and willing to go to any lengths to advance what he perceived as the requirements of Israel's national security. Revealingly, the leading American diplomat charged with resolving the Lebanese crises, Ambassador Philip Habib, later subtitled his memoirs: "The American Diplomat Versus the Israeli General, Beirut 1982."[37]

After the September 11 attacks, Americans' views of Sharon changed dramatically. Bush, who now saw the United States and Israel as "in the same boat," came to admire Sharon's decades-long experience as an anti-terrorism warrior. While this close relationship allowed Sharon unprecedented freedom to pursue his policy preferences, it also presented him with a serious constraint. Israel's prime minister now had an important stake in maintaining close ties with Washington, which he was not going to risk for short-term tactical gains. Thus, for example, when in April 2002 President Bush made clear that Israel must bring Operation Defensive Shield to an end, Sharon promptly complied.

Yet the same Sharon who played a crucial role in the eruption and escalation of the violence, now underwent a huge personal change if not a complete metamorphosis, leading him to play an equally critical role in the Intifada's abatement. Indeed, the longer Sharon served as prime minister, the greater the changes in outlook regarding the Arab–Israeli conflict he experienced. Referring to the unique perspective that comes with finding oneself responsible for the nation's wellbeing and future – in contrast with opinions one could hold as an opposition leader – he observed: "What you see from there is not what you see from here."[38] What were the important changes that Sharon experienced?

In the first instance Sharon now abandoned all notions that the Palestinian problem could be solved outside the Israeli–Palestinian realm. Ideas he previously cherished to the effect that Palestinian national aspirations could be satisfied by toppling the Hashemite regime and creating a Palestinian state in its stead – in the early 1980s this idea was referred to as "Jordan is Palestine" – were now completely abandoned. As prime minister, Sharon sought close strategic cooperation with Jordan, which he now considered an important buffer against residual threats from the unstable Gulf region.

Second, in sharp contrast to the views he held for over three decades after the 1967 War, Sharon now concluded that Israel's indefinite control of the West Bank – against the will of its Palestinian population – was not realistic. The most dramatic illustration of this was Sharon's adoption of the most important element of the Palestinians' narrative about this reality: namely, that it comprised Israeli "occupation."[39] Once Sharon adopted this term, it became clear that he gave up all hope that Israel's 1967 conquest of the West Bank could be made permanent.

Third, at the tactical and operational levels, Sharon now abandoned his decade-long conviction that the only defense against terrorism and insurgency was aggressive offense. Until 2003 Sharon's extensive experience in counterinsurgency warfare led him to reject any suggestion that Israel should augment its offensive operations with an effective barrier. Thus he continued to resist what appeared to him to be proposals that Israel should "hide behind" an anti-terror Maginot Line. By mid-2003, however, Sharon could no longer ignore the public demand for effective defense. In a dramatic reversal, he embraced the proposal for a "security fence" and began overseeing its construction.

Finally, in the aftermath of the Iraq War, Sharon seemed to have supplemented his reversal with regard to tactical and operational defense with a revised national threat assessment. Sharon had believed for decades that Israel had to retain control of the West Bank against possible challenges on its "Eastern Front"; he now seemed to embrace the view previously held by Labor leaders: namely, that the West Bank was a demographic liability from which Israel should disengage.

Beginning in a speech delivered at a Herzliya Conference on December 18, 2003, Sharon advocated that Israel begin disengaging by a complete withdrawal from Gaza – including all military installations and civilian settlements – as well as from an area in the northern part of the West Bank. Fears that such a withdrawal would constitute a "prize for terrorists" and would be interpreted by Palestinians as yielding to the pressures created by the Second Intifada's violence – Sharon had warned against such concessions throughout his political life – were now set aside in the face of a higher priority.

While Sharon resisted for a long time any acknowledgement of the demographic threat – probably fearing that admitting this dilemma would increase the Palestinians' bargaining power – some of his closest aides felt less inhibited about articulating this view. Most explicit was vice prime minister and minister of trade and commerce, Ehud Olmert. In an interview he gave to the weekend edition of *Yediot Aharonot* on December 14, 2003, Olmert said that Israel should adopt the "unilateral alternative" to the Israeli–Palestinian conflict.[40]

Concluding Notes

The period described here witnessed an enormous setback to Arab–Israeli and particularly Palestinian–Israeli peacemaking. In the physical sense, not since 1948 had Israelis and Palestinians experienced such horrific forms of violence and terrorism and measures to suppress them. And not since 1948 had the two peoples inflicted such high levels of casualties on one another.

This setback was particularly devastating given the high hopes that both peoples had attached to the efforts made to resolve their conflict during the months that preceded the eruption of the Second Intifada. Indeed, these efforts and the subsequent eruption of the violence were connected: Palestinian frustration with the failure of these efforts seems to have been an important contributing factor to the eruption of the Intifada. Thus, in both a physical and historical sense, this is a period of triumph for the forces ensuring the resilience of the conflict over the forces seeking to resolve it.

For the PA the Second Intifada resulted in a series of strategic setbacks. The Israeli peace camp – the PA's partner in the Oslo Process – was discredited by the Israelis' inclination to place the blame for the violence squarely with Yasser Arafat. Another setback for the PA was the deterioration experienced in its relations with the United States. Conversely, Israel now became more popular in the corridors of the White House, as its efforts to suppress Palestinian violence were seen through the prism of America's own War on Terror. In addition, the PA's embryonic post-Oslo attempts at institution-building were now set back, as conditions no longer allowed the normal functioning of these institutions and as the PA's security sector was now largely destroyed. A final strategic setback for the nationalist PA was the rise of Hamas, first legitimized and strengthened by its new alliance with Fatah's young guard and later strengthened by Israel's unilateral withdrawal from Gaza. The latter was presented by Hamas as a victory for the violence it exercised against Israelis and, contributed to its success in the January 2006 Palestinian elections.

But not all was lost for the Palestinians or for the process of peacemaking. The triumph enjoyed during this period by the forces of resilience of the conflict was not complete. Despite the breakdown in Washington's relations with Arafat, in June 2002 President Bush endorsed the pursuit of Palestinian independent statehood as American policy. Similarly, the formation of the Quartet and its adoption of the road map in 2003, the Arab League adoption of the Saudi-inspired Arab Peace Initiative, and Israeli disengagement from the Gaza Strip all contributed to taking both sides slightly away from conflict and violence and slightly closer to peace and reconciliation.

Moreover, the formation of Kadima served to weaken the more hard-line Likud. The Palestinian parallel to this positive development was the appointment of Mahmoud Abbas as prime minister and later his election as President of the PA after Arafat's death – an important turnabout from violence to negotiations, as Abbas was known as a critic of the "militarization of the Intifada." Thus, the period addressed here, which began with violence and a major setback to peacemaking efforts, ended with some very positive developments among the Palestinians and in Israel. These developments had important consequences, addressed in the next chapter.

Readings

Bickerton, Ian and Carla Klausner, *A History of the Arab–Israeli Conflict* (Prentice Hall, 2010) 333–368.

Caplan, Neil, *The Israel–Palestine Conflict: Contested Histories* (Wiley, 2010) 206–218.

Dowty, Alan, *Israel/Palestine: Global Political Hotspots* (Polity, 2012) 170–198.

Eisenberg, Laura Zittrain and Neil Caplan, *Negotiating Arab–Israeli Peace: Patterns, Problems, Possibilities* (Indiana University Press, 2010) 222–252.

Gelvin, James, *The Israel–Palestine Conflict: One Hundred Years of War* (Cambridge University Press, 2007) 240–249.
Lesch, David, *The Arab-Israeli Conflict* (Oxford University Press, 2008) 382–427.
Smith, Charles D., *Palestine and the Arab–Israeli Conflict* (Bedford/St.Martin's, 2007) 492–536.

Historical Documents

Arab League Summit Beirut Declaration: Walter Laqueur and Barry Rubin, *The Israel–Arab Reader: A Documentary History of the Middle East Conflict* (London: Penguin Books, 2008), 583.
Israeli Prime Minister Ariel Sharon Speech at start of Gaza Pullout: Laqueur and Rubin, *The Israel–Arab Reader*, 594.
U.S. President George W. Bush, "A New Palestinian Leadership:" Laqueur and Rubin, *The Israel–Arab Reader*, 584–588.
The Cairo Declaration 2005: available online at http://www.miftah.org/display.cfm?DocId=6938&CategoryId=5.
The Quartet Road Map: available online at http://www.mideastweb.org/quartetrm3.htm.

Notes

1. Samuel Huntington, *The Clash of Civilizations and the Remaking of World Order* (New York: Simon and Schuster, 1996).
2. "Palestinian Unrest Wanes – Death Toll Rises to 24," *Deutsche-Presse Agentur*, October 1, 2000; "Temple Mount Visit Sparks Violence," *The Toronto Star*, September 29, 2000; Leo Hockstader, "Israeli's Tour of Holy Sites Ignites Riot; Palestinians Angered by Test of Sovereignty in Jerusalem's Old City," *Washington Post*, September 29, 2000; Joel Greenberg, "Sharon Touches a Nerve and Jerusalem Explodes," *New York Times*, September 29, 2000.
3. "Section 2: The Development and Progress of the Events: Chapter 1 – The Events of October 1, 2000," *State Commission of Inquiry to Clarify Conflicts Between Security Forces and Israeli Civilians in October 2000*, State of Israel Judiciary, http://elyon1.court.gov.il/heb/veadot/or/inside2.htm [In Hebrew].
4. See Khalil Shikaki, "Palestinians Divided," *Foreign Affairs*, 81, 1 (January/February 2002), 89–105. On the Tanzim, see Graham Usher, "Fatah Tanzim: Origins and Politics," *Middle East Report*, 217 (Winter 2000), 6–7.
5. "Fatalities," *B'Tselem*, http://www.btselem.org/English/Statistics/Casualties.asp.
6. "Israeli–Palestinian Fatalities Since 2000 – Key Trends," *OCHA Special Focus: Occupied Palestinian Territory*, United Nations Office for the Coordination of Humanitarian Affairs. August 2007, http://www.ochaopt.org/documents/CAS_Aug07.pdf. "Summary of Palestinian Fatalities: 28 September 2000–28 February 2010," The Palestinian Human Rights Monitoring Group, http://www.phrmg.org/pal_fatalities_list.htm.
7. The first known use of suicide bombing within Israel occurred on April 16, 1993 near Mechola in the Jordan Valley. Two people were killed and five were injured. Earlier use of this weapon in other conflicts includes the bombing of the US Marines headquarters in Beirut on October 23, 1983 by the nascent Hezbollah organization.
8. "Suicide Bombing Terrorism During the Current Israeli–Palestinian Confrontation (September 2000 – December 2005)," *Intelligence and Terrorism Information Center at the Center for Special Studies*, January 1, 2006, http://www.intelligence.org.il/eng/eng_n/pdf/suicide_terrorism_ae.pdf, 2.

9. *Ibid.*, 5.
10. *Ibid.*, 2.
11. Khalil Shikaki, *Willing to Compromise: Palestinian Public Opinion and the Peace Process* (Washington, DC: USIP, Special Reports, January 2006), 7–9.
12. *Report of the Secretary-General Prepared Pursuant to General Assembly Resolution ES-10/10*, United Nations General Assembly, July 30, 2002, http://www.un.org/peace/jenin/.
13. "Thirteen IDF Soldiers Killed and 7 Wounded in IDF Operations in Jenin - 9-Apr-2002," Israel Ministry of Foreign Affairs, April 9, 2002, http://www.mfa.gov.il/MFA/Government/Communiques/2002/Thirteen%20IDF%20soldiers%20killed%20and%207%20wounded%20in%20IDF.
14. See Avi Issacharof and Amos Harel, *The Seventh War* (Tel Aviv: Yediot Aharonot, 2004) 257 [In Hebrew].
15. "Document 501: Final Communiqué of the Extraordinary Arab Summit Conference, Cairo, October 22, 2000," in M. Cherif Bassiouni, ed., *Documents on the Arab–Israeli Conflict: The Palestinians and the Israeli–Palestinian Peace Process*, vol. 2, 767–771.
16. "Fifteen Months - Intifada, Closures, and Palestinian Economic Crisis: An Assessment," The World Bank, March 2002, http://unispal.un.org/pdfs/WB_24931.pdf; "Twenty-Seven Months - Intifada, Closures, and Palestinian Economic Crisis: An Assessment," *The World Bank*, May 2003, http://www-wds.worldbank.org/external/default/WDSContentServer/WDSP/IB/2003/07/14/000160016_20030714162552/Rendered/PDF/263141270monthsoIntifada10Closures.pdf; "Four Years - Intifada, Closures, and Palestinian Economic Crisis: An Assessment," *The World Bank*, October 2004, http://siteresources.worldbank.org/INTWESTBANKGAZA/Resources/wbgaza-4-yrassessment.pdf.
17. Thomas L. Friedman, "An Intriguing Signal From the Saudi Crown Prince," *New York Times*, February 17, 2002, http://query.nytimes.com/gst/fullpage.html?res=9801E3D6133FF934A25751C0A9649C8B63&n=Top%2fReference%2fTimes%20Topics%2fPeople%2fA%2fAbdullah.
18. The Summit was held on March 27–28, 2002.
19. George W. Bush, *Decision Points* (New York: Crown Publishers, 2010), 401–404. In his narrative, former President Bush makes an indirect link between his relationship with Saudi Arabia and his policy towards Israel and the Palestinians.
20. "President Bush Calls for New Palestinian Leadership" The White House, June 24, 2002, http://georgewbush-whitehouse.archives.gov/news/releases/2002/06/ 20020624-3.html.
21. Reportedly, in June 2002 Bush expressed outrage at Arafat's behavior to the Saudi Ambassador to the United States, Prince Bandar. See Bob Woodward, *State of Denial* (New York: Simon & Schuster, 2006), 47.
22. Carol Migdalovitz, "Israel's Disengagement from Gaza," *CRS Report for Congress*, September 16, 2005, http://www.usembassy.it/pdf/other/RS22000.pdf. Costs after the disengagement continued to mount, as evidenced by recurring Knesset actions to compensate the evacuees. One example from as late as 2010 is from Jonathan Lis, "New Compensation Bill for Gaza Settlers Passes First Knesset Reading," *Ha'aretz*, June 23, 2010, http://www.haaretz.com/news/national/new-compensation-bill-for-gaza-settlers-passes-first-knesset-reading-1.297917.
23. For the election process and outcome, see European Union, *Final Report on the Presidential Elections*, February 2005. http://www.eeas.europa.eu/eueom/pdf/missions/finalreport5.pdf. For public attitudes, see, "In the Presidential Elections, Mahmud Abbas Won Because he was Perceived as the Most Able to Improve the Economy and Make Progress in the Peace Process; In the Local Elections, Hamas Won

Because its Candidates were Seen as Uncorrupt," Palestinian Center for Policy and Survey Research, 11 February, 2005 http://www.pcpsr.org/survey/polls/2005/exit05.html.

24. For the text of the declaration, see "Text of the [Cairo] Declaration by Palestinians," Miftah, March 21, 2005. http://www.miftah.org/display.cfm?DocId=6938&CategoryId=5. For an analysis of the implications of the declaration on Hamas, see, Graham Usher, "The New Hamas: Between Resistance and Participation," (Washington, DC: MERIP (Middle East Research and Information Project) Report, August 21, 2005) http://www.merip.org/mero/mero082105 .
25. Khalil Shikaki, "Palestinians Divided," 95.
26. Khalil Shikaki, "Willing to Compromise," 13–14.
27. *Ibid.*, 8–9.
28. "Palestinian Public Opinion: Poll No. (21): Despite Dissatisfaction with the Performance of the Hamas Government, Especially Regarding Salaries, and Despite Public Preference for a National Unity Government in which Fateh and Hamas are Equal, Hamas' Popularity Remains Largely Unchanged and the Majority does not Think it Should Recognize Israel," Palestinian Center for Policy and Survey Research, September 30, 2006, http://www.pcpsr.org/survey/polls/2006/p21e1.html.
29. Khalil Shikaki, "With Hamas in Power: Impact of Palestinian Domestic Developments on Options for the Peace Process," Working Paper 1, February 2007, Crown Center for Middle East Studies, Brandeis University.
30. For Arafat's popularity in July 2000, see "Public Opinion Poll #1: Camp David Summit, Chances for Reconciliation and Lasting Peace, Violence and Confrontations, Hierarchies of Priorities, and Domestic Politics," Palestinian Center for Policy and Survey Research, July 27–29, 2000, http://www.pcpsr.org/survey/polls/2000/p1a.html. For his popularity in September 2004, see "Results of Poll # 13: After Four Years of Intifada, an Overwhelming Sense of Insecurity Prevails Among Palestinians Leading to High Level of Support for Bombing and Rocket Attacks on One Hand and to High Levles of Demand for Mutual Cessation of Violence and Questioning of the Effectiveness of Armed Attacks on the Other," Palestinian Center for Policy and Survey Research, September 23–26, 2004, http://www.pcpsr.org/survey/polls/2004/p13a.html.
31. "Poll Number (14): First Serious Signs of Optimism Since the Start of the Intifada," Palestine Center for Policy and Survey Research, December 1–5, 2004, http://www.pcpsr.org/survey/polls/2004/p14epdf.pdf. For optimism in the Palestinian society after Arafat's death, see Khalil Shikaki, "The Palestinian Elections: Sweeping Victory, Uncertain Mandate," *Journal of Democracy*, 17, 3 (July 2006), 116–130.
32. For the IAF reservists petition, see "Army Reserve Pilots: We Will Not Attack in the Territories," Ynet, September 24, 2003, http://www.ynet.co.il/articles/1,7340,L-2767679,00.html [In Hebrew]; for an interview with Yiftach Spector, the most renowned pilot among those who signed the petition, see Neri Livne, "The Refusenik," *Ha'aretz*, December 4, 2007, http://www.haaretz.co.il/misc/1.1463239 [In Hebrew]; Suzanne Goldenberg, "12 Dead in Attack on Hamas," *The Guardian*, July 22, 2002, http://www.guardian.co.uk/world/2002/jul/23/israel1.
33. For an English version of the document, see "The Geneva Accord: A Model Israeli–Palestinian Peace Agreement, Draft Permanent Status Agreement," http://www.geneva-accord.org/mainmenu/english.
34. Shlomo Brom, "Is the Jordan Valley Truly a Security Zone for Israel?" *Strategic Assessment*, 3, 4 (January 2001), http://www.inss.org.il/publications.php?cat=25&incat=&read=673.

35. Jacob Shamir and Khalil Shikaki, *Palestinian and Israeli Public Opinion: The Public Imperative in the Second Intifada* (Bloomington: Indiana University Press, 2010), 75, 94–97.
36. "Ariel Sharon Timeline," NPR, January 6, 2006, http://www.npr.org/templates/story/story.php?storyId=5127808. "Document 243: Report of the Commission of Inquiry into the Events at the Refugee Camps in Beirut (Kahan Report), February 8, 1983," in M. Cherif Bassiouni, ed., *Documents on the Arab–Israeli Conflict: Emergence of Conflict in Palestine and the Arab–Israeli Wars and Peace Process, vol. 1*, 702–773. The Kahan Commission wrote the following about Sharon: "In our opinion, it is fitting that the Minister of Defense draw the appropriate personal conclusions arising out of the defects revealed with regard to the manner in which he discharged the duties of his office – and if necessary, that the Prime Minister consider whether he should exercise his authority under Section 21-A(a) of the Basic Law: the Government, according to which 'the Prime Minister may, after informing the Cabinet of his intention to do so, remove a minister from office'." (771)
37. John Boykin, *Cursed is the Peacemaker.*
38. "A Conversation with Ehud Olmert, Interim Israeli Prime Minister," *Washington Post*, April 9, 2006.
39. Kelly Wallace, "Sharon: 'Occupation' Terrible for Israelis, Palestinians," CNN, May 27, 2003, http://www.cnn.com/2003/WORLD/meast/05/26/mideast/. Sharon expressed this view in a meeting of the Likud faction in the Israeli Parliament (Knesset) on May 26, 2003.
40. See also "Israel Debates Going it Alone," CBS News, February 11, 2009, http://www.cbsnews.com/stories/2003/12/18/world/main589250.shtml.

12 From the Second Lebanon War to the Arab Awakening

This chapter in the history of the Arab–Israeli conflict begins with Hamas's victory in the January 2006 Palestinian elections and ends in mid-2012. Two eruptions of terrible violence took place during this timeframe: the summer 2006 war between Hezbollah and Israel, and the December 2008–January 2009 war waged by Israel against Hamas in the Gaza Strip. Conversely, the period also witnessed two significant efforts at peacemaking: Palestinian–Israeli bilateral negotiations launched at the November 2007 Annapolis Conference, and the Israeli–Syrian proximity talks facilitated by Turkey in 2008. Both efforts failed, as did all subsequent attempts by the Obama administration to revive effective negotiations during its first term.

On the global scene, this period witnessed a subtle but significant change in American foreign policy associated with the Bush administration's second term. Philosophically, the administration inched gradually away from the more crude forms of the neoconservative approach to the world that characterized its first term and closer to the more familiar world of realism. Thus, attempts to increase long-term global and regional stability through the orchestrated, if not forced, spread of democracy was now de-emphasized if not altogether abandoned.

Beginning in early 2009, the Obama administration launched another major change of emphasis in American policy in the Middle East: an attempt to positively affect the prevailing perceptions of the United States in the region. The main thrust of this effort was a number of speeches delivered by President Obama – notably an April 2009 speech to the Turkish Parliament and a June 2009 speech in Cairo – in an attempt to convince Muslim and Arab audiences that the United States was not an enemy of Islam and that it was prepared to open a new page in its relations with the Arab people. These attempts, however, met with skepticism in the Arab street.

In the Middle East this period witnessed a further expansion of the Islamists' reach and a further deepening of their roots, with the 2005 election of Mahmoud Ahmadinejad as President of Iran, Hezbollah and Hamas becoming even more entrenched, and Islamic political parties faring better than ever in locations ranging from Gaza to Egypt to Turkey. Yet these changes in the Middle East region were far less dramatic than what the region was to experience by the end of the first decade of the 21st century – changes which were then interchangeably referred to as the Arab Spring or the Arab Awakening.

In the early years of the 21st century, the regional players increased their involvement in Arab–Israeli issues, with the Arab League affirming in 2007 the Arab Peace Initiative (API). During the second half of the decade, Egypt, and to a far lesser extent Saudi Arabia and Qatar, also became increasingly involved in the efforts to craft internal Palestinian reconciliation between Fatah and Hamas.

Among Palestinians this period witnessed further fragmentation, and a growing schism between Hamas and Fatah, culminating in Hamas's violent takeover of Gaza in June 2007. Hamas then institutionalized its control over Gaza while Fatah entrenched itself in the West Bank, together producing the nearly complete territorial split between the two Palestinian areas. Finally, while support for unilateralism waned on the Israeli side, this period witnessed great progress in Palestinian unilateral state-building efforts, orchestrated by PA Prime Minister Salam Fayyad.

Following the formation of a Hamas government in March 2006, the international community, led by the United States and Israel, boycotted the new government and ceased all financial support for the PA while continuing to maintain contacts with the PA president. A year later, the formation of a national unity government led to even broader international diplomatic boycott of the PA. However, following Hamas's violent takeover of Gaza in June 2007, and the resulting breakdown of the Palestinian national unity government, the Bush administration overcame its previous inhibitions against playing an active role in Palestinian–Israeli peacemaking and, in November, launched the Annapolis process.

Main Developments

The main developments witnessed during the period addressed here include the rise and fall of American efforts to facilitate and encourage Palestinian–Israeli negotiations; the rise of political Islam throughout the Middle East; the challenge to Middle East regional security presented by Iran's nuclear efforts; the demise in Israel of the Kadima-led government headed by Ehud Olmert and its replacement by the Likud-led government headed by Benjamin Netanyahu; Palestinians' reconciliation efforts and their focus on building state institutions and gaining international recognition of their statehood; the eruption of the Arab Awakening; and the rising importance of Turkey as a regional power.

The United States in the Middle East

In the global scene affecting the Middle East the two most important developments during this period were the evolutionary transformation of the Bush administration from its first to its second term and, four years later, the ascent of Barack Obama to the presidency of the United States. The general decline of the neoconservatives' influence in the second term of the Bush administration resulted in a subtle but important change in American policy in the Middle East: reduced emphasis on the pursuit of democratizing the region.[1] With Condoleezza Rice moving from the post of National Security Advisor to Secretary of State, diplomacy now seemed to be resurrected and the use of force de-emphasized. In turn, the return of realism was associated with tacit acknowledgement that the United States would probably not become the imperial power that some neoconservatives had sought

Figure 12.1. Condoleezza Rice with Mahmoud Abbas, 2007. *Source*: Getty Images

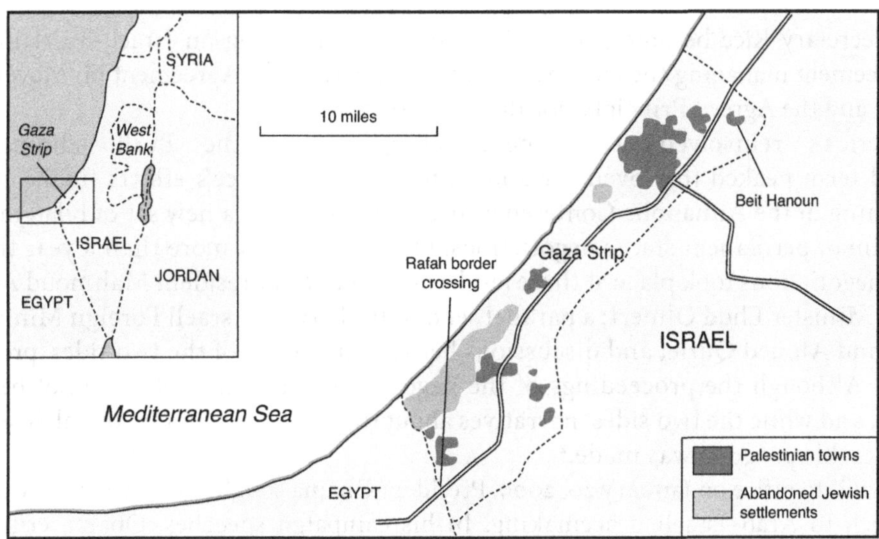

Figure 12.2. The Rafah Crossing

or imagined possible. Diplomacy having been resurrected, the United States now began to engage Iran, although at a low level.

In the Arab–Israeli arena, the Bush administration's earlier abandonment of a role in peacemaking was now itself abandoned in favor of renewed contact with the Palestinians. This process began immediately after Israel's disengagement from Gaza when for the first

Figure 12.3. Olmert, Bush, and Abbas at Annapolis. © Brooks Kraft/Corbis

time Secretary Rice became personally involved in brokering an Israeli–Palestinian deal: an agreement managing the entrances to the Gaza Strip (the "Agreement on Movement and Access and the Agreed Principles for Rafah Crossing").

America's reinvolvement in peacemaking during the Bush administration's second term peaked in November 2007, when Secretary Rice's efforts finally led to the convening of the Annapolis Conference, designed to launch a new set of bilateral Israeli–Palestinian permanent status negotiations. Over a period of more than a year thereafter, these negotiations took place at three levels: talks between President Mahmoud Abbas and Prime Minister Ehud Olmert; a parallel set of talks between Israeli Foreign Minister Tzipi Livni and Ahmed Qurie; and discussions between members of the two sides' professional teams. Although the proceedings of the negotiations held in 2008 have not been made public, and while the two sides' narratives about these talks are not identical, it seems that considerable progress was made.[2]

Sworn into office on January 20, 2009, President Obama sought to transform the American approach to Arab–Israeli peacemaking. In his campaign speeches, Obama criticized the Bush administration for having neglected this project and for having postponed any serious engagement in the process until the last year of its two-term presidency. By contrast, Obama promised serious engagement early in his first term. Signaling his commitment to this goal, on his second day in office he nominated former Senator George Mitchell as Special Envoy to the Middle East.

In an historic speech President Obama delivered at Cairo University in June 2009 and in a testimony given by General Petraeus, then Commander of the United States Central

Command (CENTCOM), the new administration linked Arab–Israeli peacemaking to two other American projects: building bridges to the Muslim people and containing Iran and its nuclear project. In both contexts, the continuation of the Arab–Israeli conflict was seen as an impediment to America's ability to address the other challenges it was facing in the Middle East.[3]

Attempting to contribute to Palestinian–Israeli peacemaking yet facing the Palestinians' lack of trust in incoming Israeli Prime Minister Netanyahu, Obama urged Israel to help create an environment more conducive to progress by agreeing to freeze all further settlement-construction activities. While seeking to persuade the Palestinians to return to direct negotiations, the United States also sought to win Arab states' cooperation in an effort to induce Israel to accept a gradual construction freeze; the aim was to persuade Arab states to implement partial normalization with Israel as a reward for Israeli steps toward a complete freeze.

In November 2009 the Obama administration succeeded in extracting Israel's consent to a 10-month partial settlement construction freeze. Yet this did not lead to serious direct Palestinian–Israeli negotiations. The Republican Party's success in the November 2010 mid-term elections – resulting in their assumption of the leadership of the House of Representatives – further limited Obama's room for maneuver. However, in May 2011 he made another attempt to launch negotiations by inviting Israeli and Palestinian acceptance of terms of reference for such talks, particularly in the realms of borders and security.[4] But after this effort failed as well, in a September 2011 speech to the UN General Assembly, Obama made clear that he had abandoned any serious effort to achieve a breakthrough in Palestinian–Israeli peacemaking during his first term.[5]

Hamas and the Broader Rise of Political Islam

In June 2005, Mahmoud Ahmadinejad was elected President of Iran. This ushered in a new level of militancy, in style if not in substance, in Iran's role in the region and in international affairs. Predicting Israel's early demise and denying the Holocaust, Ahmadinejad moved to strengthen Iran's ties to its regional clients: Syria, Hezbollah and Hamas. This coincided with a shift inside Iranian governing circles in favor of those most closely tied to Hezbollah and Hamas: Iran's Revolutionary Guard Corps.

Meanwhile, parties representing political Islam fared better than before in the electoral processes of Middle Eastern states: in the 2005 parliamentary elections in Egypt[6] and in elections at all levels in Turkey in 2007.[7] In the Palestinian parliamentary elections in January 2006 Fatah was beaten by Hamas, which won 44 percent of the vote compared with Fatah's 42 percent. The PA's electoral system translated this victory into 74 out of 132 seats in the Palestinian legislature, compared with Fatah's 45 seats.[8]

In turn, Hamas's victory posed a threat to any hope of resuming negotiations with Israel, as the Islamic movement made it clear that it would not negotiate with Israel or accept the agreements that the PLO had previously concluded. Hamas's success also presented Egypt with an array of national security challenges: terror cells in the Sinai were found to have links to Hamas and other groups in the Gaza Strip, and Hamas's link to the Muslim Brotherhood and Hezbollah underground cells worried Egypt's security services. In addition, the tunnels dug underneath Gaza's borders with Egypt challenged Egypt's sovereignty by making its borders permeable.

The Hamas government formed after the 2006 elections was boycotted not only by Israel and the United States but also by the European Union. The Quartet (representing the United States, the UN, the EU, and Russia) presented to Hamas three preconditions for engagement: that it renounce terrorism and violence, that it recognize Israel, and that it agree to fulfill all obligations undertaken by previous Palestinian governments.[9]

Relations between Hamas and Fatah began to deteriorate immediately after the elections. In an attempt to soften international reaction to its electoral victory, Hamas invited Fatah to joint it in a government coalition. But Fatah preferred to sit on the sidelines rather than make Hamas's task of governing easier. Indeed, Fatah leaders publicly predicted that, given time, Hamas would fail. They conditioned their acceptance of the coalition offer on Hamas's willingness to recognize the PLO as the sole legitimate representative of the Palestinian people and demanded that the new government's platform included PLO peace obligations – conditions that Hamas rejected out of hand. Relations between the two factions deteriorated further when PA security services showed no inclination to obey orders given by the Hamas government. Indeed, Hamas accused Mohammad Dahlan, President Abbas's security advisor and the former head of the PA's Preventive Security in the Gaza Strip, of conspiring to crack down on its military wing. Hamas then established its own security service, the so-called Executive Force, which led to frequent clashes with the existing security services that reported to President Abbas.

The rift in the Palestinian camp sparked a number of efforts to reconcile the differences between Fatah and Hamas. The first of these, seeking to formulate a common program for the two movements, came from the Prisoners' Document released in May 2006. This was drafted by prisoners in various Israeli jails, led by Marwan Barghouti, leader of Fatah's young guard, and several Hamas senior leaders. It was later revised, incorporating several reservations by Hamas that significantly diluted its main message, and renamed the National Conciliation Document. The revised version contained elements of Hamas's traditional discourse, rejecting existing peace agreements and other instruments of international legitimacy as "unfair to the Palestinian people," which Hamas interpreted as rejection of the Oslo Accords and recognition of Israel.[10]

The second such reconciliation attempt was negotiated by Saudi Arabia – the February 2007 Mecca Accord. The two parties committed themselves to end factional violence, to form a national unity government in which Fatah and Hamas would share power along with other factions and to set up a power-sharing arrangement in the security sector that would allow for the integration of Hamas's Executive Force into the legal structure of the PA's security forces. Fatah agreed to reforms within the PLO, paving the way for Hamas to become a member of the organization. For its part, Hamas agreed that the PLO and President Abbas would be responsible for negotiations with Israel and that negotiations would lead to the establishment of a Palestinian state within the 1967 borders. In June 2007, complaining of lack of implementation of the security clauses, Hamas took control of Gaza violently, dismantled the Fatah security apparatus and purged certain governing institutions in the Gaza Strip of any senior Fatah personnel.

A third effort to reconcile Fatah and Hamas during this timeframe was launched by Egypt in February 2009, immediately after Israel's Operation Cast Lead (see below) and followed earlier low level Egyptian-sponsored talks that began immediately after the Hamas coup. This effort culminated in October in an Egyptian-proposed "Reconciliation Agreement." Fatah accepted the Egyptian proposal but Hamas demanded revisions, which led to a standoff that remained unresolved until May 2011 when, in a surprise move, Hamas agreed to sign the reconciliation agreement. However, disagreements over the selection of a prime minister of the reconciliation government persisted. Even when those were eventually resolved in the Doha Agreement in February 2012 by a Hamas–Fatah understanding that Abbas would, in addition to being the president, become the prime minister, disagreement within Hamas prevented the implementation of the Qatari-orchestrated progress. Hamas's leadership in the Gaza Strip was strongly critical of the Doha Agreement and succeeded in delaying its implementation.

The Emerging Threat of a Nuclear Iran

Another set of important developments affecting the Middle East region during this period concerned Iran's nuclear project. International efforts in this realm focused on attempting to roll back Iran's enrichment program through a set of UN Security Council resolutions. These efforts suffered a setback in 2009 when Western intelligence agencies discovered another secret site intended for uranium enrichment, this one dug into a mountain near the city of Qom.

Low-level talks with Iran conducted during the Bush administration's second term by the representatives of the five permanent members of the UN Security Council and Germany (called the P-5 + 1 Talks) were upgraded in early 2009 by the Obama administration. These upgraded talks focused on the possible removal of low-enriched uranium from Iran in exchange for fuel for the small isotope-producing research reactor in Tehran (TRR). While at first Iran seemed to accept the negotiated agreement, it later rejected it. In talks held with Turkey and Brazil in May 2010 Iran finally accepted a version of the proposed deal, but the trilateral arrangement was rejected by Washington.

Economic sanctions applied in an effort to compel Iran to roll back its enrichment activities were undermined by the reluctance of two members of Security Council – Russia and China – to cooperate. Nonetheless these sanctions were gradually tightened during this period, particularly after the UN Security Council adopted Resolution 1929 on June 9, 2010. This was enabled by greater Russian cooperation associated with a worsening of Iranian–Russian relations. In parallel, the United States, the European Union, and a number of other states ranging from Canada to Australia began to apply economic sanctions and other pressures on Iran unilaterally, particularly through the international financial system. These measures made it increasingly difficult for Iran to trade with the outside world. However, the effects of the sanctions were diminished in late 2010 by higher oil prices, which increased Iran's revenues.

The escalating tension with Iran over its nuclear project triggered a number of different reactions and responses in the Middle East at large. The Gulf States – particularly Saudi Arabia – viewed the project as a direct threat to their national security. Arab worries about the possible acquisition of nuclear weapons by Iran and its allies were discernable in the complete silence with which these states reacted to Israel's alleged bombing of a nuclear facility in northeastern Syria in November 2007. In July 2010, the idea of conducting a similar military strike against Iran's facilities seemed to be endorsed by the UAE's Ambassador to the United States.[11] The failure to halt Iran's nuclear efforts – particularly its uranium enrichment program – led to an open debate in Israel and the United States throughout 2011 and 2012 on the efficacy and wisdom of a possible military strike against Iran's nuclear installations.[12]

Two Wars with Non-State Actors

The Arab–Israeli arena witnessed two wars during this period: in the summer of 2006 between Israel and Hezbollah, and in December 2008–January 2009 between Israel and Hamas in Gaza (Operation Cast Lead).

Hezbollah and Hamas had a number of features in common. Although they crossed the Sunni–Shi'a divide they were both connected to Iran. Both were much more than an armed organization: they were social movements that attracted considerable public support. In addition, to different degrees both became proto-states with broad control over territory. Indeed, after June 2007 Hamas's hold over Gaza became complete and unchallenged. Finally, the territories which Hamas and Hezbollah controlled comprised areas from which Israel had withdrawn unilaterally: from Lebanon in May 2000 and from Gaza in the summer of 2005.

On June 26, 2006 Hamas attacked an IDF armored vehicle, killing two soldiers and abducting one – Gilad Shalit. Two weeks later, on July 12, 2006, Hezbollah launched a cross-border operation along the Israel–Lebanon border, abducting three Israeli soldiers, who later died, and killing eight. Hezbollah's ground attack was accompanied by a Katyusha rocket barrage along the border, designed to divert the IDF's attention. Israel responded by employing its air force, initially against targets in southern Lebanon and gradually escalating to infrastructure targets deep inside the country. The Israeli attacks, which targeted Beirut's international airport as well as power stations, exacted a heavy toll on Lebanon's infrastructure, and its attack on Hezbollah's stockpiles of long-range rockets seemed to have destroyed most of the launchers and rockets stored there. Israel inflicted especially high levels of destruction on Dahiya – a Shi'a neighborhood of Beirut where Hezbollah headquarters were located.

In parallel, the IDF conducted a series of unsuccessful military operations just north of the border, aimed at dislodging Hezbollah fighters from their strongholds in the area and destroying the stockpiles of weapons they hid there. However, Israeli efforts to hunt for Katyusha launchers and to otherwise suppress rocket fire failed; until the very end of the fighting, Hezbollah managed to continue firing Katyusha and other rockets at targets inside Israel at a rate of some 200 per day.

What came to be called the Second Lebanon War ended on August 14, 2006, with Israel and Lebanon accepting UN Security Council Resolution 1701. The resolution followed extensive mediation conducted by the Arab League and was based on a seven-point plan previously proposed by Lebanon's prime minister, Fuad Siniora. It called for the complete withdrawal of Israeli forces; the deployment of the Lebanese Army to the southern part of the country – an area from which it was excluded by Hezbollah until then; the deployment of UN peacekeepers – the UNIFIL force now strengthened by an enhanced mandate; and the application of a security and monitoring regime with third-party involvement designed to prevent the rearmament of Hezbollah.[13]

Hamas, meanwhile, continued its efforts to end Gaza's isolation. A major attempt to do so occurred on January 23, 2008 when tens of thousands of Gaza residents breached the border with Egypt.[14] It took a few days for order to be restored and for the border fence to be reconstructed. A few tens of Hamas operatives were apprehended by the Egyptian security services as they allegedly attempted to form contact with terror cells in the Sinai. In parallel, throughout this period Hamas and elements with commercial interests continued to construct hundreds of tunnels underneath Gaza's border with Egypt, smuggling weapons and munitions into the Strip, as well as a wide variety of civilian commodities.

Just as Hezbollah declared victory following Israel's unilateral withdrawal from Lebanon in May 2000, Hamas, led by its charismatic leader, Khalid Mashaal, declared that Israel's unilateral disengagement from Gaza in the summer of 2005 was the outcome of its "armed resistance." Following Hamas's success in the January 2006 parliamentary elections, Israel blockaded Gaza but Hamas maintained, and indeed escalated, its Kassam rocket attacks against Israeli towns and settlements close to the border. Between early 2006 and December 2008, Israel's south was targeted by a total of 2,888 rockets and 1,974 other ordnances (such as mortar fire), bringing the economy of the area adjacent to Gaza to near-complete paralysis.[15] With Israel inflicting heavy punishment on Gaza in response to such attacks, in June 2008 Hamas accepted an Egyptian-mediated 6-month de-facto ceasefire (*Tah'dia*). But by November a new round of violence erupted and Hamas declared that it would not renew the *Tah'dia* unless the blockade on Gaza was lifted. In late December, this led Israel to launch a massive attack on Gaza, killing some 1,417 and wounding 4,336.[16]

Israel's extensive use of firepower against targets in an area densely populated by civilians resulted in an international outcry. It also led to the formation of a UN commission headed by former South African Judge Richard Goldstone to investigate the two sides' conduct. While finding that both Israel and Hamas had committed acts regarded by the commission as constituting war crimes, most of its criticism was directed at Israel.[17]

When the fighting in Gaza ended in January 2009, Hamas undertook an informal obligation to restore the *Tah'dia*: to refrain from further rocket attacks against Israel and to also prevent other smaller groups – such as Islamic Jihad – from launching such ordnance.[18] Since then and until November 2012, rocket attacks from Gaza against Israeli targets and Israeli air and other operations against targets in Gaza have been few and far between.

During the 2009 *Tah'dia*, Hamas's strategy shifted to ending Israel's naval blockade of Gaza. In June 2010 these attempts reached a climax when a flotilla organized by a Turkish group attempted to reach Gaza but was intercepted by the Israeli navy. The clash between Israeli soldiers and some tens of activists in the largest of the boats – the *Mavi Marmara* – turned violent, resulting in the death of nine Turkish citizens. This led to the setting up of another UN investigation, this time headed by the former prime minister of New Zealand, Sir Geoffrey Palmer. While the Palmer Commission found that Israel was within its rights to

KHALED MASHAAL

Figure 12.4. Poster of Khaled Mashaal at a rally in Gaza in support of the Hamas government, 2006. © Abid Katib/Getty Images

Khaled Mashaal became Hamas's leader and head of its Political Bureau in 1996. Born in Silwad in the West Bank in 1956, he spent most of his life in Kuwait, Jordan, Qatar, and Syria. In September 1997, while living in Amman, Mashaal was a target of an Israeli assassination attempt using a chemical substance. The attempt ended with Israel, under Jordanian pressure, handing over the antidote to treat him. But in 1999 Jordan banned Hamas, and Mishal was expelled from the country. He increased in political stature as Hamas gained popular support during the Second Intifada, which resulted in its victory in the 2006 parliamentary elections, and the movement continued its "armed struggle" against Israel even after Israel's withdrawal from Gaza.

prevent the flotilla from breaking the naval blockade, it also opined that Israel used excessive force when exercising its right to do so.[19]

Domestic Developments and the Arab Awakening

The 2006 war in Lebanon spurred dramatic internal developments in Israel. Criticism of the manner in which the war was conducted led to the formation of a Commission of Inquiry headed by a former Supreme Court judge: the Winograd Commission.[20] The broad criticism before and after the publication of the commission's report led to the resignation or termination of Israel's then defense minister, Amir Peretz, and many others, including the Chief of Staff, the Deputy Chief of Staff, the Chief of the Northern Command, and a number of other IDF senior commanders whose units took part in the fighting.

The criticism and the commission's findings also caused irreparable damage to the standing of then Prime Minister Ehud Olmert. He was later subjected to a number of police investigations on charges of personal corruption, mostly connected to his previous terms as Mayor of Jerusalem and minister of trade and commerce. By March 2009, the weight of these accusations had forced Olmert out of office. This was followed by a failed attempt by then Foreign Minister Tzipi Livni, Olmert's successor as leader of Kadima, to form a coalition. Elections to the Knesset took place, resulting in electoral success for Kadima – it won a plurality of Knesset seats. However, led by Netanyahu, Likud succeeded in assembling a governing coalition that won the confidence of a majority of Knesset members. The new government was arguably the most right-wing in Israel's history, with many of the more pragmatic Likud members and leaders having abandoned the party earlier in favor of Kadima and with the Israel Beitenu party, led by Avigdor Lieberman, now the most important coalition partner.[21]

On the Palestinian side, political developments in the West Bank included the convening in August 2009 of Fatah's sixth congress in Bethlehem – the first Fatah congress to convene since 1989. Delegates elected a new Central Committee and a new Revolutionary Council comprised mostly of younger West Bank- and Gaza-based leaders as most of the previous old guard members were voted out of office. Mahmoud Abbas was affirmed as the head of Fatah.[22]

Between 2005 and 2010 there were also significant changes in the domestic scenes of a large number of the region's states. Somalia and Sudan fell into a process of disintegration, while Yemen, Iraq, and Lebanon faced growing schisms in their political and social structures. Other countries, however, commenced a process of limited political and somewhat more significant economic reforms – Egypt, Saudi Arabia, other Gulf States, Jordan, Tunisia, Algeria and Morocco. All implemented drastic changes by moving towards a market economy and drew inspiration from global market development and the regional successes of Dubai and Turkey. All these countries went through a process of deregulation and privatization, though not all at the same pace. The end result of this was a growing middle class and a much more active private sector. The dramatic increase in oil prices gave a considerable boost to such developments in a number of Arab countries, while free trade agreements with the EU provided a boost to the Arab Mediterranean countries. The increased influence of the pan-Arab media could also be attributed to this growing wealth.

On the political reform side, the change was much slower and less impressive. However, the amendments to the Egyptian constitution in 2005 and 2007 led to presidential elections that, at least appeared, less rigged than before and allowed more political and social movements to enter the political arena. Similar developments took place in Morocco, allowing greater representation to the opposition. In most of the Gulf States, local elections were held for the first time and the appointed (for example, in Saudi Arabia) or half-appointed (for example, in Oman) Shura Councils experienced somewhat greater empowerment. In Kuwait, the process of democratization was enhanced by amending the constitution to allow women to participate in parliamentary elections. As a result, four women were elected to parliament in the May 2009 Kuwaiti elections. These developments were accompanied by a notable growth in the freedom of the press, greater development and sophistication of civil society, and the rise of Islamic groups of all types. They also led to growing tension between religious and secular values.

In retrospect, however, these developments proved to be merely a precursor to the enormous changes that Arab countries began to experience from late 2010 onwards. On December 17, Mohammed Bouazizi, a Tunisian street vendor, set himself on fire after having been mistreated by a policewoman, which triggered mass protests. The result was dramatic: less than a month later, on January 14, 2011, the country's President, Zine El Abidine Ben Ali, who had held that position for 23 years, fled the country for refuge in Saudi Arabia. A week later, some 5,000 people took to the streets in Amman to protest higher fuel prices. Egypt followed suit even more dramatically when on January 25, 2011 masses took to the streets of Cairo's Tahrir Square in the framework of a "Day of Rage" against the Mubarak regime. Less than three weeks later, Mubarak stepped down and ended his 30-year rule by handing power over to Egypt's Supreme Council of the Armed Forces (SCAF).[23]

The next stop of this Middle East political tsunami was in Libya, where, on February 15, 2011 mass protests began in Benghazi in response to the arrest of a human rights activist. Five days later Morocco also witnessed nationwide protests, but these called for a new constitution and an end to corruption, not for the end to the monarchy. Relative to the size of the population, the scale of protests that began in Bahrain on February 22, 2011 was the most dramatic yet: more than 100,000 people, comprising 12 percent of the population, took to the streets of Manama. That week, a similar number of people demonstrated in Yemen against the Saleh regime, some 30,000 of them in Sana'a.

By early March, the rebels in Libya took control of Benghazi and declared themselves to be the country's official representatives. At the same time, Saudi Arabia cracked down on Shi'a protesters, and on March 11 it sent its military forces into Manama to quell the protests in Bahrain. Five days later, demonstrations began in Syria, mostly in the southern town of Dara'a but also in a suburb of Damascus. This was followed on March 19 by the beginning of NATO air strikes in Libya, after the UN Security Council authorized the implementation of a "no-fly zone." The seven months of civil war that followed resulted in the end of four decades of Qhaddafi rule with the flight of most members of his family and his death on October 20, 2011. A month later, on November 23, President Saleh of Yemen avoided a similar fate by resigning and then leaving the country.

That month, Tunisia celebrated the first truly democratic transformation resulting from the Arab Awakening, with the country holding its first real elections. The Islamist party Al Nahdda won the elections, garnering 41 percent of the vote. Three months later, on January 11, 2012 Egypt completed a similar process with a three-phase parliamentary election that delivered a sweeping victory to the Muslim Brotherhood's Freedom and Justice Party, which won 47 percent of the seats. Even more surprising was the level of support for the more extreme Salafi party, al-Nur, which captured 29 percent of Egypt's new parliament.[24]

By early 2012, the Arab Awakening in Syria grew ever more violent and assumed many of the characteristics of a civil war. By the end of that year the death toll of the war was estimated to have reached over 60,000.[25] Meanwhile more than 400,000 Syrians fled to refugee camps in Turkey and Jordan as well as across the border to Lebanon. Thousands defected from the Syrian army to join the insurgency.

Challenges and Encouragement to the Two-State Solution Paradigm

On the Palestinian–Israeli front, a number of developments challenged the paradigm that had guided all peacemaking efforts since Madrid and Oslo: the two-state solution. On the Palestinian side, continuous Israeli settlement activities in the West Bank had bred growing doubts that such a solution, however desirable, was still feasible. In mid-2012, official figures showed that more than 350,000 Israelis lived in settlements recognized by the government in the West Bank, while close to 300,000 Israelis lived in East Jerusalem.[26] There were about 102 outposts in the West Bank not officially recognized by Israel. Thus, since the signing of Oslo, the settler population in the West Bank, not counting those in East Jerusalem, has almost tripled.[27] As a result, while a majority of Palestinians continued to support a two-state solution, even larger majorities expressed disbelief that such a solution would ever be implemented.[28]

On the Israeli side, doubts grew about whether a two-state solution could be applied without presenting a mortal danger to the country. In the aftermath of the wars of 2006 and 2008–09, Israeli fears grew that a Palestinian state in the West Bank would become another launching pad for rockets fired against Israel, except that instead of crippling Israel's north or south, this time the central core of the country, where the bulk of Israel's population and 80 percent of its industrial capacity are located, would be targeted.[29]

As a result of these developments, this period witnessed another wave of interest in alternatives to the two-state solution. On the Palestinian side – mostly in the Diaspora – this took the form of articles and statements singing the praises of the one-state solution. The discourse reflected an amalgamation of those whose case was simply that Israel's settlement activities had rendered the two-state solution inapplicable and hence irrelevant and those who had always rejected Arafat's acceptance of the two-state paradigm. On the Israeli side, ideas resurfaced reminiscent of the functional solution espoused by then Defense Minister Moshe Dayan in the late 1960s and early 1970s, which called for the granting of citizenship to all Arabs residing in the territories controlled by Israel.[30]

Parallel to these challenges, the period also witnessed a number of developments potentially making the eventual application of the two-state vision more likely. The most important of these was the effort launched by PA Prime Minister Salam Fayyad to build the institutions of state unilaterally, in much the same fashion that the Zionist movement had done under the British Mandate. In September 2009, Fayyad formulated and announced a two-year plan for building the foundations of independent Palestinian statehood.[31]

A particularly important facet of Fayyad's efforts was the reform he instituted, with American support, in the Palestinian security sector. The focus of this was the PA's establishment of a monopoly of force, outlawing the separate militias that had proliferated during the Second Intifada. The aim was to insure that no one would carry a weapon on the Palestinian side unless in uniform. These efforts were accompanied by a major project orchestrated by United Stated General Keith Dayton to train in Jordan battalions of the PA's new National Security Force. Deployment of the first of these battalions in the Jenin area in 2008, in the framework of the Jenin-First experimental approach approved by the IDF, then subsequent deployments one by one in additional areas, led to the West Bank gradually experiencing significantly higher levels of safety and security.[32]

With the IDF responding in 2009–10 to greater Palestinian competence in the security sector by lifting some road blocks and checkpoints, access and movement within and between the various parts of, and locations in, the West Bank began to improve.[33] In turn, greater safety and security and the resulting shorter travel time in the West Bank spurred greater confidence, which, in turn, translated to faster economic growth. For the years 2008–10 the IMF calculated the GDP growth of the West Bank to have averaged 9 percent. Two investment conferences held in 2008 and in 2010 in Bethlehem had attracted considerable interest, ranging from Arab investors from the Persian Gulf to Palestinian businessmen in the Diaspora.[34] Yet by 2011, the PA experienced a slowdown resulting from reduced donor support, remaining Israeli restrictions on access and movement, and reduced tax revenues and investor incentives due to the continued diplomatic impasse. As a result, growth fell in 2011 to 5.7 percent.[35]

With Israeli–Palestinian negotiations essentially frozen since 2009, and with Palestinian confidence in the ability of the Obama administration to renew such negotiations eroding, the PA decided in 2011 to seek recognition as a state and to confront Israel in various international forums as a means of increasing the costs of continued occupation. In September 2011, President Abbas submitted a request to the UN to admit Palestine as a member state. The United States Congress responded by temporarily suspending financial aid to the PA.[36] Strong American opposition and divisions within the UN Security Council kept the Palestinians' request unresolved, as they could not mobilize a majority in support of their request.[37] In October however, UNESCO's General Conference voted to admit Palestine as a member state of the organization, with 107 countries voting in favor, 14 against, and 52 abstaining.[38] More importantly, on November 29, 2012 UNGA Resolution 67\19 upgraded the status of the Palestinian mission to the UN to a "Non-Member Observer State" in a vote of 138 to 9, with 41 abstaining.

Turkey's Rising Profile

By the end of the decade Turkey's increased salience seemed of growing importance in the Arab–Israeli realm. This resulted from a broader transformation of Turkey's foreign policy from a focus on attempts to be accepted as a member of the European Union to renewed involvement in the Middle East at large. This transformation seems to have been spurred in part by the perception that Europe was shunning Turkey, and in part by a broader interest in returning to Turkey's roots – a move depicted by some as neo-Ottomanism. The political change was accompanied, if not motivated, by a dramatic increase in Turkey's economic interests abroad: its annual exports rose from $14 billion in the 1990s to some $135 billion in 2011.[39] Turkey's investments abroad also increased significantly. In this framework, notwithstanding its continued political conflict with the Kurds, Turkey's private sector now invested billions of dollars in Iraq's Kurdish region.

In 2008, Turkey's greater involvement in Arab–Israeli issues was manifested in its facilitation of the Israeli–Syrian proximity talks conducted by Prime Minister Olmert and President Assad. At the same time, Turkey's AKP-led government expressed increasing support for the Palestinians and clearly took their side during the December 2008 Gaza War. Turkey was particularly angry at Prime Minister Olmert for having launched the campaign a short time after his visit to Ankara during which talks with the Syrians had seen notable progress. Recep Tayyip Erdoğan, the Turkish prime minister, now saw Olmert as untrustworthy and as someone who had cut down a very promising process that would have brought much credit to

Turkey just as it was about to bear fruit. One result was an angry exchange between Erdoğan and Israeli President Shimon Peres on January 29, 2009 during the World Economic Forum meeting in Davos.[40]

During 2009–10, Turkey continued to assume a growing role in Palestinian affairs, through criticizing Israel's conduct of the Gaza War and in attempting to end Gaza's isolation. In this framework, Turkey deployed its diplomatic assets in an attempt to broker reconciliation between Hamas and Fatah. At the same time, it allowed the June 2010 flotilla designed to break the blockade of Gaza to set sail from Turkish ports. The violent confrontation that took place on board the largest of the flotilla boats led Israeli–Turkish relations to reach their lowest point. Although Israel offered reparations for the killing of the Turkish citizens, the crises continued to linger throughout 2011 and 2012 as Israel refused to accept the Turkish demand for an apology.[41]

As mentioned earlier, in the broader Middle East arena Turkey's higher profile translated to efforts to broker an agreement with Iran with regard to its nuclear facilities. This surprised Washington, which rejected the agreement. The Obama administration was even more dismayed, and members of the United States Congress were genuinely angered, when on June 9, 2010 Turkey voted in the UN Security Council against a new round of sanctions against Iran.[42]

Turkey's evolving relations with other regional players soon proved to be problematic. Thus, by the second decade of the 21st century the downturn in Turkish–Israeli relations was more than matched by the effects of the Arab Awakening on Turkish policy – primarily, the dramatic deterioration in Turkey's relations with Syria, as Ankara spearheaded the demand for the ouster of the Assad regime.[43] At the same time, Turkey failed to make significant gains in Egypt, where the country's security sector grew uneasy about Turkey's perceived attempts to gain a foothold in Gaza.[44] For their part, Egypt's Muslim Brotherhood was unhappy about Erdoğan's preaching the virtues of a secular state system.[45] Turkey's relations with Iran and Iraq were also far from smooth as Iran saw its strategic interests threatened by a possible Turkey-assisted downfall of Syria's pro-Iran Assad regime and as Iraq and Turkey accused each other of meddling in their domestic political scenes.[46] Finally, Turkey risked a military confrontation in the Eastern Mediterranean as it edged closer to a conflict that could have also involved Israel, Lebanon and Cyprus over a massive natural gas field.[47]

Narratives

The Israeli Narrative

The War with Hezbollah and the Gaza War

The internal Israeli debate about the summer 2006 war in Lebanon focused on the performance of the IDF as well as on the country's political leadership in managing the war. However, in the Arab–Israeli context the Israeli narrative of the war focused on the implications of the Hezbollah July 12 attack that spurred the fighting. Israelis emphasized that their country had no territorial claims in Lebanon and that it withdrew its forces from every square inch of

Lebanese territory in May 2000. For them, this meant that the conflict was not about Israel's "occupation" of the territories it conquered in 1967 but rather about Israel's very existence; that unilateral Israeli withdrawals were to no avail; and that Islamists would chase Israel beyond its borders and inside its sovereign territory.

In the broader context, with Hezbollah firing Iranian-supplied rockets deeper and deeper inside Israel, the war in Lebanon meant that Israel was now being confronted by a violent strategic arm of Iran at its doorstep. Not surprisingly, the war of summer 2006 was referred to by some Israelis as their country's "first war with Iran." It was also interpreted to mean that in confronting the prospects of Iranian nuclear weapons, Israel would need to take into account that any use of military means to deny or delay Iran's acquisition of nuclear weapons would risk a violent retaliatory war launched by Hezbollah.

In the eyes of Israelis, their country was faced with a similar reality in Gaza. In the summer of 2005 Israel saw itself as having withdrawn unilaterally from every square inch of the Gaza Strip, all the way to the 1967 lines. Israelis recalled that Sharon also insisted on accompanying this withdrawal with a symbolic evacuation of four settlements in the northern West Bank as a signal that Israel intended to continue the process of disengagement in the West Bank – that is, that its approach was not "Gaza first and last." By continuing to attack Israel after its withdrawal from Gaza, Palestinians seemed to have missed another opportunity to demonstrate to Israel that it should not fear withdrawal from the West Bank, unilaterally or in the framework of an agreement.

In both cases – the 2006 war with Hezbollah and the 2008–09 war in Gaza – Israelis felt that they were unfairly criticized for using excessive force indiscriminately. Thus, the international media, various western NGOs, and particularly the UN-appointed Goldstone Commission, were seen as paying little attention to the context within which Israel acted: that is, to the extent to which the terrorists attacking Israel were concealing themselves and their weapons amongst Arab civilian populations, forcing Israeli actions of self-defense to result in a high civilian toll. Moreover, in Israeli eyes, insufficient attention was given in these reports to the extent to which Israel's adversaries were committing war crimes by purposely targeting civilian populations.

Israelis now seemed to have drawn important lessons from these two eruptions of violence: first, that given the proximity of the West Bank to Israel's large population centers and to the country's industrial core, if it were to face from the West Bank a threat similar in weapons and ranges to that presented by Hezbollah from Lebanon and Hamas from Gaza their country would be completely paralyzed. For many Israelis this now meant that no withdrawal from the West Bank could be contemplated unless ironclad and foolproof security arrangements were implemented.

In addition, Israelis interpreted the violence that Hezbollah and Hamas continued to launch against Israel inside the 1967 lines, and after Israel had withdrawn to these lines, as evidence that for Islamic fundamentalists the conflict was not about post-1967 "occupation" – it was about their commitment to "March on to Jerusalem" and erase the Zionist entity: the Israeli state established in 1948. And, like Hezbollah, Hamas was also seen as conducting a proxy war against Israel on behalf of Iran. With Iran's President Ahmadinejad predicting Israel's early demise and supporting Islamic movements such as Hezbollah and Hamas that were committed to helping this happen, the conflict was now increasingly seen as having returned to its "existential" roots, implying that the peace process launched by President Sadat was an aberration rather than an important milestone on the road to permanent peace.

Iran's Nuclear Threat

Within this context, the prospect of Iran acquiring nuclear weapons appeared to Israelis particularly menacing. However, Israelis were not of one mind about the extent of this threat. One narrative, given frequent expression by Netanyahu, saw the possibility of Iranian nuclear weapons as equivalent to the dire consequences of Nazi Germany having such weapons at its disposal in the late 1930s. This implied that Iran would not hesitate to use such weapons and that Ahmadinejad would not be able to forgo the temptation of seeing his prediction of Israel's demise materialize. The regime in Tehran was thus viewed as driven by irrational Islamic fanaticism and as insensitive to the prospects of a very costly Israeli retaliation.

A second Israeli narrative saw the danger of Iran's future possession of nuclear weapons in broader but less apocalyptic terms. It assessed that Iran's acquisition of nuclear weapons would spur a chain-reaction in the region, with countries like Egypt, Saudi Arabia, and Turkey compelled to follow suit, thus transforming the Middle East into a multi-nuclear region, with all the complications that entailed. It also worried that Iran's possession of such weapons would at the very least tempt it to promise a "nuclear umbrella" to its allies, thus emboldening Hezbollah and Hamas.

While viewing these ramifications as very serious, proponents of the second school did not believe that Iran would launch nuclear weapons against Israel. They believed that Iran was not irrational and that knowing that Israel had the means to retaliate to a nuclear attack by devastating it, Iran would refrain from such an attack.

Another dimension of this narrative was that since Iranian nuclear weapons presented a challenge to the entire region, if not to the international community at large, preventing it from acquiring such weapons should be regarded as an international imperative, not merely an Israeli issue. In this context Israelis took particular exception to the tendency of some in the United States to link the efforts to prevent Iran from developing nuclear weapons with progress made in Israeli–Palestinian peacemaking. Israelis rejected assertions that the complications associated with the continuation of the Arab–Israeli conflict made it difficult for the United States to gain the cooperation it needed from potential Arab allies to contain Iran.

Palestinian–Israeli Negotiations

In the realm of Israeli–Palestinian peacemaking efforts, the Israeli narrative of this period included a number of assessments. The first was that the end of the Annapolis talks demonstrated that the Palestinians had not abandoned their tendency to miss opportunities and regret it. Since Olmert and his Palestinian counterparts seemed to agree that he presented them with very favorable terms, it was not clear why Abbas did not respond in a serious fashion to the Israeli offer. In this view, the Palestinians had argued that the progress made in these talks should become the starting point for any future negotiations, but at the same time avoided explaining why, if the Israeli offer was so positive, they did not embrace it.

Israeli narratives as to whether Israel could afford the creation of an independent Palestinian state in the West Bank differed widely. Aside from the narrative of the ideological and religious right – which traditionally rejected the creation of such a state as contradicting Israel's historical right to "Greater Israel" – mainstream Israelis, while continuing to support a two-state solution, seemed increasingly cautious as a result of the conflicts with Hezbollah and Hamas. As evidence that their views about the implications of an Israeli withdrawal were driven only by security considerations and that these were not a pretext hiding unrelated expansionist impulses, Israelis pointed out that their government responded to improved security conditions in the West Bank by lifting the most objectionable dimensions of "occupation."

Israelis gave a mixed review to Obama's efforts to renew Palestinian–Israeli peace talks. They were perplexed by the new administration's insistence that Israel freeze all settlement activity – a demand no American administration had presented since the Baker–Shamir tensions over this issue in the early 1990s. When the Palestinian side took this American demand and imposed it as a precondition for renewed negotiations, Israelis asked why the Palestinians were now presenting a demand they had not made a precondition for previous talks.

A second Israeli concern touched on whether their worries were taken seriously. It focused on the fact that Obama saw the need to address the Muslim world twice during his first six months in office – in Ankara and in Cairo – while refraining from visiting Israel. Israelis interpreted this to mean a lesser commitment to Israeli security concerns and the possibility that Israel was being taken for granted. Indeed, this initial impression remained remarkably immune to tens of American protestations and later speeches by Obama and his top foreign policy team to the effect that America's commitment to Israel was "unbreakable," "unshakable," and "ironclad." It even remained immune to evidence and testimonies that America's support of Israel's defense needs had reached unprecedented levels during Obama's first term.

Fayyad's State-Building Project

Equally complex was the Israeli narrative with regard to the Palestinian state-building efforts led by Prime Minister Salam Fayyad. On the one hand, Israelis seemed to admire what to some appeared to be the first Palestinian leader who was walking in the Zionists' footsteps – building a state instead of complaining about obstacles. Seen as replacing repeated verbal expressions of Palestinian victimhood, Fayyad's "can-do" mentality had earned him high marks from Israeli observers of the Palestinian scene. This was especially the case with regard to the PA's achievements in security sector reforms.

At the same time, Israelis expressed concern about two aspects of Fayyad's efforts. The first had to do with his initial intention to declare Palestinian statehood within the 1967 lines unilaterally as the final phase of his two-year plan. With Fayyad's approach earning him so much admiration abroad, Israelis feared that he was acquiring the capacity to dictate the terms of such statehood – and especially its boundaries – thus presenting Israel with a fait accompli.

The second fear focused on Fayyad's support for anti-Israeli boycotts and protest measures pursued in the West Bank and abroad. While Israelis understood that Fayyad needed to take some steps to build his political base, and while they acknowledged that most of the measures he supported were directed at Israeli settlements in the West Bank and not against Israel proper, they worried that, given his growing prestige abroad, Fayyad's expressions of support would be used as credible ammunition in the campaigns to delegitimize Israel – campaigns which were seen as proliferating in Europe.

The Crisis with Turkey

Israelis viewed the crisis in Israeli–Turkish relations as rooted in two realities: the rise of Islamists and the personal ambitions of Recep Erdoğan, Turkey's prime minister. Thus, Israelis expected that given its Islamic leanings, the rise to power of the Justice and Welfare Party (AKP) – and the corresponding weakening of the Turkish military, the bulwark of close Turkish–Israeli relations – would sooner or later result in a deterioration in the two countries' ties.

Second, Israelis regarded Erdoğan as a very ambitious individual who was bent on becoming the leader of the Sunni Muslim world and as willing to go to any length and cater to any hatred of Israel to achieve this goal. To Israelis it was, therefore, not surprising that Erdoğan sided with Hamas in its violent conflict with Israel in late 2008 and early 2009. Further, since the deterioration in Turkish–Israeli relations was viewed as a result of changes in Turkey's domestic scene, Israelis thought there was little they could do to stop the slide.

This interpretation of the general worsening of relations with Turkey also informed Israelis' perception of the Turkish flotilla affair. In Israel's view the aforementioned ambitions and goals drove Turkey to seek a confrontation with Israel. Thus its AKP-led government supported the creation of the flotilla in the hope that the IDF would be provoked to confront the boats in a way that would produce damaging television footage and depict the Turks as defenders of the Palestinian cause and Israel as unwilling to tolerate civil protests. Israelis regarded their enforcement of the blockade as a legitimate act of self-defense and they were gratified when this right was later confirmed by the Palmer Commission Report. That nine Turkish citizens lost their lives was seen as unfortunate but not a result of Israeli excessive use of force and hence not requiring an apology.

The Arab Awakening

The Israeli view of the Arab Awakening was more nuanced, indeed complicated. Israelis noted that the Arab Spring was driven by domestic circumstances and events in the affected states and not propelled by foreign policy issues. Nonetheless, they feared that while the upheavals were not motivated by issues related to Israel, in the end *they* might well become the biggest loser in the affair.

What led Israelis to this conclusion? From the outset Israelis feared that regardless of the protesters' original motivations for igniting a revolution, the Islamists were better positioned than the liberals and democrats to take advantage and then dominate the revolutions. This, in turn, entailed the risk that the Arab leaders who had over a number of decades adhered to the stipulations of peace, or at least non-belligerence, with Israel would be replaced by Islamic-leaning leaders who would regard Israel as a foreign and illegitimate entity. More broadly, it was feared that Arab leaders would now come under increasing pressure by the so-called

"Arab street." The latter was regarded by Israelis as far more hostile than Arab leaders, conditioned as it was by Arab school textbooks and the pro-Palestinian Arab mass media that spread anti-Israeli and anti-Semitic propaganda. Yet another Israeli fear regarding the possible ramifications of the Arab Awakening was that it might result in a dramatic increase in terrorist activities. For all these reasons, Israelis appeared to be far from jubilant about the dramatic events that unfolded in the Middle East in 2011–12.

Palestinian Narratives

Hamas's Electoral Victory

Palestinian narratives during this period began with disappointment and accusations of hypocrisy against the United States and the international community for their refusal to accept the outcome of Palestinian democracy as expressed in the election results of January 2006. Palestinians noted that while the international community expressed verbal support for Palestinian democracy, and in fact demanded it during Arafat's days, now that they had finally managed to create a more open and inclusive political system the international community decided to turn its back on them by boycotting the new Palestinian parliament and government simply because Hamas had won the elections. The imposition of what was perceived by Palestinians as impossible conditions on the new Palestinian majority was seen as sending a message that what mattered was not how democratic Palestinians were but what outcome that democracy produced. By doing so, Palestinians feared, the international community was destroying any basis for a genuine transition to democracy in Palestine.

The narrative of those who lost the January 2006 elections sought to defend Palestinian democracy while explaining away the rise of Hamas, an organization that had rejected the peace process since the days of Oslo. While for Hamas and many of its followers the election victory was seen as a public affirmation of support for the organization and its core values and political positions, many nationalists disagreed. For them, the vote for Hamas was an isolated instance of public disillusionment with the peace process and anger at the inability of the nationalists to end the occupation through diplomacy. Nationalists also admitted that their defeat was a consequence of huge failures in state-building: they were perceived by the public as corrupt and ineffective. In other words, the vote for Hamas was interpreted as a vote against Fatah, against corruption and mismanagement, but not against the peace process, the two-state solution or diplomacy; certainly not a vote for Islamist religious values.

Based on this nationalist narrative, public rejection of international conditions imposed on Hamas was not to be interpreted as a rejection of these conditions. On the contrary, while the public rejected the principle of *imposing* conditions it nonetheless accepted all three international demands – the recognition of Israel, acceptance of past agreements, and rejection of violence – since they were perceived as a natural outcome of PLO–Israel agreements. As the PLO had already accepted these demands in its previous accords with Israel, it was only natural that Hamas too would be bound by them, even if only implicitly. Therefore, the only demand the Palestinians had endorsed was for Hamas to accept being integrated into the PLO, as this would have implied acceptance of the three preconditions. However, for most

Palestinians, nationalists and Islamist alike, the only party that should have been asked to accept these conditions was the PLO, since it was Israel's partner in the peace process and it was the party that had negotiated with Israel. Moreover, most Palestinians did not think it was fair to ask Hamas to make an explicit and dramatic departure from its ideology and political views right at the moment of its electoral victory. For them, Hamas was capable of moderating its views if only it was allowed to do so gradually and without coercion.

Efforts at Internal Reconciliation

Within this context, the Palestinian narrative presented the Mecca Accord of February 2007 as a victory for national unity, democracy and moderation. In Palestinian eyes the agreement managed to put an end, even if temporarily as it turned out, to internal infighting by forming a national unity government and setting parameters for power-sharing. It also restored confidence in the ability of the political system to accept democracy regardless of the outcome of elections by allowing the leader of the majority to head the government. Finally, it encouraged Hamas to show greater moderation than ever by agreeing to "respect" the agreements signed with Israel. Israeli and international reaction to the agreement and to the national unity government it produced was seen as a collective punishment for the Palestinians and was viewed as counterproductive, serving only to discourage moderates and democrats and to reward hard-liners in Hamas, thus leading to its violent takeover of Gaza in June 2007.

Hamas's takeover of the Gaza Strip was seen as a grave sin and as a severe blow to Palestinian national unity. But here too, there were two Palestinian narratives. Hamas's narrative saw the unfolding of events after the Mecca Accord as confirming an Israeli–American–Fatah conspiracy to destroy the nascent Palestinian democracy, to topple the elected government, and to destroy Hamas's military wing. Most importantly, Hamas believed that while the Mecca agreement required Fatah to share power in the security sector by allowing shared control over the security services, Fatah, under threats and pressure from Israel and the United States, refused to implement those elements in the agreement. As a result, the state of lawlessness continued.

Hamas also argued that in taking the military measures it did in Gaza in June 2007 it did not seek to destroy Fatah. Instead, it merely sought to eliminate Mohammad Dahlan, whom it perceived to be in charge of Fatah's security in Gaza. It also argued that it only sought a limited military confrontation rather than a full takeover of the Strip. The unfolding of events was uncontrollable and led to a quick collapse, not only of Fatah forces but also those of Abbas's Presidential Guard and the National Security units. Hamas argued that because of this complete collapse it had no choice but to take over the whole Strip in order to prevent anarchy and chaos. After all, it had won the elections; it was the legitimate government; it could not organize a coup against its own majority. Therefore, its use of force was legitimate, intended merely to implement the will of the voters.

Fatah's narrative viewed the same developments differently. It saw the unfolding of the events leading to a "military coup" as masterminded by Hamas radicals seeking to destroy Palestinian democracy. Islamist radicals were seen as unhappy with the Mecca Accord and as determined from the outset to destroy it and topple the national unity government. While Fatah leaders acknowledged that Israel and the United States opposed the agreement with Hamas, and had threatened to impose sanctions and to boycott the new government, they argued that they did not capitulate and that progress was made in the implementation of the Mecca agreement. In Fatah's eyes, Dahlan, in his capacity as the National Security Advisor to the president, was acting within his mandate when he began an effort to rebuild the security forces. This effort took place within legitimate channels approved by the president with the purpose of building competent forces capable of enforcing law and order.

Fatah's narrative saw chaos and anarchy as a consequence of Hamas's illegal formation of the Executive Force, viewed as a Hamas armed militia that engaged in unlawful acts which led to daily confrontations with official security services. Internal violence during this period was perceived as orchestrated by Hamas, which carried out a series of assassinations targeting top leaders in the PA intelligence and preventive security services in order to weaken and demoralize these services and give a boost to anarchy and chaos that would justify its violent coup. Thus, the full takeover of the Gaza Strip was seen as having been planned from the outset. Fatah concluded its narrative by claiming that Hamas's actions were an illegal coup organized against the legitimacy of the elected president and the National Unity Government.

Hamas's narrative regarding the efforts to reconcile nationalists and Islamists and to reunify the West Bank and the Gaza Strip after the split also differs from that of Fatah. Hamas believed that the chances for reconciliation would remain slim as long as Fatah remained subservient to Israel and the United States, who were said to have prevented it from making a genuine commitment to reconciliation. Hamas viewed the 2009–10 Egyptian reconciliation plans as favoring Fatah and argued that if its reservations about the plans were seriously discussed, then it would have been willing to accept them.

By contrast, Fatah's narrative was that by signing the Egyptian reconciliation plan without any reservation it had demonstrated its willingness to reconcile with Hamas and to disregard Israeli and American objections. It further argued that Hamas's refusal to sign the plan meant that the Islamist group, under Iranian and Syrian influence, had sacrificed the Palestinian strategic national interest to reunify the West Bank and the Gaza Strip for the sake of maintaining an alliance with regional forces opposed to the PA. Hamas, in this view, had opted to maintain the split until its local and regional standing enabled it either to impose its will in the West Bank as well or to fully separate the Gaza Strip from Israeli and PA control.

The War on Gaza

The Palestinian narrative blamed Israel for starting the December 2008 Gaza War, a war that need not have occurred since Hamas was fully committed to a de-facto ceasefire before the war, just as it was after the war. Palestinians argued that rockets launched occasionally from the Gaza Strip against Israel, before and after the war, were meant to pressure Israel to ease the suffocating blockade and the siege that it had imposed on the residents of the Gaza Strip. They also pointed out that, in any case, rockets launched by Palestinian factions caused only minor damage and were merely meant to send a message:

let Gaza be free. The limited harm they caused in no way justified Israeli use of massive firepower, destroying hundreds of homes and killing hundreds of innocent civilians during the war.

The Palestinian narrative viewed Israel's military behavior during the Gaza war as evidence that Israel would not shy away from committing war crimes in order to achieve its political goals: to destroy Hamas and crush the political will of Gazans. The Goldstone Report was perceived as describing accurately the conditions during the war and as documenting diligently Israeli war crimes. Many Palestinians did not share the view that the report sought to de-legitimize Israel: instead, by exposing Israeli war crimes, the report was viewed as playing a role in restraining Israeli behavior in future wars. Delegitimizing Israeli government behavior, Palestinians argued, should not be confused with delegitimizing Israel itself.

Many Palestinians also pointed out that rocket attacks forced Israel to observe a de-facto ceasefire and to ease its blockade, at least for a while. By contrast, in the West Bank, Abbas, Fayyad and the nationalists failed to convince their Israeli counterparts to agree to stop their daily incursions into Palestinian cities or to remove hundreds of remaining checkpoints even after the splendid improvement in the performance of the Palestinian security services under the Fayyad government was achieved. In other words, under no pressure from Palestinians in the West Bank, Israel seemed to do what it wanted. This was seen as clear evidence that Israel understood nothing but the language of force. If and when the Gaza siege was removed, this narrative continued, rockets would no longer be used and Israelis would enjoy the same peace and security as Gazans.

For some Palestinians, however, Hamas's use of rockets was wrong-headed, even if its goal — ending the Gaza siege — was just. Those opposed to the use of rockets believed that it provided Israel with a pretext to maintain the siege, continue to use violence against Gaza, and prolong the agony of Gazans. By contrast, the use of non-violent means to end the siege, such as the Turkish-led Free Gaza flotilla that sought to break the blockade, was fully supported by all Palestinians. The flotilla incident was perceived as a victory for Palestinians, forcing Israel to ease the siege. In the aftermath of that incident, Palestinians were encouraged by Turkey's willingness to stand up to what they perceived as Israeli arrogance and trigger-happy traditions.

Is the Two-state Solution Still Viable?

During this period, continued expansion of Israeli settlements in the occupied territories, coupled with repeated failures to reach a permanent status agreement with Israel, led many Palestinians to lose faith in the practicality of the two-state solution. While the Annapolis process was supposed to lead to the establishment of a Palestinian state in one year, negotiations were seen as producing very little progress. Moreover, once a new Likud-led Israeli government was elected in 2009, even the little progress previously made quickly vanished: Palestinians felt their future would resemble closely their past – a Sisyphean experience, compelled to repeat, endlessly, an exhausting yet futile effort. Furthermore, the failure of Obama to convince Israel to freeze settlement construction was seen as further evidence that Israel valued settlements more than peace. And, the fact that Obama ceased pressing the demand for a freeze was taken as an indication that the new president was "all talk but no action" and that diplomacy was, therefore, pointless.

Under such circumstances many Palestinians reached the conclusion that regardless of what concessions they might make, Israel would never allow them to have a truly sovereign and independent state. Some, a minority among the residents of the West Bank and the Gaza Strip but many among the Diaspora, went further and argued that, therefore, Palestinians should abandon the search for the elusive two-state solution and embrace a one-state solution. They argued that the Palestinian struggle should now shift its focus from demanding independence and end of occupation to demanding equal rights to the Jews and Arabs who lived in the area encompassing Israel and the West Bank. Palestinians argued that even if the latter demand – equal citizenship in one state – were to prove impossible to satisfy, the outcome could be useful. Concerned about gradually becoming an apartheid state, Israel might be forced by this shift in Palestinian strategy to finally make a choice, thereby making a two-state solution more feasible. However, some, mostly leftist intellectuals, had reached the conclusion that it was already too late for that – that Palestinians should abandon the two-state solution as Israel had already made its implementation impossible. "One man, one vote" was the *only* answer, they argued.

Palestinians viewed their efforts, beginning in September 2011, to gain state membership at the UN and other international organizations, as a legitimate diplomatic tool – one that might help them end Israeli occupation. They argued that the failure of the Netanyahu government to commit itself to a continuation of the Annapolis peace process, ignoring the considerable progress made in 2008 in the framework of these talks, rendered negotiations futile and provided justification for their UN bid. The Israeli rejection of progress made was seen as reflecting the commitment of Netanyahu's right wing coalition to the Greater Land of Israel – a commitment that stood in stark contradiction to the two-state vision. The failure of the Obama administration throughout 2009–11 to force Israel to freeze settlement construction was seen by Palestinians as compelling evidence that an American-led peace process was doomed to failure. Palestinians felt that this failure left them no choice but to seek wider international involvement in the search for a solution to their conflict with Israel. They also rejected Israeli claims that their UN action was unilateral, arguing that, to the contrary, it reflected a genuine Palestinian commitment to peace through multilateral international legitimacy. And, they rejected Israeli claims that they sought membership of international organizations in order to delegitimize the State of Israel. Instead, they argued that they intended to force Israel to abide by international law through the use of the International Criminal Court and the International Court of Justice, and that it was Israel, by openly violating international law, that rendered its occupation illegitimate in the eyes of the international community and organizations.

The Arab Spring

The Arab Spring was seen by Palestinians as a victory for the Arab masses against tyranny – a victory that would serve not only the cause of democracy and liberty in the Arab World but also the Palestinian cause. Arab publics were viewed as more supportive of the Palestinian cause than their regimes. Accordingly, the change was seen as weakening American ability to force Arab regimes to maintain a stable status quo, one that served the interests of the United States and Israel but not the Arab world or the Palestinians. The Palestinian public looked favorably at the non-violent nature of the uprisings in Egypt and Tunisia and saw them as worth emulating in the struggle for independence and an end of occupation. Even in countries such as Syria, whose regimes were perceived before the Arab Spring as standing against Israel and the United States, the Palestinian public and media stood clearly on the side of the demonstrators against the authoritarian regimes. Palestinian leaders from Hamas and Fatah on the other hand remained cautious, viewing the change in geostrategic terms, focusing on how it would affect their own separate interests and agenda.

Arab Narratives

The Arab narrative of developments in this period was more sophisticated, complicated and nuanced than at any previous period of the Arab–Israeli conflict. The general rise in the level of education and the growth of civil society and political pluralism in some of the Arab states, empowered Arab public opinion. What had been often referred to as the "Arab Street" was now much more connected to a large variety of information sources, which included some 600 pan-Arab satellite TV channels as well as the now widely available internet. In turn, these led to the creation of much more independent electronic journalism and the rise of bloggers, bringing state hegemony over information sources to an end.

More than in previous eras, the period addressed in this chapter requires differentiation between the Arab collective narrative, state-specific narratives, and Arab public opinion. With the Palestinians' Second Intifada having ended, the Arab collective narrative about the Arab–Israeli conflict became more moderate during this period. The 2007 reaffirmation by the Arab League of the 2002 Arab Peace Initiative (API) was the most salient feature of such moderation. Responding to the criticism that in 2002, when the API was first adopted, the League failed to communicate it to Israelis, the foreign ministers of Egypt and Jordan, Ahmad Abu Ghait and Abdel Elah al-Khatib, respectively, traveled together to Israel to seek the latter's response.

While maintaining the central features of the Arab narrative – such as arguments about Israeli aggression, its excessive use of force, and its conduct in Lebanon and Gaza comprising violations of international law – the Arab narrative now focused on Israel's failure to respond positively to the API. Israel's latter failure also featured in the Arab narrative connecting Israel with the perceived threat of Iran. Arabs, particularly those who entertained doubts about Iran's regional ambitions, wondered: If Israel was really threatened by Iran, why did it not seek cooperation with Arab states by embracing the 2002 Arab Peace Initiative?

Arabs emphasized that whereas the Arab states signaled their support of peace by attending and endorsing Annapolis, Israel had shown "its true face" by unleashing the wrath of its military superiority against Lebanon in 2006 and Gaza in late 2008. Moreover, the Arab collective narrative now stressed that these events showed that Israeli aggressive behavior could only be contained by heroic Arab acts of resistance. In the aftermath of Lebanon and Gaza the Israeli electorate is said to have further exposed "Israel's true face" by electing a Likud-led coalition headed by Netanyahu. With non-Arab states and leaders such as Turkey's

Erdoğan and Iran's Ahmadinejad expressing strong criticism of Israel's conduct, Arabs felt they could do no less.

A More Nuanced Narrative

While the specific narrative of some Arab states – notably Syria, Yemen and Algeria – continued to see Israel as a colonial enterprise, other countries now adopted a somewhat different narrative. Without abandoning the colonial perspective, this more nuanced narrative was also critical of Palestinian internal divisions and infighting, especially after Hamas's violent takeover of Gaza in June 2007. Thus, voices in the Arab world began to ask why the surrounding Arab states and societies should take the conflict with Israel seriously when Fatah and Hamas seem more intent on fighting one another.

Another dimension of the more nuanced Arab narrative was its corresponding focus on the dangers entailed in the rise of Islamists and on the latter's responsibility for the continuation and further radicalization of the conflict. Accordingly, until the summer 2006 Lebanon War escalated, Egypt and Saudi Arabia both accused Hezbollah of causing and initiating the war by its July 12 cross-border attack on Israel. Although Egypt and Saudi Arabia denounced Israel's attack on Gaza in late 2008 as excessive and as another example of Israel's responsibility for the continuation of the conflict, both found Hamas's behavior troubling, as causing the split in Palestinian ranks, and as encouraging radicalism in their own countries, as well as in the region at large. And when both Egypt and Saudi Arabia failed to bring about internal Palestinian reconciliation, both tended to blame Hamas for this failure and for its broader responsibility for the fragmentation of Palestinian politics. The two countries also led a broad Arab consensus that included Syria, that insisted that the Palestinian National Authority (PNA) be considered the only legitimate representative of the Palestinians, including in the Arab League.

Egypt

While continuing to blame Israeli intransigence for the persistence of the conflict, Egypt moved to greater cooperation with Israeli governments led by Sharon and Olmert and even Netanyahu. This seeming contradiction stemmed from Cairo's attempt to keep open channels with Israel in order to moderate its reaction to Palestinians residing in Gaza, particularly in times of crisis. In parallel, Egypt blamed Hamas for the deteriorating humanitarian conditions in Gaza, focusing especially on Hamas's refusal to meet the conditions set for the reopening of the border crossings.

Clearly, Egypt was also unhappy that the humanitarian crisis that Hamas helped create in Gaza invited an assortment of foreigners – such as Turkey's Erdoğan – to intervene to "save Gaza." Egyptians were also bothered by the breach of their border by tens of thousands of Palestinians from Gaza in January 2008. Nor were they content with the tunnels that Gazans dug underneath the Egypt–Gaza border for the purpose of smuggling arms in and out of the Strip. Moreover, as evidence began to accumulate that terrorist groups operating in the Sinai were trained by operatives of *Geish al-Islam* (Army of Islam), an al-Qaida affiliate in Gaza, some Egyptians now began to regard Gaza as a national security problem. These concerns were intensified by the discovery of a Hezbollah terrorist cell operating in Egypt which was preparing for an attack that would have disrupted navigation in the Suez Canal in the name of "helping Gaza."

On Iran

Increasingly because of their connection with Iran, Hamas and Hezbollah were seen during this period by a number of Arab states, including Egypt and Saudi Arabia, as a threat and a source of destabilization. While Iran under the presidencies of Rafsanjani and Khatami had not been seen as a great threat, Iran with Ahmadinejad as president was viewed once again as attempting to export its revolution. Moreover, its accelerated missile and nuclear programs were viewed as compounding the threat that Israel's nuclear weapons posed to the Arab world. Iran was also seen as playing a destabilizing role in Iraq, as providing assistance to every radical Arab group, and as providing safe haven to Egyptian members of al-Qaida. By contrast, Turkey was seen by Arab publics as playing a positive role during this period, despite the fact that it competed with Egypt for influence.

Arab Publics and the Arab Awakening

The Arab Awakening which spread in a number of Arab countries in 2011 and 2012 was seen as having created fundamental changes in the environment of the Arab–Israeli conflict. This changing environment was expected to continue for the rest of the decade as revolutions were expected to evolve into various stages and phases. The most immediate impact of the awakening, however, was the marginalization of the conflict with Israel in Arab political narratives and discourse. Instead, domestic issues now dominated political discourse and media coverage.

However, the conflict with Israel did not completely disappear from Arab discourse. Former regimes were accused of being "soft" in their response to Israeli atrocities, particularly in Gaza, as well as with respect to Israel's settlement policy. In addition, the future of the peace treaty with Israel was put on the agenda during the 2012 Egyptian presidential elections, particularly by some Islamic and Nasserite candidates. Still, the vast majority of parties, including Islamic ones, affirmed their respect for the treaty insofar as Israel continued to respect it.[48]

The general prevailing narrative of the Arab Awakening was that the Arab–Israeli conflict was important and that Israel was a villain that usurped Palestinian rights, occupied Arab land, and sought to maintain a nuclear monopoly over the region. Such sentiments were reflected in Egyptian public support for the attacks on the gas pipeline in the Sinai and on the Israeli embassy in Cairo, as well as in the call made by a number of presidential candidates for a review of the treaty with Israel, particularly the security protocols, which had proved dysfunctional for protecting Egyptian and Israeli security interests in the Sinai.[49]

Whereas Arab governments' perspectives were affected by this complex set of often competing considerations, for the Arab publics at large the Palestinian issue remained salient. In the eyes of these publics Israel continued to be seen – in the standard frame of reference in media talk shows and as the basic premise of civil society groups – as the oppressor who dispossessed the Palestinians of their homeland. This attitude continued to fuel the boycotting of Israelis and Israeli goods by the Arab general public, including in

Jordan and Egypt. Thus the change in Egyptian governmental circles did not translate to a changed attitude in the country's general public, which continued to adhere to the notion of "cold peace" with Israel. Similarly, while seen as a threat by Arab governments and some elites, Arab public opinion tended to view Iran as "a balancer" to Israeli power, both nuclear and conventional, and as a long-term asset in the historic struggle against Israel. Likewise, following its harsh public criticism of Israel, Turkey's leaders now became the Arabs' favorite, and Hamas and Hezbollah were viewed as shouldering the day-to-day responsibility for resisting Israel's dark designs.

Analysis

The following section seeks to explain two important sets of developments that took place during the timeframe addressed in this chapter: first, the eruption of violence in July 2006 and December 2008; and second, the attempt and failure to resolve the Israeli–Palestinian conflict through the Annapolis process. The latter was significant as it was the first time the parties returned to permanent status negotiations since the January 2001 talks at Taba – almost seven years prior.

Wars in Lebanon and Gaza

The International System

At the *global-systemic level*, Israel's reaction to the Hezbollah cross-border attack of July 12, 2006, and its attack on Hamas in Gaza in December 2008, were both made possible by a permissive environment created by the United States, which tolerated a forceful Israeli response to the challenges presented by Hezbollah and Hamas. This permissive environment was manifested in the attitude toward Israel's conduct adopted by international forums in which the United States had decisive influence, such as the G-8 Summit which took place immediately after hostilities in Lebanon began in July 2006. It translated into a willingness to provide Israel with the requisite freedom of action to "finish the job" by warding off international pressures to end the fighting before Israel's objectives were met.

The first and most important cause propelling the United States to create this permissive environment was the continued propensity of the Bush administration to view Hamas and Hezbollah almost exclusively through the prism of the War on Terror in which the United States had been engaged since the September 11 attacks. A second dimension was the neoconservative view – which still informed the action of central figures in Washington, especially those associated or allied with Vice President Cheney – which did not ascribe great importance, let alone urgency, to resolving the Arab–Israeli conflict. Since this school viewed Hamas and Hezbollah only as terror organizations, and did not see the conflict as affected in any way by Israel's behavior, it was sympathetic to strong Israeli reactions to terrorist attacks. Indeed, Cheney and his followers did not think that such action complicated the chance of resolving the conflict as they neither believed that the conflict could be solved or that the United States should invest significant resources in the efforts to resolve it.

Rather, the Bush administration saw Iran as the region's great menace and the need to weaken Iran as of utmost importance. And since the Bush administration saw both Hezbollah and Hamas as allied with Iran, as Tehran's proxies, it was prepared to support any Israeli action that promised to weaken the two movements.

A number of factors seem to have contributed to the Bush administration's tendency to view Iran as a great menace. First, Iran was seen as avoiding all international efforts to dissuade it from continuing its nuclear program and, especially, to stop and then roll-back its enrichment activities. Second, the United States greatly feared the reach of Iran's demagoguery: its capacity to contact every corner of the region, using every conceivable form of media, directly and through its proxies, such as Hezbollah's Al-Manar television. Within this framework, Iran was seen as presenting itself as the Arabs' guardian and as seeking to increase its standing by promising that Israel was fated to disappear.

For the United States, Iran's President Ahmadinejad appeared to possess the same propensity for hyperbole that characterized the rhetoric of Egypt's President Nasser in the 1950s and 1960s: pronouncements that transcended state boundaries. Thus Ahmadinejad's passionate speeches predicting Israel's early demise were assessed as appealing to Arabs throughout the region. Indeed, Ahmadinejad seemed to be more popular in Arab countries, whose populations do not have to suffer the consequences of his rule, than in Iran.

In addition, Washington saw Iran as having created alliances with radical Islamists and as having established a network of cells of supporters throughout the region, even in the Sinai. From the American standpoint a particularly worrisome dimension of this reach was Iran's perceived involvement in Iraq – particularly its push for the creation of a political system that favored forces sympathetic to Iran. This was viewed as having brought Iran to closer proximity to American forces in Iraq and exposed these forces to deadly Iranian retaliation in the event of an attack by the United States against Iran's nuclear installations.

Regional Realities

At the *regional-systemic level*, Iran's regional reach, which was perceived as a global threat by the United States, also emboldened Hezbollah and Hamas. Indeed, Hamas was heartened during this period not only by Iran but also by Hezbollah. For some in Hamas, Hezbollah's experience in the Second Lebanon War showed that it was possible to lose militarily, and for the population to suffer considerably, and yet to emerge stronger politically. As these Hamas members saw it, Hezbollah was forced to accept a ceasefire but was rewarded in the Lebanese internal scene. The conclusion was that the risks entailed in rocketing Israel were not so great: even if the outcome were to be a massive Israeli military response, as was the case in Lebanon, Hamas would survive.

Iran's regional ambitions and reach, the bold behavior of Hezbollah and Hamas, and the balance of their power as non-state actors, vis-à-vis Israel, could together be seen as the causes of the violent confrontations of 2006 and 2008. But a coalition of the so-called "moderate" pro-Western Arab states in the region created the permissive environment that allowed Israel, in both cases, to take such strong military action. Egypt, Saudi Arabia and, to a lesser degree, Jordan enabled these wars to erupt by providing Israel time to crush Hezbollah and Hamas.

Indeed, moderate Arab states reacted similarly in the context of both wars. The governments in Egypt and Saudi Arabia shared a perception of Hezbollah and Hamas as a menace, and they both blamed the two movements for the fighting: Hezbollah for the cross-border attack and Hamas for failing to renew the *Tah'dia* – a decision that Egypt warned against during the weeks prior to Hamas's decision in December.

However, Israel's failure to bring the violent conflict to a swift, decisive conclusion placed the governments of Arab states, particularly those that initially provided the permissive environment, under growing pressure to increase their criticism of Israel's conduct. The means employed by Israel only intensified these pressures. Since in both cases Israel made massive use of airpower, the new regional media broadcasting from Lebanon and Gaza were able to transmit innumerable images of death and destruction to every home in the Arab world.

The permissive environment at the global and regional level also figured in miscalculations made by both Hezbollah and Israel. Hezbollah leader Hassan Nassrallah seems to have counted on, at worst, a brief military confrontation, discounting the possibility that Israel would be permitted to continue its devastating response for as long as 34 days. On its part, Israel failed to understand that the tacit encouragement provided by some of the region's states would not last more than a few days and that it was contingent on Israel's use of low-signature, rather than spectacularly destructive, means.

Domestic Scenes

At the *unit level*, Hezbollah's willingness to risk a violent confrontation with Israel derived from its perceived imperative to roll-back the consequences of the Cedar Revolution.[50] Within this context Hezbollah had two strategic objectives in Lebanon's internal scene: first, to obtain a veto power over Lebanese domestic politics; and second, to avert pressure on it to disarm. With Syria's military forces withdrawn, Hezbollah came under increased internal pressure to allow implementation of the most important unfulfilled clause of UNSC Resolution 1559, which stipulates the disarmament of all militias. Another military confrontation with Israel was probably seen as a means of reducing such pressures by providing Hezbollah with a justification for continuing to bear arms.

Also at the unit level, the road to war in Gaza began with Hamas's attempt to improve its position vis-a-vis Israel by playing a game of brinkmanship. The question for the Islamist group was whether to renew the de-facto ceasefire with Israel that was due to expire in November 2008. Earlier that year, when agreeing to the Egyptian-mediated ceasefire, Hamas limited its duration to six months and conditioned its acceptance on the easing of the blockade imposed on the Gaza Strip. By the end of the six-month period, it was clear that Hamas was frustrated with its inability to improve conditions for Gazans, as it saw access and movement in border crossings becoming more and more restricted. Consequently, Hamas resolved not to renew the ceasefire without gaining an explicit Israeli commitment, guaranteed by Egypt, to ease such access considerably.

Hamas now felt increasing pressure: it was seen as unable to improve living conditions in Gaza whereas conditions in the West Bank were improving considerably under the government of Salam Fayyad. Seeing itself and presenting itself as a resistance movement,

Hamas took pride in its ability to force the Israelis to do what it wanted through coercion. It became clear that Hamas was adhering to a ceasefire that was not producing the declared intended outcome. It now believed it had only two options: renew the ceasefire after forcing Israel to agree to the easing of the blockade or risk going to war. Hamas assessed that its status within Gaza and in the region would improve considerably in either case.

Hamas's game of brinkmanship incorporated an element of miscalculation: it assessed that Israel needed the ceasefire more than it in fact did. Moreover, Hamas carefully read all the press reports of the debate within the Israeli defense community about the merits and drawbacks of a major military assault on Gaza. It knew, therefore, that both Defense Minister Barak and IDF Chief of Staff (CoS) Lieutenant General Gabi Ashkenazi opposed such an operation, doubting that Israel could achieve much through it. In its worst-case analysis, the Islamist group believed that even if Israel decided to go to war rather than ease the blockade, it could only benefit by diverting blame on to Israel for the miserable conditions Gazans found themselves in under Hamas's control.

Two additional forms of domestic pressure pushed Hamas to continue its confrontational behavior. First, Hezbollah was pressing Hamas to follow its example, both by using its media to extol the virtue of "confrontation with the Zionists" and by influencing groups in Gaza that were more extreme than Hamas. Second, elements of Fatah were baiting Hamas by arguing that now that Hamas had taken over Gaza, it was adopting the behavior that it had criticized Fatah for pursuing: de-facto peaceful co-existence with the Zionists in the framework of the Egyptian-negotiated *Tah'dia*.

Hamas's continued launching of Kassam rockets against Israel and the abduction of the Israeli soldier Gilad Shalit in late June 2006 contributed to Hamas's popularity in the Arab street by seeming to damage Israel's image of invincibility. Equally important, Hamas used these successes skillfully to taunt its Fatah opponents by asking: What have years of engagement with the Israelis and the concessions of Palestinian rights achieved? But Hamas's success also bred arrogance, complicating its reading of reality. Thus, it failed to anticipate that the successful abduction of the Israeli soldier and Israel's perception that the 2006 war with Hezbollah had damaged its reputation-based deterrence, would combine to create an Israeli imperative to exploit Hamas's decision not to extend the ceasefire by striking hard against the Gaza Strip.

In Israel, the government's slide toward war seems to have been propelled by a number of cross-pressures: the population in the south pressed the government to put a stop to the unrelenting rocket attacks. The IDF was of two minds on this issue: the Chief of the Southern Command, Major General Yoav Galant, was pushing for a major assault on Hamas, arguing that under the protective umbrella of the *Tah'dia* Hamas was using the tunnels to accumulate massive quantities of arms and munitions, ensuring that a later military confrontation would be far more costly. But most leaders of the defense community, including Defense Minister Barak and CoS Ashkenazi, resisted the pressures to attack, arguing that it was impossible to liquidate Hamas, a mass movement, and that, therefore it was not clear that the reality after the operation would be different than before it.

The Israeli internal debate altered somewhat in late 2008 when Hamas began to announce conditions for extending the *Tah'dia*. With this taking place in the midst of an election campaign, Israel's Kadima-led government would not allow Hamas to dictate the terms of such an extension by conditioning it on the easing of the blockade. But this also involved a miscalculation by Israel's intelligence community: mirroring Hamas's estimate that Israel would not dare attack, Israeli intelligence assessed that in the end Hamas would renew the *Tah'dia,* de-facto if not formally.

Hassan Nassrallah

At the *individual level,* Iran's President Ahmadinejad and Hezbollah's leader Hassan Nassrallah appear to be the stars of this period. To some extent, both were a throwback to the charisma and demagoguery of Gamal Abdul Nasser in the 1950s and 1960s. Ahmadinejad gave expression to Iran's regional reach. In his attacks on Jews, Israel and the United States he gained a considerable following in the Arab street. And indeed, his defiance of the great powers was reminiscent of Nasser's earlier defiance of the imperialists–colonialists.

Nassrallah was even more charismatic, but in a different manner than is normally associated with Arab leaders who excel in fiery rhetoric. His speeches were examples of coolness: using dry humor, he mocked and taunted his adversaries. Yet this was also a period of a serious drop in the quality of Nassrallah's leadership of Hezbollah. Until the summer of 2006, his conduct was extremely impressive. Understanding the strengths and weaknesses of Israel as well as those of his own movement, and sensitive to changing circumstances in the Lebanese domestic scene as well as on the Israeli front, Nassrallah seemed to be advancing Hezbollah's interests in a purposeful and deliberate fashion, without making a major mistake.

Hezbollah's "winning streak" ended during the period addressed in this chapter, with Nassrallah making three major errors. The first, to which he openly admitted, was his failure to anticipate the ferocity of Israel's response to the cross-border attack that Hezbollah launched under his direction on July 12, 2006. The root of this miscalculation seems to have been Nassrallah's failure to understand that Hamas's successful cross-border attack two weeks earlier created a strong Israeli imperative to restore deterrence.

The resulting heavy toll exacted on the Lebanese population complicated Hezbollah's position in Lebanon: while being part of the Lebanese government – there were three Hezbollah-affiliated ministers in the Lebanese Cabinet at the time of the attack – Hezbollah attacked Israel without seeking government approval. Thus, Nassrallah appeared to be subjecting the wellbeing of Lebanon's population to his movement's interests. The resulting anger of the Lebanese forced him to apologize for the mistake he made.

Nassrallah's second mistake was to create underground cells in Egypt in an attempt to increase Hezbollah's reach. For a non-state actor battling the formidable power of Israel, adding Egypt to its adversaries – thereby also increasing the motivation of Egypt's defense community to cooperate with Israel in the efforts to battle Islamic extremism – could not be considered a smart move.

Finally, in the framework of a Lebanese internal dispute, in May 2008, Nassrallah sent Hezbollah's armed units into western Beirut neighborhoods. This was a clear violation of the 1989 Taif Accords in the framework of which Hezbollah was exempted from the accords' general stipulation that all Lebanese militias must be disarmed. The exemption was given exclusively in the context of Hezbollah's role as a "resistance movement" battling Israel. Now, however, Hezbollah was seen as turning its weaponry against its Arab neighbors in a cynical attempt to secure its political position in Lebanon in the aftermath of the 2006 debacle.

Ehud Olmert

On the Israeli side, the particular attributes of Israel's then prime minister, Ehud Olmert, played an important role in triggering the eruption of violence and war in Lebanon in mid-2006 and in Gaza in late 2008. By the mid-2000s, Olmert had undergone a complete metamorphosis from right-wing hawkishness to the realization that without an end to Israel's occupation of the West Bank, Gaza, and East Jerusalem, Israel would not be able to survive as a Jewish-democratic state. Thus, whereas until the early 2000s he regarded the creation of a Palestinian state as an existential threat, Olmert now came to view it as an absolute imperative. Finding himself earlier explaining Ariel Sharon's decision to disengage from Gaza, in the aftermath of Sharon's stroke and his own assertion of power, Olmert was determined to continue the process of disengagement, now in the West Bank.

In his quest to apply the two-state-solution unilaterally, Olmert was thwarted by a number of developments. First, Hamas's decision to continue rocket fire following Israel's disengagement from Gaza was making it exceedingly difficult for Olmert to make the case that Israel could safely withdraw from the West Bank. Second, Hamas's daring attack on June 26 undermined the argument that following Israel's withdrawal, Palestinians in the West Bank could be deterred from attacking Israel.

It was, therefore, not surprising that when two weeks later Hezbollah launched the cross-border attack on the Lebanese front, Olmert assessed that his plans for continued Israeli unilateral withdrawals would totally collapse if he did not react forcefully. From this perspective, Israel's reaction to the attack could not be separated from Olmert's enormous personal investment in unilaterally implementing a two-state solution to the Palestinian–Israeli conflict and his fear that the effort would "go down the drain" without decisive military action to restore Israeli deterrence.

Another contribution to the escalation to war in mid-2006 was Olmert's inexperience in managing a major military confrontation. While over the previous decades he had every opportunity to closely observe Israeli leaders make momentous decisions, this was not reflected in the dysfunctional way in which he navigated Israel through the war. A civilian with limited experience in the military, Olmert seemed reluctant to question the IDF Chief of Staff, deferring to him on critically important issues. This may have played a significant role in the escalation to war in 2006, as Olmert seems to have been persuaded by the IDF that Israel's objectives could be achieved through the use of airpower. Thus, unwilling and\or unable to initiate and orchestrate a debate on operational plans, he failed to mitigate the less than competent manner in which the IDF conducted the war.

Failure of Peace Negotiations: the Annapolis Process and Beyond

The Global Dimension

At the *systemic-global level*, the American interest in initiating the Annapolis process seems to have been part of the broader change of emphasis in its policy in the Middle East during the Bush administration's second term: from unilateralism and the use of force to diplomacy. Within this context, the United States identified what appeared as an opportunity: Hamas's June 2007 violent takeover of Gaza, which resulted in the demise of the Palestinian national unity government, appeared to have released PA President Abbas from the constraints entailed in the partnership with Hamas. Consequently, Abbas was now viewed as a legitimate partner in a peace process.

The new diplomatic effort also received broad international support. This was particularly the case with other members of the Quartet, who viewed the negotiations launched at Annapolis as part of a broader "West Bank first" strategy – namely, an effort to produce a new more positive reality in the West Bank with which the expected failure of Hamas rule of Gaza would be compared. The hope was that this contrast would produce public pressure in Gaza to roll-back Hamas's takeover. For this reason, in December 2007 the Quartet followed-up the Annapolis conference with a very successful donor conference in Paris that yielded over $ 7 billion in pledges – more than Prime Minister Fayyad had asked for. The Quartet took a number of additional measures designed to create an environment conducive to the Annapolis process's success: it bestowed upon Fayyad prestige and stature, it encouraged improved cooperation between Israel and the PA, it pressed Israel to lift checkpoints and roadblocks to improve the Palestinians' access and movement, and it encouraged both sides to resume security cooperation.

Ultimately, however, important factors at the systemic level condemned the process to failure. First, the Annapolis process was launched just as the Bush administration entered its last year in office, which left insufficient time to achieve a historic breakthrough. Moreover, although it now became more engaged in attempting to ease if not actually resolve the Palestinian–Israeli conflict, the administration was still reluctant to produce and present the parties with ideas of its own or with bridging proposals, let alone to use its leverage on the parties to have its proposals adopted. Thus Washington accommodated the Israeli and Palestinian requests – conveyed by Palestinian negotiator Qurie and Israeli Foreign Minister Livni – that the United States refrain from presenting the parties with its ideas. But left to their own devices the two parties could not overcome the gap between their positions.

The global-systemic causes of the continued failure to achieve any breakthrough in Palestinian–Israeli negotiations during the Obama administration's first term seem to be rooted in a number of features of its approach to the issue. First, there was a failure to utilize leverage to compel the parties to continue negotiations from the point they reached at the end of the Bush administration's second term. Instead, the Obama administration focused on attempting to improve the environment for such negotiations by pressuring Israel to implement a complete settlement construction freeze. Also, while communicating to Muslim and Arab constituencies what it was trying to achieve, the administration failed to similarly communicate the rationale and logic of its efforts to the Israeli public. Finally, during the short period of direct Israeli–Palestinian talks in September 2010 the Obama administration was reluctant to use its leverage to compel the parties to engage in serious and detailed negotiations on borders and security. Like the Bush administration, it also avoided presenting any ideas of its own and refrained from presenting proposals designed to bridge the gaps between the parties' positions.

While seeming to give priority to Palestinian–Israeli peacemaking, President Obama's ability to invest considerable resources in attempting to resolve the two peoples' dispute could not but be affected by the unique circumstances challenging his administration during its first term: first, the imperative to stabilize the American economy and financial institutions which faced the most serious crisis encountered since the 1929 Wall Street collapse. And second, its decision to invest time, energy and political capital in a heroic effort to obtain the requisite Congressional support for a massive reform of the healthcare system. By the time both issues were addressed, Obama's Democratic Party suffered a massive defeat in the 2010 mid-term elections. Now facing a much more hostile Congress, the administration's ability to use leverage to achieve a breakthrough in Palestinian–Israeli talks was seriously constrained.

Regional Circumstances

Circumstances at the *systemic-regional* level initially seemed favorable for a breakthrough in Palestinian–Israeli talks. A coalition of moderate Arab states, including Egypt, Saudi Arabia, and Jordan supported the launching of the Annapolis process and were willing to bless the talks by attending the summit. By doing so, these important regional players provided cover to the PA's decision to participate. Another expression of this regional support was the Arab League's 2007 decision to reaffirm the 2002 API and to communicate the initiative directly to Israel.

Hamas's June 2007 violent takeover of Gaza also seemed to improve the environment for Palestinian–Israeli talks, as Israel and the PA now shared a common enemy: Hamas. As a result, Israel now also seemed more willing to become a partner to a "West Bank First" strategy – hoping that the PA's success would help roll back Hamas.

Ultimately, however, these positive factors could not overcome a number of negative features of the regional environment. First, with Abbas and Olmert trying to exert pressure on one another by arguing that the other was failing to show sufficient flexibility, they failed to share with Arab leaders the progress they were making in their bilateral talks. In turn, this discouraged these leaders from creating an even more supportive environment for these talks. Second, while initially hoping to gain from Israel's December 2008 attack on Hamas in Gaza, the Arab media's coverage of the death and destruction associated with the attack made it impossible for the PA to appear complicit with Israel's action. The result was a political environment which dashed any hopes for progress in the operation's aftermath. Finally, key regional players failed to support the Obama administration's efforts by going beyond a reaffirmation of the 2002 API and offering Israel incentives to implement the proposed settlement construction freeze.

Domestic Scenes

At the *unit level*, Hamas's violent takeover of Gaza, which resulted in the demise of the national unity government, released Abbas from the constraints entailed in the partnership with Hamas, thus creating the conditions for peace negotiations. As a result, he was now perceived by Israel as a legitimate partner to a peace process. Initial conditions within Israel itself also seemed more favorable to renewed negotiations. The Israeli government was led by

Kadima. The common denominator of those who had defected from Likud to form Kadima, such as Sharon, Olmert, and Livni, was the realization that the Greater Land of Israel was an unrealistic dream and that the demographic trends between the Mediterranean Sea and the Jordan River would destroy Israel as a Jewish and democratic state, instead producing an apartheid state, which would devastate Israel's legitimacy. For these reasons, Olmert now became the architect and political front-line of Sharon's unilateral disengagement project. But with Hezbollah's attack and Hamas's continued rocket threat discrediting unilateralism in the eyes of the Israeli public, Olmert and Livni became convinced that there was no choice but to try to achieve the same goals through negotiation. In turn, this motivation was compounded by a legacy issue: Olmert wanted to undo the damage to his reputation inflicted by his imperfect conduct of the Second Lebanon War.

However, other aspects of their domestic scenes caused both protagonists to hesitate and hedge their bets. On the Israeli side, the complete rupture between Hamas and Fatah, and particularly the former's takeover of Gaza, raised questions as to whether President Abbas could implement any agreement signed. This problem was exacerbated by what seemed to Israel to be an unprecedented degree of fragmentation within Fatah itself, as the rift between the old guard led by Abbas and the young guard led by Marwan Barghouti seemed greater than ever.

Indeed, Abbas was weakened not only by the rupture with Hamas and the fragmentation within Fatah ranks but also by a series of mistakes he made – mistakes that led to the questioning of his resolve. The most important of these was his mishandling of the Goldstone Report on the 2008 War in Gaza: he yielded to American pressure to refrain from pursuing the report in the UN Human Rights Council. Abbas's decision in September 2010 to accommodate President Obama by reentering direct negotiations with Israel – albeit for a short period – after he had been insisting for months that his participation was conditional upon Israel's acceptance of a complete settlement construction freeze, further undermined his position by presenting him as too susceptible to pressure from the United States.

A mirror image of this was Abbas's worry that shaken by the lingering effects of the Second Lebanon War and the continued police investigations, threats of indictments, and the resulting pressures on him from Livni and other leaders of his own party, Olmert might not stay in office long enough and with requisite authority to see through the implementation of any agreement with the Palestinians. Indeed, these Palestinian concerns were later affirmed and exacerbated by the collapse of the Olmert administration and its replacement by Netanyahu's Likud-led government. In the Palestinian leadership's estimate, this change prohibited any movement on permanent status negotiations.

Other dimensions of Israel's domestic scene also produced impediments to the Annapolis process: the tense relations between Olmert and Defense Minister Barak resulted in (or possibly from) the exclusion of the defense community from the Annapolis talks. In turn, this resulted in the community's failure to cooperate in helping create a more conducive environment for the talks – for example, by helping fulfill Israel's commitment to the United States to remove checkpoints and illegal outposts at a faster pace. By contrast, Israel's senior defense officials supported negotiations with Syria, arguing that a deal with Damascus was essential to complicate Hezbollah's ability to arm itself and to deprive Iran of a political context for challenging Israel

The Israeli domestic scene became even less conducive to a breakthrough in the country's relations with the Palestinians following the demise of the Olmert government, the failure of Livni to form a government, the elections that brought Likud back to power despite granting Kadima a plurality of Knesset seats, and finally Livni's decision that Kadima would not join Netanyahu's coalition, which she saw as not one conducive to ending Israel's conflict with the Palestinians.

Leaders

Condoleezza Rice seems to have been one of the most consequential individuals during the Annapolis process. Paradoxically, the negative developments in Iraq in the aftermath of the 2003 War weakened the relative positions of the most important advocates of the war within the Bush administration, notably Vice President Cheney and Secretary of Defense Donald Rumsfeld. This in turn strengthened the hand of Rice who, once relocated from the National Security Council to the Department of State in January 2005, began to shift the emphasis in American foreign policy from over-reliance on the unilateral use of force to diplomacy. Without this personal conviction and Rice's close relationship with the president, it is difficult to see how the skepticism of many administration officials about the wisdom of investing in Palestinian–Israeli peacemaking could have been overcome. And without such skepticism being overcome, the United States could not have orchestrated the launching of the Annapolis process.

Another individual whose personal attributes were an important factor in affecting the developments addressed here was Israeli Prime Minister Ehud Olmert. In the personal-ideological realm, Olmert's positive contribution to the Annapolis process seems to have been propelled by the major ideological shift that he had experienced in the mid-2000s – away from the dream of the Greater Land of Israel. The most important impact of the shift was to persuade Olmert to support Sharon's orchestration of the disengagement from Gaza. Now Olmert became a strong proponent of a negotiated or unilaterally applied two-state solution to the Palestinian–Israeli conflict.

However, other aspects of Olmert's personality seem to have undermined his ability to bring the post-Annapolis talks to a successful conclusion. His personal ambition as well as fondness for the high life affected his conduct in a manner that made him a target of repeated police investigations, which eventually resulted in indictments. It also exposed him to competitors and forced him to shift his time and energy from negotiating with the Palestinians to preparing himself for criminal litigation.

Some of the personal characteristics of PA President Abbas contributed positively to the prospects for the Annapolis process. Unlike Arafat, Abbas viewed violence as a non-option, indeed destructive to Palestinian interests, and negotiation as the only means of ending Israeli occupation. Equally importantly, in Abbas the Palestinians had for the first time a leader who was almost universally seen as committed to a peaceful resolution of the conflict with Israel – a true man of peace.

Other aspects of Abbas's personality, however, were less conducive to success in the Annapolis process. He lacked Arafat's charisma and his ability to unify Fatah and the Palestinian people behind him. He also lacked the former Palestinian leader's willingness to take bold steps and far-reaching initiatives. Thus, throughout the Annapolis process and into the Obama presidency it was not entirely clear whether Abbas was psychologically strong enough to make the historical compromises that a grand-bargain with Israel required. In retrospect, it seems that Abbas was more effective when operating as an associate of a charismatic leader like Arafat than when he was in the front line and needing to take the ultimate responsibility for the national decisions made.

Concluding Notes

The period addressed in this chapter gave reasons for both hope and despair with regard to the prospects of resolving the Arab–Israeli conflict on the basis of the two-state paradigm. On the positive side, the international community remained committed to resolving the conflict on the basis of the paradigm. More important, at least for a limited time during this period, the United States demonstrated that it could play a positive role – convening the Annapolis Conference in late 2007 and nurturing the post-conference bi-lateral Israeli–Palestinian talks in 2008. Being the first permanent status negotiations since the collapse of the Camp David process in 2000, the post-Annapolis talks were important to inject a sense of optimism into the search for peace. Equally significantly, the talks seem to have narrowed the gaps between the parties' positions on key issues. And, in a completely different fashion, in its first year in office, the Obama administration showed real interest as well as a willingness to invest time, energy, and political capital in the creation of a more positive environment for Palestinian–Israeli talks.

At different points during the period addressed here, Arab states also showed their interest in resolving the conflict by reaffirming in 2007 the 2002 Arab Peace Initiative, thus showing their willingness to accept Israel as a neighbor, albeit under specified circumstances.

Among the Israeli and Palestinian publics, there remained a clear preference for resolving the conflict on the basis of the two-state paradigm, notwithstanding the concessions that would be required of them. Moreover, despite behavior that often indicated otherwise, the top leaders of Israel and the PA remained during this period formally committed to the two-state solution. Just as importantly, neither side proposed a viable alternative to this paradigm. Thus, substantial majorities among Israelis and Palestinians alike – even if for very different reasons – continued to reject one-state solutions as viable bases for ending the conflict.

Finally and most significantly on the positive side, Fayyad's two-year plan to build the institutions of state was a huge leap forward. Injecting energy and a "can-do" mentality, Fayyad's plan exemplified the Palestinians' replacement of the "all or nothing," top-down stance that the PLO had initially adopted by a pragmatic approach that sought to build Palestinian independent statehood "bottom-up," one brick at a time.

On the negative side, during most of the period addressed here the United States proved unwilling or unable to create a breakthrough in Arab–Israeli peacemaking. For a long time the Bush presidency remained skeptical, if not hostile, to Israeli–Syrian talks – a position it only reversed in late 2007. During the post-Annapolis talks, it remained unwilling to offer bridging proposals let alone creative ideas of its own, instead it complied with Israeli and Palestinian requests that it avoid micro-managing the process. And while the Obama administration initially demonstrated far more willingness to jump into the Palestinian–Israeli peacemaking arena, its efforts were ineffectual due to a series of tactical, if not strategic, mistakes. As a result, during the second half of his first term, Obama scaled down his expectations considerably and effectively washed his hands of any serious attempt at a breakthrough.

In the region at large, while the beginning of this period saw Arab states' willingness to reengage at least to some degree in efforts to resolve the conflict, by late 2010 and early 2011 this no longer remained the case. The Arab Awakening saw the most important Arab states consumed by domestic upheavals or by fear that upheavals in neighboring states would spill over to their own polity.

While one of the most interesting aspects of the Arab Awakening was that the Arab–Israeli conflict played no role in its eruption and development, the potential consequences of the Awakening for the conflict were considerable. Not only did the upheavals draw the Arab states' energies away from any possible positive role in resolving the conflict, the Awakening in Egypt resulted in the assumption of power by the Muslim Brotherhood – a movement that until then had rejected Israel's creation and legitimacy. Earlier, the rise of Hamas and Hezbollah had led to two violent confrontations: in Lebanon in 2006 and in Gaza in late 2008.

The turn inward of the Arab states and the violence associated with the Awakening in certain Arab states, notably Syria, served to further marginalize the Arab–Israeli conflict. Such marginalization was only exacerbated by the threat that Iran seemed to pose not only to Israel but also to key Arab states.

On the Palestinian domestic side, the violent rupture between Hamas and Fatah in June 2007 resulted in a political and territorial division of the Palestinians between Gaza and the West Bank. This prevented the Palestinians from uniting around a stance for negotiating their conflict with Israel.

The Israeli domestic scene produced different negative developments. The return of Likud to power in 2009 cast serious doubts on Israel's commitment to a two-state solution of its conflict with the Palestinians. Although a few months into the new government's first term Prime Minister Netanyahu committed Israel to the paradigm, his government's actions seemed inconsistent with this pledge. This was particularly the case with regard to continued construction activities in West Bank settlements as well as in East Jerusalem. Indeed, settlement construction expanded considerably not only in areas close to the 1967 Green Line, but, more troublingly, in other settlements deep inside the West Bank.

As a result of these negative developments, the public on both sides, while continuing to prefer a two-state solution, grew increasingly pessimistic with regard to the odds of this solution ever being implemented. Despair about the prospects for this solution led the PA to take unilateral action – seeking international recognition of Palestinian independence outside a negotiated deal. The punitive action Israel threatened to take in reaction to this move only served to further threaten the viability of the PA as an infrastructure for a future state. By mid-2012 where all this would lead remained very much an open question.

Readings

Bickerton, Ian and Carla Klausner, *A History of the Arab-Israeli Conflict* (Prentice Hall, 2010) 361–389.

Dowty, Alan, *Israel/Palestine: Global Political Hotspots* (Polity, 2012) 198–219.

Harub, Khalid, *Hamas: A Beginner's Guide* (Pluto Press, 2006).

Lesch, David, *The Arab-Israeli Conflict* (Oxford University Press, 2008) 427–460.

Levitt, Matthew, *Hamas: Politics, Charity, and Terrorism in the Service of Jihad* (Yale University Press, 2006).

Tessler, Mark, *A History of the Israeli-Palestinian Conflict* (Indiana University Press, 2009) 827–847.

Historical Documents

Doha Agreement: full text available online at: http://www.middleeastmonitor.com/news/middle-east/3397-full-text-of-the-doha-declaration-signed-between-hamas-and-fatah.

Hamas-Fatah 2007 Mecca Agreement: text of the agreement and the program of the Palestinian National Unity government available at:
http://www.alzaytouna.net/en/resources/documents/palestinian-documents/109086-mecca-agreement-amp-program-of-the-palestinian-unity-government-2007.html#.URSwAWca98E.

President Obama Cairo Speech 2009: full text available online at http://www.whitehouse.gov/the-press-office/remarks-president-cairo-university-6-04-09.

Prisoners Document: text available at: http://middleeast.about.com/od/documents/a/me080403.htm.

UN Security Council Resolution 1701: full text available online at: http://www.un.org/News/Press/docs/2006/sc8808.doc.htm.

UN Security Council Resolution 1929: full text available online at: http://www.un.org/News/Press/docs/2010/sc9948.doc.htm.

U.S. President George W. Bush Annapolis Conference: Walter Laqueur and Barry Rubin, *The Israel-Arab-Arab Reader: A Documentary History of the Middle East Conflict* (London: Penguin Books, 2008), 625–626.

Notes

1. The other departures tilted the balance in the second Bush term away from the neoconservatives: Paul Wolfowitz and Douglas Feith left the Pentagon, and I. Lewis "Scooter" Libby was removed from the Vice President's Office following his indictment and later conviction.
2. PLO Chief Negotiator Saeb Erakat, "The Political Situation in Light of Developments with the U.S. Administration and the Government and Hamas's Continued Coup D'État, Ramallah, December 2009, (excerpts)" *Journal of Palestine Studies*, 39, 3 (Spring 2010), 197–201; Bernard Avishai, "A Plan For Peace That Still Could Be," *New York Times*, February 7, 2011. http://www.nytimes.com/2011/02/13/magazine/13Israel-t.html?_r=2&ref=middleeast&pagewanted=all; Greg Sheridan, "Ehud Olmert Still Dreams of Peace," *The Australian*, November 28, 2009, http://www.theaustralian.com.au/news/opinion/ehud-olmert-still-dreams-of-peace/story-e6frg76f-1225804745744; Ethan Bronner, "Olmert Memoir Cites Near Deal for Mideast Peace," *New York Times*, January 27, 2011, http://www.nytimes.com/2011/01/28/world/middleeast/28mideast.html?pagewanted=all. See also Condoleezza Rice, *No*

Higher Honor: A Memoir of My Years in Washington (New York: Crown Publishers, 2011), 656, 723–724; George W. Bush, *Decision Points*, 408–409.

3. The White House: Office of the Press Secretary, "Remarks by the President on a New Beginning," Cairo University, Cairo, Egypt: June 4, 2009; "Statement of General David H. Patraeus, U.S. Army Commander, U.S. Central Command, Before the Senate Armed Services Committee on the Posture of U.S. Central Command," Senate Armed Services Committee, March 16, 2010, http://armed-services.senate.gov/statemnt/2010/03%20March/Petraeus%2003-16-10.pdf.
4. Mark Landler and Steven Lee Meyers, "Obama Sees '67 Borders as Starting Point for Peace Deal," *New York Times*, May 19, 2011, http://www.nytimes.com/2011/05/20/world/middleeast/20speech.html?pagewanted=all.
5. The White House: Office of the Press Secretary, "Remarks by President Obama in Address to the United Nations General Assembly," United Nations, New York, New York: September 21, 2011.
6. "Parliamentary Elections 2005," *Al Ahram Weekly Online*, http://weekly.ahram.org.eg/2005/parliamentary_elections.htm.
7. "Turkey: 22 July 2007 – Election Results," BBC Turkish, July 23, 2007, http://www.bbc.co.uk/turkish/indepth/story/2007/07/070719_election_results_en.shtml.
8. Khalil Shikaki, "Palestinian Elections: Sweeping Victory, Uncertain Mandate"; see also Aaron D. Pina, "CRS Report for Congress: Fatah and Hamas: The New Palestinian Factional Reality," Congressional Research Service, March 3, 2006, Order Code RS22395, http://www.fas.org/sgp/crs/mideast/RS22395.pdf.
9. Paul Morro, "CRS Report for Congress: International Reaction to the Palestinian Unity Government," *Congressional Research Service*, May 9, 2007, Order Code RS22659, http://www.fas.org/sgp/crs/mideast/RS22659.pdf.
10. "The Full Text of the National Conciliation Document of the Prisoners," Jerusalem Media and Communication Centre, May 26, 2006, http://unispal.un.org/UNISPAL.NSF/0/CE3ABE1B2E1502B58525717A006194CD; "National Conciliation Document of the Prisoners – June 28, 2006," *Bitterlemons.org*, June 28, 2006, http://www.bitterlemons.org/docs/prisoners.html.
11. Ian Black, "UAE Ambassador Backs Strike on Iran's Nuclear Sites," *The Guardian*, July 7, 2010, http://www.guardian.co.uk/world/2010/jul/07/uae-envoy-iran-nuclear-sites.
12. Shai Feldman, Shlomo Brom, and Shimon Stein, "What to Do About Nuclearizing Iran? The Israeli Debate," (Waltham, MA: Crown Center for Middle East Studies, *Middle East Brief* No. 59, February 2012) http://www.brandeis.edu/crown/publications/meb/meb59.html; Colin H. Kahl, "Not Time to Attack Iran," *Foreign Affairs*, March/April 2012, http://www.foreignaffairs.com/articles/137031/colin-h-kahl/not-time-to-attack-iran.
13. Ze'ev Schiff, "Israel's War With Iran," *Foreign Affairs*, 85, 6 (November–December 2006), 23–31; "PM Siniora's 7-Point Plan," The National Archives, The Foreign and Commonwealth Office, August 3, 2006, http://collections.europarchive.org/tna/20080205132101/www.fco.gov.uk/servlet/Front%3Fpagename=OpenMarket/Xcelerate/ShowPage&c=Page&cid=1153392753889; "Arab League Seeks Changes in Draft Resolution," CNN, August 8, 2006, http://edition.cnn.com/2006/WORLD/meast/08/08/siniora.plan/; "UN Vote Backs Lebanon Ceasefire," BBC News, August 12, 2006, http://news.bbc.co.uk/2/hi/middle_east/4785001.stm.
14. "Palestinians Breach Border, Pour Into Egypt," MSNBC, January 23, 2008, http://www.msnbc.msn.com/id/22794305/ns/world_news-mideast_n_africa/t/palestinians-breach-border-pour-egypt/#.T8klJlLC-ZR; Isabel Kershner, "Hamas and Egypt to Work on Sealing Gaza Border," *New York Times*, February 3, 2008.

15. "Terrorism from the Gaza Strip since Operation Cast Lead: Data, Type and Trends," *The Meir Amit Intelligence and Terrorism Information Center*, March 3, 2011, http://www.terrorism-info.org.il/malam_multimedia/English/eng_n/html/ipc_e169.htm.
16. "Damage to Palestinian People and Property During Operation Cast Lead," *Journal of Palestine Studies*, 38, 3 (Spring 2009), 210–212, http://www.jstor.org/stable/10.1525/jps.2009.XXXVIII.3.210.
17. "United Nations Fact Finding Mission on the Gaza Conflict," UN Human Rights Council, September 29, 2009, http://www2.ohchr.org/english/bodies/hrcouncil/specialsession/9/factfindingmission.htm.
18. "Hamas, PIJ: 'Tahdia' in Exchange for Opening Crossings," *Al Hayat*, January 28, 2009, in MEMRIBlog, http://www.thememriblog.org/blog_personal/en/13288.htm.
19. "Report of the Secretary-General's Panel of Inquiry on the 31 May 2010 Flotilla Incident," United Nations, September 2011, http://www.un.org/News/dh/infocus/middle_east/Gaza_Flotilla_Panel_Report.pdf.
20. "Winograd Commission Final Report," Council on Foreign Affairs, January 30, 2008, http://www.cfr.org/israel/winograd-commission-final-report/p15385.
21. "Elections in Israel – February 2009," Israel Ministry of Foreign Affairs, February 10, 2009, http://www.mfa.gov.il/MFA/History/Modern+History/Historic+Events/Elections_in_Israel_February_2009.htm; "President Shimon Peres Tasks MK Binyamin Netanyahu with Forming Government," Israel Ministry of Foreign Affairs, February 20, 2009, http://www.mfa.gov.il/MFA/Government/Communiques/2009/President_tasks_MK_Netanyahu_forming_government_20-Feb-2009.htm.
22. Michele K. Esposito, "Quarterly Update on Conflict and Diplomacy: 16 May–15 August, 2009," *Journal of Palestine Studies*, 39, 1 (Autumn 2009), 104–141.
23. Abdel Monem Said Aly, "The Paradox of the Egyptian Revolution," (Waltham, MA: Crown Center for Middle East Studies, *Middle East Brief*, No. 55, September 2011). http://www.brandeis.edu/crown/publications/meb/MEB55.pdf. See also, Abdel Monem Said Aly, "State and Revolution in Egypt: The Paradox of Change and Politics," (Waltham, MA: Crown Center for Middle East Studies, Crown Essay, No. 2) http://www.brandeis.edu/crown/publications/ce/ce2.html.
24. Sources: Gary Blight, Sheila Pulham, and Paul Torpey, "Arab Spring: An Interactive Timeline of Middle East Protests," *The Guardian*, January 5, 2012, http://www.guardian.co.uk/world/interactive/2011/mar/22/middle-east-protest-interactive-timeline; Greg Myre, ed., "Timeline: The Major Events of the Arab Spring," NPR, January 2, 2012, http://www.npr.org/2012/01/02/144489844/timeline-the-major-events-of-the-arab-spring; "Timeline Arab Spring: A Brief Summary of Key Events Up Until December 23, 2011," Uppsala Conflict Data Program, Uppsala University http://www.pcr.uu.se/digitalAssets/87/87711_chronologic_timeline_arabian_spring.pdf; Cosima Ungaro and Paul Vale, "Arab Spring Timeline: 17 December 2010 to 17 December 2011," *Huffington Post UK*, December 16, 2011, http://www.huffingtonpost.co.uk/2011/12/16/arab-spring-timeline-_n_1153909.html; "Egyptian Elections: Preliminary Results," *Jaddaliya*, January 9, 2012, http://www.jadaliyya.com/pages/index/3331/egyptian-elections_preliminary-results_updated-; "Muslim Brotherhood Tops Egyptian Poll Results," Al-Jazeera, January 22, 2012, http://www.aljazeera.com/news/middleeast/2012/01/2012121125958580264.html; Gamal Essam El-Din, "Egypt's Post-Mubarak Legislative Life Begins Amid Tensions and Divisions," *Ahram Online*, January 23, 2012, http://english.ahram.org.eg/NewsContent/33/100/32384/Elections-/News/Egypts-postMubarak-legislative-life-begins-amid-te.aspx; "Tunisia's Islamist Ennahda Party Wins Historic Poll," BBC News, October 27, 2011, http://www.bbc.co.uk/news/world-africa-15487647; Avi Issacharoff, "Final Results Give Egypt's Islamist Bloc 70 Percent of Parliamentary Seats," *Ha'aretz*, January 22, 2012, http://www.haaretz.

com/print-edition/news/final-results-give-egypt-s-islamist-bloc-70-percent-of-parliamentary-seats-1.408528.

25. Reuters, "Factbox: Rising Syrian death toll, refugee wave, January 30, 2013."
26. "Number of Jewish Settlers in the West Bank Passes 350,000 Mark," *Los Angeles Times*, July 26, 2012. See also, "Settlements in the West Bank," Foundation for Middle East Peace, http://www.fmep.org/settlement_info/settlement-info-and-tables/stats-data/settlements-in-the-west-bank-1; "Settlements in East Jerusalem," Foundation for Middle East Peace, http://www.fmep.org/settlement_info/settlement-info-and-tables/stats-data/settlements-in-east-jerusalem.
27. "Land Grab: Israel's Settlement Policy in the West Bank," *Be'Tselem*, May 2002. In 2009 there were 33 settlements in the Golan with a population numbering 20,000.
28. PSR's poll # 43, in March 2012 showed that 68 percent of Palestinians surveyed believed that the chances for the establishment of a Palestinian state alongside Israel in the next five years to be slim or non-existent and 58 percent believed that the two-state solution was no longer practical due to Israeli settlement expansion. Nevertheless, only 29 percent supported giving up the two-state solution in favor of a one-state solution. See "Palestinian Public Opinion Poll No. (43)," Palestinian Center for Policy and Survey Research, April 3, 2012, http://www.pcpsr.org/survey/polls/2012/p43efull.html. See also: Khalil Shikaki, "The future of Israel–Palestine: a one-state reality in the making," NOREF Report, May 2012 http://www.peacebuilding.no/var/ezflow_site/storage/original/application/c56efad04a5b8a7fa46b782fda33d74f.pdf.
29. Yehuda Ben Meir and Olena Bagno-Moldavsky, "Vox Populi: Trends in Israeli Public Opinion on National Security, 2004–2009" (Tel Aviv: Institute for National Security Studies, Memorandum No. 106, November 2010), 20–23, http://www.inss.org.il/upload/%28FILE%291291193491.pdf.
30. Moshe Arens, "Is There Another Option?" *Ha'aretz*, June 2, 2010, http://www.haaretz.com/print-edition/opinion/is-there-another-option-1.293670. About two thirds of the Israelis surveyed in 2012 opposed a one-state solution. See, "Joint Israeli Palestinian Poll, March 2012," The Hebrew University of Jerualem, The Harry S. Truman Research Institute for the Advancement of Peace, Konrad Adenauer Stiftung, Ford Foundation, Palestinian Center for Policy and Survey Research, March, 2012. http://truman.huji.ac.il/.upload/Joint_press%20release_March2012_250312%20%282%29.pdf; Asher Susser, *Israel, Jordan and Palestine: The Two-State Imperative* (Waltham, MA: Brandeis University Press, 2012), 148–149.
31. "A Palestinian State in Two Years: Interview with Salam Fayyad, Palestinian Prime Minister," *Journal of Palestine Studies*, 39, 1 (Autumn 2009), 58–74.
32. "U.S. Security Coordinator Keith Dayton, Address Detailing the Mission and Accomplishments of the Office of the U.S. Security Coordinator, Israel and the Palestinian Authority, Washington, 7 May 2009 (excerpts)," *Journal of Palestine Studies*, 38, 4 (Summer 2009), 223–229.
33. "West Bank – Access Restrictions," United Nations Office for the Coordination of Humanitarian Affairs, December 2011, http://www.ochaopt.org/documents/ochaopt_atlas_westbank_december2011.pdf; Philip J. Dermer, "Trip Notes on a Return to Israel and The West Bank: Reflections on U.S. Peacemaking, the Security Mission and What Should Be Done," *Journal of Palestine Studies*, 39, 3 (Spring 2010), 66–81.
34. "Palestine Investment Conference," 2012, http://www.pic-palestine.ps/.
35. Oussama Kanaan, Udo Kock, Bahrom Shukurov, and Mariusz Sumlinski, "Recent Experience and Prospects of the Economy of the West Bank and Gaza: Staff Report Prepared for the Meeting of the Ad Hoc Liaison Committee," International Monetary Fund, Brussels, March 21, 2012, 5; Oussama Kanaan, Javier Gomez, Udo Kock, and Mariusz Sumlinski, "Recent Experience and Prospects of the Economy of the West Bank and Gaza: Seventh Review of Progress, Staff Report Prepared for

the Meeting of the Ad Hoc Liaison Committee," International Monetary Fund, Brussels, April 13, 2011; Oussama Kanaan, Javier Gomez, and Mariusz Sumlinski, "Recent Experience and Prospects of the Economy of the West Bank and Gaza: Fifth Review of Progress, Staff Report Prepared for the Meeting of the Ad Hoc Liaison Committee," International Monetary Fund, Madrid, April 13, 2010.

36. Alistair Lyon and Arshad Mohammed, "Abbas Stakes Palestinian Claim to State at UN," Reuters, September 23, 2011, http://www.reuters.com/article/2011/09/23/us-palestinians-israel-un-idUSTRE78H28J20110923; "Steps in the Palestinian Bid for UN Membership," *New York Times*, September 23, 2011, http://www.nytimes.com/interactive/2011/09/23/world/middleeast/steps-in-the-palestinian-bid-for-un-membership.html; Mohammed Daraghmeh, "Palestinians Say Freeze in US Aid Taking Effect," Yahoo! News, October 3, 2011, http://news.yahoo.com/palestinians-freeze-us-aid-taking-effect-210008923.html.
37. Neil MacFarquhar, "Palestinian Bid for UN Membership Faces Near-Certain Defeat," *New York Times*, November 8, 2011, http://www.nytimes.com/2011/11/09/world/middleeast/palestinians-united-nations-bid-faces-near-certain-defeat.html.
38. "US Cuts UNESCO Funds Over Vote for Palestinian Seat," BBC News, October 31, 2011, http://www.bbc.co.uk/news/world-middle-east-15527534.
39. "Direction of Trade Statistics," International Monetary Fund, May 2012.
40. "Turkey and the Middle East: Ambitions and Constraints," International Crisis Group, Europe Report No. 203, April 7, 2010, http://www.crisisgroup.org/~/media/Files/europe/turkey-cyprus/turkey/203%20Turkey%20and%20the%20Middle%20East%20-%20Ambitions%20and%20Constraints.ashx.
41. "Israel to Deport Gaza Activists After Increased Pressure," FoxNews, June 1, 2010, http://www.foxnews.com/world/2010/06/01/israeli-flotilla-activists-deported/; "Q&A: What Happened in the Gaza Flotilla Seizure, What's Ahead?," Reuters, June 3, 2010, http://uk.reuters.com/article/2010/06/03/us-israel-flotilla-qa-idUSTRE6522NU20100603; Conal Urquhart, "Israel Offers Compensation to Mavi Marmara Flotilla Raid Victims," *The Guardian*, May 23, 2012, http://www.guardian.co.uk/world/2012/may/24/israel-compensation-mavi-marmara-flotilla.
42. "Iran Signs Nuclear Fuel-Swap Deal with Turkey," BBC News, May 17, 2010, http://news.bbc.co.uk/2/hi/8685846.stm; "Text of the Iran-Brazil-Turkey Deal," *The Guardian*, May 17, 2010, http://www.guardian.co.uk/world/julian-borger-global-security-blog/2010/may/17/iran-brazil-turkey-nuclear; Neil MacFarquhar, "U.N. Approves New Sanctions to Deter Iran," *New York Times*, June 9, 2010; Mark Landler, "Clinton Says Opponents of Penalties Can Still Aid Diplomacy," *New York Times*, June 9, 2010.
43. Jonathan Burch, "Turkish PM Calls on Syria's Assad to Quit," Reuters, November 22, 2011, http://www.reuters.com/article/2011/11/22/us-turkey-syria-idUSTRE7AL0WJ20111122.
44. Thomas Seibert, "Turkish Premier Seeks Influence During Arab Spring Tour," *Deutsche Welle*, September 15, 2011, http://www.dw.de/dw/article/0,,15388922,00.html; Shahira Amin, "Erdogan to Try Reaching Gaza Via Egypt," *Egypt Independent*, September 12, 2011, http://www.egyptindependent.com/news/erdogan-try-reaching-gaza-egypt.
45. "Egypt's Muslim Brotherhood Criticizes Erdogan's Call for a Secular State," *Al Arabiya*, September 14, 2011, http://www.alarabiya.net/articles/2011/09/14/166814.html.
46. Alex Vatanka, "Syria Drives a Wedge Between Turkey and Iran – Analysis," *Eurasia Review*, May 19, 2012, http://www.eurasiareview.com/19052012-syria-drives-a-wedge-between-turkey-and-iran-analysis/; "Iraq Summons Turkish Envoy Again As Tensions Grow," Reuters, May 17, 2012, http://www.reuters.com/article/2012/05/17/us-iraq-turkey-row-idUSBRE84G0K720120517.

47. Meghan L. O'Sullivan, "Israel's Undersea Gas Bonanza May Spur Mideastern Strife," Bloomberg Views, May 21, 2012, http://www.bloomberg.com/news/2012-05-21/israel-s-undersea-gas-bonanza-may-spur-mideastern-strife.html.
48. Even independent candidates like Abdel Monem Abo Al-Fotouh, who declared Israel as the "principal enemy" of Egypt said that this does not mean going to war with Israel. See The Debate, On TV channel, May 10, 2012.
49. Amr Musa, "Egypt Electing the President", Talk show, CBC channel, May 14, 2012.
50. The Cedar Revolution, also known as *Intifadat-al-Istiqlal* (Independence Uprising), erupted in February 2005 in the form of peaceful demonstrations in the aftermath of the assassination of former Lebanese Prime Minister Rafik Hariri. Demonstrators demanded sovereignty and democracy and an end to Syrian military presence in their country. They also demanded an investigation to reveal who was behind the assassination of Hariri and other Lebanese politicians.

13 Conclusion – A Conflict that Never Ends?

What can be learned from this textbook? What characterizes and what is unique about the Arab–Israeli conflict? What explains why the conflict has remained so resilient despite repeated attempts to resolve it? And what does the historical record tell us about the relative explanatory power of the different prisms used here to understand the most important developments in the conflict – explanations located at the global-international and regional levels, in the realm of domestic politics and the particular personality traits of the individuals who led Israelis and Arabs through war and peace? And finally, should one conclude from the analysis provided here that the conflict is resolvable? And if so, what would it take? What kind of international and regional environment, domestic politics and leaders' qualities are necessary in order to finally end what could otherwise be viewed as "a conflict that never ends"?

Through the book's twelve chapters we have attempted to describe and analyze over 110 years of rich history, spanning the period from the awakening of Arab nationalism and Jewish nationalism in the 19th century to the Arab Awakening that began in late 2010. We have focused on a subset of the dramatic events experienced in the region during this timeframe, namely those related to the Arab–Zionist and later the Arab–Israeli conflict. However, we also took account of other important developments that the region has seen during this period, because these developments impacted the Arab–Israeli conflict.

During this history the Arab–Zionist conflict evolved considerably from what were initially merely sporadic and relatively mild expressions of Arab discontent about Jewish immigration to the area, particularly during the period preceding the First Zionist Congress of 1898. It gradually evolved into a protracted and bitter conflict that involved states, peoples, movements, and individuals.

As we have seen, what is remarkable about this conflict is its refractory nature – its amazing resistance to any and all efforts to resolve it. Its resilience seems to be rooted in a surprising ability to adapt to changes – even dramatic changes – and to reinvent itself repeatedly by changing its form and by assuming new forms in response to changing international and regional circumstances while preserving its essence and remaining as insoluble as ever.

The persistence of the Arab–Israeli conflict is especially surprising given the dramatic changes that the globe and the region have experienced during this period. Arguably, the global scene has seen greater changes within the period addressed here than in any historical period that spanned a similar length. At first the conflict developed through colonial times: the world was divided among a small number of empires which could mitigate the effects of anarchy by keeping the peace through colonial rule. After the First World War, however, this colonial world order was replaced by a more multipolar system – breeding instabilities that led to the Second World War. In turn, the latter produced a bipolar system in the context of which the two principal protagonists – the United States and the Soviet Union – competed for over half a century in the framework of a Cold War. Indeed it was under this global system that decolonization and the independence of the new states created regional theaters for competition which were utilized by local powers to their advantage. In the late 1980s, however, the United States ended up defeating the Soviet Union, thus ascending to the position of sole world power in what was broadly viewed as "the unipolar moment." And finally, during the last of the periods described here, the world was faced with a great paradox and irony when the United States, the only surviving superpower in a new, globalized world, suffered a brutal attack on September 11, 2001 by al-Qaida, a relatively small non-state actor, thus opening a new page in history that has yet to be fully defined.

The Middle East could not remain indifferent to these dramatic changes in the world scene, nor could it be immune to the effects of these changes. For hundreds of years, the Ottoman Empire kept peace among its constituent units. This remained the case after the First World War, when the colonial system of the Mandates allowed Britain and France to enforce a division of the region under their rule. But when colonial rule in the Middle East began to disintegrate in the aftermath of the Second World War, the region became at least as multipolar as Europe had been less than thirty years earlier. And just as European multipolarity was associated with great instabilities that led to the Second World War, the Middle East in the aftermath of that war bred fierce competitions and acute security dilemmas that resulted in one war after another.

While remarkably resilient, the Arab–Israeli conflict also underwent dramatic transformation during this history: from an existential conflict in which the Arab side refused to even acknowledge that it was facing a formidable opponent, and the Israeli side rejected the possibility that something called "the Palestinian people" existed, to a non-existential conflict that focused on the terms under which Israel and its Arab neighbors could co-exist. Within the latter period the conflict went through a further evolution, as the Arab states and the Palestinians moved from de-facto acceptance of Israel to a willingness to accommodate it and to formalize this willingness in the framework of peace treaties such as those signed first by Egypt, then by the PLO, and, after that, by Jordan. Parallel to that, Israeli perception of Palestinians as mere "residents" or "inhabitants" of the land changed, as they have increasingly come to be seen as having a distinct national identity and as deserving a state of their own.

Judging whether the Middle East on the whole has become more moderate during the history of the conflict is more difficult. The radical nationalist Arab regimes that came to power in the 1950s and 1960s are now largely gone, with their leaders departed: from Saddam Hussein of Iraq to Muammar Qhaddafi in Libya. But the rise of militant Islam now ruling Iran and manifesting itself in an array of radical non-state actors makes it difficult to judge whether the region at large has become moderate. This judgment is made even more complicated by the fact that Islamic militancy did not replace nationalism in the Middle East but rather added to it. Thus, the core beliefs in the region remain nationalist but political Islam now competes against and challenges the nationalists. This is reflected in the electoral success of Hamas in Palestine and later of the Muslim Brotherhood in Egypt. Religious militancy has also gained ground in Israel, where the social democratic labor movement that established the state has been in retreat throughout the first decade of the 21st century and is challenged by the growing strength of nationalist-religious parties.

The character of the region's constituent states has also changed during this period: from units of the Ottoman Empire to colonies of the French and British, then experiencing considerable instability manifested in frequent coups d'etat as they became nation-states in formation, especially Syria and Iraq. The exceptions to this are Israel, whose democracy evolved during the history of the conflict, and the Palestinians, who at this writing were still denied statehood.

Another big change that the region has experienced over the years involves the nature of the leaders: from formative revolutionary leaders like Haim Weizmann, David Ben Gurion, Gamal Abdel Nasser, Anwar Sadat, King Hussein, and Yasser Arafat, to managers and custodians like presidents Hosni Mubarak and Bashar Assad, and kings Abdullah of Jordan and Abdullah of Saudi Arabia. But, of course, this transformation was not complete, and at this writing the region continued to feature at least one revolutionary leader: Hassan Nassrallah of Hezbollah.

Finally, it is important to note the dramatic change that the dominant macro-narrative in the region has undergone during the history of the conflict. This is particularly the case with respect to the manner in which this narrative referred to Israel: from one that viewed Israel solely as a threat to one that accepted that at least under some circumstances, conditions, and contexts – for example, when facing the perceived threat from Iran – Israel could and possibly should be considered an ally, even if only tacitly.

What Characterizes the Arab–Israeli Conflict?

As noted earlier, the most amazing aspect of the Arab–Israeli conflict is that it has persisted in the face of all the aforementioned changes. Indeed, few internal or international conflicts have proved as resistant to efforts to resolve them as this one. One reason for this resilience is the wide distance between the parties' positions and the fact that the disputes span a wide array of issues in varied realms that include history, religion, politics, and security. Not surprisingly, the conflict is associated with diametrically opposed narratives – often referred to as "the war of the narratives." The sharpest disagreements concern the origins of the Arab refugee problem, but what each of the national movements stood for proved equally contentious. Thus, Israelis often viewed their Arab and Muslim detractors as genocidal, while Arabs depicted the Israeli project in terms such as "Zionism is Racism" and even went so far as to enshrine this narrative in a UN General Assembly resolution. Less emotional but not less consequential, Israelis viewed their relationship to their Arab neighbors as summarized by the term "the few against the many," while for their Arab opponents their larger numbers were often seen as a liability, with more mouths to feed and more jobs to be created. Thus Arabs depicted the same reality as "the many against the few," noting that the fewer Israelis were adept at making the most of their smaller number and compensating for it by maintaining a "qualitative edge" through vast and intense support from the West, which Arabs could never match.

Another cause of the conflict's resilience seems to have been the parties' frequent miscalculations, which have produced a trail of unintended consequences. One realm in which this was apparent concerned the difficulty of calculating the distribution of capabilities, a term often referred to as the Balance of Power, although this distribution was rarely balanced. Not surprisingly, calculating the distribution of power between countries possessing highly asymmetric capabilities has proved to be extremely difficult. This often allowed all sides to think that time was on their side and that therefore there was no reason for them to compromise.

Another unique aspect of the conflict concerns the involvement of the world's great powers. Very few conflicts in modern times have sustained the interest and involvement, if not fascination and obsession, of the great powers over such a length of time. During the second half of the twentieth century this seems to have resulted from the region's strategic value: beginning with the Second World War, large armies needed huge quantities of oil in order to move the massive quantities of mobile platforms that they possessed. Thus, the Middle East became a central stage on which the global powers waged their Cold War. So much so that in the 1960s the region developed its own version of the global competition – the so-called Arab Cold War: the polarization of the global arena affected the regional competition and vice versa.

Associated with the involvement of the great powers is the unparalleled extent of involvement of international organizations in the Arab–Israeli conflict. Indeed, no other conflict in the 20th century has been the subject of as many UN Security Council and General Assembly resolutions. On top of that, the conflict motivated the birth of new international organizations, the best example being the United Nations Relief and Works Agency (UNRWA).

Toward the end of the 20th century the stakes involved in the Middle East for global stability were no longer limited to oil. Increasingly, the proliferation or threat of proliferation of weapons of mass destruction (WMDs) assumed at least as much importance as oil as the great powers contemplated the consequences of the possible acquisition of nuclear weapons by a number of the region's states, beginning with Israel's Dimona project in the 1950s, then Iraq's Osiraq project in the 1970s, and Iran's nuclear program since the early 1990s. And, at the doorstep of the 21st century, another global threat, that of international terrorism, was seen to be emanating primarily from the Middle East, bred by the Arab–Israeli conflict as well as by other malignancies of the region such as the absence of democratic and good governance, and arrested economic development.

Explaining the Conflict's Resilience

What explains the resistance of the Arab–Israeli conflict to the many efforts to resolve it? The most basic of these explanations concerns the nature of the *international system* in which the states of the Middle East reside. The most important characteristic of this system is its anarchic nature, manifested in the absence of strong international institutions that could impose peace among its constituent units. Unfortunately, the United Nations has proved no substitute for the Ottoman Empire – it has proved too weak to compel its constituent units to abide by its resolutions. Thus the UN General Assembly could endorse the partition of Palestine into two states – as it did on November 29, 1947 in the framework of UNGA Resolution 181 – but it could not prevent some of its member states from going to war by invading Palestine on May 15, 1948 in an effort to annul this resolution. Similarly, the UN could not compel its members to accept other relevant resolutions such as 194 or to negotiate peace based on Security Council Resolutions 242 and 338.

Equally, in sharp contrast to the instruments of hierarchical state structures – police and other public safety and security institutions – UN peacekeeping, peace enforcing, and monitoring instruments were inherently weak. They functioned on the basis of narrow mandates and operated at the pleasure of the member states. Thus, in May 1967, Nasser could order the small UN force deployed in the Sinai into its barracks, triggering their removal, and UNIFIL has been unable to keep the peace in southern Lebanon throughout the past three decades.

Neither could the United States serve as a substitute for world government and impose regional peace. In unique circumstances, when conditions allowed a President of the United States to be fully engaged in peacemaking efforts, directly or by fully backing a senior government official, significant breakthroughs were achieved. Such breakthroughs bred hopes that the conflict might after all prove susceptible to resolution. This was the case when Kissinger corralled Israel, Egypt, and Syria into three disengagement agreements, and when Carter used the full force of the presidency to extract the concessions that the Camp David Accords and later the Egypt–Israel Peace Treaty required. But such moments were few and far between. Mostly, the United States could facilitate but it could not or would not force an agreement, even when such an agreement seemed within reach.

Not only was the United States incapable of compensating for the absence of a world government and of imposing peace on its own, during much of the second half of the 20th century it did quite the opposite when together with its competitor, the Soviet Union, it fueled a Middle East regional arms race. By transferring massive quantities of weapons and munitions to their respective clients, the two superpowers exacerbated the conflict, often bringing it to a boiling point. Thus the nature of the international system and its injections into the Middle East contributed greatly to the remarkable resilience of the Arab–Israeli conflict.

The anarchic nature of the Middle East regional subsystem did its share to immunize the Arab–Israeli conflict from the efforts to resolve it. Thus, in the aftermath of the breakdown of the imperial system, no one enjoyed a monopoly of force that would have allowed it to impose peace as the Ottoman Empire was able to do among its constituent units or the colonial system was capable of doing when Britain and France ruled the region. The impact of such anarchy is best illustrated by the fact that war in the region was avoided for the many, many years that the same constituent units co-existed under the umbrella of a hierarchical Ottoman empire.

While in the 1950s, and even more so in the 1960s, there was hope that the Arab League could mitigate the effects of anarchy and play a meaningful role in conflict resolution, this was not to be. Instead, the league proved to be merely another arena for competition among its constituent states. Even in those rare occasions when it took bold steps to reduce conflict – the Fez Plan, the Taif Accords, or the Arab Peace Initiative – it failed to implement its initiatives effectively.

With anarchy prevailing in the region and consequently each party fearing for its security, none could see that the environment produced not only risks but also opportunities. One result of this was that the parties were driven to behavior based on the perceived requirements of deterrence and not on affecting their neighbors' incentive structures.

Moreover, under conditions of anarchy regional tensions were exacerbated by the "security dilemma": each side taking steps designed to enhance its security but at the same time undermining the security of its neighbors, thus leading them to take measures that in the end undermined one's own security. A good example was Israel's pursuit of "defensible borders" in the aftermath of the 1967 War, which threatened the capitals of Egypt and Syria, thus causing them to mobilize all resources to dislodge Israel from the territory it acquired.

The Arab–Israeli conflict is a difficult one. Its structural pathologies include the fact that the protagonists are vying for the same piece of real estate. This imparts a zero-sum character to the conflict. In addition, the asymmetric "few against the many" quality of the distribution of power in the region has made measuring the balance of power difficult and hence its use as a yardstick or "conflict solver" problematic. This was further exacerbated as motivation became a critically important but hard-to-measure component of the balance of power: favoring Israel between 1945 and 1967; favoring Egypt between 1967 and 1979; and favoring the Palestinians in both Intifadas. Thus, the "balance of interests" or "balance of determination" proved at least as important as the distribution of capabilities in determining the overall balance of power between contending parties.

While the systemic global and regional factors are important in explaining the unique resilience of the Arab–Israeli conflict, no less significant was the *contribution of unit-level factors*. At this level one important factor has been the role of religion in the conflict. Religion played a role in the conflict even in its early years, with Izzeddin al-Qassam introducing an Islamic dimension in the 1930s by defining Palestine as Muslim land that could not be ceded to non-Muslims, just as some Zionists saw Palestine as "the Promised Land." But in recent years the growing role of religion in the conflict seems to have induced the parties to think in terms of absolutes, not in relative terms that allow compromise.

Indeed, religious extremists seem to be perpetuating the conflict in a number of ways: first, by assassinating the peacemakers – Sadat in Egypt and Rabin in Israel. Secondly, by rhetoric that implies a willingness to go "all the way," as in the case of Hezbollah leader Hassan Nassrallah's talk of "going to Jerusalem." Third, by movements in the region – Hezbollah and Hamas – that associate themselves with a leader like Iran's President Ahmadinejad, who has predicted Israel's imminent demise. And on the Israeli side, by movements and leaders such as the national religious settlers (notably, *Gush Emunim*) who also speak of the conflict in religious and existential terms and make every attempt to sabotage the two-state solution. Taken together, these developments have invited suspicions that the conflict may be returning to its existential mode. In turn, such suspicions serve to perpetuate the conflict because they breed reluctance to make concessions in what may become once again a "zero sum" arena.

Another source of the conflict's resilience at the unit level is the parties' tendency to see time as favorable to them, or at least not operating to their detriment. When they expect that things will only get better, or at least not get worse, parties have little incentive to compromise. Arabs tend to assume that time is on their side based on geostrategic determinants. In their view demography will ultimately topple Israel's sources of power. Ultimately, they assume, "the many" will overcome "the few" and that all they need to do is to narrow the qualitative gap just enough to allow their larger numbers to defeat Israel. In this estimate, Israeli power reached a plateau in the aftermath of the 1967 War and has been contracting ever since the 1973 War. Indeed, the Arabs' larger numbers are expected to be particularly decisive in the Israeli–Palestinian realm, where the combination of the Palestinians' population growth and Israel's continued occupation will allow the Palestinians to demand participatory rights in Israel (as the occupying state) and, if denied such rights, to argue that Israel is an apartheid state.

Conversely, many Israelis seem to assume that time is on their side. If Arabs base their optimistic assessments on geopolitical considerations, Israelis seem to rely on geoeconomic factors to carry the day. That is, many Israelis seem to assume that their ever-expanding economy will make their state-building project so robust as to make it immune to the effects of the Arabs' larger numbers. They further assume that the larger populations of the neighboring Arab states will continue to be a primary liability rather than an asset, since these populations need to be fed. Indeed, they see Arabs as preoccupied by other worries and as consequently chronically unable to transform their potential or latent sources of strength into deployable power that can affect the regional balance. Some Israelis – especially in the settler community – also think that with "facts on the ground" solidifying every day to their advantage, time is working in their favor.

A third malignancy at the unit level which contributes to the conflict's resilience is the parties' ignorance of one another. Each is largely unaware of the other's narrative and motivations, and in the absence of relevant knowledge they attribute to one another the worst of intentions and designs. And with such levels of ignorance, measures taken as a result of a sense of insecurity and fear, if not sheer terror, are often interpreted as evidence of aggressive designs. Yet such ignorance is not accidental: the conflict is infused with, and perpetuated by, the belief that acknowledging the other's narrative and motivations will appear as a sign of flexibility, and thus will weaken a state's bargaining power.

A closely related unit-level factor is the contribution of narratives to immunizing the conflict against the efforts to resolve it. While the narratives adopted by the parties to explain their positions internally and externally are *a measure* of the conflict, they also comprise an important factor affecting the conflict's longevity. For example, since Arabs see Zionism as an innately expansionist doctrine, the extent to which their narratives focus on Zionism and not on Israel per se makes the conflict resistant to efforts to address it.

Stabilizing relations in a manner that might facilitate conflict resolution is also made difficult by the parties' pathological asymmetries and propensity for periodic role changing. For example, whereas until 1967 Israel – and prior to that, the Zionist movement – demonstrated pragmatism and flexibility while the Arabs remained wedded to militancy and dogmatism, after 1967 Arab decision-making became increasingly reality-based while Israeli decision-making became increasingly ideological and religiously motivated. Meanwhile, the parties' temperaments seemed to experience similar reversals: thus, while in 1948 the Arab side tended to vastly underestimate the Zionist movement – referring to Jews residing in Palestine as gangs – the 1967 War had a humbling effect on the Arabs, propelling them toward far greater modesty. Not surprisingly, the Israelis' victory in the War had the exactly opposite effect, inducing them to become so arrogant as to be blind to clear evidence in 1973 that things were not going their way.

The parties' very different political systems introduced another asymmetry which made it difficult for the parties to understand one another. With a proportional-representation parliamentary system, the Israelis subscribe to what could be depicted as the most extreme form of democracy. By contrast, their Arab neighbors have experienced various forms of authoritarian rule – from the "softer" authoritarianism exercised by most Arab monarchies to some of the world's most tyrannical rulers, like Saddam Hussein of Iraq. While democracies are said to be less prone to war, this did not prevent Israel from shooting first in 1956, 1967, and 1982. Moreover, the dysfunctional coalitions that their proportional elections usually produce have often made breakthroughs in peacemaking impossible. By contrast, while authoritarian Arab leaders could be very bellicose, they could also launch peace offensives, as Egypt's Anwar Sadat did in 1977.

Another factor complicating the efforts to resolve the conflict and thus accounting for its resilience is that Arabs and Israelis differ in the nature of their goals. While Israelis seek security, Arabs tend to emphasize the pursuit of rights.

A final dimension of the asymmetry between the parties to the conflict concerns the longevity – and thus relative stability – of the parties' leaderships. With governments in Israel changing so rapidly, peacemaking efforts have often needed to begin from scratch – a Sisyphean endeavor. As a result, the Israeli electoral cycle has always been a consideration, frustrating Arab interlocutors. While this factor has also affected American calculations as to what can and cannot be achieved, the electoral cycle of the United States, and changes in legislative and executive branches every two, four, and eight years has proved an equally important limiting factor. Occasionally, this has meant that the learning curves in Jerusalem and Washington, DC begin at the same time, as was the case in early 2009, when Netanyahu's cabinet and the Obama team were assembled more or less simultaneously.

The contribution of global and regional systemic factors and the contribution of the nature of the region's constituent units to the conflict's resilience should not hide the importance of the human factor – the nature of the protagonists' leaders – in affecting the conflict's resistance to resolution. In this context one important factor has been the propensity of despotic leaders to perpetuate the conflict by adopting bellicose positions in order to distract their publics from the miserable objective realities that characterize their daily lives. Thus for leaders suffering a "legitimacy deficit" war could sometimes be seen as providing legitimacy. An excellent example was Jordan's King Hussein who felt on the eve of the 1967 War that his throne would be threatened if he did not join Nasser in confronting

Israel. Yet as noted earlier, despots are also more capable of making peace: less constrained by public opinion they can make a "grand leap" and the compromises necessary for peace.

Relative Explanatory Power

In this section we seek to reach some general conclusions regarding the *relative* explanatory power of the different prisms we have used to explain the most important developments in the history of the Arab–Israeli conflict. Following the conceptual framework suggested by Kenneth Waltz, this book seeks to explain major turning-points, outcomes or consequences in Arab–Israeli relations by exploring and examining different causes found at three levels of analysis: systemic, domestic and individual. This approach, however, has serious limitations: it neither proves causality (namely that *B* was actually the consequence of *A*) nor eliminates the possibility that some consequences might have been unintended. For example, we did not explore the extent to which one or more of the "causes" at the aforementioned three levels was sufficient or necessary to produce the outcome, or "effect," in question.

So what can be deduced from the analytical sections of this book about the relative explanatory power of the different perspectives utilized? Have developments at the global realm and at the regional level provided the most robust explanations for developments in the Arab–Israeli conflict? Or, instead, were such developments propelled to a greater extent by domestic developments in Israel, the Arab states, and among the Palestinians? Or is it that individual leaders and their particular personality traits have had greater influence on how developments in the conflict have unfolded?

Judgments about the relative explanatory power of the three levels are difficult to make because it seems that in different periods actions at these different levels have had different effects on the evolution of the conflict and on the efforts to resolve it. Thus, if during the height of the Cold War developments in the global realm have had extremely consequential effects on the evolution of the Arab–Israeli conflict, during other periods domestic politics appeared to have outweighed all other considerations in determining developments in the conflict. And then, during other times, the unique personality of particular Middle Eastern leaders has seemed to provide the most robust explanations for such developments. Consequently, only one conclusion seems indisputable: that none of the prisms utilized here to explain the conflict can be ignored; factors at all the levels employed here have been at play, affecting significantly the evolution of the Arab–Israeli conflict.

Clearly, *global-systemic factors* played a significant role in affecting critically important developments in Arab–Israeli interactions. Israel's creation would not have been deemed legitimate without the newly created United Nations adopting Resolution 181 in November 1947. In turn, it is difficult to see how such international support could have been garnered without earlier developments in the international system: the Second World War was associated with the Holocaust which persuaded many governments that, lacking a state of their own, Jews might continue to be victims of the most hideous crimes. This was especially the case in the United States where there was understandable regret, if not guilt, over America's refusal to allow entry to Jewish refugees fleeing continental Europe in the late 1930s. At the same time, without the Cold War spurring the competition between the United States and the Soviet Union in the immediate aftermath of the war, it is difficult to see how and why these two powers came to cooperate in the short-lived coalition that presided over Israel's creation.

The Cold War competition also propelled the Soviet Union to supply masses of advanced weapons to Egypt (the 1955 Czech Arms Deal) which factored significantly in spurring Israeli fears that led it to cooperate with France and Britain in launching the 1956 Sinai–Suez War. Meanwhile, other global developments – primarily the desire of Britain and France to avert the international and regional effects of their decline as global powers – led these two countries to cooperate with Israel in launching the war in a desperate and misguided hope of maintaining their influence in the Levant and the Maghreb.

Global competition between the United States and the Soviet Union also played a major role in other important developments in the Arab–Israeli conflict. Yet to be fully explained is the Soviet Union's calculation in May 1967 that it might gain ground by supplying false information to Egypt about a supposed Israeli deployment of forces to its border with Syria, which propelled Egypt to take a series of steps that eventually made the 1967 War inevitable. And, if it were not for the parallel escalation of the Vietnam War, the United States might well have been more active and more effective in preventing the escalation in Israeli–Arab tensions in late May and early June 1967 that led to that war.

Equally important during different periods has been the effect of global factors in creating breakthroughs in Arab–Israeli peacemaking. The shift from "limited war" (1969–73) to "limited accommodation" (1974–77) could not have occurred without the United States during the Nixon and Ford presidencies launching a major effort to pull Egypt away from the Soviet bloc by demonstrating its superior capacity to help Egypt meet its most important objective: restoring its sovereignty over the territories it lost in 1967. Indeed, the same consideration also led the United States to play an indispensable role in engineering the 1978 Camp David Accords.

Nevertheless, it is impossible to be certain that these systemic-global factors provide the most robust explanations for developments in the evolution of the Arab–Israeli conflict. This is because a number of highly significant features and events of the conflict seemed to have been equally propelled by systemic-regional factors. Thus, the *Nakba* – the defeat of "the many" Arab states and the armies they deployed in Palestine in May 1948 – cannot be explained without reference to the fierce regional competition and security dilemma experienced by key Arab states – Egypt, Jordan, Iraq, and Syria – in the aftermath of the Second World War.

Other considerations related to the regional balance of power seemed equally important in determining developments in the conflict. Thus, Israeli fears of the impact of Egypt's anticipated integration of the masses of arms it received in the 1955 Czech arms deal played a role in propelling it in October 1956 to launch what some saw as a "preventive war." Similar preventive logic – fearing the consequences of Iraq's development of the capacity to produce nuclear weapons – propelled Israel in June 1981 to abort such efforts by destroying the Osiraq nuclear reactor.

Without the regional competition driving Jordan, Syria and Egypt to bait one another in the mid-1960s, it is also difficult to explain the escalation that led to the 1967 War. And what about explaining the results of that war? It is unlikely that Israel could have defeated the armies of

Egypt, Syria, and Jordan so easily and within a span of only six days if a large part of Egypt's army had not been deployed in Yemen during the two years preceding the May 1967 crisis. Similarly affected by the regional balance of power was Israel's launching of the 1982 Lebanon War. Without this balance favoring Israel due to Iraq's preoccupation with its war with Iran, and without the Egyptian–Israeli peace treaty securing Israel's southern front, would Israel have attacked Lebanon in 1982?

Regional developments and the impact of these developments on the regional balance of power were similarly important in allowing peace breakthroughs. Thus, Iraq's defeat in the 1991 Gulf War seems to have tilted the regional balance of power against the Arab rejectionist states and in favor of the more pragmatic Arab regimes. Without such a shift, it would have been more difficult, if not impossible, for the United States to convene the post-Gulf War Madrid Peace Conference. Equally, two years later, it would have been unlikely that Yasser Arafat would part with long-standing Palestinian positions and make the concessions necessary for concluding the Oslo Accords.

Yet at other junctures unit-level explanations, focusing on the domestic politics of key players, seem to provide equally robust explanations of developments in the Arab–Israeli conflict. Thus, the defeat of the Palestinians in the war with the Yishuv in late 1947 and early 1948 – leading to the intervention of the Arab armies in May 1948 – seems to have been rooted in the total fragmentation of Palestinian society. Such fragmentation had already characterized the 1936–39 Arab Revolt: it was a cause of the Palestinians' defeat in the Revolt but it was also amplified by the Revolt as the British authorities sowed division among Palestinians in an attempt ease the task of controlling them.

Just as pivotal was the effect of domestic factors in propelling developments in the conflict during the 1950s. For example, the perception that their newly assembled society was very fragile seems to have played an important role in propelling Israeli leaders to exercise "escalation dominance" in response to the *Fedayyin* attacks, thus contributing to the factors that led to the 1956 war. At least equally, however, the same escalation was the result of the unrestrained competition among Israel's top leaders, between the "moderates" or the "diplomats" led by Sharett and the "activists" led by Ben Gurion.

The interplay between Nasser and Field Marshal Amer in the mid-1960s, and Nasser's earlier neglect of commanding the country's armed forces – allowing Amer to monopolize these forces and orchestrate their growing involvement in the country's social and economic life – all played a role in Nasser's loss of control during the run-up to the 1967 War. Equally, if it were not for the weakness that Eshkol projected during the same period – and the resulting loss of public confidence in his ability to lead in times of crisis – there would not have developed the domestic pressures to bring Dayan and Begin into a government of national unity in the closing days of May 1967. And without the formation of this government it is far from certain that Israel would have launched the war on June 5, 1967.

Equally important was the impact of domestic factors in affecting breakthroughs and potential breakthroughs in Arab–Israeli peacemaking. Thus, the opposition to peace with Israel which played a role in Sadat's assassination must have affected Mubarak's decisions regarding the content of Egyptian–Israeli relations in the 1980s – whether "warm" or "cold." Similarly, domestic opposition in Israel to the Oslo Accords which led to the assassination of Prime Minster Rabin resulted in a chain of reactions that culminated in the return of Likud to power in 1996, thus affecting future Palestinian–Israeli interactions. Equally, fear of public opposition to a withdrawal from the Golan seems to have limited the ability of various Israeli leaders – Rabin, Peres, Barak, and Olmert – to bring talks with Syria to a successful conclusion.

On the Palestinian side, just as negatively, the rise of Hamas in the last two decades has contributed its share in shaping Palestinian–Israeli outcomes. Hamas's role in launching suicide attacks in 1996 and, on a larger scale, during the Second Intifada, its electoral victory in 2006, and its continued launching of rockets from the Gaza Strip even after the Israeli withdrawal from the Strip, all contributed to convincing the Israelis that the Palestinians have not abandoned "armed struggle" and that Israel cannot afford to extend disengagement to the West Bank. The role of Israeli religious nationalists in building settlements in the West Bank has had a similar impact on Palestinian perceptions that the Oslo process actually helped Israel to consolidate rather than end occupation, and that Israel is not truly committed to a two-state solution.

The parties' narratives about the conflict and the peace process at times have also played a critical role, although this is clearly an area where caution is required because it is easy to confuse causes with consequences. In this case it must be asked: To what extent have narratives actually contributed to the conflict rather than merely reflected its state? In the early years of the 20th century, Zionists' narratives about Palestine as "a land without people for people without a land," and Palestinian narratives about Jews as constituting a religious community but not a national group, contributed to mutual denial of national identities. Later, in the aftermath of the wars of 1967 and 1973, Arab narratives about the impracticality of military solutions contributed to the emergence of realism and pragmatism, hence the move toward "limited accommodation."

More recently, Palestinian and Arab narratives about Israel's unilateral withdrawal from southern Lebanon in May 2000 – as having been "chased out" by Hezbollah fire – contributed to the eruption of the Second Intifada. And, in the aftermath of the failure of the 2000 Camp David Summit and eruption of the Intifada, the Israeli narrative about "the absence of a Palestinian partner for peace" contributed to the weakening of the Israeli peace camp, as well as to the Palestinian public's belief that diplomacy was futile.

Competing with the role of global and regional factors and the importance of domestic politics in affecting developments in the Arab–Israeli conflict is *the role of individual leaders* in these developments. While individual leaders are always involved, in attributing explanatory power to the behavior of such individuals we ask: To what extent has the particular psychological or other personal traits of the individual involved made a difference in propelling these developments? Inevitably our judgment of this issue involves conjectures bordering on counterfactual as we ask: Would such a development have taken place even if the individual leader involved was replaced by a different leader? Or, was there something about the particular leader involved that explains what happened – something without which the development simply would not have taken place?

The history of the Arab–Israeli conflict is replete with examples pointing to the pivotal role of individual leaders. Thus, it is nearly impossible to imagine that the Zionist project could have succeeded without the unique characteristics of three individuals in successive order: Herzl, Weizmann, and Ben Gurion. While Herzl did not invent the idea of Jewish statehood, his capturing of the waves of nationalism and transforming them into a marketable narrative was unique. With personal charisma and a capacity to market his ideas as a political platform ("The Jewish State") as well as in fiction form ("Altnueland") Herzl was able to appeal to Jews close and afar and to create the nucleus of a political movement that would flourish only after his lifetime.

Just as surprising is the unique role of Weizmann. What exactly it was about Weizmann's personality that gave him unique access to the British elite, and hence the opportunity to present the Zionist case to anyone who mattered in the British hierarchy, remains a mystery. But that these traits were truly consequential in advancing the Zionist cause is indisputable.

Equally important in determining the success of the Zionist project were the unique attributes of Ben Gurion. Beginning with his compelling the Zionist movement to adopt the policy of *Havlaga* [restraint] during the 1936–39 Arab Revolt, negotiating in 1937 a majority which would accept the partition plan offered by the Peel Commission, then identifying as early as 1942 that the United States would emerge as the great power in the aftermath of the Second World War, and then preparing the Yishuv's security forces beginning in 1946 for the possibility of an invasion of Palestine by the conventional armed forces of the neighboring Arab states, Ben Gurion proved remarkably astute in reading global and regional trends and remarkably effective in propelling the movement to adopt appropriate responses.

An equally compelling example of the critically important role of individual leaders was provided by the Palestinians' Hajj Amin al-Husseini. Betting on the wrong horse – Nazi Germany during the Second World War – al-Husseini tarnished the Palestinians' case in all corners that really mattered in the war's aftermath. In the 1960s Nasser provided another great example of the force of personality: with his great charisma, the impact of his rhetoric and the message he effectively communicated to every corner of the Arab world, Nasser showed how an individual leader can multiply the weight his country carries in determining regional and even global developments. No less important was Arafat's unique role in the annals of the Palestinian national movement. When in 1974 he addressed the United Nations General Assembly it was easy to forget that this individual, who played a critical role in molding a scattered people into a national movement, was not a leader of an existing state.

While individual leaders like Ben Gurion, Nasser, and Arafat played a decisive role in their nations' struggles, no less important has been the contribution of individuals to Arab–Israeli peacemaking. Clearly, neither the Egyptian–Israeli and Syrian–Israeli disengagement agreements of 1974–75, nor the 1978 Israeli–Egyptian Camp David Accords, nor the ground-breaking 1991 Madrid Peace Conference could have occurred if it were not for the forceful personalities of three American leaders or senior officials: Kissinger, Carter, and Baker.

Truly unique in this respect was the force of personality exhibited by Egypt's Anwar Sadat, who proved to be an outstanding war leader and an ultimate peacemaker in rapid succession. Sadat's intuitive understanding of the interplay between force and diplomacy, his resulting conclusion that the war envisaged for 1973 must be one of "limited aims," that Egypt should follow-up its limited military gains by a diplomatic offensive, and finally that this diplomatic offensive must break the internal deadlock in Israel to create sufficient public support for the concessions that he demanded of its government, was truly unique. No other member of Egypt's governing elite came even close to possessing Sadat's talents as a grand strategist and peacemaker.

On the Israeli side, the defense credentials of individual leaders proved absolutely critical to peacemaking, but they were not always sufficient to achieve such breakthroughs. Thus, it is difficult to see how Rabin could have broken a three-decade taboo to recognize the PLO and sign the Oslo Accords in 1993, how Ehud Barak could have unilaterally withdrawn the IDF from southern Lebanon in 2000, and how Ariel Sharon could have disengaged Israel unilaterally from Gaza in 2005 if it were not for their impeccable defense credentials. Of course, such credentials were never enough – they were not enough for Rabin or Barak to overcome the domestic difficulties entailed in a possible deal with Syria, nor were they sufficient to allow Barak to overcome his fears at the 2000 Camp David Summit.

As the previous paragraphs make clear, alongside global and regional systemic factors and the domestic politics of the region's states, the personal characteristics of the region's leaders often played a crucial role in affecting the Arab–Israeli conflict and the efforts to resolve it. Equally, what the previous pages demonstrate is that it is impossible to judge which of the prisms provides more compelling insights and greater explanatory power for the Arab–Israeli conflict. Factors at all these levels – the global, the regional, the internal, and the individual – have played a role in causing negative and positive developments in the history of the conflict, and at different periods factors at some of these levels have influenced the conflict to a greater extent than others. Hence, if anything is clear it is that it is impossible to understand the conflict and the successes and failures in the efforts to resolve it without reference to causes at all these levels.

Is the Conflict Resolvable?

Given that the Arab–Israeli conflict has lasted for more than 110 years and has proven so resilient in the face of repeated efforts to resolve it, it is hardly surprising that many – Israelis and Palestinians alike – have reached the conclusion that the conflict is not resolvable. But is this really the case? Are Arabs and Israelis condemned to live with the conflict forever? Are all future efforts to resolve the two peoples' dispute doomed to failure? This question cannot be answered in definite terms. Instead, a close approximation to an answer must be based on an assessment of the assets available for resolving the conflict and the liabilities and obstacles that such an effort would need to overcome.

Pessimism about the prospects for Arab–Israeli peace is associated with a belief strongly held by Israelis and Palestinians alike, namely that "there is no partner for peace on the other side." And among Palestinians, this is reinforced by two equally strong beliefs: first, that the "facts on the ground" – namely, the construction of Israeli settlements in the West Bank and Jerusalem at large – have made peace impossible. And second, that the history of the conflict teaches us that "violence pays" – that is, that Arabs extracted Israeli concessions only when the latter was forced to experience "pain and suffering."

A second cause for pessimism is that instead of "unity of purpose" in pursuit of peace, the parties to the conflict have experienced growing fragmentation. At this writing Palestinians continue to be politically and geographically torn between the Fatah-led, PA-governed West Bank and Hamas-governed Gaza. The two movements represent not only competing views with regard to relations with Israel, they represent completely different visions as to what the Palestinian society should be all about. Syria, the most important of Israel's Arab neighbors that still lacks a peace treaty with the Jewish state, is in the midst of a civil war. And in Egypt, the Muslim Brotherhood – a movement that for many decades has been hostile to the idea of a Jewish state – has won the elections to the National Assembly as well as to the country's presidency. And Israeli policy towards its neighbors seems paralyzed as Israeli opinion has become increasingly polarized between a relatively passive majority that continues to favor peace while fully aware of the costs and risks entailed, and a growing minority committed to opposing any such concessions and to continuing Israel's occupation of the West Bank and East Jerusalem.

In recent decades, the opposition to the compromises that peace would require seems to have been enhanced by the growing role of religion in the conflict. Forces representing political Islam have become ever stronger in key Arab countries and among the Palestinians. And, in Israel national religious parties and movements seem to have gained a veto power over its policy toward its Arab neighbors.

Third, while the differences between Israel and Syria and Israel and the Palestinians – particularly those related to the future borders between these entities, and the security arrangements that would need to be put in place following the instatement of such borders – do not appear insurmountable, other issues remain intractable and some have become even more contentious. This is particularly the case in the Palestinian–Israeli realm; notably intractable issues include refugees' Right of Return (in contrast to the practicalities of resolving the refugees' problems), sovereignty in Jerusalem, especially in the Holy Basin (in contrast to the practical division of control over these sites), and Israel's more recent demand that Palestinians recognize it as "the national home of the Jewish people."

A fourth liability facing any prospects of resolving the Arab–Israeli conflict is the absence of requisite leaders. In general, at the beginning of the 21st century the Middle East does not seem to possess the imposing individuals that led it during the second half of the 20th century. While the new crop of regional leaders seem less inclined to embroil their people in the kind of reckless behavior that led to the wars of 1948 and 1967, they also seem less prepared to take the risks for peace that Sadat and Begin took when signing the 1978 Camp David Accords and that Rabin and Arafat took when signing the 1993 Oslo Accords. Peacemaking is not a job for the faint-hearted: its success depends on the availability of those who can conclude the "peace of the brave." Finally, at the beginning of the second decade of the 21st century it is also not clear that the United States would or could perform the critically important role that it has played in previous successful and less successful Middle East peace efforts: from Kissinger's 1974–75 "shuttle diplomacy" to the 2007–08 Annapolis Process.

While the combined effect of the aforementioned considerations may seem sufficient to keep the Arab–Israeli conflict in a state of irresolution, the considerable progress that has been made toward resolving the conflict in the past few decades generated assets that are likely to be available for future peacemaking efforts and as such deserve equal attention. Most importantly, the region does have a positive track record of Arab–Israeli peace or at least armistice agreements that have held over many decades, despite being challenged repeatedly. This has been the case with the 1974 Syrian–Israeli disengagement agreement, the 1979 Israeli–Egyptian peace treaty, and the 1994 Israeli–Jordanian treaty.

A second important asset for any attempt to resolve the conflict is that it has already been transformed from an existential conflict – in which Arabs and Israelis rejected one another's right to a state of their own – to a non-existential conflict that focuses largely on concrete matters: borders, security, refugee resettlement, etc. The Arab world no longer rejects Israel's right to exist – in the framework of the 2002 Arab Peace Initiative the Arab League went so far as to offer Israel the chance to be integrated in the region, subject to certain conditions. Similarly, operating within the Olso framework in 1996–99 Netanyahu, a Likud leader, signed two important agreements which transferred to Palestinian control parts of the "Land of Israel" – the 1997 Hebron Agreement and the 1998 Wye River Memorandum. In 2005, another Likud leader, Sharon, withdrew all Israeli civilian settlements and military installations from the Gaza Strip. And beginning in a speech delivered at Bar Ilan University in June 2009 Netanyahu formally accepted the two-state solution as the framework for resolving the Arab–Israeli conflict.

The transformation of the conflict from an existential to a non-existential one, and the consequent acceptability of the two-state solution to Arab and Israeli leaders and elites, are matched by its acceptability to the general publics. Thus, a majority of Israelis and Palestinians have accepted this paradigm as a framework for resolving the conflict for some years. And more recently, public opinion polls in Egypt revealed that only a small minority of Egyptians support the abrogation of the Israeli–Egyptian peace treaty. A related important development is that the gap between Israel and the Palestinians on all issues that arose from the 1967 War – the future borders between the two entities, security arrangements that would allow the two states to co-exist peacefully, and practical arrangements for refugee resettlement and dividing control of Jerusalem – have narrowed significantly during the past two decades.

Another significant asset available to future Arab–Israeli peacemakers is the considerable impressive experience gained in the use of Track-II channels to explore possible compromises. The 2002 Geneva Document is a case in point. Indeed, if there is one thing that Arab and Israeli leaders and negotiators do not lack it is at least three decades of experience in the use of all forms of negotiations: Track-I direct public and direct secret negotiations, all forms of mediation and facilitation including the art of "proximity talks" as a possible prelude to direct negotiations, and finally Track-II talks and Track 1½ – that is, informal talks that include private individuals and officials operating in a "private capacity."

A final important asset available to any serious future Middle East peacemaking effort is that the gap between Arab and Israeli narratives about the conflict has narrowed significantly in recent years. In part, this narrowing is associated with a related development: namely, the willingness of a growing number of individuals in each side to view the conflict from the perspective of the other side. On the Israeli side, this process began with the appearance of the so-called "New Historians" who, in part based on material available for the first time following the opening of previously closed archives, presented a new interpretation of past events that came somewhat closer to the Arab accounts of these developments. Since the collapse of the 2000 Camp David peace talks and earlier failure of Israeli–Syrian negotiations, this has been supplemented by accounts of former Israeli negotiators who were extremely critical of their own leaders' conduct of these talks.

For many reasons, Palestinians were more reserved in providing "revisionist" accounts of their own leaders' conduct in the conflict, and we are yet to see a single Syrian account that is critical of the Assads' contribution to the failure to achieve an Israeli–Syrian accord. However, in the past decade Palestinian historians also began to acknowledge that their leaders also had "agency" in the disasters that befell upon their people - notably the *Nakba* of 1948. With this, responsible individuals on both sides began to refocus their energies from blaming "the other side" for every disastrous outcome to seeking ways of resolving the conflict.

What would it take?

In view of the insights gained by this textbook, how can peace be achieved? How can the obstacles to peace be overcome? How can the spoilers be stopped from preventing the eruption of peace? What kind of international involvement would be required? What kind of regional involvement? What kind of domestic politics and what kind of leaders would be required if peace is to be achieved?

The answer to this question is far from straightforward because the experience with Arab–Israeli peacemaking is varied and yields competing interpretations and conclusions. A number of historical breakthroughs in this realm were associated with deep international involvement, almost exclusively by the United States. Thus, American mediation was critical to the 1974–75 Egyptian–Israeli and Syrian–Israeli disengagement agreements, and American facilitation was the key to the success of the 1978 Camp David Accords and the 1979 Egyptian–Israeli peace treaty. The United States was also the key to the convening of the 1991 Madrid Conference which spurred so many important bilateral and multilateral Arab–Israeli talks. Equally, the American launching of the Annapolis process provided the broad framework for the Abbas-Olmert 2007–08 talks as well as to the Turkish facilitation of Israeli–Syrian "proximity talks" at the same time.

Yet on other occasions Arab–Israeli breakthroughs were made without international intrusion and sometimes even as an act of frustration with the impotence manifested by global actors. Thus, in November 1977 irritation with the conduct of the Carter administration and specific concerns about its plan to reconvene the American-Soviet co-sponsored Geneva Peace Conference seems to have motivated Sadat to launch a heroic effort to "break the ice" by traveling to Jerusalem. Equally, the American input in the 1993–94 Israeli–Jordanian peace negotiations seems to have been minimal. Even more pronounced was the absence of any American input into the Israeli–PLO negotiations of the Oslo Accords.

A final note regarding American contributions to successful Middle East peacemaking: it almost always required a willingness to use leverage. The United States obtained Israeli acceptance of the 1975 second Egyptian–Israeli disengagement agreement only after announcing a "reassessment" of its policy, which was broadly understood to mean a reassessment of its relations with Israel. It similarly obtained dramatic changes in the PLO's stance in 1988 by making the opening of a dialogue with the organization contingent upon such changes. In 1991 it made the provision of $10 billion of government loan guarantees to Israel contingent on a more accommodating Israeli policy, forcing its reluctant prime minister, Itzhak Shamir, to take part in the Madrid Peace Conference. And in 1994 the United States made clear to Jordan's King Hussein that a "mending of the fence" following Hussein's siding with Saddam Hussein during the 1990–91 Gulf Crisis and War would require that the king demonstrate his sensitivity to American priorities by signing of a peace treaty with Israel.

Regional contributions to Arab–Israeli peacemaking are also important but not sufficient. By making peace with Israel, Egypt paved the way for future Arab acceptance of frameworks for accommodation. Without providing such leadership, it is inconceivable that Saudi leaders would soon thereafter offer the Fahd and Fez plans. By contrast, regional criticism of Arab negotiators – as when Arafat was criticized in many Arab quarters for his perceived willingness to place Jerusalem on the negotiation table – can have a devastating impact on the prospects for such talks. In turn, the experience with the 2002 Arab Peace Initiative provides mixed conclusions: on the one hand, the Initiative was an extremely important attempt to change the incentive structure for Israeli–Arab negotiations. On the other hand, it showed that when presented in a negative environment – the Arab Peace Initiative was proclaimed at the height of the Second Intifada when Israelis were barely coping with a wave of suicide bombings – even ground-breaking initiatives will fail to affect the basic dynamics of the conflict.

What kind of domestic politics and what kind of leaders are required if peace is to be achieved? Clearly, the far reaching compromises required for peace cannot be made without requisite domestic support. Thus domestic "coalitions of the willing" encompassing constituencies ranging from the pragmatic right to the moderates, are essential. For these to be formed, leaders must be willing to face their publics and level with them to the effect that not all their dreams can be fulfilled and not all their aspirations can materialize. Moreover, the same leaders must also be willing to face specific constituencies that might oppose the agreement reached. Indeed, it should be expected that such constituencies may even produce individuals who will be prepared to take any measure to derail the peace breakthrough, including assassination attempts. This is the heritage of the murder of two Arab–Israeli peacemakers: Sadat and Rabin. Peace, as already noted, is not for the faint-hearted.

Avoiding such catastrophes requires that leaders prepare their publics to the concessions that would need to be made if peace is to be achieved. This means that leaders must not only be courageous enough to make the required great leap forward – they must also be able to market their decision successfully. In turn, this requires that leaders prepare a narrative that addresses at least two dimensions of the steps they must take: first, a convincing case that the risks entailed in the required compromise are not intolerable and unacceptable. And second, an equally convincing case that the benefits that can be expected to derive from the agreement reached justify the concessions and the risks entailed. Ideally, leaders should be prepared to help one another in the latter cause. This is what Sadat did when traveling to Israel in November 1977: Assuring the Israelis that their quest for security was understandable and could be addressed, and persuading them that the benefits of peace would make it worthwhile for them to change their defense doctrine to one that did not require the retention of Egyptian land.

Appendix: Separation Barrier Map

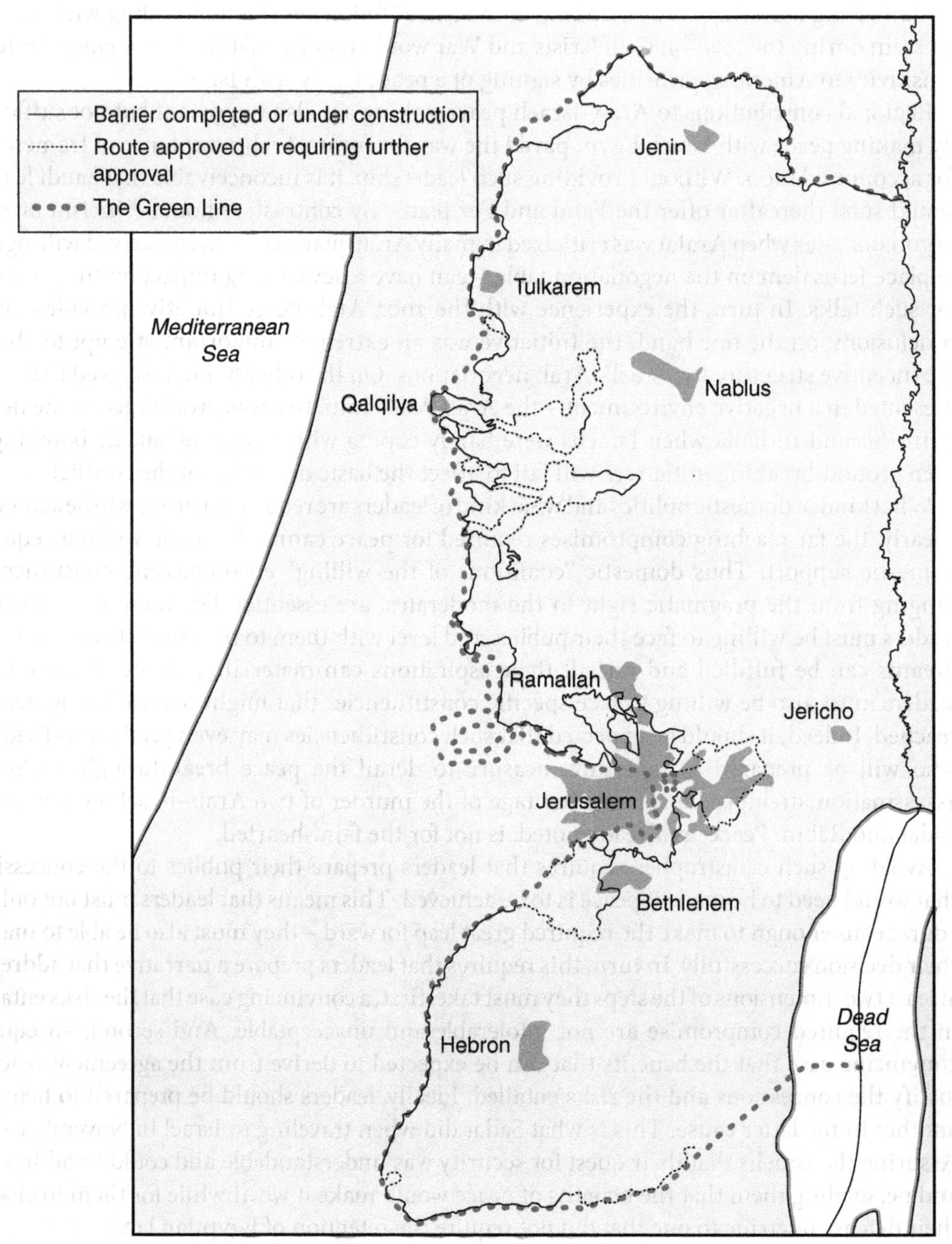

Index